SOCIETY

A DOCUMENTARY HISTORY OF HONG KONG

SOCIETY

Edited by David Faure

Hong Kong University Press
香港大學出版社

Hong Kong University Press
The University of Hong Kong
Pokfulam Road, Hong Kong

© Hong Kong University Press 1997

ISBN 962 209 393 0

All rights reserved. No portion of this publication may be reproduced or transmitted in any form or by any means, electronic or mechanical including photocopy, recording, or any information storage or retrieval system without permission in writing from the publisher.

Printed in Hong Kong by ColorPrint Production Co.

CONTENTS

Series General Editors' Foreword	vii
Acknowledgements	ix

Introduction	**1**
Chapter One: Early settlement	**15**
a. Villagers and immigrants	16
b. Respectability	19
c. Residential segregation	22
d. In retrospect	47
Chapter Two: The Chinese community in early Hong Kong	**57**
a. The temple and its community	58
b. Chinese guilds and other voluntary associations	61
c. The Chinese community's politics	85
Chapter Three: A city of entrepreneurs	**117**
Chapter Four: The people's livelihood in the 1920s and 1930s	**149**
a. Food, wages and other statistics	150
b. The strikes of the 1920s	160
c. The sale of women	174
d. Depression, livelihood and reform	180
Chapter Five: The Second World War and the Japanese occupation	**209**
a. War experience	210
b. Life in occupied Hong Kong	225
Chapter Six: The return to immigrant society, 1945-1966	**233**
a. Restoration of traditional communal institutions	234
b. Poverty and the need for welfare	248

c. Changes in personal characteristics	268
d. Industrialization in the 1950s	274
e. Social mobility	278
f. Professionalization	280

Chapter Seven: Crisis and consolidation, 1966 - 1981 — 285

a. Riots	286
b. Language	293
c. The population transition	299
d. New hopes and bold beginning	300
e. Hong Kong workers	317
f. Transforming the rural family	335
g. The new poor	347
h. As they kept coming	348

Chapter Eight: Affluence and beyond — 351

a. Out of apathy	351
b. Rich and poor	352
c. The local people emigrate	367
d. The survival of customs	370
e. How satisfied have Hong Kong people been?	372

Index — **383**

SERIES GENERAL EDITORS' FOREWORD

Impending changes in the political status of Hong Kong have in recent years brought about considerable interest in Hong Kong studies. Despite the very active publication of academic works and general books about Hong Kong in the last few years, there is still a need for a good scholarly general history which takes account of overall changes in Hong Kong's politics, society, external relations, education, economy, culture, and many other aspects of life. Indeed many recent publications are rather narrowly focused on either the Sino-British negotiations of the early 1980s or the transition of Hong Kong from a British Crown Colony to a Chinese Special Administrative Region. These are subjects that must be understood within the broad trends of Hong Kong's history, which has remained relatively neglected.

The future of Hong Kong cannot but be built on its past. It is our belief that as Hong Kong looks forward, it must also make a dispassionate assessment of its experience under British rule. No doubt, opinions about this assessment will vary; it will take time and discussions for Hong Kong, as China's Special Administrative Region, to come to terms with its colonial past. However, in our opinion, not only should such discussions be well informed, they should also not be restricted to specialists. For this reason, we think it best to produce these volumes that allow important documents to speak for themselves. The existing literature has not allowed easy access to most of the basic documents on Hong Kong history for non-specialists, and it is the object of this series to fill this gap.

We hope this series of a documentary history will be sufficiently detailed and authoritative for specialists, but will remain comprehensible to general readers. It should be a ready reference which is also readable as a general history. In our conception, a good documentary history is more than a selective reprint of documents. It should present relevant documents with introductory comments that will explain their context and highlight their significance in an interpretative framework. In this series each volume is self-contained and is edited by one or two specialists in the chosen subject. It is our intention that each volume will bring to the ready grasp of the reader documents that are normally accessible only in the archives and major libraries in Hong Kong, the United Kingdom, China, Taiwan and the United States.

Steve Tsang
David Faure

ACKNOWLEDGEMENTS

For permission to cite from their publications, the editor acknowledges with thanks Professor Chien Chiao, Professor Nelson Chow, Dr Elizabeth Johnson, Professor Ambrose Y.C. King, Rev Eric Kvan, Mr M.K. Lee, Mr Kenichi Ohashi, Professor Janet Salaff, Dr Janet Scott, Mrs Elsie Tu, Dr Thomas P. Wong, the Centre of Asian Studies of the University of Hong Kong, Chinese University Press, Columbia University Press, the Commercial Press (Hong Kong), the Department of Social Work of the Chinese University of Hong Kong, the Department of Applied Economics of the University of Cambridge (for the use of document VII.e1), the *Far Eastern Economic Review*, the Hong Kong Branch of the Royal Asiatic Society, the Hong Kong Council of Social Service, the Hong Kong Government, the Hong Kong Institute of Asia-Pacific Studies of the Chinese University of Hong Kong, the Hong Kong Management Association, Lingnan College (Hong Kong), the Royal Philatelic Society (London), the Hong Kong Museum of History, Hong Kong University Press, the Urban Council of Hong Kong, and *South China Morning Post*.

For permission to cite from material in their holdings, the editor thanks the Public Record Office (London), Rhodes House (Oxford), and Hong Kong University Library.

Dr James Hayes' continuous support and generosity should be noted, and in this present work, the editor is particularly grateful to him for making available the war diary cited in translation in document V.a1. The editor wishes also to acknowledge with thanks permission granted by Mr Kenneth Ting for a citation from Mr H.C. Ting's recollections for use as document VI.d1. Like others who have made use of the Clementi collection at Rhodes House, he is most grateful to Mrs A.I. Ovenell for making the collection readily available for research. Most of the material that goes into this book, however, was found in the Hong Kong Collection at Hong Kong University Library, and no-one who has worked there should forget the tremendous energy that past librarians, in particular, Mr Anthony Rydings and Mr Peter Yeung, had put into building up the collection, and the admirable effort in continuing that tradition made by their successors, Dr L.B. Kan as the university librarian and Mr Y.C. Wan in overall charge of the Hong Kong Collection.

Some holders of copyright have specified how acknowledgements should be worded. I am glad to comply here. I gladly acknowledge that document I.c1 is in the custody of the Public Record Office; that documents I.c2 and I.c3 are cited from Crown copyright material in the Public Record Office, London and are reproduced by permission of the Controller of Her Britannic Majesty's Stationery Office; that document VI.f1 is reprinted with permission from the January/February 1965 issue of *The Hong Kong Manager*, the official journal of The Hong Kong Management Association; and document VII.e2 is cited from *Working Daughters of Hong Kong* by Janet W. Salaff, copyright © 1995 by Columbia University Press, and reprinted with permission of the publisher.

Document V.b1 has been cited from a translation published in Course Unit 6 of AW213, A History of Hong Kong 1842-1984, by the Open University of Hong Kong. The editor is grateful for permission given for its use.

The editor has made every effort to locate copyright holders and authors for the passages cited in this volume. In the few cases where he has not succeeded in doing this, he would be glad if they would contact him.

The editor is also grateful to the British Academy for providing funding for the editing of this volume, and much heartened by further funding by the Lord Wilson Heritage Trust in Hong Kong for four forthcoming volumes.

Thanks are also due to the many colleagues who generously shared information and offered advice, in particular to Dr Elizabeth Sinn, Rev Carl Smith, Dr Steve Tsang and Professor Wong Siu-lun. At an early stage of his research into this book, the editor received much help from Dr Stephanie Chung in the collection of material. While in his last minute rush to complete the manuscript, he was given assistance by Dr May-bo Ching, Dr Henrietta Harrison and Dr Susanna Thornton, all of whom at the time were in an equal rush themselves finishing their doctoral theses.

For all the help that he received in the preparation of this volume, the editor is immensely grateful.

INTRODUCTION

HONG KONG, COLONIAL SOCIETY

Hong Kong was a China coast city. It was by and large a Chinese city. It was a metropolis. But above all, it was a colony.

Hong Kong became a British colony from 1842. It outlasted most British colonies. Post-Second World War Britain lost its world power status and gave up most of its colonies; in the pursuit of an open door into Europe, it gave up even the British Commonwealth. But colonial status lingered on in Hong Kong because, as it was said in the 1960s, China tolerated it, Britain saw no alternative to continuing and the Hong Kong people wanted it. By the 1980s, that situation changed.

Even at its mightiest, Britain had no social policy on Hong Kong as such. It applied British justice and periodically enforced standards that had been tried in Britain, whether or not they had succeeded in Britain or were suited to Hong Kong. It is hard to understand why the Hong Kong government would have promoted a Housing Society together with a Resettlement Department in the 1950s unless one realizes that the British home government sought to provide housing in Britain through the combined efforts of building societies and local councils. It is also hard to understand why in the 1970s Hong Kong should have adopted a sudden spate of labour legislation until one sees that a Labour government had come to power in London and that British Members of Parliament and the British press in the 1960s had been painting Hong Kong as a sweatshop. Hong Kong people did not demand housing, social welfare, legislation, police, not even universal education; but, in post-war Hong Kong, they had been granted by acts of benevolent government. Once granted, however, many Hong Kong people delighted in having these provisions. In this way, the benevolent provisions of the Hong Kong government, together with other provisions that were less benevolent, wove their way into Hong Kong society.

A superimposed government was the mark of the colonial status. But there must have been a society on which it was superimposed.

Society and the Realm of Politics

To describe Hong Kong society, one must return to the fundamentals of the concept. The concept 'society' was a creation of the European Enlightenment, created to represent a movement that informed kings that their subjects should suitably be governed by the laws of nature rather than their will. Subsequent to the Enlightenment, the concept went through a strange history. Because no government was willing to acknowledge that its will had been imposed in total ignorance of the demands of nature, governments have taken various means to ensure that nature and policy might meet. Dictators argue that their theories tell them what nature might demand; democrats say that they would ask the people. The theory of benevolent government to which both subscribe argues that the test of the theory lies ultimately in whether it works.

Nature being a silent partner to this relationship between governments and their people, whether governments and their policies work can only be discussed in relation to ends that are held to be worthwhile in themselves and that are vocalized. Such ends as justice, nationhood, equality, liberation, fairplay, liberty and now human rights have dominated political discourse at various times in recent history. Where society is not looked upon as a mere receipient of benevolence but an active participant in the generation of these aims, public debates concern themselves with the matching of policies to aims. However, in Hong Kong, until the 1980s, few fundamental ends of government were ever the subject of public debate. Hong Kong's commentators were not idealists but pragmatists, and there was neither the arena for nor the interest in a public discourse on the rights and wrongs of social policies on fundamental principles. After the Cultural Revolution in China, in which Hong Kong's vociferous left-wing lost, first its principles, then its nerves, not even communism provided an ideological threat. The very few champions of the needy and the powerless, among whom one must include the indefatigable Mrs Elsie Elliot (now Mrs Tu), made their mark in the 1960s and the early 1970s. They were superceded when by the 1980s even the poor took off into economic growth.

The Hong Kong government was a very successful government. It was successful because it did not bulldoze its way in social policies. It listened to the voice of the Hong Kong people, but it also selected the mouthpiece. Sir Murray Maclehose (now Lord Maclehose) might well have congratulated himself when he recruited 'grassroots' communal organizations into the vast advisory network that the Hong Kong government built up in the 1970s, much of it on his personal initiative. His Secretary for Home Affairs, Mr Denis Bray, put his finger on the communal pulse when he said in the Legislative Council on 29 November, 1973:

But it has only recently become clear that the most important change in society is not its increasing wealth nor its increasing expectations of Government performance but its new sense of purpose. The new society no longer expects everything to be done for it by a paternalistic government. It is a society on the move, prepared to act on social issues with the same vigour that the old refugee society displayed in the pursuit of private prosperity.

But hear the next sentence:

> How else can one explain the public response to the two campaigns of social awakening — Clean Hong Kong and Fight Violent Crime?[1]

In the 1970s, Hong Kong did not see any major extension to electoral politics.[2] Government benevolence depended on a choice of policies that the government would find practical and society would be willing to accept. When the formula worked, as it often did, there would have been participation. Cleaning Hong Kong and fighting violent crime would have been issues that members of the public might willingly participate in.

Nevertheless, the advisory network of communal organizations that might lend the Hong Kong government administrative support was genuine. The Hong Kong government needed a buffer between itself and the British home government. The Hong Kong government had to be able to report to the home government that there were laws of nature that even the home government should not upset. For this reason, society in Hong Kong was created in the same fashion as it was created in Englightenment Europe.

To see this line of thinking evolve, one returns to 1869. Sir Rutherford Alcock, British Minister in Beijing, had suggested that the Chinese government appoint a consul in Hong Kong and it seemed that he might receive the support of the Foreign Office. The Governor of Hong Kong, Sir R.G. MacDonnell found no merit whatsoever to the proposal and decided there were disadvantages to the interests of the Chinese people who were resident in Hong Kong. He could not put the case more eloquently than a memorial from the inhabitants of Hong Kong to the Foreign Secretary:

> In this colony there are upwards of 120,000 Chinese residents, all of whom are colonists, subject to our laws, the great majority of them tax-payers, and a very large number of them landholders, and entitled as such to Colonial Registers for vessels (owned by them) flying the British Flag, who have been for many years peaceable, well-conducted citizens, with a considerable stake in the welfare of the colony, and who, by being promoters and managers of the large emigration to the United States and Australian colonies, the principal exporters and traders, shareholders in our banks, steam, insurance and other public companies, and eager adventurers in new manufacturing projects, under our rule and are free, at present, from the extortions and squeezes to which they would indubitably be subjected, through their families or relatives living in China, if a Chinese consul were placed here.[3]

This was the first occasion, but not the only occasion, when as defender of the Chinese in Hong Kong the Governor presented his case to the home government.

A Chinese person was represented on Hong Kong's governing machinery only from 1880, when Ng Choy was made a member of the Legislative Council followed soon by the appointment of Ho Kai (later Sir Kai Ho Kai) to the Sanitary Board.[4] The decisions institutionalized the process whereby Chinese people were represented in Hong Kong politics, and for that reason, became an estate (or, to borrow a term from Hong Kong's political reforms of the 1980s, a 'functional constituency'). The politics of appointment was particularly suited to the workings of interested estates: the government itself and the Western commercial interest were the estates that the Legislative Council began with, to which was added the Chinese representation. The issue of sanitation control highlighted the other reason for bringing it into existence. After all, as Ho Kai observed when houses had to be demolished as a measure of plague prevention, it was the Chinese people's houses that were to be demolished.[5] The Sanitary Board and the Legislative Council, with the occasional knighthood, created the upper class of Chinese people in Hong Kong society.

The small Chinese upper class stood by the Hong Kong government. Ho Kai supported the advance into the New Territories. When he defected to the Chinese Revolution in 1911, he soon lost his seat on the Legislative Council.[6] It went to Mr Lau Chu Pak, who held steadfastly to the government of Hong Kong in the intricacies of the four-cornered politics between London, Hong Kong, Guangdong province (that was becoming increasingly independent in its actions after the 1911 Revolution) and Beijing. In the 1922 seamen's strike, the Hong Kong government drew on the prestige of Lau Chu Pak, Robert Hotung and R.H. Kotewall (who was Eurasian) to intervene on behalf of the Hong Kong community, and in the 1925-26 general strike, it had the support also of Chow Shou-shan. After the Second World War, Sir Man-kam Lo stood up against widening the electorate.[7] In 1971 over the very sensitive issue of the adoption of Chinese as an official language, itself a rare outburst of nationalist sentiments in Hong Kong, Sir Kenneth Fung Ping-fan wrote the very mild report that pleased all parties.[8] The rise of the Chinese upper class might be traced to the 1870s and its replacement in the 1970s. By the 1970s, the Shanghainese financier, the grassroots representatives, and more recent upstarts representing Western or Chinese interests, found their hearing in the Legislative Council. The new-comers might have created another Hong Kong upper class, but time ran out.

Mercantile Community

The Hong Kong Chinese upper class was always uncomfortable with its position. It was too small to make an impact on the Chinese community's lifestyle, and too weak to show itself as Hong Kong's communal leaders. In the absence of an upper class, the merchant and the civil servant took over leadership of the community.[9] Understandably, the Hong Kong government supported trade and the merchant stability.

The Hong Kong mercantile community was an anachronism by the 1950s. To find its parallel, one has to go to the treaty ports on the China coast, none of which survived the Second World War. The treaty ports were founded to facilitate trade. Unlike Hong Kong, they were not colonies, and there the merchants and rate-payers had a stronger say in the running of their own affairs than the foreign governments. The treaty port mercantile community as such declared no stakes in Chinese politics: the rising tide of nationalism in China through the 1920s and 1930s was at odds with its continuation as a community. The China coast mercantile communities survived, therefore, not by affiliating themselves with the national government but by dissociating themselves from it. But they lost their battle with Chinese nationalism. In 1927, foreigners were driven out of Hankou, by the end of the Second World War, all foreign rights to Shanghai were renounced, while Chinese merchants were absorbed more and more into the state's economic orbit. By the 1950s, the Hong Kong mercantile community stood alone on the China coast, in support of the free market as all of China came under economic control. Through ingenuity, hard work, luck and connections, it created the economic miracle of the 1970s and then 1980s. When it came to the crunch, it compromised. When the Hong Kong government decided that it had to provide low-cost housing for the poor, on a scale that by the 1990s was to make available housing for 40 percent of the population, Hong Kong private land-developers acquiesced. In effect Hong Kong land-developers divided the housing market with the Hong Kong government: private business managed the upper end of the market while government provided public housing for the needy, the same needy being workers in commerce and industry and the housing subsidy making up for the low wages of the 1950s and 1960s. Civil servants and the merchants managed Hong Kong with a strong business sense.

From early days, the mercantile community developed a social hierarchy whereupon power and privilege might merge. Standing in Government House, one might place at the top of the hierarchy the established merchant or civil servant who had 'come out' from Great Britain, and who would 'go home' upon retirement. The merchants and civil servants who came to Hong Kong for life-long residence recreated in Hong Kong respectable society as they might know it: St John's Cathedral on Garden Road, built to look like the church that one might find in most parts of Britain, the clubs and the annual balls, residences on the Peak (kept until the Second World War by law as a reservation for Western-style houses). Most did not learn to speak Chinese and an aversion to inter-marriage with Chinese people was common until the 1950s. A rung down the social ladder one might find the Westernized Chinese. Many wore Western suits, even before the Second World War — Ho Kai appears in photographs dressed in the Western suit, but Sir Robert Hotung, whose features betrayed his part-Western origins, was fond of appearing in Chinese dress. The Westernized Chinese might be mercantile or professional, but the less Westernized Chinese who mingled with this community would have been mercantile. Those who aspired to community leadership involved themselves in charitable institutions. Since 1870 the Tung Wah Hospital directors stood at the top of its hierarchy.

To say that Hong Kong was a mercantile community that was not dominated by an upper class, one acknowledges that while the rich were obviously distinct from the poor, the mercantile community was not divided socially from the rest of the population. Trade permeated the whole of Hong Kong society and social fluidity followed from the rapid economic development that Hong Kong experienced. Hong Kong abounds with stories of the self-made man (and woman) with every economic boom, in real estate at the end of the nineteenth century or the early years of the twentieth century, in industry in the 1920s and 1930s, in industry again in the 1950s and 1960s, and in finance and real estate in the 1980s and 1990s. The ideology of the really successful Chinese merchant in the harsh competitiveness of Hong Kong went beyond self-help; there was also a strong sense of comradeship and responsibility to his fellow men. Mr Fung Ping-shan, himself an exemplar of this tradition, described it as *lipin* (*laap-ban* in Cantonese) which may be loosely translated as 'establishing one's character'.[10] Mr Fung was a philanthropist, not only in Hong Kong, which he made his home, but also to his home village and county in China where he was born. The character *pin* in Mr Fung's term incorporates a hidden agenda which can be understood in the light of the Confucian classics: the Chinese gentleman subscribes to the principle that social harmony can be achieved only by putting one's character and then one's household in order, and putting them in order means behaving in propriety to one's social station. The importance of this maxim rests not in how much one is paid, but in whether one is paid as an employee. To be the free man, one's objective in life is to be the free agent. High and low in Hong Kong, the working man would have wanted to be the director of his own company. This is not the ideology of the yuppie of the 1980s, but the ideology of traditional Chinese entrepreneurship.

The traditional ideology that provided the common language of the self-made Chinese merchant such as Mr Fung Ping-shan, and the Westernism that would provide the avenue for moving socially ahead in Hong Kong, reflected fully the ambiguity of twentieth-century Chinese culture. Sir Robert Hotung, writing about the achievements of the Chinese people in Hong Kong, emphasizes the 'progress and intellectual development' of the Chinese community rather than its obvious financial success. He refers to their making great strides in education, but qualifies it by saying 'from a Western standpoint'. He was proud of the educational achievement of the Hong Kong Chinese, particularly because some of them had succeeded 'to such centres of learning as Oxford and Cambridge Universities for the completion of the courses of studies first begun in Hong Kong'.[11] Fair enough,

Sir Robert was writing for a Western readership, and Mr Fung Ping-shan did not speak English and was brought up in the Chinese classical tradition. Nevertheless, the Chinese mercantile community fell precisely between those two stools when they pursued recognition from seats of learning in Britain while maintaining their Chinese cultural contact by appealing to tradition. In the new China of the 1920s, the classics were giving way to the vernacular, where literary giants such as Lu Xun made waves that were to pass Hong Kong by. Shanghai became China's literary haven, some of its merchants investing in and benefiting from the publications that flowed from the new culture. Hong Kong in the 1920s as in the post-Second World War decades until the 1980s, was cultural wasteland.

Surely, one might say, one looks to intellectuals to make culture, not the mercantile community. Hong Kong had its share of intellectuals but Hong Kong did not produce an intellectual tradition. The impact that Hong Kong society made on Chinese intellectual life was made through its public media, and its content was heavily determined by the mercantile interest. Before the Second World War, the Cantonese opera was its habitual entertainment; after the war, it was the cinema, and then television. When one looks below the surface, one sees within the media elements of a Hong Kong culture, but the Hong Kong way of life was lived rather than discussed, and when it was, it was dominated by the sense that the Hong Kong way of life was really Chinese, which was only partly true.

China, Tradition and Revolution

The Chinese person living in Hong Kong has, since the fall of the Qing dynasty in 1911, known two Chinas: cultural China and national China. Cultural China one sees in Hong Kong in the temples and shrines, in the annual festivals, in speech, in manners and gestures, and in ingrained habits. National China one sees in Hong Kong as elements of unwanted politics, potential threats to the colonial regime. The Hong Kong government from the 1910s has been comfortable with cultural China; it prefers to keep national China at arm's length.

It is a common misconception that Chinese culture had stood still within Hong Kong's history. Although it is true that the British government had, on the whole, honoured its pledge in 1842 to leave Chinese customs alone, there had been times when it saw fit to intervene and intervene it did. In no area did it intervene more than in the family. From the 1870s, the Hong Kong government had had to be concerned with the position of bonded women. They were found in prostitution, but when they escaped from it, they needed a home to go to. The Chinese merchants had founded a loose organization known as Po Leung Kuk to give them assistance. In 1890, the question was raised as to what this organization was and in what sort of form help was being made. A committee of enquiry was set up, and it is clear when one reads the proceedings, that the committee of enquiry was suspicious of the Po Leung Kuk's intentions. Did the committee members of the Po Leung Kuk seek concubines among the poor women who were in its custody? Why did the Po Leung Kuk consent to these women being taken out as concubines at all; why were their weddings not given the pomp that was fitting for weddings of the first wife?[12]

Humanitarian principles do not always win in Hong Kong, but time, economic opportunities and ideologies slowly and surely bring Chinese customs into step with Western trends. Child labour was brought to an end by the labour legislation and compulsory education of the 1970s, but rising standards of living would have contributed. In the case of the *mui-tsai*, bonded women in domestic positions,[13] pressure had been exerted from the Western quarters in Hong Kong as in Britain. By the 1920s, Britain could not condone slavery within its colonies and the practice must be banned, whatever difficultes the Hong Kong government might have to face in banning it, and however impractical it was to let loose the many bonded women domestics, mostly in their teens, onto the streets of Hong Kong. Few issues caused as much outcry within Hong Kong as the freeing of the *mui-tsai*, but it was passed into law by the Legislative Council in 1923. Nevertheless, much less public interest was aroused over removing the rights of concubine in the 1950s. By the 1950s, concubines belonged to a way of life that had passed, and the law was concerned, in any case, with the awkward question of the distribution of inheritance for persons who died intestate. The law, in any case, could not rule on the keeping of mistresses, which became more an issue as Hong Kong businessmen and factory owners set up their businesses in China as they continued to maintain their abodes, and hence families, in Hong Kong. The occasional cases of bigamy were brought to justice, but only if the second union was considered and registered as a marriage.

Not even in the management of temples and sacrifice therein did customs stand still. Until recent years, the Wong Tai Sin Temple and its popularity was almost wholly a Hong Kong phenomenon. Yet, religious ceremonies conducted at temples and shrines convey a sense of timelessness: the deities had been sacrificed to from time immemorial and might, for all we know, continue unto the end of time. In much the same connotation, one might say the Chinese family, despite changes to the status of women, despite changes to the style of living created by closely packed flats in tower blocks in the Hong Kong environment, did not give up entirely the basic tenets that allowed it to hold together. The predictions of some social scientists in the 1970s notwithstanding, Hong Kong people did not give up the values of the extended family. Sociologist Lee Ming-kwan summed the attitude in his study from the 1988 indicators of social development survey: '[People] expect siblings to perform obligations, but are less insistent about supporting their parents. Many believe that sons and daughters should not be treated differently, but would think twice when asked to depart from traditional sex-roles.'[14] The conclusion does not call for optimism for the continuation of traditional values; it suggests that the values are passing but have far from departed.

The sluggish persistence of cultural China in its timeless continuity contrasts with the shockwaves that national China generates at every abrupt turn. The dates stand out as outstanding events in Hong Kong's history: 1912, 1927, 1949, 1967, 1982 and soon 1997. In both 1912 and 1949, when a revolution heralded a new era in China, the Hong Kong government watched with premonitions but Hong Kong society remained calm.[15] The impact of the revolution came a decade later. In 1922, the seamen's strike signalled the new nationalism that would have backed what it considered a working class in Hong Kong, and in 1925-26, it was an incident that offended nationalism rather than a demand on wage or working conditions that sparked the general strike. In 1956, the riot that gripped parts of Kowloon and the New Territories began as a continuation of the Guomindang - Chinese Communist antagonism that was inherent in the revolution of 1949, and it was in 1967 that in the extremism of the Cultural Revolution China's populist movements spilled into Hong Kong. There was a riot that arose from home-grown social tension; that took place in 1966 but it was mild in comparison to the mass actions of 1925-26 or 1967. Significantly enough, no attack on the colonial presence, either in 1925-26 or in 1967, actually demanded its withdrawal. The demonstrations of strength were precisely that. The colonial regime was vulnerable because the Chineseness of its subjects provided a bond that would resonate with any nationalist appeal. Yet, when it came to the crunch, it was the Chinese government that decided if Hong Kong was to be part of China. And when it did in 1982, popular sentiments would rather colonialism stay.

It has often been said that the Hong Kong population of the 1950s and 1960s was a population of refugees. This generation had moved into Hong Kong from China in escape from war, political persecution, poverty and famine, and it had good reason to be apprehensive of the post-1949 Chinese government. The same should not be said of the generation that grew up in Hong Kong and reached adulthood in the 1970s and 1980s. This younger generation found China as it emerged from the Cultural Revolution and as Deng Xiaoping's modernization policies generated economic growth and investment opportunities on the mainland, especially across the Hong Kong border at the Shenzhen Special Economic Zone. It was this generation that had to relearn and rebuild its relationship with China as a nation. The return of Hong Kong to China spelt political uncertainty but the economic opportunities, and the very high salaries that Hong Kong was to pay its administrative and executive elite in the 1980s and 1990s, were too much to turn down. The solution that was found by a substantial portion of this generation was to approach the opportunity with a foreign passport tucked away in the belief that if the very worst came to the very worst, there might be an opportunity to emigrate.[16] Hong Kong had become a lifestyle that was not easily reproduced elsewhere. Some emigrated, but many more wanted the opportunity of emigration only as an insurance policy, for by choice, they would rather live in Hong Kong.

Immigrant Society and Its Lifestyle

To discuss Hong Kong's lifestyle, one can really never be far from the fact that throughout its history, Hong Kong was an immigrant society. Many Hong Kong people were first-generation settlers; but at various times in its history, such as the 1980s and 1990s, many more were into the second generation in Hong Kong. Because of the disruption of the Japanese occupation, only a minority had roots that went three or more generations back.

First-generation settlers remember the experience of settling down in a new and unfamiliar surrounding. A vivid illustration of the opportunities that open up with length of stay may be found in the report of the Hong Kong government's first Labour Officer, H.R. Butters, which appeared in 1939. Possibly frustrated by the lack of opportunities to come into direct personal contact with Hong Kong's workers as people, it seems that Butters went into the street and interviewed workers whom he came across. A man who had come to Hong Kong at age 16 had after nine years' stay become a joiner at the Taikoo Dockyard. He also rented a flat where he lived with a wife and a son, and he sub-let two rooms to tenants. Another man, 'found buying cigarettes from a stall in Hing Lung Street after carrying vegetables', had stayed in Hong Kong for only a year and a half, worked as a coolie, lived in a cockloft which he shared with two other men, kept his wife back in the village and regularly sent her half his income.[17] Such vivid descriptions of the lives of working men in the 1930s are rare in Hong Kong records. They show that the extra resources that the longer-term resident could muster made the difference between maintaining a family in Hong Kong and living apart from the family.

It goes without saying that wealth and income made a great deal of difference to lifestyle. Nevertheless, despite the difference in material comfort, the sense of precarious achievement pervaded the mentality of the first-generation migrant. One sees it in the lifestyle of these working men and women as in the war diary of the unknown shop-owner who in the midst of the fighting over Hong Kong Island in 1941 felt most saddened by the thought that his life-time savings would, in a literal sense, go up in flames.[18] But one sees it also in the Shanghainese industrialists starting out afresh in Hong Kong in the 1950s, who like the self-made men who had succeeded before them, who drew upon for support the ideology of self-help and in a very conscious way practised the Hong Kong ethos of keeping clear of issues that might seem political.[19] It is possible that the roots for this tendency of the first-generation settler to look inwards for the resources that might change his economic and social status were part of traditional Chinese culture, as the Chinese imperial state (but not the post-1911 Chinese nation) had long advocated personal introspection and family control as the cornerstones of its social policies. However, the inward-looking character of the first-generation resident in Hong Kong contrasts sharply with his agility in seeking out opportunities outside the family. The much vaunted Chinese dependence on the family in the social science literature is probably no more than a short-hand for the discrepancy between the traditional ideology which encourages the family to withdraw from the state, and the nationalist ideology of the Chinese nation which wants to draw the family in.

It makes sense, therefore, to speak in terms of a family strategy, in those Hong Kong families that, as anthropologist Janet Salaff found out in the 1970s, would have a daughter start early in her factory work career so that her income might supplement family resources to support a son through education.[20] The description agrees with the findings of economist H.A. Turner in the same period that Hong Kong workers had only limited aspirations for themselves but they wanted their sons to do very much better, by which they meant that they should qualify for professional or managerial jobs.[21] It also agrees with the conclusion that sociologist Thomas W.P. Wong, arrived at by re-examining the survey findings of the 1970s and 1980s, that while Hong Kong people believed in the openness of and the opportunities available in Hong Kong society, they also felt pessimistic and powerless in relation to their work.[22]

No-one would dispute that Hong Kong had made great material progress in the decades from the 1930s to 1990s. In no other area would progress be as evident as in housing. One needs only compare reports on housing conditions of the poor in the 1950s with Osbert Chadwick's report in 1882 to see how a rapid increase in population without adequate sanitation enforcement could create slums. The suggestion that government should concern itself with the provision of housing for the poor was made in the Housing Report of 1935; it developed into enforceable policy in the 1950s in spite of objections from the local Chinese leadership, and it was pushed to its extreme by an energetic governor in the 1970s.[23] The net result was that 40 percent of Hong Kong's population by 1980 lived in some form of public housing. But the aspiration to upward mobility, and the actual opportunities available, meant that the public housing population was never really cut off from the rest of society. Entry into public housing, for the majority, was entry into the dream of upward mobility.

Given the aspiration and the mobility, should one speak of the working class in Hong Kong? Was the Hong Kong population more aptly described as a pool of refugees, coming from varied backgrounds but all being caught up in the upward ladder afforded by economic growth where only the handicapped and the aged found little room to stand? Surely, this was not a society that cherished equality and just as surely, some outsiders, such as Filipino domestics and Vietnamese refugees (renamed 'migrants' because many were said to have left Vietnam for economic and not political reasons), were not to advance beyond the lowest rung.[24]

Hong Kong society produces no diplomat, no military general, no international civil servant, no ideology and therefore no ideologue. That is as it should be for being a colony. Successful Hong Kong people aspire to be what they would be best at, the mercantile princes of the twentieth-century international scene. Those

Hong Kong people who are not successful are contented with a low-key existence. But that is not unique to Hong Kong's history. Being low-key has been the style of the common man (and woman) of all ages. Shred off its colonial past, Hong Kong will be a city, where surely people mix only anonymously among the crowds.

The Selection of Documents

A social history of Hong Kong has to be an account of the common people as much as the elite. But, of course, the elite is everywhere more evident in the historical sources. I try to strike a balance in this compilation, and it has not always been easy. In bringing to the fore the historical experience of what I think would have been the majority of Hong Kong people, I have probably not given enough weight to the minority. Ethnicity in Hong Kong will eventually have to be a subject of research in its own right, so that the experience of the European, Indian, Filipino, Chaozhou, Shanghainese communities may be recorded. I have also probably not given enough weight to the changing conditions of work, a complex subject because the term 'work' itself is value-loaded and any discussion will have to bring into the concept the difference between whether the worker is paid or unpaid, whether work is conducted legally or illegally, and whether indeed, the nature of the work is such that it is 'work'. Subsequent volumes in this series may be able to remedy some of these shortcomings, but they should be borne in mind by anyone who searches in this volume for a view that even remotely resembles a complete social history. Ultimately, this volume represents the bias of an age: a concern for economic success, social mobility and integration. Rapid movement of population into and out of Hong Kong keeps alive the image of Hong Kong as a success story, but one has to be constantly reminded that the same image leaves out much of consequence in the lives of common people.

In this volume, beyond the luxury of this 'Introduction', the compiler tries to keep his own voice to the minimum. The documents selected will be read if they are found engaging. Where he interrupts the flow of the sources, usually by way of introduction or explanation, his comments are either consigned to the footnotes or indicated by a vertical line in the left-hand margin. No compilation of sources can be free of the compiler's biases; the compiler of this volume will be happy enough if, despite his own biases, the voices of Hong Kong people are heard through this volume.

---

[1] Document VII.d2 below.
[2] It would, however, be fair to say that government policies in the 1970s led up to the White Paper on District Administration in 1981, although the reforms proposed therein took quite a different turn when by 1982 the Sino-British negotiation on Hong Kong's future became the driving force in the evolution of electoral politics. On the White Paper, see Volume 1, Document V.c7.

3   Correspondence Relating to the Proposed Appointment of a Chinese Consul at Hong Kong, 1908, p. 15.
4   Volume 1, Document II.b1-4, V.a3.
5   Document II.c1 below.
6   Volume 1, Document V.a4.
7   Volume 1, Document II.d2.
8   Document VII.b2 below.
9   See in particular Volume 1, pp. 72-81.
10 Document III.8 below.
11 Document II.c3 below.
12 Document II.b1 below.
13 Document IV.c1 below.
14 Document VIII.d1 below, see also Document VII.f1.
15 See Documents II.c2, IV.b1, IV.b2, VII.a1 and VII.a2 below for these incidents.
16 Documents VIII.c1 and VIII.c2 below.
17 Document IV.d2 below.
18 Document V.a below.
19 Document VI.d below.
20 Document VII.e2 below.
21 Document VII.e1 below.
22 Document VIII.e below.
23 Documents IV.d6, VIb2 and VI.b3, and VII.d1 below.
24 Documents VIII.b4-6 below.

CHAPTER ONE

EARLY SETTLEMENT

It is often said that Hong Kong was a fishing village before the British arrived on the island in 1841. The description raises the image of fishing boats and stakenets along the waterfront, ramshackle houses beyond the reach of high tide, fish — dead, rotting, salted — and shrimp and seaweed being dried on the beach, and men, women and children, many living on rather than off the boats often side by side with their cooped chickens in their holds. There must have been such villages on the island, for it is known that they existed in many inlets on the outlying islands of the Hong Kong region, such as Tai O, Cheung Chau, Leung Shuen Wan, or Kat O. But settlements of Chinese people on Hong Kong Island were more than fishing villages. There was farmland, even by seaside villages such as Chek Chu (later Stanley) and Shek Pai (Aberdeen). Some of the villages were located inland, at Wongneichong (Happy Valley) and Pokfulam. Farming congers up a different image of the village: the seasonal rhythm of crop growing, land rights and taxes, village alliances for the safeguard of water, access, firewood, grave sites. Into this setting came the Westerners. They were not new to the China scene, having withdrawn to this forlorn island from the hustle and bustle of Guangzhou where the foreign 'factories' had been established. There in Guangzhou they had mixed in the company, not of the officials, but of the 'Hong' merchants, who were among the wealthiest people in the whole of the Chinese empire. Having been wined and dined in the fine private gardens of Guangzhou, they had come upon Hong Kong with the firm conviction that little culture was to be found among its rustic population. The colony was to grow in isolation from this unrecognizable community, the native Chinese population to come attached to the foreign establishment as hangers-on, along with many others soon to follow from across the harbour on the mainland. This sense of disdainful disregard of the Chinese community was to continue until some among the Chinese new-comers proved that in the realm of business, they were at least the foreigner's equal.

a. Villagers and Immigrants

By the nineteenth century, land rights tied many out-of-the-way communities to the Chinese imperial administration. But the imperial administration had worked only because powerful families might, working through it, vie for influence and exchange compliance for tax privileges. The British entry onto the scene upset long-established patterns of power relationships, to the detriment of the land-holder who had claimed ownership on the strength of registration at the county government, and to the benefit, perhaps, of the tenant who found himself transformed into the resident owner of land he had tilled. Understandably, the original land-holders protested. Had the observer been present in the preparation of the following document submitted to the county magistrate in 1844, he might have heard the original owner of the farmland at Wongneichong Village exclaiming, 'My land', as he made his claim.

DOCUMENT I.a1: My land, 1842 (source: *Guangxu ershi nian chongchao Daoguang ershi er nian buzheng liangdao Guangfu Xin'an chenggao zhaolu*, (A record of the petition submitted to Provincial Administration Commissioner and the Grain Intendant from Xin'an county in Guangzhou prefecture in the 22nd year of Daoguang, recopied in the 20th year of Guangxu), photocopy of manuscript included in *The Historical Literature of the New Territories: Kam Tin*, vol. 1, deposited at Hong Kong University Library)

A petition from Military Student Tang Chi-cheung and others begging, on the grounds of evidence here presented, for the grace of a memorandum directed to the English officer Pei Shun:

Your students and others inherited from their ancestor Tang Tin-luk land to which they had by petition moved upon return from the evacuation of Kangxi Year 10 [1671]* by the local place names of Fuk Tam, Wang Lek, Yim Tin, Tai Lo Ha, Lok Tz Lung etc., for which a tax on 368.75925 *mu* has been registered, land to which they had by petition moved upon return from the evacuation of Kangxi Year 23 [1684] known by the local place names Tai Tam, Wang Lek, Heung Kong, Tai Lo Ha, Lok Tz Lung etc. for which a tax on 332.16 *mu* has been registered, and land to which they had by petition of Tang Wing-kui** moved upon return from the evacuation of Kangxi Year

---

* In the 1660s, while the regime of Zheng Chenggong continued to hold out in Taiwan, the imperial government evacuated the entire coastal region in south China including Hong Kong Island. The local population was allowed to returned when the command was rescinded in 1671.
** Tang Wing-kui, literally 'Permanently occupied by the Tang surname' was obviously a fictitious name. The use of such names in the registration of lineage properties, however, was not uncommon in the Qing dynasty.

30 [1691] known by the local place names Kong Ts Leng, Wang Leng, Tsung Wo Kong etc. for which a tax on 102.7 *mu* has been registered. The total amount of land registered for tax is 803.61925 *mu*, and evidence for this may be found in stamped registers deposited at the county. The tax is registered under the name of household head Tang Tin-luk of the sixth *du* seventh *tu*. In addition, [they held land] purchased by Tang Chun-fui in Kangxi 59 [1720] from Hoh Ting-fong of Dongguan [county] located in Xin'an county at the local place name Wong Nai Chung amounting to third-class tax on 33 *mu*, [land] bought in Qianlong 26 [1764] located in Xin'an at local place names Wong Nai Chung, Kwan Tai Lo, Sheung To, Tai Shek Ha, Tai Hang, Ham Wai, amounting to third-class tax 62 *mu*, [land] bought in Qianlong 7 [1742] located at Wong Nai Chung and other places amounting to 72 *mu*, [land] bought in Qianlong 27 [1762] by Tang Tsit Yat from Hoh Chiu-ping located in Xin'an at local place names Wong Nai Chung, Wat Shek Hang, Wai Kon Tang, Kwai Tau Shek, Wong Tuk Shek, Yeung Mui Hang and other places amounting to third-class tax 22 *mu*, coming to a total of a tax of 189 *mu*. Evidence for these holdings may be found in volumes of stamped deeds. All tax is payable under the name of Tang Chi-fu of Dongguan county 2nd *du* 18th *tu* last *jia* and Tang Yuan-tsun of 3rd *du* 50th *tu* last *jia*. All this tax land was leased to tenants for rent, and peace had endured for many years. Now it has been found that these tax-registered properties had been used for building houses, leading to the consequence that rent might not be collected and taxes not paid. This is an unbearable situation. Under the force of circumstances, this full account is hereby reported in petition, accompanied by three stamped deeds that are attached. We humbly beseech the kind magistrate to take pity on us, to grant a document that may be sent to the English official in evidence, so that the land holdings detailed here may be returned for rent to be collected and taxes paid. Your honour's great virtue will be deeply felt. A petition is made hereby for this purpose.

Daoguang 24th year, tenth month eighteenth day [27 November 1844]

The founding of the British colony on the northern shore of Hong Kong Island (facing the promontory of Kowloon) soon attracted Chinese immigrants from China. The British colonial government of Hong Kong had proclaimed from its first arrival that the Chinese would be allowed to maintain their own laws and customs, and in the first two decades of Hong Kong's history, the proclamation served to maintain separate communities for the British and for the Chinese. But it was not only custom that divided the two communities: in those early days, the British were disappointed with the Chinese population that they found attached to their colony. Aside from the missionary interest to convert them, the practical need to hire their labour as builders, porters and servants, there was little interest in the lives and livelihood of the Chinese. Like the Chinese officials of the county of Xin'an, of which Hong Kong Island until 1842 had been a part, British colonial officials were superior to the people they governed. It was easy in these circumstances for such words as 'pirates' and 'secret societies' to be applied loosely to the local population. No doubt, there were pirates, but such words came to be used indiscriminately for Chinese voluntary associations as well.

DOCUMENT I.a2: Kwok Ah-man and Chow Chau-chi, pirates, 1848 (source: *Zhong-Ying waijiao wenjian chaoben* (manuscript copy of Sino-British diplomatic documents), held in Cambridge University Library)

The testimony of Kwok Ah-man: I am also known by the name Mow Kam, and the nickname Blind Man. I am a person from Pingshan Village in Panyu county, aged 51 *sui*. My parents have both passed away and I have no brothers. My wife, nee Leung, has given birth to one son. I am employed to operate salt-fish boats. I am now a member of the Alliance Righteous Hall at the peak of Taipingshan.

The testimony of Chow Chau-chi: I am a Tanka from New Market, Chencun, Shunde county, aged 31 *sui*. My parents are both dead. I have no brothers. My wife nee Cheung has no children. I am employed to operate sailing boats. I am now a member of the Alliance Righteous Hall at the peak of Taipingshan.

They both alleged that on the thirteenth day of the eleventh month in the year Daoguang 26, Wong Ah-dak, alias Chan Ah-dak, who was known to them but who had not yet been arrested, told Kwok Ah-man that he worked on an Englishman's schooner lighter as compradore and cook. He said that opium and private goods might be found on board and that it was going with another English lighter carrying opium to sell on the coast of Xiamen in Fujian Province. I, Kwok Ah-man thought of gathering a gang of men to loot them and take a part of the spoils. Wong Ah-dak agreed that he would return to the ship to provide the inside lead. Kwok Ah-man then asked me, Chow Chau-chi, and . . . altogether over twenty people, to come prepared with guns and food, to go by Leung Yik-foon's big sailing junk . . .

The trial testimony of bandit Kwok Ah-man has provided the following list of lodges (*tang*) in the area of Taipingshan in Hong Kong:

The Luen I Tong set up by Blind Head, who has not yet been arrested;
The Uet Loi Tong set up by Bald-head Chan who has been arrested;
The Tin I Tong set up by Lee Hung I who has been arrested;

. . .

The botanist, Robert Fortune, who stayed in Hong Kong in the mid-1840s, left a grim view of the colony:

DOCUMENT I.a3: The population of Victoria (source: Robert Fortune, *Three Years' Wanderings in the Northern Provinces of China, including a Visit to the Tea, Silk, and Cotton Countries*, London: John Murray, 1847, pp. 27-29)

The native population in Victoria, consist of shopkeepers, tradesmen, servants, boat-people, and coolies, and altogether form a most motley group. Unfortunately there is no inducement for the respectable Chinese merchant to take up his quarters there, and until that takes place, we shall always have the worst set of people in the country. The town swarms with thieves and robbers, who are only kept under by the strong armed police lately established. Previous to this, scarcely a dark night passed without some one having his house broken into by an armed band, and all that was valuable being carried off or destroyed. The audacious rascals did not except the Governor even, for one night Government House was robbed; and another time they actually stole the arms of the sentries. These armed bands, sometimes a hundred strong, disappeared, as they came, in a most marvellous manner, and no one seemed to know whence they came or whither they went. Such attacks are fortunately now of rare occurrence. In all my wanderings on the island, and also on the mainland hereabouts, I found the inhabitants harmless and civil. I have visited their glens and their mountains, their villages and small towns, and from all the intercourse I have had with them, I am bound to give them this character. But perhaps the secret of all was, that I had nothing for them to take, for I was always most careful not to have any thing valuable about me, and my clothes, after scrambling amongst the rocks and brushwood, were not very tempting even to a Chinaman.

Since the island of Hong Kong has been ceded to England, the foreign population in it has been much changed. In former days there were only a few mercantile establishments, all known to each other, and generally most upright and honourable men. Now people from all countries, from England to Sydney, flock to the Celestial country, and form a very motley group.

Viewed as a place of trade, I fear Hong Kong will be a failure. The great export and import trade of southern China must necessarily be carried on at Canton, as heretofore, there being at present, at least, no inducement to bring that trade to Hong Kong. It will, nevertheless, be a place of great importance to many of the merchants, more particularly to those engaged in the opium trade; and will, in fact, be the headquarters of all houses who have business on the coast, from the facilities of gaining early information regarding the state of the English and Indian markets, now that steam communication has been established between this country and the south of China. Moreover, with all its faults, its importance may yet be acknowledged in the event of another war. Our countrymen cannot have so entirely forgotten the kind of protection which used to be afforded them by the Portuguese at Macao, as to make them wish to be put in the same circumstances again; and it is of no little importance to know that their lives and property are safe under the British flag.

b.   Respectability

In its early days, respectable society on Hong Kong Island was restricted to the Western enclave. Chinese people gained entry into it only very gradually. Colonial society was made up of the administration, the business community and the church, all with their hangers-on, English, Scottish, Irish, American, European, Indian, and Parsee. But nineteenth-century British society, being itself strongly status-oriented, would have carved the cosmopolitan community in Hong Kong into minute sections on a social hierarchy. The report of the Anglican Bishop of Hong Kong to the Christian Missionary Society in London in 1864 on the occasion of the ordination of the first Chinese deacon allows a glimpse of what must have been a rather open-minded view of social mingling.

DOCUMENT I.b1: The Church, Western and Chinese (source: George B. Endacott and Dorothy E. She, *The Diocese of Victoria, Hong Kong, A Hundred Years of Church History, 1849-1949*, Hong Kong: Kelly & Walsh, 1949, pp. 32-33)

I write with much satisfaction and thankfulness to inform you that I have now admitted your excellent native catechist Lo Sam Yuen to deacon's orders. More than 13 years intimate knowledge of his character and usefulness here, and at the Australian goldfields in Melbourne diocese, seemed to me fully to justify my course in admitting him to the ministry of our church.

The ordination took place in our Cathedral last week, viz. on Monday, December 21st amid a large concourse of Chinese worshippers, filling a considerable space in the nave of our beautiful structure, and joining aloud in the responses of the liturgy. About 200 Chinese were present, representing various classes among the more influential portion of the native population of the Colony, together with about forty English residents; among whom I noticed with much pleasure the ladies of His Excellency the Acting Governor, the Attorney General, and other leading persons in the British community. The pupils of St. Paul's College and the girls in our newly established Diocesan Female School, together with several native interpreters and writers in the public offices, and formerly inmates of our college, gave to our little assemblage a more than ordinary personal interest in my mind.

On Christmas Day I preached a sermon to the English congregation in the Cathedral, on behalf of the Church Missionary Society's local mission at Hongkong and more especially for the support of the recently-ordained Minister. An offertory collection was made, and nearly 400 dollars (equivalent to £90 sterling) were collected, including a few donations sent afterwards.

Lo Sam Yuen was present with the other officiating clergymen in his surplice, and assisted in administering the elements in their own language to the Chinese portion of the communicants. Out of seventy-five exactly one-third of the whole number of communicants in the Cathedral on Christmas Day, were Chinese converts.

Thus in the twentieth year of my connection with Missionary labour in this land, and having been often deeply humbled before God under a sense of my unprofitableness, I am in mercy permitted to see some streaks of hope lighting up the dark horizon.

Two native deacons, ordained by me at Shanghai and Hongkong, and sixty Chinese converts confirmed at Hongkong, Shanghai and Ningpo, have been among the happy events which I am privileged to associate with the year just closed, 1863. 'To God be all the glory'.

One of Hong Kong's earliest historians, E.J. Eitel, left an impression of the Western community in his days. Sir John Pope Hennessy, whose name appears in the following passage, was Governor of Hong Kong from 1877 to 1882.

DOCUMENT I.b2: An impression of the Western community, circa 1880s (source: E.J. Eitel, *Europe in China*, London: Luzac & Co., Hong Kong: Kelly and Walsh, 1895; pp. 563-564)

Such was the mutual incompatibility of temperament, views and ways, between Sir John and the European community, that he deliberately assumed a position of entire isolation, whilst the European community felt, year by year, less and less disposed to disturb his insularity. Apart from Sir John's general policy, there were special causes which irritated the community. Such were, for instance, his interference (October 24, 1879, and February 5, 1881) with the rules of admission to the City Hall Museum, his attempt to confiscate the steam-tug *Fame* (October 28, 1879), and his prohibition of the sale of refreshments at the City Hall Theatre (February 25, 1880). As regards amusements, however, the community was, during this period, well provided for. In addition to the established periodical treats provided by the Amateur Dramatic Corps, the Choral Society, the Horticultural Society, the Victoria Recreation and Regatta Clubs, the Liedertafel of the Club Germania, and the Race Club, this period is distinguished by some specially successful celebrations, among which mention is due to St. Patrick's festival (March 17, 1879), the centenary of the birth of the Irish poet Tom Moore (May 28, 1879), the Masonic Ball of 15th January, 1880, the anniversary of Washington's birthday (February 23, 1880), and the tercentenary of Camoens (June 10, 1880). As to other social events those deserving mention are the semi-extinction of the Humane Society (May 13, 1878), the formation of St. John's Lodge under the Scottish Constitution (November 30, 1878), a banquet and presentation of an address in honour of Professor Nordenskjold (November 3, 1879), the starting of jinrikshas in the Colony (April 22, 1880), the establishment of a Polo Club (April 27, 1880), the presentation of an address and testimonial to the Hon. W. Keswick (May 14, 1881), the arrest of Messrs. Rapp and Schmidt by a Customs cruiser while on a shooting expedition (November 26, 1881), and the appointment of Mr. C.P. Chater as Masonic District Grand Master of South China (February 2, 1882).

The charity of the Hong Kong community was, during this period, called forth and exercised to an extraordinary degree. To the relief of the famine in North China the Hong Kong community contributed (from April, 1877, until August, 1878,) an aggregate sum of $132,000. Floods in Canton necessitated (in May, 1877) a separate appeal which in a day or two produced $5,000. The Freemasons raised separately funds (October, 1877) for the relief of sufferers from famine in India, and in January, 1878, a subscription was started for the sufferers from the *Yesso* explosion, while Messrs. Douglas Lapraik & Co. headed the list with a subscription of $10,000. An Amateur Concert was given (December 12, 1878) on behalf of sufferers by the failure of the City of

Glasgow Bank. An Irish Famine Relief Committee was started (March 8, 1880) and collected $36,000. The Hon. E.R. Belilios having (October 15, 1878) placed in the Governor's hands the sum of £1,000 for the erection of a statue of Lord Beanconsfield, used this sum, when Disraeli deprecated the honour, to establish a Medical Scholarship Fund (October 7, 1879), subsequently changed (November 29, 1883) into the Belilios Scholarship Fund, and gave to a row of houses opposite the City Hall, which he erected at the time, the name Beaconsfield Arcade. A Medical Mission Committee (J.C. Edge, Dr. Young, and H.W. Davis), having, since October 1871, established a public dispensary in Taipingshan, made (January 13, 1872) an appeal to the community and commenced taking steps which ultimately resulted in the establishment of Alice Memorial Hospital.

c. **Residential Segregation**

The impetus for change came from trade. Nothing speaks louder of this development than Hong Kong's historical statistics. In 1881, the Governor of Hong Kong, Sir John Pope Hennessy (Governor 1877-1882), said as much in a speech that acknowledged the increasing contribution to Hong Kong that came from the Chinese people resident there. Yet one detects that the matter-of-fact approach in the speech hides the opposition that the Governor faced in the support he gave to recognizing the stake of the Chinese community in Hong Kong. He reminded his listeners that barely a generation before, it was a debatable question as to whether the Chinese should be allowed to purchase land from the Hong Kong Government. And he took heart in the ability of the Chinese community to look after itself, citing the Surgeon General's observations on vaccination among the Chinese in justification. No-one should accuse Sir John Pope Hennessy of taking a less than sympathetic attitude towards the Chinese people in Hong Kong, but the sympathy had been needed because the Hong Kong of the 1880s was as yet a racially segregated community.

One only has to look at the geographic distribution of the Chinese and Western houses to see that the two communities barely mixed and even the casual observer might have noticed that the residential segregation between the two was founded not only on race, but also on class. The standards of respectability governed where one lived as much as any other aspect of how one might behave: the majority of the Chinese people in Hong Kong lived in what better-off Westerners would have thought of as congested and unhygienic dwellings, but Chinese of 'the better classes' could have owned houses where the Westerners lived. The image of the Chinese encroaching upon areas where Westerners had built their houses led to the legal provision for residential segregation.

DOCUMENT I.c1: An increased Chinese community of great importance to the commercial interests of England 1881 (source: Encl. 2 in No. 42, Legslative Council, Hong Kong, Statement of His Excellency Governor Sir John Pope Hennessy, K.C.M.G., on the Census Returns and the Progress of the Colony, House of Commons Papers 1881, Vol. LXV, serial no. 42, Public Record Office, London)

I am placing upon the table a return which has been prepared in the Survey Department in consequence of a minute of mine, in which I directed attention to the publication in the 'Daily Press' of the 11th May 1881, of a statement of transactions in landed property in Hong Kong, and called upon the proper officers to have that return checked and verified. Accordingly, that return, which, no doubt you have all seen, was transmitted to the Acting Surveyor General. He has now furnished us with an authentic statement of the transactions, from the Land Office books, that have taken place in the transfer and sale of property from the 1st of January last year to the 11th of May this year. To be brief, I think, on the whole, he corroborates what appeared in the 'Daily Press,' and the summary he gives at the end is to this effect. Total value of properties bought by Chinese from foreigners, 1,710,036 dollars; total value of properties bought by Chinese from the Government, 17,705 dollars; total value of properties bought by foreigners from foreigners, 216,750 dollars; total value of properties bought by foreigners from the Government, 5,060 dollars; total value of properties bought by foreigners from Chinese, 16,450 dollars.

Now, this large item of 1,710,000 dollars on the transfer of property almost entirely for commercial purposes, to the Chinese community since January last year, is undoubtedly an event of great importance. Is it speculative, or is it justified by the returns I am now laying on the table? In the first place what do we learn from the census returns of the Registrar General? We find that the population has risen from 139,144 in 1876 to 160,402 in 1881, showing, in four years and four months, an increase of 21,258, and of this increase the Chinese population account for 20,532. The Registrar General adds, that the European and American community is larger by 273; that the increase is among the British, Portuguese, Germans, and Italians, and is that of women and children; that the male adult population of Europeans and Americans has decreased. This fact is of interest, because, whilst taking the male adult British subjects from the United Kingdom there has been a decrease from 342 to 336, there has been an increase in the number of women and of boys and girls. So, too, with the Portuguese; there is a falling off from 418 adult males in 1876 to 384 at present, but an increase in the women and children. So, too, with the Germans; there is a falling off in the adult German population, and in the American population, and in the French population, but in each case there is an increase in the number of women and children. This fact, I say, is of interest, because the tropical Colony where European children flourish cannot be very unhealthy. The vitality of a foreign child is a delicate test of climate, and I believe we can point to this particular item in the census returns affording some indication that Hong Kong is growing more healthy. And, now, proceeding to the question of the 20,000 additional Chinese, we have to consider this:- Has the increase in the various mercantile occupations of the Chinese been such as to justify the remarkable transfer of landed property I have referred to? The census returns furnish us with an opportunity of testing how far in the harbour of Victoria itself the means we have of commercial movement — that is, the transference of goods from steamer to steamer, from steamer to shore, and *vice versa* — how far that has been facilitated since the year 1876. From the returns, I find that the movement is conducted by steam launches, cargo boats, and sampans. The steam launches have increased from eight in 1876 to 37 in 1881, the cargo boats from 494 to 656, and the sampans from 1,357 to 2,088. So far for the machinery that we have in our harbour for conducting the commercial movement of the Colony, it has substantially increased. The returns I am laying before you are identical in form with the returns prepared in the time of Sir Arthur Kennedy,* and probably his predecessors, and amongst these returns there is one which answers the question I have been asking, and that is a return of the occupations of the Chinese adult male inhabitants of the Colony. On analysing that return, I find that the following are the changes that have taken place since the last census with respect to Chinese merchants and other Chinese directly concerned in the trade and commerce of the Colony.

The Chinese trading hongs, that is, the Nampak hongs and other wealthy merchants who now send the manufactures of England into China, have increased form 215 to 395. Chinese traders have increased from 287 to 2,377; Chinese brokers, from 142 to 455. Taking the Chinese engaged in dealing in money; the shroffs have increased form 40 to 208; the teachers of shroffing have increased from 9 to 14; the bullion dealers, who do not appear in any former census, are now returned at 34; the money changers, 111 in 1876, still remain at 111, but in 1876 there were no Chinese bankers returned, and now we have in this census 55 Chinese bankers. The piece-goods dealers have increased form 78 in 1876 to 109, and cotton and yarn dealers from 38 to 58. This is of interest, not merely to Manchester, Bradford, or Leeds; these Chinese merchants of Hong Kong are now facilitating an Indian trade with China, healthier, and with a safer future, than the trade in that drug which a few years ago was the only considerable commercial link between British India and China. Since 1877 the quantity of Bombay yarn received in Hong Kong has steadily risen from 21,000 bales to 61,000. The increase in the value of this trade from 1,706,913 dollars in 1877 to 5,251,246 dollars in 1880, has been coincident with an increase in our imports of raw cotton from Bengal and Rangoon from 33,000 bales in 1877 to 86,000 in 1880. Our opium trade shows no such tendency to increase. In 1880, we imported 87,747 chests, as against 88,428 in 1877. Mr. F.D. Sassoon tells me that the value of our total trade with India last year was 67,772,937 dollars, the value of the opium being 58,248,235 dollars. Though the trade in other goods than opium is but one-sixth of the total Indian trade, yet it is so rapidly developing that I look forward with confidence to the time when it will outstrip, and, perhaps, enable the Indian Government to curtail, the trade in

---

* Hennessy's predecessor, Governor of Hong Kong 1872-1877.

opium. Tea merchants have increased from 26 to 51, rice dealers from 95 to 128, coal dealers from 16 to 20, fire-arms dealers from 15 to 20, timber dealers from 15 to 107, drapers from 101 to 156, and foreign goods dealers from 167 to 191. Compradores have increased from 77 to 95, ship compradores from 67 to 113, and ship charterers from 7 to 41. Looking to the increase I have pointed out in the ordinary machinery for commercial movement in the harbour, to this remarkable increase of the mercantile community, and to the well-known magnitude of the mercantile transactions of our Chinese merchants, it seems clear that this large expenditure since January 1880, of 1,710,000 dollars by Chinese for commercial property was a necessary expenditure.

There is another question that we may fairly ask. It has often been said, and there is hardly a directory or guide relating to Hong Kong in which you do not see it recorded, that Hong Kong has no local manufactures whatever. Is that true? Well, on turning to the census returns, I find many local Chinese manufacturers in this Colony. Bamboo workers have increased from 93 in 1876 to 121 in 1881; boat-builders from 48 to 110; carvers from 59 to 70; cigar makers from 21 to 31; engineers from 10 to 121; and gold beaters from 41 to 60. Glass manufacturers appear for the first time; there are now 16 in the Colony, and I believe at this moment the glass manufactory to the west of the town is capable of turning out such glass as some of the European storekeepers here are themselves prepared to sell; and when a service of glass may get injured, they can now send to our local glass manufactory and get tumblers to replace those broken in the set. I find image makers have increased from 10 to 15, lantern makers from 50 to 63, leather box makers from 39 to 53, lemonade and sodawater makers from 28 to 30. Watch manufacturers did not appear in the former census; they now number 13. Oar makers have increased from 30 to 43. Opium dealers have declined from 108 to 103, but that is not coincident with any decline in the revenue the Government of Hong Kong derives from the monopoly of prepared opium, which was 132,000 dollars in 1877, but was sold in 1879 for 205,000 dollars a year. Paper box makers have declined from 21 to 10, and rattan workers from 596 to 448. Of rifle makers we have five in the Colony. Sail and rope makers have increased from 100 to 141, and sandal-wood dealers and workers, from 74 to 76. Workers in sapanwood have declined from 96 to 20, and though there is apparently a decline in the number of sauce manufacturers from 49 to 41, there has been an increase in the quantity of sauce manufactured. I may mention that a short time before the late Mr. Kwok Acheong died, I went with him and two or three other Chinese gentlemen interested in the factory at Yau-ma-ti, to examine the factory, which was in a more or less rude state, the buildings not being then completed. I was glad to see what they were doing. In addition to making soy, they made ketchup for the European market, and they had also a manufactory for preserving fruits. Now, the ketchup is sent in hundreds of barrels every year direct from Hong Kong to a well-known house in London — that well-known provision merchant whose good things most of us have, from time to time, enjoyed. He sends out thousands of little bottles of his ketchup to Chinese as well as to European storekeepers here, so that, in short, the ketchup we consume as English ketchup is manufactured by Chinese in Hong Kong, sent to England, and this famous provision merchant in England returns it to us for retail. I am bound to add, that the latest advices are that the peculiar article which is produced by the Chinese manufacturer at Yau-ma-ti was regarded at the recent sales in London as the best in the market, and our little local manufactory is very successful. I find immediately following this we come to the soap manufacturers; they do not appear in the last census, and they are now only seven in number. There also appears, for the first time, one spectacle-maker. We have Chinese sugar refiners; they have declined from 25 to 15, and tanners form seven to one. Tobacco manufacturers have increased from 44 to 96. Tooth-powder makers appear also for the fist time; they number 57. Umbrella-makers have increased from 97 to 169, vermilion manufacturers and dealers from 111 to 123, and weavers, who appear for the first time in our census, number six. It is, therefore, clear that we have in this Colony numerous local manufactures which have every prospect of extending.

But apart from the question of such manufacturers, there are in this Colony, as you all know, various industries employing Chinese artisans. Carpenters have increased from 2,510 to 2,923, blacksmiths from 690 to 708, pewter-smiths from 60 to 173, tinsmiths from 88 to 172, and braziers from 488 to 864. Masons show a falling off from 845 to 542. Rice-pounders have increased from 954 to 1,083 and in stone-cutters there is a large increase — from 449 to 1,439. The number of tailors now in the Colony, who work with sewing machines mostly, amounts to 1,857. It is an interesting fact, that for these tailors drill is imported into the Colony from England; they make it up with their sewing machines, and the made clothes are then exported to New Zealand and Australia. In that way Chinese cheap labour, even without leaving the atmosphere of China, is, to a certain extent, successfully competing with Australian and English manufacturers of clothes.

There are certain special occupations of the Chinese which are worth noting, as they indicate the prosperity of the natives. We have the birds' nest sellers, who have increased from 12 to 35, the sharks' fins dealers, from 9 to 15, beancurd sellers, from 93 to 107, jadestone dealers, from 8 to 18; but cinnamon dealers have fallen from eight to seven. Sessamum oil dealers appear for the first time, and number five, and ginseng dealers also appear for the first time, and are four in number. Joss-paper sellers have increased from 30 to 47, joss-house keepers, from 17 to 41, and chair-coolies, from 859 to 980.

In addition to those who are concerned in our commerce and trades, there is a certain amount of professional life amongst the Chinese, as shown by the census returns. We had in 1876, 198 Chinese doctors; now we have 333. Well, the question has often been asked, whether Chinese doctors do much good, but I think we may, perhaps, rely upon the good sense of those who employ them and have confidence in their empirical knowledge and skill. But even the European community and the Government of the Colony owe a debt of gratitude to some of those Chinese doctors. Hong Kong is peculiarly situated with respect to the possibility of an influx of small-pox. Perhaps no other port in the world is more liable to a visitation from that disease, and yet, though occasionally I get a report from the Harbour Master of a case or two that may be brought here, it does not spread in the Colony. How does that come to pass? I was talking not long since to the Health Officer, Dr. Adams, and he tells me he has to examine the Chinese who emigrate, and he finds nearly all the young Chinese have three or four vaccination marks, or inoculation marks, upon the arms. He says he was often puzzled to know how this vaccination came to be apparently so perfect among the Chinese. Well, the fact is, that for some years past the doctors of the Tung-wa Hospital have vaccinated extensively, and some of them have been employed as travelling vaccinators, who go about this Colony, and who, since 1878, visit the mainland and vaccinate all through the neighbouring province of China. Thousands upon thousands have been vaccinated by them. The returns are printed in our annual Blue Books. Thousands upon thousands have been vaccinated during the last four years. But when I saw the annual returns sent in by the Colonial Surgeon not many weeks ago, I appended the following minute to that document: - 'I cannot find any return showing the number of vaccinations by the Medical Officers of the Colony. Ascertain how many persons have been vaccinated every year for the last four years by the Colonial Surgeon, the Health Officer, the Superintendent of the Civil Hospital, and the Deputy Superintendent.' This appears to have been sent to the Colonial Surgeon for a report. The report of the Colonial Surgeon was very brief: - 'No return has ever been kept.' Whereupon, my honourable friend on my left (the Acting Colonial Secretary) writes to the Colonial Surgeon asking him if he could from his memory, and approximately furnish the number he has himself vaccinated, and get the same information from the other Medical Officers of the Government. The reply of the Colonial Surgeon is:- 'I have the honour to inform you that 10 persons were vaccinated in the hospital by the Superintendent. I have not been able to obtain any more information from the Superintendent. The Acting Health Officer vaccinated his own child twice without success. I have performed 32 vaccinations on children, 15 unsuccessfully, and about as many more on adults.' And then he proceeds to state that he distributed lymph, which I send to him (it comes to me every mail in my Despatch bag from Downing Street), amongst his professional brethren in the Colony and at Canton. He adds, that in future he will take care that a record of the vaccinations by the Government officers is kept. It may, of course, be said that the Colonial Surgeon and the other officers of the Government were aware of the fact that this semi Administrative duty — in fact, a duty of no slight importance to the Government and the Colony — was actually being performed for them by the directors of the Tung-wa Hospital, and, therefore, they did not think it necessary to interfere with the Chinese doctors, who were vaccinating thousands of people, and doing it so well, and who have protected the Colony so thoroughly. Passing from the doctors, we come to the druggists, who have also increased from 164 to 243. I find, for the first time in the professional life of the Chinese in this Colony, that we have three dentists. About 18 months ago I visited one, not professionally, but for the purpose of seeing the instruments he used, and I then found he had the same apparatus we find in all dentists' establishments. In fact, he did work for the first-rate American dentists we have here, being fully capable of making or repairing sets of teeth. He was a gentleman of intelligence, and impressed me, I must say, as favourably as a dentist could. I also find Chinese architects for the first time, five in number. For the first time, we also have in the list one geomancer. I have not seen that gentleman, but I find in the list perhaps an antidote to the geomancer; for the first time we see in this list a Chinese barrister-at-law. I think we may all congratulate ourselves on his appearing not only in the census returns as a barrister, but as being also a member, by the Queen's favour, of the Legislature of the Colony. I find also on this list three newspaper editors, but there were three in 1876. They are not exactly the same three, because one, a gentleman who was enumerated in 1876, was a friend of mine, the editor of the 'Chinese Mail,' Mr. Chun Ayin, and I believe that newspaper editor is now receiving a salary of 1,200 *l.** per annum as an officer of the Chinese Government in Cuba, where I understand he is the Consul General. I don't know whether I am right in classing them amongst the professional portion of the Chinese community, but I find we have 84 fortune-tellers in the Colony, instead of 46 in 1876. The schoolmasters have increased from 114 to 171, and students from 341 to 2,562. These students are not to be confounded with school-boys, who are dealt with in anther part of the census. Most of these gentlemen who return themselves as students are, no doubt, young men, but some of them possibly are old men, who devote themselves to literary pursuits. Portrait painters have increased from 170 to 200, and photographers from 30 to 45. Story-tellers have decreased from five to one. Musicians, also, I am sorry to see, have fallen from 70 to 30. If it were not one of those statistical fallacies that sometimes occur, even in the best regulated Registrar General's Office, it would be a melancholy fact, that when our Chinese bankers and bullion dealers come upon the scene, the story-tellers and musicians seem to disappear. Perhaps great material prosperity is not without some drawbacks.

On the whole, it is manifest we have in this Colony an increased Chinese community of great importance to the commercial interests of England, and, therefore, we may at once answer the question as to this large dealing in land, and may admit it was a just and natural process, and that this transfer of property from European to Chinese was not of a merely speculative kind.

Now, does Hong Kong fulfil the object for which it was established? That I need hardly ask you, gentlemen, after the brief *resume* I have given you of our census returns. But it has sometimes been discussed what the object of this Colony is, and in my time I have heard it said that it is a military object, or a naval object, I have generally been of opinion myself it was commercial, but I find on referring to a Despatch of the Secretary of State to Sir John Davis,** where this question was raised, that there it is briefly and clearly laid down for what object this Colony was really established, Sir John Davis had to forward to Her Majesty's Government a memorial from the foreign merchants complaining of the taxation of Hong Kong. They represented that Hong Kong had been established, as they thought, for military objects in China, and on that account they begged the Imperial Government would undertake to pay for the cost of the

---

* *liang*, ie tael.
** Governor of Hong Kong, 1844-1846.

establishments, and that they themselves should be relieved from taxes. The Secretary of State who had to decide this question was a man of great ability. It was in the year 1846. He was then a young man, but he evidently gave due attention to the subject, and, having reviewed the whole question, he expresses his opinion that the occupation of Hong Kong was decided on solely and exclusively with a view to commercial interests; and, in a word, his Despatch said it was established in the interest of trade alone, and that the traders naturally should pay the expenses of the Colony. I find that this same Secretary of State had in a previous Despatch requested the Governor to have land sales in the town of Victoria at which none but Chinese could bid. Representations came from the Governor — either Sir Henry Pottinger, or Sir John Davis — that there was a certain class of Chinese who would be peculiarly suitable for commercial operations, but that, owing to land jobbers, they could not compete at the land auctions in Hong Kong, and therefore the Secretary of State took the rather strong course of saying there should be some land sales at which none but Chinese could bid. Well, he incurred a little local criticism for doing that, but when this Despatch of his was published laying down the purely commercial objects of Hong Kong, and stating that the Colony should pay for itself, the newspapers then printed here commented on it in these terms: 'The answer of Mr. Gladstone is universally regarded by everyone with whom we have conversed since it was published as sealing the fate of Hong Kong. We do not believe it will be met by any violent recrimination or outcry, but the disgust it has excited is such as will not be speedily eradicated. What little trade we ever possessed here has been all but extinguished.' Well, a generation has passed since that criticism was published in the Colony, but I am bound to say, every year since then has justified Mr. Gladstone's policy; and, at this moment, we are in a Colony whose commercial prosperity is perhaps unrivalled. Who now will venture to say that he was not right to encourage the Chinese to buy land and settle in Hong Kong? Who now will differ with Mr. Gladstone as to the true character and object of this Colony?

DOCUMENT I.c2: Hong Kong in 1882, a description (source: *Mr Chadwick's Report on the Sanitary Condition of Hong Kong*, November 1882, pp. 8-10, Colonial Office, *Eastern* No. 38, CO 882/4 Public Record Office, London)

The city of Victoria extends along the shore for a distance of about 3-3/4 miles running back inland for about half a mile. Viewed from the opposite shore of the Kowloon peninsula, on the extreme left or eastern extremity, a projecting promontory of reclaimed land would be seen, occupied by sugar works. To the westward of this the Wong-na-Chong valley enters the sea. At its mouth is one of the largest pieces of flat land in the island, which is occupied inland, by the racecourse, and harbourward by building lots, at present but partially built upon. Westward of this again, the foot of the hills re-approaches the shore. For a distance of about three quarters of a mile, or up to 1-1/2 miles from the eastern extremity, the harbour front is occupied by warehouses, with a few second-class Chinese dwellings. At this point the naval and military establishments commence, occupying about half a mile of the water frontage, the barracks being on the slopes of the hills in rear.

Next to this is the City Hall, behind which are the public gardens. For about half a mile westward of the City Hall, the water front is occupied by the stores and offices of the principal European mercantile houses. Behind this the town climbs the side of the hill, terrace above terrace, to a height of 400 feet and more. Here are the majority of European-dwellings and the Chinese houses of the better class.

A further length of half a mile is occupied, in front, by the principal Chinese warehouses, in rear is the densely packed Chinese quarter. This portion of about one mile west of the City Hall may be said to be the heart of the town. In front of it are anchored seagoing and river steamers of all sizes, sailing vessels and junks, whilst inshore, alongside the wharf, is a dense mass of boats and barges. The Praya here presents a scene of the greatest activity. To the west of this, again, the movement rapidly diminishes. Towards the western extremity, Slaughter-house or Belchers Point, Chinese warehouses line the shore, behind are dwellings, chiefly Chinese, but the whole has the appearance of a district but partially developed.

Slaughter-house Point may, for the present, be considered as the western extremity of the city. Beyond this is Belchers Bay, or Lap-sap-wan ('Rubbish Bay'); works of reclamation are actually in hand.

The streets running up the slopes of the hill, at right angles to the shore line, are far too steep for wheeled vehicles. In some cases, indeed they are formed into steps; carriages drawn by horses are virtually unused. For passenger traffic a large number of 'Jinrickshaws,' small carriages drawn by men, have been recently introduced, and ply for hire in the Queen's Road and Praya. Chairs carried by coolies are still, however, the usual means of locomotion. Burdens of all sizes and weights are carried by men.

The accompanying table (Table 1.1) derived from the census returns of 1881, gives an abstract of the statistics of the City of Victoria. The village and rural population is not included. Asiatics are notably unwilling to give any return of their true numbers, and therefore it is impossible to say how far these figures are to be relied on. They are certainly under, not over, the true numbers.

The Chinese form by far the majority of the population, and of them the men greatly preponderate, being more than three times more numerous than the women. Hence this large section of the community is not normally constituted. A very large proportion consists of working men, temporarily residing in Hong Kong for purposes of industry and trade. This is clearly shown by the very small number of Chinese families; 9,724 families to 68,000 men and 19,000 women.

Like the Europeans, few of the Chinese are permanent settlers, but only temporary residents, coming to Hong Kong to avail themselves of the facilities offered by British rule, for earning money, with which they propose to return to their own country, to end their days amongst their own people. Even the richer Chinese, who possess much housing property in the Colony, do not, as a rule, settle there with their whole family. Their first or principal wife remains at the home of their ancestors, in their native country.

The small number of really permanent Chinese settlers is due, to some extent, to the want of suitable sites on which they could build houses and plant gardens such as

Table 1.1
Statistics of the City of Victoria, from Census of 3rd April, 1881

	Resident Population				Temporary Population—Naval; amd Military Establishments Police, Crews of Shipping, Prisoners				Chinese Boat Population	Totals
	European and American	Goa, Indian and Mixed Blood	Chinese	Total	European and American	Goa, Indian and Mixed Blood	Chinese	Total		
Men	935	426	66,928	68,289	4,564	735	2,527	7,826	7,635	83,750
Women	768	174	18,003	18,945	131	7	64	202	3,440	22,587
Boys	629	185	8,774	9,658	158	6	98	262	3,061	12,981
Girls	638	183	8,680	9,501	97	6	21	124	2,551	12,176
Totals	3,040	968	102,385	106,393	4,950	754	2,710	—	—	—
Grand Totals								8,414	16,687	131,494

Number of houses tenanted 6,402
Number of inhabitants per house 16.6
Number of Chinese families 9,734

Total Europeans and Americans 7,990
Total Indian, Goa, and Mixed 1,722
Total Chinese 121,782

Total population 131,494

Chinese deaths in 1880 recorded Victoria 3,358

Chinese death-rate on census of April 1881 = $\dfrac{3{,}358}{122}$ ——— mille = 27.52 per mille.

they like. It would appear, however, that even in their own country, the Chinese prefer to have their permanent dwelling in some country village, the home of their ancestors, rather than in great cities. Even in Canton, a considerable number out of the vast population of that city are only temporary residents, their wives and families residing elsewhere, in their native villages. This strong attachment to the native place is probably due to the joint family tenure of land which obtains throughout China. Real property does not descend to one heir, but is administered by the senior member for the benefit of the whole family.

From 1872 to 1876 the population increased at the rate of about 2-3/4 per cent per annum; from 1876 to 1881 the increase was at the rate of 3 per cent. Seeing that the proportion of women is so small, this increase cannot be due to births, but must be caused almost wholly by immigration.

The Chinese population of Hong Kong comprises representatives of several distinct races or tribes, respectively different in appearance, habits, and speech. The written language is practically the same, but in speaking, the pronunciation and even construction varies so much, that one tribe cannot understand the other.

The following are the three principal tribes:

(1) The Pun-tees or Cantonese merchants, shop keepers and artisans.

(2) The Hok-lo, from Amoy and Foochow. These men are chair-coolies, boatmen, etc.

(3) The Hakkas, from the north-east of the province of Canton. They are stone-cutters, barbers, smiths, and labourers. They bring with them many women, who shun the sight of foreigners less, and appear in public more than those of other races. They inhabit principally the district near West Point. It is most important that all these peculiarities be remembered when comparing the vital statistics of Hong Kong with those of other places.

The city of Victoria, with upwards of 130,000 inhabitants out of the total 160,000 is virtually Hong Kong. A few small patches of garden cultivation in the valleys are the only agriculture. The bare slopes of the hills afford pasture to a few goats and cattle. With these exceptions the island is uncultivated, and judging from the soil, and from the state of the adjacent and similar country on the mainland, it does not appear likely to come under cultivation, to any great extent.

Most of what may be said as to the sanitation of Victoria, applies equally to the villages, only in them the task is simpler, for they are less crowded, and the proximity of cultivation, facilitates the proper disposal of sewage.

The larger villages owe their existence either to European dock establishments, or to the large fleet of fishing and trading junks which resort to the bays on which they are situated, for shelter, or to refit and victual.

The Kowloon peninsula, however, merits special consideration; the irregular and broken nature of the soil, forbids it to be called a first-rate building site, except comparatively to the still more rugged slopes of Hong Kong. Nevertheless, in the absence of any large extent of better ground, it affords space for future extensions as a suburb, and room for manufacturing and commercial establishments.

The peninsula consists of a mass of low but steep hills, tumbled together in so irregular a manner as to baffle description. Between the hills are narrow flat valley soles, but little above sea level. The geological formation is the decomposed granite which is here seen in the greatest perfection. In some places large masses of sound granite exists, which are quarried, and afford an excellent building stone.

No stream of importance enters British territory from the mountains on the mainland.

The rain falling on the peninsula, percolating through the porous soil appears in the form of rivulets in the valleys, in which wells of no great depth give a good supply of pure water. The valleys are under cultivation with rice and vegetables, and are irrigated from the said streams.

DOCUMENT I.c3: Chinese houses (source: *Mr. Chadwick's Report on the Sanitary Condition of Hong Kong*, November 1882, pp. 10-14, Colonial Office, *Eastern* No. 38, CO 882/4 Public Record Office, London)

On account of the slope of the ground on which the city of Victoria is built, most of the houses stand on artificial prepared sites, part in bank, part in cutting. Frequently an underground floor or basement of a house facing one street is entered as a ground floor from the street or alley next below. With this partial exception, basements or cellars under houses are unknown.

The usual building material is a blue Canton brick, not unburned, as often stated, but fired in a closed kiln, whereby the blue colour is produced. As ordinarily imported these bricks are soft and very porous, but they can be procured of good quality.

Red bricks can be obtained, but being more expensive, are rarely used. Granite from the local quarries is largely employed for door jambs and lintels over shop fronts. It is also used in the form of ashlar in the fronts of the more pretentious buildings.

Most houses are plastered, a few are faced with selected blue bricks rubbed smooth and neatly pointed according to Chinese custom.

The usual roof is of segmental tiles, with semicircular tiles covering the vertical joints, forming ridges, which often terminate at the eaves in ornamental glazed earthenware finials. In better classes of house an inner layer of segmental tiles is laid, with butt joints on the battens, to form a ceiling; on this is a course of tiles laid with lap joints. The vertical joints of this layer are covered with ridge tiles as before described.

For the ground floor unglazed red tiles are used; frequently, however, there is nothing but rammed earth. Cookhouses and alleys are paved with granite blocks. Upper floors are made of China fir planks supported on round rafters, flattened above and below, to receive the planks and ceiling, if there be one.

Concerning European dwellings little need be said. They are substantial structures, often standing detached, with arched masonry verandas. The observations to be made on the drains of Chinese houses, but too frequently apply with almost equal force to them also.

The usual type of Chinese house in Hong Kong is essentially different to that in use on the neighbouring mainland. This is due to some extent, no doubt, to European influence and example, but principally to the necessity for economy of space on account of the high price of land and the great cost of preparing level sites for building. This shows that the Chinese are not so averse, as commonly supposed, to change their habits to suit altered conditions.

According to immemorial custom, in one respect at least, the street frontage of the house is narrow, being 13 to 16 feet only. The depth back from the street is large, varying from 30 to 60 feet. Even the houses of the wealthy are formed by uniting several of these narrow units by doors or archways in the party walls.

If the site be level the houses are often built back-to-back, no lane or space being left between them. If the ground be sloping there will be a lane or gully at the back, often not more than 5 feet wide, sometimes less, and frequently this lane will be at or near the level of what is the first floor in the street in front.

Figures 1, 2, 3 give the general appearance and leading dimensions of a house in Kai-ming Lane, Canton Bazaar, the district so frequently referred to in the correspondence with the military authorities. Between Kai-ming Lane and that next and parallel to it, are two rows of houses built back-to-back, having a common back wall, and no open space between them. This is by no means an unusual method of building, especially in the flatter parts of the town. The house depicted in this sketch is a fair specimen of its class, and was selected quite at random. The ground floor in front is completely open to the street, and is used as a shop or workshop, but in it the shopkeeper or some of his assistants usually sleep. At night the front is closed by upright wooden bars, fitting into sockets in the threshold and lintel, behind which again, in cold weather, shutters are placed. The floor in this case is of rammed earth.

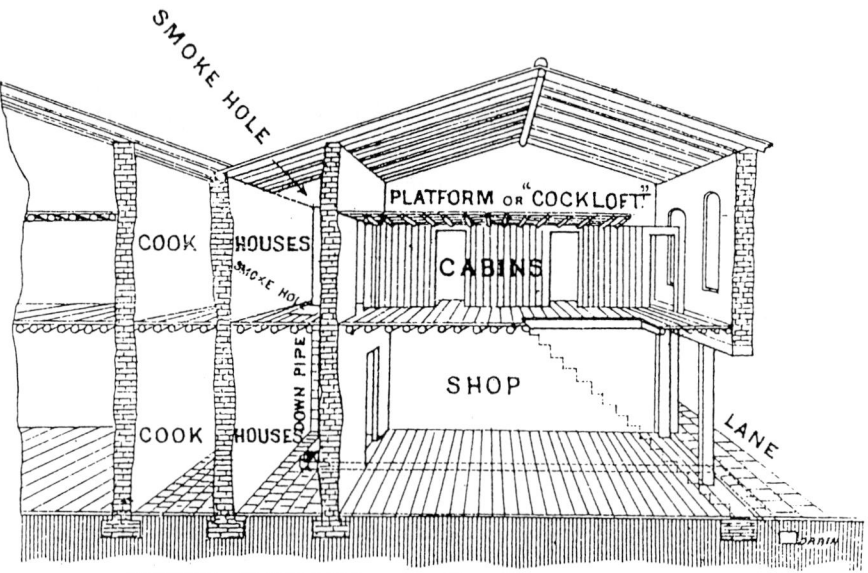

Figure 1

FRONT ELEVATION.

Figure 2

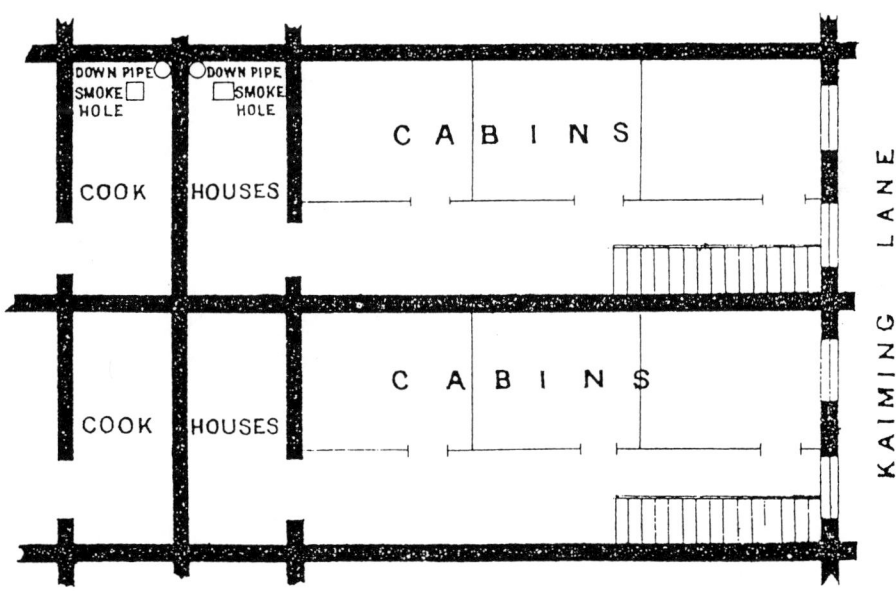

PLAN OF UPPER FLOOR.

Figure 3

In the house shown in the drawing, as in almost all other dwellings at the rear of the building, on each floor a portion about 7 feet deep is separated from the rest of the house to form the 'cookhouse.' For the inhabitants of the floor the cookhouse has to serve as kitchen, latrine, urinal, and general backyard, and in it not unfrequently may be found the bed of some member of the family. The floor of the cookhouse is of granite blocks. Usually it is broken up and disjointed by the efforts of the cook to raise the sink stone to clear the drain or by splitting firewood.

In back-to-back houses, as well as in some of other construction, the ground floor is ventilated and the smoke escapes by a 'smoke-hole' in the first floor, usually about 4 or 5 feet square. There are similar smoke-holes in the floors above, and in the roof. In the house shown in the sketch, however, the smoke hole in the floor was but 12 inches square. Chimneys are the exception. If they exist but little smoke goes up them, the greater part, if there be no smoke-hole, escaping by the windows, blackening the walls in a most unsightly manner.

Very frequently a space is boarded off on the ground floor in front of the cook house, forming a store or bedroom. Often a sort of platform or gallery is erected above this, on which several artisans work at their benches, or on which several beds are made. From the ground floor again, a further portion is cut off, containing the narrow steep stair, leading to the upper floors.

In the house in Kai-ming Lane, like the great majority of dwelling-houses, the upper floor is divided off by board partitions into cabins about 9 feet long and 10 feet wide. Each of these forms the dwelling of an individual or family. These cabins do not extend to the full height of the storey. On the contrary they are but about 7 feet 8 inches high; for in order to economise space a platform or floor, locally known as a 'cockloft,' is constructed above them. The cockloft is almost universal in dwellings of the middle and poorer classes.

In this house in the upper floor only there were five families including 16 souls. There were here three cabins and a platform extending over them, and over this passage. Hence the total cubic space per head was 437-1/2 cubic feet, and this includes the *whole* domestic accommodation, with the exception of the cookhouse, and not sleeping room only, which in the case of the cabins does not exceed 130 cubic feet per head. It must be remembered that the lower floor rarely belongs to the inhabitants of the upper floors. Very frequently each floor is leased separately from the owner, or from his 'comprador,' and sublet again to individual lodgers.

The wooden floor of the upper storey is usually encrusted with mud, for the boards are so loosely jointed that it could not be washed without deluging the people below, even were water available for the purpose, which is seldom the case.

In some parts of the town the ground floor also is used as a dwelling. In a house in Peel Street having a frontage of 15 feet and a depth of about 50 feet, the ground floor was divided into four cabins about 10 feet by 10 feet each, inhabited by a family. The head man of this floor was a fireman aboard a local steamer; he paid the rent to the landlord for the whole floor ($8.50 a month). Inhabiting one cabin himself, he sublet the remaining three. The first floor also was divided into four cabins and occupied by

13 persons; the second floor was occupied by 11 persons, small traders from Shanghai. This house, situated in one of the better streets, is certainly above the average in point of accommodation.

Notwithstanding that Ordinance 8 of 1856 directs that, 'every house shall be provided with a latrine or privy and ashpit . . . to the satisfaction of the Surveyor General,' anything satisfying the most modest requirement as to such appliances, is very rarely to be found. In the houses of the poorer classes they do not exist, unless indeed a pot placed in the corner of the cookhouse, sometimes enclosed by a few boards, may be considered to be a latrine within the meaning of the Act.

To carry off slopwater, a drain leads from a sink in the cookhouse to the public sewer. The arrangement of these house drains varies so considerably, that it is impossible to determine any general rule of construction, for very often their course and position cannot be ascertained.

Sometimes each house has an independent drain, running out under the floor to the street in front. More often the drain runs from cookhouse to cookhouse, under the party walls of adjacent tenements, till it reaches the end of the row, or is brought out under some one house to the front. Sometimes, but very rarely, the drain runs along a back alley. Not unfrequently private house drains traverse several distinct lots, or properties, on their way to the public sewer. It does not appear to be the practice to make provision for this state of things by easement or otherwise in deeds of transfer. Consequently, if one or more houses out of a row having a common drain are sold and reconstructed, the remaining houses may be deprived of their outlet to the sewer.

For house drains, brick (often the inferior blue brick), is the usual material. It is set in common mortar, and sometimes bedded in concrete, but not often. The best form of house drain in use is a 9-inch half-barrel drain covered with a flat tile. Square brick drains are more common, with flat tile soles and covered with flat tiles. Down some alley-ways a private drain about 2 feet 6 inches by 1 foot 6 inches runs, the granite covering slabs forming the pavement of the alley, the open joints of which freely permit the escape of the emanations from the filthy black deposit with which they are filled.

Of late years the Government have made the connection to the main sewer, and constructed the house drain up to the front wall of the house. The remainder of the drain has been left to the uncontrolled intelligence of the Chinese builder. No care whatsoever is taken as to line, gradient, or workmanship.

In February last a *new* drain was being constructed in the following manner. the drain was square 1 foot 2 inches wide by 1 foot 3 inches high. The sides were of brick *on edge*, and did not rest on the tile which formed the sole. Under these circumstances it need hardly be said that a great proportion of house drains are but elongated cesspools, the greater part of their fluid contents filtering into the subsoil. In one case a drain was found having no bottom but the natural soil.

Instances are to be found, where the outer wall of one property is built so close to that of the adjacent house, as to leave an inaccessible space between them, which services as an open drain. In one case the space between two houses was but 8 inches wide, and it received the filth from windows of cookhouses looking into it.

Something similar was found in Josi Lane opening from Ladder Street. . . Here a drain certainly went down into the gully, but what became of it afterwards could not be discovered.

The slops from the upper cookhouses are conducted down by a pipe of rough earthenware, coated with plaster. Frequently this is inside the house, in which case it simply delivers its flow on to the floor of the cookhouse below, as in the case of the house shown in Figs 1-3, Sheet I.

At other times it is put outside the house. As the upstairs lodgers have no convenience for getting rid of rubbish, much is stuffed into the down pipe, choking it, causing it to leak, and saturate the walls with the filthy fluid, oozing from its imperfect joints. For the same reason, the house drain also is frequently obstructed.

Trapping, disconnection and ventilation of house drains, may be said to be unknown. The sewer gas has a free channel to the interior of the house, except when the drain is blocked up with filth. Even houses of Europeans may be found, where waterclosets and baths within the house or in a veranda, are connected to the drains, without ventilation or disconnection of the soil-pipe, and without any proper trap.

The following examples will give an idea of the principal varieties of house construction. They are by no means extreme cases, some of the houses are quite new, and not yet fully occupied. These will illustrate the working of the Building Ordinance at the present time.

Figures 4 to 12, Sheet II, show the arrangement of a block of four houses in Taipingshan Street. They are of a somewhat different type to that just described, having a lane at the back of them, which is much lower than the street above, so that the basement is entered at the ground level from it, Figs. 9-10. The cross section, Fig. 9, shows the intermediate floors or 'cocklofts,' A and B, that have been constructed between the original floors, and the ground plans, Nos. 4, 5, 6, 7, 8, show the way in which they have been subdivided into cabins.

The following is the number of inhabitants and the cubic space per head: -

		No. 25	No. 23	No. 21	No. 19
	No. of occupants	11	11	10	0
Basement	Cubic space per head	604	604	665	-
Ground fl	Do do do	shop	7	15	30
	Do do do	-	822	383	192
2nd floor	Do do do	20	-	17	14
	Do do do	308	-	339	441

Early Settlement

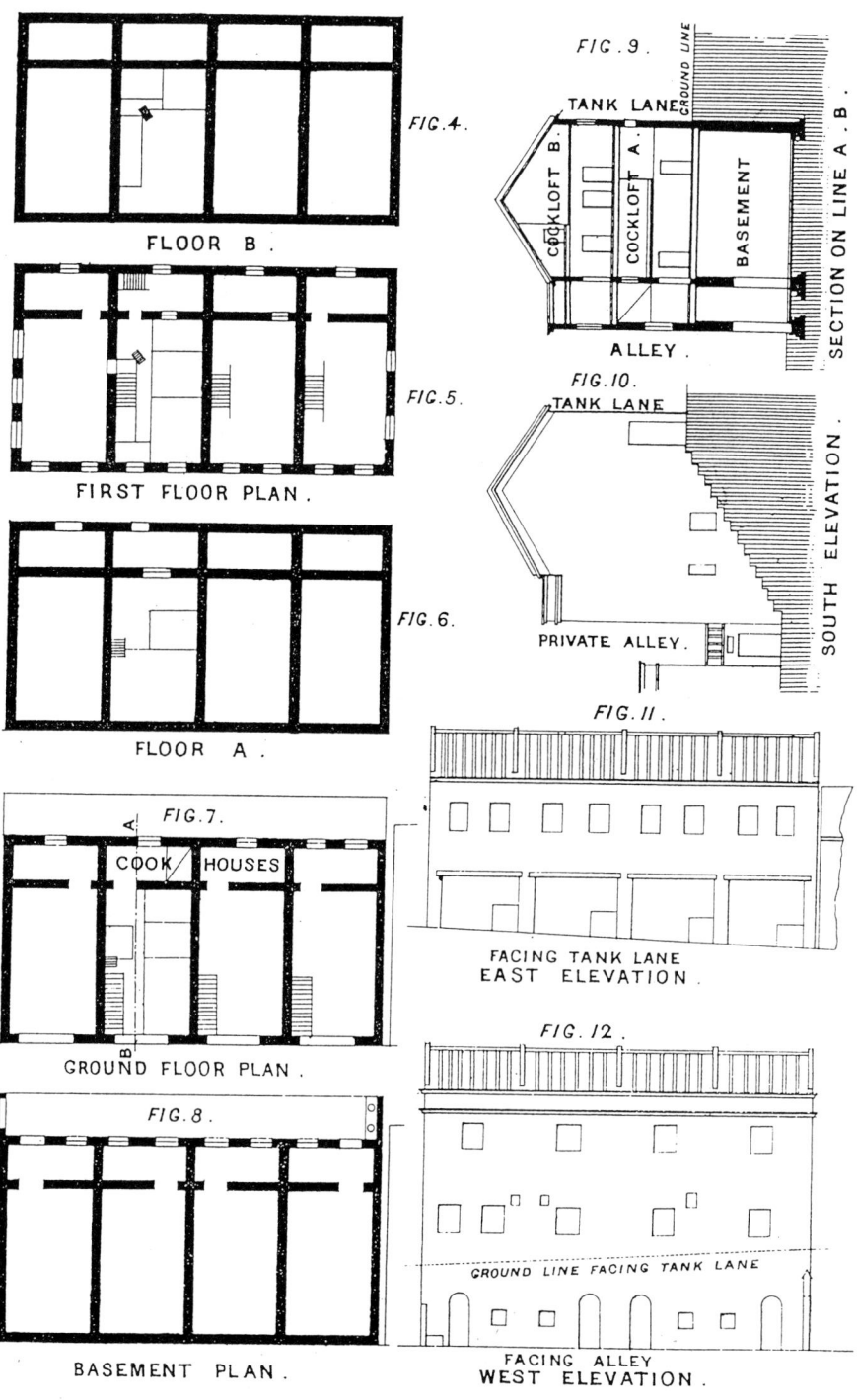

Figures 4 - 12

Here each floor is lighted by two windows in front, and the cookhouse has also a window, by which the smoke principally escapes, but which is of little use to the main room.

Bed spaces were found in the cookhouses. In one of these houses a space of not more than about 2 feet 6 inches square was boarded off beneath the narrow stair to serve as a latrine, that is to say, a pot was kept there. In other houses even this scanty accommodation was absent. The down pipes from the upper storey lead into the basement, one was burst and had flooded the place. The house drains lead out into the gully at back, and thence their course could not be positively ascertained.

The pair of new houses shown in Figs. 13-20, Sheet III, are not yet fully occupied. They give a good illustration of the manner in which additional accommodation is gained by introducing floors after the building has been constructed. An ample space between floors is shown on the plans sent in for the approval of the Inspector of Buildings, which is after construction, halved by the introduction of the cockloft. In this case it will be observed that in the rear elevation there are *two* rows of windows on the ground floor. It seems more than probable, therefore, that the introduction of a 'cockloft' was contemplated from the first and provision made for it in the design.

The number of inhabitants, &c was —

	Basement	Ground floor	1st floor	2nd floor	Basement	Ground floor	1st floor	2nd floor
Number of rooms	8	12	Unoccupied	5	8	14	10	-
Number of people	10	22	Unoccupied	11	16	41	15	8
Cubic feet per head	592	388	Unoccupied	769	370	208	638	1,058

On revisiting, after the drawing was made, it was found that several new partitions had been put up.

There are no chimneys at all to the house. All the smoke escapes by the windows into the narrow lane at the back. The only light which penetrates into the basement is that which finds its way through at the cookhouse, and that which enters by the small area grating about 4 feet by 2 feet, in the street in front. Not only these basement or cellar dwellings, but also those on the ground and upper floors, are so dark, on account of the obstruction in the way of cabins and 'cocklofts,' that in making one's way through to the cookhouse much care is requisite to avoid falling over things.

Fig. 21, Sheet IV, shows No. 22, Station Street. The number of inhabitants is given in the drawing and the cubic space per head, exclusive of the cookhouse, which is separated from the main building by an alley, spanned by a narrow gangway. It seems almost impossible to conceive how so many inhabitants could be stowed away in so small a space. Indeed, some had come out into the street to do their work, namely picking oakum.

Fig. 22, Sheet IV, gives the section of a somewhat less crowded building. In the

Early Settlement

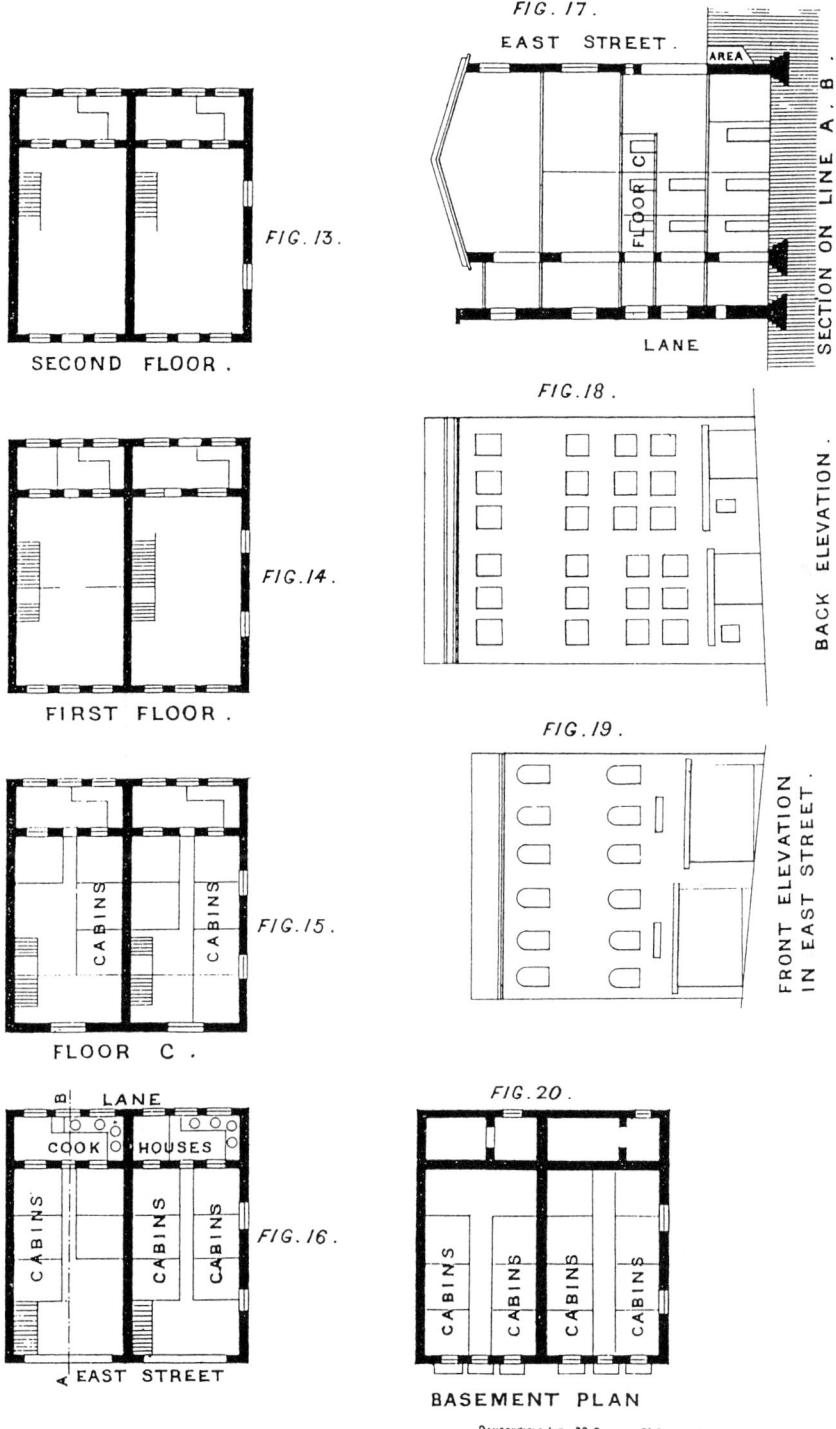

Figures 13 - 20

upper storey 25 chair coolies lodged, having erected bunks to sleep on. Here the cubic space per head amounts to 400 on the upper floors. The lower storey was occupied by seven chairmakers, who used it as a workshop and dwelling. It should be noted that the only ventilation for the ground floor cookhouse is a hole 3 feet square in the floor above, so that the whole of the space, nearly 50 feet long, is lighted form one end only. In one of these buildings is there any such thing as a latrine.

Figs. 23-27, Sheet V, show the details of a block of buildings in the district of Taipingshan. It will be observed that there are two floors below the level of the ground on the one side. Also that the middle of the block derives its sole light and ventilation from a narrow central alley arched over at both ends.

The ground or basement floors which open off this alley are chiefly tenanted by hawkers of vegetables. They wash their wares in the alley, and, as the central channel is carelessly laid, the whole place is continually damp and offensive.

The dwellings of these unfortunates are quite dark. The drainage intended by the architect is shown in the section, a square channel running from cookhouse to cookhouse. Some of these dens were untenanted, so it may be supposed that even poor Chinese shrink from inhabiting such holes as these.

These buildings are recent.

Figs. 28, Sheet VI, and 29, Sheet VII, show the plan and section of a new block of buildings abutting on Queen's Road. Here again the ground and part of the first floor as seen from that street are below the level of the interior alley. In this case some improvement may be seen in the open space which ventilates the cookhouses of the double block of buildings facing Gough Street. In practice, however, such narrow openings are of little use, as they soon become blocked up with temporary erections.

This block is new and of decidedly superior construction, and on the whole well kept. The drainage, however, was remarkably defective; the drain from the central portion of the block passed down behind the retaining wall forming the back of one of the houses facing Queen's Road, and out under its floor to the main sewer. Being badly made, leaky, and untrapped, a most abominable nuisance ensued. This house was intended as an hotel for Europeans.

Figs. 26, Sheet V, and 28, Sheet VI, give a fair idea of the way in which access to the interior of large blocks by means of narrow alleys , the inadequate amount of light and ventilation which they afford to the surrounding buildings. Instances are to be found where the backs of two rows of buildings are separated by an alley about 4 or 5 feet wide, and where this narrow space has been divided up by boarded partitions. In one instance the alley thus obstructed, is public property.

In some instances, chiefly on the level ground, near the harbour, two rows of houses face a central lane, which runs completely through the lot from street to street, and which is used as a thoroughfare. These lanes, as well as the narrow gullies, are private property and not scavenged by Government. In blocks built on in this manner inaccessible gullies too often exist between the backs of the houses on one lot and of those on the next.

In Queen's Road and some other streets, permission has been given to construct

N.º 22 STATION STREET.

First Floor   33 persons   144 cubic feet each
Ground Floor 36 . do   133   do · do
Exclusive of Cookhouse

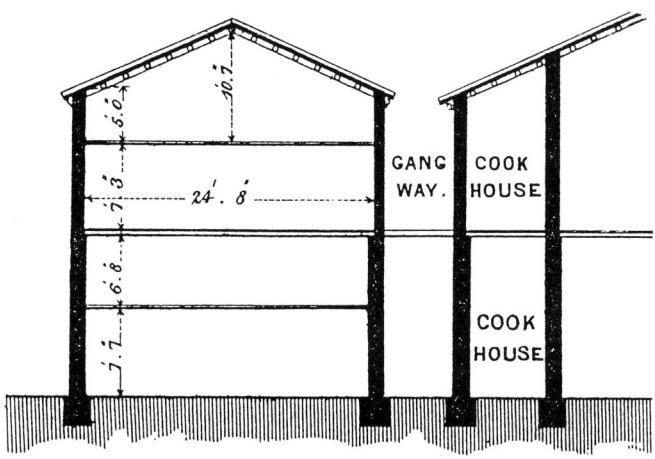

Figure 21

N.º 22 MARKET STREET.

First Floor   25 persons   400 cubic feet each
Second Floor 7   do   1337   do   do
Exclusive of Cookhouse

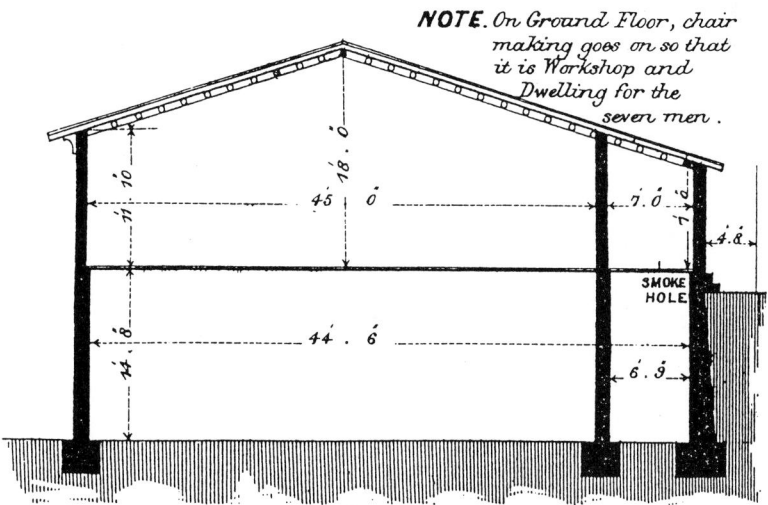

Figure 22

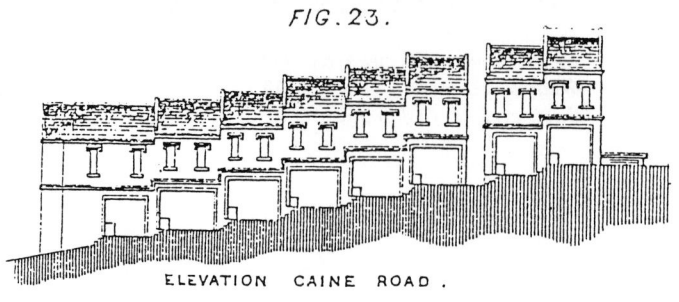

FIG. 23.
ELEVATION CAINE ROAD.
FIG. 24.
ELEVATION TAIPINGSHAN STREET.
FIG 25.
SECTION ON LINE A.B.
B
TAIPINGSHAN STREET.
FIG. 26.
TAIPING LANE
CAINE ROAD
ALLEY.
A
FIG. 27.
ELEVATION TAIPING LANE.

SCALE. 40 Feet - 1 Inch.

Figures 23 - 27

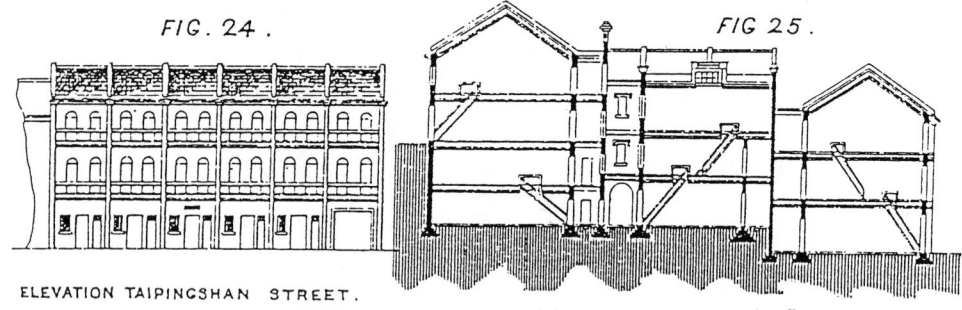

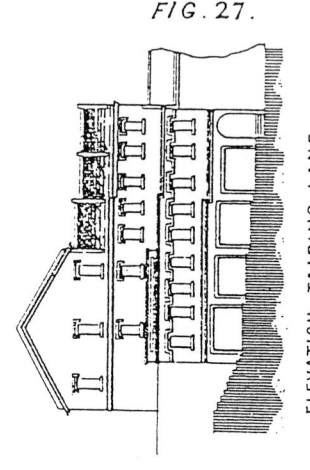

Early Settlement

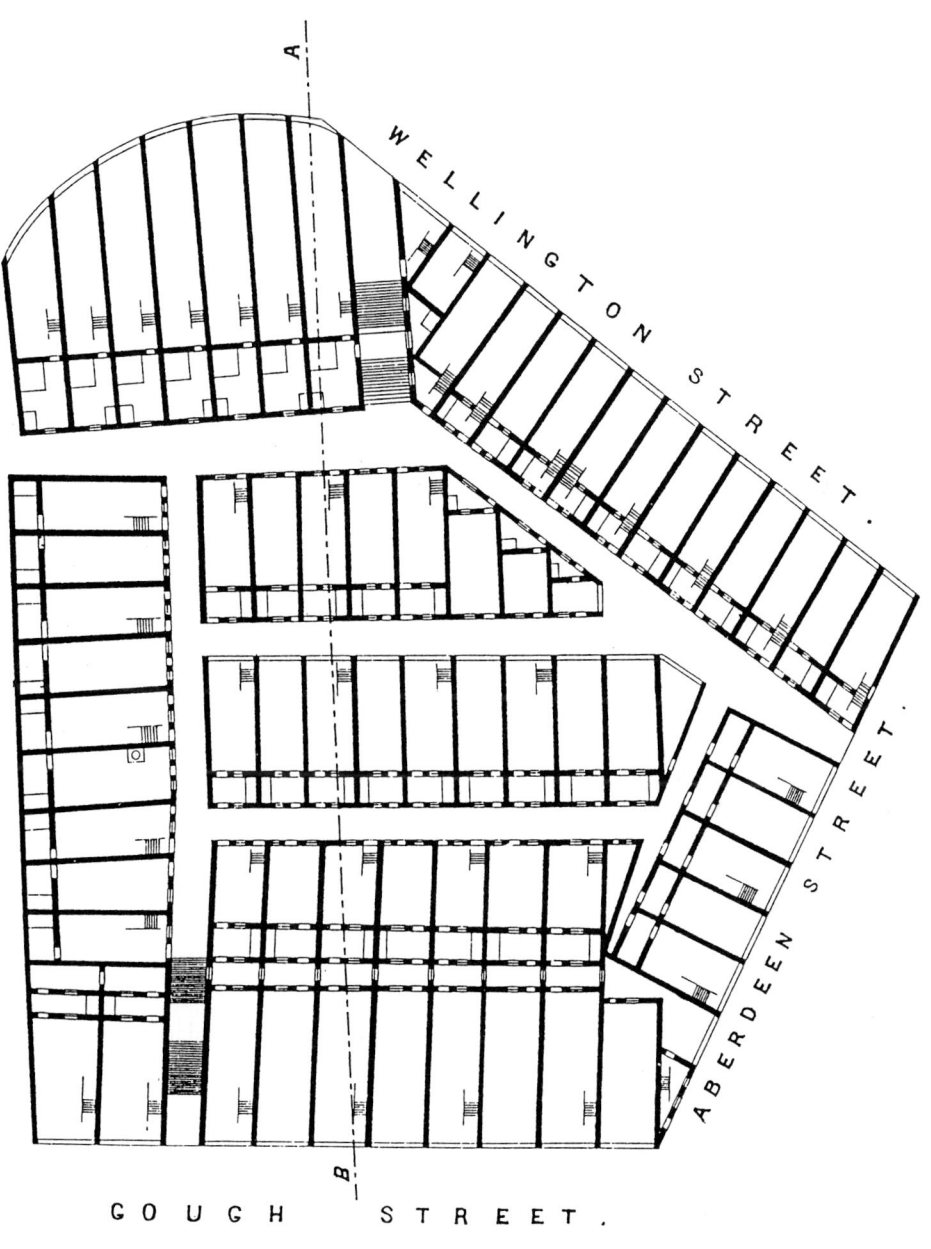

Figure 28

verandas over the public sidewalks. These would afford agreeable shade to foot passengers. Being but narrow, and much obstructed either by persons looking into shops or by goods temporarily deposited, they are of but little advantage to the pedestrian, whilst the veranda above are so substantially built, and so enclosed with blinds, that they amount to inhabited spaces, and thus the width of the street is diminished by the depth of the veranda.

The lodging houses of common labourers are often very much crowded. In a row of eight small houses 428 inhabitants were found, having but 230 cubic feet of space per head, exclusive of the cookhouse. These houses were exceedingly filthy. They were built close to the scarp of the hill, from which they were separated by a narrow gully only, which was wet and very dirty, and without proper drainage.

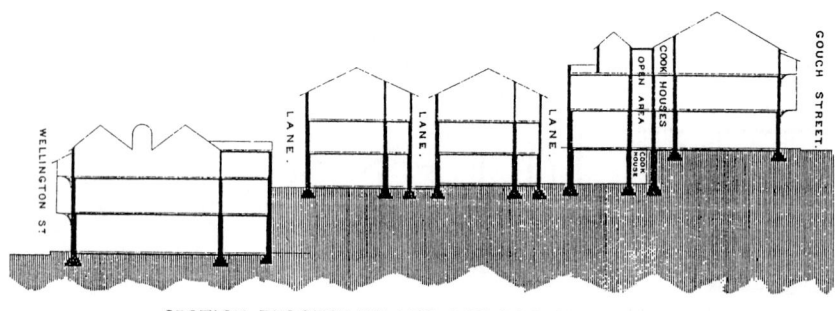

SECTION THROUGH INLAND LOT No 8 ON LINE A.B.

SCALE 40 Feet - 1 Inch.

Figure 29

DOCUMENT I.c4: The European District Reservation Ordinance 1888 (source: H.E. Sir G. William Des Voeux, Governor &c., 'Report on the Condition and Prospects of Hong Kong', *Sessional Papers*,* 1889)

The 'European District Reservation Ordinance' deals with an evil which has been recognised by successive Governors for years past, but for which this represents the first effort to provide a remedy. The close packing of the Chinese in their houses which is the normal condition of all classes among them, including in some degree even the well-to-do, enables a much larger rent to be obtained from land in Chinese occupation than from that inhabited by Europeans, whose health in a climate unfavourable to them (not to mention their comfort) requires much more breathing space in connection with their residences. Thus the large influx of Chinese in recent years, and the

* *Papers Laid Before the Legislative Council of Hong Kong*, annual, Hong Kong.

comparative advantage to land owners in providing residence for them, has caused a continually increasing intrusion of Chinese houses upon the quarter of the Town formerly occupied exclusively by Europeans. This result would have been comparatively endurable if it were possible for Europeans to live in health or comfort when surrounded by such houses. But unlike the Chinese who have, probably by a long process of natural selection, become inured and insensible to the conditions inseparable from extreme density of population, they are rendered ill and miserable by the effects of habits which such insensibility produces. Thus little by little, and at a gradually increasing rate, the Europeans were being, so to speak, pushed out of the Town of Victoria; and it seemed probable that before long there would be no suitable area for their residence there, and that such as remained in the Colony would have to choose between the alternative of living under most disagreeable and unhealthy conditions, or of incurring the heavy expense, possible only to the comparatively wealthy, of residence in the Hill District.

Had the above state of things been allowed to continue, there can be no doubt that it would have brought about a diminution, if not actual at least relative, of the already small European population, a result which could not be otherwise than prejudicial to the Chinese themselves. For though possessed of many valuable characteristics, the latter are still, and are likely to be for a long time to come, lacking in some of the qualities which are essential to true progress; and I can scarcely think there is any opening for rational doubt, that without the presence of a considerable complement of Europeans (apart form those engaged in Government) this Colony could no more maintain, than it could ever have reached, its present condition of prosperity.

By the Ordinance in question, a certain portion of the Town is reserved, not for exclusively European occupation, but for houses built according to European models, and occupied in much more limited numbers than is usual with Chinese. If Chinese choose to live under these conditions, as I am informed they commonly do in the neighbouring Penang, there is nothing in the Ordinance to prevent their doing so; and the provisions of this Law are simply directed to secure for Europeans a prescribed portion of the Town in which they can live in reasonable comfort.

d. In Retrospect

> Some features of the early years of Hong Kong's history remained long-lasting. Stamped on the early character of Hong Kong from its early days was the transitory nature of its population and its very Chineseness. Apart from the Chinese population, Westerners and Indians took their respective places in the Hong Kong social hierarchy. These various communities crossed but did not mix. Nevertheless, however much racial difference might contribute to the social divide, race itself was seldom an issue that galvanized organization. It was often remarked in the years to come that the relationships that held among the different communities had continued to improve.

DOCUMENT I.d1: An impression of the Chinese in Hong Kong c. 1917 (source: 'The Romance of Hong Kong, the Progress of Sixty Years', in *The Hong Kong Daily Press, 1857-1917*, Hong Kong, 1917, p. 15)

Nothing could be more remarkable than the change of attitude of the Chinese towards the British during the last sixty years. Then, as now, the security of life and property assured by the Colony attracted large numbers from the Kwangtung province, but the feeling of the officials in those days to 'the outer barbarians' was one of hatred and contempt. Sixty years ago our naval and military forces captured Canton and took the Governor of the City a prisoner. In these days the Governor of Canton attends official ceremonies in the Colony and is an honoured guest at Government House. The relations between Canton and Hong Kong are most cordial. While the Chinese appreciate to the fullest extent the advantages of many ideas and customs of the British, we, on our part, have learned to understand and respect many of their sterling qualities. Nor must we forget that among the citizens of the British Empire there are some 3,000,000 of the Chinese race. They have taken no insignificant part in the development of British Malaya, Sarawak and Hong Kong, and we believe they are destined to take a still larger part in the future. They have given freely of their wealth to War funds, and in other ways have assisted the causes of the Allies. We may recall, with pride, the fact that the British Empire offers its citizenship to all who conduct themselves properly and qualify by residence, irrespective of race, creed or colour. Among the subjects of all kinds in our variegated Empire none are more loyal than those of the Far East. We are also glad to believe that there are no greater admirers of the British than the Chinese traders and officials who come into contact with our kith and kin in China.

In this Colony we can see many great contrasts between the Chinese residents of sixty years ago and those of today. Then they were all, more or less, of the social status of the present house-boy or coolie, or very small shop-keeper. Many were closely associated with, if not actually engaged in, piracy, and all were terrorised by the Chinese officials on the mainland, who incited them to commit murder and robbery. Nowadays the Colony attracts wealthy ex-officials of even the Peking Government, while there has grown up in our midst a moneyed class of Chinese merchants who own a great proportion of the property in Hong Kong. They have also extensive interests in local industries, and there can be no doubt that their interests will grow.

DOCUMENT I.d2: A Description of the Population of Hong Kong c. 1921 (source: *China Mail* 76th Anniversary Number, Hong Kong, March 1921)

The following figures extracted from the census of 1911 show the different nationalities inhabiting the Colony, how they are divided between the urban and rural divisions, and the numerical proportion of children to adults:-

	Urban Division	Rural Division	Total	Percentage of children between 5–15 years of age
Non-Chinese:				
Europeans and Americans	5,185		5,185	13
Portuguese	2,558		2,558	24
Indians and others	3,482		3,482	10
Chinese:				
Land population	273,364	110,352	383,716	12 Urban; 20 Rural
Boat population		55,157	55,157	21
			*450,098	

* This total of 450,098 excludes the Naval and Military forces and the Mercantile Marine.

Upon consideration of the numerical ratio of children of school-going age to the total population, two distinct groups emerge. This ratio is in the cases of the Portuguese and the rural Chinese about double that which exists among the Europeans and the Americans, the urban Chinese and the Indians, a phenomenon due to the conditions of transience and impermanence affecting the races of the latter group. There follows immediately a short description of each of the various sections of the population.

English

The *Europeans* and *Americans* (hereafter for convenience called 'English') are all classified as being in the urban division: this is not quite accurate: but they are of it and generally near it, and may conveniently be considered as belonging to it.

The low proportion of children to adults indicates the transitory nature of this section of the population. It consists largely of young bachelors; many men come out to a temporary employment leaving wife and children at home; often the mother and children are sent home for climatic or other reasons, while the father remains here. Indeed with respect to the most firmly rooted, the cycle of their life may be described as ten years of bachelordom, ten of married life, and ten of family remittances and expectation of the hour of retiring. Nevertheless the number of English children is considerable, though the census figures probably include a number of Eurasians.

Those of the English population who can afford it usually live on the Peak. The next category usually includes the sons of lower grade Government officials, such as subordinate officers of the Police and Sanitary Departments, and junior employees of firms in receipt of incomes of £150 a year to £500 and upwards, as well as all others whose duties or choice confine them to the lower levels. While most of the English inhabitants of Hongkong feel the heavy cost of living, it may be said that of 'the poor' as the expression is understood at home, there are none.

Portuguese

The *Portuguese* belong entirely to the urban population. Of them it has been said, 'There is a sufficient distinction between the Portuguese population and other Europeans to make this division advisable and interesting.' The Portuguese of Hongkong form a European community settled in the tropics, thoroughly acclimatised, and apparently not recruited to any extent from Europe.

In one sense therefore they are indigenous; but in another alien, as they retain their allegiance to their own country, and their connection with the Portuguese Colony of Macao. The adults are almost entirely in business or employed as clerks: even the poorest are unwilling to do manual labour. While a few of the better educated like to cultivate the literary language of their country, they attach greater importance to a knowledge of English, so much so that there is no demand for the study of Portuguese in the schools which their children attend. The speech of the lowest classes is a degraded form of Portuguese mixed with Chinese, of no literary possibilities. The Portuguese learn English early in life and quite readily; and the education given in the schools which they attend assumes that this is so. The high percentage of children is evidence of the settled nature of this section of the population.

Indians

The Indians, like the English, are an alien and unstable element. But a considerable number have married, sometimes to Chinese wives, and settled here quasi-permanently. Their sons do well at school and afterwards in business. Special facilities have been made for their education.

The *Others* classified with Indians are Filipinos, Asiatic Jews, Japanese, Eurasians, etc., to whom no special reference need be made.

Chinese: Boat Population

In dealing with the *Chinese* population it may be well to be rid at once of the *boat population*. These live, marry and die in the thousand sea-going junks and slipper-shaped boats called *sampans* so characteristic of the Hongkong harbour. I have classified them as 'Rural,' because they have the characteristic of permanence. At any rate they are not townspeople. Very little is known about them. They have big families as the figures show, and no education, unless it is education which teaches a child of ten how to gybe a crank, round-bottomed craft in a gale. A few of their grubby urchins may attend the vernacular schools intermittently for a year or two. It should be understood that these people are a class apart from the other Chinese. The educational scheme of the Colony is open to them, but has not caught them hitherto.

Rural Population

Some description of the *Chinese rural population* proper has already been given. They are, fishers and farmers alike, hard-working, ignorant, narrow and superstitious, as may well be imagined. What is more surprising is their desire for education and the respect in which they hold it.

Urban Population

There remains for consideration the most important section of the community, the *Chinese urban population* of all sorts and conditions, merchants, clerks, shopkeepers, and skilled and casual labour. To the number of 270,000 and upwards it has been attracted to our shores in the last seventy years by opportunities of business and its appreciation of security, but in the main not as to a home but as a miner to his camp, a place where gold is won to be enjoyed elsewhere. The average urban Chinese never regards Hongkong in any other light: he returns to his village every festival day of his life, and if he dies here, retires thither for burial. This does not prevent him from establishing domestic ties with us; but the proportion of children to adults as already shown is little more than one half of what it is in the case of his compatriots of the rural and boat population. The inference is fairly clear that half his wives and children are absent in China.

Educational Policy

It will next be convenient to explain briefly the policy adopted with reference to the education of each of these sections of the population, before describing the schools and other educational institutions which are the embodiment of that policy.

English children born in the tropics have the same right to a wholesome education as have their happier home-born brothers, though the circumstances of climate and tropical environment must in any case weigh heavily against them. In the words of the Committee of Education of 1901, 'it is undesirable that they should in their most impressionable years be associated with the children of alien beliefs and other ethical standards.' It is particularly undesirable that they should get an insight into mixed and illegitimate establishments. Further it is not possible to yoke young English children, who have a knowledge of their own speech but little else, with much older children who know a great deal else, and wish to begin the study of English.

It is upon these considerations that the British schools were founded. It is believed that these schools are pioneers in the history of education of the Empire. The Government realises the justice of making the ratepayers contribute as little as possible towards the cost of this school, and the fees are therefore put as high as the parents can afford.

These schools are conducted on a Protestant-Christian basis and are visited by the clergy of the Anglican and Union Churches.

The obligation to supply a good education to our Indian fellow-subjects is strongly felt. A small school under Indian masters has long been maintained for their exclusive use, and a still smaller one was recently opened at Kowloon. They act as feeders to the district schools and Queen's College, where the Indian boys hold their own without much difficulty among the ablest Chinese. No particular description of these schools is needed.

The establishment of a superior school for Indians is under contemplation. Scholastically speaking, the difficulty of combining the education of Chinese and Indians is that while each Class needs to learn its own written language (Urdu in the case of Indians), Chinese is by far the more exacting and lengthy study.

Indigenous, yet of alien nationality, domiciled half here, half in Macao, it might be hard to establish the precise educational claim of the Portuguese. Fortunately the question does not arise. Their schooling is amply supplied by the various Roman Catholic Missions. In any case the demand for a good supply of educated Portuguese to fill clerkships, especially the higher ones, would have to be satisfied.

The case of the boat population is this. They are indigenous, which gives them a moral claim to education. On the other hand, they have no natural desire for it. The alternative seems to lie between compulsory education with its vast attendant difficulties in Hongkong, and the policy of masterly inactivity which the Education Department has hitherto adopted.

Until 1913, hardly anything was done for the Rural population except the establishment by the Missions of one or two vernacular Grant schools. Three small Government schools where English is taught are also maintained in the New Territories: but they are of little importance, and not worth a detailed description. An indigenous population and one with a deep respect for education, the New Territories have urgent claims, and the obligation of the Government to meet them is heavy. That so little has hitherto been done is due to two causes - lack of funds and the preponderant need during the past twelve years of establishing a sound secondary system of education in Hongkong. The beginning of an elaborate system has been made under which the best private schools in the New Territories are to be encouraged by small subsidies.

But the main educational problem attaches to the urban Chinese. It has been shown how they all, with the partial exception of the poorest, are bound to the Colony by the easiest of connections. This ephemeral quality of merchant or shopkeeper very greatly relieves the sense of responsibility with which an educator must regard him.

There need be no talk of free, much less of compulsory education. The Chinese, as a rule, comes here for what he can make; so we must educate his sons for what we can make of them. How much is that?

Demand for an English Education

Since Chinese is so difficult a language that it is only studied by Government officials, missionaries and Sikh policemen, English must be the general medium of communication. Thus at the very outset, we are committed to the establishment of English schools for the Chinese, not as a moral obligation, but as a commercial necessity. Such schools cannot be worked at a lower fee than between $5 and $10 a month for each pupil. But this is more than very many Chinese of the most desirable classes can afford. It follows if such schools are to be established, the ratepayers must share the cost, and, as a matter of fact, they halve it. The great majority of the ratepayers being Chinese, this really means that those of them who have no children at school pay in part for those who have.

It has been objected that though local taxes are fairly spent on the education of Chinese connected with the Colony, others should be carefully excluded who come to Hongkong for that education alone, and without any intention of making a lengthy settlement. In theory this position is reasonable: in practice nothing short of a Commission upon the antecedents of each applicant would arrive at the truth. And so it is necessary to console ourselves with the facts, first, that Chinese boys utterly unconnected with the place would really find their way here; and secondly, that Chinese who have received a good English education and been impressed with the stamp of a Hongkong school are an asset sooner or later to be realised, whether they settle down in China as merchants, or pass examination and become members of the Chinese Civil Service.

A Matter of Expediency

This, and the insatiable demand among the Chinese to attend English schools makes the way very clear. No sentimental feeling for instance, need rap the judgement in carrying out the statesman-like advice of the Indian Education Commission of 1882.

'We think it generally desirable that even in primary schools fees should be raised as far as is consistent with the spread of education . . . . The whole educational fund is inadequate to the supply of schools for every group of villages, and those who enjoy the advantage of a school should contribute towards its cost so as to promote the establishment of similar institutions elsewhere. But we do not overlook the wants of the struggling poor, nor of exceptionally backward races and tracts.'

Some exception from this doctrine of expediency must be made in the case of the poorest of classes. In the first place, cost of travel has somewhat reduced their tie with the mainland. And then, because they are less aware of the value of education, the more need is there to give it to them. Their requirements are very modest.

Chinese Must Study Their Own Language

Another axiom on which our educational policy rests, is that Chinese are not educated unless they possess a reasonable facility with their own written language. This has been the better opinion among both English and Chinese authorities for many years. Attempts have been made to blur the argument by references to the controversy over the value of Latin or Greek. The cases are not parallel. A Chinese engineer will find himself in difficulties if he cannot read a specification when ten miles inland, or a doctor who cannot write a prescription.

Conveniently for the Department it is the habit of the better class Chinese to give their sons a few years Chinese education (usually in their own villages) before they bring them into our sphere. It is thus only necessary to hold Chinese entrance examinations in the English schools, and to maintain and improve this so to speak pre-natal knowledge. The great number of small vernacular schools in Hongkong both Missionary and private are supported on the contrary by the poorer part of the urban population, who do not desire an English education for their sons. Thus broadly speaking, Hongkong is concerned with the English education of the wealthier of the urban Chinese, and the vernacular education of the poorer. Further reference will be made to an educational ladder making it possible for the sons of the very poorest to obtain a free education through the English schools into the University.

Some description has now been given of the two main classes of the population which lie receptive to the hand of the educationist, the urban, and the rural.

Of these the Urban Division falls naturally into three divisions. First, the English and Indians who, while alien to the Colony are native to the Empire and claim their rights as such; second, the Chinese Urban population which has claims based less on a moral right than urgent expediency; third, the Portuguese who hold a position between the first two, being neither altogether residents of the Colony, not altogether alien to it. The education of the Urban population is by now fairly established.

The rural population proper although possessing great claims has hitherto received but little attention.

The boat population which is classed with it drifts along contentedly ignorant, and unaware whether it is a loser by its ignorance or not.

DOCUMENT I.d3: Mutual toleration (source: Geoffrey Robley Sayer, *Hong Kong, 1862-1919, Years of Discretion*, edited and with additional notes by D.M. Emrys Evans, Hong Kong: Hong Kong University Press, 1975, pp. 128-129. The manuscript for this book was completed in 1939. The author came to Hong Kong in 1910 and retired as Director of Education in 1938.)

It is a considerable development to have taken place in a brief fifty years, and parallel with it is to be found also a progressive change in the relationship of the Chinese to the English community. We need not describe it in all its aspects. The history of the residential reservations, real and so-called, sufficiently illustrates the point. Originally without part of lot in the centre of the town, for the simple reason that Elliot's original land sales were (not unnaturally) open only to Europeans, the Chinese were in their turn soon allotted sites in contiguous areas. In fact the old factory system so familiar in Canton by which the visitor from overseas was strictly confined without the gate was closely reproduced (excepting the physical barrier) in Hong Kong, with this difference, of course, that in the Colony it was the English who occupied the centre of the stage, the Chinese who took the wings. A generation or so later, in the consulship of Hennessy, the hard and fast line drawn around this de facto European reserve was in part relaxed, the business section of the Central District being officially pronounced accessible to Chinese purchasers and Chinese occupants.

Ten years later, the European main body having meantime retired to the hills, the position of the residential section on the mid-levels was in turn reviewed by Governor Des Voeux and a 'European reservation' was created — a reservation which, so far from excluding Chinese, expressly admitted them on terms (namely the acceptance of European conditions) — to territory hitherto closed to them. In 1904, Nathan's first year in office, the exclusively European retreat on the Peak was in turn accorded de jure recognition as such. But in 1918 Sir Henry May reversed the step, substituting for the Peak Reservation Ordinance a new Ordinance of the same name which demanded of all who desired to reside in the old European reserve that they submit their claim to do so to the Governor's decision.

Here indeed is a striking change, but in these fourteen years, and notably in the years following the Chinese revolution, many new things have occurred and among them is to be detected a palpable rapprochement in the relationship of the two communities. The blind instinct to exclude, the blind resentment at exclusiveness, yields to a conscious desire to find common ground, and from that desire springs naturally a mutual respect for privacy and a sensitive disinclination to intrude.

It is on this note that I close. After all it is the keynote of the piece. Had this small island been kept as a purely European retreat — on the pattern, for example, of Shameen, its history, though perhaps curious, would inevitably be trivial. It is as the point of impact of the scientific West upon the philosophic East, of military Europe upon civilian China, that Hong Kong claims our real interest. Here — at her own doorstep — China, and here — after traversing half the world — England, abruptly confront their antitheses. Here two peoples, each profoundly confident of its own superiority, meet face to face. The onlooker, stepping back a pace or two, watches the reaction of the one upon the other with curiosity, and not without a smile.

CHAPTER TWO

THE CHINESE COMMUNITY IN EARLY HONG KONG

For most of the Chinese people who lived in Hong Kong, Hong Kong was not home until they made it their home. Like the foreigners, they had come to Hong Kong as outsiders. Like the foreigners, they started out detached from their village and family, uncertain of the future in this foreign land, but hopeful that one day they might go home — home, from where they had come — enriched.

The village society from where the Chinese came, as one can see it today in the New Territories of Hong Kong, was dominated by the religion of place and descent. Ancestral halls would be built where people of the same surname settled together. In the urban and refugee environment of Hong Kong, few people had the fortune of staying in a group with a substantial number of people of their own surnames. But temples and shrines were dedicated to territorial deities, from whom protection might be sought for all affairs in life and in death. Temples and shrines, therefore, dotted the Chinese settlements of Hong Kong as they dot, even now, the villages of the New Territories.

The community away from home that the temple provided mattered a great deal to the Chinese people. The Chinese deity was sacrificed to because he or she was able to protect. Many offerings would have been made by individual worshippers, and little organization would have been needed in such individual offerings. However, in order to ensure that the temple might be looked after, and in order to invite the deity to bless not only the individual, but also the community, some organization would have been needed. In the village, villagers might take turns to serve the deity; but even in the village, it was not uncommon for managers to be appointed every year, and for the worshippers to organize themselves into a society that came together on the occasion of the deity's birthday for a feast after the offering. In worship, therefore, was derived a sense of comfort that came from the sharing of an activity. One does not have to assume that religion must matter to all immigrants to see the prominence of the temple as a focus of the communal bond. The successful who attributed their success to the glory of the god would have contributed to the grandeur of the temple. The temple, architecturally unique and ideologically distinct from beliefs of the Western tradition, symbolized the independence of Chinese culture in Hong Kong. Yet, surely that was not all there was to Chinese society. Surely, that Chinese people could be so used to handling their own affairs did not imply that government might or needed be kept at arm's length.

a. The Temple and Its Community

Nevertheless, for all its managerial independence, the temple was never very far away from the imperial system. Emperors granted titles to deities, deities were officials to an emperor of all deities, temple liturgies imitated imperial practices, the temple was the deity's court. When Chinese people invited their village deity to Hong Kong, they re-enacted the ritual relationship that the village had established with the imperial regime, and the deity would only gradually lose its local connection as it took on the new urban clientele. Such was the case of Lord Shek Lau in Quarry Bay. The deity was known among the Hakkas for his ability to cure disease, but he stayed on, gathered a reputation for his ability to deal with venereal disease and developed a clientele that came to him for its cure. When the following passage was written, the respect due to him for that ability was yet to come. In 1889, newly installed, he was remembered for his connection to home and village.

DOCUMENT II.a1: Deities from home: a dedication to the Venerable Shek-lau, 1889 (source: Stone inscription found at the Quarry Bay Yi Paak Kung Temple, recorded in David Faure, Bernard Luk and Alice Ngai-ha Lun Ng, *Historical Inscriptions of Hong Kong*, Hong Kong: Urban Council, 1986, pp. 231-232)

> Clouds fly over rock surface, adding miracle to miracle.
> On the moon beyond the tower, there you trace his immortal steps.

A summary of the propitious deeds that defended the nation and sheltered the people:

At Fou Tong Pui Range of Wang Po Yeuk at Cheung Lok county is located the grave of our lineage uncle the venerable Wo Chen. He was also known by his other name, Shek Lau. And, because he was the second-born, the people in the lineage called him Second Uncle Shek Lau.

He was clever and willing to learn. He was very knowledgeable and knew all there was to know in the classics and the histories.

He attended the junior official examination but did not pass. He met an extraordinary man who taught him the craft of the extraordinary, and he learnt all its mysteries.

At the time, an uprising took place in the county city. So he gave up the idea of seeking advancement, and attended to the high intentions of becoming a hermit. He knew how to bring about changes, and he did much that benefited the people. The people in the village acknowledged his benevolence, and when he died, they set up an altar at his grave to sacrifice to him. Day by day, the number of people who prayed there increased.

In the Qianlong period,* the Maau Shan sect used its teachings to harm people. People who were bewitched were suppressed by the incense that came from the venerable gentleman and the sect came to an end. Thereafter, people practised spirit writing and cast divining blocks at his altar, and all who asked for medicines or protection received the most propitious responses. Especially notable was the incident in the winter of the Yimao year in the Xianfeng reign [1855]. The Red Turban Chak Fo Ku came with thousands to disturb the county, and they were very fierce. At the battle of Kau Leng, all living things panicked. Our lineage went with the medium to seek advice from the venerable gentleman, and speaking through the medium, the gentleman said, 'Do not fear, for the troops are coming. You should be united in your hearts, and wait for them at the Filled-in Tin Mine-shaft. [At that spot], you will have in front of you the natural grandeur of the mighty river, which the bandits cannot cross easily. On the range, there will be many flags, while on the banks of the river, you will make many embankments. I shall lead the spirit troops to help you, and the bandits will depart in a few days.'

Our lineage did as we were told. The bandits watched our forces from afar, and saw that our fortification was orderly and that we were stationed all over the place. Moreover, they saw that we were many and well-fortified, we had no fear. So they gathered themselves and said, 'Wherever our flags pointed, we destroyed all as if it were dead branches, and all surrendered at the sight of us. Only this place has mounted an iron-clad defence. How would it be easy to defeat it?'

We fought three skirmishes and on all three occasions we won. Countless bandits were killed. Our men chased them until we reached Siu To. On that day at the *yin* hour, heavy fog blocked out the sky, and a strong wind whirled across the ground. The rebels heard drums in their dreams. They panicked, and could barely get dressed. Their tents and all were discarded, emptied. By the *chen* hour, the fog had become so dense that you could not see the face of the man standing in front of you. The rebels cried out in fear, 'These people are helped by the gods. We must not fight them.' After that,

---

* 1736-1795

they dispersed and crossed the ranges into Lung Chuen. In the Bingchen year [1856], the rebel Lo Ah Tim came to disturb our place. The venerable gentleman again revealed to the medium how we should defend ourselves and our lineage following his instructions set our men at the Tin Mine-shaft to mount the defence. Our initiative was overwhelming. When the rebels heard of it they escaped. In these two actions, Shiu[*] and others personally served, and that is why we can describe these events in detail. Magistrate Lo, who was known by his posthumous name, Hon Lung, came to Cheung Lok with the rank of a Hanlin, and he said to Shiu and others, 'On these various occasions when the rebels attacked our county, if it had not been for the power and propitiousness of the venerable Shek Lau, we would have been defeated. Great is his achievement in defending the nation and sheltering the people. I shall write a detailed account of it and petition for an award so that he may be sacrificed to. This is how we should thank the god.' For this purpose, the god was granted an honorific board, as an award for the peace of the land. The board read, 'Defence of the village.'

On this present occasion of a new altar being built in Hong Kong, to prepare for his propitiousness, we record his history in brief and carve it on stone, so that those who sacrifice to the venerable gentleman may know of his propitiousness and military might. By showing his propitiousness . . . , the liturgy for the sacrifice may be determined. We invite him, and petition for an award to be granted to him. How can this [temple] be treated as an illegal temple and his sacrifice be treated as wild sacrifice?

To be appended is Lord Ma, known also as Yi Yam, a nephew of Second Uncle. In life, his nature was honest and straight and his body strong and handsome. He thought little of serving as an official, and wanted to travel afar. He helped people to sort out their differences, helped the weak and suppressed the strong. At the time of the beginning of the dynasty, there were many bandit disturbances. The gentleman led the militia to dispel them. He was brave and marched ahead of others. His strength was such he could fight a hundred men. People relied on the gentleman as they would rely on a great wall, and he was willing to defend them. He rode on a bamboo horse, and he went not towards the capital but to Jiangxi. Because he was a good runner, he was known as Lord Ma. Most Jiangxi people who had asked the gentleman to save them do not forget his benevolence. He is sacrificed to in the temples to this day. People call him 'Father'.

In the 15th year of Guangxu in the Qing dynasty, the year of Jichou [1889], in spring . . . , by 18th generation descendant Ngai Shiu, alias Lai Shang, student of the sixth military rank, recommended for the post of deputy police chief.

> Few temples succeeded as much as the Man Mo Temple on Hollywood Road. Built in 1847 and dedicated to the literati deity Man Cheung and the warrior deity Mo Tai, who respectively oversaw fortune in the official examinations and the sense of righteousness, the Man Mo Temple was given

---

[*] Author of this essay.

pride of place among temples in Hong Kong. Yet temples and their deities were at most curiosities to the Western community of Hong Kong. The procession of the deities on the occasion of the repair of the Man Mo Temple in 1893 shows that the Western and the Chinese communities met but did not mix.

DOCUMENT II.a2: Procession of the deities of the Man Mo Temple (source: *China Mail*, 1 and 2 March 1893)

March 1, 1893
The streets have been so croweded with Chinese today that it is almost impossible to get about the busier thoroughfare. Not only have thousands of visitors arrived from Canton and the nearer villages to witness the great three-day procession, but the Chinese places of business in different parts of the town have been closed to enable the workmen to prepare for the carnival, which is likely to be one of the most noisy and distracting ever held in the Colony. Permission has been given to begin the din at 9 o'oclock tomorrow morning. As a matter of fact the beating of gongs and other noises have begun already.

March 2, 1893
The procession in connection with the Man Mo temple commenced in all its noisy hideousness this morning, and in some parts of the town business was practically suspended for several hours. About tiffin hour a protest was at last raised by the banks and business houses in Queen's Road, and an order was given for the Police to divert the procession from making a second jouney along Queen's Road from Pottinger Street to the City Hall. The execution of this order nearly gave rise to a riot . . . .

b. Chinese Guilds and Other Voluntary Associations

The temples and their committees were typical of the associations that Chinese people founded among themselves. Trade and regional associations were never really very far from some religious affiliation. Representatives elected by the guilds and the merchants, in a process that nobody seemed to know very much about, made up the committee of the Tung Wah Hospital that was founded in 1870. The committee of the Tung Wah Hospital served as spokesmen of the Chinese community. Until a prominent Chinese person was appointed to the Legislative Council from 1880, they were the community's only spokesmen.[*]

---

[*] See also *Government and Politics* Documents V.a1-a3 and b1-b6 on appointment to the Legislative Council and traditional channels of communication with the Hong Kong government.

The Hong Kong government was uncomfortable with these associations: for a long time, it did not quite know what they were, and by the time it did, it was suspicious that the Chinese leadership that was involved in voluntary associations might have harboured ulterior motives. The Po Leung Kuk, set up by Chinese merchants to protect women who had been sold into prostitution, would have been a case in point. The Hong Kong government agreed that poor young women snatched from their native villages should be saved,* but did the Chinese directors of the Po Leung Kuk treat as well as they should the women it saved from prostitution? In the interview below, the Westerners appointed to the commission to examine the activities of the Po Leung Kuk in 1892 were highly suspicious of the arrangements that had been made to marry off its inmates while the director of the Po Leung Kuk found the sense of fair play exhibited by these Westerners uncalled for even if not confrontational. Yet the voluntary association thrived, for government needed the contribution of these voluntary efforts as much as the voluntary bodies needed the support of the government.

DOCUMENT II.b1: Questions of trust and mutual convenience (source: 'Reports of the Special Committee to Investigate and Report on Certain Points Connected with the Bill for the Incorporation of the Po Leung Kuk, or Society for the Protection of Women and Girls', pp. 31-39, *Sessional Papers, 1893*)**

Mr. Ho Fook called ....
Q. — how are these cases [i.e. cases of women referred to the Po Leung Kuk — Ed.] investigated now?

---

* For more on these women, see chapter 4.
** The history of the Po Leung Kuk up to the time of the enquiry is outlined in the minority report given by T.H. Whitehead, a member of the special committee appointed in 1892: 'There is no evidence that there ever were any subscribers to the Po Leung Kuk as a separate and distinct Society. For 1878 and 1879 there are no lists and no accounts; the cost of providing food was borne by the Tung Wah Hospital; any other costs and expenses were borne by Mr Fung Ming Shan and others, the first members of the Committee, out of their own pockets. There are accounts from August, 1880, or thereabouts to August, 1892, and they show that the total receipts of the Society during these twelve years amounted from subscriptions and contributions *from the Directors* to $1,330. In addition there have been loans from the Tung Wah Hospital and the Man Mo Temple to the amount of $2,600, and from the Government grants or gifts of $1,050. No Home has ever been established or attempted to be established. The women and girls were housed in the Tung Wah Hospital to the great inconvenience of patients there and to the very doubtful advantage of the women and girls themselves, and food and clothing has been found by the Tung Wah, a separate and distinct Corporation. There have been no annual meetings of subscribers to the Po Leung Kuk, for there were none, and of course no proper elections of members of the Committee. The meetings have either been meetings of members of the Tung Wah, or of the general public, and the persons elected have

A. — By the Committee.
Q. — By the members of the Board?
A. — By as many as are present.
Q. — How many are present?
A. — Three or four.
Q. — Never only one member?
A. — No, always more than that.

Honourable C.P. Chater — I was told there was sometimes only one.

The Chairman — Who was your informant?

Honourable C.P. Chater — I do not remember.

Honourable Ho Kai — I can say there are generally two or three as far as I know.

Honourable T.H. Whitehead — But sometimes only one?

A. — I have never seen only one. There are generally two or three.

The Chairman — I may say that every letter sent to me as Registrar General is signed by two members. We had that in evidence last time. It came out during the examination of Mr. Wai Yuk.

Honourable T.H. Whitehead — As regards that subscription for $30,000 did you aid the Society in collecting it?

A. — I did nothing at all.
Q. — Did you know who did?
A. — I think the members of the Committee for last year and the year before collected it.
Q. — Do you think that the whole of the money will ultimately be paid.
A. — Yes, certainly, unless they allow some to hang on for a few years and then times may have changed.
Q. — And people may go away?
A. — Yes.

---

been generally the Tung Wah Committee men. It is not even certain . . . on what principle or how the Chairman of the Po Leung Kuk was elected or appointed or whether there was an election or a mere nomination. A book containing the names of the original members of the Society in 1881 has been produced . . . , but there is no register of later date. It is evident that the book cannot be correct because if there were 122 members there must have been at least $1,220 to the credit of the Society, but in 1880-1882 nothing appears in the accounts but subscriptions from the Directors, receipts from the former Emigration Enquiry Office, and a subscription of $100 from the Lai Hing firm.' (p. xii of the report)

Q. — Did any man outside the Po Leung Kuk assist in the collection of this money?
A. — I don't know.
Q. — You haven't heard?
A. — No.
Q. — Have you heard that the Registrar General assisted in the collection of it?

The Chairman — That has nothing whatever to do with the question before the meeting. Any accusations against the Registrar General can be made outside this committee.

Honourable T.H. Whitehead (to witness) — The Po Leung Kuk is practically governed by the Registrar General, isn't it?

A. — Yes.
Q. — In fact, the Po Leung Kuk is the Registrar General?
A. — No, not that.
Q. — As a matter of fact he decides everything?
A. — He decides everything; but these people have to find out everything for him.
Q. — He sits in judgement on the Committee?
A. — Yes.

The Chairman — Under the present rules of the Po Leung Kuk has the Registrar General any control over the Society?

A. — No control, but they choose to work with him.
Q. — Does not the Registrar General invariably consult the Po Leung Kuk with regard to any girls sent to the Po Leung Kuk?
A. — Yes, he asks for recommendations.
Q. — And is it not his rule to adopt these recommendations?
A. — Yes, as a rule.

Honourable T.H. Whitehead — There have been exceptions?

A. — Yes, certainly.
Q. — That being the case does it discourage the Po Leung Kuk from carrying on their work?
A. — If the Registrar General was right it would not discourage them.
Q. — If he happened to be wrong?
A. — Then, of course, they wouldn't like it.

The Chairman — Have you ever known a case where there has been a serious disagreement?

A. — No, not a serious disagreement.

Honourable T.H. Whitehead — You told us of one.

The Chairman — I will explain that to the Committee.

Mr. Ho Fook — That was in 1883 or 1884.

Honourable Ho Kai — It was a matter of form I think. There was some disagreement about the form of marriage, wasn't there?

Mr. Ho Fook — Yes, the Po Leung Kuk Committee objected to bridal chairs being used.

The Chairman — Do you remember Dr. Stewart having a discussion with the Po Leung Kuk on the question of the bridal sedan? The Po Leung Kuk differed from him on that question, didn't they?

A. — Yes.
Q. — The point was finally carried by the Registrar General. The opinion he combated was that a girl rescued from distress was not entitled to the same respect shown to other girls?
A. — Yes. Of course, if you marry a girl you must go through the proper ceremony.
Q. — That includes the use of the bridal sedan?
A. — Yes.
Q. — The Registrar General wished to show as much respect for the girls as possible?
A. — Yes.

Honourable Ho Kai — Prostitutes and such like?

A. — Yes, he made no distinction.
Q. — The Chinese are all against it?
A. — Unless you want the girls to be taken as concubines. I don't see why they should not use the bridal chairs.
Q. — You know that it is sometimes impossible to get rid of them as first wives. You know that the Po Leung Kuk Committee, or some of them, considered that the girls would do very well as second wives to respectable men?
A. — The English law does not permit bigamy.
Q. — I know that, but some of your friends and relations have concubines in this Colony?
A. — Yes.
Q. — They are in an English colony?
A. — Yes, but if the Society was associated with the Government would they permit it?
Q. — They are permitting it every day, aren't they?
A. — If they will permit these girls to be taken away as concubines that is all right.
Q. — That is, if they are comfortable and well provided for?
A.— Yes, but the Government might not allow such a thing to go on.
Q. — I know that, but I only ask whether that was not the point of dispute between the Committee and the Registrar General.

The Chairman — And the rule laid down by the former Registrar General has been carried out?

A. — Yes.

The Chairman — In Chinese marriage customs the bridal sedan is an indispensable accompaniment of a marriage. No legal marriage is complete without it. The Committee of the Po Leung Kuk of that day went to Dr. Stewart and said — 'These girls have led improper lives, why should we treat them in the same way as respectable girls?' Dr. Stewart said, in reply, that he would not allow them to be treated in any way different from respectable women. They come, he said, under the protection of the Society and he intended to show his respect for them as much as he would for his own daughter had he one. That was the difficulty. But afterwards the matter was arranged and now whenever a marriage is celebrated it is insisted that the document for hiring the bridal chair should be produced and then filed in the Office with the other documents. With regard to the other point, as to taking girls as second wives, the Registrar General from the very start set his face against it. Ever since I have known the office, and up to the present day, we have never sanctioned the taking of a girl as a concubine, because it was felt that you have no security in such a case, that the girl will not be got rid of. A respectable Chinaman treats his concubine well; but it might be possible for a man, so disposed to get rid of his concubine more easily than his wife, for among the Chinese the union with a concubine is not considered so binding as the union with a legal wife. For that reason the Registrar General set his face against the system of concubinage, and also because concubinage is not recognised by our law.

Hon. C.P. Chater — The Po Leung Kuk have never given these women away as concubines?

The Chairman — No, never.

Honourable Ho Kai — The mother sometimes gets the girl out and ultimately she is given away as second wife, but it is not done with the Registrar General's knowledge and consent.

The Chairman — If a girl is given out under security the surety must arrange to have her properly married, and, so far as I am aware, they are always married as first wives. There may be cases outside in which the girls are given as concubines.

Honourable Ho Kai — Yes, there are cases in Hong Kong in which girls are taken, though not from the Registrar General's Office, as concubines.

The Chairman — Then they must be out of our control because one of the provisions of handing them over is that they should be married as a first wife and brought up properly. The case you refer to, I think, is where the girl was detained in Hong Kong and sent to the Po Leung Kuk and it was then found out that she had already been sold to a man as his concubine. She was handed back to the mother to arrange for her marriage. The mother came down and took the girl away. She came from the country. We really had nothing whatever to do with the girl.

Honourable T.H. Whitehead — What happened to the girl?

Honourable Ho Kai — She was married as a concubine.

Honourable C.P. Chater — Are there many cases like that?

Honourable Ho Kai — The account given by the Chairman is correct, but what induced the Po Leung Kuk, in the first instance, to approach Dr. Stewart was that they experienced considerable difficulty in getting rid of those girls who had been prostitutes. A large number of the Chinese, in fact practically the whole of the Chinese Community, do not care to take a second-hand girl, as you may call her, as first wife. It is a kind of article of faith with them.

Honourable T.H. Whitehead — Then as regards these girls who have formerly been prostitutes, is there any difficulty placed in the way of their being made concubines?

Mr. Ho Fook — The Registrar General does not sanction it, and therefore they cannot do it.

Honourable C.P. Chater — The Registrar General tells us that he insists that there is a clause in the bond that the girls should be married as first wives. Dr. Ho Kai tells us that they do not get married as concubines.

The Chairman — Do you know, Dr. Ho Kai, whether the girl was married under the auspices of the Society?

Honourable Ho Kai — I do not say under the auspices of the Society. When they are handed back I know that sometimes they have been married as concubines and not as first wives.

Honourable C.P. Chater — You say that it is almost compulsory that the first wife should be a respectable woman?

Honourable Ho Kai — Certainly.

Honourable C.P. Chater — Then all these bonds given to the Registrar General have been violated?

Honourable Ho Kai — I don't know that, I don't know whether the bonds have been violated in any way. The Registrar General explained in this particular case that I mentioned that he had taken no bond. I can mention one or two cases. One case I know where a Committee man's brother took a girl out and she became his concubine. I think that it was during the present Registrar General's absence.

The Chairman — That does not matter whether I was absent or not as long as it was done in connection with the Po Leung Kuk.

Honourable Ho Kai — I have witnesses to prove that it was done.

The Chairman — I should like to know about it.

Honourable T.H. Whitehead (to the witness) — Do you know anything about this?

A. — No, I do not.
Q. — Or any similar case?
A. — No, I don't. There has been a good deal of talk that some of the bonds were violated in some way or another.

Honourable Ho Kai — Understand me. I don't mean to say that it was in connection with the Registrar General, but when the Registrar General has let them go outside, I know of cases in which they were married as concubines.

Honourable C.P. Chater — In one case you say that she was taken out by a brother of a Committee man of the Po Leung Kuk?

Honourable Ho Kai — Yes.

The Chairman — If he has violated the bond he has of course rendered himself liable.

Honourable C.P. Chater (to witness) — Do you know of any other members of the Committee, or their relatives, who have taken as concubines girls who have been inmates of the Home?

A. — No.

Honourable Ho Kai — I remember these cases because, at the time, I thought it was not quite proper, because if the Registrar General holds one rule it ought to be binding. I don't quite approve of the rule myself personally. Among the Chinese a girl, who is a reclaimed prostitute, has no chance of being married as a first wife.

The Chairman — It has not been found to be impossible. Many girls have been married as first wives who have come down here as prostitutes for a short time.

Mr. Ho Fook — It would take a longer time.

The Chairman — You must remember that the fact the man gets his wife for nothing weighs a good deal.

Honourable Ho Kai — But such a wife would have no status at the house in the country, and they would degrade her. If any Chinese is known to have taken a prostitute as first wife, he would lose caste.

Honourable F.H. May — Are you of opinion, Mr. Ho Fook, that we ought to do away with that restriction on concubines?

Witness — Yes, privately of course. But there is the question of expediency.

Honourable T.H. Whitehead — Therefore that the decision should rest with the permanent committee of the Po Leung Kuk?

A. — Yes, you might find a few men to take some of the girls as first wives, but if you have a girl who is old or ugly you will find some difficulty in disposing of her.

The Chairman — Have you ever heard of a case in which one of the Committee has got possession of one of these girls improperly?

A. — No, I have never heard; I don't remember, but I may have heard it. If the name of the man was given to me it might refresh my memory.

Honourable C.P. Chater — You don't know of your own knowledge that any member of the Committee, past or present, has as his concubine any woman who has been released from the Po Leung Kuk under the bond which the Chairman has spoken of?

A. — I haven't heard of any case.

Honourable Ho Kai — I don't know whether she was released under a bond in this particular case.

Honourable T.H. Whitehead — Who signs and is responsible for the bond?

The Chairman — I will show you a copy of the bond.

Honourable T.H. Whitehead — Who are security?

The Chairman — That depends. Satisfactory security has always to be found. When the people go away to the mainland, it is rather difficult to keep any check on them. We can only do our best and we try to prevent ourselves being deceived. (To the witness). Have you any extra checks to suggest which would secure the liberty of these girls more than at present?

A. — No. Whatever check you may provide, if the people themselves desire to deceive they generally carry out their object.

Q. — Then is it your opinion that what is done now cannot be improved upon?
A. — No, it cannot.
Q. — You think there has been an improvement in this respect during the last 10 years?
A. — Yes.

Honourable T. H. Whitehead — That is that at the beginning it was not such an easy matter to deal with these cases as it is now?

The Chairman — The checks have still to exist.

Honourable T.H. Whitehead — They have been increased from time to time?

Witness — Yes. I am not suggesting anything, but, as a matter of fact, people can deceive the Registrar General, and the Po Leung Kuk too, if they choose.

Honourable C.P. Chater — You would prefer the ordinance to be passed so as to enable the committee to decide, even if the Registrar General is against them?

A. — Yes.

Honourable T.H. Whitehead — Suppose the Government will not grant you that concession, what do you propose to do then? If the Government will not permit the cases to be decided by the majority of the members of the Po Leung Kuk, what do you propose to do?

A. — Let the Government manage the thing themselves.
Q. — In that event would the Police be capable of undertaking the work with the assistance of the Chinese?
A. — What Chinese? What Committee could you get?
Q. — Are there no Chinese here who would be in a position to assist the Police in the work?
A. — No.
Q. — The Registrar General would be helpless?
A. — Yes, without the assistance of the Po Leung Kuk.
Q. — If you do not get the power to deal with these cases into your own hands you propose to abandon the good work which has been carried on?
A. — Yes, unless the Government take the work on their own shoulders.

Honourable F.H. May — I do not understand you to mean that the proceeding you refer to would turn on that point alone. I consider you to mean that it will happen if the Po Leung Kuk does not receive assistance in money and get the ordinance?

A. — I mean both together. If you don't give the Committee a voice in their affairs, what is the good of having a Society? At the same time if the Government is not going to vote the money, how can the Society be kept up?

Honourable T.H. Whitehead — But this is a benevolent work and the Society is carrying on this work for the benefit of their own countrywomen, and as the Government are incapable of doing it without the aid of the Po Leung Kuk, surely the Society will still assist. If the Government refuses to grant the Society the power to overrule the Registrar General by the majority of votes, what will the Society do?

A. — The Society will throw up the whole thing.

Mr. Wai Long Shan examined, interpreted by Mr Ho Fook.

The Chairman — You were Chairman of the Po Leung Kuk Committee?

A. — Yes.
Q. — How long did you serve as Chairman?
A. — One year.
Q. — You are compradore in the Telegraph Company?
A. — Yes.
Q. — There is a document here, a memorandum from the Po Leung Kuk Committee with your signature?
A. — Yes.

Honourable C.P. Chater. — How long have you been Chairman?

A. — One year.
Q. — Have all cases which have gone to the Po Leung Kuk been brought before you?
A. — Yes.
Q. — Every case?
A. — When I had time I used to go up every night, but my business sometimes prevented me.
Q. — Do these investigations take place every night?
A. — Nearly every night.
Q. — How many are present as a rule?
A. — Two men at least.
Q. — Always two men?
A. — At least two.
Q. — Do the Committee arrange between them who are to be there, so as to ensure the presence of two men?
A. — There are no arrangements about it. According to rule two must be present. Sometimes one man may be a little late and then the clerk would be present with another member of the Committee.
Q. — Who is the clerk?
A. — He looks after the correspondence.
Q. — He is a servant of the Po Leung Kuk?
A. — Yes.

Q. — He makes the second when there are no other members present?
A. — If another member happens to be late.
Q. — Does that happen often?
A. — Only occasionally.
Q. — Is the second member ever entirely absent?
A. — Never absent, only late. The report must be signed by two.
Q. — Do you not know of a single instance in which there have been only one member of the Committee and the Clerk present?
A. — No, not a single case.
Q. — After the investigations you send the particulars in to the Registrar General?
A. — Yes.
Q. — And are guided by the Registrar General as to what should be done with the girls?
A. — We make recommendations.
Q. — Which would you prefer — the state of things as it is at the present moment or getting the majority of votes to decide as to what should be done with the girls?
A. — I should prefer that we might decide by the majority of the members of the Board.
Q. — Has not the business of the Society been carried on in a satisfactory manner heretofore?
A. — Yes.
Q. — And everything has worked well?
A. — Yes.
Q. — Then why ask for a change?
A. — The thing would not be right unless the majority decide it.
Q. — Then the thing has not been right heretofore, but you contend that everything has been satisfactory.
A. — We have made our recommendations to the Registrar General and they are generally accepted by him.
Q. — Why should not that be done in the future?
A. — You see, we are business men. We may get hold of kidnappers, and, if we work without the Government, they may go for us in our commercial affairs.

The Chairman — You have read the new Ordinance?

A. — Yes.
Q. — You desire that the Society should be associated with the Government, and not be able to act, as at present, independently of the Government?
A. — That is so.
Q. — That is one of the chief advantages?
A. — Yes.
Q. — The other advantage is with regard to the permanent Committee?

Honourable C.P. Chater — Why do you want these changes?

A. — Under the old rules the Committee could act independently. There is no mention of the Registrar General in the old rules and we want him to be associated with us. We desire that the Registrar General should be associated with our work, but we do not want to give the full power to him.

DOCUMENT II.b2: A Chinese guild in 1912 (source: Extracted from 'Information concerning the Guilds of Masons, Bricklayers, Shipbuilders, Carpenters & Contractors', in Miscellaneous Papers 1902-1911, Clementi Papers, Rhodes House Library, Oxford)

Bricklayers

The Bricklayers' Guild, known as the 'Kwong Yi T'ong,' is a guild of artisans numbering about 3,000 members. Its meeting place is at No. 2 Upper Rutter Street. The committee-men of the guild are known as Nga Shau and are elected annually on the 13th day of the 6th moon. Their number varies between 4 and 10, and their duty is to collect guild-fees and control unruly members. In February, 1903, the committee consisted of 4 men:-

> Ch'an Yau   No fixed address, but can always be found
> Kwan Kit   by reference to No. 2, Upper Rutter Street
> Kwan Yu   of the shop, No. 8 Moon Street, ground floor.
> Tsang Ch'ong Ke   No. 10 Station Street, Yaumati, first floor

The retiring Nga Shau recommend to the guild candidates for the committee of the ensuing year. Influential members are Tsa Weng Kwai, of No 2, Upper Rutter Street (ground-floor), who has belonged to the guild for more than 20 years and is one of the original members, and Ch'an Sheng, of No. 2, Upper Rutter Street. The guild is established in Hong Kong only, and has no connection with the bricklayers in Canton. No distinction is made of masters and artisans, and there is no separate guild of masters in the Colony corresponding to the artisan-guild.

Rules of the Bricklayers' Guild

Governments have codes and guilds have customs. Governments by merciful administration gives peace to the world, workmen by the use of rules and compasses make squares and circles. We bricklayers are disciples of Lo Pan, apprentices of Duke Pak Sheng, dexterous in making houses. In seeking for prosperity we all rely on the patron saint as our secret ally. We would require his help but cannot do so to our satisfaction. Eagerly we erect a tablet to our patron, with a whole heart we worship him. Hence we have set up rules which we all obey, in order that man and God may rejoice together. But unfortunately our means are small; and for this reason, after consulting together in general meeting, we have decided to open a ledger for recording contributions: thus by united exertion the load will easily be lifted, though one man's strength is insufficient. It is expected that you will unanimously give your assistance, open your purse-strings and help whole-heartedly the consummation of this worthy object. Is it not worthy? So much by way of preface.

Our guild is styled the Kwong Yi syndicate. Every year in the 6th month on the 13th day we must with reverent heart joyfully worship our patron Lo Pan wishing him a thousand birthdays; thus will the saint be pleased, men happy, and joy boundless.

The master-members of our guild must make an initial payment of $1, the artisan-members a similar payment of 10 cents: payment to be made by the 13th day of the 6th moon at latest. Those who join the guild later than that date must pay $2 if masters, and 30 cents if artisans: payment to be made by the 30th day of the 8th moon. Those who join later still must pay 50 cents and an additional $1 on the first day of the following year. Men of 60 years' age or more need not contribute. Contractors must pay at the same rates.

Rules:- (1) Members of the guild engaged for odd jobs must enter the facts every month in the guild-ledger, stating the wages they receive. For a job worth $2 or more, the guild-fee is at the rate of one per cent. If a contract is entered into for a whole piece of work, the guild-fee is at the rate of one per cent for a job worth $5 or more: but if the contractor has to pay for the materials, the fee will be 1/2 per cent only. If the fee paid to the syndicate is $25 or more, the syndicate shall make the payee a present of 30 catties of roast pork, a thousand K'ai-hung crackers, artificial flowers, red cloth, paper-money and candles. If the fee is even greater, the present will be increased in proportion.

If a member of the guild is already engaged on the spot for an odd job, no other member may underbid him and oust him from employment: but a member of the guild may accept engagement for an odd job close by and not on the spot where the other member is engaged. No quarrelling is permitted.

Similarly no member of the guild is permitted to eject another from employment under contract, plan, or specification.

Offences will be investigated by general meeting of the whole guild and a fine payable to the syndicate will be imposed of 5 per cent on the wage of the offender.

(2) Members of the guild entering into contract for work must within 10 days register the contract in the ledger of the guild. If they fail to do so, they incur a fine payable to the guild of 5 per cent on the value of the contract.

(3) Members of the guild receiving work from other members are distinguished as 'Sub-contractors' and 'Contractors.' If a contractor carries out completely the terms of the contract, but there are one or two small things which are not to the taste of his employer, then the contractor will make the requisite alterations: but if many alterations are required, additional wages must be paid. If the work is done too coarsely, or the roof is not waterproof, then the work must be done over again. If a sub-contractor is dilatory and does not do his work, the contractor will complete it himself deducting the expense from the wage due to the sub-contractor. If the sub-contractors give up the work when half finished, the contractor will complete it himself, and will cut the sub-contractor

to the full extent of the contract money which he the contractor shall have retained in his hands, becoming himself responsible for the payment of guild-dues. If the contractor's workmen steal the property of the employer, then the contractor will himself adjust the matter: but if the sub-contractor's workmen steal building materials, etc., the money will be cut out of the sub-contractor's contract.

(4) If a workman is permanently engaged, he must enter into a contract and begin work at once. If within one or two days he does not make a start, the contractor will do the work himself or depute another man to do it in his stead. Obstruction is not allowed. The contract will be treated as waste paper. Stirring up strife is not permitted, and any man who does stir up trouble will be tried and punished in general meeting of the guild.

(5) A man, who has not yet joined the guild but takes odd jobs in Hong Kong, should be invited to join our guild. If he refuses to join, should our guild procure labourers for him, he will be charged guild-tax at the rate of .04 tael per head, if he is a contractor, or .02 tael if he is a labourer. If a man not in the guild is employed by the guild as a master-workman, he must pay .01 tael as guild-money: if employed as an under-workman, at a daily wage of .08 tael or more, he must pay .005 tael as guild-money. If his daily wage is less than .08 tael, no charge will be made. All these charges are daily. If a stranger comes to Hong Kong from another port, no charge will be made for 7 days after his arrival: but after the 7th day, the full fee from the date of his arrival must be paid. If he works for a month he must enter the guild. Evasion of this rule will be considered and punished in general meeting of the guild.

(6) If owing to change in the contract-plans the additional employment of about one man for 10 days or 10 men for one day becomes necessary, the required change must be made. But if more labour than this is required, then additional payment must be made and an account rendered of the extra labour necessitated. If additional payment is refused, the contractor must temporarily stop work in expectation of the employer's obtaining another man for the work. Offenders will be tried in general meeting of the guild and will be fined one per cent as guild-tax. If the employer is in a hurry and wishes to engage another contractor, such contractor, if a member of the guild, can undertake the work only with the consent of the previous contractor, not otherwise. If he takes the work by force into his hands, his punishment will be decided upon in general meeting of the guild. But if the work is not included in the contract, a member of the guild may undertake to do it, and the previous contractor cannot under our rules bring force to bear upon him. Offenders will be punished in general meeting of the guild.

(7) The big contractors have an easy time, but the small contractors a bad time. First ascertain whether a labourer is honest, then whether he is skilful. It is most necessary that contracts should be precise in order that subsequent disputes may be avoided. If a sub-contractor completes the work according to contract and hands it over to his employer, then being a subordinate artisan of small means his account should be settled and his wages paid up to date as soon as possible. At most the employer should not delay more than a month in settling the account. If the employer delays

payment for more than a month, and some work remains incomplete, no member of the guild may do the work until the arrears of wages have been paid off in full. If any one disobeys this rule and takes over the work by force, then he must make good to the previous contractor the full sum still owing to the latter. Should he be unwilling to do so, the guild will deliberate on his punishment. The big contractors deal necessarily with the big employers, but these latter usually have a number of master-bricklayers with whom they deal year after year, and whose wages will frequently be in arrears: but it is scarcely possible to keep distinct the accounts of the different works on which they are engaged: hence the above rule must be obeyed.

(8) Members of the guild, if employed on odd jobs by an individual or by a shop must be paid, if master-bricklayers at the rate of 216 taels a day, if under-bricklayers at the rate of .144 taels a day. Therefore, on the average, employing master-bricklayers and under-bricklayers together, the wage of four workmen will be one dollar. From the present year, 1884 A.D., the calculation of wages must be made in accordance with this rule, and members of the guild are not at liberty to accept lower rates. If they do so they will be fined 10 per cent on their wage.

(9) The above guild-dues are heavy in the case of those who get most work, and light in the case of those who get little. They must be paid at regular intervals, in order that the collectors may not be obliged to pay frequent visits.

(10) The guild in engaging its accountant and its treasurer must insist on their giving security in money. Four collectors of guild-fees will make collections four times a month, and on each occasion every collector will be paid 216 tael for food and wages, including their refreshments while collecting. They must all four meet together at 8 a.m., to start on their round, they must walk [sic] hard and collect the fees. They may not, through favour, remit any one's fee. The chop of our guild will be evidence of payment, and any one who pays carelessly, without demanding a receipt, will only have himself to blame. Sums collected must at once be paid over to the treasurer, and the collectors must see with their own eyes that the entry is at once made in the ledger, so that mistakes may be avoided.

(11) Every bricklayer, engaged for a job, must within 3 days make a correct entry of the amount of this wage in the wage-book. If he fails to do so, the guild will enter his wage as being at the rate of 12 tael[*] per diem: and if the employer is not prepared to pay at that rate, the bricklayer must throw up his job and have his wages paid up to date. If the bricklayer is unwilling to accept the wage, he should not do the work. Force and compulsion must not be used on either side.

(12) Every bricklayer must be industrious and law-abiding: if he is not, but steals property in the store or the clothes of his fellow-guildmen, he must on arrest and conviction by the guild make good the theft and will be fined $3, half of which will be taken by his fellow-guildsmen to purchase wine and make merry. If the culprit stubbornly refuses to pay the fine, he must be given up to Government, and no member of the

---

[*] Chinese text gives 1 *qian* 2 *fen*, that is .12 taels.

guild may in future employ him: or, if engaged without knowledge of his disgraceful antecedents, his master must on discovery dismiss him, and his name must be posted in all the labour yards and shops, so that he may not be allowed to mingle with members of the guild: and he may not spend the night in any building belonging to the guild, so that all may be protected against possible injury from him.

(13) Englishmen fix a limit to the number of hours' work that may be done in a day: we must do the same. The hours of work are therefore to be as follows:-

From the 1st day of the 3rd moon to the 30th day of the 6th moon, from 6 a.m. to 6.30 p.m.

From the 1st day of the 7th moon to the 30th day of the 8th moon, from 6 a.m. to 6 p.m.

From the 1st day of the 9th moon to the 30th day of the 2nd moon, from 6.30 a.m. to 5 p.m.

The interval for luncheon and rest to be one hour.

(14) If, after working till 10 a.m., rain falls, it shall be reckoned that the half day's work has been done. If again in the afternoon, after working till 4 p.m., rain falls, it shall be considered that the half day's work has been done. If there are sudden showers, which clear off and come on at intervals, work must be continued till noon and again till 6 p.m., in accordance with the rules: if not continued, it shall be reckoned as short time.

(15) Every bricklayer must be paid .015 tael for food daily, that sum not including salt fish, oil and salt. But on the 2nd and 16th days of the month, which are days of sacrifice to Lo Pan every bricklayer must receive .05 tael for food and vegetables: and on each of the 4 annual solstices, every bricklayer must be paid a ration allowance of .07 tael, exclusive of wine.

(16) Each apprentice must come to an agreement with his master in the first instance and draw up a deed of apprenticeship. The term of apprenticeship will be 3 years, and the apprentice must attach himself to his master for the full period before he can set up on his own account. If, before the term expires, he hires himself for employment at another shop, no member of the guild may engage him. If this rule is broken the runaway apprentice must repay his board to his master at the rate of $3 a month and the man who has unrightfully employed him will be fined $5 to be used by the guild for the celebration of Lo Pan's birthday.

(17) If a member of the guild has a matter which he wishes to lay before the guild, he must first pay .36 tael in tea and smoke* money to the headmen and the members of the guild for the expenses of advertisement. No member may accept bribes to support an unjust cause, but just decisions must be given. Persons giving help to an unjust cause will be punished in general meeting of the guild.

---

* That is, tobacco.

(18) Any offence against the rules must be considered in general meeting. The offender's district must be ascertained and the chief member of the guild for that district will exert his authority over the offender and reprimand him. Quarrel and assault are not permitted. If a member of the guild fights and is arrested by the Police and fined, the guild will not be responsible.

(19) Obey these rules and make early payment of the guild-fees: this will be the high road to prosperity.

Made by the Kwong Yi Syndicate in the 6th moon of the 10th year of Kwong Sou (July-August, 1884 A.D.)

DOCUMENT II.b3: A Report on the Chinese guilds of Hong Kong, 1912 (source: A.E. Wood, *Report on the Chinese Guilds of Hong Kong, compiled from material collected by the Registrar General*, Hong Kong; Noronha & Co., 1912)

The guilds of Hong Kong may be divided into three classes:

(a) Those formed for the establishment of business regulations and rules governing apprenticeship and the proper conduct of appropriate religious ceremonies. These are akin to the craft guilds of medieval Europe, and are mostly law-abiding. The regulations are frequently very minute, and one may trace in them the influence of the 'father and mother' attitude which is so pleasant a feature of ideal Chinese administration. The Artisan Tailor rules, for instance, forbid the introduction of rainhats and other dirty articles into the guild hall, and prohibit work there as an insult to the Patron Saint. Most guild rules contain regulations about food and premises, and discountenance misbehaviour of any kind. The Nam Pak Hong rules are a good type of those based on a desire for commercial honesty.

(b) Those that possess many of the characteristics of a modern Trades Union. These are formed by Masters or by Employees, or sometimes by both in concert, as a weapon for enforcing their terms on opponents. Such guilds appear to be the result of Hong Kong conditions of trade and association with Western methods, rather than typically Chinese institutions. They are sometimes turbulent, and often powerful, and are the guilds that call most for the attention of the Government. Important modern problems, e.g. strikes and a minimum wage, are introduced. Certain guilds employ professional fighters to do their persuasion for them, put compulsion on masters to engage none but guild-men, and retain lawyers for defence of members who get into trouble on account of the guild.

(c) Those that are mutual benefit societies and Clubs rather than guilds in the ordinary sense of the term. They are usually inoffensive and do good work, but sometimes, as in the case of the Blackwood Trade, contain the germ of potentially powerful institutions.

Object of formation

Common to almost every guild of whatever class is the practice of granting burial money to the relatives of deceased members. Originally, perhaps, this, together with the observance of religious customs, was the chief object of Chinese guilds, and it still forms an integral part of the guild's economy. It is interesting to note that Sandalwood Men's Guild was originally the 'long life association', that is to say it was a Burial Fund Club which grew into a Guild. Other objects have since supervened, and Table [2.1] gives a detailed list of those that stimulated the formation of Hong Kong guilds.

Guild funds

Many of the guilds have considerable funds at their disposal, invested either in their own trade or elsewhere. Sometimes they have real property, and possess their own guild-halls, but these are usually rented.

Those guilds that are connected with Canton branches of the same trade may have a twofold source of wealth: e.g., the Tinfoil Guild rejoices in the possession of a house near the West Gate in Canton, where out-of-work Hong Kong members go to rest themselves.

The chief sources of funds are as follows:

(1) Entrance Fees. There has been a gradual and general rise in these of late, but they vary very much from guild to guild, ranging from $1.00 to $20.00 or more. Some guilds make a practice of paying expenses out of entrance fees, but this is a bad system, since the raising of the fee tends to frighten away new members, masters cannot get all the men they want, and trouble follows.

(2) Regular subscriptions, which are payable monthly, or on two or more Feast Days, or annually. In these again there is no uniformity: they may be anything from 10 cents to $1.00 a time. Under this heading may be placed such sources of income as percentages on commissions, as in the Coal Sub-contractors' Guild, on wages, as in the Masons', and on sales, as in the Rattan (公和堂).

(3) Special Subscriptions to meet special needs.

The usual expenses of a guild are: -

(1) Hire of guild hall, something like $40.00 a month. This item is not, of course, incurred by guilds that own their own hall. Others again have no hall, but meet in members' shops in rotation, or hold their feasts in a restaurant.

(2) Periodical feast in honour of the patron saint or saints. Each dining member pays a special subscription of 40 or 50 cents, but any deficit is met by the guild.

(3) Payment of burial money, and in some cases, honoraria to the aged on retirement. Special subscriptions are, however, frequently levied to assist the guild funds in making these payments. Burial money may be anything form $5.00 to $40.00.

(4) Subscriptions to charitable institutions, such as the Po Leung Kuk, and the Tung Wa Hospital.

Table 2.1
Object of Guild's Formation*

Note:- Provision of burial money is among the objects of almost every guild. It is therefore omitted below, for the sake of convenience.

Tiffin Houses	Provide quarters for employees.
Artisan Tailors	Get rise in wages.
Barbers	Fix prices.
Blackwood	Not yet formulated as a guild, but might become an effective one.
Boat	To meet difficulty of wages in advance.
Brass-smiths	(1) Self-defence of Yaumati against Hong Kong branch of the trade. (2) Represent interests of employees.
Bricklayers	Represent interests of employees.
Brothel-waiters	Religious customs: a club.
Californian Merchants	Fix rules.
Carpenters	Fix wages and rules: unite masters and men.
Coal Contractors	As result of, and in opposition to, Coal Sub-contractors' guild.
Coal Sub-contractors	Get rise in wages.
Boys and Stewards	A club.
Steamers' Cooks and Boys	A club.
Chinese Compositors	To represent employees' interest and find work for members.
European Compositors	Do
	To combat grievance of dismissal without notice.
Compradores	Fix business rules and customs.
Builders	Improve conditions of trade, promote harmony, and, if funds permit, subscribe to charitable institutions.
Coopers	Represent employees' interests and support them during strikes.
Copper-smiths	(1) As result of, and in opposition to, employees' guild. (2) Represent interests of employees.
Dyers	To strengthen the hands of masters against employees.
Eating House Employees	To provide substitutes, when leave required.
European Tailors	(1) Old guild: one object was to prohibit the use of sewing machines. (2) New guild: to strengthen the hands of employees, and fix rules.
Fish (sea)	A club. Religious customs and charitable subscriptions.
Fish (pond)	Do
Nam Pak Hong	Fix business rules. (The preamble is typical.)
Masons	(1) Religious. Maintain good relations with employees. (2) Fix rules for men v. masters.
Master Tailors	'Peaceful Deliberation Society.' Provide means for settling disputes between masters and men.
Piece Goods	A club. Provide fire-brigade.
Pig-buyers	Unite masters and men and fix prices.
Pig-dealers	Fix amount of commission.
Rattan Chairs (skin)	Fix rules and tariff.

(Table 2.1 cont)

(Table 2.1 cont)

Rattan Chairs (pith)	Do
Restaurant Employees	(1) Assist unfortunate members. (2) Fix rules of labour and wages.
Salt Fish	Fix commission.
Sandalwood	(1) Fix hours and wages. (2) Originally purely a burial fund club. Rules since added.
Servants	Mutual help, and social intercourse.
Society for Improvement of Engineering	Largely educational.
Tin Foil	Solidarity of masters and men.
Washermen (West)	Combination of masters and men.
" (Wanchai)	Unite masters and men against Washermen (West).

*This table has been abbreviated. — Ed.

(5) Purchase of pork for distribution to members on festal occasions. To these may be added two rarer items;-

(6) Employment of professional fighters. (e.g., Blackwood, Teahouses)

(7) Engagement of lawyers when a member gets into trouble on the guild's account. (Rattan)

Where the guild has only small funds, or none in hand at all, these expenses cannot, of course, be lavishly maintained, but every guild should be able by subscription to raise enough money to hold a periodical feast, to worship its patron saint, and to provide pork and burial money. It is curious that there are a few guilds (Carpenters, Coopers, Masons (men), Master Tailors and Tinsmiths) which do not give burial money, but lack of funds does not appear to be an explanation in any of these instances.

Administration of the guild

The administration of the guild is generally in the hands of a committee on which members may serve in rotation. The usual term of office is one year. It is the duty of the committee to keep accounts and post balance-sheets, to administer funds, to prevent quarrels, and sometimes to draw emoluments (cf. Californian Merchants, who make a special grant of $100 travelling allowance per annum 'that (the manager) may be vigorous in well-doing.')

Sometimes a permanent clerk is paid to look after the books. (Coal Sub-contractors.)

Strength of the guilds, and their weakness

(a) Many of the guilds are effective and powerful. They maintain a rigid authority over members, and insist on strict adherence to the rules. As might be expected, they are in many cases the very guilds that have come in contact with the Registrar General or the Police. Certain of them employ professional fighters, or are connected with powerful political societies, and discipline is encouraged by rewards for information of disobedience, and fines for offenses against the rules. The Bricklayers' and Carpenters' Guilds insist on all contracts being reported to the committee, and no alteration can be made in any contract except through the guild. Where a guild is strong and yet orderly, its firmness is largely due to tradition, and the stiffening afforded by several tens of years of old custom.

(b) Their weakness is liable to come from the absence of real advantage to be gained, and from the difficulty of supervision.

Strikes

Strikes, as the Registrar General remarks, seem to occur chiefly in expanding trades where there is a scarcity of skilled workmen.

Table [2.2] sets forth the strikes that are on record in Hong Kong and gives the date and object in each case. It will be seen that most of the disputes have been connected with wages, but about 20 % originated from insistence on the unity of the guild.

Table 2.2
Guilds Which Have Strikes on Record, and the Occasion of Each Successful Strike

Guild	Date	Cause or object of strike
Artisan tailors	1883	Demand for small rise in wages.
	1905	Force recalcitrant tradesmen to join the guild.
Barbers	1895	Raise price of shaving.
Blackwood	1911	Failure of one master to keep promise of New Year pay.
Brass-smiths (employees)	1900	Prevent removal to Yaumati and consequent reduction in wages.
Carpenters	1891	Raise wages.
Coal sub-contractors	1909	Raise 'shovel-money'
European compositors	1910	Demand double-pay for overtime.
Coopers	1894-5	Resist employment of outsiders.
	"	Two strikes, arising out of reprimand to workman.
Masons (employees)	1889	Protest against inferior quality of rice supplied by masters.

(Table 2.2 cont)

(Table 2.1 cont)

Trade	Year	Cause
Painters	1909	Rise in wages (only partially successful).
Rattan chairs (pith)	1891	Shorten hours of labour.
Rattan splitters	1903	Raise wages.
Sandalwood (employees)	1901	Raise wages.
Shipwrights	1911	Raise wages.
Tea boxes	1904	Raise allowance for 'Sung,' (i.e. fish, pork, or other accompaniment to rice).
Brass-smiths (employees)	1882	Raise wages.
Bricklayers	1900	Shorten hours of work.
	1902	Trouble with Roman Catholic Cathedral contractors.
Coopers	1895	Protest against dismissal of member.
	1908	Shorten hours.
Dyers	1908	Strike of workmen's guild, which was dissolved on failure of strike. Connected with distinction between permanent and job workmen.
Masons (employees)	1902	Trouble with Roman Catholic Cathedral contractor.
	1907	Failure of sub-contractor on Kowloon-Canton Railway, No. 4 Bridge.
Master tailors	1910	Quarrel with workmen.
Rattan chairs (pith)	1910	A quarrel.
Society for Improvement of Engineering	1910	An unauthorized strike, which the guild committee soon crushed.

In some instances petty quarrels were the excuse, if not the reason, for a strike, while in three cases the cause was a demand for European hours of labour, i.e. from 7 to 5, with an hour for tiffin, as opposed to the native hours of 6 to 6, with no stated intervals for refreshment.

Strikes are usually settled by the Registrar General, with the assistance of Chinese gentlemen, by means of a compromise, and frequently the opportunity is taken to draw up new rules. On the whole, masters and employees are remarkably willing to listen to reason, and serious strikes have been few.

It is interesting to note that the Coopers' Guild, which is one of the most firmly organized, will pay its members five cents a day during a strike.

DOCUMENT II.b4: The Tung Wah Hospital, election of committee (source: Man-kam Lo, later Sir Man-kam Lo, in *South China Morning Post* 1934 or 1935, included in Vincent H.G. Jarrett, 'Old Hong Kong', deposited at the Hong Kong Collection, Hong Kong University Library.)

Europeans in the Colony must have frequently heard of the Directors of the Tung Wah. In view of the responsibility of their work, and the honoured tradition of their office, they occupy a highly esteemed position in the Chinese community, and the Chairman for the time being may more or less be regarded as the unofficial mayor of the Chinese community. How are they elected. What is the procedure of the election? Well, the procedure is shortly as follows:

In the 8th moon of every year a notice is posted up outside the Hospital, and also in some public place near the old fire Brigade Station, announcing the fact that the term of office of the directors would soon expire (i.e. the end of the year), and asking the Kai Fong* to proceed to elect new representatives to serve. The language of the announcement, like so many other things connected with the Tung Wah, is strictly in accordance with precedent, and is couched in deprecatory terms as to the inability of the current directors to accomplish anything for the Hospital — however much such language may be at variance with the directors' achievements!

About this time notices would be sent out by the hospital to the various guilds who for the time being have the right to nominate representatives to serve as directors. On receipt of such notices, each guild would proceed to call a meeting of its members and to nominate one to serve. The guild would inform the hospital of the person nominated. The hospital would then write to the person in question telling him that he had been elected by his guild to serve, and inviting him to do so. According to old custom, if he intended to accept, he would first write a letter to the hospital declining on account of his imaginary unfitness and incapacity. Another letter from the hospital would be sent to him extolling his accomplishments and virtues, and pressing him to accept. He would probably write a second letter declining. Another letter would be sent to him and he would then write in reply to accept. In more recent times, however, the practice of going through a formal refusal twice is not adhered to. If he really wished to decline, the hospital would then notify the guild, requesting the guild to proceed to another person to serve.

Eventually the representatives elected by the guilds would all have signified their agreement to serve, and their names would then be posted up in the big hall of the hospital as notice to the public in case anyone should like to raise any objection to the nominees.

The number of guilds sending representatives varies from time to time. Besides the yan sheung, to which I will refer, the following guilds nominate representatives to serve as directors. — Pawnbrokers' Guild, Piece-goods and Silk Guild, Californian Merchants' Guild, Chinese Bankers' Guild, Chinese Insurance Guild, Importers of Foreign Goods Guild, and the Chinese Medicine Guild.

The above guilds are guilds properly so called. There is one special body which is not strictly a guild, but which has always had the right of sending representatives, namely the yan sheung, literally meaning 'wealthy merchant'. Anyone who subscribes either $50, or $100 to the hospital becomes a member of this body, but he has to continue to subscribe such sum annually, otherwise he ceases to be such a number. The

---

* Neighbourhood committees

number of directors elected by the yan sheung varies from time to time. This year the yan sheung elected 8 out of the 20 directors serving. The mode of electing a representative of the yan sheung is the same in principal. But as the body is necessarily vague and fluctuating, the exact method of election is as follows:- About the time when letters would be sent out to the various guilds, but usually a little later in the year, a public advertisement is inserted in the papers stating that the election of representatives of the yan sheung would be held at the hospital on the date therein stated.

On the day in question, usually a few of the yan sheung would be present, but in any case the current directors representing yan sheung would be present, together with their colleagues. Those who were willing to stand would have been previously ascertained, and the election would be merely a matter of formality.

Such, in brief, is the way in which the directors of the Tung Wah are elected annually.

c. The Chinese Community's Politics

At some stage, feelings for home and temple were converted into an identity with the Chinese as a people and China as a nation. Expressions of this identity took many forms: Ho Kai's opposition to the Public Health Bill of 1887 fell within the realm of opposition that was acceptable to the Hong Kong Government; Tse Tsan-tai's liaison with Chinese revolutionaries fell on the edge of acceptability.*

Ho Kai was, after all, appointed to the Sanitary Board so that there might be a Chinese voice at its meeting. By now he had qualified as a barrister and he represented a Chinese view that had been enlightened by Western values. He was not necessarily opposed to the need of government setting sanitary standards, but, he was opposed to what he considered the imposition by law of Western standards on on-going Chinese practices. His opposition was, however, quite harmless. The Sanitary Board's rejoinder to his opposition was signed by seven Westerners, who in answer to Ho Kai's opposition, appealed to universal standards that community health demanded. 'These [that is, the provisions of the bill] fall far short of European sanitary provisions on the one hand, while on the other hand nothing has been adduced to warrant the assumption that the constitution of the Chinaman is so far different from that of the rest of the human race, that his dwelling may do with less light, less air, and less ventilation, than the minimums provided in the Bill.'** Nor did the protest bring Ho Kai a great deal of harm. In 1890, he was appointed to the Legislative Council.

---

* In *pinyin*, Tse Tsan-tai's name would be spelt Xie Zantai.
** 'The Sanitary Board's rejoinder,' in *Sessional Papers of the Legislative Council*, 1887, p. 409.

Tse Tsan-tai's remarkable account of attempts by him and his friends to bring about uprisings in south China in oppostion to the Qing dynasty government addresses a much more complicated period in Hong Kong's history. The sentiments that Tse Tsan-tai's account reveals show that political activism was made of very different stuff from internal lobbying that depended on the Hong Kong government's appointment. The political activist at the turn of the nineteenth century in Hong Kong had his eyes set on China, and his activism developed in the crevice that was created by the remote chance that the Hong Kong government might allow him to pursue an agenda that would be at odds with the toleration of the British home government in London. In 1899, the chance came about because as the Boxer Rebellion was breaking out, it looked as if political activism might pry Guangdong province away from the Chinese government. That opportunity passed, but the aspiration towards political reform in China lingered. Despite Tse Tsan-tai's claims, it is unclear to what extent he was involved in subsequent uprisings, but the Qing government took seriously enough revolutionary groups such as the one that had formed around his friend Yeung Ku-wan[*]. Yeung paid for his activism with his life. However, Sun Yat-sen, an associate from this time, moved on to fill the role of the revolutionary leader.

DOCUMENT II.c1: In defense of the Chinese community, Ho Kai's protest against the Public Health Bill, 1887 (source: Ho Kai, 'Memo of objections', 22 December 1886 in 'Dr Ho Kai's protest against the Public Health Bill, submitted to the Government by the Sanitary Board, and the Board's rejoinder thereto', *Sessional Papers* August 1868- September 1887, pp. 404-405)

Some Sanitarians are constantly making the mistake of treating Chinese as if they were Europeans. They appear to forget that there are wide constitutional differences between a native of China and one who hails from Europe. They do not allow for the differences of habits, usage, mode of living and a host of other things between the two. They insist upon the theory of treating all nationalities alike however much they may differ from one another physically, mentally, and constitutionally. Hence arise the several provisions in this Ordinance and Bye-laws in question which I have no hesitation in characterizing as wholly unnecessary. One might as well insist that all Chinese should eat bread and beefsteak instead of rice and pork, just because the two former articles agree better than the latter with an English stomach. One favorite argument must here be stated and refuted. It has been stated by some advocates of this Bill that the Government is always adverse to anything like class legislation and that any recommendation of the Sanitary Board to that effect would not likely be entertained. This I must confess does remind one of old times when all class legislation was earnestly

---

[*] In *pinyin*, Yang Quyun.

sought for to be abolished, but with what results I need not mention. Look over our local Ordinances, how many there are still in force which make clear distinctions between Chinese and Europeans. It would only be a wasting of time to quote instances. As long as we govern the Chinese according to our promise given while this Colony was yet in its infancy, viz., to govern them as much as possible in accordance with their manners and customs, and to respect their religion and prejudices, we must of a necessity modify our laws in order to meet their peculiar requirements. Besides, does not common sense alone indicate to us the advisability of legislating especially in many cases to suit circumstances and surroundings?

From an economical point of view, the idea of sacrificing the millions of square feet at an average price of $6 to $7 per square foot is even more ridiculous. What is this enforced sacrifice for? Simply for the sake of a theory that the Chinese public require all such Sanitary improvements to promote their health and welfare. But I challenge the soundness of that theory: I say the Chinese in general do not require this sacrifice or even desire it. Let the Government ascertain the views of the Chinese in this matter. I have often been told that I was almost always in a minority in the discussion of the various sections of this Bill, but I was and am confident that the public at large, without distinction of races, will support me in most of my contentions. I was often charged also with looking too exclusively after the interest of landlords, but I always denied that charge. I do not only represent the interest of landlords, and personally I am not a landlord, I care for the tenants as much as the landlords, and the poor as well as the rich. It is not for the welfare of the poor to have the valuable space occupied by their small rooms narrowed, in order to provide for a model of a privy, a superb kitchen and a sumptuous backyard of 10 feet wide, while at the same time the wicked landlords continue to charge the same rent or even a higher one for improvements and increased capital necessary to effect such improvements. I am not aware of any law, except in Ireland perhaps, which will compel landlords to lower their rent to an equitably low amount. Perhaps such law will be enacted here, but for the present at all events, all landlords, like everybody else, will want to get from 7 to 8 per cent net interest on their capital. What is the price of land now per square foot? In the central and most populous parts of China-town, like Queen's Road Central, and Bonham Strand, it is something like $9 or $10 or more, and even in the more distant and less valuable quarters, it is something like $3 or $4. Just fancy the position of the poor tenant if this Bill becomes law, he would be forced to pay an enormous rent for less space than before, plus all sorts of Sanitary improvements which, however good in themselves from a European stand point, they do not care for, and which they think at least their constitutions do not require. They may say that they are habituated to such cities like Canton, Kowloon city, &c., compared to which Hong Kong as it now stands is a paradise, a model of cleanliness, a perfect Sanitarium, and that if any more improvements are required, let those who advocate it pay for them and not they. Here two adverse arguments must be noticed. The first is that the Chinese are so ignorant of what is good for themselves that they must be taught, and forcibly too, by means of severe legislative measures. I hardly expected to hear of such an argument, if such it may be termed, at the end of the nineteenth century. It reminds one of the Star Chamber and the Inquisition. Those who advance this argument had better take care, lest some wiser heads might act upon the same principle and enforce something unpleasant upon themselves. Let me give a few illustrations of this dangerous but with some persons most plausible argument. (1) The established religion of England is Protestant Christianity, the Chinese are mostly heathens, but as they are ignorant and should be taught, let us legislate for enforced Christianity. (2) The Chinese doctors do not know anything about the European practice of medicine and the Chinese public constantly go to them for advice; but then they are so ignorant — let us legislate for the total expulsion of Chinese trained practitioners and forbid all Chinese under heavy penalties from consulting any one but European doctors. (3) Many Chinese are inveterate opium smokers, that if long continued, must be injurious to their health as well as a waste of their money; but they are so dreadfully ignorant — let us legislate and force every one to abstain from opium smoking. I may multiply examples, but these will show what I mean. No European will deny that the Chinese urgently need reform in their religion, their system of medicine and their opium smoking habits, but who will advocate that such reform should be wrought by means of harsh and sweeping legislation? Their ignorance should be enlightened no doubt, but not by penal law. The second argument is more reasonable and it is this, that as habitable rooms get smaller and rents go higher in directly opposite proportion, wages will get higher too and that will compensate the poor tenants. This would be perfectly true, I admit, if Hong Kong were hundreds of miles away from China. But fortunately or unfortunately, we are close to the mainland, where thousands of poor Chinese are struggling for a bare subsistence. The labour market is always in excess of the demand, and there are many able bodies who are willing and even anxious to get their 10 or 20 cents a day. Those who stick out for higher wages on account of increased rent and less house accommodation will be supplanted by those who will be content with less. For example, if a man gets say $15 a month and has to pay $5 per month for two small rooms for his wife and children and $10 for food and clothing &c., but on account of higher rent he has to pay $6 for the same two rooms smaller than before on account of the sacrifice of building for backyard and other spaces, he would, according to the law laid down above demand $16 per month for his services. He would certainly succeed in this if there were no one to take his place for less, but let us say there are plenty who will take it for less, then what must the poor man do but to pay the $6, or resort to overcrowding or to stinting himself and his family of food and clothing. Now allow me to ask whether building four feet away from retaining walls, the leaving of a ten feet wide backyard and the establishing of a 3/6 feet brick privy and spacious kitchen, are more necessary than food and clothing, or more desirable than overcrowding?

DOCUMENT II.c2: Political activism, promoting China's revolution in Hong Kong (source: Tse Tsan Tai, *The Chinese Revolution, Secret History of the Revolution*, Hong Kong: *South China Morning Post* 1924)

SOWING THE SEED

Arrival in China

In the year 1887, when sixteen years of age, I left Sydney for China with my mother, two younger brothers and three sisters. What struck me on first landing in Hong Kong on the 20th May, 1887, was the cramped pigeon-holed houses, the narrow insanitary streets, and the total absence of shade trees.

My father's old friends welcomed us all ashore, and we quickly found ourselves at home in a strange city with strange surroundings. Shortly after settling down, I was introduced to Hon. Mr. J. H. Stewart Lockhart, now Sir J.H. Stewart Lockart, K.C.M.G., retired ex-Commissioner of Wei-hai-wei, who was then Registrar General of Hong Kong. He received me very kindly and advised me to enter Queen's College preparatory to joining the Hong Kong Government service.

During my stay at Queen's College, I made the acquaintance of a number of promising and patriotic young men inside and outside the College, and it began to dawn upon me that the time was ripe and opportune for planning and organizing a movement for the reformation of China's millions, and for the expulsion of the usurping Manchu Tartars from China.

Chief of those of my sixteen friends who were in my confidence and knew my secret were Yeung Ku-wan, Chan Fun, Chau Chiu-ngok, Wong Kwok-u, Lo Man-yuk and Lau In-bun. The remainder were not let into the secret, as it was too dangerous to openly preach revolution at the time, and besides, the Colony of Hong Kong was full of spies and secret agents of the Manchu Canton Government.

Accordingly we used to meet surreptitiously at Ping Kee shipping office, Praya Central, where Lau In-bun was chief shipping clerk, at the China Merchants Steam Navigation Co., where Yeung Ku-wan was chief shipping clerk, at Gon Kee, the shipping office of Woo Gon-chi, Compradore of Messrs. David Sassoon & Co., and at my own house, No. 11, Wing Shing Street.

Difficulties and Dangers

So feared and dreaded were the Manchu Canton officials and their spies and informers, that the people dared not talk of revolution or associate with people of revolutionary tendencies. Such was the state of public feeling during the years 1887 to 1895, when it was extremely difficult to gain recruits or even sympathisers.

We always met the taunts and ridicule of our chicken-hearted and doubting 'friends' in silence. But nothing discouraged us, and we fearlessly and silently struggled on.

During all these long years of secret planning and organizing, I always used to mix up with the spies and secret agents of the Manchu Canton Government, and pay visits to their 'haunts.' I was persistently putting my head in the tiger's jaws!

How I bluffed and blinded them is a long story, and cannot be told in the pages of this short history.

My English friends and colleagues were just as careful and shrewd as myself, and we managed to keep everything secret and to ourselves.

The Seed Germinates

On the 13th March 1892, we established our Revolutionary Headquarters on the first floor of No. 1 Pak Tze Lane, Hong Kong, the second floor being occupied by Luk King-fo and his friends of the 'Iu Kui' Club.

Luk King-fo is, at present, an official of the Foreign Affairs Department at Canton, but was formerly a teacher of Queen's College, Hong Kong.

We adopted as our motto 'Ducit Amor Patriae,' and named our meeting place the 'Foo Yan Man Ser,' but this did not prevent it from being visited from time to time by European Police detectives, who were always welcome!

In the year 1894, Japan declared war against China, and the disgraceful defeat of China, followed by the 'Boxer' rising, increased the growing discontent of the Chinese against the Manchu regime in China, and from this time onwards a new spirit was abroad in the land.

16th May, 1894 — I advocated in the *Hongkong Daily Press* the suppression of the Indian opium trade, and widely distributed my pamphlets in England and in China, I took a leading part in the formation of the Anti-Opium Society of South China in the year 1898.

30th May, 1894 — I protested in the *Hongkong Daily Press* against the slandering of the Chinese community; and for 'dabbling in politics,' whilst in the Government Service, I was reprimanded by the Colonial Secretary.

In the spring of 1895, Yeung Ku-wan conferred with me, and we joined hands with Dr. Sun Yat-sen and his friends and established the Hing Chung Whui revolutionary party. We established our new headquarters at No. 13, Staunton Street, and named the meeting place the 'Kuen Hang' Club.

We frequently interviewed the late Sir Kai Ho Kai, Kt., C.M.G., and he secretly promised us his support. We also succeeded in obtaining the secret support of the editors of the *China Mail* and *Hongkong Telegraph*.

Thomas H. Reid, Editor of the *China Mail*, and Chesney Duncan, Editor of the *Hongkong Telegraph*, were the first to openly and fearlessly champion the great cause in their newspapers, and at a time when nearly everybody ridiculed the movement.

On one occasion, Chesney Duncan was called before the Colonial Secretary, who reprimanded him for what he had published, claiming that it amounted to incitement of the Chinese to revolt against a Government with which Great Britain was on friendly terms. In spite of such warnings, I am proud to record that their faithfulness and loyalty has never swerved.

Organizing the Revolution

12th March, 1895 — Dr. Ho Kai's 'Reform' article published by the *China Mail*. Dr. Ho Kai was a Barrister and a member of the Hong Kong Legislative Council, representing the Chinese. He was a man of sound judgement and ripe experience.

13th March, 1895 — Yeung Ku-wan, Dr. Sun Yat-sen, Wong Wing-sheung, and

Tse Tsan-tai confer together re organization of the movement to capture Canton. Wong Wing-sheung was the second son of the late Hon. Wong Shing, member of the Hong Kong Legislative Council.

16th March, 1895 — Yeung Ku-wan, Dr. Sun Yat-sen and Tse Tsan-tai discuss plans for an attempt to capture Canton with 3,000 picked men.

We obtain the secret support of the Japanese Government through the Japanese Consul.

We adopt as the design of our flag, a white sun on a blue ground.

Dr. Ho Kai accepts responsibility for the work of drafting proclamations, etc.

Thomas H. Reid, Editor of the *China Mail*, interviewed, and he promises us his support.

18th March, 1895 — The *China Mail* publishes a lengthy article in our support.

21st March, 1895 — Yeung Ku-wan, Dr. Sun Yat-sen, Wong Wing-sheung and Tse Tsan-tai confer with Chesney Duncan, Editor of the *Hongkong Telegraph*, at No. 13 Staunton Street. He assured us of his support.

The *Hongkong Telegraph* supports our movement.

Manifesto to Emperor Kwang Hsu

30th May, 1895 — Tse Tsan-tai's 'Open Letter' to the Manchu Emperor Kwang Hsu published in the *China Mail*, *Hongkong Telegraph*, and other newspapers of Singapore and the Far East. This 'manifesto' was broadcasted by means of the English and foreign newspapers in order to search the hearts of the Chinese at home and abroad.

27th August, 1895 — Plans for the capture of Canton being completed, orders were given for the closing of the 'Kuen Hang' Club at No. 13, Staunton Street.

29th August, 1895 — Yeung Ku-wan, Dr. Sun Yat-sen, Wong Wing-sheung, Chan Siu-pak, Dr. Ho Kai, Thomas H. Reid and Tse Tsan-tai meet at Hang Fa Lau Hotel. Dr. Ho Kai acted as spokesman, and we outined the policy of the Provisional Government. Thomas H. Reid agreed to do his best to work for the sympathy and support of the British Government and the people of England.

9th October, 1895 — Our proclamation to the Foreign Powers drafted by Thomas H. Reid and T. Cowen, and revised by Dr. Ho Kai and Tse Tsan-tai.

President of Provisional Government

10th October, 1895 — Yeung Ku-wan elected President of the 'Provisional Government,' preparatory to the attempt to capture Canton.

Note: The election of Yeung Ku-wan as President greatly displeased Dr. Sun Yat-sen, and it always rankled in his breast. On the 12th October, 1896, Wong Wing-sheung (second son of Hon. Wong Shing) remarked, when strongly censuring Dr. Sun Yat-sen for his incapacity: 'I will have nothing to do with Sun in the future.'

On the 26th October, 1895, we made our first attempt to capture Canton, but owing to our plans being divulged to the Canton authorities by traitors in Hong Kong, the attempt ended in failure. Numerous arrests and executions followed. Yow Lit and others escaped.

Dr. Sun Yat-sen and Chan Siu-pak succeeded in escaping to Macao, and from thence they proceeded to Japan.

Dr. Sun Yat-sen was subsequently kidnapped in London on 11th October, 1896, by the Manchu Chinese Legation officials, and rescued by his friend Dr. James Cantlie, who was his old teacher in the Medical College in Hong Kong.

Party Split Up

On the 13th November, 1895, Yeung Ku-wan left Hong Kong for Saigon, after returning from Macao. From Saigon Yeung Ku-wan proceeded to Singapore, Madras, Colombo and South Africa, where he established revolutionary juntas of the 'Hing Chung Whui,' as advised by me. Before Yeung Ku-wan left for the Straits Settlements and South Africa, it was agreed between us that in order to preserve secrecy all our letters should be numbered.

On his way back from South African, Yeung Ku-wan established revolutionary juntas in Singapore and the Straits Settlements, and obtained the co-operation and support of the anti-Manchu secret societies. Immediately after Yeung Ku-wan reached Japan, emissaries were despatched to the Yangtze Valley provinces and the United States of America with copies of our 'manifesto' and other revolutionary literature, and they succeeded in obtaining the co-operation and support of all the anti-Manchu 'Tongs' and secret societies in these places.

It was from these sources that much of the fighting material was obtained, during the stirring days of the revolution.

During Yeung Ku-wan's absence in the Straits Settlements and South Africa, Dr. Sun Yat-sen and his partisans had been busy organizing the 'Tung Meng Whui' in Japan. As I know very little about the affairs of this organization, I leave Dr. Sun Yat-sen and his followers to fill up the gap.

UNIFICATION OF PARTIES

Meeting between Kang Yu-wei and Tse Tsan-tai

On the 21st February, 1896, I met Kang Yu-wei's brother Kang Kwang-jin and other members of Kang Yu-wei's party at a dinner at the Bun Fong restaurant given by my friends and colleagues Chan Kam-to (Dr. Chen Chin-tao), and Leung Lan-fan (Liang Lan-hsun). Dr. Chen Chin-tao was at one time Minister of Finance, and Liang Lan-hsun, Chinese Consul for Australia.

We discussed 'reforms, and the importance of union and co-operation.' Not being a 'party' man myself, I strongly advised the union and co-operation of the different political parties working for the salvation of China, and this has always been my policy. 'Unification of parties and Unification of China' has always been my watchword.

On the 4th October, 1896, I met Kang Yu-wei at the Wai Shing Tea Hong in Queen's Road Central by arrangement. We discussed the political situation in China, and I counselled union and co-operation in the great work of reform. Kang Yu-wei outlined his scheme of reform, which is too long to be recorded in these pages. It will appear in the complete history.

We agreed to unite and co-operate, after a confidential exchange of views.

Kang Yu-wei

The following pen picture of Kang Yu-wei is from my diary of this date:

'Kang Yu-wei is 43 years of age and a native of the Nam-hoi district of Kwang Tung province. He appears to be a man of superior intelligence. He is learned and experienced, and possesses an excellent all-round knowledge. He possesses a highly retentive memory, and is a great lover of books. He is always busy investigating, and searching for knowledge, in all its branches. He is the most learned progressive "Chinese scholar" of modern China. It is said that he remembers all that he reads. He is often styled by his disciples and pupils "Kang Fu-tzu." — the 'New Confucius'! The Chinese literati hate him.

'He has reviewed the works of Confucius, in many volumes, and for this he has been censured by the Throne. The publication of his works has been forbidden in China.

'Kang is of middle stature. He is stout and strong, and looks healthy. His eyes are dark and brilliant, and his glance is quick and sharp: his eyebrows are black, well-arched and high. His complexion is dark, and his forehead is high and well-formed, as also are his nose and thick lipped mouth. His upper lip is surmounted by well trimmed black moustaches, and his ears are small but well formed. Some of his fingers (third and fourth of his left hand) grew long nails! His head and hands are not large, but are well formed and shaped. The expression of his face is keen, intelligent and fascinating. The glitter of his dark eye-balls was striking. His bearing is proud and independent. At a glance one can see that he is not a "man of the common herd."' '

Meeting between Tse Tsan-tai and Kang Kwang-jin

On the 21st March, 1897, Leung Lan-fan brought Kang Yu-wei's brother Kang Kwang-jin and a follower named Ho Jeong to see me.

We discussed the political situation and the importance of union and co-operation. On the 29th, September, 1897, Kang Kwang-jin and I met by arrangement, and had a long confidential chat in the Public Gardens in Hong Kong, under the big pine tree in the East corner below the fountain. We agreed to work for union and co-operation and Kang Kwang-jin promised to discuss the matter seriously with his brother Kang Yu-wei. The following is from my diary of this date:

'Kang Kwang-jin said: Yes I quite agree with you, let us unite. What is the use of a body without a leg and a hand? I shall be glad to place your views before my brother, and I am certain he will be pleased to favour them. Yes, we should get the 'superior' men of both parties together, and hold a conference. We desire to see a 'peaceful' revolution for the good of the Empire and its millions, but still we must be prepared to act at any moment! I do not favour 'desperate' attempts at 'reform'.

'Men like Sun Yat-sen frighten me — they spoil everything. We cannot combine with such rash and reckless men. Yeung Ku-wan is a good man, and I hope to meet him yet. It is a pity we cannot get more good and able men to push the movement. My brother and I are doing our best, but we are afraid that we cannot accomplish much. There is an understanding between Chang Chih-tung, Viceroy of the Liang Hu provinces, and us. And besides him there are many other sympathisers amongst the officials. My brother is afraid to make himself too conspicuous, and is consequently working very quietly. It would be ruinous to our party if my brother got into trouble. My brother has numerous enemies, and they would seize any opportunity to bring about his downfall. So you see we must be very shrewd. No one must be able to say that ours is an anti-dynastic or revolutionary movement! We can save China!'

A Political Confession

Kang Kwang-jin confessed to me that he was not pro-Manchu, and that he and his brother were trying to bring about a 'peaceful' revolution in favour of the Chinese. This confession has been verified by the Ta Tung revolutionary movement of August 1900.

Before separating, Kang Kwang-jin exclaimed: 'What is our duty? We are born in this world to do our duty, which is to do all we can for our fellowmen before we die.'

Alas, my poor friend Kang Kwang-jin was one of those reformers who lost their lives during the Empress Dowager's coup d'etat of 21st September, 1898. Little did he dream that his last words to me would come true so soon!

Kang Kwang-jin was honest and sincere, and a true patriot.

1st October, 1897 — Kang Kwang-jin leaves Hongkong for Shanghai by s.s. 'Loong Moon' to meet his brother and Liang Chi-chao. Liang Chi-chao is a noted Chinese scholar and politician, and the chief disciple of Kang Yu-wei.

3rd October, 1897 — I communicate the result of my interview with Kang Kwang-jin to Yeung Ku-wan in South Africa, he having announced to me his safe arrival in a letter dated 7th January, 1987.

20th October, 1987 — I receive a letter from Yeung Ku-wan (28/8/97) informing me of the date of his departure for China, and reporting the establishment of a revolutionary junta in Johannesburg.

8th November, 1897 — Kang Kwang-jin informs me by letter from Shanghai that Liang Chi-chao is in favour of union and co-operation.

25th November, 1897 — Yeung Ku-wan leaves Durban, South Africa, for Colombo, the Straits Settlements, Rangoon, Hongkong and Japan.

The Hongkong Chinese Club

9th January, 1898 — I founded the Hongkong Chinese Club with Cheung Tsoi, Luk King-fo and Leung Lan-fan. See Hong Kong newspapers of 9th January, 1898.

2nd February, 1898 — I meet Dr. Timothy Richard LL.D., at the London Mission House in Bonham Road. We discussed reform in China, and he promised to give the reform movement his strong support.

11th March 1898 — Yeung Ku-wan arrives in Hongkong Harbour on board the s.s. 'Wakasa Maru.' I meet him on board ship and inform him of the result of my interview with the brothers Kang Yu-wei and Kang Kwang-jin. I also give him advice regarding the organizing of the Revolution, and remind him of the importance of obtaining the co-operation and support of the anti-Manchu secret societies in the Straits Settlements, and the Yangtze Valley provinces, and the United States. (See also my letters No. 12 of 4th March, 1898; No. 25 of 13th October, 1898; No 26 of 22nd September, 1898, and No. 33 of 7th August, 1899.) Yeung Ku-wan sailed direct for Japan to confer with Dr. Sun Yat-sen.

Anti-footbinding Society

12th March, 1898 — Kang Kwang-jin writes to me from Shanghai asking me for Yeung Ku-wan's address. I reply and at the same time advise the formation of a society for the suppression of footbinding in China.

21st March, 1898 — Yeung Ku-wan arrives in Yokohama.

25th March, 1898 — I interview Thomas H. Reid, and the *China Mail* publishes a leading article in support of the reform movement.

29th March, 1898 — Kang Kwang-jin writes to me from Peking expressing his anxiety to meet Yeung Ku-wan.

24th July, 1898 — Kang Kwang-jin writes to me again from Peking expressing his anxiety to hear from Yeung Ku-wan, to whom I had already written conveying to him Kang Kwang-jin's friendly desires.

Empress Dowager's Coup D'etat

21st September, 1898 — Empress Dowager's coup d'etat.

Kang Yu-wei and Liang Chi-chao succeeded in escaping from Peking, but Kang Kwang-jin, Tan Sze-tung, Liu Kwang-ti, Yang Tze-wei, Yang Shih-shen, and Lin Shio were seized and executed without trial.

I will leave the story of the Empress Dowager's coup d'etat and the events which followed to be written by my old friend Kang Yu-wei and his chief disciple Liang Chi-chao.

29th September, 1898 — Kang Yu-wei arrives in Hongkong and after a short stay leaves for Japan by s.s. 'Kawachi Maru,' on 19th October, 1898.

When Kang Yu-wei landed he was befriended by my old friend Ho Tung, now Sir

Robert Ho Tung, Kt., who extended to him his friendly hospitality, in spite of the hostility of the Manchu Peking Government and its myrmidons at Canton.

Sir Robert has always been the friend of the reformers, and he is still unsparing in his time and energy in China's welfare.

8th October, 1898 — I discuss with Dr. Ho Kai the political situation and our prospects of success.

Martyrdom of Kang Kwang-jin

5th December, 1898 - In reply to my enquiries of 17th October, 1898, regarding my friend Kang Kwang-jin, Dr. Timothy Richard writes to me from Shanghai informing me of the safe and satisfactory disposal of Kang Kwang-jin's body, and he also deals with the question of the salvation of China as follows:

Shanghai, Dec. 15th, 1898.
Tse Tsan-tai, Esq.,

Dear Sir, — I am in receipt of your letter of the 6th inst. making enquiries about your friend.

I did all I could through a friend in Peking and since then I have written to him (your friend) direct saying that everything has been arranged satisfactorily about his poor brother for the present.

I gave him details.

As to the other question for the salvation of China, I am doing all in my power. But the Manchus refuse light and will not invite the help of friendly foreigners. Some of the leading Chinese also have published documents in which they insult the best men of the West.

They want to learn foreign military and naval affairs: they want to open mines in order to have funds to fight the foreigners and drive them all out of China. It is this want of friendliness on the part of the Manchus and some of the leading mandarins and even hatred of all foreigners which makes it impossible that God should give power to them.

It is such principles which destroy China most of all. The salvation of China as well as of the whole world lies in the cultivation, not of militarism, but of friendship. Let the best people of China and of the West persevere in their good work of making peace, and goodwill, and goodness their chief aim, and then prosperity will in due time follow.

But if nations only seek their own national interests first, then no matter how great they are, and whether they are Chinese or European nations, they cannot last long when they make righteousness a secondary aim. Be not weary in well doing.

With best wishes for yourself and your country, I remain, Yours Sincerely,
Timothy Richard.

(This letter is mentioned in Professor William E. Soothill's book 'Timothy Richard of China' (Page 242). Professor H.E. Soothill is Professor of Chinese in the University of Oxford.)

UNION AND CO-OPERATION.

Progress in the Yangtze Provinces

9th December, 1898 — Letter No. 29, dated Yokohama, 24th November 1898, received from Yeung Ku-wan informing me of the success of our plans, and the co-operation of the Hunan 'reformers.'

Yeung Ku-wan also informs me that there may be difficulty in uniting the two parties owing to selfishness and jealousy.

24th December, 1898 — I send a letter to Kang Yu-wei in Japan outlining my policy and strongly advising union and co-operation in the movement for Freedom and Independence.

9th January, 1899 — Kang Yu-wei writes to me from Japan expressing his concurrence with my policy of union and co-operation in the work of 'reform.'

1st March, 1899 — I write to Kang Yu-wei urging upon him the importance of union and co-operation and advising him to come to an understanding with Yeung Ku-wan and his friends in Japan.

28th March, 1899 — Liang Chi-chao writes to me from Tokio, Japan, expressing his concurrence with my policy of union and co-operation and informing me of Kang Yu-wei's departure for the United States.

17th April, 1899 — I send a reply to Liang Chi-chao's letter impressing upon him the great importance of union and co-operation.

23rd April, 1899 — Yeung Ku-wan writes to me from Yokohama informing me that the members of Kang Yu-wei's party favour union and co-operation, and that Japanese friends and supporters have also advised the union of the two parties.

Meeting between Yeung Ku-wan and Liang Chi-chao

19th June, 1899 — I received from Yeung Ku-wan letter No. 31 dated Yokohama, 6th June, 1899, informing me of a meeting between him and Liang Chi-chao in the office of Messrs. Kingsell and Co., in Yokohama.

Yeung Ku-wan writes:

'He (Liang Chi-chao) advised me to try my best to go on with the work of our party and he will try his best to go on with the work of his party. He does not like to co-operate with us yet. Hong's party are too proud and jealous of our Chinese English scholars. They don't like to have the same rank as us; they always aspire to governing us or want us all to submit to them. They do not know what justice means, as Mr. U Lai-un remarked in the 'Sun Ching On Hang' (book), and I have heard several wise Hunan men make similar remarks concerning them.'

Note. — My old friend the late U Lai-un was a great thinker and philospher, and collaborated with the late Sir Kai Ho Kai in translating and writing many works on reform, which were read with avidity by Kang Yu-wei and his disciples.

He led the life of a recluse, and was a staunch supporter of the Cause of Reform and Independence in China.

I succeeded in bringing the 'leaders' together, and did my best to unite two parties, but their failure to bring about the much desired union of the two parties is most regrettable. It has all been a game of selfish political chess and scheming to become top dog!'

A Political Cartoon

19th July, 1899, — I design and publish a political cartoon — 'The Situation in the Far East' — which appeared in many foreign illustrated newspapers. This cartoon was designed to arouse the Chinese nation, and to warn the people of the impending danger of the partitioning of the Empire by the Foreign Powers.

I allowed Yeung Ku-wan to publish in Japan a coloured travesty of my cartoon, which led to my being questioned by the Colonial Secretary of Hongkong.

3rd August, 1899 — I receive letter No. 32, dated Yokohama, 27th July, 1899, from Yeung Ku-wan enclosing copies of revolutionary propaganda, which have been circulated broadcast exhorting the people of China to rise and rebel against the Manchu usurpers.

31st August, 1899 — I receive letter No. 33, dated Yokohama, 19th August, 1899, from Yeung Ku-wan, informing me that revolutionary 'exhortations' have been sent to partisans in America, Honolulu, Australia, the Straits Settlements, Bangkok, Saigon, and Canada, in the name of the Republican Party ('Chung Kwok Hop Chung Ching Fu Ser Whui') of China.

The 'Po Wang Whui' Society

4th November, 1899 — I write to Kang Yu-wei severely denouncing his 'Protect the Emperor' (Po Wang Whui) Society.

6th November, 1899 — Letter No 34, dated Yokohama 28/10/99, received from Yeung Ku-wan enclosing printed copies of revolutionary manifesto and circular letters, and reporting the successful progress of the work of partisans in the Yangtze provinces, and other parts of the world. Kang Yu-wei's 'Po Wang Whui' (Protect the Emperor Society) is also denounced and exposed by Yeung Ku-wan.

19th Novemebr, 1899 — Hung Chun-fei, alias Hung Wo, alias Hung Chuen-fook calls to see my father, and I make his acquaintance, my father having previously spoken to me about him.

Hung Chun-fei was a nephew of Hung Hsiu-chuan, the 'Tai Ping' king. He had travelled rather extensively, and possessed a thorough knowledge of men and world affairs.

(Note: Later on I sounded Hung Chuen-fook, and he agreed to join me and undertake the task of organizing a force for the capture of Canton City.)

21st December, 1899 — Imperial Edict issued for the arrest of Kang Yu-wei and Liang Chi-chao.

SECOND ATTEMPT TO CAPTURE CANTON

A Commonwealth Government

On making Hung Chuen-fook's acquaintance on the 19th November, 1899, and discovering he had considerable military training and experience in the armies of his uncle Hung Hsiu-chuan, the 'Tai Ping' king, I decided to plan and organize another attempt to capture Canton and establish Commonwealth Government under a 'Protector,' as I was of the opinion that the 'Republican' form of government was too advanced for China and the Chinese. Accordingly I consulted my father, and he approved of my decision to entrust Hung Chuen-fook with the task of organizing the revolutionary army.

The sinews of war were supplied by Li Pak, alias Li Ki-tong, who had already sacrificed a fortune in the revolutionary cause. Li Pak was one of the greatest financial supporters of the Revolution, a fact which it is my pleasing duty to record.

24th January, 1900 — Yeung Ku-wan arrives in Hongkong from Japan per s.s. 'Kamakura Maru.' He informed me that the Hunanese members of the revolutionary party were actively organizing in Hunan and Hupeh provinces in the disguise of monks, and that many Japanese were also supporting us.

Yeung Ku-wan surprised me by telling me that Dr. Sun Yat-sen had demanded that he should resign the leadership of the party in his favour. He said: 'We were dangerously near being split up into two parties some time ago. Dr. Sun Yat-sen informed me one day that the 'Ko Lao Whui' party of the Yangtze provinces had appointed him 'President', and hinted that as there could not be two Presidents, it would be obligatory for me to work independently, if I would not recognize him in his new position. I confessed to Sun Yat-sen that I was quite pleased to resign my position, and advised him not to encourage separation. I also informed him that I was always willing to sacrifice my life, let alone my position, for the good of the cause. We must obey the people's will, I said. I also told him that I was not particular who was appointed President so long as the movement progressed successfully under his leadership. Dr. Sun has requested me to ask if you are in favour of this change and recognize his appointment.' (See my diary.)

In order to prevent party strife, I advised Yeung Ku-wan to resign the Presidency in favour of Dr. Sun Yat-sen.

6th February, 1900 — Yeung Ku-wan invited me to join the new Revolutionary Party — 'Tung Meng Whui', which had been organized by Dr. Sun Yat-sen and his partisans in Japan. Owing to the usurpation of Yeung Ku-wan's position by Dr. Sun Yat-sen, I declined this invitation to join his new party. And disapproving of Dr. Sun Yat-sen's high-handed behaviour, I decided to act independently.

9th February, 1900 — I broadcasted my letter 'Liberty, Freedom and Reform' from Canton, in anticipation of the success of the second attempt to capture Canton City, and in order to 'blaze the trail' and 'clear the way'. Those were the days, when things had to be accomplished in round-about ways!

THE RESCUE OF KING LIEN-SHAN*

Tse Tsan-tai Meets Mrs. Archibald Little

26th February, 1900 — I meet Mrs. Archibald Little at the Chinese Club (Hongkong), where she lectured on the evils of foot-binding. Mrs. Little appointed my wife local Secretary of the Anti-Footbinding Society. Mrs. Little helped me to obtain the release of the reformer King Lien-shan from 'Monte Forte' Prison, Macao, by influencing H.E.Sir Henry Blake and Lady Blake to send friendly representations to the Governor of Macao. My friends D. Warres Smith and Alfred Cunningham, Editors of the *Hongkong Daily Press*, and Thomas H. Reid, Editor of the *China Mail*, also interested themselves in the case, and published strong leading articles in their newspapers advocating the early liberation of the prisoner.

King Lien-shan was Manager of the Imperial Chinese Telegraph Administration at Shanghai, and was arrested in Macao by the Portuguese authorities on the false charge of embezzling the funds of the Administration which was made by the Chinese authorities. King Lien-shan was the man who sent the telegram from Shanghai urging the Empress Dowager not to depose the Emperor Kwang Hsu. This telegram was signed by 'King Lien-shan and 1,231 others.'

The news of King Lien-shan's arrest and imprisonment was brought to me by my old friend Tsu Sien-ting, who was a staunch supporter of the cause of Reform and Independence.

The following letters from Mrs. Archibald Little and Mr. D. Warres Smith are interesting:

Government House, Hongkong,
Tuesday, (27/2/1900)

Dear Mr. Tse Tsan-tai, — The meeting on Thursday is for all Chinese ladies bound and unbound who will like to come. And Lady Blake particularly hopes to see your wife as I do too.

I am writing two letters to high officials at Macao about your friend.
Therefore excuse haste. — Yours sincerely,

ALICE LITTLE.

Hongkong Daily Press Office,
Hongkong, 3rd March, 1900.

---

* Better known to historians as Jing Yuanshan.

Tse Tsan-tai Esq.,

Dear Sir, — I am afraid that there is not a ghost of a chance of anything any or all of the foreign papers may say, having the most distant effect, direct or indirect, but we will do our best.

I hardly think the Macao Government will defy both European and Chinese public opinion by giving up Mr. King Lien-shan. I am going to endeavour to send a reporter to the trial in Macao. We happen to have no suitable man on our staff, but will write to Macao to-day to see if I can get a man there to do it. — Yours truly,

D. WARRES SMITH.

28th February, 1900 — My father, Yeung Ku-wan and I hold a conference, and we discuss the political situation in China, and the cure for China's ills.

5th March, 1900 — Li Pak calls to see me, and we discuss the political situation.

31st March, 1900 — I meet Dr. Yung Wing, LL.D. at Thomas's Hotel, and we discuss the political situation.

2nd April, 1900 — Dr. Yung Wing and I have a long confidential talk. Dr. Yung Wing agrees with my policy of union and co-operation under able Christian leadership.

Dr. Yung Wing said: 'I have not met Dr. Sun Yat-sen yet. What is his age? I don't think much of Sun as he is too rash.'

Dr. Yung Wing, LL.D., was a graduate of Yale University, and was a true lover of his people. He was the man who brought one of the first relays of Chinese students to the United States to be educated, amongst them being the well-known statesman and politician Tang Shao-yi, and it was mainly through his influence that the famous Educational Mission was sent to the United States in 1870. This may be considered the great work of Dr. Yung Wing's life. In 1864 he prepared the way for the foundation of the Kiang Nan Arsenal, and the China Merchants Steamship Co. (1870). In 1876 he was appointed Associate Chinese Minister together with Chin Lan-pin to Washington, U.S.A.

3rd April, 1900 — I arrange a confidential meeting between Dr. Yung Wing and Yeung Ku-wan with the object of hastening union and co-operation.

4th April, 1900 — Dr. Yung Wing leaves for the United States by the 'Empress of China.' I write to Dr. Sun Yat-sen advising him to meet Dr. Yung Wing in Japan.

11th April, 1900 — Dr Ho Kai and I discuss the political situation, and the prospects of the success of the revolutionary movement.

The Wei Chow Movement

18th April, 1900 — Yeung Ku-wan calls to see me. In order to prevent selfish rivalry and jealousy between the leaders of the different parties, I strongly advised that Dr. Yung Wing LL.D., be elected President of the United Reform Parties. Yeung Ku-wan informs me that the work of organizing the Wei Chow movement is progressing rapidly and smoothly.

22nd April, 1900 — Li Pak joins the revolutionary party.

26th April, 1900 — Yeung Ku-wan leaves for Japan by s.s. 'Awau Maru,' to confer with Dr. Sun Yat-sen.

6th May, 1900 — Chan Siu-pak, Li Pak and I confer re the Wei Chow movement.

6th June, 1900 — Letter dated Yokohama 26/5/1900 received from Yeung Ku-wan informing me of his decision to visit Australia and the United States.

17th June, 1900 — Yeung Ku-wan and Dr. Sun Yat-sen arrive in Hongkong from Japan by the s.s. 'Indus,' and are accompanied by a party of Japanese friends and supporters. Yeung Ku-wan, Dr. Sun Yat-sen, Chan Siu-pak, Cheung Sau-por, Hiriyama and I meet in a sampan alongside the s.s. 'Indus' and hold a one hour's conference.

Yeung Ku-wan and Dr. Sun Yat-sen assured us of the support of the Japanese Government.

It was decided to start active operations without delay. Yeung Ku-wan landed in Hongkong and Dr. Sun Yat-sen proceeded to the Straits Settlements.

Li Hung Chang's Trap

On the day of their arrival in Hongkong, Li Hung-chang, Viceroy of Canton, laid a trap for the kidnapping of Yeung Ku-wan and Dr. Sun Yat-sen.

They were invited to a 'conference' on board the Canton gunboat 'On Lan,' but were warned in time by their Japanese friends, who frustrated their attempt to kidnap them.

25th June, 1900 — Colin McD. Smart of the *China Mail* editorial staff called to see me. He assured me of his support, saying that he would follow in Thomas H. Reid's footsteps.

1st July, 1900 — Yeung Ku-wan and I meet our Japanese friends and supporters, M. Fukumoto, Macamoto Ntoo, Y. Osaki, Capt. S. Hara, M. Itoh, and H. Iwasaki at the Hongkong Hotel. We discussed the political situation in China.

M. Fukumoto assured us of the support of himself and his friends and said, 'We are prepared to shed our blood for your cause.'

2nd July, 1900 - M. Fukumoto and his friends leave for Saigon by the s.s. 'Laos' to meet Dr. Sun Yat-sen.

17th July, 1900 — Dr. Sun Yat-sen and his friends arrive in Hongkong by the s.s. 'Sado Maru,' but he is forbidden to land by the Hongkong Government.

20th July, 1900 — Dr. Sun Yat-sen leaves for Japan by s.s. 'Sado Maru.'

21st July, 1900 — Dr. Ho Kai reports that Sir Henry A. Blake* is in favour of a Southern Republic for China.

1st August, 1900 — Dr. Ho Kai's article based on the terms of our political programme is published by the *China Mail*.

---

* Governor of Hong Kong 1898 – 1903.

2nd August, 1900 — Dr. Ho Kai and I discuss the terms of our Programme and the Appeal to the Foreign Powers.

21st August, 1900 — I advocate religious toleration and the establishment of an independent Christian Church for China. See letters to Rt. Rev. Bishop Hoare, D.D., Dr. Timothy Richard, LL.D., and Pastor Kranz.

22nd August, 1900 — Dr. Ho Kai's 'Open Letter' signed 'Sinensis' appears in the *China Mail*.

26th August, 1900 — Kang Yu-wei and his followers unsuccessfully planned a revolutionary movement at Ta Tung in Anhui province and Hankow in Hupeh province. Dr. Yung Wing, LL.D., and his nephew Yung Sing-kiu were connected with this movement, and narrowly escaped with their lives.

11th September, 1900 — Owing to the failure of the Ta Tung movement Dr Yung Wing flees from Shanghai, and arrives in Hongkong by s.s. 'Empress of Japan.'

Tang Tsai-chang, the leader, and others were captured and beheaded.

5th October, 1900 — Flag of Independence unfurled at Wei Chow by General Cheng Put-san.

The movement is supported by the *China Mail*, *Hongkong Telegraph*, and *Hongkong Daily Press*.

28th October, 1900 — Sze Kin-yu attempts to blow up Viceroy Tak Sau's yamen at Canton, and is arrested and executed.

7th November, 1900 — The Wei Chow movement collapses through shortage of ammunition and men.

28th November, 1900 — Viceroy Tak Sau issues a proclamation, denouncing Yeung Ku-wan and other reformers.

Assassination of Yeung Ku-wan

10th January, 1901 — Yeung Ku-wan is assassinated in his schoolroom at No. 52, Gage Street, Hongkong. The assassins escaped to Canton.

Yeung Ku-wan was a noble-minded man, and was heart and soul a devoted adherent of the Cause. It may be truthfully said of him that he was one of the noblest of China's patriots, who suffered martyrdom in the cause of Freedom and Independence.

Yeung Ku-wan's body has been buried in the Protestant Cemetery at Hongkong, and the story of his life and work has still to be written.

1st March, 1901 — I receive a letter from Dr. Sun Yat-sen dated Yokohama, 13/2/1901, deeply regretting the assassination of Yeung Ku-wan, and forwarding obituary notices for distribution.

25th May, 1901, — I have a confidential talk with Alfred Cunningham, Editor of the *Hongkong Daily*, re the movement for Freedom and Independence.

23rd September, 1901 — King Lien-shan calls personally to see me, and to tender thanks to all those who interested themselves in his case, and helped to obtain his release from 'Monte Forte' prison, Macao.

Second Attempt to Capture Canton

26th September, 1901 — I confer with Li Pak, who expressed his willingness to join me in organizing another attempt to capture Canton City and establish a Provisional Government with Dr. Yung Wing LL.D. as President.

We decide to place the task of recruiting and organizing the fighting forces in the hands of Hung Chuen-fook.

3rd October, 1901 — Ng Lo-sam, alias Ng Sui-sang, is banished from Hongkong for being connected with the assassination of Yeung Ku-wan.

7th October, 1901 — I discuss with Hung Chuen-fook the plans for capturing Canton.

13th October, 1901 — I discuss with my father the organization of the movement for the capture of Canton.

25th October, 1901 — I discuss with Dr. Ho Kai the organization of the movement for Freedom and Independence.

30th October, 1901 — Hung Chuen-fook, Li Pak and I meet to discuss plans for the capture of Canton and the establishing of a provisional government.

Interview with Dr. G. E. Morrison

22nd November, 1901 — I meet Dr. G.E. Morrison, *London Times*, correspondent, at the Hong Kong Hotel.

We discuss the movement of Freedom and Independence and he assured me of his friendly sympathy and support. He said: 'I am quite willing to help you and shall do my best to further and support the movement. My support means the support of the *Times*, and the support of the *Times* means the support of the British people. My policy is the *Times* policy.'

Dr Morrison advocated in strong terms the removal of the old Empress Dowager. He told me of his friend J.O.P. Bland's timely rescue of Kang Yu-wei at Woosung.

The following is my pen-picture of Dr. G.E. Morrison:

'Dr. Morrison is a man who commands attention by his distinguished appearance and fine presence. He is tall and close-shaven, with a bold, broad and commanding brow, large eyes with a piercing look, straight eye-brows, long nose, and firm mouth with thin lips.

He hair is light, and he is a fine looking type of Australian manhood.

I found him polished, genial and affable, and a man possessing great common-sense and decision of character.'

26th December, 1901 — Dr. Yung Wing LL.D. arrives in Hongkong bound for the United States. I send him confidential instructions through Li Pak.

16th January, 1902 — I receive a letter from D. Warres Smith, dated London, 13th December 1901, acknowledging receipt of King Lien-shan's letter of thanks and gratitude.

18th January, 1902 — I receive a letter from Dr. Timothy Richard, dated Shanghai, 13th January 1902. He wrote:

'May all your efforts on behalf of Reform in your country be also abundantly blessed.'

28th January, 1902 — Dr. Sun Yat-sen arrives in Hongkong by the s.s. 'Yawata Maru,' and stays at No. 24, Stanley Street.

3rd February, 1902 — Dr. Sun Yat-sen leaves Hongkong.

1st April, 1902 — I receive a letter from Dr. G.E. Morrison, dated from Peking 17th March, 1902, sending me his address and enquiring for 'news' of the movement.

16th April, 1902 — My letter 'Manchu Rule' appears in the *Hongkong Telegraph*.

As we descended upon the anti-Manchu secret societies to furnish the fighting material for the Revolution, I frequently contributed articles and letters to the foreign newspapers in their support.

16th May, 1902 — Dr. Yung Wing leaves for the United States by the s.s. 'Gaelic.'

23rd May, 1902 — I receive a letter from D. Warres Smith, dated *Hongkong Daily Press* office, London, 25th April, 1902, assuring me of his support.

6th June, 1902 — I advocate popular representation for Chinese in Hongkong. See *Hongkong Daily Press* of 6th June 1902.

9th June, 1920 — Alfred Cunningham, Editor of the *Hongkong Daily Press*, helps me to draft our Proclamation and Appeal to the Foreign Powers.

The Rottenest Government in Existence

4th July, 1902 — I receive a letter from Dr. G.E. Morrison, dated Peking, 25th June, 1902, asking for 'news.' He writes:

'The Government of this country is the rottenest in existence with the possible exceptions of Persia and Turkey.'

11th August, 1902 — I receive a letter from D. Warres Smith, of the *Hongkong Daily Press*, dated London 7th July, 1902, assuring me of his support. He writes:

'But of course a reformation and that a very complete one in the system of Government is absolutely necessary. That may be brought about by a big revolution, but I question it much; I fancy it will be a thing of slow growth. Anyhow, a beginning must be made some day and the sooner the better.'

13th August, 1902 — I write to Dr. Yung Wing, LL.D., instructing him to organize a junta in the United States, and work for the co-operation and support of American friends and sympathisers.

9th October, 1902 — I write to Dr. G.E. Morrison warning him to be in readiness for the coming Revolution. I also write to D. Warres Smith in London.

16th October, 1902 — I discuss with my father the progress of Hung Chuen-fook's organization work.

19th October, 1902 — I warn Thos. H. Reid Editor of the *China Mail*, to be prepared for the coming Revolution, and also Alfred Cunningham, Editor of the *Hongkong Daily Press*.

2nd November, 1902 — I advocate the suppression of slavery in China. See English and Chinese newspapers.

6th November, 1902 — I receive a letter from Dr. Yung Wing, LL.D., dated No.

12, Myrtle Street, Hartford, Conn., 21st September, 1902. He writes:

'I hold myself ready, at this end, to do all I can to meet your wants at the other end. Send on the cipher or secret code as soon as possible. It is an indispensible adjunct to our correspondence.'

13th December, 1902 — Dr. Sun Yat-sen arrives in Hongkong by the s.s. 'Indus' and proceeds to Saigon.

24th December, 1902 — Alfred Cunningham, Editor of the *Hongkong Daily Press* secretly prints our Proclamation of Independence, and in order to preserve secrecy, it is written and lithographed on stone!

25th December, 1902 — My brother Tse Tsi-shau (Tse Tsan-ip) arrives from Singapore by the s.s. 'Korea,' and I appoint him my Deputy.

Meetings with Dr G.E. Morrison

26th December, 1902 — Dr. G.E. Morrison arrives in Hongkong from Haiphong by s.s. 'Hoihao.' We hold a secret consultation at the Hongkong Hotel, and meet again on the 28th, two days later. I hand him copies of our Proclamation of Independence.

27th December, 1902 — Hung Chuen-fook and my brother Tse Tsi-shau leave for Canton on a special mission.

29th December, 1902 — Dr. G.E. Morrison leaves for Australia by s.s. 'Chingtu.' Before parting he assured me of his staunch support, and promised to return to China immediately on receipt of my telegram.

30th December, 1902 — I receive a letter from my brother Tse Tsi-shau dated Canton, 29th December, 1902, reporting the results of a secret conference of eight of the important leaders of the movement at Fong Chuen.

1st January, 1903 — Hung Chuen-fook and my brother Tse Tsi-shau return from their mission to Canton.

9th January, 1903 — Alfred Cunningham calls to see me and reports that General Gascoigne and the Commodore are in favour of supporting our movement for Independence.

13th January, 1903 — Hung Chuen-fook calls to see me, and reports that he will make the attempt to capture Canton City on the night of the 28th January, 1903 (Chinese New Year's Eve).

20th January, 1903 — I discuss the situation with my father and brother Tse Tsi-shau.

The Betrayal

25th January, 1903 — Hung Chuen-fook and my brother Tse Tsi-shau leave for Canton via Macao to direct the operations for the capture of Canton. Not long after their departure, the Headquarters of Hung Chuen-fook at No. 20 D'Aguilar Street, were raided by the Hongkong Police, and a number of arrests made.

26th January, 1903 — I despatch a message to Rev. A. Kollecker of the Berlin

Mission at Fong Chuen requesting him to warn all friends and sympathisers in Canton and Fong Chuen. I discuss the situation with Alfred Cunningham and Thomas H. Reid, and we watch developments. I sent a special messenger to Macao to search for and warn Hung Chuen-fook and my brother Tse Tsi-shau of the betrayal of our movement.

27th January, 1903 — My father falls ill through anxiety and worry due to the betrayal and the failure of the attempt to capture Canton City. Perhaps it was well that the attempt failed, and God, in Whom I have always trusted, knows best.

27th January, 1903 — My brother Tse Tsi-shau returns from Macao. Arms, uniforms, etc., at Canton and Fong Chuen seized by the Canton authorities and numerous arrests made. Hung Chuen-fook shaves off his beard and escapes in disguise. J. Scott Harston, of Messrs. Ewens and Harston (Solicitors) is retained to watch the case of the arrested and imprisoned reformers.

31st January, 1903 — The *Hongkong Daily Press* publishes a leading article counselling protection for all reformers and their sympathisers. Alfred Cunningham and J. Scott Harston working in their behalf, all the prisoners are liberated, which causes a great sensation.

The S.C.M. Post, Ltd.

6th February, 1903 — I discuss with Alfred Cunningham the promotion of the South China Morning Post, Limited, for the furtherance of the cause of Reform and Independence.

7th February, 1903 — The *China Mail* publishes a lengthy leader in support of the 'Reform' movement.

14th February, 1903 — I discuss the situation with my father, and in order to prevent useless bloodshed, we decide to disband the different forces in the interior.

17th February, 1903 — My father expressed fears that he will not have long to live and blames Hung Chuen-fook for not listening to his advice. Hung Chuen-fook was lacking in discretion, and my father suspected him of selfish designs.

Death of Tse Yet-chong

11th March, 1903 — Death of my father Tse Yet-chong in Hongkong at the age of 72.

16th March, 1903 — I meet Dr. G.E. Morrison at the Hongkong Hotel, and we discuss the political situation in China. He assured me of his unswerving support.

1st April, 1903 — The South China Morning Post, Limited, is successfully promoted, and I am appointed to be Compradore of the Company.

Owing to the failure of the attempt to capture Canton City, and the death of my father, I decide to allow Dr. Sun Yat-sen and his followers a free hand, and to devote my time to the furtherance of the cause of Freedom and Independence through the columns of the *South China Morning Post*, and other newspapers.

28th April, 1903 — My letter 'Russia and Manchuria,' signed 'Indignation' is published by the *Hongkong Daily Press*.

7th August 1903 — The *China Mail* and *Hongkong Daily Press* publish at my request strong leading articles in support of the 'Supao' prisoners, who were arrested in Shanghai.

22nd July, 1904 — I published the first Chinese Diary of the Russo-Japanese War, and received appreciations from high Japanese officials.

22nd August 1904 — I advocated the formation of an International Society for the protection of Ancient Historical Relics, and the universal suppression of vandalism. See world's newspapers and Hongkong newspapers of 22nd August, 1904.

The World Chinese Students' Federation

1st October, 1904 — I advocated the formation of the World's Chinese Students' Federation. See letters to my old friend Wu Lien-teh, M.A., M.D., LL.D. Dr Wu Lien-teh is the world-famed Plague Expert of China, and the founder of the Peking Central Hospital and Medical College. He is one of the brightest gems in China's medical history.

28th December, 1905 — I advocated a scheme for the termination of the United States boycott movement in China. See *South China Morning Post* of 28th December, 1905.

26th April, 1907 — Dr. Sun Yat-sen, Wong Hing and others raise the flag of revolt at Wong Kong and Yam Lin in S.W. Kwang-tung.

18th July, 1907 — I receive a letter from Dr. Yung Wing, dated South Windsor, Conn., 7/6/1907, assuring me of his continued staunch support.

24th September, 1907 — In order to frustrate Russian designs, I urged the immediate colonization of Manchuria and the development of its mineral resources. See *Sheung Pao* of 24th September, 1907.

Dr. Yung Wing's scheme

22nd October 1907 — I receive a letter from Dr. Yung Wing, dated 771 Asylum Avenue, Hartford, Conn., 17/9/1907, submitting his scheme for a successful revolution in China.

15th January, 1908 — I meet Dr. G.E. Morrison at the Hongkong Hotel, and we discuss the political situation in China. (See lengthy interview in my Diary.)

12th May, 1908 — Dr. Sun Yat-sen, Wong Hing, Wu Han-man, Wong Chin-wei and others raise the flag of revolt at Ho Hau, on the borders of Yunnan province.

17th August, 1908 — I receive a letter from Dr. Yung Wing, dated No. 310 Sargent Street, Hartford, Conn., 14/7/1908, advocating the union of the reform parties, and condemning Kang Yu-wei and his Po Wang Whui (Protect the Emperor Society) Party.

30th June 1909 — Claimed that the Chinese were the first to discover Northern Australia during the Ming Dynasty, and advocated an investigation by the Chinese Government. See *China Mail* of 30th June, 1909.

17th May, 1910 — I receive a letter from Dr. Yung Wing, dated 16 Atwood Street, Hartford, Conn., 13/4/1910, strongly denouncing Kang Yu-wei and his disciple, and informing me of his meeting with Dr. Sun Yat-sen.

24th, October, 1910 — I advocated a closer understanding between the United States and China, and discussed the future control of the Pacific.

See *South China Morning Post* of 24th October, 1910.

22nd February, 1911 — My Open Letter 'Russia and China' is sent to the Governments of the Foreign Powers, the Foreign Ministers at Peking and all the Foreign newspapers, in order to pave the way for the Great Revolution in China.

8th April, 1911 — Tartar General Fu Chi, of Canton, assassinated.

27th April, 1911 — Attack on Viceregal Yamen and attempted capture of Canton by Wong Hing and others. Seventy-two revolutionaries lose their lives in this attack.

Sir Hiram S. Maxim

14th June, 1911 — I receive a long letter from Sir Hiram S. Maxim, dated London, 13/5/1911.

He offers China a new rifle, and refers to the importance of flying machines.

He discusses flying machines viv-a-vis dirigibles.

Sir Hiram always supported the Chinese in speech and writing. He greatly sympathised with the Chinese in their struggle for Freedom and Independence, and went so far as to offer his valuable services to the Republican Government of China.

In a letter to me, dated 14th April, 1913, he wrote: 'I could do a great deal for China if the Chinese would give me the opportunity.

'I am regarded as the greatest expert on fire-arms in the world.

'I took the personal Grand Prix for artillery at the last Paris Exposition.

'Notwithstanding that I am an old man I am still very active and able to do a lot of work.

'I have long been in strong sympathy with the Chinese, and I would like to finish up my career by making myself very useful to them.'

I strongly recommended Sir Hiram to President Yuan Shih-kai direct, and also through my friend Dr. G.E. Morrison, but Yuan Shih-kai failed to take advantage of Sir Hiram's offer. It was to Sir Hiram that I sent my plans of a dirigible airship in 1899. The problem of aerial navigation by dirigible air-ships, propelled by motor-driven fan-propellers fore, aft and deck, was solved by me in 1894. The three deck propellors embodied the gyroscopic principle of ascending and descending. Sir Hiram beleived in flying machines and had no faith in dirigibles. The design of my dirigible air-ship was published in many of the world's illustrated newspapers and magazines of this period.

25th August, 1911 — I expose 'Lin Shao-yang,' the author (European) of 'A Chinese Appeal to Christendom,' in the *Hongkong Daily Press*. He apologises in the columns of the *North China Daily News*.

THE REVOLUTION

The Wuchang Revolt and Li Yuan-hung

10th October, 1911 — The foreign-drilled troops of Hupeh province mutiny, and co-operating with the revolutionaries succeed in capturing Wuchang.

The Revolution spreads quickly throughout the whole Empire, from Chihli in the north to Kwang-tung in the south, and from Shan-tung in the east to Sze-chuan in the west. So swift and overwhelming was the progress of the Revolution that consternation reigned in Peking, and in despair the Manchu court turned to Yuan Shih-kai for assistance in quelling the rising and saving the dynasty.

In fifteen days, all the lower Yangtze provinces were lost to the Empire, and by mid-November, fourteen provinces had declared their independence.

Li Yuan-hung is elected by the Revolutionary Committee to be President of the Provisional Government at Wuchang.

25th October, 1911 — Tartar General Fung Shan is killed by a bomb at Canton.

3rd November, 1911 — I reply to Sir Hiram S. Maxim's letter of 29th September 1911, thanking him for his support and offer of a new rifle.

4th November, 1911 — Shanghai captured by the revolutionaries.

9th November, 1911 — Independence of Canton declared.

21st November, 1911 — Dr. Sun yat-sen arrives in Hongkong by the s.s. 'Devanha.' We meet on board and exchange greetings.

Dr. Sun Yat-sen leaves for Nanking.

Dr. Sun Yat-sen Elected Provisional President

29th December, 1911 — Dr. Sun Yat-sen is elected Provisional President of the Republic of China by the Military Assembly at Nanking.

15th January, 1912. — I interview my Editor friends Thomas Petrie of the *South China Morning Post* and B.A. Hale of the *Hongkong Daily Press* and urge them to advocate the early recognition of the Republic of China by Great Britain. I also write to Dr. Yung Wing, LL.D., Dr. G.E. Morrison, *London Times* Correspondent, D. Warres Smith and Sir Hiram S. Maxim.

DOCUMENT II.c3: A sense of complacence, The Chinese in Hong Kong, by Sir Robert Ho Tung, Kt. (source: W. Feldwick, *Present Day Impressions of the Far East and Prominent and Progressive Chinese at Home and Abroad*, London: Globe Encyclopedia, 1917, pp. 527-530)

The population of the colony, which consisted of a handful of fishermen and peasants in 1841, is now (1916) about half a million, of whom 97 per cent are Chinese. No part of this population can be described as purely indigenous. It is essentially transient, composed for the most part of Chinese from the adjacent populous and wealthy province of Kwangtung and the maritime province of Fukien. The former may be classed as the merchants, the traders, the shopkeepers, and the domestics in the employ of the well-to-do Chinese and foreign residents. The latter are birds of passage, who pass through on their way to the tin mines and rubber plantations of the Malay States and the Dutch East Indies. In the early days it was the natives of Sunning, Sunwui, and other districts of Kwangtung in the vicinity who repaired to California, Australia, and the Mexican ports, and, in lesser numbers, to the South American republics. Such is the enterprise of the Sunningese that the first railroad in south China to be designed, built, and managed entirely by Chinese was the Sunning-Kongmoon lines, constructed in 1910. The money for this undertaking was found for the most part by Chinese merchants returned form California. The emigration to South Africa was of short duration, and may be left out of consideration, since the coolies have all been repatriated. A good proportion of the men from the districts in the neighbourhood of Swatow, in Kwangtung, come to Hong Kong, and from this class are partially recruited the coolies for the vehicular traffic of the city and the labour required in connection with the loading and discharging of steamers. Tungkun and the districts in the neighbourhood of Canton also supply a fair proportion of this class of labour. These coolies are for the most part a hardy and sturdy lot, and can be seen in hundreds any day handling loaded trucks in the quays and in front of the warehouses at Kowloon.

A special Commission on behalf of the French Government during 1916 passed through Hong Kong en route for Peking to investigate local conditions with a view to recruiting Chinese labour, with the concurrence of the Government of China, for France. It is understood that this labour will be temporarily employed to make good the deficiency caused by the war, and to repair the havoc and damage wrought by the enemy in the cities and towns of France. From French Indo-China native artisans and mechanics have already departed for France. It is not too much to expect that in the course of time south China will also supply its quota of labour for Europe, including Russia. When this time does arrive, Hong Kong may be expected to be the headquarters for the southern recruiting field. New possibilities of Chinese emigration for Europe loom large in this connection.

It is with the commercial and domiciled Chinese community in Hong Kong that this cursory review is mainly concerned. It is their progress and material and intellectual development that it is desired to emphasize. That progress has been remarkable, and in some respects even astounding, if one goes no farther back than the past ten years. In no department of human activity among the Chinese in Hong Kong have such wonderful strides been made as in that of their education, considered from a Western standpoint. Nor has that progress been limited to the male population. It has shown even more remarkable development among the women. This is the more surprising when the old-time conservatism of China, in regard to the 'weaker sex,' is considered. Denominational and private schools have vied with a paternal Government to foster female education among the Chinese. The Church Missionary Society and London Missionary Society; and the Society of the Propaganda Fidei (better known as the Italian Mission in Hong Kong) have done more in the direction of education in Hong Kong than the efforts of all the other organizations combined. These efforts have been made possible by reason of a system of grants-in-aid from Government, which, judiciously worked, has produced the maximum results with the minimum of cost to the ratepayers in general. No district or hamlet in Hong Kong is without a vernacular school for primary education. These schools act as feeders to the higher-grade schools, and lead successively through the colleges to the Hong Kong University. Is it surprising, then, that a perfect revolution has been wrought on the moral and physical life of the Chinese by well-directed efforts for considerably more than half a century?

If those who have done all the spade work like the early leaders of Christian thought could have lived to see the result of their indefatigable labours, they would have been well rewarded by a knowledge of the fact that their later disciples have succeeded to such centres of learning as Oxford and Cambridge Universities for the completion of the courses of studies first begun in Hong Kong. The broader outlook which such a system of liberal education has imparted into the native mind has already left its impress on the social, religious, and domestic life of the Chinese. And what has been written as regards female education can be as truthfully recorded of male education. The Trimetrical Classics once learned by rote by the Chinese child have now given way to the standard spelling books and readers of the recognized Western schools. From these early beginnings the male students are taken by progressive stages from form to form until they complete their elementary course and are in turn matriculated. Then follows their course as undergraduates in the Hong Kong University, where, by dint of characteristic application, they qualify themselves for diplomas in the faculties of medicine, engineering, and arts. There are nearly 200 of such students in the Hong Kong University today.

It has been remarked that this system of education has brought about a wonderful revolution in the social, religious, and domestic life of the Chinese in Hong Kong. One example alone will illustrate the point. When the liberty now enjoyed by Chinese girls, in association with male companions, is contrasted with the attitude that prevailed not so many years ago, one cannot refrain from observing that, however beneficial the assimilation of Western thoughts and manners may be, there is danger of the girls losing that decorous reserve which is such an admirable Chinese characteristic in the views of members of the older school of thought, but is not so much admired by the Young China party. The same may be said of the dress affected after the Revolution of 1911. When the old regime was cast off for the new, it was thought the proper thing to discard all that appertained to national custom. Thus, for instance, the national costume — economical, comfortable, and eminently suitable from a hygienic point of view — was hurriedly discarded for foreign clothing. Even in the matter of footwear the Chinese, generally speaking, rushed to adopt the Western style. This exuberance of spirit has somewhat subsided, although the hybrid fashion of the Chinese coat with foreign skirt now worn by Chinese ladies on ceremonial occasion still offends aesthetic taste. On no ground can the absolute denationalization of Chinese customs be defended. Radical changes are also noticeable in the matter of social observances; in none are they so prominent as in the matter of the bridal party. Fashion has apparently ordained, as the correct thing in the eyes of the Chinese world, that the contracting parties to a marriage shall be driven in motor-cars, and that the wedding guests shall employ the same mode of conveyance to and from the reception, after the style of European countries. Ostentatious display appears to be the keynote of every wedding ceremony, and there is danger of such display being carried to the border-line of the ridiculous. It is left to the leaders of Chinese society in Hong Kong to set up some standard of correct observances that would not offend any code of morals or good taste. Admittedly, such a task is not easy of accomplishment. Better far to make an early attempt than to delay until objectionable practices have received the sanction of usage. In this connection, expensive funeral ceremonials have as little to commend themselves as lavish expenditure on the living.

Closely associated with the subject of marriages is that of the religion of the Chinese in Hong Kong. As a natural corollary to the denominational system of education prevailing, there can be little wonder that the Chinese are coming more and more to embrace Christianity as one of the forms of religion. Especially is this the case with the womenfolk, among whom the most active form of Christian propaganda is being carried on. Where Christianity is embraced from a conscientious belief that it is the safe course to pursue for the life hereafter, there is nothing to be said against the individual or the community choosing it as the guiding principle in morals; but when communion with the congregations of the established Churches is sought as a means towards social or material advantages or for personal aggrandizement, the hypocrisy of the adoption of an alien religion cannot be too strongly condemned. In modern times liberty of conscience appears to connote the setting up by any religious sect of mushroom growth of a doctrine ostensibly justified upon biblical authority. Oftentimes the most strenuous of such sectarian preachers have adopted religion as the easiest calling or profession, and rely upon the 'gift of the gab' to prevail upon the credulity of the Chinese for the converts. This is a very real danger, and is even now apparent in Hong Kong.

Turning from a highly controversial subject to one for the amelioration of the human race, the adoption by the Chinese in Hong Kong of the system of Western medicine and modes of healing may be cited as a mark of progress. A quarter of a century ago, at the time of the first outbreak of plague in its most virulent epidemic form, the Government had to combat the deep-rooted prejudice and ingrained ignorance of the Chinese populace in its attempt to minimize the dreadful ravages of the disease. The most difficult task was to bring the lower orders of the Chinese inhabitants to realize the benefits of Western medicine and preventive hygiene. It was at this parting of the ways, when the Hong Kong Chinese stood at the threshold of the gates to Western medical science, that the Tung Wah Hospital performed one of the most beneficent of the many acts of benevolence which this fine institution has rendered to the Chinese people during nearly three-quarters of a century. For the first time in the history of the colony, Chinese patients were given the option of choosing between their own method of treatment by Chinese medical practitioners, with their concoctions of herbs and dried roots, and that followed by licentiates who had obtained their diplomas from the Hong Kong College of Medicine, before that institution was merged in the Faculty of Medicine of the Hongkong University. The experiment has proved a great success. Statistics compiled at the hospital show that Chinese have come, in increasing numbers, to prefer the benefits derivable from Western treatment to their own more primitive and unscientific methods. Moreover, the coolie class now submit even to surgical operations without demur, whereas at one time, in their ignorance, they believed that the body, in its process of transmigration to the world beyond, would not be admitted if it had been subjected to any process of mutilation such as a surgical operation was supposed to involve. At one time the belief was also general with the Chinese that the application of the surgeon's knife meant certain death. Except for a small annual monetary grant by the Colonial Government, the Tung Wah Hospital is wholly maintained by voluntary subscriptions from the Chinese in Hong Kong and abroad. Besides this institution, which enjoys a reputation amongst the Chinese of world-wide fame, there are the Kwong Wah Hospital at Yaumati, the Infectious Diseases Hospital at Kennedy Town, the district dispensaries, and the Po Leung Kuk Society for the protection of women and children, all of which owe their foundation to the liberality of Chinese residents, and are administered wholly by Chinese committees and governing bodies under the aegis of the Government of Hong Kong. The newly formed Ambulance Corps of the Chinese Section of the Police Reserve is also quite a useful organization. That the Chinese do not shirk their civic duties is proved by the formation, wholly on their own initiative, of the Company of Police Reserves since the outbreak of the European war. Numerically, the Chinese is the largest of any of the companies composing the Hong Kong Police Reserve.

The list of purely Chinese institutions would not be complete without the inclusion of the District Watchmen's Committee, an elected body composed of some of the leading members of the Chinese community in Hong Kong, whose duty it is to advise the Secretariat of Chinese on all Chinese matters in Hong Kong. This subject leads to the consideration of the political status of the Chinese. In this matter, as in all others, they have no reason to complain that the Government does not extend to them a fair measure of equality of treatment with the other races in the island, for two unofficial members, nominated by the Government, enjoy the distinction of representing the Chinese there on the Legislative Council. The senior has had the honour conferred upon him by the King of a Companionship of the Order of St. Michael and St. George. Similarly, on the Sanitary Board there are two unofficial Chinese members, both Government nominees. In the list of justices of the peace for the colony, quite a representative number of prominent Chinese names also appear. Two leading members of the Chinese community have received the honour of knighthood.

Another very conspicuous feature of Chinese progress in Hong Kong is the remarkable growth of the Chinese press. Although the art of printing — not from movable types, but from woodcuts — was first discovered and put into practice by the Chinese, no nation has been so backward in the dissemination of news by the printing press. Within recent years, however, there has been a wonderful transformation. Today the printing press is to be found throughout the country, and in no direction has private and joint enterprise been so active as in the matter of newspaper printing. With the greater enlightenment of the masses and a more intelligent interest taken in political affairs, printing presses have been erected broadcast in Hong Kong. Under a Government which concedes much latitude in regard to the freedom of the Press, Chinese newspapers have, generally speaking, thriven in a remarkable degree. The unbridled freedom which the Press has enjoyed in the hands of novices led to the enactment of a legislative measure against the publication of seditious matter, and prosecutions under this law have been instituted, but fortunately they have been few and far between.

Thus far the commercial success and material prosperity of the Chinese have been touched upon only incidentally. No one, however superficially acquainted with the importance of Hong Kong as a great entrepot of trade and the third shipping port in the world, can withhold a meed of praise from the Chinese who, in greater measure than any other section of the community, have stood to benefit by the prosperity of the colony. The Chinese are excluded from no department of commercial activity in Hong Kong. The natives of Kwangtung, renowned for their business acumen, have availed themselves to the full of the rare opportunities which intercourse with the foreigners have brought within their reach for profitable trade between their wealthy province and the outside world. The result is apparent in the accumulated wealth and influence of the Chinese of the commercial class in Hong Kong. Wealth with them is diffused instead of, as in some other countries where the doubtful system of trusts prevails, becoming concentrated in the hands of a few and producing socialistic tendencies and conflicts between capital and labour. The innate shrewdness of the Chinese and the extent of early correct intelligence of conditions in the consuming districts which they are capable of controlling give them an advantage not to be despised where business success is concerned. The natives of Kwangtung excel as shopkeepers. In the retail trade they hold today the pride of place in successful competition even with the first-class European establishments in the colony. The department store is a plant of recent growth in Hong Kong, but it has taken root in fertile soil. Such stores are amongst the most successful business places in Hong Kong. Consular reports have chosen them for special mention. Their self-contained buildings, specially designed and adapted, occupy most prominent positions on the water-front. The principal department stores combine with their retail trade the business of fire and marine insurance, and to this end their memoranda of association have recently been revised and have received the legal sanction of Court. In every case the working capital of the concerns has been doubled, and represents in the aggregate several millions of dollars. Chinese-capitalized, Chinese-managed, and Chinese-staffed joint-stock companies doing business in fire, marine, and life insurance, shipping, land and estate business, and shipbuilding and repairing, are no longer isolated instances of native enterprise. They rank today amongst the successful companies operating in friendly rivalry with similar British companies. Another notable fact is the inclusion of Chinese names in the directorate of British companies. This is not confined to companies of minor importance or of strictly local operation. The companies that have thought fit to relax the rigid policy of exclusivism are amongst the largest capitalized and most influential of those registered in Hong Kong.

It can no longer be said that the Chinese resort to Hong Kong for sordid motives only. If their patient industry and frugality have been the means of amassing for them considerable wealth, it cannot be denied that a large proportion of their accumulated savings is invested in and spent in Hong Kong. So great is their faith in the permanent prosperity of the colony, and the safety of domicile under the folds of the British flag, that the Chinese are said to own more than three-fifths of the landed property in Hong Kong. Outside the Peak Reservation, Chinese families of the well-to-do class own and live in some of the largest and finest residential properties on the island. Their standard of living has also been considerably raised. European luxuries are freely indulged in, whether in the matter of wearing apparel or the creature comforts of the household. Of the hundred or so motor-cars licensed in Hong Kong, omitting those of the garages for public hire, the greater number belong to the Chinese monied class.

It is singular that the Chinese, who have such an enviable reputation as successful agriculturists, should show such little progress under this head in the New Territories since their occupation by the British under the Kowloon Convention of 1898. Under the auspices of the Botanical and Forestry Department, Government has endeavoured in every way possible to help the Chinese with imported seeds and technical advice to improve their primitive agricultural methods. Better sugar-cane, tea plants, tobacco, and fruit-seeds have been imported and freely distributed to the farmers. The results have been disappointing. Excepting for a slightly improved quality of pineapple and of one or two English seasonal fruits, like the strawberry, the Chinese have not progressed in agriculture as they have done in other departments of their varied activities. Those activities have been remarkable in their success, and they are a tribute to the genius of the Chinese, who have helped to make Hong Kong what it is today.

CHAPTER THREE

A CITY OF ENTREPRENEURS

Hong Kong survived on its ability to trade; and trade thrived because the institutions for trade were put in place and because a mercantile community grew up in Hong Kong that actively sought opportunities for trade.

Among Hong Kong's early merchants were the taipans of Western companies, the compradores who served as intermediaries between Western trading houses and the Chinese population, and Chinese merchants from the Nam Pak Hong (the North-South Guild) of importers and exporters. These well-known stereotypes, however, do not tell the full story of trade. They say little, in particular, of the linkages between Hong Kong, other parts of China, and, indeed, other parts of the world. They are silent about the importance of real estate in the building up of the capital base of Hong Kong's prominent merchants. Nor do they say very much about merchant networks built upon common origins, interests and social life.

Chou Show Son and Sir Robert Ho Tung, whose contemporary biographies are reproduced below, went easily between the Western and the Chinese communities. Lau Chu Pak, long-standing Legislative Councillor from 1913 to 1922, sat on the boards of public service companies both Western and Chinese. The Sassoon family, which came originally from India, owned spinning mills in Bombay and real estate in Shanghai, but also traded in Hong Kong. Hong Kong and Whampoa Dock Co. and Dodwell & Co. were owned by Westerners and managed along Western lines. The Hong Kong Chamber of Commerce, which represented the interests of Western merchants in Hong Kong, was formed in 1861. The Hong Kong Chinese General Chamber of Commerce was formed much later, in 1913.

This chapter also includes a detailed year-by-year autobiography written by Fung Ping-shan, a Chinese merchant and philanthropist who settled in Hong Kong in 1910. Fung Ping-shan was in many respects a traditional merchant. Like many Chinese merchants, he moved to Hong Kong because it provided safe haven for his business. His commitment to Hong Kong grew as his business depended more and more on Hong Kong. But his circle maintained its very Chinese characteristic: it was concerned, in particular, with the promotion of Chinese education in Hong Kong and welfare services in their home county.

In political outlook, one might say the entrepreneurs accepted quite readily a conservative working relationship with the Hong Kong government. No serious constitutional demand was ever made in the name of the mercantile community. No impetus for social reform was driven from its imagination.

DOCUMENT III.1: Mr. Chou Show Son (source: W. Feldwick, *Present Day Impressions*, pp. 578-579)

Mr. Chow Cheong-ling, or, as he is known to his intimates, Mr. Chow Shou Son, was born in Hong Kong 55 years ago.* After his early education in China he was sent by the Chinese Government to America, where he entered the Columbia University, New York. On returning to his native land he received in 1881 a Government appointment on a deputation to Korea to assist in the establishment of the Korean Customs. He remained in this service for about 10 years, after which he was transferred by Yuan Shihkai, the late President of China, to the Consular Service. At that time Yuan was the Minister Resident in Korea, and he held that post, with Mr. Chow as one of his assistants, until the outbreak of the Chino-Japanese War.

Mr. Chow then left for China, and after occupying various official positions he became managing director of the China Steam Navigation Company in Tientsin. He held that post for a number of years, and was then appointed managing director of the Peking-Mukden Railway. For four years he was in this highly responsible position, and on his relinquishing it he was the recipient of a most gratifying testimonial from the European staff, acknowledging in the highest terms the services he had rendered. This was a rare distinction, only one other such instance having been known.

Afterwards he was sent to Newchwang in the capacity of Customs Taotai. This is a position involving many official duties besides those directly connected with the Customs service. Mr. Chow was responsible for a territory of several hundred square miles, and had control of all foreign intercourse there. For three and a half years he served in this district, which lies between Shanhaikwan and Hsin Min Fu, on the Liao River. Then he was recalled by Prince Ching, and given the appointment of councillor or secretary at the Foreign Office in Peking. He was later offered the high position of Minister to one of the European countries, but this he declined, feeling that he needed a rest after many years of strenuous work.

During this time the Revolution broke out, and he returned to Hong Kong, where he was when this book was compiled. Since coming to Hong Kong he has been

---

* 1862

associated in business enterprises with the Hon. Mr. Lau Chu Pak. He has become a member of the committee of the Chinese General Chamber of Commerce. He is proud of the fact that he has been asked to return to Peking and resume official work. Mr. Chow is the owner of very considerable property both in the north and the south of China.

As will be seen by a photograph in this section,* Mr. Chow, as the representative of the viceroy at Mukden and senior official at Newchwang, entertained the late Earl Kitchener when his lordship visited the battlefields of Manchuria after the Russo-Japanese War. In the picture in question Mr. Chow may be seen on the deck of a steamer engaged in conversation with Earl Kitchener.

Mr. Chow Cheong Ling is a member of the North British Academy of Arts, Literature, Science, and Music, and also a member of the Society for the encouragement of Arts, Manufactures, and Commerce, London.

DOCUMENT III.2: Sir Robert Ho Tung (source: W. Feldwick, *Present Day Impressions* pp. 582-583)

Sir Robert Ho Tung . . . was born in the colony fifty-two years ago, and has spent practically the whole of his life on the island. He received his education in Chinese privately, while he pursued his English studies at the Central School (now Queen's College). Starting business at the age of seventeen, he joined the indoor staff of the Imperial Maritime Customs. He left that service to take the post of assistant compradore to Messrs. Jardine, Matheson & Co., Ltd., and also became manager of the native branches of the Hong Kong Fire Insurance Company and the Canton Insurance Company. During this period he opened up on his own behalf a very extensive trade in raw and refined sugar with Shanghai and the Yangtse ports. His health failing, Sir Robert handed over these business responsibilities to a brother. He retired from Jardine, Matheson & Co. in 1900 (having been appointed chief of compradore in 1894), after twenty years' association with that firm.

Sir Robert Ho Tung is one of the most extensive property owners in the colony, and he also possesses lands and houses in the Macao district. His Hong Kong residence, 'Idlewild,' occupies one of the finest sites in the island, with an enchanting harbour view. It is surrounded by an extensive garden, and Lady Ho Tung is annually a winner of many prizes at the Hong Kong Flower Show.

The business ability of Sir Robert Ho Tung is well shown in his dealings with the Hong Kong Hotel Company's affairs. At one time the shares of that company were as low as $ 5 and unmarketable, as the concern had paid no dividend for years. Sir Robert, being a shareholder, suggested the appointment of a Committee of Investigation, which suggestion was acted upon. The result was reorganization, and incidentally the present flourishing condition of the concern. Sir Robert is a director of the Hong Kong Land

---

* Omitted here.

Investment and Agency company, the Hong Kong, Canton, and Macao Steamboat Company, the Kam Hing Knitting Company, and of the Indo-China Steam Navigation Company. He has, in addition, accepted a seat on the board of the Consulting Committees of the Hong Kong Fire Insurance Company, Ltd., and the Canton Insurance Office, Ltd.

Sir Robert takes keen interest in all matters relating to Chinese social life, and he was the first president of the Chinese Club, an influential organization founded mainly through his efforts.

Sir Robert Ho Tung has served on several notable committees: that which organized the local celebration for Queen Victoria's Diamond Jubilee, and that which received H.R.H. the Duke of Connaught at Hong Kong. He also served on the Committees of the South African War Fund (1890), the Kwong Sai Famine Fund, and the Tung Wah Hospital.

Sir Robert is proud of the fact that he was able to be of service to that great Irish sailor, Lord Charles Beresford, when he was commissioned by the Home Government and the Associated Chambers of Commerce to furnish an exhaustive report upon British trade in the Far East. He also offered the farewell banquet to the world-famous engineer and contractor, the late Sir Thomas Jackson, on the occasion of his departure form Hong Kong.

During the Administration of Sir William Robinson*, Sir Robert was invited to fill a vacancy on the Legislative Council when Dr. Ho Kai (now Sir Kai Ho Kai) went to Shanghai to join His Excellency Sheng Kung Po. However, Dr. Ho Kai returned to Hong Kong before the expiration of his leave, and thus resumed his seat on the Council. During the Governorship of Sir Henry Blake** , Sir Robert was invited to become a member of the Sanitary Board, but did not accept the invitation as he was about to proceed to Europe and America.

It is, however, by his endeavour in the world of philanthropy that Sir Robert has won such an honoured name. Any scheme having as its aim the betterment of the condition of the Chinese or European population is sure to enlist the sympathies of this warm-hearted knight, who, especially in matters of public health and public education, has been munificent in his gifts. He promoted the Tung Wah Hospital Extension Scheme, and was largely instrumental in the collection of the $150,000 necessary for its completion. His sound advice has been of particular value to the Government in matters dealing with plague prevention. The erection of the finely equipped Plague Hospital is largely due to Sir Robert's efforts, and most of the $100,000 which the institution cost was donated by him. For many years he has been on the Committee of the Po Leung Kuk, that splendid organization for the protection of native women and girls. He gave largely to the Canton Flood Relief Fund, and has supported the Helena May Institute; indeed, his gifts and acts have been innumerable.

---

* Governor of Hong Kong, 1891-1898.
** Governor of Hong Kong, 1898-1903.

In the realm of public education Sir Robert's generosity has been no less remarkable. He presented to the colony the Kowloon School for children of British parentage, the first civil school for European children in Hong Kong. The foundation stone was laid by Governor Blake in 1900, and the school was declared open by Sir W.T. Gascoigne, K.C.M.G., on April 19, 1902. Sir Robert also presented a valuable scholarship to Queen's College. When the University scheme was mooted he was one of the largest contributors to the Endowment Fund. Early in 1915 he made still further munificent donations to the funds of the University. Of these, one was an immediate gift of $50,000, the income of which is to be devoted to the establishment of a Chair of Clinical Surgery tenable at the Civil Hospital. The second gift took the form of an annual subscription of $5,000 for ten years. Altogether, in ten years, the University will have benefited by Sir Robert's donations to the extent of $110,000.

When the Great War broke out Sir Robert showed his loyalty by offering his services in any capacity to the Colonial Government. He gave $10,000 to the Prince of Wales's Fund, and offered to import rice from Bangkok and Saigon and sell the same in the colony at cost price. In a dispatch from Sir Henry May to the Home Government, in which the splendid loyalty of the Chinese residents of Hong Kong was placed on record, Sir Robert's philanthropic offer received special comment. In conjunction with his brothers and three more Chinese gentlemen Sir Robert made the gift of an aeroplane to the British Government; and still more recently he has presented to the Government, as a contribution to the War Fund, the sum of $50,000. This amount, which is equivalent to £4,908, His Excellency the Governor decided to dispose of as follows; £3,000 for the purchase of two aeroplanes to be presented to the War Office, and £1,908 to be paid to the British Red Cross Society for the purchase of motor ambulances.

As a mark of appreciation of his many services Sir Robert has been elected a a member of the Peace Commission of the colony, and the Government of China has conferred upon him the Order of the Chao Ho (Third Class). His greatest reward, however, was at the hands of His Majesty, who graciously bestowed upon him the coveted honour of Knighthood. The news reached the Governor of the colony in the following telegram: 'It gives me much pleasure to inform you that His Majesty has been pleased to approve of a Knight Bachelorship for Mr. Ho Tung.' The news was received by foreigners and Chinese alike with feelings of great appreciation.

DOCUMENT III.3: The Hon. Mr. Lau Chu Pak, J.P. (source: W. Feldwick, *Present Day Impressions* pp. 574-575)

In all South China no name is held in greater respect, by Chinese and foreigners alike, than that of Mr. Lau Chu Pak, who, by his abilities, tact, and the soundness of his views, has obtained the high esteem of all with whom he has come in contact. He brings to bear upon all questions a sound common sense, and on more than one occasion his advice has been of the greatest value to the Government when delicate questions relating to Chinese affairs have arisen.

Mr. Lau is especially noted for the great interest he takes in all matters connected with the welfare of his countrymen. This is especially the case in relation to education. A man of scholarly attainments, he has taken up enthusiastically the question of the education of the rising generation. His view is that a young Chinese should not only acquire a sound knowledge of English to enable him to take part in the business life of the country, but that he should also be well instructed in Chinese literature and learning. This plan is admirably carried out in the schools of the Ellis Kadoorie Chinese Schools Society in Canton and Hong Kong, and those of the Confucian Society of Hong Kong. Mr. Lau was one of the founders of these societies, and is their honourary secretary and president respectively.

The great scheme of controlling the course of the West River, and thus preventing the terrible devastation of villages, destruction of crops, and the drowning of untold numbers of people which has been going on annually for centuries, may be justly attributed to Mr. Lau. The Chinese Chamber of Commerce has decided to support this scheme, which will cost millions of dollars. The far-sightedness of Mr. Lau has enabled him to make clear to his countrymen the enormous benefit that will accrue from the execution of the design, not only in the increased happiness and security of the inhabitants of the West River Districts, but in the largely augmented trade that is bound to follow the completion of the scheme. The increased prosperity of the agricultural districts will also contribute greatly to the solidity of the State, for it is a well-known fact that the risings, rebellions, and periods of unrest occurring so often in south China have their origin in the vast majority of cases in the distress caused by floods, famine, and other calamities, which evils the West River scheme will go far to eradicate. Whether the Chinese Government will fall in with Mr. Lau's views or not is still a pending question.

The secret of Mr. Lau's popularity with all classes of the community lies in the fact that, although he is a man of advanced views, and one possessing sound grasp of Western methods and ideals, he remains essentially a Chinese. He does not affect the Westerner in dress or customs, and he is bold and fearless in putting forth his views, which are always supported by sound and logical argument. This is especially the case where he is advocating schemes for the welfare of his countrymen. He is a great supporter of the contention that the Chinese should be allowed to control their own affairs, and he always figures prominently in charities, whether foreign or Chinese.

Mr. Lau has been a prominent member of the Hong Kong Legislative Council since 1914, and he is always listened to very seriously by the official members of that Council when any question of Chinese importance is on the agenda. He speaks so eloquently and is so clear in thought that it is a pleasure to listen to him. He is in every sense a practical politician, with fixed aims and definite purposes. He has served for twelve years on the Sanitary Board, and his advice in delicate matters arising from the necessity of plague control has been of the very greatest service to the Government.

The extent of the Hon. Mr. Lau Chu Pak's influence and the esteem in which he is held are admirably shown by the positions he holds, and which embrace (1) Justice of the Peace (having previously served 12 years on the Sanitary Board); (2) member of the Law Committee; (3) member of the Architects Committee; (4) member of the

Food Committee; (5) member of the District Watchmen's committee; (6) member of the Public Dispensaries Committee; (7) member of the Council and the Court of Hong Kong University; (8) member of the Advisory Board of the Tung Wah Hospital; (9) member of the Finance Committee of the Alice Memorial Hospital; (10) chairman of the Chinese General Chamber of Commerce; (11) chairman of the Confucian Society of Hong Kong; (12) chairman of the Po On Chamber of Commerce; (13) president of the Federated Athletic Sports Association; (14) hon. sec. to and a founder of the Ellis Kadoorie Chinese Schools Society; (15) vice-chairman of the Po Leung Kuk (a society for the protection of women and children); (16) member of the Selection Committee of the Chinese Police Reserves; (17) member of the Committee of the Chinese Recreation Club.

Business positions: (1) director of the Tramway Company; (2) director of the Anglo-Chinese Education Trust, Ltd.; (3) director of the Gold Mine Company of Manila; (4) director of the Shanghai Life Insurance Company, Ltd.; (5) member of the Consulting Committee of A.S. Watson & Co.; (6) managing director of the Spirit Farm of Canton; (7) managing director of the Ping Wu Trading Company; (8) managing director of the Cheong Yue Finance and Commission Company of Ping Wu; (9) managing director of the Cheong Yue S.S. Company, Hong Kong; (10) a managing partner of the Tai Yuen Bank; (11) general manager of Lau Chu Pak & Sons (finance and general agents); and (12) managing director of the Hong Kong Mercantile Company, Ltd.

DOCUMENT III.4: Hongkong and Whampoa Dock Company, Ltd. (source: W. Feldwick, *Present Day Impressions*, p. 543)

The history of this famous company, its origin, early struggles, gradual development, and present proud position, forms a romance which is an integral part of the story of the spread of British influence in China. The advent of the company took place in those early days when the Eastern seas were first furrowed by the steamers of the P. and O. Company and the speedy vessels of the great opium houses. The various companies were loath to trust their valuable ships for docking and repairing to the Chinese of Canton and the mud docks there. The demand for better docking accommodation was recognized by Mr. John Couper, of Aberdeen, who had been appointed by the P. and O. Company as overseer of their vessels while in Chinese hands. By his enterprise and foresight the Couper Dock was constructed, but this was fated to partial destruction by the native troops in 1856, an incident in the *Arrow* affair. The progressive Scotsman lost his life at the same time. When peace was restored the dock was rebuilt, and from the Couper family it passed into the hands of a company which has since become the Hongkong and Whampoa Dock Company. The company soon afterwards took over an undertaking which had been started at Aberdeen, on the south side of the island, by Mr. John Lamont, and which contained two larger docks. Mr. David Gillies, a partner in this enterprise, entered the service of the new owners.

In 1865 the company was formed with a capital of $240,000 and two years later this was increased to $750,000. The original founders were Mr. Jas. Whittal (head of

Messrs. Jardine, Matheson & Co.), Mr. (now Sir) Thomas Sutherland (of the P. and O. Company), and Mr. Douglas Lapraik. Extensive additions to the docking accommodation were soon made, notably that of a large dock at Whampoa for the repair of the mail steamers of the P. and O. Company and the M.M. Company. During this period the company had to cope with formidable rivals, but following the opening of the Suez Canal it was enabled to acquire the property of the Union Docks Company. Shortly afterwards the slips and docks of its two leading competitors — Captain Sands and the cosmopolitan Dock Company — were absorbed by the company.

Mr. Gillies had now assumed the secretarial management of the whole concern, and he initiated vast developments in the way of new docks and workshops, which proved the foundation of the company's subsequent prosperity. The ever-increasing size of merchant vessels and warships in Far Eastern waters necessitated yet larger docking space. The No. 1 or Admiralty Dock in Kowloon was accordingly built in 1888. It cost over $1,000,000, of which £25,000 [sic] was granted by the British Government in return for priority of entrance for 20 years. The supremacy of the Hongkong and Whampoa Company in Chinese seas was thus permanently established, and it is impossible to say what benefits to the colony have accrued from the company's enterprise in providing for vessels of such large capacity.

The retirement of Mr. Gillies, after 26 years of splendid service, took place in 1901. His successor, Mr. W. Dixon, held the post for three years, followed by Mr. Wilson and Mr. Mitchell, who acted as chief manager until the former retired in 1909. The present manager is Mr. R.M. Dyer. A survey of the properties controlled by the company may now be given:

Kowloon:	No. 1 Dock, Kowloon
	No. 2 Dock, Kowloon
	No. 3 Dock, Kowloon
	Patent Slip No. 1, Kowloon
	Patent Slip No. 2, Kowloon
Tai-kok-tsui:	Cosmopolitan Dock
Aberdeen:	Hope Dock
	Lamont Dock

DOCUMENT III.5: David Sassoon & Co., Ltd. (source: W. Feldwick, *Present Day Impressions* pp. 554-555)

The firm of David Sassoon & Co., Ltd. ranks among the three or four oldest houses in the colony, for it has been closely and prominently connected with the business of the island from the earliest days of its existence as a British possession. David Sassoon, the founder of the house, was born in Bagdad in 1792, and settled in Bombay about 1832. His father, who bore the title of Nassi (Prince of the Captivity), was head of the Jews in Mesopotamia.

The opium trade has always been one of the principal interests of this house, and it was in order to extend his activities in that article that David Sassoon sent his sons to open branches in China. He was thereby enabled to keep in direct touch with the producing and consuming centres, and David Sassoon, Sons & Co., as the China firms were formerly styled, were the leading opium merchants. Of recent years the shipments of opium from India for consumption in China Proper, have been entirely stopped under treaty, and the firm's representatives in India and China have taken a prominent part in the delicate negotiations connected with the disposal of the accumulated stocks. In the old days the house had its own opium clippers.

The company owns cotton mills and a silk mill in Bombay, the product of the former being widely used in the neighbouring country. The firm's activities embrace trade of almost all descriptions, particular attention being devoted to Manchester goods and to metals, whilst in exports the company also does a general business. The first Far Eastern branch of the firm was at Canton, but the advantage of transferring it to Hong Kong under British rule was soon apparent, and the principal south China branch was established there.

The head office is now in London, and all the directors of the firm are resident in England. There are branches in Manchester, Bombay, Calcutta, Karachi, and Bagdad, as well as in Hong Kong, Shanghai, and Hankow. The present chairman of the company is Sir Philip Sassoon, M.P., the third baronet. The present managers of the firm in Hong Kong are the Hon. Mr. Edward Shellim and Mr. A.H. Compton, the former being a member of the Legislative Council and of the Committee of the Chamber of Commerce, and having a seat on the board of directors of the Hong Kong and Shanghai Banking Corporation. He is also a director of many of the principal Hong Kong companies, in which the firm are shareholders, such as the Hong Kong and Kowloon Wharf and Godown Company, the Hong Kong Land Investment Company, the Hong Kong Tramways, the Hong Kong Land Reclamation Company, the China Sugar Refining Company, the Canton Marine Insurance Company, the China Fire Insurance Company, etc. The firm controls considerable properties in Hong Kong, Canton, and North China. For many years the firm has been agent of the well-known Apcar Line of Steamers, and on the purchase of this by the British India Steam Navigation Company, the agency was left in the hands of Messrs. David Sassoon & Co. A regular service is maintained between Calcutta, the Straits, China, and Japan, and first-rate steamers, with ample cargo space and up-to-date passenger accommodation, run about three times a month. The firm is agent for the Norwich Union Fire Insurance Society, Ltd. (founded in 1897), both in fire and marine insurance, and also represents the Lancashire Insurance Company, Ltd. (now merged in the Royal Insurance Company, Ltd.)

DOCUMENT III.6: Dodwell & Co., Ltd. (source: W. Feldwick, *Present Day Impressions* p. 562)

This firm is of long standing and well known in Far Eastern trading circles, as well as in Europe and America. It was formed in 1891 to take over the interests of Messrs. Adamson, Bell & Co., the style then being Dodwell, Carlill & Co., and as such it was known until 1899, when the existing company was established. The head offices of this important house are at Exchange Chambers, St. Mary Ave, London, and there are branches at Hong Kong, Canton, Shanghai, Foochow, Hankow, Kobe, Yokohama, Colombo, San Francisco, Portland Tacoma, Seattle, Vancouver, Victoria, B.C., and New York. The activities of this firm are well shown under the following headings:

Shipping. — Messrs. Dodwell & Co. run a line of steamers, the Dodwell Line, to New York and Boston, via the Suez Canal and the Panama Canal, and they are agents for the Nanyo Yusen Kaisha, running between Japan and Java via ports. Other lines for which they hold the agencies are the Barber Line, the Mogul Line, the Warrack Line, the American and Oriental Line, and the Natal Line.

Imports. — In addition to the general import trade, this house makes a specialty of the importation of machinery and flour. Representing several of the most prominent manufacturers in the United Kingdom and the United States, large quantities of hardware, metal, and machinery are brought in. It is sole agent for the well-known Sperry Flour Company of San Francisco, and a large stock of that company's flour is always carried.

Exports. — All kinds of merchandise and produce from Hong Kong and Canton are handled, among which are rice, metals, rattancore, ginger, fire-crackers, essential oils, wood and bean oils.

Insurance.— The company does a large business in insurance, representing some of the leading houses operating in life, fire, and marine risks. Besides being general agents for the Phoenix Assurance Company and the Standard Life Assurance Company, Messrs. Dodwell & Co. hold the agency for the Thames and Mersey Marine Insurance Company, Ltd., St. Paul Fire and Marine Insurance Company, and the Providence Washington Insurance Company.

General agencies. — (1) The Underwood Typewriter Company, Incorporated: Dodwell & Co. are sole agents for this company in the Far East. Stocks of machines of all standard sizes, as well as accessories of all kinds, are carried by all branches of the firm in China and Japan, and special mechanics are retained to attend to all matters in connection with this branch of business. (2) The Kailan Mining Administration: The Company is sole agent in Hong Kong for this important mining concern, and supplies of bunker coal are always obtainable, while the other produce of the administration, such as coke, firebricks, fireclay, stoneware piping, glazed tiles, etc. can be quoted for on application. (3) The United Asbestos Oriental Agency Company: Dodwell & Co. act as general managers of this company, which deals in all goods composed of asbestos and the requirements of steamers generally. (4) The Union Waterboat Company: This concern, for which Dodwell & Co. act as general managers, has an efficient fleet of steel-built steam water-boats, and is a contractor for the British Admiralty and for all the principal mail-boat companies visiting the colony. (5) Other important concerns represented by Messrs. Dodwell & Co. are: Suter Hartmann and Rahtjen's Composition; the Johnson Picket Rope Company, Incorporated; the Harrison Patent Knitting Machine Company (a stock of whose machines and accessories are kept); the Phoenix Insurance Company; the Imperial Fire Office; the Standard Life Assurance Company; Messrs. Douglas and Grant, Ltd; the Selby Lead and Smelting Company; the Expanded

Metal Company, Ltd; Francis Webster and Sons; Samuel Osborn & Co., Ltd; Fairbanks, Morse & Co.; Waygood-Otis, Ltd.; and Tuck & Co., Ltd.

DOCUMENT III.7: The Hong Kong General Chamber of Commerce (source: *China Mail 76th Anniversary Number*, March 1921, pp 45, 49, 51–2, 53)

June, 1862

A Special Committee at this time was appointed to confer with H.E. the Governor as to introducing a new system of coinage into the Colony. The coinage at this time in circulation was the Carolus, or Spanish pillar dollar, the Mexican dollar, Indian rupees, English sovereigns, shillings, sixpences and three-penny bits, Chinese broken silver and Chinese cash.

A record of the report of the Committee on this subject is unfortunately not to be found in the archives of the chamber.

A form of bond and award to be used in cases of arbitration submitted to the chamber was prepared at this time, while attention was also directed to the necessity for having a Bankruptcy Law in the Colony.

It was also decided to publish for each Mail a market report, the members generally being in favour of such a proposal and willing to furnish the necessary information.

Arrangements were also made to transfer the offices of the Chamber from the Court House to the premises of Messrs. Marsh and Boyers.

In September 1862, it was decided in view of the intimate relations which existed between Hongkong and Lancashire to raise funds by public subscription to assist the cotton operatives who were suffering from the closing of the mills.

This was agreed to; the Chamber contributed $500.00 and the total sum raised came to £5,000.

In October the Attorney-General (Mr. Smale, later Sir J. Smale C.J.) under instructions from the Governor appeared before the Committee and read a draft he had prepared for submission to the Law Officers of the Crown in England dealing with the proposed Bankruptcy Law. The draft ordinance was explained to the Committee and left for their consideration.

A dispute having arisen as to a judgment given by the British Consul at Canton in regard to some goods belonging to a British firm at that port, the Committee decided to address her Britannic Majesty's Minister (Sir F. Bruce) on the subject. This was not the first time that the Chamber had addressed the Minister, as in August 1861, representation had been made to Peking on the subject of the Chinese Customs, a question which for many years previously had been continual bone of contention between the British traders and the Chinese officials.

The matter is worth recording as from that date onwards the Chamber has repeatedly communicated direct with the British Minister at Peking. It is perhaps as well to direct attention to this point as now after 50 years the question has been informally raised by a member of the Consular service who complained of the action of the Chamber and endeavoured to dogmatize that the Chamber should not communicate with British officials except through the Hongkong Government.

A ruling which it is needless to say has been rejected by the Chamber.

Towards the end of the year, some correspondence passed between the Shanghai British Chamber of Commerce and Hongkong with regard to attempts made by the Chinese Government to interfere with the freedom of trade on the Yangtze. Correspondence of a similar nature has been carried on between the two Chambers from that date till now with wearisome persistency.

The first annual meeting of the Chamber was held on 22nd April, 1862, under the chairmanship of the Vice-Chairman, Mr. Walkinshaw.

The result of the year's working was laid before the members of the Chamber and among other matters already mentioned correspondence was referred to which had passed between the Committee and the British Minister on the subject of the detention of vessels at the treaty ports by the Imperial Customs until all import dues on their cargoes had been actually paid, a question which subsequently engaged the attention of the Committee for many years. The surplus funds in the hands of the Chamber at the end of the first year amounted to the very considerable sum of $8,100.00 and it was decided therefore that the Committee should be empowered to use these funds for 'charitable subscription or other purposes tending to promote the interests of commerce.' The charity which appears to have been in mind was the Sailors' Home.

At the present date times have changed and with increasing expenditure and a shrinking revenue, the Chamber finds charity with them begins, and ends, at home — and does not even extend so far as the Sailors' Home. . . .

1892

In the summer of 1892, the Governor requested the Chamber of Commerce to give an expression of their views on the Shares Bill, which had now been in force for a twelvemonth. Two meetings were held in August and September at which long and able speeches were made by several of the leading merchants of the Colony. The speeches were at times unfortunately of a distinctly personal and acrimonious character. Opinions differed very widely from leaving the bill as it was, amending it in one way or another, or in rescinding it in toto. In the end it was agreed by a small majority to ask the Governor to give the bill a further six months trial and then again refer the question to the Chamber.

In November Mr. O'Conor, the New Minister at Peking passed through Hongkong when the Committee had an interview with him and discussed several matters of interest, the chief being the Telegraph Convention and preferential duties by Chinese craft from Kwangtung.

The next question under consideration of the Chamber was that of exchange and at a meeting held in November a resolution was adopted to the effect 'that H.M. Government be urged to take such steps as may be possible' in conjunction with other Governments to lessen if not remove the serious 'uncertainty which existed in exchange between silver and gold.' This resolution was telegraphed to the London Chamber of Commerce.

1893

Early in 1893, the unofficial members of the Legislative Council decided to forward a petition to the Secretary of State protesting against the great increase in cost of the administration of the Colony, and asked the support of the Chamber. After full consideration it was agreed that while certain parts of the petition were somewhat beyond the scope of the Chamber's operation, it was decided to support the request for the appointment of an independent Commission to report on the cost of administration of the Colony and to address the China Association in London on the subject.

In May, H.E. Herr von Brandt, German Minister at Peking, and Doyen of the Diplomatic Body, passed through Hongkong and granted an interview to the Committee of the Chamber, at which the gratitude of the merchants of Hongkong was conveyed to His Exellency for the many services rendered to trade by the interest he had displayed and the energy shown in endeavouring to force the Chinese Government to carry out its treaty obligations while great regret was expressed at His Excellency's retirement. In reply, His Excellency dealt with several matters of importance specially pointing out the desirability in the interests of trade both Chinese and foreign for opening inland waterways of South China, more particularly the West River.

The Governor having asked the opinion of the Chamber as to the desirability of making the Japanese yen legel tender in the Colony, a largely-attended meeting was held in July when it was unanimously agreed that this should be done. During the discussion which was a full one, the question of a British trade dollar was brought up, but no resolution was taken on the subject, owing to the divergent opinions held by those present.

Considerable attention was given during the year to the advantage to be gained by the opening of the West River to foreign trade, the question being strongly supported by the British Minister.

1902

In January the question was raised as to the right of the Taotai at Amoy to levy a tax of $1.00 per head on all Chinese embarking at that port by foreign vessels. The British Consul supported the Taotai and, owing to his representation had obtained the sanction of the British Minister at Peking. It was urged that the latter probably had only given his consent on imperfect information. It was contended that unless the Chinese brokers agreed to be responsible for the payment of the tax, native emigrants would be prevented from embarking, thus interfering with the coolie trade. This amounted to a breach of the treaties.

In consequence of the 'Boxer' rising of 1900 against the foreign representatives in the capital of China and the consequent disturbances in North China, accompanied unfortunately in many instances by the cruel murder of a number of foreign residents in the Empire, the Peace Protocol was signed in Peking on 7th September, 1901.

As a corollary to this, a new commercial treaty was subsequently drawn up between

Great Britain and China and Sir James Mackay was despatched to China as a special Commissioner to draw up the new commercial treaty in conjunction with the British Minister, Sir Ernest Satow. The question of the new treaty naturally occupied a good deal of the attention of the Committee and was specially dealt with by the Chairman (Sir T. Jackson) in his annual address on the 24th March, 1902.

In the summer of this year, the opium Hongs stated that the Canton authorities had imposed an increased duty on all kinds of opium. Reference to the acting British consul at Canton confirmed this report and stated that a proposal had been put forward to form a syndicate to farm the new tax. In consequence however of the opposition shown to this movement by the British officials, instructions were shortly sent down from Peking forbidding the new impost.

The question of so-called Chinese 'pilots' during this year engaged the attention of the Committee and certain regulations were drawn up and submitted to the Government with a view to preventing Chinese from boarding vessels, giving out that they were qualified to navigate steamers into the harbour, when in many instances they had not sufficient knowledge to do so.

The step thus taken by the Committee was later on made use of and an attempt was made to force an occidental pilot service on the shipping community. This would have entailed an entirely unjustifiable expense on the shipping and after some months of experiment, during which it was attempted to increase the rate of pilotage so as to bring the service within the reach of Europeans, the whole scheme fortunately collapsed.

There is no real necessity for a highly paid pilot service in Hongkong drawn from skilled and reliable officers of the Mercantile Marine and the attempt to force such a service, supported as it was by the then Harbour Master, very rightly came to grief, in the summer of 1905. The intention of the Committee had been to ask the Government to establish reasonable control over native pilots and not to inaugurate a highly paid and entirely unnecessary service of 'foreign' pilots. The Government for some considerable time declined to accede to the request of the Chamber, but in 1905, a bill regulating pilots was brought in and duly became law.

The Kwangtung authorities now again attempted to impose special lekin and battery taxes on yarns imported into Canton and to still further increase the duties on opium.

After reference to H.M. Minister in Peking the taxes on yarn were abandoned and the Committee therefore recorded an appreciation of the energetic manner in which the Consul-General at Canton (Mr. J. Scott) had dealt with this matter and brought it to a satisfactory conclusion: the question of the increased duties on opium however still remained unsettled and it was not until December that the Hongkong Government was able to report 'that H.M. Consul-General at Canton had been successful in securing the 'final' abolition of the tax on prepared opium in the two Kwangs.'

A prophecy which unfortunately was falsified eight years later as will be explained hereafter.

On the 5th September the new commercial treaty (generally known as the Mackay treaty) was signed in Shanghai and ratified in Peking in July 1903.

In December a special meeting of the Committee was called to consider a question put forward by the Straits Settlements, whether it would be possible or advisable, to urge on the Government to deal with the silver question with a view to bringing about some measure for stability in exchange.

The Chairman (Mr. C.S. Sharp) laid the matter before the Committee in a very comprehensive speech, the gist of which was that while a number of writers in the local press had urged that the Colony 'Go Gold,' they had passed very lightly over the numerous difficulties and objections which might be brought forward against the proposal. He added 'we seem from the nature of things, inextricably bound up with China in the matter of trade and currency, and till that Great Empire 'Goes Gold,' I fail to see how we can take such a course,' (ie. put the Hongkong currency on a gold basis).

1910

In the summer of 1910 the British Section of the Kowloon to Canton Railway was opened to passenger traffic, and later in the year the first section of the Chinese line from Canton towards the British frontier. It is anticipated that the line will be completed by the autumn of this year.

Quite one of the most important questions dealt with by the Chamber, and a burning one, has been that of the opium trade with Kwangtung.

During the greater part of the year the Committee has been very actively engaged in corresponding with the Hongkong Government, the Minister at Peking, the Secretary of State for Foreign Affairs, the London Chamber of Commerce, and others, with regard to the renewed atempts on the part of the Canton Viceroy to levy an additional tax on raw foreign opium.

The question is still under discussion between the British and Chinese Governments, and as it has not been considered advisable, under the circumstances, to publish the enormous mass of correspondence bearing on the subject until a final agreement has been arrived at by the two Governments, it is inadvisable to give details here.

In brief, however, the proposal as put forward by the Viceroy created the entire monopoly of the foreign opium trade and the levying of a special tax on all opium imported into Kwangtung. The facts of the case are fairly well understood, as reference had frequently been made to the matter in the local press and several proclamations issued by the Viceroy have also been published.

The question bore a very similar resemblance to former attempts by previous Viceroys, notable in 1902, 1903 and 1908 and in Nanking in 1907.

On each of these occasions the merchants, having appealed to the Chamber, the question was taken up, and in each case, thanks to the prompt action of the respective British Consuls on the spot, and support given by the British Minister at Peking, the contemplated interference with the trade was abandoned.

In this case, however, when it was first proposed to levy the new tax on foreign opium, protests were at once made to the Consul General at Canton, and the Viceroy therefore delayed carrying out his scheme for a month, waiting to see what attitude the British authorities would take up.

The Consul General — unlike his predecessors — did not see any breach in the treaties in the levying of the tax, while he declined to recognise in the proposed regulation the formation of an illegal monopoly. He stated that 'provided the tax was not differential' he did not see his way to make any representations on the subject to the local Chinese officials and would only do so under definite instructions from his superior officers.

Emboldened by the attitude of the British officials the Chinese extended their operation to Swatow and all other parts of the Kwangtung Province.

While at first it was stated these steps were taken to discourage the smoking of opium, the officials now frankly admit that the new tax is levied to replace the loss of revenue caused by the suppression of gambling, and the sum estimated as likely to be raised has been variously stated as from three and a half to nearly six million dollars per annum.

In spite of the strongest possible protest from Hongkong, put forward by the merchants, the Chamber of Commerce and the Hongkong Government who are now being supported by the British Minister at Peking, this illegal interference with trade and import of opium still continues.

The loss to the British merchants concerned is already enormous, while a huge sum of money has been locked up in large and accumulating stocks, money which would otherwise have already passed into circulation greatly to the benefit of all — native and foreigner alike — engaged in the trade of Southern China.

The final outcome of this lamentable state of affairs is awaited with great interest.

Other questions which have occupied the attention of the Committee during 1910 are the Trade Marks Ordinance and the proposal put forward by the Chamber that a trade convention should be signed between Hongkong and France, in order to obtain the benefit of the minimum tariff for goods imported into French territory from this Colony.

Throughout these fifty years many other questions have been dealt with by the Chamber of Commerce, but space does not admit of reference to all. I may, however, mention that among others, quarantine regulations affecting our trade, sanitary reforms, water supply, and many other matters more nearly relating to the actual Government of the Colony, have repeatedly received the consideration of the Chamber.

In the foregoing sketch I have endeavoured to give a brief outline of the work which has been carried out by the Hongkong General Chamber of Commerce during the first half century of its existence.

It will, I think, be readily admitted that the record is a good one and that successive Committees have worked hard, and in most instances successfully, in the interests of the Colony and its trade. While fearlessly advocating views which they believed to be in the true interests of the Colony as a whole, even when they found the British high officials, in the Far East or at Home, were disinclined to agree with them, they have, by strictly confining themselves to such questions as rightly fell within their province and by their moderation of expression, almost invariably gained the respect and goodwill of the officials, even when failing to secure the support they desired.

It is only right to place on record the courtesy and consideration which has, at all events of recent years, invariably been accorded to the Chamber of Commerce by the officials of this Colony, and I doubt if anyone now resident in Hongkong can recall a single instance in his own experience where the reverse has been the case.

This is a very marked advance on the bitter controversies which at times took place between the leading members of the Mercantile community and the higher local officials in the earlier days of the Colony.

The existing state of affairs will, we believe, continue, much to the benefit of the Colony in which we — official or unofficial — the residents of Hongkong, are also so deeply interested, and whose prosperity and progress we have so much at heart.

The history of the Chamber of Commerce has been the history of Hongkong for the past 50 years, and this intimate relationship between our Chamber and the Government of Hongkong must continue, if our wish for the advancement of our Colony is to be realised.

DOCUMENT III.8: A Hong Kong autobiography, Mr. Fung Ping-shan (source: Fung Ping-shan, *Feng Pingshan zibian nianpu*, The autobiography of Fung Ping-shan, undated manuscript deposited at the Fung Ping-shan Library, University of Hong Kong)

From my youth, I was taught by Mr Jingtang [my father] that, 'to be a man, it is necessary to establish one's character (*lipin*).' That was sixty years ago. I can still recall that when I was young, I once found by accident that the book *Precious Aphorisms* was really about 'establishing one's character in order to be a man,' and I became very fond of it. Everything I said and everything I did fitted well with Mr Jingtang's teaching. Whenever I made a mistake and came to realize it afterwards, I tried not to make it again.

I am getting on in years. There are things that my sons have heard of and yet do not know the truth about. In my younger days, I had wanted to write down my experience but had been too busy with my work to do it. Now, I have been invited by the Hong Kong government to attend the exhibition* in London, and I am taking the opportunity to visit Europe and America. It so happens that the General Manager of the Bank of East Asia, Mr Kan Tung-po, and Chief Accountant Mr Kwong Loi-yam, are visiting Europe and America to investigate the banking business and have asked me to join them. I can neither read nor speak English, it is a rare and invaluable opportunity for me to have Mr Kan's company and advice, and so I have joined them on the ss 'Australian Queen'. On board, we six or seven friends talk about current

---

* British Empire Exhibiton — Ed.

events, but there is time left for leisure. The boat has passed the Sea of Japan and entered the Pacific Ocean. In eleven or twelve days time we shall arrive. I am taking the opportunity of these ten or more days when I have little to do to write down for my family my experience year-by-year.

I do this for the sake of teaching my family. However, because many of these events took place a long time ago, there may well be incidents I have forgotten or that they do not understand well. If it is anything to do with our business in Chongqing, they can ask my fifth younger brother Shek-fan and my nephews Hon-sun and King-yu. The three of them have worked in our place for more than twenty years and they know everything. As for my properties or my business in Guangzhou or Hong Kong, my nephew King-yu has helped me for many years, and should know. For matters back in the village or in Siam, they can ask my third younger brother Ching-shan. As for money accounts, I have always asked people to keep them separately for me so that I only need take an overall view. For details, they can ask the chief accountant or the divisional accountants, or look up the books to find out.

I went to school at seven. At fourteen, I listened to my teacher explaining the lessons to me. At the end of the year when I was fifteen, I left school. In the middle of the twelfth month, my sixth uncle asked me to join him to do business in Siam. When we arrived, we had not found a suitable location for our shop, and so I stayed with our friend Uncle Kung who worked at the Royal Dockyard. His family treated me very well, and taught me to speak the native language.

In the next year, when I was sixteen, on the fourth day of the fifth month, my uncle found a site for his shop, and he started the Kwong Tung Hing Shop that dealt in haberdashery from the Yangzi area. This was my uncle's own business. At the time, he had not yet employed a counter attendant and wanted me to take the place. Because I had not learned to use the abacus, I did not dare accept. However, he had to open for business the next day and so the night before I delved into arithmetic. When I mounted my post, I was trembling. Fortunately, nothing went wrong.

At nineteen years, Uncle entrusted me with various purchases back in Guangzhou and Hong Kong. Every half month I could return home for a visit. I had not had much schooling and my ability to write was poor. So I consulted my parents, learned from my teachers, and started to practise writing letters. Every half a month, I went out to Hong Kong to order the goods, and once the goods had been paid for, I would return home for my lessons. It was like that every month. Thanks to the work I did these six or seven months, I learned a little about writing letters. At the end of the year, I went to Siam for the new year.

At age twenty, I returned to Guangzhou and Hong Kong to purchase supplies. At the end of the eighth month, I married. In winter, I went to Siam again to work at my post. I stayed there without a break for two years. Mr Kung wanted to give me his daughter as a concubine; but I realized I had just married and taking a concubine would not have been fair to my wife. Moreover, Mr Kung had large sums of money to leave to his daughter. If I married her, I would have to continue doing business in that place and live in Siam for ever. I also realized that there were customs and practices that I did not approve of over there in Siam, and so although Mr Kung pressed hard and time and again asked Uncle and Aunt to persuade me, I did not want to accept it and gently refused. I said I had only just married and needed my parents' agreement. So he also gladly waited for me to consult my parents. At age twenty-two, I returned to China. At the time my father was ill and that gave me the excuse to write to him to turn him down. I heard that he waited for me for two more years.

At age twenty-three, my father-in-law and I together invested capital to grow sugar cane on forty *mow* of land in Ku Ching and Tzi Kai. At age twenty-four, that was in the beginning of the sixth month of the ninth year of the Kuang Shui reign, the sugar cane was destroyed in a typhoon. I lost a lot of capital. In the ninth month, my father died of illness. His body was deposited temporarily at Feng's House Embrace in the Twenty-four Ranges, to be moved for burial at the Immortals' Range in the following year. The grave was lined with a whole foot of cement so that it might last for a very long time. I wanted to stay on in the county city to make my living; but because I left home early in life, business there did not come up to expectation. However, I did not want to return to Siam, and so I did not know what to do. At age twenty-eight, my eldest son Yu Choi was born. It was then that I remembered that Uncle Yip Wai Kwong was soon going to trade in Sichuan. So I consulted him. At the end of that year, I bought some fruit peel in Macau, and some cardamons, putchuk* and cassia in Hong Kong, to the worth of a thousand dollars. At age twenty-nine, in the first month, I went with Uncle to Chongqing to start the An Kei Company. This was my own business; there was no partner. Uncle Yip's business, known as Fook Shun Lung, had been a partnership with Wah Kei Hong for years. In the third month, I arrived at Chongqing. I went to the Ku Kong Warehouse and sold my goods. In the autumn, I bought some goods to take back to Guangzhou and Hong Kong. I traded in three places, leaving home at the beginning of the year and returning towards the end.

At age thirty-one, I spent my New Year in the Ku Kong Warehouse, learning about the businesses of various merchant groups. Business between Guangzhou, Chongqing and Hong Kong was so difficult. At the time, the telegraph between Chongqing and Hong Kong had just been built for several months and many people had not noticed its importance. I realized it was hard to succeed in competition without using the telegraph. However, it was not safe to use the open code, and it was more expensive and easier to make a mistake in using the hidden code. In the event of local disorder breaking out, you would not be allowed in any case to use the hidden code. So I made my own hidden code, and compiled another hidden code to use within the open code. It looked like the open code on the surface, but its content could be secretly coded. That is to say, when the telegraph message is passed on and read, unless the reader could have access to the code, the message could not be understood. It took me more than a year before this code could be effective, but the smoothness of my business in the years thereafter had to be related to it. About ten years later, an employee

---

* Putchuk, or *muxiang*, was used for making incense, medicine and insect repellent.

resigned to join another company and leaked it to other people in the trade. It became like any other telegraphic code and could not be used any more.

At age thirty-two, that is, in the seventeenth year of the Kwong Shui reign [1891], the Maritime Customs opened a station in Chongqing. In that year, I returned home and became resident merchant in Guangzhou and Hong Kong, entrusting the business in Chongqing to an employee to be stationed permanently there. For myself, in Hong Kong I lived at Kwong Fung Wo, and in Guangzhou at Wah Kei Hong. Later in the year, I found that it was not convenient to live at that Guangzhou address, and so I rented the shop that I now presently have at An Kung Street, which I subsequently bought.

At age thirty-three, I was resident merchant in Guangzhou and Hong Kong. Every month, I went to Hong Kong once or twice to make some purchases. As a rule, goods designated for Sichuan I left to the warehouses to transport. However, this way of handling the goods not only made their cost high, but it also made transport slow. In business competition, you do not win unless your costs are low and your transport fast. So I started despatching the goods myself. But, because it was quite troublesome to do your own transporting, I seldom went back to the village.

At age thirty-four, with my mother's permission, I took my wife and son out to Guangzhou. We first lived on the Second Lane at Chiu Yam Street, and then we moved into the upper floors above the shop. (At age thirty-five, in the year of Kap Ng [1894], Grandmother died of illness.)

In the ten years from the time I was thirty-four to forty-three years of age, the volume of goods that went between Guangzhou, Hong Kong and Chongqing increased yearly. The increase was particularly notable in yellow silk and pig bristles. Because I handled transportation myself, I often went between Guangzhou and Hong Kong. I had little spare time. I also had little else to do, and so fortunately nothing much went wrong. Several years earlier, someone at Sam Yuan Lei in Guangzhou went to Chongqing to buy Sichuan opium and made a large profit. Many people asked me to look into Sichuan opium, saying that my company stood an advantage because we did not have to provide for extra overheads or pay interest for any advance. Because we had shops in Guangzhou, Hong Kong and Chongqing, we had ready access to local news. They said it would not be difficult for me to make several hundred thousand dollars. These remarks were not unreasonable. However, I believed that in order to establish one's character, it was necessary to carry out a right and proper business. It would have gone against my conscience to go into this business. In previous years, some Sichuan groups bought Japanese ginseng to sell as American ginseng. Many people made a quick profit by selling foreign herbs that they passed off as standard herbs. However, although they made a large profit from these methods, they soon lost it. This was a pattern. The people who went into Sichuan opium at Sam Yuen Lei and made a profit, I heard, soon lost it. Although progress might be slower when you deal in proper business, you feel satisfied and at ease with your conscience. From this experience, you know you have to be careful in the choice of a trade.

At age forty-four, in the year Kwai Mau [1903], I settled down with my family in the county city. In the fifth month, Mother died. In the seventh month, I lost my wife. The two coffins were left in a coffin house, so that at the end of the year I might bury them on the ridge of the Immortals' Range. I lined the graves with a foot of cement. They were made very strong inside and outside so that they might last for a long time.

At age forty-five, in the year Kap Shan [1904], I bought a house at Xinhui county city that had been owned by the Ng surname so that I might build an ancestral hall dedicated to ancestor Cha Cheung. The reason for it is this: In the last admonitions of Mr King Tong, it was stated that if there was a day when we could build an ancestral hall, we must first build one for ancestor Cha Cheung who first settled there. This admonition was given so that we might not forget our origin. I also bought Numbers 6 and 8 on An Kung Street in Guangzhou, shops and houses facing each other.

At age forty-six, in the year Yuet Tzi [1905], Ancestral Cha Cheung's hall was completed. Although I paid for all of it, I needed the agreement of the entire lineage, and I had the help of my nephews Ah Tung and Ah Leung in supervising the construction. So, when it was almost completed, I consulted my uncles and nephews in the different branches, and we agreed that we would burn all the spirit tablets of ancestors who had derived from ancestor Cha Cheung. The ashes we would keep in a jar under the altar in the hall. People who did not understand what we were doing thought that we had become Christians. In reality, our lineage did not become Christian; we only wanted to make an improvement on old customs. (In the eighth month of this year, my fourth younger brother Yan Nam died in Sichuan.)

At age forty-seven, in the year Ping Ng [1906], I completed my mournings. I set up the An Lung Native Bank. Prior to this, I had been involved in the Kwan Shing Native Bank, but I disagreed with a partner and the manager and so we wound that up. Mak Shum Yu had started out at Kwan Shing, and was serving as a street agent. He wanted to set up another native bank, and I saw that he was reliable and experienced. So, to help him set up the bank, I contributed two-thirds of its share capital. My relatives and friends advised me to take another wife to look after the family. In view of the fact that my oldest son, Yu Choi, was still a minor and was weak, I thought that if I remarried late, step-mother and son or daughter-in-law might not know how to deal with one another. So, at the end of the year, I reluctantly took as my second wife Madam Lee.

When I was forty-eight or forty-nine, my wife gave birth more than once, but none survived. When Kei Fung Hong began, I had some shares there, but in three to four years time 70 to 80 percent of its capital had been lost. Later, we hired Kwong Tzi Ming as purchaser, and in two to three years time, we not only recovered our capital but even made a profit. I saw that he had proved that he was effective, and that his character was reliable. In the autumn of that year, the manager wanted to re-employ the buyer who had been unsuccessful and to give up Tzi Ming. I advised the Kei Fung manager to use Tzi Ming instead, but to no avail. Tzi Ming asked me to help him find another job, and even at that I was unsuccessful. So I was forced to give up my shares in Kei Fung and ask Tzi Ming to prepare to organize another company.

At age fifty, in the year Kei Yau [1909], in the first month, the Siu Fung Hong was set up. This was a partnership between myself, To Sei Tuen, Tsang Yan Po and Kwong Tzi Ming. In the next year, we gradually set up our warehouse, the shop and our pier. All additional capital was provided by myself, but I also depended on Tzi Ming's assistance. Only now do we see any result. Towards the end of the year, my second son Yu Wai was born.

At age fifty-one, in the year Keng Sut [1910], Nam Shang in Annam was set up. This came about when Mak Mo Yan came to see me through Kwok Sin Chau's introduction and spoke to me about setting up an Annam interest. At first I did not want to take part, because it was hard to find people to work with and it was not easy to have ready several hundred thousand dollars all the time. Later on, I found out that Mo Yan had worked in his old company in Guangzhou for more than ten years, and his colleague Wong Chi Ping had also worked in Annam for more than ten years, both in important posts. They were people of experience and good character. In the previous year, they came into a dispute with their young employer, as a result of which they were dismissed. He wanted to set himself up, but he also picked his partners carefully. I thought it would have been a pity to give up on them, and so we set up the company. I took thirty percent. In the sixth, seventh and eighth months, my second son was ill. He died. In the winter, my oldest son also died. At the time, my friends saw that I was at a loose end in Guangzhou and urged me to go to Hong Kong.

At age fifty-two, in the spring of the year San Hoi [1911], my friends in Hong Kong seeing that at my age I had no sons, and that there was only myself with two concubines, urged me to take another concubine. Even my concubines and their parents urged me to take more concubines, and went to Foshan to find me some prospects. I remembered that in my youth, having seen how cumbersome polygamy was for Chinese people, I had decided to be monogamous. By the time I was over thirty years old, when I had only a single son, my mother as well as my wife urged my relatives and friends to poke fun at me for not taking a concubine. I used to brush that aside with a smile. However, I did not have my way. Finally, To Sei Tuen served as the go-between, while Tsang Yan Po put pressure on me, and so I took my third concubine. In that year, my third and fourth sons were born.

At age fifty-three, which was the first year of the Republic, the year of Yan Tzi [1912], I realized that foreign countries were wealthy and powerful because they put family education in an important place. They considered it urgent that women be educated. This was because women were mothers of the nation. If women became literate and knowledgeable, they would be able to bring up their children educated. When children had first been educated at home, and subsequently cultivated by their teachers, they would be able to meet the world with a knowledge of science and speak for the wealth and power of the nation. For this reason, in this year, I employed Miss Leung to come to my house to teach my two concubines to read. She taught them for two years. The year after she left, I employed Misses Wong and Lee, teachers, to teach them for many years. In summer, epidemic broke out in Hong Kong. In the fourth month, we went up to Guangzhou. In the autumn, the situation quieted down. I had just bought a shop at No. 106 Jervois Street. I renovated it and moved back to live in Hong Kong in the winter months.

At age fifty-four, the year of Kwai Chau [1913], I became chairman of the Tung Wah Hospital. Hong Kong law required Chinese people to exhume the corpses they buried in the seventh year after burial so that the bones might be moved to another site. This requirement was at odds with Chinese custom. So, I suggested to the government that land might be set aside for a permanent Chinese cemetery. This was finally approved. The government set aside a hill in Aberdeen for a cemetery. Anyone who wanted it might pay 500 dollars for a plot. I put my name down for a plot of land under the character 'cheng'. In the tenth month that year, I set up the Wai Kat Native Bank. Fung Yee Chai had worked as a manager in a native bank in Guangzhou and, having gone down to Hong Kong at the time of the revolution, he had also worked in a native bank there for two to three years. Later, because he disagreed with the chief manager in the Guangzhou office, he resigned. I had worked with him for many years and knew that he was experienced. So to give him our support, I asked Wang Hing, Sze Tuan, Yan Po and Yee Chai to take out half the shares, and I contributed half. I became chief manager and Yee Chai served as deputy manager.

At age fifty-five, in the year Kap Yan [1914], I became chairman of the Po Leung Kuk. In that year, epidemic broke out in Guangzhou and Hong Kong. In the third month, I took my family to live in Macau. We returned to Hong Kong in the eighth month. At the end of the year, my second daughter was born. My first daughter was born of my first wife, but she died in infancy and so I did not record her birth. In these years, because my business activities were closely intertwined with my social activities, I wanted to delegate my business to lighten my burden. Realizing that the Sichuan business was the achievement of my brothers and nephews, as well as my employees Leung Ying Chou, Kwong Tzi Ming and others, I decided to give them each a share in the On Kei Company that I wholly owned. On the one hand, I wanted to thank them for their hard work; and on the other hand, the business might last long only if many people supported it. So I wound up On Kei and reorganized my business. I kept 40 percent, and out of the annual profit, gave a share each to my third younger brother Ching Shan, fourth younger brother Yan Nam, fifth younger brother Shek Fan, and Kwong Tzi Ming. I wanted really to also give a share to Leung Ying Chau, but he firmly declined. He had worked in my company for more than twenty years. His honesty was highly commendable, and you could see he was clean from the way he declined my offer. It was hard to find someone like that. However, because he was becoming old, he took the opportunity of the reorganization of the company to resign. I gave him 20,000 dollars for his pension. I pressed him several times before he accepted it.

At age fifty-six, in the year Yuet Mau [1915], the Guangdong Government Property Office sold the Xinhui county county office. The Yu family of Taishan [Xining county], resting on its wealth, bought it for its ancestral hall. The people of the county were very angry. I was friendly with the Yu family, and I advised them not to go against public anger. Sometimes, even wealth was not sufficient to fall back on. The Yu family woke up, and allowed the county people to buy back the land. However, it was hard to find such a large sum of money all of a sudden and so a loan had to be raised. When there was not enough, I made it up for them. The Xinhui School was built as a result. In this same year, my third and fourth daughters were born.

At age fifty-seven, in the year Ping Shan [1916], I became a long-term adviser to the Tung Wah Hospital. Fire broke out every year on Jervois Street; there was a fire on the ground floor where we lived. Members of my family were worried about this and did not come down to live in Hong Kong. I had for some time wanted to buy a house in Hong Kong, but had not found anything suitable. But I was afraid of another fire downstairs, and so towards the end of the year, in the twelfth month, I moved up to Bonham Road and rented a house across the road from Hong Kong University.

At age fifty-eight, in the year Ting Tzi [1917], I employed Mr Chiu Tin Hing to come to my house to teach my son and my two concubines. On the first day of the first month, Mr Lee Tam Yu came to Hong Kong from Victoria, and I asked him to immediate start a private school for poor children in Xinhui county city. At the same time, I joined with the Confucian Association in Hong Kong to run three charity schools for boys and girls. In the fourth month, I bought a house on Park Road. I moved in in the seventh month. Because I was renovating the house in the fifth, sixth and seventh months, I seldom went to Wai Kat. The inside manager and some employees were not doing their jobs. Because they were unreliable, comments were being made by people outside as well as outside partners. When the accounts were drawn up at the end of the year, I was also careless and so could not put the blame on them. Fortunately, when the accounts were completed, there was still a profit of several per cent for the shareholders. That was gratifying. At the end of the year, my fifth daughter was born.

At age fifty-nine, in the year of Mo Ng [1918], I became once again chairman of the Po Leung Kuk. In the fourth month, the Yick On Native Bank opened for business. I was getting on in years and did not want to be involved in a new business. But Yee Chai and Tzi Ming asked me several times and so I did it. They said there was much money coming and going among the allied businesses, and so even if I did not want to take a part in this business, I had to manage the comings and goings in the accounts. This would have been even more of a hassle. So it was better to set up a side entrance at Siu Fung Hong and start from small. This would be easy to manage and could reduce overheads. I thought this argument was reasonable. At first, Tzi Ming also took out some shares. He had already paid his share of the capital, but two to three months later, he said back in the days of the Wai Kat Company, Sei Tuen and Yan Po also had shares. Now that they did not, he was afraid there might be misunderstanding later on. So time and again, he asked to be given back his capital. There was not much I could do about it, and so I allowed him to withdraw. One might say he was righteous even at the sight of wealth.

At age sixty, in the year Kei Mei [1919], the Yung Hang Pawnshop and the Yung Hang Native Bank were set up. I was chairman of the District Watch Committee. There were many people from Xinhui who were living in Hong Kong, and they had a good reputation in business. However, they were not as united as other people. Sometimes they came together, but they did not have a definite meeting place. I always thought that was regrettable. So, this year, I worked hard to explain to people from our county why it was important to purchase our own meeting place. Many people agreed. I donated 1,000 dollars, and the rest of the purchase price of the meeting place was advanced by Yick On. Fortunately, capable people had been in charge of it year after year. So, besides the meeting place, we started a charity school, and there was money to spare. This was gratifying. People of our county often ascribed all this to my reputation, and many a time nominated me chairman. However, I turned that down, and agreed only to serve as adviser. This was all my duty: there should be no talk of achievement. But this made me think of the Chinese Chamber of Commerce, to which I once donated 1,000 dollars towards the establishment of its premises. At the time, many people wanted to accept titles of office, but I only wanted posts that I could manage. I served variously as committee member or treasurer, and dared not accept other important posts. Two more incidents in this year related to my county are worth recording. Firstly, we repaired our ancestral graves. The ancestral graves from founding ancestor Cha Cheung downwards had not been repaired for years. Some of them were not marked, and in time it was hard to find them. So I asked my third younger brother Ching Shan and my nephew Leung to look after this matter. We set up honorific pillars next to the graves so that they might be easily recognizable. Secondly, we added some scenic areas. In our county, Chan Pak Sha was a Ming dynasty neo-Confucian master, and Cheung Cheung Shan was also a well-known character of our county in the Ming.* On Mr Lee Tam Yu's suggestion, we built the Pak Sha Memorial Park and the Cheung Shan Memorial Park. In order to let later generations admire these early notables, I donated more than 6,000 dollars for constructing these parks and building pavilions in them.

At age sixty-one, in the year of Keng Shan [1920], I visited Hangzhou and Beijing. In the second month, the Shanghai branch of the Bank of East Asia was opened. Chow Shou Shan, Mok Ching Kong and myself went together to the opening ceremony of the Shanghai branch. We took advantage of the trip to visit the West Lake in Hangzhou and also Beijing. In the third month, we returned to Hong Kong. On the nineteenth day of the fifth month, I was firmly installed as the chairman of the Defense Corps. The term was to be five years.

At age sixty-two, in the San Yau year [1921], in the sixth month, I employed Tam Lai Woon to teach my sons and nephews at home for two to three years. Lai Chak Man served as assistant teacher. I had not returned to the village for more than ten years. This was because after the change at the end of the Qing dynasty, the place was not peaceful and I dared not go. In the autumn of this year, it was relatively peaceful, and so I could go. At the Double-Ninth Festival in the ninth month, I returned to the county to sacrifice at the ancestral hall and to tidy the graves. I inspected the charity school for poor children, and I bought the big house that belonged to the Tam surname on Yan Shou Street. In the spring of this year, I saw that the poor among my relatives and friends in the county, including many elderly people and women, had difficulties making a living and were short of food. I felt sorry for them. So I provided monthly subsidies of three to five dollars, or eight to ten dollars. At the end of the year, I doubled this amount. This was done in the spirit of being good to one's relatives; that would only be right. In this year, some people followed the practice of the Shanghai

---

* Chen Baisha and Zhang Hui, early Ming scholars in Xinhui county.

stock exchanges and wanted to set up similar speculative businesses in Hong Kong. I knew they would be harmful in the long run and so asked the government to ban them. They had tempted me with shares worth 20,000 dollars, but I was not taken in. I tried my best to block them. Soon, these businesses failed.

At age sixty-three, in the year of Yam Sut [1922], the Yu Hing Company was set up. The King Tong Library was set up in a new building that was built on land cleared by dismantling the Tam surname house on Yan Shou Street that I bought.* Also, because educational activities in the county city had been deteriorating, I consulted Mr Lee Tam Yu to establish a senior primary school. Mr Tam Yu became the headmaster. In the fouth and fifth month, I agreed with Lee Wing Kwong, Wan Man Kai and Choi Kung Po to visit Yokohama, Tokyo, Kyoto and Kobe in Japan. In the eighth month we returned to Hong Kong. Early in the ninth month, I returned to the county to sacrifice at the ancestral hall and to inspect the senior primary school, the charity school, and the work on the library. On the next day, my fifth son was born. In the middle of the month I returned to Hong Kong, and then I went with Mr Lee Tam Yu to Guangzhou to visit an orphanage and a secondary teacher-training school. Right after that, I donated a large sum towards the building of a senior primary school that was affiliated to the teacher-training school. In this year, I wound up the Yung Hang Native Bank. The reason for winding it up was that although the Yung Hang Native Bank was profitable, the manager was too agressive and lacked caution in his business. I was afraid that one day it might bring me a loss and that would not be worthwhile. So I declared that it would be closed, and after returning the share capital, there was a profit to distribute. After the Yung Hang Native Bank was closed, I also withdrew my shares from the Yung Hang Pawnshop. This was because although pawnshops were meant to to provide relief for the sudden needs of the poor, people who were engaged in this business in Hong Kong usually went against this principle. When I was engaged in business, I did not want to invest in anything that went against my conscience. So I withdrew my shares. I also withdrew my shares from other pawnshops. I hope my descendants will pay attention to this. Since our founding ancestor Mr Cha Cheung settled in Xinhui in the early Qing dynasty, our lineage had expanded there. There were many descendants and the branches of the lineage were complex. If we did not have a genealogy that set out our generations, in time some people would be forgotten. So some people in the lineage suggested that a genealogy be compiled. My fifth younger brother Shek Fan was put in charge of this. It was completed after a year.

At age sixty-four, in the year Kwai Hoi [1923], I employed Messrs. Mok Yuen Hing and Lai Chak Man to teach my sons and nephews Chinese. In the next year, they also taught them English. I also employed Mr Au Tai Tin to lecture on the classics and history for two hours every week. In the winter, my fifth daughter died in hospital. This year, I became a permanent council member of Hong Kong University. This was because I donated 50,000 dollars in addition to 2,500 dollars for the library. I was given

---

* In Xinhui county city.

for perpetuity four free places at the university that I could give to friends and relatives. I bought the former garrison office and the government building at Xinhui county city, which I demolished to turn into a school. Also, Chuen Yuk and Wing Kwong asked me to set up the Shiu On Wing Real Estate Company, Ltd. I was getting old. Several years earlier, I had put a limit on the business I had been conducting and I did not want to start a new business. However, this company was to build shops for rent on land leased from government for forty years, and it was easier to manage. I held a quarter of the shares. I also set up a vocational school in Xinhui county city, and asked nephew Shui Chau to serve as honorary headmaster, to be in charge of everything. In this year, in memory of ancestor Yuk Fong, I donated 500 dollars in his name to the Sai Nam Middle School in the county city.

In the Kap Tzi year [1924], I visited Europe and America, and while travelling I had the spare time to write down what happened to me year by year. This is recorded above. After Kap Tzi, at the end of every year, I continued to write down in the same manner what was worth noting or what I did or said during the year. I append these records below.

At age sixty-five, in the year Kap Tzi, in the first month, I transferred to the Cho Cheung Ancestral Trust the management of my shop properties in Xinhui county city at Tai Sun Street, South Gate Straight Street, Chan Wan Street, and Pig Sty Street in Honam, so that the rent might be credited to it. The charity school for poor children was also transferred to the Cho Cheung Ancestral Trust. The rent collected every year was to be used for expenses within the lineage, for the maintenance of the charity school, and as scholarships for male and female descendants in the lineage. On the eighteenth day of the fourth month that year, I went with the manager of the Bank of East Asia, Kan Tung Po, and its secretary, Kwong Choi Yam, on the Queen of Australia to attend the exhibiton in London, and while on this trip, I went around the world. I went first from Hong Kong to Shanghai, to Kobe, Yokohama and Tokyo in Japan, I crossed the Pacific Ocean, reached Vancouver, at Victoria Street, changed into a car to go to San Francisco. I stayed there for ten days, and then went to Chicago, Washington and New York. At New York, I stayed for about a month, and then crossed the Atlantic to go to London to attend the exhibition. After eight or nine days, I went to the French capital Paris, Belgium, Holland, Hamburg in Germany, the German capital Berlin, Lausanne and Innsbruck in Switzerland, and then from Marseilles in France I took a boat to Port Said, went on the Suez Canal and the Red Sea to the island of Aden in Arabia. Then I took another boat across the Indian Ocean to go to Bombay. I stayed there for two days and took another car to Madras in India. I took a boat to reach Ceylon, and took a car to British Colombo. I took the French steamer Pa Shi La to reach Annam in one day. I stayed in Saigon for two days. On the 28th day of the ninth month I reached Hong Kong. On this trip, I took special note of commerce, schools and libraries. However, these are subjects beyond this essay and so I shall not elaborate. I have been feeling this year that in Hong Kong, students pay attention to English and neglect Chinese. Moreover, now that war is common on the mainland, the younger generation who want to continue into middle school after they have graduated from primary school find that there is no school that is suitable. So I decided to start a Chinese middle school in Hong Kong which should be a subsidiary of the Confucian Society. Its expenses would be taken care of by myself and three to five colleagues. This will make it possible for the younger generation to study. In this year, I was made a Justice of the Peace.

At age sixty-six in the year Yuet Chau [1925], in the fifth month, a wave of strikes suddenly broke out. The whole of Hong Kong was shaken. Business became very quiet. Many who could not cope collapsed. As banks were institutions for the transfer of finance they were particularly affected. I was chairman of the board of directors in the Yick On Native Bank, and so I found all matters rather taxing. Fortunately, in my daily business activities, I have always been in favour of caution. Moreover, I lead a frugal way of life, and so even in difficult situations, I have sailed through. It so happened that the few days of the strikes coincided with the opening ceremony of the King Tong Library in Xinhui county city. The Ping Shan new school that was under construction was also almost completed. Because transport was interrupted, I could only tell the people in charge to do the best they could. Towards the end of the year, because the senior middle school that I had established in Xinhui county city had been rather boisterous and had succumbed to evil doctrines, and because I did not want to be known to have donated towards education only to harm other people's children, I decided to suspend it and to move into it the charity school for poor children. In the third month of the same year, Tung Nam Hing in Saigon opened for business. In the eleventh month, the Kwong Hing Company was set up. A ship was newly fitted out from England, known as Fu Shun[*], to ply between various places in Sichuan. I had some shares in both. In the eleventh month, construction on the plot of land owned by the Yu Hing Company in Mong Kok was completed. The whole building was made of cement. Formerly, houses and staircases were made of wood. When there was a fire, there was no escape. Many people died from this. This was no way to protect one's tenants. This was why in recent years, I advocated using cement in building. In this year, I continued to serve as chairman of the District Watch Committee.

At age sixty-seven, in the year Ping Yan [1926], the Confucian Association Middle School had been set up from the Kap Tzi year for two years. When the strikes broke out, the students were also involved. So, in spring this year, I asked the government to take over the school, and it was renamed the Government Chinese Middle School. This was so that students in Hong Kong could have a good Chinese school to go to. I also told my sons Ping Wah and Ping Fan to continue to study in this school. I continued to serve as a member of the school council, and I also donated some money towards scholarships. Mr Lee King Hong exerted himself in making this development possible. For some years, my house was not very suitable for my use. Moreover, the floor was made of wood and there were termites. I was also worried about fire hazards. I wanted to renovate it somewhat, but that cost several tens of thousands of dollars. I decided to rebuild it. So on the eleventh day of the twelfth month, I moved into No. 52 Robinson

---

[*] 642 tons, taken over by the Minsheng Co. in 1932.

Road, and then we cleared the old building in preparation for the new one. My eighth daughter was born at this time. The carpentry school in Xinhui county city had been established for some yers, but in recent days, strikes on the mainland led to the unions interfering in the equipment of the school. For this reason, the school could not advance. The headmaster resigned and refused to continue. His successor was hard to find. So at the end of the year, I declared that it would be closed. In Hong Kong, I had always had three charity schools attached to the Confucian Association. Later, I saw that the people in charge did not have the energy to manage them, and so I closed them.

At age sixty-eight, in the year Ting Mau [1927], towards the end of the year, my sons Ping Wah and Ping Fan graduated from the Chinese Middle School and at the same time matriculated into Hong Kong University Chinese Department to further their studies. The political situation on the mainland was changing unpredictably; politicians counted extortion among their capabilities, so I was not optimistic about commerce there. The On Lung Native Bank was affected by the political situation and business had not been as good as it used to be. If I did not bring my shares there to an end, I was afraid I might be quite encumbered. So I declared that my interest there was at an end.

At age sixty-nine, in the year Mo Shan [1928], my fifth younger brother Shek Fan and my old friend Yee Chai both passed away. Feelings for my brothers and friends wounded my heart. Moreover, at the Yick On and Cheung Wo Companies, I also lost my assistants. I was very much saddened when I thought of all this. This year, it was the Yick On Company's turn to provide a person to serve as a director of the Tung Wah Hospital on behalf of the banking sector, and so I asked my nephew Kang Yu to do it. I wanted to reorganize the schools run by the hospital and so I recommended Mr Chan Chiu Mei to be its honorary inspector of schools. His travelling expenses were to be paid by me and not to cost the hospital anything. Fortunately, my wish was granted. The schools were also somewhat improved, and the directors of that year were quite satisfied. I was quite gratified by this.

Libraries were a source of social education. The King Tong Library that I had established was making progress, but Hong Kong did not yet have a library of scale. I proposed to the Chinese Chamber of Commerce that it should set up a library. Fortunately, that proposal was accepted. I donated 1,000 dollars towards its establishment.

In order to promote national scholarship and preserve the national essence, it was certainly necessary for the university to set up a Chinese Department. The university in Hong Kong and people who were enthusiastic towards this objective discussed this matter several times. Finally, as the government had intended, Chinese merchants would donate 200,000 dollars to the government to set it up. So donations were asked for, and I donated 10,000 dollars in order to expedite it. Many people nominated me to be treasurer. I accepted the post gladly.

In my life, most of my time was spent in commerce and little in scholarship. However, it was thanks to Mr Kam Lan Shang's book *Precious Aphorisms* that I was able not to have caused any harm in my dealings with people. When I had time, I read it aloud. This book was becoming hard to find, and so I reprinted 5,000 copies to distribute to friends and colleagues.

The Hong Kong government this year announced that it would finally abolish improper temples. I had often suggested to government that I had often heard that these temples not only bred superstition but also hid many dirty things, and that unless strict measures were imposed to abolish them, supervision could not be destroyed and propriety maintained. Fortunately, the government had now determined to carry this out. No doubt this measure would be greatly beneficial to the people's intelligence.

In the seventh month this year, my new house was completed. On 27th day I moved into the new house.

The Yu Hing Company was engaged in four business activities: (1) rebuilding the shops on An Kung Street and Yat Dak Road in Guangzhou; (2) building sixteen Western-style houses on High Street; (3) withdrawing shares from Kwong Tai Cheung and buying into Ho Nam Warehouse; and (4) buying a few plots of farmland in Lower Village.

DOCUMENT III.9: Indian pioneers (source: *Hong Kong Centenary Commemorative Talks, 1841-1941*, n.d. n.p., first published in the *Radio Review*, pp. 108-110)

India's contact with China goes back twenty-three centuries when Buddhism was introduced into China from India, and India's association, mainly economic, with the colony of Hong Kong dates from the very date of the foundation of the Colony in 1841.

Prior to this year (1841) Indian firms were carrying on business in Macao and Canton, the pioneer in recent Indo-Chinese trade being the late Sir Jameshetji Jeejeebhoy, Bart, a Parsee adventurer from India. In collaboration with the late Mr. Jardine, they carried on a lucrative trade between India and China, and the Parsee knight introduced into India Chinese bangles, glass bottles, silks, tea, cassia and sugar from China. He almost monopolised the bottle trade and even to this date his House is known in India as 'bottlewala' (owner of bottles). From India, they brought hand-woven cotton piecegoods, cotton yarn, spices, and unfortunately also opium.

This trade was continued by other Indians who followed in his footsteps, and they carried on trade from Canton and Macao, but shifted to Hong Kong as soon as the Colony was founded by Great Britain in 1841.

From 1841 to 1880, the firms which did a good deal of business in Hong Kong were N. Mody & Co. (1842), Abdoolally Ebrahim (1842), who are still carrying on their business in the Colony and will celebrate their centenary next year, Ghandy & Co. (with which were associated the brothers of Sir Pherozshaw Mehta, the great Indian leader of late nineties of the last century and early years of the present century), Currimbhoy Ebrahim & Co., D. Naoroji & Co., Cawasji Pallonji & Co., Bomanjee Karanjia & Co. and others. Messrs. D. Naoroji & Co. were the original owners and pioneers of the ferry service beteen Hong Kong and Kowloon on the mainland, and the later development of this effort is the present Star Ferry.

Messrs. Naoriji & Co. were pioneers in several other lines, as they were the principal bakers and general caterers in those days, and also owned one hotel called Parsi Hotel, Hong Kong. During this period the business of the Indian firms, amongst whom the Parsees from India took almost the leading part, was mainly in the import of cotton yarn and cotton piecegoods, gunny bags and opium which were the staple products imported from India even by all other non-Indian firms into Hong Kong.

But also during this period, the foundation was laid (in 1868) by an Indian firm from Sindh (Hyderabad), Messrs. Wassiamull Asoomull & Co., of a business which was later to assume a great importance in the economic life of the Colony.

This firm, as did all Sindhi firms from India, engaged itself in the local sale and export of Chinse silk piece goods, raw silk, curios and several other Chinese products, and also sold Indian piece goods. They were not interested in other lines like grains, yarns, opium, cassia etc. They specialised in the line of silk, curios and other Chinese products which they exported in large quantities to all parts of the world including India. They had about fifty-two branches throughout the world, and did and are still doing a large business in their specialised lines. The lead given by them was followed later by a large number of Sindhi firms which have grown up since in number, extent and importance in the Colony.

Passing on to the period from 1880 onwards to the close of the century, we find further establishment of Indian firms in Hong Kong. In this period, Mr. Hormusji Ruttonjee, the founder of the firm of Messrs. H. Ruttonjee & Son, came to Hong Kong in 1884 and was followed in 1886 by Mr Hormusji Sorabji Kavarana. Both these gentlemen are fortunately alive. Mr Kavarana later shifted his centre of activities to Canton; but Mr. Ruttonjee, who at the age of about 21, first came as a clerk in the firm of Messrs. P.F. Davar & Co., wine and provision merchants, on a monthly salary of HK$13.00, remained in Hong Kong and made a large fortune by painstaking struggle, doggedness of purpose and transparent honesty. Within three years of his arrival, he founded his firm 'H. Ruttonjee & Son' in 1887 and the business of the firm is still being carried on by his son and grandson in a very flourishing condition. Other firms of this period were M.P. Talati & Co., Sir Hormusji Mody as Exchange Broker, Pohoomull Brothers and Tarachand & Co., D. Chellaram, G.W. Ramchaud whose successors are W. Boolchand, Kayamally & Co. and others which were the five other Indian firms to follow Messrs. Wassiamulls, who carried on their business along with others established earlier in Hong Kong.

Since the beginning of this century, especially from the second decade, the cotton and cotton yarn trade between India and China dwindled considerably owing to the competition of yarn from the United Kingdom, Japan and Shanghai. Up to the end of the last century, the Chinese were using mainly the rougher count of yarns which India produced.

But the introduction of finer counts from the United Kingdom and the cheaper prices of yarn made in Shanghai and Japan ultimately ousted Indian yarn from Hong Kong (that is from the Chinese market served by Hong Kong), and the business of the Indian firms was greatly reduced, only to be revived since 1938.

But the foundation laid by Messrs. Wassiamull Assomull & Co., bore fruit and there was a rapid growth in the rise of these Indian firms from Sindh. Since about the time that the business in cotton, cotton yarn and cotton piecegoods and other lines, was lost by other Indian firms, the Sindhi firms kept up the pace of Indian business in silk in the Colony and today, they control, if they do not monopolise, the trade of the Colony in silk and curios.

The social and communal 'life' as such, as it is understood in the modern sense, is of a more recent origin amongst Indian residents of Hong Kong though a good deal of progress had been made by the colonial Indians (locally born). When the writer came here at the end of 1931, each of the religious sections of the community had its own organization and a joint and fuller 'life' of the community as a whole had yet to be developed. This development, however, soon became apparent and from 1934 onwards there has been a tendency to combine the different sections of the Indian community together. In the sporting and literary spheres, these attempts were made earlier, as seen by the foundation of an Indian School and an Indian Recreation Club. But outside these there were hardly any social gatherings of Indians to warrant the name, unless distinguished Indians passed through the Colony.

But from 1934 onwards, almost every Indian felt the need of promoting some organization which would represent and combine all Indians, irrespective of creed and locality. In 1935, an attempt was made to establish a merchants' chamber, but the organizers felt the time was inopportune and postponed the project. However, that gave a fillip for further intercourse and the idea was never given up. Ultimately on April 21, 1939, representatives of the Indian community met and decided to establish a central Indian organization, 'The Indian Association of Hong Kong & South China' which came into being on March 4, 1940.

The other organizations in the community are:
1. The Khalsa diwan (or 'Gurudwara') for the Sikhs, which maintains a boarding house for travellers and destitutes.
2. The Hindu Association for the Hindus, which maintains a Crematorium and Cemetery, and a temple under construction.
3. The Zoroastrian Club, which maintains a Parsee Cemetery.
4. The Indian Muslim Society, mainly for Indian Muslims.
5. Three Mosques, two of which maintain two cemeteries.
6. The Sindhi Merchants Association & Club (for business purposes).
7. The Indian Recreation Club (cricket, tennis, lawn bowls, and indoor games).
8. The Kowloon Indian Tennis Club (tennis, hockey and indoor games, etc.)
9. The Ellis Kadoorie Indian School.
10. The Indian Ladies Club.

The general position of the Indians in Hong Kong is that of peace-loving and law-abiding citizens engaged mainly in trade, commerce and industry, co-operating with the government of the Colony and other communities for making the Colony's life fuller and richer.

CHAPTER FOUR

THE PEOPLE'S LIVELIHOOD IN THE 1920s AND 1930s

When the First World War broke out, in 1914, Hong Kong had a population of 500,000. When the Japanese invaded Hong Kong in 1941, the population had surpassed 1,500,000.* It was not at all easy for Hong Kong to accommodate this very rapid increase in population, but a rapid increase in population was as much as asset for some as a liability for others. The general low standard of living for the many dislocated men, women and children, working intermittently at odd jobs, often in building construction, should not be confused with the steady income that was being received by an up-and-rising working class. And, in the midst of a thriving economy, the very genuine bondage of servant girls that was permitted by time-honoured Chinese custom looked increasingly out of tune with humanitarian ideals that the British home government found itself committed to. The social and economic needs of the dislocated, the bonded servant and the working class fitted into the Hong Kong social structure in very different ways, yet the political situation in China in the 1920s was such that for a while, their aspirations seemed united. Popular Chinese nationalism possibly reached its height in the 1920s, and for a time, especially during the general strike of 1925, it looked as if all other interests might be subsumed under the feeling that Chinese people in Hong Kong might stand up for their own interests.

In 1922 and 1925, Hong Kong experienced industrial strikes on an unprecedented scale in its history. The strikes arose from very different origins. The 1922 strike, which involved in the main Hong Kong's seamen, was called primarily as the result of a dispute on wages. The strike demonstrated

---

* Census figures for the Hong Kong population at various times are: 1921: 625,166; 1931: 840,473; and 1941: 1,639,337.

the ability of the seamen to bring Hong Kong trade to a standstill, and ended in victory for the strikers. The 1925 general strike, that lasted into 1926, was an expression of nationalist sentiments that traversed economic interests. It was part of a much larger series of events unfolding in Guangdong province and elsewhere in China, that involved China's relationship with the foreign powers, especially Japan and Britain. Mounting nationalism had been evident in China from the end of the First World War, and it became very much an integral part of the ideology of the nationalist government that was being built by Sun Yat-sen in Guangdong in the 1920s. This was the period when the Guomindang Party, under the leadership of Sun Yat-sen, was supported by the Comintern in its effort to defeat the warlords and unite China. Under the policy of the United Front, members of the Chinese Communist Party cooperated with the Guomindang, many of them being active in China's labour movement. Nationalist sentiments took a drastic turn in 1925 when on 30 May, Chinese demonstrators were killed in Shanghai by the police in the International Settlement. Like the people of many other Chinese cities, a substantial number of Chinese people in Hong Kong went on strike in protest.

Subsequent events, especially another incident that involved firing on demonstrators in Shameen, Guangzhou, complicated the situation. After extensive negotiations that went on between the Hong Kong government and the Chinese government in Guangzhou, the strike was brought to an end only in 1926. It is unclear if the strikers received what they demanded, but the strike, no doubt, left a strong impact on the Hong Kong government. By the 1930s, the Hong Kong government made serious effort in various social reforms, which, in turn, set the course for some of its policies in the 1950s.

a. Food, Wages and Other Statistics

At the end of the First World War, the price of rice rose substantially on the international market. Hong Kong was dependent on its supply of rice from abroad, and the Hong Kong government had good reasons to be alarmed. To face the crisis of rising prices in 1919, the Hong Kong government purchased a substantial quantity of rice which it was prepared to sell at a loss. Supplies from China provided relief, but the price of rice remained high throughout the 1920s.

Hong Kong's prosperity in the early 1920s allowed its people to weather the pressures of inflation. Hong Kong wages were higher than Guangzhou's and surrounding areas, which should be reason enough to explain the influx of population. Among the signs of prosperity were features that Hong Kong had become used to: increasing government revenue and rising land sales. A substantial portion of the government's income in the 1920s, however, still came from taxes levied on opium. In 1920, over a quarter of the Hong Kong government's income came from opium; in 1925, about 11 percent did.

DOCUMENT IV.a1: The supply of rice, 1919 (source: Preliminary Report on the Purchase and Sale of Rice by the Government of Hong Kong during the Year 1919, pp. 1-6, *Sessional Papers*, 1920)

From the beginning of last year it was realised that owing to the extensive purchases of rice that were being made to meet an abnormal situation in the Straits Settlement and Ceylon the Hong Kong rice market was sure to be affected. At the end of the year 1918 the Government received an intimation from the Secretary of State that owing to the exports form India having been restricted the Colonies mentioned were endeavouring to obtain rice from Siam, and the Secretary of State was informed on the 4th January that the Government of Hong Kong had never contemplated official purchases of Siamese rice, but could not prevent local merchants from placing orders in Siam if the state of the market there was favourable. On the 13th January information was received from the Government of Ceylon that arrangements had been made for the supply of rice to Ceylon which would not necessitate buying in Siam or French Indo-China.

Early in February Japan began to buy rice in large quantities in the Hong Kong market, while at the same time the Government of Indo-China fixed the amount of rice for export as follows:

February — March	120,000 tons
April	60,000 "
May	60,000 "

On the 28th of May the Secretary of State enquired whether the Government of Hong Kong was negotiating for the purchase of rice from Siam, and on the 5th June he suggested that in order to avoid competitive buying in Siam the Government should prohibit import of rice from Siam on private account as had been done in Ceylon and the Straits Settlements. In reply the Secretary of State was informed that Hong Kong was an entrepot for a very large rice trade with all parts of the world, local firms buying as agents for all countries and buyers in foreign countries transhipping in Hong Kong. It was pointed out that if an embargo were to be placed on the importation of rice it would seem probable that the result would be to divert trade round the Colony without achieving the object in view, and that the result to the large rice trade in the Colony would be most serious. That arrangements had been made to have sufficient rice for three months local consumption always in the Colony, estimated at about 27,000 tons. That careful watch was being kept on exports the endeavour being to prevent the export of abnormal amounts to ordinary destinations and to limit the exports to countries which did not normally draw on Hong Kong to the lowest limits. In these circumstances the opinion was expressed that it would be very inadvisable to impose restrictions on importation. The Secretary of State replied on the 11th June that the matter of dealing with the rice situation was left to the discretion of the Officer Administering the Government.

Before proceeding further it will be convenient to explain in some detail the paramount importance of the rice trade to the Colony of Hong Kong. Rice is much the largest commodity dealt with in the trade returns and a large number of ships is employed in bringing it to the Colony and in carrying it away after it has been dealt with. The handling of the cargoes both at the ships and on shore gives employment to a large portion of the floating population as well as to a large number of the coolie class. The companies and individuals who own godowns also derive great benefit from the storage of the rice while in course of preparation for export. For the year 1918 the value of rice imported was no less than £12,904,321, while the exports for the same period were valued at £11,608,509.

As has been often pointed out the Colony of Hong Kong is in the unique position among the great ports of the Empire of producing practically no raw materials, but on the other hand of possessing in its geographical situation and in its splendid harbour unrivalled opportunities for dealing with an immense transhipment trade. It is in fact in the nature of a great wharf and godown where every class of goods can be handled expeditiously provided the machinery for doing so is kept at the highest pitch of efficiency and without any unnecessary restrictions retarding smooth working. Nothing could be more fatal to local trade than for an impression to be created in the great markets of the world that the Hong Kong Authorities might place obstacles in the way of the quick despatch of cargoes, or interfere with contracts connected therewith.

With regard to the rice trade a step in the right direction was taken not long ago by the standardizing of rice by the Exporters and Dealers Association of Hong Kong in accordance with the repeated request of the California Rice Association. Prior to the adoption of this measure no limit was placed upon the amount of broken grains mixed with good whole rice, with the result that serious complaints came from American buyers. It is expected that the action taken by the Exporters and Dealers Association will have the effect of restoring confidence among buyers in America and elsewhere, whereby this valuable trade will be retained in Hong Kong.

The bulk of the imported rice comes from Saigon and Bangkok, and is usually packed in single gunny bags of about 160 catties weight (213 lbs.), and, with the exception of some shipments to Japan, is never re-exported from Hong Kong in the original bags. The principal grade of rice exported is known as 'Siam usual', and is ordinarily made from a mixture of Siam rice and Saigon long rice in equal parts. Before mixing, the rice is screened so as to bring the amount of broken grains down to the standard. In the case of brown rice, especially when the season is advanced, it is the custom to winnow the rice before packing as it generally contains a quantity of dust and husks. The American market takes rice in 100 pounds double gunny bags and sometimes in double bags of 240 pounds. The Cuban market also takes the latter packing, but shipments intended for South America are usually packed in double bags of 193 pounds gross weight. It is this work of standardizing and re-packing, which makes the trade of such importance and gives employment to the large number of persons referred to.

There is only one crop a year in Siam and Indo-China, the Siam crop being available in December and January and the Saigon crop about a month or so later. Rice is, however, exported from Hong Kong all the year round according to demand. Japan has been recently the largest customer, the United States of America coming next. Until a short time ago shipments for the Cuban market went to the Pacific ports of the United States, and were transhipped thence to their destination; but latterly Cuban buyers appear to have preferred to make direct shipments.

It will be clear from the account given in the foregoing paragraphs that the situation presented considerable difficulties, and the receipt of a telegram on the 14th June from H.M. Charge d'Affaires at Bangkok to the effect that the Government of Siam had prohibited the export of rice from Siam as from the 12th July except under licence did not tend to improve matters. The price of both Siam and Saigon rice continued to rise the former to $15 a picul and the latter $13 a picul, the poorer grades being rather less. To show how sensitive the feeling was in other countries it may be mentioned that on the 26th June a telegram was received form H.M. Minister at Tokyo stating that the Japanese Minister at Bangkok reported that transhipment of rice at Hong Kong was to be prohibited shortly and enquiring whether the report was correct. An assurance was given immediately that it was not intended to prohibit transhipment of rice at Hong Kong. At the same time acting on the report above quoted a Japanese firm was about to make arrangements to divert two ships loading in Saigon so that they would proceed to Japan direct without calling at Hong Kong. This was averted.

It was obvious that with a view to controlling the price and preserving the trade immediate action was necessary, and after some discussion it was decided to call a meeting of the principal employers of labour to consider the whole question. After two meetings it was decided that the only feasible course was for the Government to purchase rice and, subject to the approval of the Councils, this situation was accepted by the Government. A telegram was sent to the British Consul at Saigon on the 1st July enquiring whether it would be possible for the Government of Hong Kong to buy Annam rice from the 1st August up to a maximum of five thousand tons a month for six months for the purpose of local consumption, and on the 4th July the Consul suggested that the best course would be for the Government to approach the Food Controller at Singapore with a view to buying 27,500 tons of rice which he was willing to resell, the price being about $13 a picul (Saigon currency) f.o.b., the market price at the time being considerably higher. This suggestion was adopted, and on the 11th July a telegram was received from the Colonial Secretary, Straits Settlements, stating that the Food Controller could sell 27,500 tons Saigon rice July allotment for October delivery at $13.30 Saigon dollars ex mill, and requesting the Government, if it wished for this rice, to remit to the British Consul at Saigon $1,500,000 Saigon dollars for the necessary advances.

The Officer Administering the Government thereupon summoned a meeting of the Unofficial Members of the Executive and Legislative Councils on the 15th July at which the Colonial Secretary and Mr. R.O. Hutchison were present, when it was decided to purchase the 27,500 tons of rice offered by the Food Controller, Singapore.

It was realised that the Government would have to face a considerable loss of money in giving effect to the decision to purchase rice, and it at once became apparent that the loss would be increased owing to the high rate of discount on the Hong Kong dollar at Saigon. The discount at first was 23-1/2 per cent, but on subsequent purchases was somewhat lower. The Treasurer arranged with the Hong Kong and Shanghai Banking Corporation for the financing of the purchases in Saigon, and the Government is much indebted to that institution for the valuable assistance rendered in this matter and for the moderate rate of four per cent interest that has been charged on the overdraft. On the 26th July a telegram was received from the Colonial Secretary, Straits Settlements, to the effect that owing to an error the Food Controller had offered 27,500 tons whereas 13,750 tons only were available, the balance having been sold to the Netherlands Indies. As no further supplies could be got from Saigon except at a prohibitive price it became necessary to make purchases locally and this was done to the extent of about 10,000 tons principally of broken rice to mix with the Saigon rice on arrival.

Mr. R.O. Hutchison was put in charge of the general control of the rice position and five of the leading Chinese rice merchants were invited to act on a Committee to arrange the purchase and price of rice for local consumption. Sufficient godown space was rented and everything was in order to begin sales on the 1st August.

Unfortunately at the end of July typhoon weather prevailed and it was impossible to convey rice across the harbour to Yaumati. The result was that a portion of the population started looting rice shops and a riot took place outside the Yaumati Police Station. The Naval Authorities lent the tug 'Cherub' and the Military Authorities the tug 'Omphale' on the 28th July, which made it possible to send some rice to Yaumati and Hunghom. With the exception of some looting no other disturbances occurred. The rice was guarded by military escorts for two days while being conveyed from the tugs to the shops. In Victoria looting on a rather serious scale took place for about a week, and it became necessary to start the Government sales of rice before the organization was completed.

It will be convenient to deal now with other measures taken to obtain supplies of rice. The July crop in the New Territories was a good one, and in order to ensure that the rice did not go into Kuangtung all export except to Hong Kong was prohibited, and it was notified that the Government would be prepared to buy rice at $10.14 a picul. It has been the custom for the New Territories to export their rice and buy cheaper rice in Hong Kong for their own use. In the abnormal conditions prevailing this year this practice had to be abandoned.

An endeavour was made to obtain rice from Kuangtung, and after much correspondence the Government at Canton permitted the export of 10,000 piculs of Wuhu rice by the Kuangtung Food Relief Association to the Tung Wah Hospital at

Hong Kong at a price of $6.70 a picul. The Tung Wah Directors showed great energy in erecting a number of matsheds in Victoria, Shaukiwan and Aberdeen where many thousands of very poor people were supplied free of cost with a mixture of boiled rice and salt, known as congee, twice a day. This system of relief continued for several weeks and was most useful in preventing a great deal of distress.

An attempt was also made to get rice from the Hunan Province of China *via* Shanghai. H.M. Minister at Peking and the Consul at Changsha did all they could, and the Government at Peking was favourable to the project, but owing to the stipulations for the Governor of Hunan the price demanded was prohibitive so that the offers made had to be refused.

The Indian Government sanctioned the export of 3,750 tons of rice from Rangoon and this rice has recently arrived in the Colony. Through the generosity of the firm of Messrs. Nemazee & Co., about two-thirds of this rice is being carried free of freight to Hong Kong.

The rice purchased was divided into three classes under the designations Hong Kong No. 1, No. 2 and No. 3, and the recommendation of the committee to fix the price of the three grades at 20, 16 and 12-1/2 cents a catty respectively was adopted. These prices were altered a few days later to suit the usage of Chinese buyers to 5 catties = $1, 7 catties = $1, and 9 catties = $1, and before the end of August the price was further reduced to 5-1/2 catties = $1, 7-1/7(sic) = $1, and 10 catties =$1. No. 1 rice was Saigon round or long, No. 2 a mixture of Saigon round or long with an equal amount of broken rice, and No. 3 a mixture of one-fifth Saigon round or long with four-fifths broken rice.

Sales of Government rice took place up to the 3rd September as follows:

No. 1 .... 2,853 piculs
No. 2 .... 8,838 "
No. 3 .... 56,124 "

About the 3rd September sales suddenly ceased and it was found that rice had begun to come into the Colony from Kuangtung. An excellent quality was thus available for consumption in the Colony at the comparatively low price of $8 a picul.

In view, however, of the appearance of this rice on the market, the question immediately arose as to what was to be done with the rice imported by the Government and bought locally. Some of the latter already showed signs of deterioration and it was decided to sell the rice bought in the New Territories at $8 a picul and to make enquiries as to the best markets in which to sell all the remainder with the exception of a few thousand tons. Japan had ceased to buy any rice in Hong Kong and the Straits Settlements did not require any. The sterling value of the dollar had continued rising so that the price to be obtained in countries with a gold standard was becoming less when reckoned in dollars. Eventually arrangements were made to sell 10,000 tons on consignment to America and about the same amount locally. A careful examination of the rice stored in the godowns in Victoria showed that much of it was discoloured and full of weevils, but notwithstanding this prices were obtained which were quite good considering the state of the market. In fact the sales were made just in time to avert very serious losses indeed owing to the rice becoming practically unsaleable.

On 19th September an Ordinance was passed providing for the acquisition and disposal of rice by the Hong Kong Government, and for validating acts previously done.

The situation dealt with in this report is happily without precedent in the history of the Colony, and this is not surprising. Only events of a most unusual character could produce such a crisis. First, a world shortage of cereals combined with a partial failure of the rice crop in Siam, one of the principal producing areas; secondly, an abnormal trade situation in Indo-China leading to such a rise in exchange rates as to make the price of rice in the currency of the Colony almost prohibitive; thirdly, the increase in the sterling value of silver during the critical period from about 18 pence to 75 pence an ounce; and lastly, the unexpected arrival in the Colony of abundant supplies of good and cheap rice from a source supposed to be closed, which rendered the large supplies of rice bought under adverse conditions useless for the immediate purpose for which they were intended.

DOCUMENT IV.a2: The cost of labour, 1920 (source: Economic Resource Committee, Hong Kong, Factory, Home and Cottage Industries Sub-committee, 'The Report, with Minutes of Proceedings, Appendices and Illustrated Memo on Sericulture, Pig-breeding, Tobacco, Cotton, Fruit and Vegetable Growing', 1920, pp. xiv - xvi, *Sessional Papers*, 1921)

It has been our endeavour to ascertain how the cost of labour compared in Hong Kong with that in Canton, and to this end Question S was framed in the following terms: -

> What is the cost of labour compared with labour to be obtained on the mainland and Canton and its vicinities?

With only very few exceptions the answers received force us to the conclusion that wages all round are higher in Hong Kong than in Canton and the mainland. A British firm tabulated the comparative wages hereunder reproduced:-

Hong Kong	Canton	Mainland
50 cents to 90 cents	50 cents to 70 cents	40 cents to 60 cents

The knitting factories definitely assert that wages are twice as much here as in Canton. The foregoing statements go to prove the correctness of the view taken by the members of the Sub-Committee as expressed in the following Resolution, proposed by Mr. Andrew Beattie, and seconded by Mr. Chow Shou-son, and unanimously adopted at a meeting held soon after their appointment:-

> That, in view of the increased advantages which will obtain as soon as a stable government is instituted in South China, it behoves the Authorities in

Hong Kong to very carefully watch the situation. We believe when settled conditions exist in Kwangtung advantages for conducting factories will be superior (considering all circumstances) to Hong Kong, labour, land rentals and building conditions all being on a much lower basis.

The evidence given by Mr. Yip Woon-nam, late manager of the Loong Kee Match Factory, now out of operation, and that voluntarily tendered by Mr. Chow Shou-son, when examined by us establishes beyond a doubt the advantages afforded by Canton in the matter of wages as against Hong Kong.

The percentage of increase in the cost of labour during the last ten years has been on the whole not under 20 %, but in several cases as high even as 50 %. Three Chinese machinery shops record varying rates of increase of wages. Our considered opinion is that all things considered the average rate of increase is approximately 35 %. A local tobacco factory, probably the largest employers of labour in this particular branch of industry, pay wages equivalent to an increase of 50 %. By contrast with the Philippines, it is interesting to observe how the question of exchange operates in the matter of wages. The tobacco factory at Yaumati having experience of conditions in the Philippines, states:

> The only comparison we have is that of our Manila competitors and owing to the high rate of exchange our labour costs are practically the same as theirs.

On the other hand, if exchange between Hong Kong and the Philippines should attain to its normal pre-war level it stands to reason that imported cigars and cigarettes from the Philippines would cost in dollars so much more. High exchange is, therefore, not an unmixed blessing for the local tobacco industry.

It has to be observed that higher wages do not obtain in Hong Kong alone. The same ratio of increase has been maintained on the mainland. In such branches of industries as oil-pressing, wine-distilling, and iron-mongering, the increases have been substantial. They vary from 30 to 50 per cent.

On the whole the reasons assigned have been two, *viz.*, higher rent and higher cost of living. The lower cost of rice today as compared with the cost prevailing a few months ago has not shown any tendency to lower the cost of wages.

In probably no other direction than a sufficiency of housing accommodation at cheap rentals for the working classes can the general tendency towards increases in wages be satisfactorily checked. In this connection, we would like the Committee appointed by the Imperial Government,

> take the opportunity of observing that, while we have not regarded the investigation of housing questions as within the terms of our reference, we have been impressed in the course of our enquiries with the urgent importance to the future industrial development of the Colony of the provision of increased and improved housing accommodation for the working classes on a considerable scale.

In many cases no answer was returned to our direct question as to —
What control do the guilds exercise on labour generally?

A large proportion of the industries report that they are not affected by the influences of guilds known to be existing, but recent events regarding the tendency of the labour question show considerable influence of the guilds.

DOCUMENT IV.a3: Financial and other statistics, 1897-1926 (source: 'Financial and other statistics showing the development of Hong Kong during the thirty years 1897-1926', *Sessional Papers*, 1927, pp. 111-119)

Table 4.1
Population

Year	Total civil population
1897	243,565
1898	239,210
1899	252,405
1900	277,740
1901	290,124
1902	303,116
1903	317,130
1904	352,487
1905	370,325
1906	318,304
1907	323,280
1908	329,650
1909	337,160
1910	344,180
1911	464,277
1912	467,777
1913	489,114
1914	501,304
1915	509,160
1916	529,010
1917	535,100
1918	561,500
1919	598,100
1920	648,150
1921	686,680
1922	662,200
1923	681,800
1924	799,550
1925	874,420
1926	874,420

Table 4.2
Revenue of the Hong Kong Government

Year	Revenue
1897	$2,687,000
1898	2,918,000
1899	3,610,000
1900	4,203,000
1901	4,214,000
1902	4,901,000
1903	5,239,000
1904	6,809,000
1905	6,918,000
1906	7,035,000
1907	6,602,000
1908	6,104,000
1909	6,823,000
1910	6,961,000
1911	7,497,000
1912	8,181,000
1913	8,512,000
1914	11,007,000
1915	11,786,000
1916	13,833,000
1917	15,058,000
1918	18,665,000
1919	16,525,000
1920	14,690,000
1921	17,728,000
1922	22,291,000
1923	24,784,000
1924	24,210,000
1925	23,244,000
1926	21,132,000

Table 4.3
Revenue Derived from Opium, Liquor and Tobacco

	Opium	Liquor duties	Tobacco duties
1914	$2,819,000	$657,000	
1915	3,812,000	627,000	
1916	4,929,000	794,000	$211,000
1917	5,274,000	781,000	500,000

(Table 4.3 cont)

(Table 4.3 cont)

1918	8,047,000	715,000	545,000
1919	6,106,000	740,000	619,000
1920	3,941,000	780,000	632,000
1921	3,484,000	1,041,000	1,062,000
1922	5,067,000	1,197,000	1,475,000
1923	4,946,000	1,240,000	1,829,000
1924	4,460,000	1,229,000	2,007,000
1925	2,568,000	1,141,000	1,797,000
1926	2,140,000	1,186,000	1,835,000

Table 4.4
Land Sale Figures for the Years 1919-1926, Illustrative of the Land Boom

1919	$ 264,000
1920	556,000
1921	1,634,000
1922	2,722,000
1923	3,489,000
1924	1,909,000
1925	570,000
1926	286,000

b. The Strikes of the 1920s

The seamen's strike in 1922 was brought about by the breakdown of wage negotiation. The progress of this strike demonstrated a strategy that could be followed by the general strike of 1925-26. The strikers would leave Hong Kong, return to China, where much sympathy and support would be given by the Guangdong government and Chinese unions. Hong Kong's trade would be paralysed.

This strategy was effective only in the 1920s, when the Chinese revolutionary government in Guangdong was interested in enlisting workers' support in favour of its Northern Expedition. After 1927, when the Guomindang was firmly established in Nanjing, Guangdong ceased to be a viable retreat for Hong Kong's workers.

Chen Ta, the writer of Document IV. b1 below, was a social scientist who wrote extensively about the conditions of Chinese workers. Deng Zhongxia, the writer of Document IV. b2, was a Chinese labour organizer and a member of the Chinese Communist Party.

DOCUMENT IV. b1: Seamen's strike in Hong Kong (source: Ta Chen, 'Shipping strike in Hong Kong', *Monthly Labour Review*, May 1922)

In recent years commodity prices in this colony have advanced faster than in any of the other commercial cities in China. For instance, the cost of polished rice in Shanghai has increased 125 per cent since 1914, but in Hong Kong it has increased 155 per cent. Being an industrial centre, in order to meet the daily needs of its 528,090 inhabitants, the colony imports necessaries from other towns; these include fowls from Wuchow, Kwangsi, beef and pork from Canton, fruits and fish from Swatow, and textiles and clothing material from Shanghai. Freight charges and customs duties on these goods make the cost of living relatively higher in Hong Kong, which has worked hardship on its labouring classes.

Repeated triumphs of labour in recent strikes have given Hong Kong's seamen courage and confidence in their present struggle for a fair compensation for their toil. During the year 1921 a successful strike occurred in almost every important industry in Canton. The printers' strike of last December left the whole city without newspapers for three days and compelled the publishers and newspaper companies to grant their employees a 40 percent increase over the prevailing wages. About 60,000 workers in some 100 trades in Hong Kong are unionized, some following the rules of craft guilds while others have adopted those of labour unions. Fully 30,000 of them are natives of Canton, who have been in constant touch with labour conditions in their home community and who are prime movers in the present strike.

Ever since the Hong Kong strike of April 1920, which involved 9,000 workers, local labourers have been dissatisfied with capitalists. This class feeling was greatly intensified when toward the end of last year foreign seamen in the colony, who already had a comparatively higher scale of wages, were granted a further increase of about 15 per cent, whereas most of the Chinese were still paid at pre-war rates. Because of this discrimination the Chinese seamen had a general grievance against the shipowners. In a recent interview the president of the Chinese Seamen's Union summarized the situation accurately when he said: 'The Chinese have taken a stand against deprivation of their rights, rough treatment, 14 hours' work a day, and an existence bordering on semistarvation. The majority of these men have families averaging three or four persons, and they find it impossible to live on $20 a month, and are therefore determined to obtain a minimum of $29.50 a month.'

Extent of the strike

Since the shipping companies had twice refused to consider the seamen's demands for a wage increase, the Chinese Seamen's Union presented its third petition on January 12 and demanded a reply within 24 hours. Failing again to receive a satisfactory answer, 1,500 deck hands and stokers 'downed tools' on the morning of January 13. A week later the number of strikers reached 6,500 and shortly after the Chinese New Year

(Jan. 27), it grew to about 30,000, including pilots, tallymen, lightermen, carriers, stevedores, wharf coolies, cargo labourers, and coal coolies, in addition to the deck hands and stokers already mentioned. When on February 1 the British Governor of Hong Kong proclaimed the Chinese Seamen's Union an unlawful society, a general sympathetic strike was declared, which increased the strikers to about 50,000, and included cooks, domestics, bakers, pastry men, office boys, delivery men, dairymen, tramway employees, ricksha and chair coolies, bank clerks, compositors, newspaper employees, printers, cable company employees, and employees of shipbuilding and repairing yards.

Up to the middle of February, 166 steamers carrying 280,404 tons of shipping were held up in the port of Hong Kong. This tie-up of cargo caused direct losses of about $5,000,000 to shipping companies.

At first the strikers were almost all Cantonese. Seamen and coolies from Shanghai and Ningpo, Chekiang, who had their own unions, did not join. Gradually, however, they refused to take jobs which were vacated by their Cantonese comrades. As the shipping companies were sustaining heavy losses by having their ships tied up in Hong kong, they recruited Filipino coolies from Manila and Ningpo coolies from Shanghai at from $1 to $1.20 a day. But this small number of recruits did not materially improve the shipping situation.

Most of the strikers were sent by their union to Canton, partly because of the relatively cheaper living there and partly in order to prevent possible disorder or violence in Hong Kong. During the strike each striker whether he belonged to the union or not received a subsidy from it varying from 45 cents to $1 a day, as the union had raised about $300,000 to sustain the strike. Voluntary contributions came from many parts of the country. Railway workers of the Peking-Hankow, Tientsin-Pukow, Peking-Mukden and Peking-Suiyuan lines contributed one day's pay. Seamens' unions in Tientsin and Shanghai held mass meetings to solicit contributions on behalf of the Hong Kong strikers. The Returned Labourers' Union, together with the Labourers' League of Shanghai, sent telegrams of sympathy and relief funds to Hong Kong.

Dissolution of the Seamen's Union

On January 16, the strike had assumed such alarming proportions that the Hong Kong Government deemed it necessary to declare martial law in the colony and to place armed military and naval guards at important points to preserve order and to demand passes of those going in and out of the territory. Fearing that scamps might disturb the peace and the strikers be blamed for it, the Seamen's Union organized 8 squads of 10 men each, under a captain, to patrol the streets.

Gradually the actions of the strikers went beyond the control of their leaders and cases of improper picketing and intimidation were alleged to have occurred. On February 1, the Hong Kong Government declared the Seamen's Union an unlawful organization with an explanatory note stating that 'the order in council was made not because the members of the Seamen's Union had struck for higher wages, but because attempts had been made by the union to paralyse the life of the colony by creating strikes in other employments of workmen who themselves had no grievances against their employers. Were this permitted it would cause widespread distress by interfering with the food supplies of the community and with the carrying on of essential services.'

Two days later, two other Chinese labour organizations were declared unlawful on similar grounds. However, evidence of coercive persuasion and intimidation to induce a sympathetic strike seemed meagre. Disapproval of the Hong Kong Government's action was expressed by The China Press, a leading American daily in Shanghai (Feb. 5, 1922) in these words:

> ... Immediately after the governor of Hong Kong issued his order the police raided the Seamen's Union's headquarters, seizing the office furniture, books, and papers, and closing the premises and putting them under a police guard. This is exactly the kind of procedure that, formerly, Englishmen were accustomed to associate with the police of czardom and the autocratic Hohenzollern regime. Not so many years ago English workingmen fought a long and strenuous battle to obtain the legal right to strike and they now possess that right. Combination of workmen to secure better conditions for themselves from employers is the only constitutional method they possess, and the united strike is the only effective way for attaining better conditions.

Demands and efforts to arbitrate

Shortly after the strike was declared, the seamen's demands were presented to the Governor of Hong Kong for a settlement. The rates of increase demanded by the strikers were based upon the prevailing scale of wages, of which the following is an example:

	Monthly wage
Baker	$22-25
Boatswain	25-35
Carpenter	25-30
Compradore	30-35
Cook	20-25
Deck steward	20-25
Dollar examiner[#]	25
Fireman	40-65
Kitchen helper	20-30
Letter carrier	20-22
Oiler	28-31
Sailor	22-25
Servant	20-30
Waiter	10-15

[#] Detector of counterfeit money.

The above table shows the monthly wages of a Chinese crew on an ocean-going steamer. It is reported that the highest monthly wage of a Chinese seaman is $65 which is not quite one-fourth that of an European employee of the same rank on another steamer.

On January 17, E.R. Hallifax, Secretary for Chinese Affairs, issued a proclamation setting forth the shipowners' terms of settlement. The increases demanded and the terms offered are shown below:

Type of steamer	Increases demanded	Shipowners' terms	Difference
	per cent	per cent	per cent
1. Coastwise steamers	35.0	15.0	20.0
2. Chinese river steamers	32.5	25.0	7.5
3. Other Chinese steamers	32.5	25.0	7.5
4. Canton, Macao & Hong Kong Co. steamers (British)	25.0	15.0	10.0
5. Other British steamers (taking scale of 4 as base)	25.0	15.0	10.0
6. Java lines	17.5	12.0	5.5
7. Pacific lines	17.5	7.5	10.0
8. European lines	17.5	7.5	10.0
9. Australian lines	20.0	10.0	10.0

Since there was too much discrepancy between the shipowners' terms and the strikers' original demands, the Chinese Seamen's Union on January 27 passed four regulations modifying their demands:

1. For the time being the arrangement shall be as follows:
    (a) An increase of 40 per cent shall be given for wages under $15 a month.
    (b) An increase of 30 per cent for wages under $25.
    (c) An increase of 20 per cent for wages over $25.

Resolution 4(b) must be first recognized in respect of these arrangements. If, however, these arrangements are recognized by the shipowners, all seamen will return to work at once and leave resolution 4 to be considered by an arbitration board.

2. The arbitration board shall be established in Canton.
3. The arbitration board shall consist of the following:
    (a) Representative of the Canton Government.
    (b) Representative of the British consul general.
    (c) Representative of the European shipowners.
    (d) Representative of the Chinese shipowners.
    (e) Representative of the Chinese seamen.

The number of the members of this board shall be decided by the Chinese and British Governments after due consideration, and this board shall have the full power to settle this strike.

4. The Seamen's Union will lay the following eight demands before the board for consideration:
(a) The increase shall be 30 per cent for all monthly wages over $30, and 40 per cent for those under $30.
(b) No seaman who returns to work after the strike shall be dismissed or degraded for any reason.
(c) The increase shall be applied to all steamers at present anchored at Hong Kong or en route to Hong Kong from other ports.
(d) All seamen shall be employed through the union, so that no commission is to be paid to the compradores.
(e) No agreement in connection with the employment of the seamen shall have effect unless the Chinese Seamen's Union has been a witness to it.
(f) No seaman or officer of the Seamen's Union in Hong Kong shall be banished for any charge which has no proof.
(g) The full increase shall be retroactive to January 1, 1922.
(h) No discrimination shall be practised against Chinese seamen after they have returned to work and they shall be in no way maltreated.

Terms of the agreement

Mediators along the line suggested by the strikers were appointed and held frequent meetings in Hong Kong and Canton. They reached an agreement on March 5, the terms of which were as follows:

Type of steamer	Terms of settlement	Strikers' original demands	Difference
	per cent	per cent	per cent
1. Coastwise steamers	20.0	35.0	15.0
2. Chinese river steamers	30.0	32.5	2.5
3. Other Chinese steamers	30.0	32.5	2.5
4. Canton, Macao & Hong Kong Co. steamers (British)	20.0	25.0	5.0
5. Other British steamers (taking scale of 4 as base)	20.0	25.0	5.0
6. Java Lines	15.0	17.5	2.5
7. Pacific lines	15.0	17.5	2.5
8. European lines	15.0	17.5	2.5
9. Australian lines	15.0	20.0	5.0

On March 6 a gazette extraordinary was issued by the Hong Kong Government rescinding the order in council of February 1 which declared the Chinese Seamen's

Union an unlawful society. Immediately a fife and drum band led thousands of Chinese seamen in a parade to celebrate their 'victory' and to replace the signboard at their old headquarters. Firecrackers and a feast completed their memorable celebration.

Effects of the strike

During the strike, namely between January 13 and March 5, there was a complete paralysis of industrial life in Hong Kong. The manager of a leading restaurant was compelled personally to attend to the provision of food for resident visitors there. Boy scouts operated the electric elevators and acted as messengers. High class Europeans performed their own personal services. Children carried lunches into the city to their elders. Privately owned cars were impressed for public use, and Government employees of British birth volunteered for janitor service in government buildings.

Ships having no southern Chinese crews were able to come and go as usual, but the strike of the coal coolies and stevedores rendered it almost impossible to move freight, and cargoes generally were either left in idle ships or carried on to other ports. No river steamers were running and trade with the interior was out of the question.

The importation of food stuffs being stopped temporarily, prices in Hong Kong rose suddenly. Describing business conditions during the strike, an eyewitness says: 'The Chinese shops as well as European are mostly only partially open. The banks are functioning with armed volunteers within the vestibule. The business houses are staffed as usual but are partially depleted of their Chinese employees, and there is an absence of transactions. A few straggling rickshas and chairs are the only visible evidence of public vehicular traffic.'

On the whole, the strike was carried on in an orderly manner. Only on March 4 was a case of violence noted. After the dissolution of the Seamen's Union, the strike situation became more serious and the Hong Kong Government closed the passenger traffic of the Canton-Kowloon Railway in order to prevent more strikers from leaving the colony. On March 4, about 2,000 domestics decided to go on foot to Canton. On reaching the Kowloon frontier, they broke through the British cordon without the required passes. As the strikers refused to come back, a warning shot was fired. This proving ineffective, several volleys were fired which killed three strikers and wounded eight. The Seamen's Union now demands a satisfactory and just settlement of this case.

DOCUMENT IV. b2: The general strike of 1925-26 (source: Deng Zhongxia, *Zhongguo zhigong yundong shi*, 1919-1926 (A history of Chinese trade unionism, 1919-1926, published in 1930)

Preparation

The Hong Kong-Guangzhou strike was brought about as a protest against the May 30th Incident in Shanghai. It continued for as long as two years, and it became the last bastion of the anti-imperialist tide since the May 30th.

The Hong Kong-Guangzhou strike could not be started immediately after the May 30th Incident in Shanghai because at the time in Guangzhou there was the Liu-Yang War. Guangzhou was in a state of war, and so when the All China General Union received the news of the May 30th Incident, it could only hold a mass meeting and not decide on the strike in Hong Kong and Guangzhou. Nevertheless, the All China General Union was prepared to call for the strike in response to events in Shanghai immediately after the end of the war. Consequently, while the war was going on, it had sent representatives to Hong Kong to prepare for action.

The situation in Hong Kong at the time was as follows: although there were more than a hundred unions in Hong Kong, they were either 'yellow unions' or trade guilds. Although we had some influence in the the Seamen's Union, especially since Lin Weimin and Su Zhaozheng joined the Chinese Communist Party, the chairman of the union was an extreme rightist. At the time, there were barely ten Communist Party members in Hong Kong, and most of them were the lowest dock labourers. There were several more Communist Youth League members than Party members, but most of those were students. Clearly, from our own subjective assessment, we could not predict with confidence whether the strike could be organized. So when we promoted the strike, we did it from both the top and the bottom ends. On the one hand, we distributed leaflets in the factories, and, on the other hand, we approached the leaders of the unions.

At the time, anti-imperialism was riding high in Shanghai and it provided much impetus for workers in Hong Kong. In a few days time, our promotion brought results, for the feeling for the strike continued to intensify. The trouble we had to face was that the Hong Kong unions were not united. At the time, they were divided into three groups. Firstly, the faction around the General Association of Labour of Hong Kong consisted of over seventy unions, mostly handicraft. Within this faction, the Seamen's union was a major union. Secondly, the faction around the Chinese Labour General Association included over thirty unions. Again, most of these were handicraft unions. Only the Tramway Workers' Union was an important union in this faction. Thirdly, about twenty unions did not belong to any faction. Most of these were big unions, such as engineers, loading workers, coal and charcoal and foreign goods. Under such circumstances, how could the strike be united? Fortunately, in the Second All China Labour Congress, the All China General Union had been established. The Hong Kong unions had taken part in the All China Labour Congress and so they showed some trust in the representatives of the All China General Union. So when the All China General Union called a meeting of representatives of the trade unions, in the meeting it passed the decision to strike unopposed, and also adopted the communique to be issued for the strike as well as the strikers' demands. A day later, a second joint meeting was held and decided on the name and membership of the united command for the strike, which was called the Hong Kong Confederation of Labour.

As I said, the Hong Kong trade unions were either 'yellow unions' or trade guilds. Why did these 'yellow' union leaders agree to the strike? They did because they had their own intentions and wishes. These 'yellow' union leaders were really people who had no occupation. They lived on the union fees they collected. They believed that taking part in the strike did not go against their interests, because, they thought after the strike, leadership would rest in their hands. They would enjoy on the one hand the vanity of being patriotic, and, on the other hand, also the pratical benefit of taking a slice of the strike expenses. We knew this at the time, and so when we approached these 'yellow' union leaders in Hong Kong about the strike, we took a tolerating attitude in their fight over what positions to occupy in the strike leadership. We did this because at the time, if we wanted the strike in Hong Kong to succeed, we had to have them involved. Without them, the strike would be sabotaged. We wanted the strike to take place, and so we had to adopt the policy of tolerating these people. Nevertheless, when it came to the crunch, the 'yellow' union leaders were afraid, and they raised many difficult questions: First, there was the question of food and lodging for strikers, for they said before the end of the Liu-Yang War, how could the strikers find food and accommodation. We told them that within three days the war would be over, and that food and accommodation in Guangzhou would prove no problem. Indeed, news came the next day that Liu and Yang had been put down. However, the 'yellow' union leaders still did not believe we had a grasp on the problem of food and lodging, and they wanted to send representatives to Guangzhou to negotiate. Because after the Liu-Yang War, the Guangdong government on the advice of the Communist Party was in support of the strike in Hong Kong, the Hong Kong union representatives were given satisfactory assurance. Second, how should we handle the question of the Hong Kong government obstructing the exit from Hong Kong? They said, the Hong Kong government would impose a curfew and stop the train so that strikers could not leave. What could we do about that? We said, if the train stopped, there were several routes by sea and overland that we could take to reach Guangzhou. In the unlikely event that the Hong Kong government would block all transport, by sea or on land, and we rioted, we had the support and sympathy of all workers the world over. Finally came the third question. The 'yellow' union leaders raised the question of the strike schedule. They suggested that the strike should be staggered; it was clear that they were afraid of striking. We demanded that all workers strike at the same time. During the meeting, they reluctantly accepted our proposal, but we expected these 'yellow' union leaders to be slow in implementing the decision. At this critical moment, on that night, the Communist Party corps decided in its meeting that the strike should be initiated by unions that were under our direction (seamen, tramway, Chinese and English type-setting, foreign employees*), so that the hands of the 'yellow' unions would be forced. So, this great historic Hong Kong - Guangzhou strike began, on the night of 19th June.

---

* Chinese domestic workers employed in European residences

The outbreak of the strike

Before the strike began, the Hong Kong unions jointly presented a document to the Hong Kong government, explaining the reasons for the strike and listing out their demands. There were two sections. Under the first section, the document stated its support for the seventeen conditions made by the Shanghai Federation of Workers-Merchants-Students. Under the second section, it made six demands on the Hong Kong government: (1) political freedom, (2) equality before the law, (3) popular election, (4) labour legislation, (5) rent reduction, and (6) freedom of residence.

When the strike was announced, the gist of what was said was as follows:

> Since the Opium War, imperialism not only mounted an economic, political and cultural invasion of China, but also added to it mass slaughter. This cannot be tolerated! For this reason, by a joint meeting of all labour union representatives in Hong Kong, we have decided to take the course of action adopted in Shanghai, Hankow and other places, to fight imperialism to its death. For the sake of the survival and dignity of our nation, although we know that the rapid guns and mighty cannon of the imperialists may kill us, but knowing also that our Chinese nation will die whether or not we struggle, we have decided to die after a struggle rather than dying without a struggle so that our blood can be cast into the glory of our national history. So we are not afraid and are willing to fight to our death with force.

From the night of 19th June, like a big earthquake, the strike broke out in Hong Kong. The seamen, tram workers and printers made the first move, and they were followed by foreign employees, cargo loaders, coal and charcoal workers, and many other workers. Finally, machinists and dock workers also joined in the strike. In a matter of about fifteen days, all workers were on strike. About 250,000 workers took part and the scene was set. The workers all went by train and steamer to Qianshan, Jiangmen, Sanshui and Hekou back to Guangzhou.

Foreign employees on Shameen in Guangzhou also went on strike at the same time.

I must supplement the following. What I said about the 'yellow' union leaders being afraid at the last moment was real. If the strike had not been initiated by the seamen, tram workers and printers, I am sure the strike would have taken a different turn. In actual fact, the 'yellow' union leaders delayed their decision on a simultaneous strike, and only when the masses of the workers of their own will stopped work that they knew they had to follow suit. So, the decision of the Communist Party corps was correct. The most amusing thing was that the chairman of the Seamen's Union was a rightist of the highest order and he was shaken at the last minute when the strike broke out. The seamen forced him to order the strike, saying, 'Are you going to order it or not? If you don't, we'll give you our fists.' So he had to order the strike. Even more amusing, the Hong Kong Chinese Machinists Association was a pro-Hong Kong imperialist organization, and it had refused to attend the joint meetings of all labour union representatives or to issue the order to strike even after the strike had started. However, the working masses of machinists and dock workers under it went on strike without waiting for the union's order. This was why the machinists and dock workers were especially late in joining the strike.

The Hong Kong government had known about the strike in advance. It sent out its spies to arrest the strike leaders. It also issued a notice to say, 'The Shanghai incident had nothing to do with Hong Kong. Workers should continue to work and not make any rash move. All trouble-makers would be punished.' This sort of threat made no impact at all on the striking workers. When the strike broke out, the Hong Kong government went into panic, and announced a curfew that had been made possible by a law passed during the time of the European War. It announced a ban on the export of food, specie and paper currency. The marines landed, and military boats patrolled back and forth on the sea. Immediately, Hong Kong went into a state of seige. But the workers were unafraid and rushed to leave Hong Kong.

The Shakee massacre

The strikers all returned to Guangzhou. On 23rd June, they went with workers from Guangzhou, peasants from the suburb, young soldiers and students, totalling 100,000 people, on a massive demonstration. When they passed Shakee that was on the other side of the Shameen international settlement, the British and French imperialists ordered their sailors and policemen to take aim at the demonstrating masses from behind their sandbags and fire on them with machine guns. At the same time, their gunboats fired to demonstrate their might. After twenty-five minutes, 52 Chinese people lay dead from gunshot, more than 170 were seriously wounded, and innumerable people were hurt. The massacres that had taken place in Shanghai, Hankou and Qingdao were re-played in Guangzhou. However, this feat by the imperialists stirred up the determination of the Chinese people to resist. As a result, people from all walks of life fervently supported the Guangzhou-Hong Kong strike.

The strikers' organization

When the strikers arrived in Guangzhou, the All China General Union called a meeting of representatives of the Hong Kong and Shameen unions and adopted an organizational law for the strike committee. The strike committee was made up of thirteen members, of whom Hong Kong was given nine members and Shameen four. The strike committee was governed by the general assembly of strikers' representatives. These were elected on the principle of one representative for every 50 people. This was the highest consultative body and it was made up of more than 800 representatives. It held a meeting every two days. Under the strike committee was set up a secretariat, which was divided into seven sections, that is clerical affairs, propaganda, reception, general affairs, transport, social activities and entertainment. A separate finance committee was set up to raise and keep the funds needed for the strike. Later was added a court, to try the running dogs who sabotaged the strike, who smuggled food and enemies' goods. There was also a prison to keep criminals in custody. Then a stores and auction department was set up, to keep and auction enemies' goods that had been intercepted by the strikers' patrols. A drafting department was established, to draft the organizational laws and regulations for the various departments. An audit department was set up, to audit departmental accounts. A road-building committee was set up, to take charge of road building and repairs. Then there were the patrols (more later), land-and-sea patrol groups, the strikers' hospital, and the propaganda school. Also set up were dining halls and hostels; these were converted from gambling and opium dens as well empty houses in Guangzhou. The whole of Guangzhou was divided into eight districts. In each district was set up a registration point. Registered strikers were given certificates and sent to the hostels. They might have their meals anywhere, as long as they had the certificates and meal coupons. Still later, there were other departments, too many to describe here. Yes, this strike committee, in reality, was no less than a government. It had absolute power to take charge of all matters related to the strike. The Guangdong government had no authority to intervene. This was why later on the Hong Kong imperialists said in their propaganda that it was a 'second government.'

The chairman of the strike committee was Comrade Su Zhaozheng. It happened that when the committee agreed to pass the strike organization laws, the 'yellow' union leaders objected. First, they opposed the establishment of a united strike committee, saying that there should be different organizations handling affairs in Hong Kong and Shameen. But this opinion was knocked down by the meeting. Then they objected to the numerical basis for the selection of strikers' representatives, saying that the unit of representation should be the union. (The 'yellow' unions were for most of them trade guilds with small membership.) This was also knocked down by the committee. Third, the All China General Union had expressed the wish to the Hong Kong trade unions that the nine members from Hong Kong on the strike committee should include a member each from the seamen, cargo loaders, machinists, coal and charcoal workers and foreign employees, and two members each from the General Association of Labour and the Chinese Labour General Association. They objected to that, suggesting that there should be a free election. But the result of the election was that victory went to the wish of the All China General Union, and so they lost. With these failures, the intentions of the 'yellow' union leaders in Hong Kong came to nothing. Comrade Su Zhaozheng became chairman with the support of the masses.

In major areas, although we did not yield to the intentions of the 'yellow' union leaders, in secondary places we were quite tolerant. For example, we allowed them to continue the organization that they set up in Hong Kong to initiate the strike, the Hong Kong Conferation of Labour, and we gave it a subsidy every month. Many departments also involved them in their work, in order to divide them. These 'yellow' union leaders were widely engaged in corruption during the strike. Later on, they were punished by the general assembly of representatives. Many were tried and sentenced to fixed term imprisonment.

We must point out that the eight-hundred people general assembly of representatives made an unimaginable impact on the strike. Through collective discussion, the policies of the strike were given unity. Many internal disputes were solved through the power and authority of the assembly. The schemes of the 'yellow' trade union leaders and other reactionaries were effectively curtailed by the assembly. All the intentions of the working masses were taken to the assembly by the representatives. News of the strike was taken by the representatives to the masses of workers. Reports were made regularly in the assembly of general affairs and finance, and they dispelled outside rumours. All important posts in the strike organization were filled by election in the general assembly, and people who were incapable were removed at any time by the assembly. In this way, the strike organization did not deteriorate. Really, the general assembly was the foundation of the strike. It was in the strike that for the first time we had this experience.

It should also be said that the strike committee had all manners of power but not the power to kill. It was precisely over this issue that a fierce struggle took place. After the strike was started, the Hong Kong imperialists sent a large number of running dogs into Guangzhou, to spread rumours and stir up trouble in order to sabotage the strike. A reporter by the name of Lin He tried to induce the seamen to return to work. The court found this a very serious issue and sentenced him to capital punishment. When this news was known, the Chief of the Guangdong Prosecution Bureau objected on the grounds that 'the law must be respected and human rights must be guaranteed,' and that 'the punishment for sabotaging the strike should not be death.' The strikers were very angry, because they believed that the strike brought about an extraordinary situation in the anti-imperialist revolution that should not be governed by ordinary law that might be lenient to traitors. Finally, the Guangdong government set up a 'special court' to sentence such criminals.

Blockading Hong Kong

Blockading Hong Kong was an experience learned from the 1922 seamen's strike. Once the strikers reached Guangzhou, the unions organized the patrols to blockade Hong Kong. When the strike committee was set up, it coordinated the patrols. It reorganized and expanded them, set up the headquarters, appointed a commander and an adviser, and these were the brains of the entire force. (Later a seven-man patrol committee was set up.) A chief instructor was appointed, who was in charge of military training. There were five large patrols, each patrol having a senior captain, a deputy captain and an adviser. Each large patrol was divided into three branches, each branch having a branch captain, a deputy branch captain, and an advisory instructor. Each branch was divided into three small patrols, each small patrol coming under a small captain. Each small patrol was in charge of three groups, each group having a group leader and twelve members. (Later on, this structure was slightly changed.) At first, the patrols were made up of more than 2,000 people. Later they were expanded. The responsibilities of the patrols were to maintain order, arrest running dogs, stop the transport of food and intercept enemy goods. After the patrols were set up, they were stationed in various ports. As a result, transport between Guangzhou and Hong Kong was totally cut off. Then, because Macau supported Hong Kong, transport to Macau was also stopped. Before Guangdong was united, the blockade was limited to the mouth of the Pearl River, starting from Shenzhen in the east to Qianshan in the west. Later on, when the Guangdong government had retaken the Eest River and the south, the blockade extended to Shantou in the east and Beihai in the west. On the entire Guangdong coastline, patrols were stationed in all the ports. They stretched out for several thousand miles, and they could see one another's banners and hear one another's drums. The patrols also had twelve small boats and several motor boats to assist its duties. They were said to have had more than 400 guns, but only 200 could be used. (We put a lot of energy into getting more guns but did not succeed in adding many.) Under this blockade, Hong Kong had no supply of meat or vegetable. The price of pork increased to more than $1 per catty, and eggs were 50 cents each. Beef went out of existence. Markets might as well not open. Rubbish piled high in the streets, while people wrapped their faeces in paper and threw it into the streets. In the hot summer sun, the stench reached the sky. Hong Kong at the time came to be known as 'smelly harbour.' However, the most painful experience for Hong Kong was the unprecedented set-back on the economy.

Hong Kong's unprecedented economic losses

After the Shakee massacre, the British Consul in Shameen sent us a letter, which said more or less, 'It is good enough to boycott English goods. Why should you go on strke!' At the time we were amazed by that. Later, we learnt from the Chinese Maritime Customs Trade Returns that every year, Hong Kong's import and export amounted to 150,000,000 pounds sterling, equivalent to 2,520,000,000 Chinese dollars. After the strike started, all transport and trade came to a halt, and the loss for a month amounted to 210,000,000 dollars, or 7,000,000 dollars per day. British goods imported into Guangzhou amounted to no more than 30 to 40,000,000 dollars. In this way, 5 or 6 days on strike would be equivalent to a year's boycott. What an effective weapon the strike was! That was why we insisted on striking, boycotting and blockading in our encounter with Hong Kong's imperialism.

Yes, since the blockade was imposed, Hong Kong suffered unprecedented losses. We can see this from the news disclosed in Hong Kong newspapers at the time.

Let us consider exports. In 1924, exports amounted to £8,810,000. In 1925, they were only £4,700,000. The difference was £4,110,000. . . .

Let us consider other areas of Hong Kong's losses, for example, shipping. In 1924, 76,492 ships reached Hong Kong, adding up to a tonnage of 57,000,000 tons, or 210 ships a day of 156,154 tons. However, from July 1925, on average only 34 ships reached

Hong Kong, making up 55,819 tons. Compared to 1924, the number of ships arriving in 1925 went down by 5.5 times, that is, it was only 16 percent of 1924. Tonnage declined by 1.8 times, that is, it was 36 percent of 1924.

Or, for example, many shops went bankrupt. After the strike started, Hong Kong newspapers and the Hong Kong government's gazette reported every day shops that were burgled. In November and December 1925 alone, more than 3,000 shops went bankrupt.

Or, take the banks. After the strike started, sources of deposits stopped, and withdrawals increased. Nobody wanted the paper currency, and there was a drain on ready money. Although the newspapers of the time did not say anything about the losses suffered by the banks, we can see that shares had fallen. For example, from 22nd June to 19th October, 1925, the shares of the Hong Kong and Shanghai Bank fell from 1,290 dollars to 1,140 dollars, a decline of 11.5 percent.

As for government income, after the strike started, the government lost more than half of its customs from imports and exports, land value fell by 50 percent, rent by 40 percent, and so tax revenue certainly dropped. But expenses increased sharply, because the government had to face the strike and add to its military preparation. Yes, the Hong Kong government withdrew from the banks all the 17,000,000 dollars it had in reserve, and drew up a new budget that made a lot of noise about 'dismissing staff and reducing salary.'

This was why the Hong Kong imperialists were so angry with Guangdong. . . . .

c. The Sale of Women

If the strikes of the 1920s demonstrate that new ideologies fermenting in post-First World War China were bound to have an impact on Hong Kong, the dispute over the abolition of the *mui-tsai*, Chinese girls sold into domestic servitude, indicates that Chinese traditions persisted in Hong Kong, and, deeply rooted in the family system, they were not to be readily purged.

The abolition of the practice was made the subject of legislation in 1923. The Hong Kong government fully realized the ineffectiveness of legislation in curbing the practice, but had succumbed to firm decisions made by the Colonial Office in London. In Hong Kong, the Colonial Office's decisions became the subject of heated emotions. Supporters of the legislation formed themselves into an Anti Mui-tsai Society, opponents set up the Society for the Protection of the Mui-tsai. Gatherings were held by both supporters and opponents. Considering the administrative difficulties of abolishing a practice that had deep roots in Chinese custom, successive Governors of Hong Kong sided with the opponents. But the British home government could in no circumstance tolerate the continuation of a practice that could be construed as slavery. The law was passed in 1923, and supplemented in 1929 and 1938.

The use of domestic servant girls, no longer known as *mui-tsai*, continued in Hong Kong into the 1950s. Eventually, it gave way, probably less to legislation than to rising wages from the factories.

DOCUMENT IV.c1: In defence of the *mui-tsai*, 'small sister', domestic or bond servant? (source: 'Expert opinion given by the Hon. S.W. Ts'o, O.B.E., LL.D., Chinese member of the Hong Kong Legislative Council, in a mui-tsai case tried before the Hong Kong Police Magistrate on 26 September 1929', *Sessional Papers*, 1930, pp. 255-260)

In order to understand the answers to the following questions it is necessary first, to have some knowledge of the real *mui-tsai* system in China. The term *mui-tsai*, literally translated into English, is 'small sister.' The reason for employing such a term for a class of servant girls is partly explained by the Chinese method of teaching young children to be polite and to treat those below them with consideration. *Mui-tsai*, though a servant, is not considered to be like a paid servant and merely a member of the household, but a member of the family. It is difficult to trace the origin of this system, but from descriptions in old Chinese books this class of young girls was probably the daughters of paid servants employed in rich or powerful families. For the advancement of their young daughters these servants would deem it fortunate if their daughters were allowed to be admitted into such families as attendants to the ladies of the house, where they would be well looked after, having good food and good clothing, and where they could acquire good manners and gentleness and, as personal attendants or companions to the young ladies of the house, they could also learn needle-work, embroidery, reading, writing and other accomplishments. Being personal attendants to the ladies they were never required to perform any domestic or menial work, as in such families there were plenty of paid servants to do the menial work. Having attained a certain degree of accomplishment, these girls acquired a status far above that of their parents. When they grew up to a marriageable age, they might and invariably did, through the influence of the master, marry into well-to-do families. In such cases the parents would be too thankful for what was being done for their daughter to interfere with the arrangements made by the master or mistress for the girl. A connection by marriage with a well-to-do family would mean also the advancement of the family of the parent, although the girl might not be married as a wife but as a concubine. Girls having been brought up in such a way became deeply attached to their mistresses and were greatly trusted by them and the whole family. Instances have occurred, we are told, of such girls making great personal sacrifices for the sake of their mistresses when the master's family got into trouble.

This system of servant girls or *mui-tsai* became so satisfactory and beneficial to both sides, particularly to the girls, that poor parents were quite willing to part with their daughters to any well-to-do family to be a *mui-tsai*, leaving absolutely in the hands of the master or mistress the care and control of their daughters. On the other hand the well-to-do families, finding this class of servant girls so trust-worthy and so much attached to the family, being reared up in the family from quite a tender age, began to appreciate this class of girl servants. Hence the *mui-tsai* system came into vogue. Poor parents being in need of money would, on parting with their daughter, ask for some compensation for the expense they had incurred since the child's birth, not as a price or value of the girl, but as a refund of such expense. The amount was usually a nominal sum. Unfortunately by taking money the transaction became at once a case of buying and selling of children. However, in such transactions the following conditions attached even to this day by tradition, that is to say :-

(1) That the master or mistress should be responsible for the welfare and the person of the child by giving her proper food and clothing, and in case of illness, medical attendance.

(2) That the girl should be considered to be a member of the family, and not as a paid servant.

(3) That when she is old enough to be married, she must be properly married by the master or mistress as a wife or concubine.

(4) That no girl should be sold as a prostitute and this should apply to a *mui-tsai* as much as to any girl.

(5) That by custom, when a *mui-tsai* is engaged to be married, if her parents be then living, the master or mistress should notify them of the fact and the circumstances attending hereto. If the parents desired to do so they would associate with the family of the girl's husband as if she had been married by them. In such a case the responsibility of the master or mistress would cease but if her parents be dead the girl, after her marriage, would be treated in her master's house as a 'quasi daughter' and her husband as a 'quasi-son-in-law'; and all the thousand and one Chinese ceremonies relating to child birth and annual festivities etc., would be performed by and at the expense of the mistress as a mother-in-law.

There is one point I omitted to mention in my memorandum to H.E. the Governor on the question of *mui-tsai*, that is (6) a *mui-tsai* wears mourning on the death of her master or mistress for the same period as that of a daughter. This is custom and is usually done but is not provided by law, as the law only prescribes the period of mourning of persons related to the deceased within the 5 degrees of consanguinity. This point is very important as it shows that a *mui-tsai* is treated by the Chinese as a foster-daughter.

Now I will proceed to answer the following questions.

Question 1. Is the document exhibit 'A' consistent with:-

(1) An intent that the child should be adopted as the daughter of first defendant (Lei Wong Shi), or,

(2) An intent that the child should render to the first defendant services as a domestic servant?

Or, is the document equally consistent with either such intention?

Answer. Exhibit 'A' is the usual form of a document presenting a daughter to another family as a *mui-tsai*. With the explanation of the meaning and position of a *mui-tsai* in a family as above, a *mui-tsai* is neither an adopted daughter in the strict legal sense of the word 'adopted' according to Chinese law, nor is she a domestic servant in the ordinary sense of a menial or paid servant. She is rather in the position of a foster-daughter liable to do such domestic service as a natural daughter might be called upon to do at any time. The amount of degree of household work to be performed by her depends entirely on the social position of the family to which she is attached. When there are plenty of paid servants in the house she is only called upon to do the very light kind of household duties. Therefore Exhibit 'A' is equally consistent with the intentions of 1 and 2 in the question.

Question 2. Is it customary or usual among the Chinese to adopt daughters?

Answer. No. It is unusual to 'adopt' daughters among the Chinese but they are in the habit of having foster-daughters. The world 'adopt' has a special meaning in the Chinese law. There is only one kind of adoption in the Chinese law, that is, the adoption of an heir male (there is no such thing as a female heir in China) to carry on or continue the line of lineal descent for the purposes of ancestral worship. The law regulates the poorer class of male persons to be adopted as an heir but no regulation exists to provide for the adoption of a daughter. To use the word adopt loosely and to apply it to females is rather misleading and confusing.

Question 3. Would such adoption be usual for an elderly lady whose own only daughter had died? Would the fact that the lady had a son and several grandchildren affect the position?

Answer. To use the word 'fostering'. Yes. Particularly with old spinsters or old ladies whose children are all married — more so if the only daughter had died. The fact of having grand-children does not affect the position. The object of having a foster-daughter is so that the old lady might have some one constantly near her and that she might receive the little attentions, care and affection of some one like a daughter. When one foster-daughter is married, she would look for another.

Question 4. If a daughter were to be adopted would it be customary or usual to adopt some female relative?

Answer. As answered in question 2 it is very unusual to adopt a daughter in the strict sense of the word. There is no object in adopting a daughter in the whole fabric of the Chinese Constitution. In the case of relatives, if the family of a relative be in affluent circumstances no daughter would be given to another man as an adopted or foster-daughter. If the parents of a relative be poor then they would ask compensation for 'rice, ginger and vinegar money'. If that happens, it at once places the child in the same position as a foster-daughter or *mui-tsai*. Besides, to adopt (using the word in a loose sense) a relative as a daughter one has to be very careful as she must be of a generation next below that of the adopter, otherwise a person of a higher generation (that is, the Aunt Class) might inadvertently be made to become a daughter, which is punishable by law for upsetting the natural family relationship. With regard to strangers no such precaution is needed.

Question 5. Would it be in accordance with Custom to adopt the child of persons entirely unrelated to and unknown to the adoptive parent?

Answer. Yes. See answer 4.

Question 6. Assuming that such an adoption was not contrary to custom, would the adopted child's surname be changed to that of the adoptive parent?

Answer. As there is no legal adoption of a daughter in China, the change of the surname is not absolutely necessary. Some do, however, and it all depends on the degree of attachment and affection between the adopter and the adopted.

Question 7. Would it be in accordance with custom for the surname of a *mui-tsai* to be changed for that of its adoptive parent?

Answer. A *mui-tsai* is in the position of a foster-daughter and the answer to question 6 applies to this question.

Question 8. Is it customary or usual in the case of *bona fide* adoption for a 'rice, ginger and vinegar fee' to be paid to the child's parent by the adoptive parent?

Answer. As there is no legal adoption of a daughter in the same sense as that on an adoption of a son, it is usual in the case of a *bona fide* adoption of a foster-daughter for a rice, ginger and vinegar fee, to be paid to the child's parent by the adoptive parent.

Question 9. Is such a fee ever or usually paid in the case of the adoption of a male child?

Answer. No. The adoption is done by law. The adoptive parent only decides the person to be adopted among the class of persons adoptable by law.

Question 10. Is it customary or usual to insert in a document evidencing a transaction of adoption double the amount actually paid for a 'rice, ginger and vinegar fee?'

Answer. No. The fee paid in such cases is nominal and not the ascertained expenses.

Question 11. Is it customary or usual in the case of a *bona fide* adoption to have any document evidencing the transaction?

Answer. In the case of a *bona fide* adoption of a son, No. The announcement in the family of the decision of the adopter is sufficient. In the case of a *bona fide* adoption of a foster-daughter, Yes.

Question 12. Is it customary or usual to stipulate that if the adopted child is found disobedient to instructions the adoptive parent shall have the right to present the child to any other person?

Answer. The clause is unusual. But it seems there is an inherent right of parents or an adoptive parent to present the child to any other person on the same terms as those of the original deed of presentation if the child turns out to be unmanageable.

Question 13. Is it not the essence of adoption that the transaction shall be irrevocable and that the child thenceforward at all times stands in the relation of a child to the adoptive parent?

Answer. No. Even the adoption of an heir is not irrevocable. If an adopted heir turns out to be disobedient to the adoptive parent, his adoption may be revoked upon application to a court of law.

Question 14. If such is not the essence of adoption is it not foreign to the conception of adoption that in case of disobedience the adoptive parent should have an unrestricted right to present the child to whomsoever such adoptive parent may choose?

Answer. The answer to question 13 applies to this question. In China the parent or the adoptive parent who is in *loco parentis* seems to have such unrestricted right.

Question 15. Is such an unrestricted right of presentation in case of disobedience consistent with the child being handed over as a *mui-tsai*?

Answer. Yes, it may be so. But the terms of such presentation must be the same as that of the original deed of presentation. That is, either to be a servant, if the original terms meant her to be servant, or a foster-daughter, as the case may be.

Question 16. Is it customary or usual in the case of *bona fide* adoption to stipulate that the adoptive parent shall have the right to get the child married at her discretion?

Answer. The adoptive parent being a person in *loco parentis* has the inherent right of a natural parent of making arrangements for the marriage of the adopted or foster-daughter. This stipulation need not be inserted in the deed of presentation but is usually inserted.

Question 17. Is not such a right one which is incidental to the relationship of employer and *mui-tsai*?

Answer. The right of marrying a *mui-tsai* is incidental to the relationship of the master or mistress and a *mui-tsai* who is in the position of a foster-daughter; but it does not exist between and employer and a paid servant girl, that is *Chue Nin Mui* (住年妹).

Question 18. What is the strict meaning of the word which is translated as 'presented'?

Answer. The word translated as presented means 'given as a gift'.

Question 19. Is it a word which one would expect to find used in connection with adoption and/or the establishment of the relationship of employer and *mui-tsai*?

Answer. The word (送) is used in order to distinguish the relationship between the master or mistress and the *mui-tsai* who is to be treated as a foster-daughter and as a member of the family from that of the relationship between an employer and a paid servant say, the *Chue Nin Mui*. If an agreement had to be made between an employer and a paid servant the word used would be (請)or (僱), that is 'to engage'.

Question 20. Is it customary or usual for an employer to provide for a *mui-tsai* an ample wardrobe, including silk garments and ornaments such as a gold ring and a pair of ear-rings?

Answer. If the master or mistress is well-to-do and is in the position of a foster parent of a *mui-tsai*, Yes. If the master or mistress is not rich or is in the position of employer of a paid '*mui-tsai*', No.

Question 21. Is it customary among the Chinese for the younger daughters of a house to participate in the duties ordinarily performed by domestic servants such as the sweeping of floors, the cleaning of spittoons, dusting of rooms and the like?

Answer. Yes. Not only the younger ones but all daughters. Unless the family employs many servants daughters do perform household duties. It is considered by the Chinese to be a virtue in their daughters to do household duties.

Question 22. Has the parent of a *mui-tsai* a right to redeem his child and if so upon what terms?

Answer. Yes. The Chinese have the greatest respect for the natural affection between parents and children. If parents desire the return of their daughter after being presented to another family as a *mui-tsai* for a reunion of their family, a Court of Justice would order the return of the daughter subject to payment of compensation. But in most cases the natural feeling among Chinese in such cases would not oppose the return of the girl provided it is a *bona fide* case of reunion. Compensation would be paid for the up-keep of the girl calculated in a nominal sum upon the number of years she has been in the master's or mistress' family.

Appendix 'B'#

I, Lam Yung, native of Shek Tsui village, San Wui District, Kwongtung, now residing at No. 453 Shanghai Street, Mongkok, Yaumati, 2nd floor, am the maker of this Deed for the presentation of my daughter. It happens that I have fallen ill, and have no money to pay for medical expenses. Further the price of rice has gone up and I cannot earn enough to pass my days. Therefore I, after due discussion with my wife, am willing to leave my own daughter named Lam Ah Tseung, aged 7, born on the 21st day of the 12th moon, to be introduced by my acquaintance Li So Man to Li Wong Shi. It was stipulated and agreed between the 3 parties that a 'rice, ginger and vinegar fee' of $190 in Hong Kong notes should be given me as compensation. The money was personally received by me and the girl Lam Ah Tseung was handed over to Li Wong Shi to be brought up. If the girl is found disobedient to her instructions, Li Wong Shi shall have the right to present the girl to any other person and when the girl grows up in the future, Li Wong Shi shall have the right to get her married at her own discretion. After the girl is presented, each party shall acquiesce in Heaven's decree in case of any misfortune. This is a mutual trust between friends, and has been agreed between both parties; and it is in no way a case of kidnapping. To avoid the unreliability of a verbal promise, this deed is made as proof.

A 'rice, ginger and vinegar fee' of $100 has been personally received by me as compensation for the presentation of my daughter.

> Finger-print of Li So Shi — the witness.
> Finger-print and personal signature of Lam Yung, maker this deed for the presentation of his daughter and recipient of the money.

Finger-print of Chan Shi, wife of Lam Yung, who is also a recipient of the money.

(Dated) 4th November, 1924.

d. Depression, Livelihood and Reform

> Just who were the workers of Hong Kong in the 1930s? Is it possible to put some faces on this nondescript word 'work'? Is it possible to pry into the livelihood of people who performed hard physical work in Hong Kong?

Translation of Exhibit 'A'.

The first Labour Officer appointed in Hong Kong probably had the same questions in mind when he wrote his report on labour and labour conditions in 1935. He included in the report notes on twenty workers he seems to have met randomly in the street. One man, for instance, was found buying cigarettes, a woman was hawking peanuts, and a ricksha man was plying for hire. The man buying cigarettes had worked in Hong Kong for only one and a half years. He shared a cockloft with two other workers, each paying one dollar a month. He had been a farmer, but now in Hong Kong he was a tea-carrying 'coolie'. He earned about five to six dollars a week, but every month he sent ten dollars home to his wife and his mother. One could almost hear the Cantonese spoken when he said, possibly in response to a question asking him how he spent his leisure time, that 'when no work, fellow workers come together and discuss affairs.'

But compare this man with the Taikoo Dockyard worker, employed in Hong Kong for nine years. He was principal tenant for a flat; that is to say, he kept one cubical and a sitting room for his family and rented out two rooms to subtenants. He made 45 dollars a month. His family stayed with him in his flat, even though he still remitted about ten dollars a month to his mother. One can see the difference made in the family budget by being principal tenant. He paid 14.50 dollars per month towards his flat, but received 4 dollars each from his two tenants.

The difference of a few dollars a month mattered to Hong Kong's workers, because it was only a few dollars that divided them in the social hierarchy. Economic depression in the early 1930s accentuated the difference, while housing congestion, created by the large influx of refugees added to the social divide. One might almost visualize the categories: the flat-owners, the one-flat principal tenants, the one-room sub-tenant, the homeless . . . . In 1937 alone, the police found 1,353 dead bodies on the streets in Hong Kong.

The shortage of housing became acute. The report of the Housing Commission of 1935, which was appointed by the Governor of Hong Kong to 'enquire into the housing difficulties . . . with special reference to overcrowding and its effect on tuberculosis . . . ' commented boldly on the need for a subsidized housing programme for the poor. This very important report, which preceded the Hong Kong government's housing programme in the 1950s by twenty years, also made the important argument that provision of housing should take account not only of the human need for light and air, but also the use of space in the family setting.

DOCUMENT IV.d1: Economic depression, 1935 (source: 'Report of the Commission appointed by His Excellency the Governor of Hong Kong to enquire into the causes and effects of the present trade depression in Hong Kong and make recommendation for the amelioration of the existing position and the improvement of the trade of the colony, July 1934 - February 1935', Sessional Papers 1935. pp. 75-76)

After the Great War and until 1924 the trade of Hong Kong in common with that of the rest of the world appeared to be steady and prosperous. During that time there ruled a high rate of exchange with sterling. It will be remembered that trade was badly hit by a big shipping strike in 1925. When we come to 1931 we perceive an increase in the Hong Kong dollar value of both imports and exports but the sterling value of the dollar had become less than half what it was in 1924. Since 1931, while there has been a gradual rise in the average rate of exchange there has been a persistent drop in the dollar value of both imports and exports. Thus in 1931 imports were valued at 652-1/2 million dollars or 34-1/2 million pounds sterling, while in 1933 the dollar value of imports had decreased to 432 millions an equivalent of 29 million pounds. This decrease has been accentuated in 1934 and an estimate based on the first nine months of the year gives for the whole year a dollar value of imports of only $402.8 millions, a rough equivalent in sterling being 29.7 millions.

The same tale is told with regard to exports which in 1931 amounted to 542 million dollars or 29 million pounds, in 1933 to 403 million dollars or 27 million pounds and in 1934 only 316.8 million dollars or about 23.3 million pounds.

Perhaps the trend of depression as assessed by trade figures may be more accurately shown by those of the first nine months of 1934 compared with those of the same period of the previous two years as follows:-

	(Millions)	
	Imports	Exports
1932	$477.8 = £31.4	$352.3 = £23.2
1933	$381.1 = £25.5	$307.0 = £20.5
1934	$302.1 = £22.3	$237.6 = £17.5

It will be seen that in terms of Hong Kong currency imports in the first nine months of 1934 declined by 20.7% as compared with the corresponding period of 1933; and 36.8% as compared with the corresponding period of 1932, while exports in the first nine months of 1934, declined in value by 22.6% as compared with the first nine months of 1933; and 32.6% as compared with the first nine months of 1932.

Another indication of depression is the fall in wholesale prices. The price index for Hong Kong has been constructed on the basis of the declared quantities and c.i.f. values of commodities imported into Hong Kong, the year 1922 being taken as 100. In 1931 the index stood at a peak of 136.6 whence it has annually increased until for the first half year of 1934 it stands at 95.9.

Further signs of depression are not wanting. If we turn to the Treasury figures of Revenue for the years 1932-1934 we find therein a steady progressive decline in every item and a strongly marked steep decline in those items which may be said to be the fruits of luxury expenditure.

The world wide depression, a reaction from the post war boom, was bound to touch China and therefore Hong Kong somewhat later than the western and more highly organised countries. It would, of course, be impossible to prescribe a special antidote to this for Hong Kong and as far as the Colony's present position is the result of world depression so far must we await the general improvement in world trade which the more optimistic of us believe now to be commencing, albeit slowly and under the doubtful aegis of economic nationalism.

DOCUMENT IV.d2: Workers of Hong Kong in the 1930s (source: H.R. Butters, Report on Labour and Labour Conditions in Hong Kong, Sessional Papers, 1939, Hong Kong: Norohna & Co., 157-163)

I have taken statements from twenty individuals chosen at random as representative of various classes of workers.

(1) YIU SUN, male, age 30 (found buying cigarettes from stall in Hing Lung Street, Hong Kong, after carrying vegetables)

In Hong Kong one and a half years, came from Kong Moon, Kwangtung Province, to look for work; in Kong Moon was small farmer and gardener; now tea-carrying coolie for Douglas boats; employed by coolie foreman Ng Pui who is employed by Tea Guild. Wife in country, no children, married four years, supports mother in country. Lives 10 Chinese Street in cockloft on first floor which he shares with two fellow workers at one dollar each month. Five families, eighteen adults and six children, on floor.

Employment regular, paid once a week according to number of boxes carried; earns five to six dollars a week. When no tea ships, no tea-carrying, carries vegetables at thirty cents to a dollar a day.

Has two meals a day from street stall at twenty cents a meal. Wears clothes he brought from the country. Can sometimes make two dollars a day. If sick, female cousin, 9 Chinese Street, whose husband is also a coolie, looks after him; if very sick would go to hospital. Wife in Kong Moon weaves at home, can earn very little, mother also weaves. Sends them about ten dollars a month. They spend six to seven dollars and save the balance in case children are born.

Since arrival in Hong Kong never been back to country, wife never been to Hong Kong. Clansman writes for him two or three times a month. Travelling trader on board Kong Moon boat arranges his remittances and pays them in Chinese currency. Expects to go home on visit in a few months at Ching Ming Festival. Better off here than in Kong Moon; does not smoke opium but spends three cents on cigarettes a day (six cigarettes).

Hours of work: 8 a.m.- 5 p.m., sometimes works late till 9 p.m.

Average earnings when working $1.60-$1.70 a day; Sunday a holiday — walks about the streets.

In the country worships idols, Gods of the sky; in Hong Kong does not care. Cannot read or write. When no work fellow workers come together and discuss affairs.

Winter clothing — two singlets, two jackets and two trousers (one short); does not wear shoes.

Rises 6 a.m., goes to bed 8 p.m.; 5 p.m. - 8 p.m. takes a walk; has a bath at home every two days.

Clansman introduced him to Ng Pui (his immediate employer) half month after arrival in Colony; clansman fed him for that half month. Does not gamble; occasionally drinks five cents wine after hard work.

(2) LAM YEE, female, age 60, (found hawking peanuts in Connaught Road, Hong Kong). In Hong Kong fifteen years, unlicensed hawker, formerly street seamstress but sight failed. Husband died over twenty years ago; after his death came to Hong Kong from Fa Yuen, near Canton, with son, age 23, and daughter. Son emigrated after a year; never hears from him, thinks he has been kidnapped. Daughter married into family in country. No relatives in Hong Kong. Lives in Des Voeux Road West, number unknown. Occupies bedspace, principal tenant has pity on her, no fixed rent, pays on average of about a dollar a month. Cooks her own meals, two meals a day — rice, salt fish, vegetables — cost ten cents a day; eats very little. Clothes she wears ten years old. Has been arrested twice for hawking without licence, fined fifty cents each time, lost her capital. Borrowed fresh capital. No news from daughter in country for over a year; daughter is a widow; daughter's family would not allow her in. Was paid between twenty and thirty dollars and some pork and cakes when daughter married. When weather bad stays at home — five families in flat, ten adults, five children. When a seamstress made about the same as hawking peanuts — fifteen cents a day. Came to Hong Kong as could not make a living in country; when worked in fields did not get enough to eat. Better off in Hong Kong, seldom sick; life in Hong Kong is wonderful in comparison with the country. No expenses beyond food and rent.

(3) CHENG KWAI YING, female, spinster, age 22, outworker, Fung Keong Rubber Factory, Shaukiwan, Hong Kong; lives with brother and sister-in-law at 5 Tai Cheung Street, Sai Wan Ho, rent over four dollars a month. There are four cubicles on the floor, and over twenty persons on the floor. Family occupies one cubicle. Brother has daughter, age three, brother skilled worker in Taikoo Dockyard.

Occupation: stitching uppers together; owns sewing machine for which she paid eighty dollars second-hand. Has made ten dollars deposit with Fung Keong Company; receives sixty to seventy pairs of uppers a day; sister-in-law assists her to certain extent in work; paid according to size and kind. Earns 70 cents to $1.00 a day; ten pairs require from two and a half to three hours. She herself stitches about fifty pairs a day, works every day.

Four years in Hong Kong, came from Canton where she worked in silk factory but market was poor and it was difficult to get work. Earns more here than in Canton. Brother earns over a dollar a day. Family income in all over fifty dollars a month. Family sends $10 Cantonese ($5 Hong Kong) per month to parents in country and elder brother. They are farmers in Shun Tak. Can read a little but cannot write, never been to school. Goes to pictures sometimes, cannot read newspaper. Not member of any union or guild.

(4) PANG SO FONG, female, spinster, age 24, employed at Fung Keong Rubber Factory, Shaukiwan, Hong Kong.
   Work: Gumming soles and uppers together.
   Lives 35 Kam Wah Street, 3rd floor, Shaukiwan, with brother and sister-in-law; brother employed in office at Fung Keong at $150 a month. In Hong Kong since childhood, parents in country. Brought up by brother; was back in country for two years. Can read a little and write very little. Was two years at charity school.
   Hours: 7 a.m.-12 noon, 1 p.m.-6 p.m., 7 p.m.-8 p.m. Been employed for five years, day's work — forty to fifty pairs at three cents a pair, average earnings over $1.20 a day; takes a day off after seven or ten days.
   Brother's family occupy a whole floor, rent unknown; sometimes gives brother six dollars towards it, sometimes nothing. Younger brother and sister and cousin and brother's daughter, age four, and two servants, cook and amah, also reside there. Brother sends money home to parents in country. Spends ten dollars per month on herself — amusements and cosmetics; goes to pictures once or twice a week. Not engaged to be married but saves a little against marriage. Has been trained as first-aid nurse in factory by St. John Ambulance; when she acts as such, receives one dollar a day.

(5) WONG TAI, female, married woman, aged 36, (found carrying sand in Cheung Sha Wan Road, Shamshuipo, Kowloon), husband mason; they occupy half a cockloft; ground floor of Tai Nan Street, Shamshuipo, number unknown, rent $2.20 per month, no children; two children dead.
   Carries sand daily for building contractor at forty cents a day, paid twice a month.
   Hours: 7 a.m.-12 noon, 1 p.m.-5:30 p.m.; husband employed on odd jobs 70-80 cents a day when working. She eats on the street while at work, sometimes sends $2-$3 home to brother in country. In Hong Kong eight to nine years; came from Wai Chau, Kwangtung Province, as could not find work in country. Not member of any guild or union.

(6) SO FUK CHOI, female, spinster, age 17, employed Lo Kwok Po weaving factory, 43 Cheung Sha Wan Road, Shamshuipoo, Kowloon. (unregistered), lives 170 Nan Chang Street, 2nd floor, Shamshuipo, with elder sworn sister (i.e. friend) age 22 years, who does similar work in another factory; parents in Shatin, New Territories, working as farmers; came to Sha Tin seven or eight years ago; born and educated at Shiu Hing, near Canton, and can read and write; employed here for two years, working hand weaving machine; piecework, twenty to thirty cents a day.
   Hours: 7 a.m.-10 a.m., 11 a.m.-5 p.m., 6 p.m.-8 p.m., can occasionally have a holiday on private affairs, no pay, generally works seven days a week.
   Shares a bedspace with sworn sister, formerly $2.30, now $2.40 a month; they buy and cook their own food. Food costs $4-$5 each per month. Sometimes buys clothes,

sometimes receives them from mother who assists with one to two dollars twice a month. Has to pay for kerosene lamp in house. Not member of any union or guild.

(7) CHEUNG YAU LIN, female, married, woman, age 31, employed at Wah Nam Battery Company, Pine Street, Taikoktsui, Kowloon.

Husband, unemployed seaman, three years unemployed, works occasionally, ten to fifteen days a month, as ship's painter and earns about ten dollars per month.

Three children, husband looks after childern while wife works; while husband is also working eldest child, boy, age eleven, looks after the others and cooks the food.

Lives in cubicle at 128 Yee Kuk Street, Shamshuipo, Kowloon, for which they pay $3.60 per month.

Came to Hong Kong four years ago from Toi Shan, Kwangtung Province, as ship on which husband was employed furequently called at Hong Kong.

Work: Wrapping paper round manganese batteries (electric torch) and carbon sticks.

Wages: 21 cents a day. Hours: 7 a.m.-12 noon, 1 p.m.-5 p.m., 6 p.m.-8 p.m.; works every day.

Cannot read or write. Is not a member of any union or guild.

(8) CHEUNG SIU, female, spinster, age 19, employed at Leung Wing Shing Joss Stick Company, 896 Kremer Street, Taikoktsui, Kowloon.

Came from San Wui, Kwangtung Province, four years ago to look for work; lives with elder sister in Ash Street, Taikoktsui, number unknown — shares cubicle and pays one dollar per month rent.

Employed four years in joss stick factory, piecework.

Wages: Three and a half cents per thousand joss sticks rolled, earns about 30 cents a day.

Hours: 7 a.m.-8 p.m. with intervals of about forty minutes off at 10 a.m. and 4 p.m. Is not a member of any guild.

(9) YAM SIU YING, female, spinster, aged 25, Moonlight Torch Factory, 11-27 Yen Chau Street, Shamshuipo, Kowloon.

Works machines (various) that stamp out parts of electric torch cases; in present employment two years.

Wages: 25 cents a day, paid fortnightly.

Hours: 6:45 a.m.-11:45 a.m., 12:45 p.m.-5:45 p.m., occasionally works late till 8 p.m. with extra day's pay in three. Works every day of the week.

Lives in Pei Ho Street, Shamshuipo, number unknown, with mother, who works in knitting factory; shares bedspace with mother. Rent for the two women, two dollars a month.

Three years in Hong Kong; came from Canton, where she worked in a similar factory at 35 cents Cantonese a day, until factory closed.

Mother and she have just sufficient income to live on. Does not remit any money to country. Cannot read or write. Is not a member of any guild or union.

(10) LEI PIU, male aged 48, fisherman (found on water front at Aberdeen, Hong Kong).

At present unemployed, living with friend in Aberdeen; born in Macao, four years in Hong Kong since master's boat was dismantled at Aberdeen, now generally on junk fishing in Chinese waters, away from Aberdeen three days to a month at a time.

Wages: $18.00 per month and food together with certain perquisites in respect of small fish worth three to five dollars a month. When in regular employment used to be paid six months' wages in advance.

Wife dead, two sons now at work, one daughter married in Macao. Normally spends on an average about twenty days a month afloat: when employed sleeps board. Wife when alive stayed in Macao. Junk carries over twenty persons including women and children — these consist of wife and children of owner and some fishermen's wives who do cooking.

(11) LAU SAU, male, aged 57, ricksha collie (found plying for hire in Conaught Road, Hong Kong).

In Hong Kong four years, from Swatow, Chiu Yeung District, Kwangtung Province, where he was farmer; was never a ricksha coolie till he came to Hong Kong; no work in country. Wife died last year in country. One son aged 27, farming in country (Chiu Yeung District).

Lives 100 Second Street 3rd floor — coolie lodging house, thirteen coolies divide rent of floor, $17.00, between them.

Hires ricksha from owner (licensee) at twenty cents a day, other coolie hires it at twenty eight cents a night.

Total earnings 70 cents to $1.00 a day out of which he pays for hire of ricksha and repairs.

Hours of plying for hire: 5 a.m.-3:30 p.m., night coolie then takes over ricksha.

Four meals a day: At home before starting out, cost fifteen cents; in street at 8 a.m., ten cents; in street at 12 noon, ten cent; 5 p.m., at home, 15 cents. Meals at home cooked by himself on charcoal fire.

As it is wet, wearing oilskin coat; material and tailoring cost $1.70. No expenses beyond food, clothing and rent. Sends five to six dollars home each month to son in country. Son does not earn enough. He is too poor to marry.

Is better off in Hong Kong than in Swatow. Cannot read or write. Not a member of any union. When he came to Hong Kong looking for work clansman introduced him to ricksha owner.

(12) CHING YUK, male 31, salesman, Men's Department, Wing On Department Stores, Des Voeux Road Central, Hong Kong.

Wages $30.00 per month, free food and quarters on premises. Free laundry, shaving and hair-cutting. Employed by Wing On Company for fifteen years. Came from Chung Shan, Kwangtung Province, educated from Chung Shan, can read and write Chinese and a little English. Not married. Sends no remittance home. Spends nearly all income on clothes and entertaining friends; dresses in European fashion.

Hours of work: 9 a.m.-8 p.m. with half an hour off for lunch 11:45 a.m.-12:15 p.m.; 1 p.m. to 8 p.m. on Sundays. Holidays when store is closed — on Chinese festivals and public holidays.

Three meals a day but morning meal is only congee. If ill, leave without pay. Company provides doctor and maintenance expenses in hospital; pays himself for medicine dispensed.

Not member of any union.

(13) FUNG SHU PING, male, 24, of Chekiang Province, employed in hand press sub-department, Banknote Department, Chung Hwa Book Company, Pak Tai Street, Mataukok, Kowloon.

Employed by Chung Hwa Book Company in Shanghai, about nine years in photographic department. After hostilities Shanghai works closed, came to Hong Kong October, 1938, on written contract, time indefinite, entitling him to two months' wages and twenty dollars fare to Shanghai in event of determination [sic] of contract.

Wages: $15.00 per month, free food ($7.50 rice money), free lodging and light in quarters provided by company, Sung Wong Toi Road, free medical treatment at factory by Chinese doctor qualified in Hong Kong University. If seriously ill sent to Government hospital, employers paying fifty cents per day. Full wages continue during illness for two months, thereafter half wages. If permanently unfit will be sent back to Shanghai. Earns also bonus on production.

Hours: 7.30 a.m.-12 noon, 1 p.m.-5:30 p.m. Works occasionally on Sundays. Nine men to one press, standard day's work nine hundred sheets; bonus one cent per sheet additional divided between the nine men; for sheet spoiled fined five cents divided likewise. Can print seventeen hundred sheets per day with certain number spoiled. Share of bonus last month $11.26.

Not married. Expenses chiefly on clothing; remits $10 Hong Kong to Shanghai monthly. Can read and write Chinese and speak and write a little English. Educated at Provincial Government School at Chekiang as day boy, fees about $40 per half year. In Shanghai earned about $70 (Shanghai) before the war. Member of the Chung Hwa Branch of the Hong Kong Printers Union. Was not a member of any union in Shanghai.

(14) LAM SANG, male, aged 34, joiner, Taikoo Dockyard:

Employed there for last nine years. Married, one son four years, residing 61 Main Street, Saiwanho, 1st floor. Principal tenant of floor, rent $14.50 (formerly $11.00), retains for self one cubicle and sitting room, has two subtenants at four dollars each. Born San Wui, Kwangtung Province. Came to Hong Kong, aged 16, with a clansman as was poor in country. Apprentice for three years in furniture shop, Wanchai, Hong Kong, no pay, free board and lodging; then nine dollars per month with free lodging but not free food. After two months left shop to look for odd jobs as pay was too low. After several years obtained work at Taikoo, at first under contractor; three years ago joined permanent staff. Time work, $1.26 a day—both under contractor and directly employed.

Hours: 7 a.m.-12 noon, 1 p.m.-5 p.m. Sunday work — time and half; over-time — time and half.

If ill, leave but no pay.

Wages amount to about forty five dollars a month, paid monthly. Wife does no work except house work—no servants. Not member of any union or guild. Food for family about eighteen dollars per month. Remits seven to ten dollars per month to mother in country. Can read and write Chinese: learned in country when boy. No savings.

(15) CHAN PUI, male, 48 years, plater, Taikoo Dockyard:

Married: two sons, four daughters eldest aged 22, 48 Saiwanho Street ground floor. Principal tenant paying $11.50 per month, four sub-tenants from whom he collects from $8 to $9, retains one cubicle and bedspace, no servants. Two daughters work at Fung Keong Rubber Factory, earning thirty to sixty cents a day each which they hand over to him; he provides them with house, food and clothing.

Came to Hong Kong, aged 29, from Toi Shan, Kwangtung Province, as no work in country, learned trade for three years at Bailey's Shipyard at forty cents a day — then in Kowloon Docks from two to three years — fifteen years at Taikoo Dock, employed through a contractor, time work.

Hours: 7 a.m.-12 noon, 1 p.m.-5 p.m. Wages $1.50 a day. Overtime — time and half, Sundays — time and half.

Sent remittance to country monthly when mother was alive. Can read and write Chinese. Not member of any union. Eldest son, aged fourteen, goes to private school — fees thirteen dollars a year. Only eldest girl went to school. Food for family forty dollars per month.

(16) CHAN YIN, male, 60, coolie in coppersmiths shop, Taikoo Dockyard:

About thirty years in Hong Kong, came from Ching Yuen, Kwangtung Province, to look for work. Formerly employed as ship's painter, Taikoo Dock, but work too hard and dangerous, so became coolie. Employed as such for last seventeen years, wife dead. Resides with son, aged 17 years, apprentice in machine shop at fifteen cents a day, in Dockyard Quarters paying $1.50 per month for one bunk. Son resided with wife in country until three years ago.

Wages: 9 cents an hour — 81 cents a day.

Hours: 7 a.m.-12 noon, 1 p.m.-5 p.m. Overtime and Sunday work — time and half.

Can read and write a little. Son can read and write as he went to school in country. Son now studying English at night school. When a painter was member of painters' guild. Was not skilled worker. Food for self and son $17 per month. Used to remit money to parents when alive. Saves four to five dollars per month which he spends on relatives who borrow but never repay.

(17) WONG SIK PO, male, 26, foki of Sheung Chit Fat rice and oil shop, 158 Tam

Kung Road, Kowloon City.

Came from Chiu Chow, Kwangtung Province this month as no work in country owing to war. Left wife and daughter, aged two, in Chiu Chow. Master of shop, also from Chiu Chow, pays him six dollars a month, free food; sleeps on premises.

Hours: 7 a.m.-9 p.m. with half hour off for meals at 8 a.m., 12 noon, and 7 p.m.

Can read and write a little. Not member of any guild or union. Remits four dollars per month home.

(18) LEUNG SAM, female, 40, (found shovelling sand at house being erected along Customs Pass Road, eight miles beyond Kowloon City).

Widow, came from Hoi Ping nine months ago to make living in Hong Kong leaving son aged 13 and daughter aged 15 with mother-in-law in country. When in Hong Kong lives with sister-in-law, whose husband is a seaman, at 18 . . . [sic] Street, name unknown, near temple, Kowloon City; pays no rent. Was small farmer in country. Has been on present job four to five months, lives in wooden shed beside work.

Wages: Thirty cents a day.

Hours: 7 a.m.-1 p.m., 3 p.m.-5:30 p.m. Feeds herself at cost about three dollars a month, goes to Kowloon twice a month for rice. Remits four to five dollars per month to mother-in-law in country.

(19) TANG HO, female, aged 32, (found turning over earth under water before rice planting between Castle Peak and Un Long).

Married as 'tin fong' or second wife (first wife being dead) to farmer, Lam Tei Village, married four years, one daughter; was born near Castle Peak, New Territories. Has three step sons, all married, and two step daughters; a third step daughter is dead. Family lives together in four village houses which it owns. They own three fields, two bullocks, chickens, vegetables. Supporting themselves on rice of their own growing and sale of surplus crop. Have no pigs this year. Only purchases salt fish, fresh fish, some vegetables and pork. Wearing clothes she possessed at time of marriage. The wives of the three sons also work in the fields — they have three children. No servants. Cooking done by step daughter, aged 12. Last year two harvests. Cannot read or write. Never been ill. Two meals a day — rice, and congee at midday.

(20) NG WAI, female, aged 34, domestic servant employed by Wong family at 6 Queen Victoria Street third floor, Hong Kong.

Master and mistress, no children, occupy one cubicle; is only servant and sleeps in camp bed outside cubicle.

Does cooking and washing, etc. Wages — $2 per month.

Born in Canton; came to Hong Kong last year as refugee. Widow, no children.

Rises at 6 a.m., goes to bed 9-10 p.m. Feeds at employer's table; three meals a day supplied. Cannot read or write.

Summary and Recommendations

It is not proposed to collate these cases but to allow them to speak for themselves. It is interesting, however, to note that of the twenty workers chosen at random only one, the New Territories farmer, is a native of Hong Kong. The Colony was described in the earlier paragraph as geographically but not politically a part of China. Many of the inhabitants ignore this distinction and that is the root trouble in respect of Hong Kong trade unions. As many cases show, the interests and loyalties which bind the workers to China are strong. However low the wages and long the hours, they are, even with a higher cost of living, better off in Hong Kong than they were in China, and many are able to remit money home to China monthly. Most of them look to China as their home. When I called at Chung Hwa Factory shortly after the strike and lockout referred to in a previous paragraph I found all parties united for the time in the despatch of a joint telegram to Chiang Kai Shek advocating the expulsion of Wang Ching Wei from the Kuomintang.

DOCUMENT IV.d3: Workers' associations and labour legislation (source: H.R. Butters, 'Report on Labour and Labour Conditions in Hong Kong', Sessional Papers, 1939, pp. 116–123, 134–135.)

The history of societies and trade unions in Hong Kong runs parallel with that in China. As early as 1845 it was found necessary to pass an ordinance to curb the activities of the Triad and other secret societies.[#] 'The ordinance was necessarily severe, branding being provided for, and causing much discussion, but in October following, doubtless upon instructions from Home, an amendment was effected by which branding was done away with and the ordinance not made applicable to any secret society other than the Triad.'

The direct descendant of that ordinance through the Triad and Unlawful Societies Ordinance 1887 was the Societies Ordinance No. 47 of 1911, which was passed in order to control the political activities of certain associations. Under the Ordinance all societies were compelled to register or obtain exemption from registration.

Section 4 (4) reads:

'The Governor in Council shall not refuse permission to any society to be registered under this Ordinance unless it shall appear that such society is likely to be used for unlawful purposes incompatible with the peace or good order of the Colony or that its action and proceedings are calculated to excite tumult or disorder in China or to excite persons to crime in China.'

[#] Norton-Kyshe 'History of the Laws and Courts of Hong Kong'.

A schedule of exempted societies was appended. This contains besides two Chinese general merchants' associations, namely the Chinese Chamber of Commerce and the Chinese Commercial Union, thirty-four Chinese masters' trade guilds and societies, three of which included workmen as well, and only seven guilds of workmen, the Brass-smith Guild, the Carpenters Guild, an Eating House Employees Guild, the Ginseng Workmen's Guild, a Gardeners Club and two guilds of Waiters.

A schedule was published annually till 1919 when there were thirty-six masters' trade guilds or societies exempted, five of which included workmen, and thirty-five guilds of workmen. In addition, twenty-four trade guilds and societies were included in the list of registered societies. Among the exempted guilds there were no less than six brass-smiths guilds, six masons guilds, and three teahouse guilds, showing the lack of organization and unity among the workmen of the various trades.

Both exempted and registered societies might at any time be ordered to furnish information to the Registrar of Societies, who was the Registrar-General, as the Secretary for Chinese Affairs was then called, concerning the constitution and rules of the society, its office bearers, and the number of its members. As a vehicle for obtaining reliable information about, and control over, the societies the Ordinance was a failure and frequently a cause of embarrassment to Government.

The Societies Ordinance No. 8 of 1920 reversed the policy. Registration was abandoned and the only societies declared to be unlawful were:
(a) the Triad Society;
(b) all societies which use a Triad ritual;
(c) all societies which have among their objects unlawful purposes or purposes incompatible with the peace and good order of the Colony.

It is lawful for the Governor in Council in his absolute discretion to declare to be unlawful any society which in his opinion:-
(a) has among its objects unlawful purposes or purposes incompatible with the peace and good order of the Colony, or
(b) is being used, or is likely to be used, for unlawful purposes or for purposes incompatible with the peace and good order of the Colony, or
(c) is by reason of its actions or proceedings calculated to excite tumult or disorder in China or to excite persons to crime in China.

The first general strike[#] in Hong Kong took place in 1922 following a dispute over seamen's rates of pay for which there was some economic justification. Most of the men's demands were granted and the Chinese Seamen's Union obtained a considerable amount of power and glory which it immediately set about to exploit. The second general strike took place in 1925. It had no economic justification whatsoever and was merely an attempt at revolution fomented by the General Labour Union and the Chinese Seamen's Union in sympathy with similar activities in Canton and Shanghai. This was the heyday of labour power in Canton and the boycott of Hong Kong continued

---

[#] A mechanics' strike involving about 9,000 workers occurred in 1920.

well into 1926. The general strike was a complete failure and in 1927, while the powers of labour unions were being drastically curtailed in China, the General Labour Union of Hong Kong was proscribed under the Emergency Regulations, and the Chinese Seamen's Union was declared unlawful under the Societies Ordinance, 1920.

In 1927 the Illegal Strikes and Lockouts Ordinance, based on the Trade Disputes and Trade Union Act, 1927, was passed. This Ordinance, Ordinance No. 10 of 1927, was the first enactment in Hong Kong dealing expressly with trade unions. Besides declaring that any strike is illegal if it has any object other than or in addition to the furtherance of a trade dispute within the trade or industry in which the strikers are engaged, and is a strike designed or calculated to coerce the Government, either directly or by inflicting hardship upon the community or any substantial portion of the community, and making it an offense for any person employed in the service of the Crown under the Government of Hong Kong or employed in certain essential public services, to break an agreement of service if the probable consequence would be to hinder or prevent the discharge of the functions of Government, it contained a section forbidding the control of any Hong Kong union by any trade union or other organization outside the Colony, and the use of union funds for political purposes outside the Colony. There are no political purposes inside the Colony to which they might be applied. This Ordinance has never been invoked.

After the failure of the general strike and boycott and the proscription of the Seamen's Union and the General Labour Union conditions rapidly returned to normal and the surviving Hong Kong unions became little more than friendly societies concerned more with the provision of funeral expenses for the dead than the improvement of the conditions of the living.

Twelve societies have been declared unlawful under the Societies Ordinance 1920 and three organizations proscribed under the Emergency Regulations.

List of societies declared unlawful under Societies Ordinances 1920:

Name	Government Notification Number
The Hong Kong and Wuchow Steamers Industrial Association	412 of 13.10.22
The Hip Tsun Tsung Kung She (Hotel Boys and Cooks Guild)	542 of 15.12.22
The Kau Lung Ch'a Kui Kung Sheung Lun Hop Wui (Kowloon Teahouses Union)	42 of 2.2.23
The Chung Wa Hoi Yuen Kung Ip Lun Hop Tsung Wui, otherwise known as the Chinese Seamen's Union	315 of 27.5.27
The Chik Tso Kung wui, otherwise known as the Chik Tso Yin Kau Wui, otherwise known as the Knitters' Union	731 of 16.12.27

The Kau Kong Luk Kwan Ping Ka Lo Tung P'ing Yi Ngoi Yu (Military employees)	71 of 10.2.28
The Kiu Kong Ping Fong Tso Tin Kung Sz (Military employees)	do.
The Heung Kong Ping Ka Kung Sheung Tsui Tsap Sho (Military employees and contractors)	do.
The Ki Tuk Kau Wui Siu Nin Tuen (Christian Youths Group)	158 of 30.3.28
The Ch'a Kui Tsung Kung Wui (Teahouses General Union)	629 of 23.11.28
The Heung Kong Kiu Sheung Sz Wo Ch'eung Shang Yee Wui (Funeral Benefits Associations)	165 of 18.3.32
The Kiu Kong Lei Fat Tung Yip Wui (Barbers Union)	417 of 8.5.36

List of organizations proscribed under the Emergency Regulations (Emergency Regulations Ordinance No. 5 of 1922):

Name	Government Notification Number
The Kiu Kong Kung T'un Tsung Ui (General Labour Association of Hong Kong)	188 of 1.4.27
The Wun Yin Kung She or Barbers Guild	636 of 9.10.31
The Hong Kong Seamen's Union	71 of 28.1.38

No action was taken against the Hong Kong Seamen's Union, which professed to be unconnected with the proscribed Chinese Seamen's Union, until it became clear that its objects were purely political. The causes of proscription though not declared have generally been subversive or political activities.

Since 1927 there has been no major labour dispute in Hong Kong. The boycott of 1925-6 left the unions impoverished and unpopular. The restrictions imposed on unions in China depressed the spirit of unionism in Hong Kong, and several years of trade depression were not conducive to their recovery.

The hostilities between China and Japan have established a common front in place of civil war between the Kuomintang and the Communist Party and the revival of unions in China as a matter of government policy has its repercussions in Hong Kong where the local unions are moved by patriotism to renewed activity chiefly of a political and nationalist character. Many unions which for ten years have appeared to be extinct have been recently revived. In addition, the imported workers from Shanghai and elsewhere have brought with them their own unions and agitations. The only dispute of any importance in the last twelve months occurred among such Shanghai workmen.

It occurred in the banknote printing department of the Chung Hwa Book Company, Kowloon, and involved about fifteen hundred workers. There had been unrest for several months, the root cause of which was a feeling of insecurity among the workers, many of whom had left their families in Shanghai, and who felt themselves strangers in the Colony, where their future was obscure. Two trivial incidents brought matters to a head. The management declared a lockout — with pay, and dismissed sixty-nine men whom it regarded as ringleaders. When the works were opened the other workers returned and, adopting an equally novel technique, seven hundred in one department commenced a combined sit-down and hunger strike.

The trouble was settled amicably on the intervention of the Labour Office whose offer to arbitrate the management had at first declined.

The peculiar circumstances of this Company, however, contain the seeds of further trouble, as the contract which affords employment for the majority of the men will be completed in a few months.

So far as is known, and for such information as is available I am indebted to the Police Department, there are at present about three hundred associations in Hong Kong with a nominal membership of 111,400. These include twenty-eight merchants' guilds with a membership of 2,700; twenty-eight craft guilds or guilds which include both masters and men, with a membership of 12,000; four clan associations or societies of persons having the same surname, membership 3,000; thirty-six district associations or societies of persons from the same district with a membership of 40,000; eighty-four labour unions, membership 44,000; and eighty-nine clubs some of which are purely social while others approximate closely to labour unions, membership 7,000, and thirty-one seamen's clubs, lodging houses and employment agencies with a membership of 2,700.

The association with the largest membership, namely 20,000, is the Sung Tsing General Association, a kind of clan association, which has been in existence for about eighteen years and whose members are Hakkas. It is the only Hakka association in the Colony. This association has branches in New York, San Francisco, Honolulu, and Amsterdam. It supports six free schools for the benefit of Hakka children.

The Chung Shan Commercial Association whose members are natives of Chung Shan has about 4,000 members; the Tung Sai Commercial Association, composed of masters of various shops, brokers and employees of European firms, 1,200; the Plasterers' Guild (Kwong Yee Tong), about 3,300; the Printers' Union, about 3,000; the Cargo Coolies Guild, 1,500; the Shing Fat Stonebreakers Guild, about 1,270; the Building Construction Workers Guild, 2,700; the Tung Tak Chung Kung Wui, a coolies guild, 2,000; the Market Stall Meat Coolies Guild, 1500; the Bricklayers Guild, 3,000; the Wai Yeung Merchants' Club, formed by merchants and workers of Wai Yeung District,

3,000; the Fong Yin Kung Wui, composed of boarding house workers, 1,400; the Wong Kong Ha Tong Clansmen Association, consisting of members of the Wong clan, 1,000; the Yeung Mo Kung Wui — Foreign Employees Guild# — composed of boys employed in European residences, 2,000; the Hong Kong Sai Yee Boat-Builders Guild, 1,250; the Hoi Ping Merchants Association, merchants from Hoi Ping district, 1,000; the Chung Wah Lam Sai Ho Tong or Lam Clansmen Association, 1,200 all surnamed Lam; the Toi Shan Commercial Association, 1,200, natives of Toi Shan District, and the Chinese Engineers Guild, which is one of the oldest trade unions in the Colony and which most closely approximates to the English model, 1,500.

Each association has its own rules and regulations regarding membership, privileges and duties, organization, meetings, maintenance expenses, and frequently funeral money.

Most of the trade unions being composed of members whose wages are small have no large funds. The Chinese Seamen's Union has in its time been wealthy and the Pork Butchers Guild supported its anti-Hong Kong activities in 1925 by funds collected from a levy of 1% of the price of pigs purchased by pork dealers (called the 'ninety-nine' system), while the proscribed Barbers Union sought to levy an additional percentage on the price of haircuts nominally to finance anti-Japanese activities.

What information is available regarding unions at the present day is largely the result of detective work. The present position is anomalous as though registration is no longer required application is still frequently made to the Secretary for Chinese Affairs for permission to establish a union, a permission which is gratuitous but which implies a certain acknowledgment of the union's activities without giving any measure of control.

History of Social Legislation in Hong Kong

'The first legislative steps—British people may be thankful for it—actually taken in the Far East for protection of Chinese workers in factories were taken by the Government of Hong Kong, not by the International Settlement of Shanghai.' ## And it might be added, not by the Government of China.

In 1919 a resolution was adopted at a meeting of the Sanitary Board (now the Urban Council) requesting in the interest of public health that the Public Health and Building Ordinance, 1903, be amended to empower the Sanitary Board to make bylaws regarding the employment of children.

During the same year the Board also made certain bylaws to prevent overcrowding in factories, but these never received the confirmation of the Legislative Council.

\# This constains a section of women members — amahs — which is the only organization of female workers in the Colony. A few unions admit women as ordinary members.

\## 'Humanity and Labour in China.' An Industrial Visit and its Sequel (1923-26) By Adelaide Mary Anderson D.B.E., M.A.

Finally, in 1921 a Commission[#] was appointed to inquire into the conditions of the industrial employment of children in Hong Kong and the desirability and feasibility of legislation for the regulation of such employment.

The Commission found that the number of children employed varied according to the nature of the industry. In some factories there were children engaged in such work as packing whose output was greater and wages smaller than those of adults. In other cases children were tolerated in factories as an act of grace as their mothers when employed in the factories had nowhere else to put the children.

The hours of labour appeared to be universally excessive and in few case amounted to less than seventy a week. Wages were paid almost entirely by piece rates and it was noted that the low wages paid to children must depress the general standard of remuneration of adults. The Commissioners commented on the absence of factory amenities such as rest rooms, eating rooms and wash houses for the workmen, and remarked that the arrangements for medical attention in case of accidents were of the scantiest. In glass factories in particular labour conditions were unsatisfactory and the physique of the workers poor. It may be noted in passing that in spite of a general improvement in conditions glass factories remain in a general unsatisfactory condition. The physique of the workers is still poor and explanation is that they were employed in China as children in glass factories before coming to the Colony.

The Commissioners animadverted on the employment of pseudo-apprentices and the system of sub-contracting both of which will be referred to later in this report. The most difficult problem which they had to face was stated to be the employment of children outside factories in casual and unskilled work, and especially in burden bearing, in particular the carrying of bricks and other materials to the Peak and Hill Districts. The Commissioners have been proved correct in their opinion that the real solution of the question lay in development of mechanical transport. I have, however, seen a number of children employed in stone breaking and carrying at a quarry in Shaukiwan.

The Commissioners made certain recommendations including the compulsory registration of children by employers; the prohibition of the employment of children under the age of eleven years (Chinese), that is, roughly ten years (European), in any factory or in any form of casual labour; limitation of the hours of work for children to fifty-four per week; the prohibition of their employment between the hours of 7 p.m. and 6 a.m. and for more than five hours consecutively, and the provision of one day's rest in seven. It was also recommended that children should not be employed in glass factories, or in engineering works on the work of boiler chipping, or in dangerous trades generally, and that accommodation should be provided which could be used by workers during meal hours, and as a rest house for children taken to factories by their mothers. While local factory legislation in the last fifteen years has advanced far beyond the desiderata of the Commissioners only one such rest house for children is known and it is of the crudest. The provision of first aid appliances and the equipment of

---

[#] *Sessional Paper* No. 11 of 1921.

factories with approved sanitary conveniences was also advocated.

The Commissioners declared that their intention was to avoid introducing a series of factory regulations which would merely lead on the one hand to 'squeeze' and on the other to police court prosecutions, and they recommended the appointment of inspectors for all classes of child labour, the inspectors to be persons of standing, knowledge, tact, and sympathy. It was suggested that they should include Chinese representatives as well as British, women as well as men, and voluntary workers as well as government servants. One of the Commissioners offered as a solution of the problem the compulsory education of Chinese children by government.

As a result of these recommendations the Industrial Employment of Children Ordinance No.22 of 1922 was passed which forbade the employment of children in any dangerous trade, under the age of ten years in any factory, and under the age of twelve years in carrying coal, or building material, or debris. A child was defined as a person under the age of fifteen years. The owner and the manager of every factory were compelled to keep a running record of all children at any time employed in such factory. Hours of work were limited to nine hours per day and five hours continuously. One day's rest in every seven was to be allowed every child and employment of children between 7 p.m. and 7 a.m. was prohibited. No child was to be allowed to carry any weight which was unreasonably heavy having regard to the child's age and physical development or any load exceeding forty catties in weight. The Ordinance also provided for the appointment of a protector and inspectors of juvenile labour. The Secretary for Chinese Affairs became Protector of Juvenile Labour and one male and one female inspector were appointed. The female inspector retired after a short time and was never replaced.

The Factory (Accidents) Ordinance No. 3 of 1927 provided for the appointment of inspectors and assistant inspectors of factories. The Governor in Council was empowered to make regulations for the purpose of preventing accidents in factories. The existing inspector of juvenile labour undertook the work of factory inspection.[#]

Ordinance No. 24 of 1929, the Industrial Employment of Women, Young Persons and Children Amendment Ordinance, 1929, included women within the scope of the Industrial Employment of Children Ordinance, 1922, which was amended accordingly, in order to regulate the employment of women in certain industries.

A consolidating ordinance entitled the Factories and Workshops Ordinance 1932 was passed as Ordinance No. 27 of 1932. In it child was defined as a person under the age of sixteen years. The employment of children in dangerous trades (boiler chipping, the manufacture of fireworks, glass working, lead processes, and vermilion manufacture)

[#] The Steam-boilers Ordinance No. 32 of 1909 providing for the periodical inspection of steam boilers and the prime movers has never been enforced owing to the lack of regulations and inspectors. Further legislation is under consideration.

The Gasholders Examination Ordinance, No. 1 of 1938, provides for the periodical examination of gasholders.

and the employment of any female young person or woman in such trades without the written permission of the Protector, was prohibited. The employment of any child under the age of twelve years in any industrial undertaking was prohibited as was also the employment therein of any woman or young person between the hours of 9 p.m. and 7 a.m. A list of factories and workshops regulations was appended to the Ordinance as Schedule B.

As from 1933 the Factories Inspectorate was increased to two by the secondment of a second officer from the Sanitary Department.

By Ordinance No. 30 of 1936, the Factories and Workshops Amendment Ordinance, 1936, the Protector of Labour was empowered to exempt any industrial undertaking from any regulation under the Factories and Workshops Ordinance or to order the adoption of additional and special precautions. The existing law is consolidated in the Factories and Workshops Ordinance No. 18 of 1937. The Protector of Labour who was previously the Secretary for Chinese Affairs is declared to mean the Chairman of the Urban Council or any person appointed by the Governor to be Protector of Labour, and the Urban Council is empowered to make bylaws in respect of industrial undertakings. No such by law has been made since the passing of the Ordinance. Dangerous trades are by law extended to include processes involving the use of arsenic, manganese,# mercury, phosphorus or any compound of any of these or of lead. Child is defined as a person under the age of fourteen years, and young person as any person of or over the age of fourteen years and under the age of eighteen years.

The following are some of the bylaws in the schedule to the Ordinance:
No. 3 No person shall employ any child in any dangerous trade.
No. 4 Except with the written consent of the Protector, no person shall employ any woman, young person under the age of 16 years or any female young person in any dangerous trade.
No. 5 No person shall employ any child in any industrial undertaking.
No. 6 No young person shall be suffered to carry any weight which is unreasonably heavy having regard to the age and physical development of such young person, and no young person under the age of 16 years shall be suffered to carry any load exceeding 40 catties in weight.
No. 7 No female, whatever her age, shall be employed on underground work in any mine.
No. 8 (1) Except as provided in paragraph (2) no woman or young person shall be employed in any industrial undertaking between the hours of 8 p.m. and 7 a.m.
(2) The Protector may in exceptional cases authorize the employment of any woman or young person of 16 years or over for not more than 60 days in any year between the hours of 8 p.m. and 9 p.m.

I have seen women preparing manganese for the manufacture of batteries for electric torches.

No. 9 No young person under 16 years of age shall be employed in any industrial undertaking —

(a) between the hours of 7 p.m. and 7 a.m.

(b) for more than 9 hours in any period of 24 hours;

(c) for more than 5 hours continuously;

(d) unless after every spell of 5 hours continuous work and before his next spell of work there is an interval for relaxation of not less than one hour, or after a spell of less than 5 hours, such interval as may be reasonable in all the circumstances;

(e) unless in every seven days he is allowed one day's rest.

No. 10 (1) The proprietor of every industrial undertaking shall keep a register of the young persons employed in such undertaking.

(2) Such register shall be in the form and contain the particulars shown in Appendix I to these bylaws.

Bylaws dealing with the prevention of accidents and notification of accidents, and the prevention of and escape from fire are also included which empower the Protector to require the provision of fire escapes in any factory in which more than twenty persons are employed and prohibit a tenement factory or workshop to be situated above a dangerous goods store. The question of tenement factories will be dealt with later.

It will be observed that these bylaws give effect to the provisions of certain conventions of the International Labour Office such as Convention No. 4 concerning the employment of women during the night; Convention No. 5 fixing the minimum age for admission of children to industrial employment; Convention No. 6 concerning the night work of young persons employed in industry; Convention No. 41 concerning the employment of women during the night; and Convention 45 concerning the employment of women on underground work in mines of all kinds.

Other conventions are given effect to by separate ordinances — Convention No. 26, concerning the creation of minimum wage fixing machinery, by Ordinance No. 28 of 1932, the Minimum Wage Ordinance, which empowers the Governor in Council to fix a minimum wage for any occupation in which he is satisfied that the wages paid are unreasonably low. To conduct any necessary inquiry a Board of Commissioners consisting of five persons may be appointed. Up to date no such Board has been appointed and no minimum wage fixed. Convention No. 7, fixing the minimum age for admission of children to employment at sea, is given effect to by the Employment of Young Persons and Children at Sea Ordinance No. 13 of 1932, which restricts the employment of children under fourteen years of age to vessels where only members of the same family are employed, or to junks or sampans where the child is placed in the charge of an approved relative who is also a member of the crew. The registration of members of crews who are under sixteen is required.

...

In the factories and workshops registered there is an estimated total of 28,470 male and 26,220 female workers, making in all a total of 54,690.

These figures of course only cover a portion of the labouring population. Apart from those engaged in fishing, agriculture, and domestic service, there are large numbers of casual workers, such as coal coolies and stevedores and street hawkers, licensed and unlicensed, and the innumerable fokis to be found in every shop who often work for little more than their board and lodging. The number of licensed hawkers was 16,087 in 1936, 13,211 in 1937, and 11,722 in 1938. An itinerant hawker's license costs four dollars per annum. Many have been paid for from the poor box at the magistracies as a form of relief to the infirm and aged. The decrease does not represent a diminution in the number of hawkers, but merely in the number of those licensed. In 1938 as a result of the influx of refugees there were probably five unlicensed hawkers for every licensed one.

Most of the labour employed in factories other than shipyards is on a direct basis, skilled labour being frequently employed at monthly rates and unskilled on piece work. This is a rough generalization only as one can find skilled labour on piece work and unskilled on time work. Some factories pay a fixed wage with a bonus on production. Coolie labour in building construction and road making is paid by the day. The shipyards retain a certain number of skilled men on a permanent basis, but the major part of ship-building and repairing is let out to contractors. Although the Hong Kong Mines at Lin Ma Hang employ all labour direct, the Marsman Mine at Needle Hill engages its labour through a labour contractor. Coal bunkering and transporting coal and stevedoring in general are let out to contractors. Sub-contracting is rampant in building construction, reclamations, and any scheme which involves the employment of large numbers of coolie labour.

Within limits there are certain advantages in the system as in shipyards where there is no constant amount of work and the labour contractor may be able to switch his men from one job here to another there as occasion demands, and to tide them over periods of unemployment with free food and lodging, but it becomes vicious in building construction where it is not a question of splitting a contract among several sub-contractors but of subletting a whole contract through several intermediaries who all take their profit until the actual contractor who does the work may receive so little that he scamps his work or goes bankrupt and is unable to pay his labourers. The standard form of Public Works Department contract contains a clause forbidding the subletting or assignment of a contract or any portion of it without the consent of the engineer, but it is to be feared that in practice this is seldom adhered to.

Labour trouble in connexion with the construction of the catchments at Shing Mun Valley investigated by the writer were found to be due to the sub-contracting system under which payment to the actual labourer was constantly in arrears and frequently deficient.

The chief vice in the sub-contracting system is the excessive commission drawn by the contractor. A recent petition from certain ricksha coolies in Kowloon, who complained that the charge for which rickshas were hired to them by the day had been increased, disclosed, on investigation, the existence of certain sub-contractors who hired the rickshas at forty five to fifty cents a day each and sublet them at seventy-five to eighty cents a day. This parasitic growth is being eliminated and action is being taken to control the rate at which contractors, who license their ricksha with the Police Department, hire them to the individual coolies.

Another questionable feature of local labour is the apprentice system which was adversely criticized by the 1921 Commission and since then has undoubtedly decreased with the elimination of child labour in industrial undertakings. While there are genuine apprentices learning their trades as in the dockyards, the system is frequently an excuse to obtain cheap labour in return for little or no wages but with the provision of food and lodging. Several years' apprenticeship may be demanded in what would appear to be largely an unskilled trade, the secrets of which could be mastered in a month. The apprentice system is for boys what the 'mui-tsai' system is for girls. It extends into domestic labour where a cook may require a 'makee-learn' to do his work for him.

It may safely be said that the employment of child labour in factories in the Colony has been eradicated, although an occasional child may still be found who has wandered in to be near his mother. In 1938 there was only one prosecution for employing children under fourteen years of age.

The employment of children, however, even to the early hours of the morning as pages and bell boys (or girls) in local hotels persists, and children are still employed to carry the paraphernalia in Chinese funeral processions. Legislation to extend the prohibition of child labour now in force in factories (age 14), in domestic service (age 12), and at sea (age 14), to all employments would not cover the many child hawkers and newspaper sellers who throng the streets: no one could be proved to 'employ' them. One form of child labour, the carrying of building material, has practically disappeared in recent years with the extension of roads and the development of motor transport.

Little is known for lack of investigation concerning the conditions of outworkers, such as seamstresses and the women and girls who stitch the canvas uppers of rubber shoes.

Conditions in factories vary considerably from those approximating to a garden city as at the Hume Pipe Company at Tsun Wan and the Hong Kong Brewery further along the coast, where the employees are excellently housed and provided with hot and cold baths, to converted tenements in what are little better than urban slums where few or no amenities are provided for the workers.

One of those inspected, a tailoring establishment, was so overcrowded that one male worker engaged in ironing was found suspended from the roof on a beam with his ironing board suspended in front of him. Conditions in printing establishments and in many Chinese newspapers, most of which are concentrated in old property in the central district of Hong Kong, are generally bad.

DOCUMENT IV.d4: Overcrowding reconsidered (source: Report of the Housing Commission, 1935, (published 11 October 1938), pp. 17-18)

In the 1931 Census Report the population for Hong Kong and Kowloon is given as 654,715. Of these, 304,664 are single, (both sexes) 189,502 are married men, 131,369 married women and the remaining 29,180 are almost all widowed. Taking the normal family as consisting of father, mother and children, with 131,369 married women, it might be taken that that would represent the maximum possible number of families. Many of the married men and some of the women have their wives or husbands and families living in the country. It is natural to presume that this would apply mainly to married men, of whom there is a surplus of 58,133 over married women. If it be assumed that 20% of the married women are living alone (a rather generous percentage) then the remaining 80% or 105,095 may be assumed to be living with their families. In other words, it seems reasonable to assume that there are round about 100,000 families requiring accommodation. The latest building returns show that there are, at present, about 75,000 tenement floors in Victoria and Kowloon. On the basis of one family per floor there is thus a shortage of about 25,000 floors or, approximately, 8,000 three storied tenements. Since the Census was taken in 1931 it is estimated that the population in Victoria and Kowloon has increased to about 750,000, an increase of 15%. Presumably, the number of families has increased in the same proportion. At the present time therefore a reasonable estimate of the number of families is say between 100,000 and 110,000 and the shortage of accommodation between 25,000 and 35,000 flats. If the widowed and single be taken as divided equally amongst the families, the average size of families would be six.

If the shortage of flats is to be made up, it is highly desirable that these new dwellings conform more nearly than do the present tenements, with the needs and circumstances of prospective tenants. They should provide for family life, for an average family of about six and the rent must, on average, not exceed $5 per month per family. Where poverty is the main factor to be dealt with minimum permissible standards are apt to become maximum possible provision. Present and possible standards therefore need careful consideration.

The question of overcrowding is dependent to a great extent on unit of occupation adopted or implied. The Hong Kong ordinances do not cater for the family as a unit; nor do they give any consideration to the question of the sex separation. The overcrowding standard is based on so many square feet of floor space and so many cubic feet of air space per person. Given sufficient floor and air space any number of people, regardless of sex, may occupy one room. Applied to the normal tenement each floor of which is capable of accommodating 10 or 12 persons, and in many cases more, then, provided those numbers are not exceeded, then the 75,000 floors can accommodate 750,000 to 900,000 people and there is no housing shortage. The fallacy is obvious. It would be quite impossible to distribute the population evenly among the available houses. Family ties would frustrate any attempt to do so.

In England family usage is recognized, as the overcrowding standards, whilst laying down minimum requirements per person, also lay down the number per room for sleeping purposes according to the size of the room, with a maximum of two persons per room, however big. In addition, the standards fix the number of people who can use a house for sleeping purposes, according to the number of habitable rooms in the house. Whilst the wording of the law refers only to persons, its provisions are based on the use of the dwelling for normal family purposes. The Hong Kong ordinances completely ignore family life amongst a people whose regards for family ties is [sic] probably stricter than that of any other nation in the world. By English standards the normal tenement floor would only permit of four adult persons living in it; i.e., less than one average family. By Hong Kong standards two normal families can occupy one floor without overcrowding. Poverty frequently compels more than two families to share a floor.

For an ordinary family it is highly desirable that parents should have a room to themselves and that there should be separate rooms for adult children of each sex. For a family of six therefore three rooms would normally be required. It is preferable that the living room should not be used for sleeping purposes but, to obtain the lowest possible rents, this double use cannot be avoided. Whilst the living room should be larger than the remainder, it is essential that it should not be so large that, to make full use of its as a sleeping chamber, the mixing of sexes would result. Children under ten years of age normally count as half an adult. A room designed to accommodate three adults could therefore be used by the parents and two children under ten years old. In a family of six the remaining two children could have a room each or if both under ten or of the same sex could share a room and leave one vacant for letting off to a lodger. For the sake of economy the combined area of the three rooms should be as near as possible to the minimum area required by law for the whole family.

DOCUMENT IV.d5: The dumping of the dead (source: Hong Kong Government, Administrative Report for the Year 1937, p. 9)

To avoid paying burial fees, and, in the case of infectious disesases, to evade the cleaning of their houses by the Health Authorities, the poorer members of the Chinese community continued to dump dead bodies in the streets. In 1937 the Police found 1,353 of these bodies.

DOCUMENT IV.d6: Towards subsidized housing, 1938 (source: Report of the Housing Commission, 1935, pp. 3-6)

A Commission 'to enquire into the housing difficulties in Victoria and Kowloon with special reference to overcrowding and its effect on tuberculosis and suggest steps which should be taken to remedy existing conditions' was appointed by Sir William Peel under the Proclamation dated 10th May, 1935.

Hong Kong is a powerful magnet drawing to itself not only the seekers after work but hangers-on and parasites of all kinds. The struggle for existence is very severe. It is only too common, especially amongst unskilled labourers, to find three men doing the work of one and sharing remuneration which might be adequate for one but is certainly insufficient for three; while the regular employee is fortunate if he is not maintaining a number of relatives out of his earnings.

The system of contracting and sub-contracting is often carried to extreme lengths, and results, in many instances, in the inability of the final sub-contractor to pay even the low wages on which he has based his contract.

Still more reprehensible is the system by which individuals or organizations levy commission in return for introduction to employment, or exact blackmail in the guise of 'fees for protection against competition'.

Conceivably the various systems by which the proceeds of every piece of work tend to filter through to the largest possible number of individuals might be regarded as an elementary form of practical socialism, without which the even more serious problem of complete unemployment of a large part of the population would have to be faced. We believe that there is no escape from one problem or the other so long as an enormous reservoir of population exists at our door, unless it is a remedy which presents very serious difficulties, namely, restriction of immigration.

For these reasons we do not believe that any measures which can reasonably be taken can, in the immediate future, have any noticeable effect on the problem of overcrowding, the problem which we were primarily appointed to consider. We consider, however, that some action is possible which, even if it will not altogether put a stop to overcrowding may eventually reduce its proportions and at least would improve the hygienic conditions of premises, even though they be overcrowded.

Our investigations have led us to certain conclusions regarding the causes of overcrowding and the conditions which are essential, if overcrowding is to be alleviated, and improved housing accommodation provided for the masses. Our conclusions are:-

(i) Overcrowding arises almost entirely from poverty which in Hong Kong is so dire that many families cannot afford any rent at all, and that, of the remainder, the majority can afford so little rent that a normal interest rate on capital outlay for housing cannot be obtained. Poverty itself is the result of an economic system over which Government has little or no control. Any attempt to alleviate overcrowding and improve housing must abide by the conditions imposed by that system.

(ii) For a great number of the population the rents which can be afforded vary from nothing to a maximum of abut $7.50 per month per family.

(iii) For those who can afford between $4.00 and $7.50 per month, it appears feasible under reasonably favourable conditions to provide improved housing without loss.

(iv) The existing standard types of tenement houses, which have been evolved from the use of the China fir pole, are now uneconomical in design and in many details of construction, and the plan is not adapted for family life under existing conditions of poverty. In consequence overcrowding, primarily due to poverty, is accentuated by the system of subletting which arises from accommodation not properly adapted to the needs and circumstances of the population.

(v) Under present circumstances it is not practicable to enforce the law against overcrowding.

(vi) To reduce overcrowding and permit the law to be enforced it is essential (a) to provide more and better designed houses until sufficient accommodation is available, (b) to decentralize the population, (c) to reduce building density.

(vii) Decentralization cannot be achieved unless means of livelihood are provided within easy reach of new housing areas.

(viii) The bulk of Chinese industries are of the 'home' variety. Factories, however, are being established in increasing numbers, but at present the majority of the concerns are small and cannot afford to build their factories in undeveloped areas. They are therefore competing with householders and housebuilders for premises and sites for their factories and tending to increase the prevailing congestion.

(ix) Before factories can be established outside the populated districts certain requirements must be fulfilled. They include the provision of public services such as water supply, light and power supply, drainage and sewage disposal, adequate communications and houses for their employees. These requirements should, if possible, be fulfilled in advance of the erection of factories or at least there should be a guarantee that such provision will be made by the time the factories are ready to operate.

(x) At the present time there is a tendency for the factories to increase in size and number. If they be permitted to become established in the congested areas decentralization would be much more difficult and expensive. The cost may well be prohibitive. It is essential therefore that, in order to prevent further congestion in built-up areas, the establishment of factories in those areas should be strictly controlled and that every possible inducement should be offered to attract them to new areas to provide work for the decentralized population.

(xi) The provision of adequate housing for the poorer classes cannot be left to private enterprise unassisted. If the housing is to conform to acceptable standards the return on capital will not be sufficient to attract private enterprise; to put it another way, the return on capital normally expected by private enterprise can only be achieved by overcrowding in houses which are below acceptable standards. If new and improved housing be provided for these classes, it will be necessary to ensure supervision and provide social services on lines similar to those adopted in many European countries.

(xii) Slum clearance envisages reduced building density and reduced population density, and in consequence a large number of the present population will eventually have to be housed elsewhere. This accommodation must be available before slum clearance can be commenced.

(xiii) Before the actual clearance of slums can be undertaken, it will be necessary to prepare a survey of local industry and housing, each in relation to the other; to prepare a survey of existing buildings, particularly houses, in order to find the number and situation of those which do not conform to acceptable standards; to prepare a key plan as a guide to redevelopment as opportunity occurs; to survey sites and prepare plans for possible new developments; and to prepare legislation and devise machinery necessary to give effect to town planning and housing schemes. This preparatory work and eventually constructional work will take many years and some form of permanent authority will be necessary to organize, carry out and control such an undertaking.

(xiv) If the provision of working class housing and the clearance of slums be undertaken financial provision will be required for:-

(a) New housing, both in new and built-up areas, for those who can afford a small economic return.

(b) New housing for those who can only be housed at a loss.

(c) Compensation arising out of slum clearance.

(xv) Of the means of raising revenue for these purposes two which most immediately occur to mind are a loan or a special tax. A possible alternative is to raise revenue by the issue of 'Housing Shares' in the same way that, in commerce, capital is raised by issuing shares. The last method, if successful, would eliminate the sinking fund for amortization of loan. Should circumstances permit funds might be provided from general revenue. For compensation arising out of slum clearance this might be feasible, but the provision of new housing will involve the annual expenditure of large sums, which may be beyond the capacity of general revenue, on its present basis, to provide. The financial aspect needs further examination by specialists.

(xvi) If and when slum clearance be decided upon, it is highly desirable that progress should be subject to as little fluctuation as possible. This would involve a steady supply of funds.

(xvii) It is also desirable that, in order to combat the evil effects of overcrowding, parks should be provided. It is not suggested that these parks should be laid out and equipped for organized games, but that they should simply be open spaces in which the population can enjoy fresh air. They should be in or close to the congested areas and should be large enough to ensure that the air is purer than in the neighbouring streets. The provision of the King George V Playing Fields is a step in the right direction, but does not go far enough. There should be many more such parks.

In view of the foregoing conclusions we recommend:-

(i) That a permanent Town Planning and Housing Committee be formed to advise Government in town planning and housing matters.

(ii) That a permanent Town Planning and Housing Sub-Department of the Public Works Department be created to carry out the work mentioned.

(iii) That, when that preliminary work has been completed, it should be subject to review and criticism by an acknowledged expert from England.

(iv) That Government should encourage and, where necessary, assist the establishment, by charitable organizations, of 'settlements' in the slum areas.

(v) That Government should consider the erection of experimental quarters for their Asiatic employees. While the provision of these quarters will, in a small degree, increase the amount of available accommodation, their special value will lie in enabling experiments to be made with a view to devising a more satisfactory type of dwelling.

(vi) That Section 167 Sub-Section (3) of the Buildings Ordinance of 1935 be deleted, and the following two sub-sections be substituted:-

(3) The provisions of Sections and 116, so far as they relate to authorized architects, shall not apply in any case in which the Building Authority shall so decide.

(4) Buildings in accordance with type plans, approved under Regulations, prepared under the direction of the Governor in Council, and contained in Schedule O, may be erected in any part of the colony (*Note:* Schedule O will, presumably, be prepared by the Town Planning and Housing Committee).

(vii) That Government shall as soon as possible put forward proposals for the provision of parks in suitable areas.

CHAPTER FIVE

THE SECOND WORLD WAR AND THE JAPANESE OCCUPATION

The Second World War took Hong Kong by storm. China went into war in 1937, Guangzhou fell in 1938 and Hong Kong fell on Christmas Day 1941. The Japanese occupation government decided upon evacuating a substantial portion of the Hong Kong population. Those that remained remembered well the 'three years and eight months' that followed.

Being shelled came as the initial shock of war. Hong Kong had prepared for battle, but the British forces in Hong Kong could not have withstood the onslaught. Most civilian accounts of war experience recount the bombing from the air that began on 8 December. For three weeks, a state of seige continued. Eye witnesses recalled the anguish, the uncertainty, the sense of loss, that came with food shortage and lawlessness. By the time Hong Kong surrendered, many people might have breathed a sigh of relief.

The events of the Japanese occupation are still a largely unwritten chapter of Hong Kong history. At present, the documents appear as snippets. Hong Kong's rice supply before the war had come substantially from Southeast Asia; it would seem that continuation of war in Southeast Asia might have brought on the shortages that led to the policy of evacuation. Among the population that remained, civilian nationals of those countries that were at war with Japan were kept in internment camps, while the Chinese population eked out a living in wartime circumstances. Some trade went across the border: second-hand clothes were smuggled into China as food was sent into Hong Kong. The East River Guerrillas were active in the New Territories, but did not make an impact on the urban areas.

Chinese voluntary associations such as the Tung Wah Hospital and the Po Leung Kuk continued to provide charity relief. Substantial donations were given by members of the Chinese elite. It is less clear how under the Japanese occupation these associations might have served as channels of social mobility.

> Many in Hong Kong did not lose hope that the occupation would come eventually to an end. The best example of this subdued optimism was possibly exhibited by the few men in the Stanley Internment Camp who prepared a postal stamp to be used upon the recovery of Hong Kong. At the end of August 1946, the stamp designed in the camp was used for the commemoration of the end of the war.

a. War Experience

DOCUMENT V.a1: The outbreak of war in China to 1941 (source: *Xianggang bainian* (A hundred years of Hong Kong) Hong Kong, 1941, pp. 60-62.)

The Sino-Japanese War broke out in the 26th year of the Republic, that is, 1937. The fire of war was lit suddenly at the Marco Polo Bridge, and Japanese aeroplanes bombed civilians all over China. From the beginning of war, Hong Kong became a haven for people escaping from disaster, and the consequences that followed were many. Therefore, from the outbreak of the war it was affected, and war brought about serious consequences.

Because many refugees escaped to this place from the mainland, the population of Hong Kong increased wildly. In Hong Kong, the residential areas were quite limited, and immediately there was a shortage of housing. Many landlords raised their rent as a result. A flat that used to cost ten dollars had its rent raised first by several tens of dollars, and thereafter to over a hundred dollars. Moreover, rent was raised time and again. So, the first consequence brought by the war to Hong Kong was a wave of rent increases.

The rent increases were not only imposed on new houses. Many incumbent residents also felt the pressure. When the landlords repeatedly demanded increases in rent, if tenants did not accept the increases, they had to move out . . . [sic].

Both residents and refugees were oppressed by the landlords in their effort to find shelter. They suffered pain beyond words. Moreover, there were rascals, who, in order to make a profit, monopolised the rental market in order to demand key money, took over houses that they would let out only at the highest fee, or who became secondary landlords and sublet. Many bad practices followed, and residents were put to more pain.

In this situation, the Residents' Association was born. It opposed the many exploitations of . . . [sic], and much social turbulence was created. Only when the Hong Kong government had issued its regulations to prevent eviction did the situation calm down.

After the wave of eviction, house rents in the whole of Hong Kong had reached a new level. A room that was barely enough to hide one's knees cost over a hundred dollars. People who had less money found it hard to pay that, and the poor had to live on the street or in refugee camps. The ranks of the lower social classes increased daily.

As war broke out in Bao'an county and refugees rushed into the New Territories, the problems of population and housing became even more serious. The Hong Kong government then set up eight refugee camps in the New Territories, Kowloon and Hong Kong to house them. However, when the population still did not come under control, the Hong Kong government had to turn to the imposition of an immigration ordinance.

The local [Chinese] residents, by their nature, are patriotic. When war broke out, the patriotism exhibited by the overseas Chinese became even more concrete. They carried out many impressive deeds. Most obviously, many organizations were set up to carry out patriotic work. The Chinese Chamber of Commerce, as the largest organization among Chinese people in Hong Kong, first set up the Chinese Merchants' Relief Association. After that, many professions set up their own relief associations, all calling for contribution towards relief.

Among women, the first organization that was formed was the Women's Concern Association. After that, there was the Women's Military Disaster Association, and then the Chinese Women's Association. These three organizations were tireless in their work, and together with the already existing New Women's Movement Association, the Y.W.C.A. and the local branch of the Shanghai Women's Frugality Association, became the six organizations which advanced this work on an established footing.

Ambulance units were also formed, and many relief associations sprang up. The work of local residents became more prominent.

Much of the work that was done was limited to fund raising. There were many ways for doing that, including dinner-and-dance parties, goods sales, drama, flower sales. Local residents were not slow in exerting their generous spirit; even dancing girls offered charity dances, and street hawkers, charity sales. Their warmth was admirable. As it was said, young and old, rich and poor, could all be patriotic. Residents in Hong Kong well deserved this claim.

As Hong Kong was on the coast of south China, when the war spread to south China, Hong Kong itself was affected by the blockade set up directly or indirectly by the Japanese military. For this reason, all industries and trades in Hong Kong were adversely affected.

Hong Kong was a port that looked towards the outside. It did not produce very much. Thus, when overseas transport was blocked, food became a problem. When the Japanese military attacked south China, trade from both the East and West Rivers was interrupted. Transport between Hong Kong and the mainland was not totally stopped, but the volume of goods sent over here dropped. Moreover, because Japanese military actions also affected port activities in Hong Kong and Vietnam, interruptions were also frequent. Food transport to Hong Kong was intermittent, and prices in Hong Kong escalated.

The price escalation experienced in Hong Kong in these few years was unprecedented. Rice used to cost one dollar for several ten catties, but, by this time, fewer than ten catties might be had. Ordinary green vegetables were sold at as high a price as 20 or 30 cents a catty on the market. There was little fish, and its price was twenty times what it had been five or ten years earlier. Clothing material also became very expensive. In the fourth year of the war, the price of woollen cloth was twice what it had been before the war.

The Hong Kong government imposed regulations on the control of food supply. An official was put in charge of such control. It actively developed agriculture in the New Territories, including the islands, such as Lantau or Cheung Chau. These measures were ineffective, and so they brought the jeer that they were very distant water for a nearby fire.

Because many people came from the mainland, Hong Kong became a cultural centre for mainland culture. When Shanghai fell, many Shanghai scholars fled to Hong Kong and started a new leaf in Hong Kong's culture. The number of newspapers and magazines published increased daily, and this was beneficial to popularizing education.

Moreover, many schools from the mainland moved to Hong Kong. Branches were set up in Hong Kong by the universities, such as the Guangzhou University, the People's University, or the Lingnan University. There were more primary and secondary schools than one might enumerate. At the time, there were schools all over Hong Kong.

The fees charged at these schools were quite high. Many Hong Kong people subjected to increasingly high prices could not afford to send their children to school, and so many children from poor families could not receive education. Refugee children, naturally, had even less of a chance to go to school. So enthusiastic people set up charity schools. These schools were overwhelmingly welcomed in Hong Kong, and many more were established than there had ever been.

DOCUMENT V.a2: War experience (source: Anon. 'An account from memory of my escape from the fire of war', manuscript*)

An account from memory of my escape from the fire of war

I have heard that it is a natural cycle that when things reach their extremes they retreat, and when things reach their most prosperous they decline.

Hong Kong was a barren island leased to Britain in the twentieth year of the Daoguang reign, which was the year 1840, when China sought peace by conceding land after losing the war in the Pearl River that had arisen from the opium issue. The British people developed this barren island into a commercial port. It was the only port in the south of China. It was grand and very beautiful. After the conclusion of the First World War, when all countries lived peacefully, Hong Kong became very prosperous. Its population increased to 800,000 or 900,000.

---

* This manuscript was discovered by Dr James Hayes at a second-hand book store in Hong Kong. It is now deposited at the Hoover Institution, Stanford.

I returned to China from Cuba in North America in 1928. I saw Hong Kong's prosperity, and, in contrast, disorder from soldiers and bandits on the mainland, and so I took my family to settle peacefully in Hong Kong. In September 1932, I left my family in Hong Kong and returned to Cuba to make my living. In January 1934 I wound up my business and returned from Cuba to Hong Kong to live with my family. In February 1935, I set up the Wah Shing Lung Company at No. 29 Tung Man Street in Central District to deal in industrial dyes. I was quite gratified. In 1936 [sic], that is the twenty-sixth year of the Republic, after the Sino-Japanese War broke out at the Marco Polo Bridge incident, the population of Hong Kong increased from 800,000 or 900,000 people to 1,800,000. Hong Kong was such a small island; with so many people, it was very prosperous indeed.

In September 1939, Britain, France and Germany declared war. Prices rose in every country and Hong Kong businesses reaped large profits. Wealthy merchants did not care to dream of life or death. They drank by the day and sang and danced all night, keeping the lights on until morning. On 23rd June, 1941, Germany and the Soviet Union declared war on each other. The world was at war. Anyone who had foresight and knowledge could anticipate that Hong Kong would not be spared from war. It was only a matter of time. But I did not expect the Empire of Japan to declare war on Britain and the United States of America on the nineteenth day of the tenth month in the year of San Tzi by the agrarian calendar.

The people of Hong Kong were fast asleep. The next day, that is 8th December, 1941, or 20th of the Tenth Month by the Agricultural Calendar, at 7.30 in the morning, Japanese planes suddenly attacked Hong Kong. I was just awake and had risen from bed to go to the toilet. Suddenly I heard the air siren and the sound of gun-fire. I came out of the toilet and went into the sitting room. My family were all frightened. I told them this was only an exercise and that they did not have to fear. After a short while, I heard the sound of bombing that was like thunder. I went out to the verandah, saw people running about in fear in the street and the air-raid wardens having been mobilised. I raised my eyes to the sky and saw Japanese planes about in the air, their silver wings reflecting a blinding glare from the sun but showing the red sun insignia on the underside. I dared not tell my family the truth for fear of adding fear upon fear. Later, Hung Nung-cheung came to visit and said that the barracks in Shamshuipo had been bombed. Then I went immediately to the Shamshuipo pier, intending to take a boat to get back to the shop. But boats were not sailing. I went to Mongkok, but no boats were sailing from there either. So I went to the Universal Metalworks Co. There, my brother-in-law Wong Pak-ho said to me that the night before Japan had declared war on the United States and Britain. . .I telephoned the shop and asked about the current situation. Hung Hau answered the phone and said it was quiet on the street and that business was going on as usual. He also said the *South China Morning Post* had reported that morning that Britain and the United States had declared war. After that, I wanted to take the boat from Yaumati to return to the shop. My brother-in-law Wong Pak-hung said if I wanted to cross the harbour, I would have to go to the Y.M.C.A. in Tsimshatsui to ask for special permission for a pass before I could get to the boat for

Hong Kong. I thought that as I was not a member of that organization, and I did not have friends there, it must be difficult to do that. So I gave up. However, because I did not have a cent on me, and now that no end was in sight for the war that had started, I asked Wong Pak-ho for the loan of one hundred dollars in case of emergency. I quickly went to the Universal to purchase two Wai-mei kerosene lamps. Halfway home, Japanese planes came again to bomb. I took shelter in a staircase and quickly went home when the alarm had ceased. However, I saw that in the war situation, with so many children, I had to have some food ready. So I went to the Garden Biscuit Co., and bought some cream crackers and tinned food. As I was going home, I saw people fighting to purchase rice. The place was very crowded. The police had come out to maintain order. Only then did I remember we did not have much rice at home. It was rumoured that Kai Tak Airport had been entirely destroyed by the bombs. I looked up and saw that in the distance, black smoke went up to the sky and did not disperse for a long time. So I took the food home, had dinner and slept till midnight when the air raid siren woke me. When I heard the sound of aeroplanes, I quickly got out of bed and went with my family down the stairs to take shelter in the Shun Tak Co. At the time, the wind was cold and pierced into the bones. It was a pitiful situation. People were trembling and had nothing to say. This was the first time in my life I had experienced something like this. I was full of emotions. After almost two hours, the alarm stopped. My family went back upstairs so as not to disturb our friends and relatives.

The next day, that is 9th December, 1941, 21st day of the Twelfth Month by the agricultural calendar, at 8.00 a.m. when we were just about to have breakfast, the air raid siren sounded again. The humming of the planes came once more. Fortunately, they did not bomb this place: they were going after military targets and did not pay attention to where the civilians were. The Japanese planes scattered leaflets, telling people to move a hundred yards away from military installations. They told them not to be afraid, for the war was waged to drive the white people out of Asia so that the new East Asian order might be established and this had nothing to do with the Chinese overseas. At 11, the alarm stopped and I went with my family upstairs to have our breakfast. Even if we had been eating the finest food, I could not have swallowed it. My eldest son, Chen-tai, perhaps understood a little of what was happening and was somewhat afraid. But my second son, Chuen-chung, and my third son, Chuen-hau, did not understand anything of the world and so they ate as usual. My fourth son, Chuen-sheng, was still being nursed. He was just about learning to say a few words and he was as playful as usual. Sometimes he came into my arms saying 'papa' and I forced myself to give him a smile. In reality, my mind was all confused at the time; I did not know what to do. I thought about my hard-earned savings that had come from my working beyond the hills and oceans overseas, my aspirations to return to the home country and now residing in Hong Kong, thinking that this might be a place for the peaceful life that would allow me to keep my family until the end of my years. Now to my surprise the god of war had descended so quickly, and I had been caught totally unprepared. The day before the war broke out, I came home empty-handed; so, at present, I had no money and no rice. I could not have imagined that the situation could be so bad. Moreover, my age was coming on, my children were small, and we did not know how the war was going to end. When I thought about all this, my grief came from my heart and tears welled up in my eyes. I looked at my family and could not say a word.

After that, I comforted myself, realizing that the present situation was a situation of a national disaster, an international situation, not one that affected me alone. In this world war, no city on earth was having peace, so how could Hong Kong? As people might say, this was a disaster I could not run away from. Although untalented, I did anticipate that, even though I had not expected it to have come so quickly.... I could honestly say that in my dealings with people, I had no competition with anybody. I could hope that the Heavens might protect me and that by being fortunate people we might, with Heaven's help, get out of this misfortune. We might even come clear of it safely. When I thought of this, I could put down my sorrows, and so as not to tire myself out, I went into the street to see if I could pick up some news.

I ran into Old Wan, an acquaintance. He said he was going to the Westerners' Y.M.C.A. to get a ferry pass and I thought I would take the opportunity to take him there. Just as we wanted to go to the bus stop at the end of the street to take the bus, the Japanese planes came again. The alarm sounded, I looked up at the sky, saw the planes and heard the humming. The guns rumbled, people on the street ran about to escape. Old Wan and I parted and went home. After about two hours, the alarm stopped. I went over next door to the Mau Shang Lung Tea Co. to telephone Universal Metals to ask what one had to do to get a ferry pass from the Westerners' Y.M.C.A. Pak-ho said in reply that it was very difficult, and told me not to waste time by going. He also said the war was getting quite threatening. I also called the shop to see what was happening. Hung Hau said things were peaceful, but on the island all the shops had closed. In any case, no business was being done. So I told him to keep calm and not to be so frightened as to get all into a mess. Hung Hau said, 'yes, yes.'

I put down the phone and went home. Hung Nung-cheung had come to visit and we sat there and talked about the current situation. I told him I had no money with me at home but only the key to my safe and wondered what I could do. He said he had a friend who worked for the government who could go freely to Hong Kong, and he asked me to give him the key of the safe so his friend could take it to Hong Kong to give to Hung Hau. He said he was sure that would be all right. I thought about it carefully but realized there was nothing else I could do and so gave him three keys. Hung Nung-cheung departed. The air raid siren went off again. Five to six air raids came on that day; we could hardly seek shelter for there were so many of them.

I was a little bored sitting at home and wanted to go to Mongkok for a walk. Having decided on that, I went out, went down Laichikok Road and turned into Shanghai Street. Soon, I had reached Tung Cheung Hing Metalworks. I thought they owed my shop several hundred dollars in unsettled accounts, and although war had broken out and business had stopped, with some good feelings I might still be able to get a favour out of them. So I went into the shop and saw the owner Chan Cheung. I spoke sweetly to him about my request, and Chan immediately gave me a hundred dollars. I was very grateful and departed.

Then I went to Universal Metalworks. Pak-ho said to me that America, San Francisco, New York, Washington, Hawaii, the Philippines and Singapore were all being bombed from the air by the Axis powers. This was a real world war, not one that would be settled soon. In any case, we had to have ready some firewood and rice.... But this had taken me by surprise and I was totally unprepared with food in the shop or at home. I said I did not know what to do. Pak-ho said, 'Yesterday, I got six bags of rice from Chung Sai Wing Co. They will deliver today, and . . . I can let your family have one to two bags. As for the shop, please call them on the phone and tell Hung Hau to quickly buy more rice.' My brother-in-law Pak-ho was really someone I could trust. I was truly grateful to him. I called the shop, and Hung Hau said that Uncle Yu-pui had bought two bags of rice on their behalf which would be delivered that day. I thought that was quite definite, but unfortunately because the situation was getting very tense, too many people were trying to buy rice, order was very bad and so the rice shops had stopped working. I told him about the safe key. He said Hung Nung had already gone to the shop. Hung Nung went to the phone and spoke to me. I was very surprised and asked him how he managed to cross the harbour. Hung Nung said . . . So I told him to ask Hung Hau for three hundred dollars to take back for my family so we could buy some rice. He agreed. So I talked to Pak-ho about what was said on the phone and then I went home. By 5.00 Hung Nung-cheung had returned from Hong Kong with the money. When I got the money, I felt more settled and less worried than before.

After dinner, because of the confusion of the war, I decided not to go out but to go to bed early for some rest. At midnight, the anti-air raid siren sounded again. I woke up from my dreams and my family wanted to go downstairs to take shelter. Having seen the leaflets that the Japanese military had distributed telling people not to run away in fear, I told my family that they did not have to seek shelter. Moreover, it was midnight and very cold, and so they did not go away and we slept till the next morning, which was the third day after the outbreak of war, 11th December by the Western calendar, and the 23rd day of the Tenth Month by the agricultural calendar.

At eight o'clock in the morning when we were getting ready for breakfast, the air raid siren went off and the Japanese planes had come round again. Because my family had little courage, I had no choice but to go downstairs with them to seek shelter. We went back upstairs when the alarm had stopped.

After breakfast, Hung Nung came to say that he was crossing the harbour to go to Hong Kong to collect some money from the Bank of Canton. As I had little money on me, and did not know when the war was going to end, I thought it would be a good idea if I could give him my little seal to take to Hung Hau to collect five hundred dollars at the Bank of East Asia to buy food for the family and the shop. I thought carefully about this, made up my mind and entrusted him with my little seal to take over to Hong Kong. I thought Hung Nung would have been able to go and return in one day. But the war continued to be very intense and so he could not return to Shamshuipo. I went to Universal to see if there was any news; Pak-hung said to me that he had heard that Tsuenwan had already fallen and that British troops were withdrawing to Kowloon. Pak-ho said Japanese troops using rubber boats were preparing to land that night at Cheungshawan. When I heard that, I went into a panic. I immediately called the shop on the telephone to ask what the situation was like, and if Hung Nung had come over to the shop. Hung Hau said in answer that he had not seen Hung Nung, but the situation was very tense. The police had gone over to say that they should disperse. But the workers in the shop had no intention of going elsewhere. By then, I knew that the British had lost and that Hong Kong and Kowloon were in danger. What could one do?

Immediately, I left the Universal and braved the danger to go home. Halfway there, the air raid sirens sounded again. I looked up and saw three Japanese planes. People on the street were running about. I chose a firm-looking staircase and took shelter. Suddenly, I saw on Laichikok Road a car fitted with an anti-aircraft gun and three gunners coming from afar firing at the Japanese planes. Without my knowing, I had put myself into the war zone. It was a very dangerous situation, and as people might say, one ran for it. So immediately I went along Pak Yeung Street to go home. I took a rest when I got home, and shortly after that I went out onto the verandah. I saw that people on the street were all in fear. I looked up towards Wong Chuk Street and saw two young women stopped by ruffians. They were body-searched and robbed. They had to take even the shoes on their feet off. . . .This was quite frightening.

At that time, I was sure Pak-hung was right about the British withdrawing to Kowloon, even though I did not know where he had found out. This was why the ruffians were so blatant. I went downstairs to go to Mau Shang Lung Tea Co. to see if I could hear anything. The owner of Mau Shang Lung, Wong Shiu, said to me that in the morning the British troops had retreated to Hong Kong Island. As the Japanese had not yet arrived, the world belonged to the ruffians.

I did not know what to do and so I went home. I was frightened and confused. From hereon, the ruffians were fiercer than ever on the street and screams became louder and louder. The wife and daughter-in-law of the resident on the first floor, Mui Yau-hong, came up to our door to ask us take pity on them by letting them in to take shelter. They had few people on their floor and were frightened that the ruffians might come up to harm them. I saw that it was a dangerous situation and so I firmly refused. My wife, woman Wong, begged me to save them on the grounds that they were good people living in the same building, and as these were women and children, there was no reason why they could do us any harm. As people might say, everyone has a sense of compassion, and so I let them in. But no sooner had I done that, Mui Yau-hong's son came to knock on my door to ask his wife, his mother and his children to go back downstairs to the first floor. I refused. This was a dangerous situation; how could we open the door so easily? But he said he had paid thirty dollars to some society for protection, and that I could let his family safely out. I was all confused and angry, blaming my wife for getting me into this mess. At the time, it was becoming noisier in the street. My family hid away our finer clothes and our rice, while my wife, seeing the situation, told Mui Yau-hong's son to arrange for me to join the society before we opened the door to let his family out. In a moment, Mui's son came back with several men who asked for a hundred dollars as admission money. They said they would write us a receipt which would give us protection. I said I would pay thirty, but they refused. They looked quite fierce. I realized that in this dangerous situation, under their coercion I had no room to manoeuvre. So, in the midst of a sense of pain, I told my wife to fetch a hundred dollars to hand over to these robbers, and they wrote us . . . Lee and Chiu kept the shop. . . . After that they left and went elsewhere.

It was night. Soon, someone came and knocked on my door again. I thought it was the ward captain and it was more likely to be bad news than good. But it was my clan-brother Lau Shing. I welcomed him in and noticed that he had come with a strong man whom I had not previously seen. Lau Shing introduced him to me as Leung somebody-or-other. He asked me for pen and paper and he wrote on a page '555 and three-three-four'. He told me to post that sheet of paper on the door, and said that if anyone wanted protection money, to say that we were all brothers and that they could go elsewhere to announce victory. He said there was no need to be afraid. I thanked him many times. Lau Shing and Leung left. I realized clan-brother Lau Shing bringing me help at this time was an uncalled-for favour. Such favours must be rare, and I should not ever forget it.

That night, the robbers came and went like the south wind. The whole city was robbed. Suddenly, you would hear from afar the cry of 'robbery', the noise of doors being broken down, or iron bars being cut. These noises were very frightening. I could not sleep, and sat there waiting for the morning. At midnight, all the electric lights went out. I was sitting on my bed with nothing to do, when I heard footsteps coming up the stairs, and people knocking on my door, shouting loudly 'Victory!' I knew what sort of people these were, and so I calmly opened the little peep-hole on the door. I saw several ruffians holding electric torches, shouting 'victory'. So I said to them that we were brothers and that they could shout 'victory' elsewhere. The ruffians said, 'You impersonate as our brother. What proof have you got?' So I told them about Lee and Chiu. Fortunately, my concubine, woman Lo, had some courage, and helped me. But there was one ruffian who would not stop. He kept speaking, and demanded two dollars before he left. These were really devils.

On the fourth day, that is 12th December by the Western calendar and 24th day of the Tenth Month by the agricultural calendar, British troops had lost all of Kowloon. The Japanese were in control and had set up their headquarters. However, they had little time to take care of the place . . . there were few troops on duty and so it was still a bandits' world. Rumours were all about. It was said that the people of a certain society were going to return tonight to this street. My wife was very worried and frightened, and asked the owner of Shun Tak downstairs to plead with the leader of this society, because the owner, Mak Chiu, had once met him. The leader wanted two hundred dollars from me before he would give me protection. I was prepared to give him a birthday present of fifty dollars, but he refused. Mak Chiu went back and forth several times and finally settled for seventy dollars for my protection. He wrote me a piece of paper ('Wo Shing Wo Hall') that I could post on my door for my safety. I knew that this so-called protection was really robbery. But in any case, because I had paid my money, the robbers did not enter my house. I heard that many people were robbed, even of their rice, their blankets and their clothes. In the midst of winter, some families were deprived of food and clothes. Readers, don't you think this is very sad!

I also heard what happened to the Tai-yik Pawnshop in Mongkok, that was worth more than a hundred thousand dollars. When the ruffians first appeared, the owner offered to pay a thousand dollars for protection, hoping that he would be safe. But they came again and again and finally all the goods were taken. These robbers were worse than tigers and wolves: they would eat all of you, bone and all. Before the war, the owner of Tai-yik was a rich man with a fortune of more than a hundred thousand dollars. He was dressed in fine clothes, he went around in a fine carriage, he was served by pretty women, and he was fed on good food. Now, he had become a hawker selling vegetables on the street, weeping whenever he came across people he knew to tell them of his disaster. How can there be such sorrow in the world! There might even be events that were more sad in this untold disaster.

On 13th December by the Western calendar, which was the 25th day of the tenth month by the agricultural calendar, the authorities had posted a notice to pacify the people. People in the district also saw Japanese troops on patrol. The bandits became more quiet and were less fierce than the day before. There were still some robberies, and we heard . . . .

On the 14th, which was the 26th day of the tenth month by the agricultural calendar, people organized self-protection units and called themselves members of hygiene committees. The situation became calmer. There were self-protection guardsmen on the streets, who wore white armbands and badges. They patrolled the place and maintained order, carrying sticks in their hands. The people became calmer. But there was panic over food. Although members of the self-government committee had in their enthusiasm asked the Japanese interior department for leniency and had bought a large supply of rice which they were selling at various stations to the people at 3 catties a dollar, it was supply enough only for four to five days. There were just too many mouths to feed. I sent my servant Ah Chai to go four times to the self-government rice station, and she bought altogether six catties of rice, at two dollars. For two days, she spent half a day waiting and came back empty-handed. There was a long queue, and some people waited all day without buying a grain of rice. It was very hard indeed. The food we had at home was being used up. One day, when I was just getting worried about it, my nephew Au Hua came to see me and asked if we had any rice. I told him it was getting used up. The next day, he went to Tsimshatsui, bought just over ten catties for ten dollars on my bahalf and brought it over. I thought that was praiseworthy of him, to be so helpful at his young age. Au Hua said to me that while he was in Tsimshatsui the day before, he saw a huge fire rising out of Central District. When I heard that, I thought of my staff at the Wah Shing Lung Store. I did not know if under aeroplane and gun fire they were dead or alive. I felt so uneasy I could hardly eat or sleep.

Two days later, not having anything to do at home, I went out onto the street. At Cheungshawan Road, I saw a passer-by with a liberation newspaper. I did not know him, but because I was worried about the shop, I asked him to lend it to me. I saw that in Central Market . . . . The news came to me like cold water being poured onto my back. . . .. I went home, and dropped into my bed, my grief coming straight from my heart and tears out of my eyes. I could not help myself, and I cried. My wife and my concubine did not know what to do. They could only tell me to look after myself. In my mind, I found it so sad that my life's savings were coming to such an end, and the employees in my shop losing their lives in this way. Heaven had not helped us! But then I thought the Central Market area was still a large place. It was still not clear where the bomb had dropped. That was not clear in the paper. If the bomb had been dropped on Victoria Street, it would have been beyond Tung Man Street. That might be frightening, but it would not have affected me. However, if the bomb had been dropped on Jubilee Street, Tung Man Street would have been affected.

Then I remembered that Hung Nung-cheung had taken my bank withdrawal seal on the 23rd day of the tenth month to Hong Kong to withdraw some money from the bank and had not yet returned. I did not know if he was still at the store or if he had been robbed and killed by robbers on the way. If the misfortune had taken place, it would not just mean his coming to a sorry end, but it would also mean bankruptcy for me. This is because he had my bank seal and if this was lost, I could not withdraw the money I had saved up in the Bank of East Asia or the house deeds that I had in its safe-deposit box. That whole night I could not sleep. The next morning, my wife burnt incense to Buddha Wong and asked for guidance, using the fortune-telling blocks and sticks. Fortunately, both the blocks and the sticks showed a good omen. They predicted that Wah Shing Lung, the employees and Hung Nung-cheung were all safe. I could only half believe this, but, as they might say, a propitious god does not lie to a man in misfortune. So I forced myself to eat some breakfast, and then I went out. I went to Tai Nam Street and went inside Fook Hing Dyes-store to talk about recent developments in the war. A friend said that the day before British troops used big cannon to shell Kowloon, and some shells fell on Yam Chau Street. At the time, a verandah fell and killed or wounded more than ten people. . . .

Then it was 23rd December by the Western calendar, or the 5th day of the eleventh month by the agricultural calendar. It was winter solstice. In former years, winter solstice was a festival. Every family and every shop would hold a feast, and people would enjoy themselves eating and drinking. Today, in the middle of this unfortunate war, with disaster looming above our heads, how could one think of a feast. But we were rearing a few fowl at home, and as rice was short, I thought we might as well take this opportunity to kill them for food and at the same time offer sacrifice to the deities to ask for an early peace in this war. At noon, while we were sacrificing to the deities, and my young child Chuen-sheng was in my arms, suddenly we heard the sound of gunfire. It sounded like a clap of thunder, frightening heaven and earth and shaking this house. It was so violent that my child started crying in fright. My family was all confused, not knowing where the frightening sound had come from. I quickly had my meal and then went out to find what news I could. I found out that the sound had come from a cannon that the British troops on Hong Kong Island had used to shoot a shell over here. The shell fell on the playground on Cheungshawan Road at our back. Immediatley, nineteen people were killed and ten people were wounded. This was because two gambling stores and a congee store were located there, and this coincidence gave rise to the casualty. After this frightening experience, I was forewarned. I felt that one could not be certain in the morning that one would still be living by night. Hong Kong Island and Kowloon were separated only by a stretch of water; with bombs flying in the sky, how could one feel safe? But one gained nothing by worrying about it, and one had to leave one's fate to heaven. The newspaper said that the day before, the Japanese commander had sent a peaceful mission to the British troops on the other side to ask them to surrender and they had refused. I thought this was very stubborn of the British; Kowloon having fallen, how could Hong Kong Island be held? All soldiers knew that when the lips had been cut the teeth would feel the cold.

I also heard that there was no water in Hong Kong. Each bottle of water sold for four to five dollars. So if people did not die from the bombs they would have died from thirst. Having no water was like having no food. It was also said that the Japanese had used rubber boats to land at Shaukiwan.

On 23rd December, which was 6th day of the eleventh month, I bought a copy of the *Hong Kong Daily* which said that from Shaukiwan the Japanese had taken Mount Cameron. Some people also said that the Japanese had taken Central and hundreds of thousands of people had been killed or wounded. These were rumours; I did not know if they were true. I was feeling frustrated at home when I heard the droning of aeroplanes. I went out to the verandah and saw across the sky three Japanese planes coming from Hong Kong. The white smoke from anti-aircraft guns had not yet dispersed. Upon a closer look, the white smoke seemed to have come from Central. That made me worry about the safety of my employees in the shop. They were in such danger! I was so sad that I wept.

It was 25th December by the Western calendar, or the 8th day of the eleventh month by the agricultural calendar, 7 p.m., the night of Christmas. Hong Kong Governor Yeung Mo-kei [Sir Mark Young] and commander-in-chief Major General Mo Yi-tat [Major General C.M. Maltby] voluntarily and unconditionally surrendered to Japanese troops. One might say this was the end to a hundred years' dream of prosperity. It was night, and people in Hong Kong did not yet know about it. The next morning, when I went downstairs, I ran into Mui Yau-hong's son on the first floor and he told me that the night before the English had surrendered to the Japnanese military and that fighting had stopped on both sides. I did not believe him immediately. I went along to Pak Ho Street and bought myself a copy of the *Hong Kong Daily* and there it was really reported that the English had surrendered to the Japanese troops the night before. I could somewhat put my mind at ease. I went home immediately and told my family the good news. My wife said, 'I couldn't sleep all night but did not hear the sound of any gun fire.' So it seemed that fighting had definitely stopped. . . .

The next day, I went up to the ferry pier on the waterfront and looked across the harbour. The atmosphere was restful and the water was calm. I thought about the busy traffic across the harbour in former days and contrasted it to the quietness. I looked around and realized that the war had caused a great deal of damage, that a dent had been made in the spirit of prosperity in Hong Kong, and wondered when it might recover. Amidst mixed feelings, my worries came and I went home. Had some breakfast and worried about the survival of the employees in my shop. I felt as if I had a load of a hundred catties put on me that I could not put down. So I went out again, walking along without spirit. I found myself on Shek Kip Mei Street. I saw a blind man, Law Yung, a fortune-teller who had a stall there, and I asked him to foretell my fortune. The blind man asked me what I wanted to know. I told him I wanted to know if my business at Wah Shing Lung and my employees had survived. The blind man then resorted to his tortoise shell several times. When he finished, he said to me that the omen was very good, but it fortold of slight changes. He said if my question had to do with people, they were unharmed; but if if it had to do with things, then there were slight losses. I thought the slight losses might mean that the goods I had in the shop were taken by robbers. But that was not so. I paid him ten cents and left, and I wandered about not quite knowing what I was doing. I wanted desperately for Hung Nung to come back and I wanted to write a letter and have someone take it to Hong Kong for Hung Hau. All these thoughts came to me, they were aggravating.

On 29th December by the Western calendar, which was the 12th day of the Tenth Month by the agricultural calendar, I was sitting in my sitting room feeling frustrated, and my eldest son Chuen-tai was on the verandah looking at passers-by in the street. He came in to say that he saw . . . . Hung Hau, Tung-sheng, Au Wah, carrying a bagful of rice and two bottles of oil, came into the sitting room. We all sat down and talked about what we went through in the war. I was both delighted and frightened. I was delighted because my employees had come through unharmed, and frightened because the warehouse of the Tung Yat Restaurant had been bombed and burnt. When I realized that the goods in the warehouse had been totally destroyed, and that several thousand dollars of my hard-earned capital had gone, I felt as if my heart was pierced through. I recalled what the blind man Lo Yung said the day before, and he was certainly very accurate. In this life, what we gain and lose is determined, and it must be heaven protecting us that has allowed us to live through all this disaster. Perhaps in future we will make a large fortune. Fortunately, Wah Shing Lung was safe, and so what we lost today we might regain tomorrow.

So we talked for a while. Hung Hau and Tung-sheng left. They wanted to go to Shun On Co. in Mongkok. Hung Nung wanted to go home. After this frightful experience, I felt more at peace with myself. I became less frustrated and worried. My only hope was that the new government would quickly put order into the new Hong Kong and that prosperity would return. This was my new hope.

The next day, Tung-shing came to say he could not return to Hong Kong because there had been a curfew. He said the Japanese authorities did not allow people to go back and forth.

Some days passed, and soon it was New Year's Day 1942 by the Western calendar. We heard that after the victory in Hong Kong, the Japanese troops had been given three days' holiday, and that they would have a good time. People here became quite frightened, fearing that the Japanese troops might be up to no good, looking for women

... Girls dared not go out, and good families took great care. The girls were frightened and dressed up like country women. But I knew all this was really worrying to no purpose. So I did not worry about it and we got through peacefully.

But there was a food shortage, which worsened day after day. After the war, ordinary rice cost a dollar a catty, and a bag of wheat flour was forty-nine *sen*, which was more than forty silver dollars. Oil was 1.20 dollar a catty and kerosene 80 cents per catty. The cost of living went up daily and so the Japanese authorities issued a notice to tell people who had no occupation to leave Hong Kong and return to the home village. The authorities would give people departing half a catty of rice each and would escort them to the Chinese border.

Hung Hau and Tung-shing could not return to Hong Kong because of the curfew and they stayed at Shun On for a week. After that, they sneaked out by boat from Shamshuipo and went back to Hong Kong. I thought at the time that the rice shortage must be only temporary, and that soon the authorities would make available large quantities for the relief of the local people. But I waited and waited and there was no news of rice being put on the market. Rice went up from a dollar a catty to two dollars, and wheat flour from forty dollars a bag to seventy dollars. After the war, things became so expensive that many people could not afford what they needed. Many starved.

On 10th January, 1942 by the Western calendar, which was the 24th day of the eleventh month by the agricultural calendar, Hung Hau wrote to report that there was only eight to ten days' worth of rice for congee in the shop, and that even though they had money there was no rice to buy. It looked as if their food supply would be exhausted. That was quite frightening. He wanted to disband the staff in the shop, and asked me for my view. I became quite frustrated when I saw that. One trouble had really come after another. With my limited energy, how could I face all that. Disbanding the staff was no problem at all, but neither land nor boat transport had resumed ... On 15th January, which was .... I received a letter from Hung Hau .... had chartered a junk from Macau to come to Hong Kong to take his family back to Macau and it was prepared to take other passengers. It charged 25 dollars for a person. He had decided to send Ah Tong, An Fai, Ah Ngau to go with Hung Shi to Macau, and had given each employee forty dollars in silver to take back to the village. I thought that was costing too much money. It was more than I could afford in the present situation, but with the present state of our food supply, there was not much to do but to disband the staff. I also realized that with ten mouths to feed in my family, I needed 6 catties of rice per day, which cost 10 dollars, and at least another 300 dollars for a month's expenses. It was not yet clear when business might resume, and I was not able to collect any rent. I wondered what was to happen to us if this situation continued for much longer. I really thought it was better to be a dog at a time of peace than a human being at a time of war.

On 15th January by the Western calendar, which was the 30th day of the eleventh month by the agricultural calendar, after breakfast, I was frustrated at home thinking about people in the shop. I asked Hung Nung to go with me to the Office of the Interior on Nathan Road to apply for a permit to cross the harbour at Tsimshatsui so that I might return to the shop for a look to see how things had become after the war. When I arrived at the Office of the Interior, it was full of people. Moreover, the process of obtaining a permit was very complicated, so I gave up my attempt. I went home with Hung Nung, and on the way went over to Yaumati for a visit, just so we did not have to so frustrated. We soon found ourselves at the Tai-ping Restaurant. Our legs were tired and we were thirsty, and so we went up to the restaurant for some tea. It so happened my old friends Kong Ping-chung and Wong Pak-ho were there and they invited us to join them. Soon, the waiter came with a plate of fried beef noodles. I saw that a plate of noodles was not enough for four people, and so I ordered another plate of beef noodles and two dishes of four lotus-seed-paste buns. Then we talked about current events. The waitress served . . . I paid the bill, we left the restaurant and parted to go home.

On 18th January by the Western calendar, which was the second day of the twelfth month by the agricultural calendar, after breakfast, I bought a copy of the *Wah Kiu* newspaper. I saw that transport between Hong Kong and Kowloon had been restored. It was possible to buy a ticket at Tsimshatsui and the local people were free to come and go. I had been thinking about the shop and so I arranged to take the bus with Hung Nung to Tsimshatsui pier to wait for a ferry. I found people to be in good order, because there were Japanese soldiers making passengers wait in the queue to buy their tickets. Hung Nung and I waited in the queue and bought two tickets, and we boarded the ferry *Man-hong*. In a minute, the ferry's siren sounded and the boat was going towards Hong Kong. Soon it reached the other shore. We landed at the entrance of Ice House Street, and we turned into the banking district on Des Voeux Road . . . The department stores were still there, but the people had changed. Some companies had been closed by the Japanese military and some hotels had become Japanese military clubs. They might be called gardens or hotels, but some of them were being used to house British soldiers who had been captured. In the shops, people played mah-jong, but there were places of music where girls were singing. One might say 'commercial women knew nothing of the sorrows of national defeat, and across the river sang the tune 'the flowers of the back garden'.'

I could remember Des Voeux Road as the only prosperous part of Hong Kong before the war. There used to be people dancing, young people smartly dressed, tourist agencies, modern women, nightless lives, like the French capital Paris. Now, after the fighting, it had become a scene of desolation. I felt sad as I walked along. I could remember the night before the war walking from the shop on the island to return to Shamshuipo where I lived, and now I was retracing my footsteps . . . . I could not forget that.

1942 by the Western calendar, the last month of the 31st year of the Republic, the year of San Tzi.

b. Life in Occupied Hong Kong

DOCUMENT V.b1: Cultural activities (source: 'Cultural activities in the new Hong Kong, a special article from the Hong Kong Broadcasting Office', *The New East Asia* September 1942, pp. 107-108.)

For someone who returns to Hong Kong after having left before the War, the first thing he will find surprising will be that all the signboards that used to be written in English are now gone. From this alone, it should be clear how the culture of the new Hong Kong is different from that of the old Hong Kong.

Strictly speaking, the Hong Kong of the past had no culture of its own. The most that might be said is that what little culture there was was a low-grade colonial culture. So, for more than a hundred years, although the British in Hong Kong wanted to win the hearts of local people by encouraging the study of the classics and respect for Confucius, ultimately, they produced such laughable Hong Kong Chinese sentences as 'If you want to stop the car, you can do it here.'

Now, Hong Kong is in the hands of the Japanese Imperial Army. It has become a Hong Kong for the East Asians. The poison of the former British colonial policy must now be thoroughly eradicated. For this reason, the poisonous remains of British cultural leftovers must also be eradicated. The new Hong Kong culture must not only include Chinese culture but also elements of new Japanese culture. Only in this way may Hong Kong bear the new responsibility of a centre of cultural exchange between China and Japan.

At present, Hong Kong cultural activities are proceeding towards this direction. Not only have these activities quite recovered, but also new life has been injected into them. They have far exceeded the former confines to move towards a new future.

The new cultural activities in Hong Kong can be discussed in several parts. First, we can discuss the newspapers.

Newspapers are the voice of the people. In the past, there were too many newspapers in Hong Kong, and their backgrounds were too complicated. On the one hand, they all reported the same news, but on the other hand, they all made conflicting comments. Every day, they fought one another with pen and ink. Such newspapers were a waste of human and material resources. Such laxity had been purposely cultivated by the British. The new Hong Kong certainly cannot permit this warped phenomenon. Since the restoration of peace in Hong Kong, this situation has been remedied. Pornographic tabloids are no longer published. The major newspapers have been negotiating mergers, and plans for them will take effect on 1st May. At present, there are four morning and one evening newspapers in Hong Kong. They are: daily newspapers such as the *Xianggang*, the *Xingdao*, the *Huaqiao*, the *Nanhua*, and the *Dongya Evening Post*. These are all published in Chinese. In addition, there is the *Hong Kong Daily* published in Japanese, and the *Hong Kong News* in English. The newspapers come out daily in a single sheet, and are sold at 5 *sen* Military Currency each.

When the newspapers have been merged, talent will be concentrated, and their contents will be more substantial. Moreover, in order to compete, everyone will do his best at what he can do well. Consequently, on the one hand, they will be coordinated, but on the other hand, they will also be less dry.

As for cultural organizations, the first organization to be established after the war was the East Asian Cultural Association. The second was the South China Film Association. At the time, they included all the notable people in the cultural spheres in Hong Kong. The chairman was Mr. Yang Qianli and the Vice Chairman Mr. Ma Jian. They contributed greatly to the promotion of early cultural activities. These organizations are now being reconstituted into a new East Asian Cultural Association.

On schools resuming after the war, the situation is more complex. This is because under British rule, all schools offered either a Western education or a 'slavery education'. The choice of subjects and the quality of teachers were often absurd. For these reasons, it was necessary to completely overthrow the old and to start all over again from the foundation. In order to do this, a teacher training school has been established to train teachers, while the quality of existing teachers is being examined. So far, two classes of students from the teachers' training school have graduated. Several dozens of private and church schools have also resumed classes. A new curriculum and new textbooks are being examined and printed.

Because there is the actual need, there has been much support in Hong Kong for learning Japanese. At one time, there were many express classes and Japanese language schools. Nevertheless, the educational authorities have not for this reason been lax in the establishment of Japanese language schools. On the contrary, they maintain very strict control on the the quality of Japanese language taeachers, and disallow all those schools that fail to come up to standard. At the same time, in order to popularize Japanese language education, on the one hand they have set up voluntary Japanese language schools in which specialists are hired to hold voluntary classes in many institutions, and on the other hand, they include Japanese language courses in the radio programmes of the Broadcasting Department, so that residents can have more chance to learn.

As for publication, there is now in Hong Kong a sizable Datong Book Publishing Co. This company has been set up jointly by Mr Au Boonho and Mr Ho Tung. The publications that are now available incude the *New East Asia Monthly* and the *Datong Pictorial*. In terms of both content and printing quality, they have broken all records of Hong Kong publications. This is something in the new Hong Kong cultural activities that one can take pride in. The company has also started to edit a book series that introduces Chinese and Japanese cultures, and they will soon be published.

On the question of other artistic activities, artists in the Chinese as well as the Western styles who have remained in Hong Kong, such as Bao Xiaoyou, Wang Taoyuan have formed the Hong Kong Artists' Association. Mr Jian Qinzhai last month staged a large-scale exhibition of bronzes, stone inscriptions, calligraphy and paintings that included well-known ancient and modern items held by collectors in Hong Kong. Thousands of spectators attended. This was a rare and exciting occasion in artistic circles in Hong Kong. Recently, artists in Hong Kong and Kowloon organized an art exhibition in aid of orphans. They collected items that they sold to provide relief for orphans. That also received much warm support.

Other branches of cultural activities have also been active. Film and drama are really holding hands, for actors in both have formed theatrical companies that perform in the theatres. Newly written plays include 'The One Hundredth Christmas in Hong Kong' that describes life during the war in Hong Kong. Ba Jin's famous 'Family' has also been dramatized. In music, the musicians who have remained in Hong Kong have formed the Hong Kong Orchestra, which has already given one performance. This is the first time there has been an orchestra of a large scale in Hong Kong.

What used to be the Fung Ping Shan Library has also actively collected paintings that used to be in public or private collections but have now scattered. It has been putting them in order and soon they will be available for exhibition. It will become a public library for the use of Hong Kong citizens.

This is the general situation of cultural activities in Hong Kong since the war. Together with other activities, under the bright sun, on the calm of the South China Sea, under the all-embracing defence of the Great Japanese Imperial Army, the new Hong Kong has taken on its shoulders one of the responsibilities for building the Great East Asian Co-prosperity Sphere, and is moving forward in peace and joy.

DOCUMENT V.b2: The Po Leung Kuk under occupation (source: Faure, Luk and Ng, *Historical Inscriptions of Hong Kong*, p. 557)

In commemoration of the Recovery

The fires of war spread to Hong Kong. Lives were put in hardship, the city was deserted. In particular, in the fourth year of the occupation, residents there led lives that were hardly fitting for human beings. Speaking about it brings pain.

Truly, the price of rice rose from just over 10 dollars per catty to more than 200 dollars. Even the rich found it hard to have enough to eat, how could the poor not starve to death and remain unburied? At this time, we succeeded into our positions in the Kuk.

More than two hundred pitiable orphaned and neglected children noisily waited to be fed. How could we bear this painful sight? We knew that our resource did not match our needs, but we would not call ourselves human if we watched them without doing something. So we exhausted our finances and our strength, first to maintain a supply of food for the orphans in our care so that there would be no shortage and their health might recover. However, when the children in the Kuk had fortunately had an abode, many weak and small children were crawling about on the streets, pitiably starved of the last grain and breathing their last.

We considered that in the realm of charity there could be no barrier. We wanted to help all as we had helped some. We developed our conscience into a source of strength, and we distributed congee in front of the Kuk, thereby saving a thousand people a day. We gave suitable relief, and looked after people both inside and outside the Kuk. From the day we took over office, to the recovery of Hong Kong, 123 days passed. This enormous expenditure came from our own donations and the support of enthusiastic men and women. With good fortune, we passed this serious and dangerous bend. We take comfort in this act and report it to gentlemen of this realm. When it comes for our term to be succeeded, our successors, will firmly and solidly present themselves as parents-of-rebirth for the foresaken. This will be their offer to us.

Directors of the year: Law Chi-hing, Ko Cheuk-hung, Wong Siu-hing, Tong Luk-kut, Law Wai-kwan, Ku Cheuk-lun, Lee Shu-yuan, Wong Ping-ying, Yeung Shu-cheung, To Tin-han, Ma To-sang, Lee Chun-nung

On a fortunate day in summer, 1946, 35th year of the Republic.

DOCUMENT V.b3: Internment (source: Type-written manuscript, in David Faure's possession)

A Message to all Christians in Stanley

'Ye that follow the vision of this world's weal afar':-

More than two years ago a message was addressed to the Camp which had as its theme the phrase, 'Redeeming the Time'. Today we face a different situation, and there is need for something else to be said.

Many people have had a clearer vision of God and of duty than was theirs before internment. High resolves have been made by many — two years ago. There is a danger that the moment of vision will be forgotten, and that resolution will weaken. Many facing the future today are aware of little but the small things of life that will be possible once again. The old round and routine is to be resumed.

Now, unless life has come to mean more to us than it did prior to internment we have not 'redeemed our time', we have wasted it. Each one must face for himself the question, 'After internment, what?'

God has nothing greater to give to man than the gift of life with its truly amazing range of opportunity and of service. Are you going to be of the type of whom Kipling wrote,

> 'But now, discharged, I fall away
> To do with little things again . . . '

or, has life awakened desires,

> 'Not to be satisfied as men appease
> Hunger of food or sex or market gain'

and are you going to give yourself to the battle that will continue ceaselessly after the present battle is over, the achievement of the Kingdom of God upon earth?

If so, you are proposing to enter a contest from which there is no discharge, and which will require reserves of energy and resolution that you should be seeking and possessing NOW!

We celebrate the third anniversary of our Camp Services on Sunday, 28th January. We invite you to the service at 9.45 a.m., that together we may seek strength and wisdom for the future that lies beyond our present sight, and that, with St. Paul, we may say -

'I was not disobedient to the heavenly vision.'
Frank Short
Chairman, Stanley Ministers & Clergy

DOCUMENT V.b4: Letters from occupation (source: *Journal of the Hong Kong Branch of the Royal Asiatic Society*, vol. 21 1981, pp. 187-190)

31 Shelley Street,
2nd floor,
Hong Kong.
22nd March, 1942.

Dear Mr. Lum,

I trust you & your family are well, as we all are here. Things have been fairly quiet since you all left, but of course prices are soaring higher. We have had several letters from Mrs. Lee since she arrived in Macao & she has given us news of things there. It seems you are suffering the same hardships as we are as far as cost of living goes.

I now have a favour to ask of you & would be most grateful if you can help me. I am now in close touch with my younger sister & brother who were living in Kowloon Tong when war broke out. They are both well, & as a matter of fact are now staying with us until things clear up a bit. We are very anxious that our mother & father should know we are safe & well & that my sister's house is intact. Since I heard that it is possible to cable to Australia from Macao, I hasten to ask this favour of you. Would you be kind enough to enquire for me the cost per word or per telegram of so many words, for cabling to Australia as follows:-
Address:

SUEON
HANIDCRAFT
SYDNEY
SAFE IN HONG KONG
LILAILDER

Please note the signature 'LILAIDER' which is a combination of our three names Lily, Aileen & Derek so that our parents will know we are all safe & well; I think it can pass for signature, I don't know the regulations in Macao.

We should like to let our parents know that they can communicate with us via Macao, so if you have a short address to which they may send a reply will you kindly add the words 'Reply (address) Macao' after 'Hongkong', i.e.:

SUEON
HANDICRAFT
SYDNEY
SAFE IN HONG KONG, REPLY MOCTO MACAO
LILAILDER

If the cost of such a cable is under HK$50 I shall be glad if you will send it off straightaway & let me know, when I will send you payment. Should the cost amount to over HK$50, will you please let me know the exact amount first? We will be waiting anxiously for your reply to this letter as our mother will be worrying terribly about us & we wish to allay her anxiety as soon as possible. If you can help us in this way, we shall be most grateful.

With best wishes & kindest regards to you all,

Yours very sincerely,
Lily Tam

31 Shelley Street,
2nd floor,
Hong Kong.
22nd March, 1942.

Dear Mr. Lam,

I have not thanked you for your letter written to me many months back & I do so now. I believe Tsuen has written to you in the meantime.

I trust you & your family are well as it leaves us at present. We are finding the new exchange of HK$4.00 to yen 1.00 very difficult. I suppose you know this was announced officially on the 24th July, i.e. 4 days ago. So now instead of one yen being worth $2 it is worth $4. Everything has gone up double the price in Hong Kong Money. Peanut oil is y. 1.80 per catty which is equal to HK$7.20, as against HK$3.40 last week. Vegetables are twice the price in H.K. currency, but remain the same in yen.

My sister-in-law (Yung Ngan) has asked me to write you a few lines for her. She asked me to say that several people in Macao have asked her to buy things for them here, which you probably already know. As she could not get the permit to leave Hong Kong & as it has been raining for the past month here, she thought she would wait until she got permission to leave before buying the goods, because if she bought them first & couldn't get a permit to leave, it would be difficult to find someone to bring them over.

Now she has fortunately received papers & has handed them in on the 25th instant. However, as you know, the yen has gone up within the last few days, & everything is twice the price, or nearly that. Sister-in-law now wants to know whether these people still wish to buy what they asked her to. If so will you please let her know immediately, as she will get the permit any day now, & will have to hurry & buy them.

She also wants to know the exchange in Macao, what is the Hong Kong dollar worth in Macao money?

Hoping to hear from you soon & with kindest regards to you all,

Yours sincerely,
Lily Tam

31 Shelley Street,
2nd floor,
Hong Kong.
19th February, 1943.

Dear Mr. Lam,

My sister-in-law, Yung Ngan, has asked me to write you a few lines to let you know her news. She wishes to be remembered to all.

Everything is very expensive now, ever since Chinese New Year the prices have gone up twice. Will you please tell Mrs. Ho that the 'Lee Kung Man' singlets with long sleeves are approximatley HK$8 per piece, & that she is not going to buy for her & asks her to buy for herself in Macao. Also the short socks which she bought last time for 80 sen at 'Shui Hing' are now Y1.20. Now the prices are going up for a third time. Prices vary from day to day, so Yung Ngan cannot buy anything. She says that if the prices are reasonable for the things you want for your family, she will buy, if not, you will have to buy them yourself, as she doesn't know how much you are willing to go up to.

I hope you & your family are well as it leaves us here. Everything is very difficult with these high prices but we struggle along somehow. I received a letter from my sister Gertie, & was very happy to get it. I hope we can all meet again soon.

Please excuse this short note. I must close now with kindest regards from us all.

Yours sincerely,
Lily Tam

DOCUMENT V.b5: Victory (source: F.W. Webb, *The Philatelic and Postal History of Hong Kong and the Treaty Ports*, London: The Royal Philatelic Society, 1961, pp. 39-40)

29 August 1946, Victory Issue; recess printed by De La Rue, Perf. 13x12-3/4; designed by E.I. Wynne-Jones and W.E. Jones; invalidated for postal purposes 1 September 1956.

The two special adhesives of the Victory Issue were designed in captivity. A full face portrait of the King surmounts a phoenix rising from flames and a motto 1941-1945 RESURGO. Values in English and Chinese appear in the lower corners.

The story behind this issue deserves to be recorded more fully, and the following is condensed from the account of Mr E.I. Wynne-Jones, Postmaster General before and after the Occupation.

The design of these adhesives was conceived and executed during internment in Stanley Camp. In 1943, it occurred to Mr Wynne-Jones that it might be a good idea to have a commemorative issued when Hong Kong was finally liberated, and he set about designing one. Though by his own account no artist, he roughed out the design which was finally adopted, choosing the Phoenix. This was not only the obvious symbol of resurrection from the flames and ashes of the years of Japanese occupation, but had the further significance that in Chinese mythology the appearance of the Phoenix is held to indicate the return of good government.

Mr Wynne-Jones then enlisted the help of Mr W.E. Jones, a fellow internee and Senior Draughtsman of the Public Works Department, who is not only a keen philatelist but an artist who had already designed the Centenary Issue of 1941. He elaborated the rough design into a large scale drawing. The original dates optimistically chosen were 1941-1944, which had subsequently to be altered to 1941-1945. The originators toyed with other designs — time hung heavy on their hands — but always came back to the original design as representing what they firmly believed would be a fact: the liberation and resurrection of the colony to its former greatness.

The two characters on the shields supported by the Lions of England represent Hong Kong, and on the side panels are inscribed Chinese characters for 'The resurrection of the Phoenix is the symbol of general peace for Chinese and British'. In the background on both sides of the King's head are two bats, symbols in China of good luck and long life.

Mr Wynne-Jones kept the design carefully, a matter of some danger, for the Japanese would not have appreciated it; on the voyage home in one of H.M. ships he showed it to a young Chinese naval officer of considerable literary achievements, who pointed out that two characters chosen for the last part of the inscription on the left panel meaning literally Great Peace were also used in classical Chinese to mean Japan! Others were therefore substituted, and on reaching home the amended design was put to the Colonial Office and duly approved.

The commemoratives were originally intended for issue on 15 August 1946, first anniversary of V.J. Day, but owing to delay in their arrival in the Colony the date was altered to commemorate the arrival of the British Fleet at the end of August.

It should be realized that Mr Jones ran very considerable risks in producing the full scale designs while in Japanese hands. When he was working, pickets had to be thrown around his hut in order to signal the approach of any of the guards. The courage, optimism and faith in victory which led to the planning of this issue under such circumstances provide an epic in the philatelic history of Hong Kong which deserves to be placed on permanent record.

CHAPTER SIX

THE RETURN TO IMMIGRANT SOCIETY, 1945-1966

From the 1840s to the 1920s, Hong Kong the Chinese city established a foothold in the south China-Southeast Asian nexus of trading cities consisting of Guangzhou, Foshan, Shantou, Hong Kong, Macau, Saigon and Singapore. Came the 1930s, when within a few years, upwards of half a million people went into Hong Kong to escape from the war in China, and equally quickly, the population was depleted as war broke out in Hong Kong itself. Many people returned quickly enough at the end of the war, for in 1947 the population stood at 1,750,000, which was slightly higher than the count conducted in 1941. Perhaps another half a million entered Hong Kong between 1947 and 1966, but Hong Kong's was a young population* and they gave birth to more than a million more people in the same period. The numbers add up to congestion, housing shortage, the need for social services, in particular, schools, and, of course, poverty, poverty and more poverty.

Social structure continued very much as it was before the war. The need for the Western community in Hong Kong to work closely with its Chinese population continued to nurture an English-speaking Chinese elite that was imposed upon statuses attained through wealth. Just as before the war, the Hong Kong government drew support from traditional communal organizations. Chinese tradition, however, was rapidly becoming an anachronism as an aid to administration. The strikes of the 1920s, and then the riots of 1956 — which arose out of an incident in which the hanging of a flag was the centre of dispute — taught the Hong Kong government to be wary of issues that involved the politics of China. Chinese tradition became the venue by which the Hong Kong government sought to relate to the

---

* 40 percent of the Hong Kong population was aged 14 or below in 1961

Chinese community at large and Chinese custom came to be preserved with a sense of pragmatic reverence that was quite out of step with changes going on in China itself.

a. Restoration of Traditional Communal Institutions

Like many other local-place associations, the Dongguan Charity Hall was founded with the avowed purpose of providing facilities for burial and sacrifice. When it diverted its focus to the provision of schooling in the 1920s, it was reacting to the increasing numbers of its countrymen that had settled in Hong Kong. In the 1950s, provision of schooling remained its focus. The association's report makes no reference to the curriculum, which was closely supervised by the Education Department of the Hong Kong government.

The involvement of Chinese communal institutions in the running of schools without a say in the content of education put the onus of coming to terms with Chinese culture on the Hong Kong government. Much too timid in the face of tradition, the Hong Kong government tread cautiously — and slowly — in areas that involved a departure from traditional Chinese values. British law dealt with legal issues the best way it could, but reforms of Chinese marriages, overdue in the 1950s, were a long time in coming. Concubinage was not dealt with by ordinance until 1971.

DOCUMENT VI.a1: The Dongguan Charity Hall (source: *The Dongguan Industry and Commerce Association Journal* (Dongguan gongshang zhonghui huikan), 1956, pp. 38-37.)

This hall, having been established in the Kuei Tzi year at the end of the Qing dynasty (1893), has had a history of sixty-three years. It was originally founded for the purpose of maintaining contact among people from the same county and promoting their common welfare. In the early days of its foundation, it set up a communal graveyard to bury the remains of their relatives and friends, it attended to annual sacrifice for them, and sent the bones of their departed friends home for burial. Subsequent to these activities, it established a charity school for the education of poor children who had no schooling. In all these activities, there was considerable achievement, as all know. When the Pacific War began, Hong Kong fell, members of the hall dispersed, and the activities of the hall were interrupted. The charity school that had been established for many years ceased to function. When the occupation was over, members of the hall met to discuss its revival. It bought a school building so that there might be a foundation for education. The achievement of today is built upon the difficulties that were overcome by the early founders, and the enthusiastic support given by the gentlemen who succeeded them. They deserve the admiration of all of us who come after them.

There was once in circulation a brief history of our hall. However, owing to changes and turmoil, few copies of that have remained. The following is a report of the work of this hall, with an account of the origin of its activities. It serves the purpose of pointing the way to all comers, to enable them to promote and improve upon its work, so that it may go from strength to strength.

A history

Our county is adjacent to Hong Kong. Transport is convenient, and so it is possible to go from one place to the other within a day. For this reason, there are 300,000 people from our county who make their living in Hong Kong. Of all counties, ours has the largest number of people living in Hong Kong.

Sixty to seventy years ago, in the days before the Kowloon-Canton Railway or even the steamer, people who came to Hong Kong came by sailing junks via Guangzhou. At the time, business in Hong Kong was not yet very prosperous. It was a time of peace, when the people lived contentedly at home and did not think about travelling afar. In those days, most of the people who came from our county to Hong Kong were coolies, hawkers and artisans. Merchants in business of scale might be counted on the fingers of one hand. There were fewer of them from our county than from other counties.

When more people stayed in Hong Kong, there were naturally those who died but whose bodies, for reasons of poverty, were not sent back home for burial. When the coffins were stored in communal mortuaries or buried on crown land, sometimes they were lost track of. In those early days, we set up a charity cemetery on Telegraph Hill, collected the bones of departed friends that were not sacrificed to, and buried them there. However, that was a small water-logged place where many graves were already located nearby, and so there was little room for expansion. In order to ensure that the bones of our departed friends might not be exposed in the wild and become lost, people of our county who worried about such matters agreed that the establishment of another charity cemetery was urgently needed. They also saw that many counties at the time had set up halls to promote charitable activities. They all had public cemeteries, and we regretted that we did not. So we followed in their footsteps.

In the autumn of 1893, the Dongguan Charity Hall was set up by [names omitted] in August. In September, under the joint names of the Managers for the Promotion of the Dongguan Charity Hall, a donation drive was mounted from door to door. A poster was also posted, which said, 'To all readers, our county intends to set up a charity site in Hong Kong for the convenience of the temporary burial of those departed friends whose coffins have not been sent [home], and to offer sacrifice annually for the repose of sojourning spirits. These activities will be costly, and the contribution of all will be necessary. Immediately upon the call for donation, many shop-owners have enthusiastically responded. However, there are still many whose whereabouts are not known, and it is difficult to approach them in person to ask for donations. For this reason, this notice is posted for their information. Friends from our county who wish to donate any amount large or small may register their names on the ground floor of Yan Wo Company. When payment is made, a receipt will be given, and the donor's name will be recorded on stone to be noted for perpetuity. In this way, philanthropy and humanity become one. . . .' Donation books were then distributed, so that donations might be asked for from prosperous merchants from our county who were residing overseas, and that small sums might gather into large amounts. Many people donated. Later, because for some years there had been an epidemic, and people in their alarm had moved away, it was not possible to hold discussions on this matter. The Dongguan Charity Cemetery at the Chinese Permanent Cemetery at Aberdeen was, therefore, completed only shortly before the Qingming Festival in 1897. This Hall was established in 1893, and until 1901, for nine years, it was managed by Mr Wei Minchai without any change in personnel. In April of that year, Mr Wei resigned when he found that he was too busy at his own business, and he was succeeded by Messrs Lo Tso-shen, Chow Siu-kei and Wong Kat-yu. The term of office was not fixed. They were responsible for the safe keeping of public funds, sacrifice at Qingming and the distribution of sacrificial pork.

In 1910, it was found that remaining funds were limited, and a donation appeal was organized. Immediately 2,000 dollars was raised, and a further 4,000 dollars was donated by our overseas countrymen. At the end of that year, the post of chairman was instituted. Every three years, the managers cast their votes to elect three persons to serve in turn as chairman-cum-treasurer. In addition, two auditors were elected.

In 1916, it was suggested that the distribution of sacrificial pork be terminated and a school be started. In 1920 a charity school was started. In order to raise funds for regular expenses for the school, all those who pledged to donate 5 dollars per year towards school expenses might become Hall managers. For this reason, the number of managers rose to 180. Out of this number, eight school managers were nominated, who were in charge of school affairs, taking turns each month to inspect all charity schools. It was also agreed that the funds being kept by the chairman should accrue an interest at 0.7 per cent per month.

From 1923, it was decided that all Hall officials be elected annually, the election being held three months before the end of term. In that year, a chairman-cum-treasurer was elected. Also elected were nineteen school managers, who formed the education department, to be managed by a section manager and deputy manager elected among the managers. Moreover, because Hall affairs had increased, a director was added who was to assist the chairman in his management of Hall affairs.

In 1926, during the election of the director, two candidates received the same number of votes. It was decided that votes would not be cast a second time. Instead, there was to be a deputy director as well as a director. From that time on, this became an established rule.

In 1930, a school supervisor was engaged to assist the education department to improve school affairs and to supervise the charity schools. By this time, the number of Hall managers had increased to 200.

In 1931, the Hall was reorganized. The number of manager-officers increased to 50. Hall affairs were decided by the council of manager-officers and executed by the chairman. Other posts remained unchanged.

In 1941, Hong Kong fell. The students dispersed and nothing was left of the school buildings. All documents disappeared. In the early years of Hong Kong's recovery, while military rule was imposed. the affairs of the Hall ceased.

In the autumn of 1946, civilian government was revived and members of the Hall gradually returned to Hong Kong. In August, Mr Yip Tsak was elected the first chairman of the Hall after the War and he sought quickly to resume its affairs. So many activities had been set aside that had now to be revived that the chairman was kept very busy, and because it was unsuitable in these circumstances for him to serve also as treasurer, another person was elected to share his labour. Because the current term was to end within a short time, it was decided that from the following year the treasurer should be separately elected. Also, because there was much work to be done, it was necessary to consolidate the internal organization of the Hall. Therefore, 63 manager-officers and 30 school managers were elected.

In 1947, Mr Lau Cheuk-kwong was elected chairman. The post of treasurer was separately filled, and in order to strengthen the education department, a department chairman was added and an honourary school supervisor was engaged. In that year, two evening charity schools were started. A site for the school building was purchased, and donations were invited for the building.

In 1949, Mr Chan Lan-fong was elected chairman. Immediately, a school-building committee was formed jointly with the Industry and Commerce Association, while efforts to raise funds intensified. Mr Chan was the first to contribute a donation to promote the cause, and he contributed both money and strength, bearing all blame and labour. From that year, two deputy chairmen were added, and the organization of the Hall became even better. Mr Chan's leadership as chairman was the wish of all our members, and he was re-elected in all subsequent years, up to the present. In May, 1952, work was begun on the new school building. In September, the building was completed. On 6th September, the new school was opened in a key-turning ceremony, officiated by Mr Chow Chun-nin, Industry and Commerce Association Chairman. After that, for the reason that there was no regular income for the school, and it was necessary to work towards providing for it, a four-storey building was built on the vacant land on the side of the school. This building was to be rented out, the rent providing an income for the school. This building was completed in 1954. By this stage, our Hall had laid a foundation for educating the young. This difficult task in the post-war era has been completed thanks to the methodical leadership of Chairmen Chow and Chan, the cooperation of the school-building committee, and the enthusiastic support of many people in society.

DOCUMENT VI.a2: British law and Chinese customs (source: *Chinese Law and Custom in Hong Kong, Report of a Committee Appointed by the Governor in October, 1948, pp. 92-108*)

> Cases in the Hong Kong Courts which Throw Light on the Application in Hong Kong of Chinese Law and Custom

Ordinance No. 1 of 1857 extended certain imperial Acts to Hong Kong. Among these was an act for the uniform administration of intestates' estates and in the column of the schedule specifying how much of the act was extended to the Colony the following appears:-

> The whole of the act except so far as it may be deemed to affect the customs and usages of Chinese people touching the distribution of the personal estate of Chinese persons dying intestate.

Nobody has given a satisfactory explanation as to why it was ever thought necessary to apply this act to Hong Kong. The effect of the act was to abolish the special customs of London and York which had been preserved by the Statutes of Distribution*. Unless those special customs could be carried to Hong Kong by persons coming here from London and York, why apply the abolition of the customs of London and York to Hong Kong and in any event how could Chinese possibly be affected? The exception made to the application of the act has, nevertheless, been relied upon by the courts in Hong Kong as an expression of the views of the legislature —

> (a) that the Statutes of Distribution did not apply to Chinese at all; and
> (b) that if it did not apply its non-application must affect leaseholds (which in English law are classed as personal estate) and should not be confined to the movable property of a Chinese intestate.

An expression of the views of the legislature which does not take the form of legislation is not a satisfactory basis of judicial decision and though the judges in Lau Leung Shi v. Lau Po Tsun appear to have realized this, there is little doubt that it influenced the decision in the leading case of Ho Tsz Tsun v. Ho Au Shi and others, 10 H.K.L.R. 69 with the possible result that insufficient heed was paid to the vital problem, namely, the true construction of section 5 of the Supreme Court Ordinance, 1873. The following references may assist those who wish to pursue the matter further — 6 H.K.L.R. at p. 164 and 172, 10 H.K.L.R. 71, 72 and 81.

Cases in Hong Kong courts

A. *Lau Leung Shi v. Lau Po Tsun*, 6 H.K.L.R. 149. In this case the deceased was a Chinese person domiciled in China. He died possessed of leasehold property in the Colony as well as of shares in companies registered in Hong Kong and in firms carrying on business in the Colony. There was a bequest of shares of his estate to ancestors sacrificial fund which infringed the Rule Against Perpetuities. The Full Court found that the Rule Against Perpetuities applied, but whereas both the Chief Justice and the

---

* The Statutes of Distribution governed the distribution of property left by a deceased person without a will. - Ed.

Puisne Judge agreed in applying it to the leasehold property, the Puisne Judge considered that it should not apply to movable property. As a result there was an intestacy and it became material to decide whether the Statutes of Distribution or Chinese law should govern the devolution of the leaseholds. Held that the Statutes of Distribution applied. Both judges concurred in holding that any movables as to which there was an intestacy should devolve in accordance with Chinese law. Both judges considered the Schedule to Ordinance No. 1 of 1857 and came to the conclusion that it could not have the effect of applying to the leaseholds the law of the testator's domicile, i.e. Chinese law, but the Puisne Judge (Gompertz J.) went further in that he said that in his view 'it was nothing more than a saving clause for Chinese customs and usages, with reference to the personal property to which those customs properly relate: that is to movables'. Had he qualified his words by saying 'so far as the saving can apply at all to Chinese persons not domiciled in the Colony', he would, in my view have stated the law correctly and there is no doubt that the decision in the particular case was correct, i.e. that the movable property only could be affected by the law of the testator's domicile and that the Statutes of Distribution must govern the devolution of the leaseholds because the *lex loci* applied, and although as we shall see, the *lex loci* in the case of Chinese domiciled in the Colony was Chinese law and custom there could and can be no justification for so interpreting selection 5 of the Supreme Court Ordinance as to make it derogate from the ordinary principle of Private International Law as applied by English courts, that no matter what the personal law of a foreigner may be if he dies intestate possessed of land within the Court's jurisdiction, that land devolves in accordance with ordinary domestic law. See Dicey, Conflict of Law, 6th Edition, p. 536. Nevertheless, in Ho Tsz Tusn's case (*infra*) a justification was found.

B. *Ho Tsz Tsun v. Ho Au Shi and Others.* No. 83 of 1910, 10 H.K.L.R. 69.

The testator in this case was apparently a Chinese domiciled in China. I say apparently, because the expression used in the report is 'domiciled Chinese' which might also mean a Chinese domiciled in Hong Kong. It seems clear from the case, however, that the Full Court was dissenting from and refusing to follow that part of Lau Leung Shi's case *supra* which decided that leaseholds in the Colony should devolve in accordance with the Statutes of Distribution. Now the testator in that case was clearly domiciled in China and if the testator in Ho Tsz Tsun's case was not so domiciled Lau Leung Shi's case would have been distinguishable on that ground and much of the judgments in Ho Tsz Tsun's case would be unintelligible. Moreover, in Ho Cheng Shi v. Ho Sau Lam, 15 H.K.L.R. 35, Gompertz J. at p. 37 says —

> I agree with Mr. Potter that the only question before the Full Court in Ho Tsz Tsun's case was what was the law governing the distribution of the leaseholds of a Chinese intestate? The importance of the decision lies of course in the recognition for the first time in this Court, of the principle that, in that connexion, domicile is immaterial, and that the Chinese law of distribution is part of the law of the Colony.

We may therefore assume that the testator was domiciled in China. The testator had made a bequest for ancestral worship which was found to be bad as offending against the Rule Against Perpetuities with the result that there was an intestacy. In consequence the Chief Justice considered himself bound by Lau Leung Shi's case to order that the leaseholds of which the estate consisted should devolve under the Statutes of Distribution. On appeal it was held by the Full Court consisting of Haviland de Sausmarez President and the Chief Justice that the Statutes of Distribution did not govern devolution of the leaseholds because the *lex loci* in such a case is the Chinese law and custom of inheritance. In other words the Court did not purport to depart from the principles of Private International Law on the question of the *lex loci* applying but held that in Hong Kong there were two such laws, one for the Chinese, namely Chinese law and custom as it existed in 1843, and another for everybody else, namely English law. The President qualified the word 'Chinese' by adding in one part of his judgment the word 'residents' and in another the word 'inhabitants'. In view of the wording of section 5 of the Supreme Court Ordinance, 1873, some such qualification was clearly necessary. It is interesting, however, that in the Chief Justice's judgment no such qualification was made and he referred merely to Chinese. In fact both judges proceeded on the footing that the Statutes of Distribution could not have been applied to the Colony unless it was confined to non-Chinese and therefore gave no meaning to the word 'inhabitants' because in their view, whether the Chinese intestate was or was not an inhabitant of the Colony was irrelevant, i.e. not only was domicile irrelevant but residence in the Colony was irrelevant. It must be frankly admitted that both judges gave extremely cogent reasons why the Statutes of Distribution could not be applied to Chinese successions and although we have seen that the difficulties were overcome in the Straits Settlements, the decision that they were totally inapplicable is obviously preferable to the confusion of the two systems that has resulted in the Straits Settlements. The fact remains that considerations of inapplicability do not prevent English law from applying the English law of succession to land owned in England by a Turk or a Chinese or by any national whose personal law may be entirely at variance with the law of England. So that unless we can derive comfort from some other sources we are driven back to section 5 of the Supreme Court Ordinance or to the general principles applicable where the inhabitants of a Colony have a law of their own and English law is introduced.

The President sought to derive support for his judgment from the following—
- (a) the proclamation of Captain Elliott;
- (b) the practice of the Supreme Court and the Chinese residents;
- (c) Ordinance No. 1 of 1857.

Let us examine each in turn.

(a) The *Proclamations*. Although the President admits that these were subject to Her Majesty's pleasure he seeks to draw comfort from the fact that the words in the first proclamation 'they are further secured in the free exercise of their religious rites, ceremonies, and social interests and in their lawful private property and interests' were not made expressly subject to Her Majesty's pleasure and are wide enough to cover succession to property. It is clear, however, that in the case of a ceded Colony the new sovereign has an untrammelled right of legislation and that even if Captain Elliott had been given authority to qualify such right in any way, it would have necessitated the clearest indication of such intention to qualify the right in the sense suggested by the learned President. Moreover, in view of the fact that immediately after the words cited the Proclamation continues to say that pending Her Majesty's pleasure the inhabitants will be governed by village elders according to Chinese law and custom subject to the control of a magistrate, it is more than clear that Captain Elliott was purporting to do no more than create an interim administration. Those persons therefore that attribute the survival of Chinese law and custom to the Proclamations are building their castles upon sand. See also in this connexion the judgment of Sir Henry Gollan in Chak Chin Hong's case 20 H.K.L.R. 1 at pp. 9 & 11, where he quite clearly was of opinion that English law in 1843 was to apply unless it was inapplicable.

(b) *The practice of the Supreme Court and the Chinese residents.* So far as the Court was concerned the President admitted at p. 73 'There is, however, nothing to guide us as to the extent to which the Courts have followed these customs', and Lau Leung Shi's case had decided that they did not apply to Chinese domiciled in China. There was, however, evidence that the Chinese had been guided solely by Chinese law and custom and would be unlikely to apply anything else and presumably such Chinese must have included Chinese not domiciled in Hong Kong, but much as one can understand the Court's reluctance to declare as the law something which was quite contrary to the way it had been applied and possibly, understood, by the Chinese inhabitants of the Colony, unless this practice was sanctioned by law it could not be the basis of a judicial decision.

(c) *Ordinance No. 1 of 1857.* (Originally Ordinance No. 3 of 1857.) It is of course admitted that the words 'personal estate' in the exception to the application of the Act for the uniform distribution of Intestate Estates is wide enough to include leaseholds and that the Statutes of Distribution applied to leaseholds. The observation of Gompertz J. in Lau Leung Shi's case that the saving should be restricted to movables, was therefore on the face of it open to criticism and both the learned judges dissented from it, but that was not the end of the matter. The real question was could the saving be read either as in fact applying Chinese law and custom existing in 1843 to any part of the estate of an intestate Chinese not domiciled in the Colony, or as indicating that the word 'inhabitants' in section 5 of the Supreme Court Ordinance in a matter of this kind should be read to include persons who had not made Hong Kong their permanent home and consequently were not domiciled here. If the saving could not be so read then Gompertz J. would be right in saying that *so far as Chinese domiciled in China were concerned*, and that was the only case before him, it must be taken as a saving for movables only. In my opinion the only reasonable inference to draw was that the draughtsman was anxious not to give the impression that an Act which amended the Statutes of Distribution was being applied to the Colony without any qualification as otherwise it might be argued that this showed an intention that the Statutes of

Distribution itself applied to Chinese domiciled in the Colony and this might be fatal to those Chinese laws and customs to which the Statute was clearly inapplicable. As the legislature must be deemed to make its own the words of the draughtsman it would also be fair to say with Sir Henry Gollan C.J. (20 H.K.L.R. 7) that it was in the contemplation of the legislature that despite the earlier Supreme Court Ordinances introducing English law, at the time of the passing of the Ordinance under discussion there were customs and usages in force referring to the distribution of the personal estate of a Chinese person dying intestate. So far so good and to this extent the judges were entitled to say that this confirmed their own view for which they gave good reasons that the Statute was inapplicable to the Chinese inhabitants, but surely it was a slender thread upon which to hang the proposition that contrary to the usual rule of English law the legislator was in section 5 of the Supreme Court Ordinance intending to legislate for all Chinese? The answer that the word 'Chinese' in the saving is not qualified is not a sufficient one. So it is also in numerous other Ordinances and in Ordinance No. 1 of 1856 passed in the previous years to validate wills in the Chinese form the legislature had been careful to say after the words 'Chinese testator' (*'whether a native of or domiciled in this Colony or China'*). It is at least equally arguable from the omission in the saving that it was not to apply to Chinese not domiciled in the Colony. Moreover, if the real intention of the legislator had been to override the ordinary rule of Private International Law as administered by English Courts would he not have used some more specific words both in the saving and in the various Supreme Court Ordinances? It may be said that the word 'inhabitants' is ambiguous but unless there is some good reason to extend it to temporary residents it should in my view be confined to permanent residents. In fact, as we shall see, there is good reason for so confining it. Meanwhile, let us examine the judgment of the Chief Justice. The Chief Justice sums up his own judgment as follows:-

> We have express sanction for the recognition of the dual system of law both in the Proclamations and in No. 1 of 1857. Further, Chinese customs are expressly recognized in a number of local Ordinances — 7 of 1875 (the Marriage Ordinance), 10 of 1905 (the Married Women (Desertion) Ordinance, now replaced by 49 of 1935), 15 of 1908 (Widows and Orphans Pensions Ordinance), 34 of 1910 (New Territories Regulation Ordinance), 42 of 1912 (Chinese Marriage Preservation Ordinance). A perusal of the law of the Colony taken collectively, shows that the object has been to establish in a British Colony a system of British jurisprudence in so far as it is not inconsistent with Chinese usage and custom. With these authorities before us, I think we shall be giving effect to the intention of the legislature in holding that the Statutes of Distribution cannot be applied to meet Chinese family law and customs, and so far it is inapplicable to the local circumstances of the Colony; that succession in the case of Chinese is governed by the aboriginal law, i.e. the laws of customs in force in that part of China of which Hong Kong formed an integral part before the cession to Great Britain; further,

that succession to the property in question by other than Chinese is governed by the Statutes of Distribution.

In substance the Chief Justice adds nothing to the reasons given by the President except that he cites in support of his view a number of local Ordinances.

The Marriage Ordinance 1875 restricted the right of Chinese persons to contract a marriage under the Ordinance and applied the Ordinance to all marriages except marriages between persons neither of whom professes the Christian religion, duly celebrated according to the personal law and religion of the parties. As the exception was a statutory exception in favour of all non-Christian marriages duly celebrated according to the personal law and religion of both parties and not merely of inter marriage between Chinese, if it can be called in aid at all, it seems a far better example of the oppression theory than of the dual system of law theory expounded by the President and the Chief Justice.

In the Married Women (Desertion) Ordinance, 1905, 'married woman' includes the first wife (kit fat) or second wife (tin fong) of any Chinese man married to him in accordance with the laws and customs of China, and any woman married to a man of Asiatic race (not being Chinese) in accordance with the rites and ceremonies of his religion.

Apart from recognizing the form of marriage the ordinance could hardly be said to support Chinese custom. It ignored the tsips[*] and gave the wife rights she never had under Chinese law. Moreover, it equally recognized marriage in accordance with the personal law and religion of other Asiatics and gave the wives of such marriages similar rights.

The Widows and Orphans Pensions Ordinance, 1908, dealt another blow at Chinese Marriage by refusing to class the tsips or their children as beneficiaries.

The New Territories Regulation Ordinance, 1910, legislated expressly for giving effect to Chinese custom in the New Territories. The fact that such legislation was deemed necessary can hardly be cited in support of the judgment that a dual system survived in the Colony as a whole. The Chinese Marriage Preservation Ordinance, 1912, was special legislation to give the husband of a Chinese marriage a right to damages for adultery against a Chinese committing adultery with a kit fat or tin fong wife.

The Ordinances cited by the Chief Justice therefore do no more to show that partial recognition had been accorded to marriage in accordance with Chinese law and custom and as in most cases the same treatment was afforded to other marriages in accordance with other personal law and religion they would not advance the theory expounded.

In fairness to the judges in Ho Tsz Tsun's case it must be admitted that as [sic] at the time they decided it the law in force in the greater part of China was that same law

---

[*] Concubines

and custom which they declared in matters of intestacy to be the *lex loci* of Hong Kong. But even at that time the effect of the decision was that if a Chinese domiciled in Singapore acquired leasehold property in Hong Kong, on intestacy his adopted son would succeed in Hong Kong and not in Singapore, whereas his daughters would succeed in Singapore and not in Hong Kong. Other examples could be given. since 1930 when the new Nationalist code was introduced in its full vigour the discrepancy is even more marked. A Chinese domiciled in China who leaves leasehold and movable assets in Hong Kong will, if he does not leave a will, find that the leaseholds in Hong Kong will devolve according to Tsing* law whereas the movables devolve in accordance with modern Chinese law. Nowadays the Statutes of Distribution would approximate more closely to modern Chinese law than the Tsing law of intestacy, so the shoe is on the other foot. There was the further explanation for the error, if it be an error, made by the Court, that the Court did not consider itself bound by Lau Leung Shi's case because —

> (a) the question of the true effect of Ordinance No. 1 of 1857 was not argued by Counsel in that case; and
>
> (b) the question whether in the case of all Chinese, including those who had not made Hong Kong their permanent home, Chinese law and custom and not the Statutes of Distribution could be the *lex loci* of Hong Kong was never argued.

The decision has in any event been the law of Hong Kong for so long that it is doubtful whether the criticisms levelled at it would be considered sufficient by the Privy Council to upset it, and if it is not to be the law the matter must be set right by express legislation. Moreover, so far as concerns Chinese domiciled in the Colony, the decision was eminently sensible in holding that the Statutes of Distribution were totally inapplicable and not applicable with modifications as was decided in the Straits Settlements, but in view of the Privy Council decisions it would be desirable to legislate expressly for the method of devolution upon intestacy of the estate of a Chinese domiciled in Hong Kong even if, as would appear to be the case, the necessity for legislation did not also arise from the fact that the Tsing law of succession is quite out of harmony with modern conditions.

(c). A series of cases, of which the leading case is *In the Estate Chak Chiu Hang, Chan Shun Cho v. Chak Hok Ping*, 20 H.K.L.R. 1, have decided that the Tsing law does not govern who is entitled to a grant of administration but only the beneficial distribution of the intestate's estate. The widow of Chak Chiu Hang, who had died intestate was admitted by the parties to have been domiciled in Hong Kong, claimed that a grant of letters of administration should be made to her whereas the defendant, who was the father of the deceased intestate, claimed that by the law and custom of China the estate of the intestate vested in him as trustee for the infant son of the intestate and that he was the proper person to administer the estate.

---

* Qing dynasty

Under Chinese law and custom no grant of administration is necessary and a good deal of evidence was also called to show that in Chinese law and custom women occupied an inferior position, that the widow was under the authority of the defendant as the senior male relative, and that, although she was the natural guardian of her children and could administer without handing over to the defendant, she was in a number of important matters subject to his control. The Chief Justice was prepared to concede that had the point been raised in 1843, it might have been argued that the position of a Chinese widow in the family under Chinese law and custom was such that she could not be entitled to a grant of administration of the property of her deceased husband. Nevertheless, for many years past the Court proceeding on the principles of English law had consistently granted letters of administration to the widows of Chinese intestates without Chinese family life having been subverted and he considered that it would be pedantic to upset a rule which had been consistently followed. In view of the foregoing, stated the Chief Justice, had a question of discretion arisen, he would have been prepared to exercise his discretion in the widow's favour.

In the course of his judgment the Chief Justice reviewed the earlier cases and pointed out that those cases had held that as a result of the various Probate Ordinances which applied to Chinese as well as to other inhabitants, the rule of Chinese law as to its being unnecessary to take out letters of administration had been expressly overruled. The Chief Justice also shared that view.

d. *The case of Ho Cheng Shi v. Ho Sau Lam*, 15 H.K.L.R., which was one of those cited by the Chief Justice in Shak [sic] Chiu Hang's case, is interesting in showing that Chinese law and custom as to the inferior status of a woman has not been accepted. In this case the plaintiff as administratrix claimed from the defendant an account of the intestate's share in a family partnership. The defendant was the deceased's brother and in the previous case between the same parties of Ho Sau Lam v. Ho Cheng Shi, 11 H.K.L.R. p. 92, he had previously unsuccessfully applied for a revocation of the letters of administration granted to the concubine as next friend of the infant son by adoption. Now he contended that under Chinese law and custom the plaintiff, who was a concubine of the intestate, was not entitled to administer the estate but that the proper persons were the nearest male relatives of the intestate. Mr. Justice Gompertz disposed of the argument of the inferior status of a woman and particularly of a concubine, as follows:-

> So much for the disabilities of a woman; especially a concubine in China. The answer is, I think, that the status of a woman is different in our law. She is competent to be administratrix, and as such to do anything that is necessary for the administration. In dealing with assets which are, *ex hypothesi*, Hong Kong assets, her status under the law of China is immaterial. In dealing with an estate in Hong Kong it cannot be material that the proper tribunal in China would be the elders of the clan, or that she must manage the property under their direction during the minority of the person entitled. The place of such tribunals is taken in the Colony by our own Courts.

It must of course be remembered that the argument seeking to exclude women from administration on the ground of their incapacity under Chinese law was in any event very far fetched. Quite apart from the general applicability of the Probate Ordinance, and the Married Women (Disposition of Property) Ordinance, 1885, which had long been the law when the argument was advanced, it is extremely doubtful whether English law would be held to be inapplicable in cases where the result of its application, so far from removing injustice or oppression, would result in removing a defect of capacity. This is really the basis for the express or implied non-recognition of slavery (express in the case of Hong Kong) as the institution is contrary to the right of individual freedom and while a refusal to recognize the disabilities of women is not such a clear case, recognition of such disabilities would certainly not be required by a necessity to remove injustice or oppression.

Similarly it is a fundamental principle of English law that the Courts should be open to all and are the proper arbiters of legal disputes. While agreements to refer to other tribunals may in certain instances be good, it is difficult to see how a mere custom whereby certain matters are dealt with or supervised by family councils could derogate from this fundamental principle. This may perhaps prove relevant in other matters customarily dealt with by the family council. A stronger case for the exclusion of the concubine might perhaps have been made not on the above grounds but on the ground that the legislature has signally failed to recognize her position. We have seen for example that she is not mentioned in any of the Ordinances relied upon by the Chief Justice in Ho Tsz Tsun's case. As against this, however, the rights of her children to succeed on intestacy have never been challenged and recognition of the marriages in accordance with the personal law and religion of the parties must, in the absence of express legislation to the contrary, include all unions in the nature of matrimonial unions which are part and parcel of the Chinese institution of marriage. Moreover, we have seen that in Singapore the divorce of a secondary wife has been upheld. There seems little doubt therefore that whether on the grounds actually expressed by the Courts or on more general grounds the arguments for not making a grant of letters of administration to the widows and especially to concubines because of Chinese law and custom, were rightly rejected.

E. *The case of Chan Yeung v. Chan Shew Shi*, reported in 20 H.K.L.R. 35, further decided that the previous practice of making a limited grant of letters of administration to a concubine in cases where a grant could be made at all, was misconceived and that she was entitled to an ordinary grant. Under the previous practice, according to the evidence of the clerk in charge of the Probate Office, where a grant was made to the concubine, it was usually made for the use and benefit of the children. In other cases it was only made during the minority of the children.

This case was decided by the same Chief Justice (Sir Henry Gollan) before whom evidence as to the limited rights of a widow in connexion with custody of the children and her right of administration had been called in Chak Chiu Hang's case. The evidence called in Chan Yeung's case was, as not infrequently occurs with expert evidence of Tsing law and custom, however, a little different in that it showed that under Chinese law and custom the kit fat or tin fong wife was designated as the proper person to administer her husband's estate. The Chief Justice further held that the law of England being clearly inapplicable (as it did not recognize more wives than one) he must look to the law of China to discover who was the proper person to be the legal personal representative of the deceased. He did so and arrived at the conclusion that on the true interpretation of section 38 of the Ta Tsing Lu Li* a Shu Mo, or compassionate mother (i.e. a surviving concubine who by order of her husband brings up the sons of the husband upon the death of the natural mother) was entitled to the grant both because she was a Shu Mo and because she was his concubine or tsip. He expressed himself thus — 'In my opinion, the widow of an intestate, if she was his kit fat or tin fong, is primarily entitled; if there is no such widow then a Shu Mo comes next in order; and if there is no Shu Mo than a concubine or concubines'. He examined the position of a concubine both in Chinese law and before the Courts of this Colony, and appears to have come to the conclusion that in the absence of a tsai** or Shu Mo the concubine was entitled to treatment similar to that which would have been accorded to a tsai or Shu Mo.

This case is also interesting for three other reasons:-

> (a) It is one of the few cases in which the Hong Kong Courts appear to have been made aware of the decisions in the Straits Settlements and of the Privy Council but the Chief Justice dismissed the matter briefly with this comment: 'Fortunately, express local enactment avoids any necessity for discussing the propriety or otherwise of the procedure adopted in Hong Kong in regard to similar case.' Although he does not specify which enactment it would seem probable he was referring to Ordinance No. 1 of 1857.
> (b) It shows the dangers of having to rely on expert evidence to prove Chinese law and custom in that there was not only a conflict of evidence between the evidence of the plaintiff and defendant in Chak Chiu Hang's case but between such case and the present.
> (c) It contains an instance where the Courts had to consider whether a Chinese family had in fact split up into two separate families, which, in the circumstances, the Court considered had occurred.

F. *In the matter of the Estate of Kishen Das*, 26 H.K.L.R. 42. the report is rather meagre, but it appears that a Hindu went through a form of marriage ceremony known as 'Anand' with a Chinese woman. This form of marriage was lawful for Sikhs and it is not altogether clear that it was lawful for the Hindu. The case was, however, decided on the ground that the exception made by section 37 of the Marriage Ordinance 1875 could only operate where the non-Christian customary marriage was shown to have

---

* Penal Code of the Great Qing Dynasty
** Wife

been duly celebrated according to the personal law and religion of *both* contracting parties. In the present case this had not been shown. The judge accordingly declined to allow the Official Administrator to apply the estate of the deceased Hindu Kishen Das for the maintenance of his son by the Chinese woman aforesaid. As had been previously mentioned the Courts in the Straits Settlements have decided otherwise and it is for consideration whether a marriage in a form sanctioned by the personal law and religion of the husband should not be made by legislation to suffice.

Effect of the Hong Kong decisions

With the exception of the case of Kishen Das which does not assist in the interpretation of section 5 of the Supreme Court Ordinance, 1873, the relevant cases in Hong Kong have all been concerned with the following topics:-

(a) *Is a formal grant of letters of administration necessary?*
Yes. — English law applicable.
(b) *Who is entitled to grant letters of administration?*
This must be determined in accordance with English law except to the extent where, e.g. because the position of a Shu Mo or tsip has to be considered, reference has to be made to Tsing law.
(c) *Actual devolution upon intestacy*
Chinese law and custom as it existed on the 1st of April, 1843, applies and, in the case of leaseholds, whether or not the intestate was domiciled in Hong Kong, provided he was of Chinese race. If, however, only movables are concerned the *lex domicilii* and not the *lex loci* applies and it becomes necessary to ascertain the actual domicile of the deceased Chinese. This last proposition would appear to follow from the reasoning in Lau Leung Shi's case and Ho Tsz Tsun's case. It must, however, be remembered that when those cases were decided the *lex domicilii* and Tsing law were for practical purposes one and the same. Inquiries addressed to the Registrar of the Supreme Court as to the practice in making grants of letters of administration have not elicited any definite reply on this issue. The Registrar is only concerned with the question as to who is entitled to a grant and he determines this in accordance with the principles of English law. Usually there is expert evidence as to who would be entitled to a grant according to the law of the domicile and this is sufficient to enable him to make a grant. He has not been able to find a case where there has been a conflict as to who is entitled which would necessitate an inquiry as to the beneficial interests under Tsing law and the law of the domicile and thus raise in a net form which of these two laws applies.

b.   Poverty and the Need for Welfare

The pressing problem of the 1950s was the provision of social services for Hong Kong's mounting population, and in no other area of social services was need as accute as in housing. Should government build the housing that members of the community needed? Member of the Legislative Council, Sir Man-kam Lo, opposed the proposal of government involvement. How many flats was government prepared to build for the poor? Could it be as many as 1,000? He asked in 1949. Little did he know that by 1966, almost 800,000 people lived in 150,000 subsidized units, mostly single rooms. It became a myth that was propagated through the textbooks in Hong Kong's schools that the fire at Shek Kip Mei in 1953 was the reason for the Hong Kong government's programme in subsidized housing. That was no more than an excuse to overcome opposition from some prominent members of the Chinese community for a policy that was suggested by the Housing Commission of 1935.

DOCUMENT VI.b1: A problem of refugees (source: Commission of Labour and Commissioner of Mines, *Annual Report*, 1957-58, pp. 60-61)

The majority of the working population in Hong Kong are wage earners and Hong Kong is basically a trading and industrial community, although there are important sections engaged in agriculture and fishing. The population is now fairly stable, although the movement into and out of the Colony during the year was over 1-1/2 million each way, out of a total population estimated at the end of 1957 to be 2,677,000. The natural increase was slightly less than 80,000 in the year 1957.

The ingress of over 700,000 refugees from mainland China since 1949 has had a marked effect on the labour situation in the Colony, the chief characteristic of which is an excess of unskilled labour. Previously the ebb and flow of the working population was closely aligned to the economic opportunities in Hong Kong and China. The refugees, however, have shown no desire to return to the mainland, even though Hong Kong is unable to offer to all the prospect of earning a reasonable living. Since 1950, with the exception of a short period in 1956, restrictions have been imposed on immigrants into the Colony from China.

The internal mobility of labour is generally high. Workers quickly acquire new skills or brush up old ones in order to adapt themselves to the best market for their services. The small geographical area of the Colony makes transport less of a problem. With the expansion of new industrial areas, such as Tsuen Wan and Kwun Tong, this mobility is becoming less marked because of the need to change place of residence with the new job.

There are, however, from the workers' standpoint, factors which prevent him from moving toward better economic opportunities, in particular the system of personal introduction and the preference to employ clansmen or fellow villagers. This does not mean that vacancies are left open, but that individuals, without the correct surname, antecedents and ancestral village, think and, in many instances, are right in thinking, that the job is not open to them. This is particularly so in the retail trade, in work such as building where sub-contractors are involved, and in the smaller commercial firms and workshops. In large industrial establishments which employ direct labour in quantity this is not the case.

DOCUMENT VI.b2: Housing (source: Address by Hon. Sir Man-kam Lo, Hong Kong Legislative Council, 30 March 1949, *Hong Kong Hansard*, Session 1949, pp. 99-100)

This question is of course one of vital importance to the public and I therefore feel I should say a few words on this matter.

To begin with I venture to think that some of the bitterness which has crept in in the criticisms of Government housing policy, especially in regard to building houses for Government employees, which have appeared in the local press, has been due to an inadequate appreciation of some of the circumstances affecting this problem, which include the following :

1. The majority of domestic premises are old buildings subject to controlled rent. (Incidentally I may mention that since the landlord's expenditure is increased, say, from 3 to 6 times as compared pre-war, and since his permitted increase in rent for domestic premises is only 30% on pre-war rentals, this arbitrary restriction in rentals represents an important subsidy to the cost of living in Hong Kong by the landlord.)
2. It costs so many times more to build a house now than pre-war.
3. A fair return on any new building must be governed by 2 above. Moreover in case of a slump in property, when there is no housing shortage, and when rentals of new buildings cannot compete with rentals of pre-war buildings, the owners of new buildings must 'carry the baby' — unless, indeed, they charge such premia and rent as will enable them to depreciate within a short time the value of the building to pre-war value.
4. A fair remuneration to an employee must be such an amount as will enable him to obtain accommodation suitable to his position by expending a reasonable percentage of that remuneration for this purpose.

It is because of the consequences and of the inter-play of these circumstances that large employers have found it expedient to provide accommodation for their employees. In so far as the rent charged to the employee does not represent a fair return on the cost of the accommodation, under 3 above, it represents a subsidy to the employee and the justification is that the employer regards such a subsidy as a necessary and proper expenditure to retain the services of a contented staff.

This policy has in fact been followed by large commercial firms in the Colony for a great number of years, and is being followed today. And it should be appreciated that, in so doing, they do make a contribution to the solution of the housing problem itself; to the extent to which new accommodation is created the shortage would thereby be eased.

I can see nothing against, and every reason for, Government as employer to adopt a similar policy and I can only hope that this policy will be continued so that in time Government may have buildings to house their white-collar employees and the labour class as well as their senior officers.

It is suggested that Government should build houses for members of the public, rather than its employees. I confess I cannot follow this argument. Let us however assume that Government is to build for members of the public. On what principle are the members of the public to be chosen for the honour of being Government tenants? Then what is the rent to be charged? If the rent is to be 'fair return' under 3 above, these tenants will get no special benefits, and the only effect of Government's enterprise is that Government will have become landlords and builders. If however the rent is to be so fixed as to include an element of subsidy, then all I can say is I do not see why the taxpayers who include the humblest artisan who smokes a few cigarettes should be made to pay this subsidy!

Finally how many houses or flats is Government to build? Say, 1,000 flats? Well, on the basis that each flat costs $100,000 the capital sum involved is 100 millions!

DOCUMENT VI.b3: Excuse for intervention (source: Address by the Governor, Hong Kong Legislative Council, 30 December 1953, *Hong Kong Hansard*, Session 1953, pp. 354-355)

Honourable Members, I am sure that I am voicing the sentiments of every member of this Council, indeed of the whole Colony, when I express my sympathy to all those who have suffered from the terrible catastrophe at Shek Kip Mei. The only consolation that we have is that the casualties were low.

In a disaster of this magnitude the first essential is to feed the people and to care for the sick. This has been done and is being done. The second essential is to clothe those who are in need of it. This again has been done and is being done. The third essential is to house those who have been rendered homeless. This is the most difficult task of all in view of the numbers involved. The total is roughly equal to the whole of the population of Tsun Wan, or of a fair sized town in England. There is little accommodation immediatley available, for we have no really large buildings that will be suitable, whilst the overcrowding that exists in all our domestic buildings is well known. Therefore all that is possible at the moment is to house the very young, the aged and the sick. This is being done. The rest will for the time being have to take shelter under verandahs. The necessary water, latrine and washing facilities are being provided. However, it is Government's intention to rehouse these people on the existing site at the earliest possible moment. This means that the site must be cleared, and clearing has already started. As soon as the site has been cleared and roads and drains provided rows of simple houses of fire-proof construction will be erected by Government and fire victims will be allocated to them. They will be required to pay a small rent, probably a good deal less than they were paying in those dreadful dwellings that have just been burnt down. If there is not accommodation on the site for all, the balance will be rehoused elsewhere.

Those are the immediate problems and plans. They will require much effort and considerable money: probably as much as $16 millions from Government funds. The greater part of this expenditure, of course, will be for feeding, site clearing and more particularly housing. None the less I am quite sure that this Council will vote whatever is necessary. Meanwhile there is still urgent need to help the victims in other ways and I therefore hope that subscriptions will continue to pour in from the public.

It has been a terrible disaster, but the help that has been given by all and sundry has been truly magnificent. Never before in Hong Kong have I seen such a display of neighbourliness. The way in which the voluntary organizations, the kaifong, the churches, the Army, private individuals, Government departments and officials, the way in which all these swung into action with speed and intelligence was most heartening and also most efficient. Truly it may be said that out of tragedy has come kindness.

Dr. Chau Sik-nin: Your Excellency, as Senior Unofficial Member and on behalf of my Unofficial Colleagues I wish to associate myself with your expression of sympathy which I know will be gratefully appreciated not only by the sufferers but by the whole Colony.

The community is gratified to learn of the swift relief that has been rendered by Government and the voluntary organizations to the victims of this tragic disaster and of the planned and practical measures that are being instituted to rehouse them with all possible speed. The stricken will be heartened by your words, Sir, just as they have been comforted by that kindness of which you have spoken — the spontaneous and overwhelming charity manifested by all sections of the community.

DOCUMENT VI.b4: Social policy — Address by the Governor (source: Address by the Governor, Hong Kong Legislative Council, 3 March 1954, *Hong Kong Hansard*, Session 1954, pp. 20-21)

I turn now to our greatest social problem, that is housing, with which is connected resettlement. Practically every civilized country in the world suffers from a shortage of low cost housing. We are not unique in this. What makes our difficulties exceptional is the proportion of our total population which is living without proper housing and the fact that such a large percentage is not our own people but the influx of a neighbouring country where thousands more are waiting to pour into houses as fast as, or even faster than, we build them. Consequently progress here is bound to be even slower than it has been in most other countries. In addition we have the further disadvantage that land here is much scarcer than it is elsewhere. As regards the size of the problem, it is estimated that at least 350,000 people should be rehoused. It is unnecessary for me to stress the scarcity of land in Hong Kong. That is so well known and so obvious as to call for no further comment from me. It may mean that we shall have to develop satellite towns outside the urban areas, but this is also bound to be a slow process because it is no good having low cost houses if they are too far away from the places of work of the people living in them. To give some idea of the high cost of low cost housing I would mention the latest scheme of the Hong Kong Housing Society to erect 1,000 flats at Hunghom. This does not sound like a tremendously large project, but when I tell you that the site preparation will cost $2 millions it does give one some idea of how much more difficult the problem is here than it is in other places. Incidentally, the $2 millions is a grant from the Colonial Development and Welfare Fund. In addition to this a loan of $72 millions from our Development Fund has been promised to the Housing Society for the erection of the flats. In out of town sites there would be lacking water and similar services which already exist in urban areas such as Hunghom. These services would have to be provided at no little cost. It is a difficult but not an insoluble problem. We have got to feel our way. At the same time we should realize, as we all do realize, that it should be pressed on with as rapidly as possible. We are gaining experience all the time and we should not throw that experience overboard. That is why it is intended that when the Housing Authority, to which I referred last year, is set up the Authority will not, at any rate to begin with, be the exclusive organization to deal with low cost housing. Schemes of other organizations such as the Housing Society will continue simultaneously, beause we want all the assistance we can get. Before, however, approval or Government assistance is given to schemes of other agencies it is essential that we should be satisifed that the particular scheme proposed is a sound one. The legislation to establish the Housing Authority is already in draft form and will, I hope, shortly be presented to this Council. One thing we should bear in mind is that low cost housing either by the Housing Authority or by other organizations which receive financial aid from Government, whether by direct grant or by loan, is subsidized housing. This means that it will compete with private low cost housing. We do not want to get to the stage where subsidized housing will kill private housing. However, this is unlikely to happen for a long, long time as there is so much to be done. Meanwhile we shall have to devote the greater part of our Development Fund to low cost housing.

DOCUMENT VI.b5: Poverty (source: The Family Planning Association of Hong Kong, *Fifth Annual Report, 1955*, pp. 9-10)

Of the 4,724 new cases [during 1955], 161 attended the clinic for wives of Services personnel, 32 the clinic for English Speaking Women, and 116 were sub-fertile cases. 4,415 over-fertile cases, therefore, attended the ordinary clinics. The following averages are based on these 4,415 overfertile cases:

Salary per month:	$136.02
Surviving children per family:	3.89
Age of mother:	30.89

The average salary of $136.02 per month does not give a clear picture of the extreme poverty of many of the patients who attend clinics on account of the fact a number of women from higher wage groups make use of the facilities offered. The average age of women attending clinics is high and the majority have already had their family before coming for advice. On study of each case it is found that the majority have had over an average of five pregnancies and in some cases as many as eleven pregnancies or more. Here, for example, are particulars of five cases, from the many in our records, who have come to the clinics for advice during the year:

> Woman aged 35, married 19 years, had 11 pregnancies with normal births. 6 children surviving, 7 died, husband a cobbler earning $100 per month.

> Woman aged 37, married 21 years, had 13 pregnancies: 9 normal births, 4 miscarriages. 9 children surviving. Husband a farmer earning $120 per month.

> Woman aged 38, married 19 years, had 12 pregnancies with normal births. 10 children surviving, 2 died. Husband unemployed.

> Woman aged 39, married 20 years, had 12 pregnancies: 10 normal births, 2 abortions. 8 children surviving (3 given away), 2 died. Husband a Foki* earning $80 per month.

> Woman aged 43, married 26 years, had 15 pregnancies: 11 normal births, 4 miscarriages. 6 children surviving, 5 died. Husband a tailor earning $100 per month.

DOCUMENT VI.b6: More poverty (source: The Hong Kong Family Welfare Society, *Annual Report for 1959*, p. 6)

A typical family receiving such assistance is that of Mrs. 'H'. Her husband died of T.B. in February 1959 leaving her with 4 young children. The family live in a very poorly constructed roof-top shelter. Mrs. 'H' tries to support her family by doing odd cleaning jobs but two of the children suffer from T.B. and she has to take them regularly for medical treatment which takes much of her working time. She herself is weak and undernourished, and cannot sustain long hours of work. The Family Welfare Society have given them extra nourishing food and clothing and a regular monthly grant to help with their daily expenses. School fees have also been paid for one of the children.

DOCUMENT VI.b7: And more poverty (source: Elsie Elliott, *Crusade for Justice, an Autobiography*, Hong Kong: Heinemann Asia, 1981, pp. 173, 186-187, 190-191)

Our pupils all lived in huts, and inevitably some were involved in fires. We would rush to the scene of the fire, usually during the night, to see how we might help. The

---

* Shop or store assistant

other children would then take the fire victim, if he was a student, to buy new books and clothes. The poor understand the sufferings of the poor and they try to help each other.

. . .

I enjoyed living in the midst of things in Kowloon. It was noisy, being in the flight funnel and very close to the airport. The first time a plane flew over the building, I fell flat as we had been taught to do during an air raid. I was sure the plane was going to land on the house, but I am not sure how falling on the floor would have helped if it had. We had to stop teaching every time a plane passed over. But eventually I became so used to the noise of planes that they left me undisturbed. Yet the sound of a single cockroach flying through the window would wake me up in a sweat of fear. I have never become reconciled to intruding cockroaches, though they no longer make my hair stand on end.

In Kowloon City I was right among the people. I came to know and respect the hawkers, and to understand their problems. I watched how they were hounded from a street on the excuse that they obstructed traffic; but as soon as they moved, their places were immediately taken over by parked trucks, whose owners could be seen paying bribes to the authorities for their privilege.

I was especially interested in the many street sleepers in the area, which is not far from the notorious Kowloon Walled City, that area which belongs to no one and is full of drug activitiy and vice. China claimed certain rights over it, while Britain denied them, until a claim in the Supreme Court decided in favour of the latter. Certainly China once had special rights there, but these are never used today. At any rate, the area was neglected, both for cleanliness, public services, and law and order, and provided a hide-out for all kinds of illegal activities and still does to some extent. Yet some of our finest students have come from that area, where rents are cheaper. I used to buy cotton quilts in the winter, and go out at night dropping them on street sleepers who had inadequate bedding. When I did this I always had to run away quickly, in case I was surrounded by many asking for quilts.

. . .

It was mid-February, the coldest February on record. A delegation of squatters came to tell me their huts in Jordan Valley had been demolished by the authorities, leaving them without shelter in the biting cold wind. . . . On this occasion I went at once to see the victims. There were about 400 of them, people of all ages, many young children and old people. Their huts had not only been dismantled, but the poles had been hacked through to prevent them rebuilding to the same height. I saw children sheltering from the cold in chicken pens; I saw a very old couple huddled on a bed in front of which some kind person had hung a sheet of iron to keep off some of the wind as it swept down the valley. I was introduced to a woman whom the villagers had just saved when she jumped to attempt suicide.

I was shaken. I knew that squatters' huts were being demolished on sight, but I could not imagine any human being demolishing huts to this extent during record cold weather.

Shocked and angry, I went straight to the headquarters of the Social Welfare Department in Causeway Bay, to ask what might be done for the homeless. I saw the Assistant Director, a Chinese. I explained the situation and asked if he could help the homeless.

'Why don't these people go and rent themselves a flat?' he asked.

'Their average wage is $150 to $180,' I replied, 'and I know that to rent a room costs that amount. What is the family then supposed to eat?'

DOCUMENT VI.b8: Environment and accommodation (source: *Journal of the Hong Kong Institute of Social Research*, vol. 1, 1965, pp. 1-8, 25-28, 33-38, 90-93)

Wanchai tenement

Wan Chai, formerly called East Point, was among the first areas to be inhabited on the island of Hong Kong and it has a long history of settlement. More than half the households visited in the Wan Chai area had been in the district for twenty-five to fifty years. Six of the household heads were born in Hong Kong. All other household heads came to Hong Kong when they were under twenty years of age. There were also fifteen households which had been in the area for eighteen years. That is to say then, that they arrived in the area right after World War II. They must have been part of the great influx of people from China immediately following the liberation of Hong Kong. Some of those who came at this time were newcomers to Hong Kong, while five had been here before the war but had returned to the homeland during the occupation.

During the war, Wan Chai suffered heavy bombing because of its proximity to the Naval Dockyard, so many people moved away at that time. As a result, many of the tenement blocks were still vacant in 1945 for the new arrivals to occupy. Only three households in the Hong Kong sample had been in Hong Kong for fourteen years or less, that is, since the beginning of the Communist regime in China. This might be related to the fact that houses in Wan Chai were already quite filled by the continued immigration during the post-war interim . . .

The houses in the Wan Chai district wherein most of the households dwell fall into three main types:—

(1) The oldest type is built on the gentle slope south of the original shoreline of the Hong Kong Island. These buildings are mainly three storeys high. A very steep wooden staircase serves two adjacent buildings. The treads are so worn that hollows are formed in the central parts, and sometimes one or two treads are missing altogether. As the cleaning and maintenance of the stairs are nobody's responsibility (caretakers are unheard of) dirt and dust have accumulated over the years. The stairways are dark even in broad daylight and artificial lighting is never installed so that drug addicts who take advantage of the protective darkness are encountered on the landings.

Each floor at the time of completion of the building was devoid of partitions either temporary or permanent, although an enclosed kitchen room was provided. When there is a principal tenant renting a premise, he usually divides the living space into cubicles by a maze of wooden partitions six feet high.[#] This leaves a wide passage on the side of the entrance along which two to three-tier bunks are usually erected. As the houses are built side by side, there are windows at the front opening into a veranda about two feet wide, if facing side streets, and about seven feet wide if facing a main road and also a window in the rear onto a backyard. The cubicles in the middle are therefore without windows and are in permanent semi-darkness so that artificial lighting (usually by 25 watt electric lights or kerosene lamps) is necessary whenever the cubicles are in use. Through-draught between the front and the rear windows is prevented by the intervening partitions. The air within the cubicles is stagnant and stuffy. This is especially so in the middle cubicle. Electric fans are thus not unexpectedly found to be a common item of capital outlay to offset the heat in summer. In one instance, the investigator visited a top floor rear room with a window. Despite the fact that there was a window an electric fan was in use. When questioned about the necessity of the fan in a room which has a window, the household head replied, 'You would not be able to stay in this cubicle for five minutes if I turned the fan off — so intense is the heat'. The only possible means of natural lighting and ventilation is through the space left between the top of the partitions and the ceiling, and there is no insulation in the roof.

The kitchen in this kind of building is always shared among all the households of the same floor. These kitchens are usually small, about thirty square feet in area. The floor is of concrete, graded to permit drainage. Cooking is done on fire-buckets burning discarded shuttering from building construction works. They are placed on a concrete bench under a smoke trap leading to the chimney. There is only one water tap to each floor. In the 1963-4 water crisis, the supply was sometimes inadequate so that many carried water home from standpipes several blocks away.[##] As the kitchens are so small and are shared between so many households, cooking utensils and water buckets have to be stored within each household's own accommodation.

There are no flush lavatories and bathrooms. Dry-pan lavatories are used by the children and the very old. These are kept under the bed. The night soil is removed by the Urban Services Department without charge. The adults avail themselves of the nearby public conveniences. The kitchen serves as the bath-space also.

The passage between the cubicles and the bunks is very narrow: seldom more than two feet wide. This serves as the sole thoroughfare for internal traffic. The investigator on several occasions while interviewing bunk-dwellers had to squeeze

---

[#] This height is in accordance with Urban Services Regulations.
[##] At the time of investigation Wan Chai received a house supply of water (for those with taps on the premises) of four hours every fourth day. In addition water was available at standpipes (intended for the use of those without taps in their homes) every other day for a period of four hours.

herself against the partitions to allow somebody to pass, often with wet washing, from the kitchen to the veranda.

The monthly rent for a bunk space in this type of building is ten to twenty dollars while that for a cubicle is twenty to thirty dollars.[#] Rent for a ground floor shop is about $150-$300. Shop-keepers included in the Hong Kong sample operated on a very small scale. Their shops occupied usually one-third of the area and frontage of a ground floor, and they paid about fifty to a hundred dollars for such premises.

(2) The second type of housing was built on the Wan Chai reclamation area after 1925. It consists of buildings grouped in blocks arranged in grid-iron pattern reaching to the existing praya. They are uniformly three storeys high with flat roof-tops. These houses are built of reinforced concrete with brick walls on both sides. The staircases and floors are also of reinforced concrete, some of the latter being tiled. The buildings have wide verandas (about eight feet). The main difference between this and the first type of accommodation is that these buildings have flush-toilets. In general, other arrangements are similar to the first type. The most notable difference to the investigator is that they are less decrepit than the previous type. A bunk space in this kind of building costs about twenty dollars a month, while cubicle costs approximately twenty-eight dollars.

(3) The third type of housing consists of multi-storey buildings constructed within the last five years. The buildings are built over sites previously occupied by premises of the above two types. They are often called in Chinese — modern 'Chinese tenement-type buildings' (唐樓). They are comparatively smaller than the first two types of building. The layout is also very different from that of the previous two types. The kitchen is tiled but without a chimney so that only kerosene stoves can be used with comfort; communal bath-rooms with bath tubs, wash-basins and toilets are available. The living space is built without permanent partitions. The arrangement of the cubicles follows no set pattern and may vary according to the shape of the living space and the number of cubicles to be accommodated. The rent for a cubicle in this type of building is eighty to a hundred dollars a month.

Apart from these main categories, there are three additional types of accommodation in the Wan Chai area and which are occupied by households in the Hong Kong sample:

(i) Some of the type (1) buildings are without partitions. The living space is occupied by two lines of two-tiered bunks with a passage six to seven feet wide between them. These premises are usually occupied by Chiu Chau rickshaw pullers who live as households. (The Chiu Chau come from the Swatow area of Kwangtung). The bunks are erected by the principal tenant and sublet to the worker-households at about ten dollars a month. Bunks down each side of the house are part of a single continuous framework. Simple boarding separates the adjacent bunks transversely.

(ii) Roof-top huts are usually built on the flat roofs of type (2) accommodation

---

[#] H.K.$16 = £ 1 Sterling.

described above. They are temporary wooden sheds built a little over ten years ago, largely by refugees from China. These structures are tolerated by the Squatter Control Section of the Resettlement Department. Roof-top squatter huts are built of timber and iron sheeting. It is usual to find the roofs of a whole block completely occupied by these huts, with a lane two to three feet wide between two rows of them down the length of the block. The huts are normally built by the occupants themselves and no rent is paid. However repair expenses after typhoons may be considerable.

Each household usually occupies two to three interconnecting huts so that the area of accommodation is roughly three times that of a cubicle-dweller's. Ventilation and natural lighting are fairly good due to the presence of windows in each hut. Electricity supply can sometimes be arranged with the tenant of the top floor of the building. Water is normally obtainable in the same way, but during the 1963-4 crisis,* such arrangements were suspended and the roof-top households had to draw water from public standpipes. Owing to the greater area available to a roof-top household it is usual to find an adjoining shed used as a kitchen. Toilet facilities other than dry pans are non-existent.

(iii) One household was found to occupy a shelter in a back lane between two blocks of houses. The lane is about six feet wide. A shelter made of iron sheeting on a wooden frame spanned the lane. Underneath were placed a narrow two-tiered bunk, a few stools and a small table. A small area, outside the sheltered space, served as kitchen. Ventilation was very poor and the air stale. Natural lighting was almost absent and it was very dark even in the early afternoon. A single kerosene lamp gave the only illumination. Water was provided free by a shop in the adjoining building.

Most of the households investigated lived in either a cubicle or bunk space, in the three main types of buildings.

(1) *Cubicles*: These are usually sixty square feet in area, i.e., about 8' by 8'. The cubicles are formed on one side by the side wall of the house, and on the other sides by the wooden partitions six feet high. The doorway facing the passage has no proper door. A piece of cotton cloth fixed over the entrance provides a little privacy. In the hot weather this is usually lifted to increase ventilation. Inside, the greater part of the cubicle is occupied by a two tier bunk either of wood or iron. The upper tier is reached by a small vertical ladder. Mattresses are never used. The bed-boards are covered with straw mats or more usually with fibre boards. Shelves are nailed on to the wall between the two tiers along the side and at the foot of the bed. These shelves provide the principal storage space. Clothing is put into large paper bags placed on the shelves. Occasionally an old suit-case can be seen. Cotton quilts and off-season clothing are wrapped in newspaper and hung from hooks driven into the ceiling. The rest of the cubicle is occupied by a few pieces of simple furniture. A small table and two or three stools stand near the doorway. Often there is a small cupboard near the bed on which water bottles, glasses, clocks, fans and transistor radios (if any) are placed. Over this

---

* This is a reference to severe water shortage at the time.

cupboard are framed photographs of the family or occasionally the family altar with soul-tablets used in ancestral worship. The remaining corner is generally occupied by the cooking utensils and water buckets. Rice, firewood and more water buckets are stowed under the bed. After accommodating all these things, generally less than ten square feet of foot-space is left in the cubicle.

(2) *Bunk spaces*: this usually measures 7' x 4'. A two-tier bunk of this size is the total accommodation available to the household. Water buckets, firewood, rice cooking utensils and tools are stowed under the bed. Clothing is put on shelves between the two tiers. Privacy is non-existent.

These people appear to live a very simple life. The wage earners work long hours in the day-time. Wives seldom work full time as they have to take care of the children as well as do all the house work. They usually take in some work to do at home in their spare time to contribute to the household budget. As the accommodation is so limited in area, such work is usually done on the beds, as is also the children's home-work. Sometimes if a child is in secondary school, he studies in another classmate's home or finds a 'quiet' spot to study, e.g., on the traffic-ridden waterfront near Harcourt Road. For the bunk-dwellers even the meals have to be taken on the bed.

As there are generally six to seven households on a floor, thirty to forty persons may crowd closely together in the small living space. The children, rather than stay on the beds all day, play in the streets until it is time to go to sleep. The adults also seek relief from the heat and congestion by sitting about in the street below, talking with the neighbours.

At night the small foot-space within the cubicle is taken up by camp beds. If a bunk-dwelling household is large, the father, and perhaps a son, sometimes sleep in the street, especially in the summer.

Income

Sources of income

A total household income is usually the combined income of two or three members. A typical situation is for the father to be the chief earning member, and the wife or a child or both to supplement his income with earnings of something less than a hundred dollars a month. Exceptions were found, however, where wives were chief earning members due to special circumstances and became virtually heads of the households, i.e., they had major control over allocation of money to be spent on household expenses. In one household in Kowloon, the husband was an ice-cream vendor who had earned about $150 a month. During the past few years he had been continuously ill, however, and as a result his earnings dropped to sixty dollars a month. The wife, after discussing their financial difficulties with the principal of the school which their children attended, went to work as a servant in the school and received a salary of $160 by working for the morning, afternoon and evening sessions. One effect of the wife becoming the chief earning member, which is not evident in the household described above was clearly demonstrated in another household in Kowloon. Here, the husband used to be a rattan-worker but he had been out of work for the past five or six years because of his failing strength. When the investigator visited the household, she found that it was the wife who went out to work while the husband stayed home to look after the children. When the investigator further asked who controlled the budget, the reply from the husband was that since he did not earn anything, he had no say in such matters.

A household with more than three earning members was unusual. This is perhaps due to the fact that most of the households had few adults and several children who were quite young.

Sometimes a man and his wife shared the task of providing income by working together. It was common to find in hawker households that both the head and his wife were engaged in the business. Hawkers had to make a daily trip to the wholesalers to get their wares and unless a hawker was content with half a day's trade, he needed another person to help with sales while he was away buying goods. Furthermore two persons could do more business than one. Wives whose husbands were tailors were often their husbands' only assistant as these tailors operated on a very small scale and could not afford extra help. The wives usually helped to sew on buttons or to make button-holes and do any other small tailoring jobs that might be required.

Sometimes a man and his wife were employed as wage earners in the same kind of work. One couple explained that both had been working in an electro-plating factory even before their marriage and they had continued doing so afterwards. There were a few cases in which a husband engaged in sewing work and using a sewing machine, taught his wife how to do the work. He was able to get work for the two of them, then. In one household, the head was engaged in removing garbage from one restaurant while his wife did the same work for another restaurant operated by the same management.

There were some instances both in the Hong Kong and Kowloon samples where there was only one earning member: the mother. Sometimes the head of the household was a widow, who, after the death of her husband, had to provide for herself and her children as best she could. Such widows were commonly unskilled and consequently had to struggle very hard to make ends meet. An instance of such a person was the widow of a rickshaw coolie. She earned money by doing ironing in the street getting about fifty cents to two dollars per day. After deducting the cost for charcoal for her iron, her net income was about twenty-five dollars a month. In addition she received twenty dollars each month from St. James Settlement for the school fees of her children. With a total income of forty-five dollars a month she had to support her family of three children. The eldest child, aged twelve, was a hunch-back. This household had been living at about subsistence level for five years and there seemed to be little prospect for improvement in the near future.

Other widows though better off in comparison with this woman, often could not earn much as they had to take care of their children. An exception was a widow who was able to work as a full time vegetable hawker because she was helped with the housework by her twelve year-old daughter. The nature of her work allowed her to visit her home at intervals during each day. Most widows however took in work that could be done at home. For example, a widow who sewed at home for a textile factory earned $120 a month. Another widow earned approximately the same by selling to the staff of a small ballroom prepared dinners which she cooked at home. For a dollar, she provided rice, a small bowl of soup and three small dishes of vegetables and meat or fish per person, but since she had to do all the cooking in a kitchen shared with the rest of the tenants on the same floor, she could provide only fifteen to twenty such meals each evening. Another widow living with her only son in Kowloon could only earn thirty to sixty dollars a month by doing handicraft work such as pasting fur on to slippers. Her health was poor and she complained of frequent dizzy spells, even when going to the market to buy food. Her son was thirteen and a half years old and was still studying. But in one sense they were more fortunate than other households headed by widows in that they had relatives, the husband's sister and her son—who helped regularly either by paying the rent for them or by buying rice they needed. In general, most of the widows visited had only themselves to depend on for income, because their children were still too young to contribute. There was only one case of a widow (in Kowloon) who had children earning: a son and a daughter. A possible explanation for the fact that there were so many young children without fathers is that quite a few of these widows were second wives. Their deceased husbands had been much older than they were.

Wives' contributions to income from work at home

When the husband was the chief earning member, the other main contributing member was usually his wife. Many wives could not take full-time employment because of the pressure of housework but most of the housewives visited augmented the household income by doing some handicraft work at home — such as sewing or making plastic flowers. Work was paid on a piece-rate basis. Wages for making a gross of plastic flowers appear to vary from fifty cents to a little over a dollar depending on how elaborate the flowers are. A woman could make from about fifteen to forty dollars a month without leaving home. A person who could devote her time entirely to making plastic flowers, as in the case of a housewife whose household was looked after by the husband's mother, was able to make $100 to supplement her husband's income as a barber. Two housewives in Shau Kei Wan assembled plastic toys at home and lived near to the factory providing such work. They earned about fifty to eighty dollars each per month.

Other handicrafts which could be engaged in at home included the making of paper bags, threading of necklaces, and the making of wristwatch bands. Some housewives who supplemented income by doing needlework earned ten to twenty dollars a month by sewing together gloves, sewing together sweaters, or by embroidering woollen gloves or sweaters. Some wives worked with sewing machines and a woman earned in one case as much as $100 a month in her spare time sewing shoes. She said that if she could work in a factory she would be able to earn $300 a month but as she had to look after the family she had to stay at home earning less.

Some housewives supplemented their husband's incomes by taking in washing and ironing. Such women can earn about thirty dollars a month. In one household where the wife shared the housework with her sister-in-law, she was able to earn about seventy dollars a month.

As can be gathered, housewives are very reluctant to work outside, chiefly because they have to look after their family and home. Exceptions were cases where the housework could be performed by a relative, for example, the husband's mother or mother-in-law, or where the children were capable of taking care of themselves. In one household where the wife worked in a factory and the husband in a mahjong school four of the five children attended school. Since one attended the morning session, two the afternoon, and one the evening session, there was always a child in the house to look after the youngest child aged three even when both husband and wife were away working. Another exception concerned a wife who worked as a binder in a printing firm. She was not regularly employed but worked ten to twenty days in a month. She could earn about fifty dollars a month and said she used the money to pay for her children's school fees. In another case, the wife of a driving instructor worked away from home as a daily amah (domestic servant) in a European household earning $200 a month. There were a few housewives in the Hong Kong sample who worked as part-time amahs during the time their children were away at school each day. This left the rest of the day for looking after their own households. They could earn about fifty dollars this way a month.

Other outside workers

When there were more than two outside earning members in the same household, the third member was usually one of the children. Traditionally in Chinese families daughters did not work outside but in Hong Kong this is changing. Daughters often work in factories. For example an eldest daughter in one household worked in a garment factory as a sewing machine operator. She worked from 8 a.m. to 7 p.m. with only an hour off for lunch and was paid a dollar for every dozen shirts finished. At the most she could earn about $4.50 a day but due to the present limited quota for export there was not always work enough to go around and on some days she was in fact given only three dozen shirts to sew. The amount of work she did each day was recorded and she was paid at the end of the month.

The eldest daughter of another household worked in a glove factory. She was also paid piece-rates. However she had two days off each month and she was paid every fortnight.

Some daughters worked at daily calculated rates paid monthly, in metalwork or plastic factories. They were paid two to three dollars a day, and were usually employed for about twenty-five days in a month.

Sons who were earning members of their households were often employed on a regular monthly basis. Several worked as errand boys in stores or restaurants. Others were apprenticed to a particular trade and though their earnings during the apprenticeship were small, they were provided with free board and lodgings.

Most children who are working contribute from about 30%-80% of their earnings towards the household budget. They usually keep something back to pay for their fares and lunches and to buy their clothes. A few however contribute their entire earnings. The proportion handed over by working children varied considerably because in some cases earnings of parents were so meagre that the household depended greatly on the child's contributions; in other cases the chief earner — father or mother — was able to take care of the main items of expenditure and the children's' supplement was not of such importance.

Sometimes older relatives living with households, such as the husband's or the wife's mother, earn a small sum by working at handicrafts in the home, as occasional hands in a factory, or selling toys at a small sidestall. When mothers and sisters of the husband or wife of a household were members they usually contributed their total earnings towards the household income.

Other contributions to income: occasional members

Sometimes the total income of a household included contributions from occasional members such as an absentee husband, who lived at their place of work.

Some husbands live away from their home because their place of work is far away — in the New Territories, or even abroad, e.g. in the Philippines. There was a case in Kowloon of a household consisting of a wife, and four sons aged thirteen, eleven, seven and four. There were three grown up daughters living in the Mainland. The woman was married as first wife in a village in China, but since the first three children born to her and her husband were girls and the husband's mother wanted a grandson, the husband had taken a concubine. When the Communists took over the Mainland, the husband and his two wives came to Hong Kong leaving behind his mother and their three daughters. Since coming to Hong Kong the first wife had borne four sons. At present the husband contributes sixty dollars a month to this first wife's household but he himself lives most of the time with his second wife and their six children in other premises.

Others contributing to income: outside sources

Sometimes members of other households contribute income, e.g. married children living elsewhere. Other relatives sometimes also contribute regularly to help out a household. For example, the wife in one household used to receive U.S.$50 six times a year from her father who was working in the United States. Recently, however, there had been no remittance and so the wife had started working as a servant in a restaurant to supplement their income.

There were two households where the income was entirely provided from outside sources. One was a household in Hong Kong which consisted of five orphans. Their father had died from an accident. The firm he was working for paid compensation and his colleagues donated money so that his widow and children received about $20,000 at that time. With this money, the widow had bought a flat which she let out at $280 a month. She died recently, however, and the children's expenses were provided for out of this rent money. This arrangement was only temporary as the Social Welfare Department was soon to place the three younger children in a children's home and their flat was to be held in trust under Government control until the eldest child was twenty-one years old. A household in Kowloon consisted of a man and wife and the two children of their son who was in China. The man had recently returned to Hong Kong after working for forty years in Canada. The whole family now depended on his monthly pension of sixty Canadian dollars. The man and his wife were over seventy and the two grand-children aged nine and ten were attending school.

The heads of some households were the principal tenants of a floor. Such households usually occupied the front portion of the floor and the veranda and the rest of the area was divided into two cubicles and two bunk-spaces which were let to subtenants. The rent received more or less covered the rent the principal tenant had to pay to his landlord so that in fact by acting as a principal tenant, he had earned for his household free or virtually free accommodation.

Charitable sources

A source of income very common among the households investigated was some form of payment from charitable and welfare organizations. Most of the households benefitting from these sources belonged to the income group which had less than $250 a month. However, it must also be pointed out that there were quite a number belonging to this group who did not receive any help. About a quarter of the households in the Hong Kong sample were given assistance by the St. James' Settlement (to be distinguished from St. James' Primary School. Many of the children in St. James' School belong to clubs run by the Settlement. Both organizations are run by the Anglican Church in Hong Kong). People send donations to the St. James' Settlement, mostly from abroad, under a Sponsorship Scheme. The personnel of St. James' Settlement visit the homes of the St. James' School pupils to investigate their financial conditions. If it is decided that they need help, each child attending St. James' School is given a monthly ten dollar subsidy by a sponsor. The money is used for school fees, pocket money and to pay for the ten cent lunch children can obtain at school each day. The Sponsor also pays for the child's stationery at the beginning of term. The assistance continues until the child leaves school. Any Sponsored child who has finished primary school and has managed to continue to secondary school will continue to receive assistance through the Sponsorship Scheme until graduation.

Daily life

In one household in Hong Kong there were eight persons: Cheng Ying, the father, his wife, and six children who were two sons and four daughters. They lived in a cubicle in the middle of the first floor of an old Chinese tenement building. The cubicle measured seven feet by eight feet, and was partitioned off from the rest of the floor by wooden boards, six feet high. There was no door, and an opening in the wooden partitions served as the doorway, over which a piece of cotton cloth was draped. There was no window. The room was dark, and artificial lighting had to be used throughout the day. The air in the room was stale and stuffy. Often the cotton cloth hanging over the door was lifted to encourage ventilation.

As the household shared the use of the kitchen with the other occupants of the floor, there was not enough space in the kitchen to store their cooking utensils and so all the pots and pans, as well as the water buckets, were stored within the cubicle. This made the living conditions very crowded. The small cubicle with a total area of less than sixty square feet was very small for the size of this family. In an attempt to accommodate every member, a seven feet by four feet two-tier bed had been made. The father and the two sons slept on the upper deck while the wife and daughters slept below.

Early every morning, at about six o' clock, the father, who was the chief earning member, got down from the upper deck of the bed, fetched some water from the water bucket under the bed, and carried it down to the street when he washed himself. Then, without any breakfast at home he went to look for work. As he was a casual, but skilled, labourer working in the building construction industry, and specialising in masonry and bricklaying, he had to wait for employment every morning outside the Southorn Playground. As he waited for the contractors to come he would perhaps buy a bun or two for ten cents from a nearby store, and this would serve as his breakfast. At about seven in the morning the contractors would come to pick the men for the day's work. For about a dozen days a month he would be chosen and told to go to a certain construction site. If the place was far, a lorry was provided to take him there, otherwise he would have to make his own way before eight o'clock. On the days that he was not chosen, he might go with others of the same trade to have something to eat at a tea-shop or road-side stall, where the group would discuss opportunities for employment. In the summer months of 1963 there were many days when he was not employed. This was because the contractors could not store enough water during the water crisis, and construction work had to be stopped on some days. On the days when he was not working, Mr. Cheng would go to a coffin shop opposite their house and collect the leftover wood chips as firewood. If it was water-supply day he would take a couple of buckets and queue for water from a standpipe in the street. Ordinarily the children took care of storing water. But they had to wait for their turn in the kitchen and this took up so much time that they sometimes could not finish their school work.

The second to leave in the morning was the first son. He was sixteen years old, and studying in a secondary school. Before he left for school his mother gave him thirty cents as pocket money, which he spent on bread or cakes on his way to school. The rest of the children were still in primary schools, which operated in the afternoon only. When Mrs. Cheng had washed her two younger children, she gave each of them ten cents as pocket money and sent them down to the street to play and to buy their breakfast while she did the laundry. Then she went and bought about a dollar and fifty cents worth of vegetables, fish or meat. She cooked half of this to go with the rice for lunch. The elder son came home for his lunch since the school was quite near. After lunch all the children walked to school together.

In the afternoon, when all her children were away in school, Mrs. Cheng went to work as a part-time amah in a doctor's home. For doing the washing and ironing every afternoon, she was paid fifty dollars a month, and was provided with an evening meal.

While Mrs. Cheng ate her dinner at the doctor's place, the children had finished school and her husband had come back from work (if he had been working that day). The eldest daughter, who was fourteen years old, cooked the rice and the other half of the food her mother had bought in the morning. When they had finished their dinner, at about eight o'clock, Mrs. Cheng returned from her work. If the father had been working that day, he would give about ten dollars of his earnings to his wife, for housekeeping. Then he would take his bamboo pipe down to the street and sit round with the neighbours chatting all evening.

The eldest son, after dinner, took his books and went to a classmate's home to do his homework as his own home environment was not conducive to study. Then the other children scrambled on to the bed to do their school work. The bed served also as their desks, for the only other pieces of furniture in the cubicle were a tiny table and a couple of stools. When the children had settled down to study, Mrs. Cheng would take out her needlework. Because her younger children were studying in St. James P.M. School, they were sometimes given old clothing by St. James Settlement which Mrs. Cheng altered for her family's use. Sometimes, when she had nothing to sew for her children, she altered clothes for her neighbours, or she sewed on buttons for some garment manufacturers. In this way she not only saved on the amount spent on clothing but she could also earn an extra ten dollars or so a month.

At about eleven, she put away her sewing and sent one of the children to buy twenty cents worth of bread. This was for the eldest son's later supper when he returned from his studies.

By midnight, every one was home, and they prepared to go to bed. On some hot and damp evenings, the heat in the crowded cubicle was very oppressive. Then the father and the younger son slept on a camp bed in the street. This left the upper deck of the bed to their elder son. The lower deck, however, was still very crowded. They tried to relieve this to some extent by spreading a mat on the small floor space still left in the cubicle, and this accommodated the two youngest daughters.

And thus the days followed one another. The parents attended to their work and the children their studies. There are few recreational activities to add variations to their lives. For this particular household, however, there was some hope for better days to come — when the eldest son completed secondary school and might be able to earn a good living. For this hope the family was sacrificing much. The mother left her home to go out to work every day. The younger children took on chores which would otherwise have been done by mother. They all had to cut down on unessential expenses. Many of the other households in the samples were less fortunate however, being without children in secondary school. They passed their lives without very much hope of future betterment...

c. Changes in Personal Characteristics

DOCUMENT VI.c1: 1966 bi-census, comments on the tables (source: K.M.A. Barnett, *Hong Kong, Report on the 1966 By-Census*, Hong Kong: Government Printer, 1968, vol. 1, pp. ix-xi)

As compared with the 1961 census the total number of households has increased less rapidly than the population (13.0 % against 18.5 %; land population 14.5% against 20.5%) and the distribution of household size shows the reason for this to have been a reduction in the number of single person households. Such households, as shown in Table 020 of the 1961 census report, then amounted to 15.5% of the total, and this was affected by the failure of new domestic building to keep up with new industrial building. As a result, a substantial number of young married men used to live apart from their families so as to be nearer to their work. This has been reduced (13.6% of all, or 13.9 % of domestic households) resulting in an apparent increase in the average size of domestic households, indicating not that households are really larger but that better opportunities are now provided for the whole family to live together. And although the phenomenon of a one-person household is now rare in the newly developed areas, it is still far from uncommon in Tsim Sha Tsui, Cheung Sha Wan, Yau Ma Tei and Wan Chai.

...

A feature of [Table 6.1] worthy of observation is the extent to which the sharing of domestic premises diminishes as you go from the older to the newer urban districts. In Sheung Wan district of Hong Kong Island and Yau Ma Tei district of Kowloon, shared domestic premises well out-number unshared; but in Ho Man Tin district of Kowloon and in Ngau Tau Kok district of New Kowloon such sharing is quite uncommon, as it is in most of the New Territories.

...

In paragraph 20.4 of the 1961 Census Report it was observed that out of 2,396,364 persons found living in houses built of permanent materials, 130,095 (5.4%) were using substandard accommodation such as basements, cocklofts and non-domestic space. Table 006 now shows that in August 1966, 3,228,600 persons were living in houses built of permanent materials and 211,000 (6.5%) of these were using substandard accommodation.

The 1961 Report went on to add in the roof-dwellers and wooden-hut 'squatters', those living in hawker stalls and similar 'non-house' accommodation and thus reached a total of 726,577 for those whose housing condition appeared to be gravely inadequate.

Table 6.1
Quinquennial Age Groups by Sexes Compared with Previous Censuses*

Age group	1921 Male	1921 Female	1931 Male	1931 Female	1961 Male	1961 Female	1966 Male	1966 Female
0 – 4	27,930	27,095	44,193	44,338	257,699	243,007	261,150	249,470
5 – 9	23,931	25,281	32,694	32,644	220,432	204,916	275,190	253,810
10 – 14	30,658	26,218	42,322	34,339	185,884	165,097	233,630	214,760
15 – 19	50,660	23,702	59,713	34,818	90,240	74,857	204,000	180,340
20 – 24	50,547	23,187	67,485	37,554	111,242	91,499	106,770	93,990
25 – 29	46,290	24,297	51,290	35,487	137,216	116,780	112,870	97,260
30 – 34	38,927	20,655	46,171	30,945	140,885	122,236	129,390	114,980
35 – 39	36,848	20,099	35,389	26,181	123,332	111,621	132,540	127,440
40 – 44	24,859	13,103	31,862	21,911	107,321	95,717	118,840	115,800
45 – 49	19,716	11,564	24,311	18,179	86,523	80,715	98,090	93,310
50 – 54	12,590	7,335	18,480	13,467	60,078	63,802	82,490	82,690
55 – 59	8,421	6,411	11,783	10,643	37,217	49,800	54,160	64,000
60 – 64	4,543	3,859	7,334	7,153	23,582	40,032	35,460	55,050
65 – 69	3,836	2,647	3,823	4,520	13,203	27,815	18,620	38,340
70 – 74	1,166	1,641	1,750	2,403	7,559	18,497	11,040	26,950
75 & over	718	1,372	986	2,155	5,366	15,478	6,630	19,860
Not stated	1,217	3,843	2,994	1,156	–	–	–	–
Total	382,857	242,309	482,580	357,893	1,607,779	1,521,869	1,880,870	1,828,050

*Simplified from original

Adding up the corresponding categories from the 1966 tables gives a total of 505,600 who then were inadequately housed. The tables show a great reduction in the number of roof-top dwellers, especially in Kowloon.

. . . .

By far the most important part of any census report on which all the other tables revolve are the tables showing individual characteristics, especially those in which the population is analysed by sex and age. These are collected in Section B.

The most useful table for general purposes is No. 023 [Table 6.01], which shows the 1966 population by sex and quinquennial age group compared with the three previous censuses. The trends observed in 1961 have continued, namely the sex ratio is approaching equality and the age distribution shows a more even gradation, except for the gap caused by the Pacific War, which was observed in 1961 in the groups 15-19 and 20-24 and therefore in 1966 has moved up to the groups 20-24 and 25-29.

Tables 022 and 022A show the sex ratio by census areas compared with the last three censuses. Table 021 shows population by sex and individual year of age, and those under one year of age by month of age. It also divides the population into Hong Kong born and those born elsewhere.

It will be observed from Table 021 that whereas in 1961 the sex-ratio among those claiming Hong Kong birth was lower than the rest (1038.9 against 1072.7) in 1966 the position appears to have been reversed. Males claiming Hong Kong birth number 1065.5 to every 1000 females claiming Hong Kong birth, whereas males born elsewhere number only 987.1 to every thousand females born elsewhere. Out of many possible explanations for this curiosity the simplest may be that our young people (aged 15 and down) are now overwhelmingly Hong Kong born and, since women live longer than men but more males are born than females, the sex ratio decreases with age. Nevertheless for a change of this magnitude to show in 5-1/2 years implies either that a significant group of males claimed Hong Kong birth in 1966 after having not claimed it in 1961, or that a significant group of females claimed Hong Kong birth in 1961 but did not claim it in 1966.

. . .

The importance of Table 026 is the light it throws on the attitude towards age of marriage, which has a strong bearing on estimates of future fertility. In the absence of a complete system of marriage registration (since Chinese customary marriages do not yet require to be registered) this information can be sought only from the census. Therefore to facilitate study, the percentages compared with 1961 are shown in a subsidiary Table 26A and area percentages in 26B. These indicate how rare, even in the New Territories, are teenaged married persons; also how the tendency, already observed in 1961, for men to defer their marriage to after 30 has continued to develop, though not to so marked a degree among the rural and marine populations as it has in the cities.

In connection with language, which is the theme of Tables 027-030, the reader is invited to study paragraph 11.2 of the 1961 Census Report, in which the reasons for

Table 6.2
Usual Language, Totals and Percentages Compared with 1961

Usual language	1966		1961	
	Total	%	Total	%
Cantonese	2,968,420	81.43	2,076,210	79.02
Hoklo	298,470	8.19	164,537	6.26
Hakka	121,430	3.33	128,432	4.89
Sze Yap	112,230	3.08	114,484	4.36
Other Chinese	101,580	2.79	95,544	3.64
English	29,300	0.80	31,824	1.21
Others	11,400	0.31	16,329	0.62

focusing attention on certain linguistic groups were explained in detail. In Appendix 13 [Table 6.2] Table 029 is summarized in percentages and compared with 1961, showing how the Cantonese language continues to spread. The only linguistic group which holds its own is Hoklo, which was already observed in 1961 to be highly resistant to assimilation.

Although English as a 'usual language' continues to be rare, ability to speak English is shown by Tables 027 to 029 to have increased greatly. Over 20% of the population can now speak some English, as against less than 10% in 1961. It can be seen, as might be expected, that English speakers are few among the rural and marine population, and commonest among young city dwellers. But little correlation can be found with place of birth, place of origin, or usual language where this is some kind of Chinese.

Table 030, 030A and 033 study place of origin crossed with language, sex, age and birthplace. The importance of this is more clearly seen in Tables 036 to 039A to be its bearing on fertility. Although paragraph 20.7.7 of the 1961 Census Report could not detect any significant difference in size of family between married women from different parts of China, subsequent analysis of 1961 census table 147 showed this judgment to have been hasty. For when the family sizes of women aged 35-39 and 40-44 (by which age childbearing would normally be completed) are analysed, it is seen that women of Chiu Chau origin have significantly larger numbers of children than women from other parts of China; always excepting the boat people, who have the biggest families of all. Table 039 shows this distinction to be still valid; and the proportion of Chiu Chau women who have already had two children before the age of 25 being no less than before, leaves small room to hope for an early reduction in the fertility of this sturdy and unassimilable group.

Tables 031 and 032 both show employment status by sex and age group, totalled in census areas, and form a useful introduction to the economic tables in Section D.

Appendix 14 [Table 6.3] is a condensation of Table 031 and the indices indicate that the Hong Kong born are more than proportionately represented in the 'modern sector' for the definition of which see notes (a), (p) and (q) to Code 12 in Appendix 4.* And since a greater proportion of unemployed at the younger ages are found in the Hong Kong born, a likely explanation is that immigrants are less reluctant than locals to accept jobs in the 'traditional' sector. This finding is in contrast with that of paragraph 21.2.6 of the 1961 Census Report. Table 032 indicates that ability to speak English does not alter the chances of obtaining employment in the modern sector, or at all, but modern sector employers and self-employed contain a higher proportion of English speakers.

. . . .

Some progress, however, has been made towards general literacy outside these two groups. It will be recalled that in 1961 all persons aged 10 and up who had been to school were found to be literate and all persons aged 10 and up who had never been to

---

* The notes state
 (a) The modern sector of the economy is distinguished by these typical characteristics:
 (1) Premises usually specially designed for the industrial undertaking.
 (2) Undertakings are often large.
 (3) Equipment often includes power-driven machinery.
 (4) Labour (i) works set hours; (ii) is paid an agreed or contracted rate per month, per day or per hour, with extra for overtime; or on piece work at an agreed or contracted rate; (iii) is union organized.
 (5) The capital is that of a joint stock (limited) company, the capital-labour ratio is high, the levels of technology and productivity are high and bear an economic relationship to the rewards.
 (p) The traditional sector of the economy is distinguished from the modern sector by these typical characteristics:
 (1) Premises usually not designed for the industrial undertaking, e.g. domestic premises, the street, a village out-house or squatter shack.
 (2) Undertakings are small, usually under 20 persons.
 (3) Equipment consists of craft tools or simple machinery; power-driven machinery is the exception.
 (4) Labour (i) is usually from one family, clan village or district; (ii) hours and conditions of work are not specified; (iii) receives no agreed or contracted rate of pay per month, day or hour; but either piece-work on a customary basis, or profit-sharing with pocket money; unpaid family help is very common; (iv) is not organized into unions.
 (5) The working capital is provided on a family or partnership basis and the capital-labour ratio is low. Productivity and rewards are related.
 (q) In the traditional sector there is usually no time-keeping. To those unfamiliar with local customs there often seems to be a lack of defined function. A farmer's wife is often both a full-time housewife and a full-time farmer. A farmer's old mother, though 'retired' is probably doing as much work on the land as anybody will let her. But the wives of a business director, who help their husband entertain some business associate and his wives, are regarded as non-working partners.

Table 6.3
Economically Active by Place of Birth

Sex	Category	Local born		Immigrant		Total	
		Figures	Index	Figures	Index	Figures	Index
M	Modern sector	135,090	54	335,640	48	470,730	49
	Traditional sector	102,080	41	348,520	49	450,600	47
	Unemployed	13,370	5	21,050	3	34,420	4
	Total*	250,540	100	705,210	100	955,750	100
F	Modern sector	76,340	48	118,710	38	195,050	41
	Traditional sector	71,080	45	187,410	60	258,490	55
	Unemployed	10,410	7	7,880	2	18,290	4
	Total*	157,830	100	314,000	100	471,830	100

*Total economically active

Table 6.4
Hong Kong Censuses 1961 and 1966: Literacy

		Aged 10-34		Aged 35 and up	
		1961	1966	1961	1966
Hong Kong	M	96.20 %	97.90 %	91.07%	90.53%
	F	82.22	92.57	41.29	43.79
	T	89.83	95.42	64.89	65.50
Kowloon	M	96.37	97.11	91.88	91.99
	F	83.57	90.47	41.74	48.41
	T	90.56	94.11	65.05	68.81
New Kowloon	M	94.98	97.34	90.12	88.28
	F	76.66	89.32	36.95	36.98
	T	86.19	93.44	62.39	61.25
Tsuen Wan	M	94.10	94.70	86.45	83.50
	F	72.57	83.24	28.97	31.43
	T	84.97	89.30	61.82	58.74
N.T. (except Tsuen Wan)	M	91.79	95.33	82.69	79.50
	F	61.69	77.37	21.36	22.30
	T	77.72	86.34	51.80	46.46
Boat people	M	39.68	42.84	31.48	22.62
	F	14.70	17.64	21.88	20.54
	T	28.46	31.53	17.69	13.73

school were (with few exceptions) illiterate. Table 159 of the 1961 Report further showed how illiteracy, except among the boat people, was chiefly a problem of the higher age groups, especially among women. Appendix 15 [Table 6.4] now contains the comparison between 1961 and 1966, showing that for those aged 10 to 34 some progress has been made, even in rural areas; but for those aged 35 and up there has been no improvement.

d. Industrialization in the 1950s

> Hong Kong not only survived the 1950s and early 1960s, its economy thrived. Associated with the opportunities that were brought about by economic growth was upward mobility for the new migrants from China. The 1950s and 1960s were characterized by weak trade unions but strong motivation for those who had found work to advance. One might detect in the new immigrant the stubborn determination to succeed knowing well that there was no alternative. A section of the population given economic opportunities and willing to learn professionalized quickly. The rewards were high for those who succeeded in advancing, but a gap in the social structure was soon noticeable.

DOCUMENT VI.d1: Recollections of a Hong Kong industrialist (source: H.C. Ting, *Truth and Facts, Recollections of a Hong Kong Industrialist*, Hong Kong, 1974, pp. 72-73, 76-77, 79-85)

For more than a hundred years after its founding, Hong Kong was mainly known as a free port and an entrepot. In the past, few had ever thought that Hong Kong would one day become a world renown industrial city. In terms of natural endowments, Hong Kong neither had the land needed for industrial development, nor the natural resources for raw materials supply, and still less a domestic market to absorb what its own factories would produce.

Lacking in all these basic requirements for industrial development, Hong Kong, in fact, had no foundation whatsoever before World War II in the area of large-scale manufacturing. Whatever rudimentary industrial processes which were carried on in Hong Kong prior to World War II were limited to the manufacture of flashlights, storm lanterns, metal-wares, a few small weaving mills and dockyards for ship repairs and the building of small boats.

Manufacturing then was not an important social and economic factor in Hong Kong's overall existence nor did the city's industrial output have any economic impact on overseas market.

This situation began to change after V J Day, and the main reason which brought about the transformation was the influx into Hong Kong of a large number of Chinese from the mainland who were unwilling to submit to the rule of Chinese Communism.

When the Communists took over the mainland, Hong Kong's population quickly rose to more than 2.5 million people.

Forced to flee in an endless stream into Hong Kong, these refugees had to find a means of livelihood on a barren island. They thus provided Hong Kong with the first essential ingredient of industrial development: skilled and inexpensive labour.

At the same time, among the people who came from the mainland, there were many who were successful and experienced in operating industries in China. They brought along with them not only their money but also their technical skill and a tremendous store of varied manufacturing experience. They immediately set to work and established spinning mills, plastics factories and other industrial enterprises which never before had operated in Hong Kong. They had planted the first seeds of Hong Kong's industrial growth. . ...

Kader Industrial Company Ltd was formally established in Hong Kong in 1947. Immediately thereafter, we built our own factory in North Point. With intensive preparation, we opened our cold storage and ice-making plant in 1948. The plastic plant started production in 1949. In 1948 I made a brief visit to Hong Kong, but returned shortly to Shanghai.

It was then my intention to make periodic visits to Hong Kong, perhaps as business-cum-pleasure trips after Kader's business got under way. I thought that I would be able to stay alternately in Shanghai and Hong Kong, with my principal enterprise still concentrated in Shanghai. At that time I never had the intention of leaving Shanghai permanently.

Toward the end of 1948, however, I heard unexpectedly that the situation in Kader was far from satisfactory. I felt that it was imperative for me to come to Hong Kong to look into the matter personally and to help solve the problems if necessary. I flew from Shanghai to Hong Kong on December 22, 1948 and found that our new enterprise was indeed faced with many problems. I stayed for several months and returned to Shanghai on March 17, 1949. But on April 28, 1949 I returned to Hong Kong again. By that time, the situation in Shanghai was already in a state of great chaos, and not long afterwards events took a rapid turn for the worse, with the Communists taking over Shanghai and the rest of the Mainland.

This sudden political change caused me to remain in Hong Kong, and I have not returned since. In the 21 years of my stay in Hong Kong, I was able to take part in the early struggle to establish Hong Kong's new industrial complex. . ...

When I came to Hong Kong in December 1948, I could already see that the situation on the Mainland was in the process of a cataclysmic change. No one could foretell at that stage what would happen to the business and the personnel left behind in Shanghai. Having spent my life in building up a manufacturing enterprise, I was perplexed and disillusioned.

I was not particularly interested in starting anew in Hong Kong. I had earlier established Kader Industrial Company in Hong Kong, but that was merely in an effort to help some friends to set up a business, although I owned some 90 per cent of the shares of the concern. Part of the other money invested in the company came from loans I made to friends.

I had the title of Chairman of the Company, and according to the customary practice in China at that time, the Company Chairman took no actual part in the operation of the firm nor did he deal directly with the company's affairs.

Although I had heard prior to my arrival that the handling of various affairs at Kader was by no means satisfactory, I had not wanted to play a personal part in the company's management. I had hoped that those originally responsible would in time be able to assume proper control over crucial matters and spare me from concern and personal participation.

However, I discovered after my arrival that although the company occupied a modern, streamlined plant, which gave an impressive appearance of prosperity, its internal administration was by no means in a state of robust health. Its monthly expenditures were in the region of $40,000 to $50,000, but its income was extremely limited.

I found that the ice-making department produced about 200 to 300 blocks of ice per month, and the revenue derived from sales was not sufficient to cover wages and the cost of electricity. The cold storage plant was cramped in space and rental derived from the storage was in the region of $8,000 to $9,000, a sum too insignificant to make the operation worthwhile.

The plastics department had already started operation, but it was only equipped with two eight-ounce machines and two small two-ounce machines. Whatever production in progress was, in fact, token in nature.

From a purely theoretical point of view, all the departments were in operation and there were some 100 to 200 workers. But in actual practice, one could not really appraise the entire operation in terms of efficiency and productivity. Even proper accounts and invoices were lacking.

There were quite a number of workers but the pay was extremely low and the morale among the employees was usually poor. There were, for instance, three watchmen on the payroll, working on three shifts, each one of them getting only $90 a month. This was not enough for a man to live on, and it was impossible to expect such low pay to stimulate his interest in his job or encourage him to work with great enthusiasm and efficiency.

I found that by 5 p.m., the plant was emptied of all employees, and at that hour it was not an easy task to find even one single staff member who had stayed behind. Under these circumstances, the company certainly did not appear to be a booming, properly-run business, endowed with a promising future.

I realized, of course, that it was by no means the intention of those in charge to cause the company to deteriorate. The situation was brought about by their lack of experience in handling the affairs of the company properly.

I knew that the company would run into grave jeopardy if the decline was to continue and if I did not seek to correct the situation by providing the proper advice drawn from my long experience in running industrial management. But I found that it was difficult to make the employees fully understand my ideas and my methods during a short period of time, and the results achieved were therefore negligible.

By June 1949, the company was faced with demands from Banque de l'Indochine to settle its outstanding loan by a certain time limit. If it was not able to make good the loan, the only alternative was foreclosure, and the company's assets must then be sold at auction.

All those who were then responsible for running the company were at a loss as to what to do. They repeatedly asked me to take personal charge of what was in fact a desperate situation. In order to save the business and also to insure my own survival in Hong Kong, I had little choice but to abandon my original intention of staying out of active business. On the 1st of July that year, I assumed actual management and full responsibility of the Company as Chairman and Managing Director.

Under my personal direction, I began, as my first task, an internal reorganisation of all the Company's various departments, correcting some of the irrational errors of the past. In terms of personnel, I did not bring in any new employees who were in any way personnally connected with me. Nor did I reduce the number of employees or slash wages.

Instead, by appraising job requirements and capabilities of individual employees, I managed to increase the efficiency of every individual and every department. Furthermore, I succeeded in bringing about an increased interest of each employee in his job by paying him a better wage and giving him better treatment.

Take the case of the watchman as an example. I reduced the original number from three to one, doubling the salary of the single watchman. The other two were transferred to other departments. I took similar steps with other departments, thus bringing about overall improvement.

I was a novice in the plastics and ice-making industries, but I spared neither time nor effort in studying the basic problems and techniques. In time, I gradually grasped the fundamental points involved in the manufacturing processes.

In ice-making, for instance, I went to work in the plant for a while and found that by adding some minor equipment, I could increase the output and improve the quality with a substantial reduction of both manpower and time. The result was an increase in production from a total of 200 to 300 blocks of ice per month to a daily output of more than 100 blocks.

I made a practice of holding discussion sessions with the staff. During these meetings I would explain clearly the principles on which we based our actions and our management policies. I especially pointed out that in dealing with our employees we entertained no personal prejudices nor did we allow provincial distinctions to influence us in our treatment of each individual employee. I urged that all employees, regardless of their position, should work with a sense of unity, that they should understand the meaning and significance of their work, and that improved productivity and efficiency were in their own interest as well as in the interest of the Company.

The Company never restrained its workers from forming or joining unions. And as a result of my handling of all matters in a democratic manner, the workers, on their own, all did not wish to form or join a union. This holds true even today. The number of workers in Kader has grown to more than 1,700, but they have continued to maintain this spirit of cooperation.

Speaking now of wages, I recall that in 1949, the usual wage scale for a female worker for a 10-hour day was from $1.90 to $2. I thought that this was very low since the average cost for food per person was in the region of $40 to $50. When I took over control of Kader, I stipulated that the lowest pay for a female worker for a nine-hour day was to be $3 to $3.50.

Although this wage level of 1949 would appear extremely low today, it was considered rare in those days. I recall during a visit paid to Kader by the then Governor, Sir Alexander Grantham, he told me that he had often heard from the Labour Department about the exceptionally high wage level at Kader. . . .

I waited for a gradual psychological improvement of the workers' attitude and a betterment of their morale before I took active steps to increase productivity, raise the quality and open up new markets. Starting from 1953, the quality of Kader products was beginning to be recognised by customers in remote markets abroad. There was a steady increase of orders from such industrially advanced countries as Great Britain, the United States and European countries.

In dealing with all my customers, whether big or small, I persisted in my principle of sincerity and good faith, always supplying them with a high quality product at a reasonable price. But I also insisted on equality and reciprocal reasonableness. Before long this was recognised and understood by all my customers, bringing satisfactory results to all parties.

At this moment, there is seldom any firm anywhere in the world which deals in plastics, especially in toys, which does not know the high quality of Kader products and the confidence we command.

Over the years, our product range has increased to some 600 separate items, with a total work force of more 1,700. We now rank as first or the second among all the plastics manufacturers in the Far East. This, of course, was the result of the cooperative efforts of all our personnel.

e. Social Mobility

DOCUMENT VI.e1: Education, self-help and social advancement (source: Hong Kong Chinese Civil Servants' Association, *Submissions to the Salaries Commission*, 1965, pp. 81-84)

The cases hereunder stated are factual. These informations were supplied by members of the H.K.C.C.S.A. who have brothers, sisters, uncles, aunts, cousins, spouses, in-laws, and other close relatives working in Hong Kong as employees outside the Public Service. They were supplied accurately but in confidence. For obvious reasons, the identities of the individual employers or employees have to remain anonymous. It is submitted that those information [sic] are relevant, and that they should be taken into consideration in determining the levels of salaries for civil servants in the Public Service.

1.   A junior executive who did not even pass the School Certificate Examination was promoted from an apprentice salesman in 1949 to salesman one year after, then to sales-manager in 1963 in a leading European Import and Export Firm, is now being paid a nominal salary of $750 p.m. His remuneration is mainly on commission basis. He gets 1/2% to 2% for every thing sold, which are attributable to his (the provisions) department. His gross income during 1964 was $70,000.

2.   Another junior executive without a School Certificate in the same firm selling building material, rose from salesman to sales manager after 10 years' service, was paid a nominal salary of $1,200 a month, but the commission he received at rates varying between 1/2% to 1%, came up to a total of $70,000 to $90,000 a year.

3.   A 3rd executive with School Certificate in a Chinese firm is paid $1,000 p.m. as his salary. On top of this, he gets 1/2% to 3% for every thing sold by his department. His monthly commission amounts averagely to $1,200 per month at his 6th year with the firm.

4.   An assistant with Form 4 standard of education in the catering department of a local airline receives $1,800 p.m. as salary. He receives 13 months salary in a year instead of 12. He is given a free trip once every 2-1/2 years, and if he were to bring his wife or parents along for the trip, he would need only to pay 10% of the fare. He is provided with free medical treatment for himself and his family.

5.   A married woman of Form 2 standard works as cashier in a tourist service firm is paid $780 for 14 months in a year. She is entitled to 20% of the tips received which averaged out to about $10 a day. She is given 3 meals a day, besides free quarters.

6.   A graduate from St. John's University, Shanghai, works as an assistant in the general department of a plastic factory, started off at $1,300 p.m. His salary was raised to $1,500, three months after joining the firm. By the end of the year, which was 7 months after he joined the firm, he was paid a bonus of $6,000. As from the 2nd year, he was provided with quarters of 760 sq.ft. at a nominal rental of $50 per month, besides with meals charged at the nominal price of 70c a meal, besides a promise of even a higher bonus at the end of the year.

7.   A married woman who plays the piano for the entertainment of customers in a hotel is earning $6,000 p.m. with free accommodation and free food. She holds no diploma nor certificate of competency and her knowledge of music is no way superior to an ordinary school music teacher in a Government or private school.

8.   A former university student from Shanghai (did not graduate) started off as a clerk in an American Insurance Company 8 years ago at a salary of $680 p.m. He has now reached the rank of Accident Insurance Producer earning both a salary and commission amounting to over $5,000 p.m. He himself and his family are covered by a provident fund scheme which will entitle him to no less than $100,000 on retirement (no age limit for retirement). Besides he is entitled to free medical treatment by 1st rate private practitioners. He is also entitled to 24 days' 'local leave'.

9.   A graduate of St. John's University, Shanghai, works as a secretary and export manager in a woollen yarn and carpet factory, receives $3,400 p.m. plus a 25% bonus of his yearly total at the end of the year. He is further provided rent free with a flat which cost the firm $120,000 to buy.

10. A former graduate of Peking University works in a factory which produces steel cutleries as the chief engineer for less than 3 years, is paid, on a 5-year contract, at $1,800 plus a flat which cost the firm $38,000. In addition, he will receive annual gratuities (averaged between $8,000 to $10,000 over the past 3 years). He is additionally privileged to travel aboard to Europe and America at the firm's expense according to costs.

11. A former middle school student from Shanghai, who learnt his English from an evening school, started off as a clerk in a foreign bank at the humble salary of $400 p.m. 12 years ago. By now he is promoted to head of the Inward Bills Department. His salary has been revised several times (and always timely). He is now receiving $2,350 p.m. with double pay at the year. He is allowed to operate private business of his own through the facilities and business connections he established through his service with the bank. He now owns a flat which cost him $60,000 to buy and can afford to send 2 of his elder children abroad for education.

12. A woman, graduated from a Chinese university, works as an accountant in a jewellery shop. She is entrusted to the safe custody of all the jewels after the closing time of every day. She is paid $1,240 p.m. plus an annual bonus of 8% of the profits of the shop. The bonus she received last year (1964) amounted to $24,000. She holds $10,000 worth of shares out of a total initial capital of $250,000.

f. Professionalization

DOCUMENT VI.f1: Hong Kong managers (source: *The Hong Kong Manager*, vol. 1 no. 1, January/February 1965)

'Today is not yesterday; we ourselves change; how can our work and thoughts, if they are always to be the fittest, continue the same?' asked Carlyle. This is a question which our managers must constantly ask themselves.

Tremendous strides are being made in science and technology, and the pace of change is faster and more rapid now than at any time in the history of mankind. Our managers must keep up with these changes and developments and adapt them to fit the conditions of Hong Kong. As the Hon. Sir Sik-nin Chau puts it in his article in this isssue, the managers of Hong Kong must cast off the shackles of traditional thinking, and if Hong Kong is to maintain its hard earned position as an industrial centre they must be inspired with dynamic and creative thinking.

The Hong Kong Management Association has been formed to promote scientific management and to assist managers to keep pace with developments and progress in this field. 'Newsletter' first published two years ago was one of the tools to further this objective.

But as J.R. Lowell once wrote, 'new time demands new measures' and so we feel it is appropriate to start off the New Year with a new publication — 'The Hong Kong Manager' to replace 'Newsletter', which has served our membership capably and enjoyably during the past two years.

'The Hong Kong Manager' will be issued bi-monthly in the first instance. It is designed to serve the needs, to reflect the views and to stimulate the thinking of the large and growing force of managers in Hong Kong, whether their activities are within the industrial, commercial or governmental sphere. It is the hope of those who have been concerned in the planning of this journal that, from the modest beginning we see today and with the support and contributions of our members, its voice will find real meaning and influence in management circles and will thus contribute towards the economic well-being of the community.

It is our intention that 'The Hong Kong Manager' fulfils its role as a medium of information and education, and as the reporter and watchdog of our progress. The publication will contain articles by leading local managers and management educationists and abstracts and condensations of articles of interst from overseas management publications. One section of 'Newsletter' which was of particular interest to readers — Aids to Management Efficiency — will continue in 'The Hong Kong Manager', as well as the sections on news items and information on courses. To enable readers to air their views on management needs and trends the publication will include a 'Readers' Forum', and readers are invited to send in their comments for publication.

We take this opportunity with our first issue to extend to all our members and readers the traditional Chinese salutation for prosperity and good fortune in the New Year, by wishing them 'Kung Hei Fat Choy'.

DOCUMENT VI.f2: The Accountants' Golden Jubiliee (source: *The Chinese Accountant, Golden Jubilee 1913-1963*, The Society of Chinese Accountants and Auditors, Hong Kong, n.d.)

Although the celebration of the Golden Jubilee of the Society is now over, the jubilant atmosphere that prevailed at the dinner party given on that occasion on November 1, 1963 at Wing On Life Building, top floor, had indelibly impressed upon the minds of those who did honour to the Institution, particularly the members themselves.

There were over one hundred guests and members in attendance. Prior to dinner, the Chairman, Mr Charles Mar Fan, extended the Society's welcome to all participants and thanked them for their presence. He gratefully acknowledged the greetings and congratulations received from friends overseas, and gave a brief resume of the circumstances leading to the birth of the Society. In his discourse into the matter, he said, in part, as follows:

Prior to the First World War, as a result of the steady increase in number of Chinese owned limited companies, most of which kept their accounts in Chinese, the Hong Kong Government was contemplating a revision of the existing Companies Ordinance, 1911, with a view to stipulating that their books be kept in the English language. Because of the many latent difficulties to be involved, a representation headed by the late Honourable Chau Shiu Kee (father of our Honorary Permanent President, Sir T.N. Chau) was made to the Authorities to reconsider their proposal. After due consideration, the proposed law was altered, whereby, inter alia, a daily summarised cash book in English was required (Section 121 of the Companies Ordinance refers). This led to the birth of Chinese auditors, the qualification of whom must be a pass through examination. The first Board of Examiners appointed by the Government composed of Messrs. Lau Chu Pak (grandfather of Mr Lau Chun Kwok, Managing Director of the Hong Kong & Yaumati Ferry Co., Ltd.), Ho Fook (brother of the late Sir Robert Ho Tung), the late Honourable Chau Shiu Kee, and Mr. Yuen Ying San, with the Secretary for Chinese Affairs to act as ex officio member and chairman.

The very first examination of auditors was held in 1913, in which about 17 candidates were successful. One of them, named Fung Lock Yuen, immediately convened a meeting of the qualified auditors and, as a result, an association known as 'Hong Kong Chinese Auditors Research Society' was formed. Mr J.M. Wong was elected the first chairman, while Mr Fung Lock Yuen, the first honorary secretary. This was in 1913.

Before introducing the Guest Speaker for the evening, Mr Mar Fan paid high tribute to Mr J.M. Wong, J.P., the founder-chairman of the Society 50 years ago, complimented him for his long life to witness the Golden Jubilee, and asked him to rise and receive the applause of the admiring gathering.

The Chairman also extolled the good work done to the Society by his predecessors, Messrs. J.M. Wong, W.S. Wong, W.S. Tam and C.C. Tso, and their colleagues, and looked forward to their continued guidance and co-operation in the years to come. He expressed gratitude to all who have helped to make the celebration a success.

Continuing, he pointed out that it was very fortunate for the Society to have the consent of Mr W.K. Thomson, Registrar General and currently Chairman of the Authorised Auditors Board, to address the gathering on this memorable occasion, and said that 'Mr Thomson has been very helpful to our profession as a whole, and to our Society, in particular.' In his few words to introduce the Guest Speaker, he incorporated the message: 'we also wish to take this opportunity to convey our gratefulness to him for his support and assistance.'

Rising amidst thunderous applause, Mr Thomson began his address commending lavishly the constant and creditable efforts of the Society to raise the standard of accountancy and auditing and its contributions to the business community. The full text of his address is as follows:

One of the advantages of being Chairman of the Authorised Auditors Board is that from time to time I am invited to attend your functions; one of the disadvantages of being Chairman, that I am invited to speak at them. Now this is a very important function, a landmark in the Society's history, for its purpose is to celebrate the Golden Jubilee of the Society, and when I look around I see many people better qualified to address you than I, for instance Mr Duffy, our able new Commissioner of Inland Revenue, who I am sure knows most of you much better than I. But he's a young man yet, and perhaps you are saving him for your Centenary dinner, since you don't think I'll last that long. But just as we are happy to see here tonight Mr J.M. Wong, who witnessed the foundation of the Society fifty years ago, so I am sure that many of your younger members will be around fifty years hence to hear what Mr Duffy has to say.

As Mr Mar Fan has outlined the early history of your Society there is no need for me to go into that. I do, however, wish to pay tribute to your seventeen or eighteen founder members who in 1913 had the forethought and the initiative to get together and lay the foundations of the thriving Society whose fiftieth birthday we are celebrating tonight. I think it is quite remarkable that the Society was founded immediately after the first examination for Chinese auditors in 1913. Unfortunately, the Society's pre-war records were lost during the occupation, but it is clear that in the pre-war years the Society steadily grew in strength and stature, having on the outbreak of war a membership of over 40. The Society was re-established shortly after the war, and since then, thanks to the enthusiasm and leadership of successive Chairmen, Vice Chairmen and Committee members, it can justly lay claim to a record of astonishing activity and progress for so small a body. Not that it is so small nowadays, for its membership has grown to 80. Progress has I think been most notable in the last decade: you have established your regular monthly meetings and discussion groups, and have latterly succeeded in producing your Handbook 'The Chinese Accountant' every two years, a really notable achievement.

Notwithstanding the marked increase in the number of companies and firms who keep their accounts in English — and with these too you have, of course, a great deal to do — it is still true to say that the vast majority of small businesses continue to keep their accounts in Chinese, and it is in relation to these that you have a special and most responsible role. You are a Society of Chinese Accountants and Auditors, and by the nature of things are in a position to give the most valuable assistance to your Chinese clients, and at the same time by converting the mysteries of Chinese accountants into forms that are familiar to Western eyes, and that are certified by you as professional men, you greatly simplify the task of your natural enemy, the Commissioner of Inland Revenue. You are therefore making a very real contribution to the community, and your Society by its constant efforts to raise the standards of accountancy and auditing among your members is indeed worthy of every commendation and encouragement.

But apart from your professional activities there is another side to your Society, the social side, and I must say it is evidence of a very nice spirit among you, competitors though you are, that you meet so often in such a friendly fashion, not merely to discuss matters of common interest, but also for the pleasure of a friendly chat and of each other's company. Your Society is, if I may say so, an extremely happy blend of youth and experience, and it is my earnest hope that in the next fifty years it will continue to exhibit that same friendly spirit and active, go-ahead management that have brought it so successfully to this Golden Jubilee. (Applause)

After Mr M.W. Kwan, Vice Chairman of the Society, has given a vote of thanks to Mr Thomson, Sir Tsun-Nin Chau toasted to the continued prosperity of the Society, while Mr J.M. Wong suitably reciprocated the best wishes to the guests on behalf of the Society.

CHAPTER SEVEN

CRISIS AND CONSOLIDATION, 1966 - 1981

The signs were probably there even in the 1950s, that the simple formula of a colonial government assisted by appointed members and supported by loosely organized traditional communal organizations would not hold. Housing estates being built by the Hong Kong government were to house hundreds of thousands of people who not only had no representation in the government, but also no effective communal organization among themselves. The trade unions of the 1950s, tied to the remnants of political hostility that had developed from before 1949, did not address Hong Kong's labour issues. While the working population was made up essentially of first-generation migrants — refugees — whose aspirations did not go beyond survival, and while the political situation remained in balance so that the Hong Kong government was under no threat to strengthen its social support, Hong Kong society continued through the 1950s and the early 1960s very much as it was in the 1930s. The first signs that the present constitutional arrangements were unacceptable came with the riots of 1966, that broke out over the unlikely cause of a 5 cent rise on the cross-harbour fare of the Star Ferry. The commission of enquiry that was established to investigate into the cause of the riots returned with a report that described the participants in the riot as young, under-privileged, low-paid workers who were ignorant but not criminally bent. From that point on, the 'youth problem' came to be recognized as an issue that Hong Kong must deal with. The 'youth problem' was, of course, much more than a problem of young people looking for outlets for their energy: it was no less than a recognition of the gap between the haves and the have-nots, the middle-aged first-generation immigrant and the generation that had grown up in Hong Kong within the 1950s, the government and what it might think of as its people.

The Hong Kong government would probably have been less pushed to re-think its relationship with Hong Kong society had it not been for the need to organize support for itself when its authority was challenged by the riots of 1967. Unlike the 1966 riots, the 1967 riots were inspired by the Cultural Revolution that was taking place in the People's Republic of China, and were organized by pro-PRC organizations in Hong Kong. The rioting was supported by stoppages of work and high tension on the Hong Kong-China border. They were also supported by political terrorism: home-made bombs were laid in public places and a radio announcer was murdered for his pro-Hong Kong government broadcasts. Some of the feelings expressed in these incidents were no doubt genuine, especially hostility towards the police, dissatisfaction with a competitive educational environment that favoured teaching in English, and frustration at working and living conditions. The terrorism, however, found little rapport in the Hong Kong population.

a. Riots

A noticeable section of the report of the Commission of Inquiry into the 1966 riot dealt with an allegation made by Urban Councillor Mrs Elsie Elliot that part of the rioting might have been police-instigated with the view of framing her. Mrs Elliot refused to disclose her source of information for the allegation and the Commission found her of contempt. When the Commission went on to argue that the riots in 1966 had been relatively spontaneous, that participants in the riots had included principally disaffected young people rather than criminal elements, it avoided the issue that Mrs Elliot's allegation focused on. In the early 1960s, the poorer sectors of Hong Kong's population were probably quite disgruntled with portions of the Hong Kong government that they were in touch with, in particular the Police. The traditional communal organizations that the Hong Kong government had relied upon to reflect public opinion had by the 1960s become inadequate. In other words, government itself was out of touch with a substantial section of the Hong Kong population.

DOCUMENT VII.a1: Kowloon riot, 1966 (source: *Kowloon Disturbances, 1966, Report of Commission of Inquiry*, Hong Kong: Government Printer, 1967, pp. 103-107)

The background and motives of participants

There was a practical limit on the numbers of witnesses we could call. These demonstrators and rioters who gave evidence were selected by our counsel as the most significant, mainly from the prisoners at Chi Ma Wan Prison, which housed those who were older or had received heavier sentences.

Data on all persons arrested

We had, however, three other sources of information throwing some light on the type and kind of individuals involved in the disturbances and, in some cases, on the reasons they gave for involvement. It will be seen [from an appendix] that 905 were arrested and charged, whilst 560 were arrested but released without charge; presumably because they had been caught up inadvertently in the curfew etc. Amongst those charged, the predominant age group is that of 16 to 20 years but amongst those released the age groups are more evenly balanced. The proportion of those with previous convictions is higher as the age groups get older which gives the impression that these groups were rougher and tougher than the youngsters. But this impression may be misleading because, given the same propensities, the older age group is inevitably liable to have more previous convictions. Those involved in offences more serious than just curfew breaking tended, as one might expect, to have a higher proportion of previous convictions but, in this category, there appears to have been no clear tendency towards a higher proportion of convictions for the older offenders, largely because the figures for the 21 to 25 year group seem to be so much out of line with those of the categories on either side of them.

The most significant feature of this appendix is the comparatively high proportion of those in the 16 to 20 years category who were involved in offences more serious than curfew breaking. This would seem to point to this age group as the main source of the violence.

Analysis of Chi Ma Wan prisoners

A more ambitious document was the analysis of the 313 prisoners held in Chi Ma Wan for offences arising out of the disturbances; more ambitious because, in addition to the facts about age etc., some details of their background were included and they were asked to state their reasons for becoming involved in these offences. Of the curfew breakers, 102 (40%) claimed they did not know that a curfew had been imposed whilst 81 (31.8%) said they did not realise the seriousness of the curfew or had insufficient time to go home. 68 (26.7%) said they committed the offence in the excitement of the moment, which was also the reason given by the majority for the commission of other offences. 194 offenders had received only a primary education, 102 had been to junior or senior middle schools, five had attended a post secondary college and 12 had never been to school at all. 146 (46.6%) had been in Hong Kong for less than ten years and only 11% were married. Only six were unemployed and 15 were students. The average number of hours worked per day was nine and the income earned ranged from nil to $2,000 per month. 170 (54.3%) were receiving under $300 a month whilst 106 (33.9%) were receiving between $400 and $600 a month.

Survey of detainees at Begonia Road

At our request, a group of social workers made a survey of those younger prisoners who were held at Begonia Road Boys Home for offences arising out of the disturbances.

As only 24 boys were interviewed, these workers stressed that they could not be considered as sufficiently representative of the hundreds of youths who actually took part in the riots. A further reason for not regarding them as representative is mentioned in the next paragraph. The workers also expressed some reservations as to the scientific validity of their survey, because of limitations of time and doubts as to whether their questionnaire was properly balanced and sufficient fully to support their somewhat ambitious aim of building up a reasonably accurate picture of the background and certain relevant attitudes of these youngsters.

Whilst accepting these reservations, we think the answers received are of sufficient interest to merit quoting some of them. They are given for their qualitative rather than quantitative value, all the more so as we were in no position to assess the real veracity of these answers or the extent to which they may have been coloured by the fact that the boys at the time of the interviews were actually paying the penalty for their recent clash with authority. Moreover the 24 came from those who had received comparatively heavier punishments, those with short sentences had already been released at the time of the survey and many of those convicted were never imprisoned at all.

Social background. The boys ranged from 13 to 17 years of age. The majority (18) had been born in Hong Kong. Most had left school at the time of the riots and the majority (14) had been away from school from two to three years. Ten gave 'lack of interest' as their reasons for leaving school and six 'financial difficulty'. Fifteen had both parents in the family. One had no parents in Hong Kong. Four had father only and four had mothers only. Three of the boys did not know their parents' income. The others gave figures between $101 and $1,000 per month; four between $101 and $200, five between $201 and $300, the remainder being above $400 a month. Twenty-one of the boys were working at the time of the riots in the following capacities:

Kitchen hand	7
Apprentice	5
Delivery boy	4
Bar boy	1
Hawker	2
Unskilled labourer	1
No information	1

Ten claimed they had chosen their jobs themselves. More than half claimed that they worked very long hours. Including the apprentices, their monthly salary ranged from

-$50	2
$51-$100	3
$101-$150	6
$151-$200	7
$201-$250	3

Seven of the boys did not have to give any of their earnings to their parents and four had to give all. Six of them felt that their working conditions were good, seven felt that theirs were passable, and another seven, poor. Twelve slept at their place of work, in bunks, camp beds etc. One slept on a board over a sewing machine.

Regarding prospects, half of them did not feel that they had very much future in their present job, while six felt a bit more hopeful. Seven of them aspired to be motor or electrical mechanics, four to catering and restaurant work. Others would like to be seamen (two), clerk (one), radio-worker (one), carpenter (one), construction worker (one) and hotel boy (one). One hoped to have his own garage and be his own boss. Five had no plans.

The majority, 20 out of 24, claimed to be in good health. Eighteen felt recreation was essential and important whilst three felt it was unnecessary and three had no opinion. Going to the cinema, loafing in the streets, swimming, ball-games and gambling were the major activities apart from work.

Attitudes to Government and public utilities. Four of them were unable to make any comments about the Government. Six were indifferent. Two felt the Government was good. Six felt it was satisfactory. Six felt it was bad. Eighteen of the boys felt there was no equal treatment for people in Hong Kong and sixteen of them that there was no justice in the Courts. Others had no opinion on these topics. Sixteen of them considered the police force bad. One said it was very bad. Five were indifferent and two were unable to make any comments.

Twenty-one of the boys had no knowledge of who owned the public utilities such as the Star Ferry Co., etc. Only two knew the correct answers. One was indifferent. In spite of their lack of knowledge, eleven of them positively stated that it was unfair to raise fares; twelve of them were indifferent and only one said that it was fair to raise fares and then salaries, in general, should be raised. To illustrate their lack of knowledge about public affairs, two boys said that the Star Ferry belonged to Mrs. Elliot.[*]

Reasons for participation. Twelve claimed they were not actually involved in the riots but happened to be passing by in the streets where the riots occurred. Of these, one said he was wandering along the street after a movie and was probing with a stick inside an already broken parking meter when he was arrested and charged with breaking it. Of the remaining twelve, four admitted yelling, four admitted throwing things, one said that he and his fellow apprentices thought it was a good chance to take revenge on the police and to let off steam, so he attacked a police van. Two said they joined the crowds for the fun of it and to get first hand experience of being in a riot. Eight of the boys said they joined in out of curiosity and eight said they joined in for fun. Two stated that the reason for their doing so was to reject the fare increase. One said his motive was 'anti-bad-government'. The rest could give no reason.

Eight of the boys felt the others were all fighting for a cause. Three felt the others were doing it for fun and three felt there was something wrong with these people. Two

---

[*] Mrs. Elsie Elliot, Urban Councillor.

felt these people were 'heroes'. One felt they were 'mad'. The rest had no idea on this matter. Seven out of the twenty-four said that they had no idea why they were arrested. Twelve said the reason for their being arrested was 'breach of curfew order'. Four felt it was because of their throwing things and one said he was accused of having damaged public property.

Seventeen out of the total of twenty-four felt that the main cause of the riots was the raising of fares. One said it was because of feelings against the 'bad-government'. One said it was because of hostility of the public towards the police. One said that the riot was stimulated by excitement over the police's brutality towards a five-year old child in Tsim Sha Tsui district. Four were unable to express any opinion.

Twelve of the boys thought So Sau Chung, Lo Kei, etc.* were 'good people', 'brave men', 'a hero,' and fighting for a good cause. Four were indifferent or could not express any opinion. Eight had never heard of them.

Summary by social workers

The interviewers expressed their general conclusions on these boys as follows:

It seems obvious that the boys interviewed were for the most part employed, had reasonably stable personalities and came from ordinary hard-working families. They were not social misfits anxious for political or other reasons to cause unrest and trouble in Hong Kong.

The interviewers felt that the type of employment many of the boys were in held little for them by way of future security or advancement and this, coupled with the long unorthodox hours they worked, as well as the low pay they received, contributed to the feeling of aimlessness and boredom which was part of the motivation behind their involvement in the riots. Because of the demands of their employment they lacked opportunity for normal teenage fun, so used the riots as one outlet for this need.

Conclusions

It seems tolerably clear from all this that, whilst the more prominent of the leaders in the early stages could be described as misfits or cranks like Lo Kei or So Sau Chung, the main body of these who joined in the demonstrations and subsequently in the riots were more or less ordinary youngsters and people no more disposed of crime than any average group of the less privileged in the streets of Hong Kong.

It would be foolish for Hong Kong society to comfort itself with the thought that it was only the severely under-privileged and discontented who participated in, or passively supported, the disturbances. The great majority of the participants came from the poorer sections of the community but they were not destitute nor were they identified with what are frequently called the criminal classes.

---

* Messrs. So and Lo were prominent participants in the Star Ferry incident in 1966.

Inspired by the Cultural Revolution in China, the riots of 1967 made use of propaganda and slogan campaigns that were by then commonplace all over China. In May and June, daily demonstrations, some of which were transformed readily into clashes with the police, the propaganda campaign, attempts to incite work strikes, bombs in the street, the obvious connection of some China-related organizations to these activities and the uncertainty of the Chinese government's stand on them added to considerable tension that was felt throughout Hong Kong society. Most of the tension passed rather quickly when it became clear that the government of the People's Republic had not been in support of drastic actions that might topple the Hong Kong government. The propaganda campaign, however, continued for some years before it slowly faded out.

DOCUMENT VII.a2: Propaganda during the Kowloon riot, 1967 (source: *Hong Kong Disturbances, 1967*, Hong Kong: The Government Printer, n.d., pp. 48-52)

In May the communists had under their control all the machinery required for a full-scale propaganda campaign. But whereas from the start of confrontation the communist newspapers at once slavishly followed the party line, the remainder, which included a number of vigorous and by no means sycophantic publications, preserved their independence. They have continued to criticize the Government when they thought criticism was justified but none of them at any time expressed any agreement with the objects and method of the communist confrontation in spite of the volume of propaganda they produced.

In May the communists had under their control all the machinery required for a full-scale propaganda campaign. Their three newspapers, the Ta Kung Pao, the Wen Wai Pao and the New Evening Post, were well established and had a good circulation; and they were backed up by about six other papers which not only followed their lead but at times ran to excesses of wild invention of their own. They had ample printing facilities for other propaganda material and the men and the equipment for newsreel production.

They also enjoyed considerable encouragement and assistance from the local office of the New China News Agency (Hsinhua) which is owned and directed by the Peking Government. This agency was largely responsible for directing the propaganda campaign in the Colony as could be seen from the identical reports of incidents that regularly appeared in communist newspapers, all attributed to the agency's reporters. It was also responsible for producing distorted accounts of the events in Hong Kong for the consumption of the authorities in Peking. Its highly-coloured and wildly exaggerated reports undoubtedly played a large part in inflaming opinion in China against the Government of the Colony.

In their campaign the communists employed every theme and every weapon, from deliberate distortion of facts and falsification of photographs to the spreading of rumour and the fabrication of non-existent incidents. Rumours put about by them ranged from the possible but untrue — rice shortages, power or water stoppages — to the wildly improbable — as for example the stories which appeared in minor communist newspapers, complete with photographs and maps, of Chinese gunboats approaching the Colony. Communist reporters and photographers were present at every incident to produce their version of events; and in many cases demonstrations were organized solely for publicity purposes. During the phase of street demonstrations in May communist newspapers produced special editions which were distributed free to the crowds and which were designed to incite them to further violence. The same presses produced leaflets and booklets giving lurid accounts of Police 'brutality'. . .

In the campaign of rumour-mongering, considerable use was made of loudspeakers mounted on communist owned buildings from which were broadcast threats and abuse against the authorities and encouragement to their supporters. The loudest and best known of these was at the Bank of China, the focal point for the disorders at the end of May. To meet this attack the Government set up its own loudspeakers on adjacent buildings whose combined output made the communist tirade unintelligible. The Government programme chosen consisted of selections from Cantonese opera and the resulting din made the area of Statue Square almost uninhabitable for the three days that the contest lasted. In the end the communists gave in and their loudspeakers were not used again. Broadcasts continued intermittently from other buildings, while communist river boats arriving in the Colony with goods from China, added their contribution while they were in port. These broadcasts tended to attract crowds and led on several occasions to clashes with the Police. There was a further addition to the communist propaganda armoury on 24th June when the Macau broadcasting station, Radio Villa Verde, passed completely into communist control and was used to direct more propaganda at Hong Kong.

The third medium of propaganda was posters. These appeared from the start of confrontation and continued sporadically throughout, reaching their height at the end of May and the beginning of June. Posters and slogans appeared everywhere, both ashore and afloat. They were pasted or written on every available wall, on ships in the harbour, and on the trains arriving at Lo Wu from China. Slogans were painted on the pavements and on the sides of cattle, while on one occasion a couple of unfortunate dogs were hung about with communist placards. These demonstrations had none of the subtlety of the newspaper campaign, the message mostly consisting of simple, and crude slogans. But the cumulative effect of such objurgations as 'Blood for blood', and 'Death to the Running Dogs' was considerable. They were reinforced on occasions by straw effigies hung on traffic lights or other convenient places and purporting to represent the Governor and other leading members of the community. To discourage removal, these effigies were often decorated with bombs, real and simulated. . .

Communist propaganda reached its peak in May and June. One of its main objectives had been to enlist the active support of the Peking Government in the struggle in Hong Kong and the exaggerated reports of the strength of the support for confrontation as well as of the 'brutal persecution' by the authorities were designed to that end. Any statement or protest from the Peking Government or any article in the

People's Daily that seemed, or could be made to seem, to support this possibility was given prominent treatment, with banner headlines and extra editions. By the end of July, the tone of the communist press was changing. Its shrill abuse of the Government continued and its exhortations to violence were, if anything, more extreme. But it began to speak increasingly of a long hard struggle ahead and pronouncements from Peking were given only routine treatment. While the protest after the events of 8th July at Sha Tau Kok was followed, at the prompting of the communist press, by widespread violence in the Colony, the ultimatum issued by Peking on 20th August and the subsequent attack on the office of the Chargé d'Affaires passed almost unnoticed in Hong Kong. After the suspension of the three newspapers, a mosquito newsheet campaign began. The newsheets were poorly produced but highly inflammatory and subversive. At first they were distributed widely but the campaign quickly lost its momentum and had died out completely by the end of the year, without achieving anything significant.

b. Language

After the riots of 1966 and 1967, the Hong Kong government, and Hong Kong society, became more conscious of the anomaly of Hong Kong's colonial status. The word 'colony' disappeared from the Hong Kong government's description of Hong Kong from the 1970s. But, Hong Kong, of course, was a colony, and nowhere was that point more clearly made in Hong Kong daily life than in the use of English in all official documents.

It should perhaps not be surprising that language should surface as the issue that university students focused on for action. It was an affront to Hong Kong's Chineseness. Moreover, as English had since the 1950s become the principal language of teaching in Hong Kong's secondary schools, as a result, what for the majority of Hong Kong students would be a second-language skill determined to a large extent educational success. In the aftermath of 1967, even if changes were not forthcoming, the Hong Kong government showed that it was willing to listen. Hence, whether or not Chinese was made an official language did not lead to Hong Kong's law being published in Chinese, or even more Chinese being used in the classroom, but there was at least a commission, headed by well-respected community leader Sir Kenneth Ping-fan Fung.

In Document VII. b1 below, Hong Kong University psychologist Eric Kvan discusses the difficulties faced by many Hong Kong secondary school students whose native language was Chinese but who had to confront English as a medium of school instruction. In Document VII. b2, the commission appointed by the Governor of Hong Kong to examine the issue of recognizing Chinese as an official language reported on the practicalities of this proposal.

DOCUMENT VII.b1: The cost of bilingual education (source: E. Kvan, 'Problems of bilingual milieu in Hong Kong: strains of the two-language system', in I.C. Jarive, ed. *Hong Kong: A Society in Transition, Contributions to the Study of Hong Kong Society*, London: Routledge & Kegan Paul, 1969, pp. 333-337)

Following a suggestion by Saer, I have tried to establish a situation where it would be directly possible to compare the strength, as it were, of the two languages in the individual.* The task is verbally to produce the first association coming to mind upon seeing a visually presented word in Chinese or English. The reaction time is registered electrically and the response itself is noted. The words are 50 words in both languages — the one set being the equivalent of the other; all the words should be present in the vocabulary of a 3-year-old. The presentation is randomized both with regard to language used and to particular words. From the investigations made so far it appears that it should be possible to place all the bilingual readers of the two languages on a continuum between monolingual Chinese and monolingual English individuals. But not only the relative reaction times are of interest, also the number of translations among the answers, of replies using the same or the other language and of course the nature of the answers when they are true associations, are very revealing.

In yet another attempt to penetrate further into the results of the bilingual education I obtained two sets of essays, on the same subject but in the two languages, from a group of students who had just completed their annual examination in their respective groups. Of the 100 participants some had come up through the Anglo-Chinese System, others through the Chinese, i.e. using English and Chinese as the medium of instruction, respectively. I asked several competent judges to assess the (anonymous) essays with regard to maturity and as far as possible disregarding the linguistic expression of detail. It seems clear that the students who had used Chinese as a medium of instruction but had studied English as a subject, were showing greater originality of thought and greater maturity in general than those who had used English as a medium and had Chinese as a subject only. This was very obvious in the English essays, in spite of the limitations on the English of the second group, and my Chinese judges said it was even more obvious in the Chinese essays. This result corresponds closely with the impressions of experienced educators that the pupils in the Chinese-medium classes are more responsive, more interested in their surroundings both in and outside of the school.

A possible explanation of this difference seems to be the change of language in Form I of the secondary school when the pupils are about 12-13 years old. If we assume that the possibility of 'being able to convey' is one of the most characteristic human traits — to establish a relationship with the persons around us rather than to convey 'information' — then it does seem more than likely that this sudden reduction of the

---

* H. Saer, *Experimental Inquiry into the Education of Bilingual People.* New Educational Fellowship, Education in a changing Commonwealth, London 1931.

possibilities for expression would cause a neurosis fully as severe as the one we find in children backward in reading and writing for reasons which can be counteracted by special training. I think the picture will be complete if I just add that one is not likely anywhere in the world to find 'better pupils' than those in the Anglo-Chinese schools — better with regard to discipline, obedience, and ability to work steadily through well-prepared material.

To the difficulties created by the change of language in the school must be added the peculiar difficulties springing from the many languages which are involved: for the Matriculation examination these pupils work mainly with texts in the classical language written in the classical period which is as different from the modern spoken language as Latin is from French or Italian, or Chaucer is from modern English. It would therefore appear that their language used for the description of the phenomena of everyday life, including scientific phenomena, does not develop on a par with their interests and general academic progress. Here we must remember that the characters in and by themselves give only very vague instruction with regard to how they should be pronounced and only little information with regard to their special meaning in this particular context. Unless a character has been learned in a formal learning situation it requires great expenditure of energy for the individual to acquire this character — leading to a high degree of compartmentalisation between the common and the specialised vocabularies, with a rather small number of characters being allotted to the first group.

This means in practice that the spoken language of these pupils stagnates at the level of the 12-13-years-old, the age at which they last used it as their only real medium of instruction and expression. What this means for the possibilities of expression and controlling the emotional forces released at about the same time as the language change will require much further study.

Furthermore, at this stage a new conflict develops — the conflict between the Chinese traditional approach to scholastic work and the less traditional western approach. The immediate conflict is undoubtedly made much less acute by the fact that most of the teachers are themselves trained in the Chinese traditional way and tend to transfer this method from the Chinese literary studies to the whole curriculum.

The ultimate conflict, however, is increased rather than decreased by this approach. So far as our students go it can with advantage be summarised in the following anecdote: a couple of years ago all Faculties and Departments were at one in their report on the Matriculation examination: 'The candidates rely by far too much on learning by heart instead of working in an independent and original way with the questions' — all except the Department of Chinese which wrote: 'it is clear that the candidates have not memorised a sufficient amount of material.'

But before we attempt to draw conclusions with regard to the difficulties involved in the two systems of education, the Vernacular and the Anglo-Chinese, it will be necessary to consider the instruction provided in the primary school — and even before. Here an inspection of two samples of Chinese handwriting would be useful to illustrate my point. Before the division takes place at age 12-13 the two groups have been in the primary school for 6 years and very many in the kindergarten before that. At all stages, when the child leaves the kindergarten (at 5-6 years of age), the primary school, the secondary (Middle) school, even the University, the Chinese language uses the expression: *bi yeh* (graduated) — and at all stages the child will receive diplomas and certificates. This is characteristic. The formal instruction begins as soon as the child enters kindergarten, most frequently at about the age of 3, counting age in the western fashion. The kindergarten lasts for two years and even if there are many activities (which is far from the case in the majority of kindergartens) the most important activity is the instruction in reading and writing. When the children sit for 'the entrance examination' (*sic*) to the primary school, most of them can read, write and take dictation in about 100 to 160 characters. Some are very complex, 20 or more individual strokes are necessary to construct them, to write them. Compare them with the school maturity tests common in the west, e.g. the test published by Charlotte Buehler. The test demands that the 5-year-old shall be able to *copy* a circle — 'the test has been successfully completed if the two ends of the circle meet!' — or note in the same test the table and chair (in profile) which the child should be able to copy to the extent of making them basically recognisable. Compare such a test with the details of the Chinese characters which the child in the Hong Kong kindergarten *must* learn by heart and be able to *reproduce* — not just copy or recognise — at the same age of 5. This result is obtained only by daily practice during the years from 3 to 5, both in school and at home. They practise at least a half-hour daily in the kindergarten — and in Primary I at least one hour must be spent at home practising handwriting. Further it must be remembered that the pencil (or soon the brush) must be very carefully controlled in a way much more elaborate than the way it must be controlled in the writing of English letters. Learning to write has always been regarded as much more than just learning to form the characters. It is at the same time an instruction in the ability to control one's temper, and to develop personal harmony.

Looking around for ways and means first to express and then assess the results of this very strictly formal instruction — a system which is so much older than anything found outside China — I noticed that among the more than 2,000 schoolchildren and the several hundred University students whom I tested with the reading tests hardly any were left-handed, writing or playing. This contrasts very markedly with the position in England. Assuming that the generally accepted views on the subject are meaningful, it seems likely that many children must have been forced to change from left to right hand and the absence of stammer and similar symptoms of particular stress would then be an expression of the general uniformity of this society and of the force wherewith the individual personality is formed and socialised.

DOCUMENT VII.b2: Chinese as an official language (source: *The First Report of the Chinese Language Committee*, Hong Kong: Government Printer, 1971, pp. 1-6)

From time to time over the years, there has been comment on the wider use of Chinese in public administration. In 1969, and more particularly in the summer of 1970, there was a determined 'campaign' for the adoption of Chinese as '法定語文'

(Fat Ting U Man) which has been interpreted as 'official language' in English in some quarters. There has been support for this movement from various individuals, organisations and student groups. There were indications that many people felt there was considerable justification for a wider use by Government of Chinese for the convenience of the public.

We decided to examine to what extent Chinese can have equal status with English under the following 3 broad aspects:

(a) In oral and written communications between Government and the public.

(b) At meetings of the Legislative Council, Urban Council and Government Boards and Committees.

(c) In Court proceedings and as a language of the law.

In order to seek the views of the community, we sent out 1,580 letters to organisations which fall in the various categories.

We have also had discussions with individuals and organisations both in relation to the general matters we are examining and in relation to simultaneous interpretation facilities specifically.

From the representations received, we have come to the conclusion that Chinese as '法定語文' (Fat Ting U Man) is intended by many to mean 'officially prescribed' or 'officially recognised' language having equal status with English. In general there would be satisfaction if Chinese is given, as far as practicable, equal status with English. We are generally in sympathy with public opinion in this regard.

Our first recommendations deal with the use of Chinese in Legislative Council, Urban Council and Government Boards and Committees. These will be followed by recommendations on the use of Chinese in oral and written communications between Government and the public and the use of Chinese in Court proceedings and as a language of the Law in that order, the latter being by far the most complex of the three.

Legislative Council and Urban Council

Standing Order No. 2 of the Legislative Council stipulates that the proceedings and debates of the Council shall be in the English language. The views of the Unofficials, as conveyed to us by the Senior Unofficial Member are in favour of introducing simultaneous interpretation (English to Cantonese and vice versa) in the open meetings so that non-English speaking members of the public can comprehend the proceedings of these meetings; at the same time, they consider all Council papers which are to be published for public information should be translated into Chinese. As regards closed meetings and papers for such meetings, the opinion was expressed to us that it would be desirable to provide interpretation and translation facilities so as to enable non-English speaking members of the community to be appointed to the Council in future.

Section 45 of the Urban Council Ordinance stipulates that the proceedings of the Council shall be conducted in English and this is repeated in Urban Council Standing Order No. 1; in addition, Section 7 of the same Ordinance requires a Councillor to possess an adequate knowledge of the English language.

In the Urban Council Meeting held on 6th October, 1970, a resolution was moved that Government be urged to consider the necessary amendments to Section 45 of the Urban Council Ordinance so that Council proceedings could be conducted in both English and Chinese. This motion was carried but the official members abstained from voting because they felt that the resolution should also have included a proposal to amend Section 7 of the Ordinance to enable non-English speaking members of the community to be eligible for election or appointment to the Council. Subsequently, we wrote individually to all the twenty Unofficial Members of the Council seeking answers specifically on the following two questions:

(a) To allow those not fluent in English to be eligible for the Council, and for the public to take a greater interest in the proceedings, do you consider it desirable that simultaneous interpretation (from English to Cantonese and vice versa) should be made available in both public and closed meetings of the Council in view of your resolution?

(b) Do you consider it necessary for papers associated with your meetings to be translated into Chinese?

Of the fourteen replies received to date, all are in favour of introducing simultaneous interpretation (English to Chinese and vice versa) for public meetings: five further suggested that consideration should be given to extending this facility to Mandarin at a later stage.

As regards the second question, the views expressed by the majority are that all papers would have to be translated into Chinese if Section 7 of the Ordinance were amended to enable non-English speaking members of the community to be elected or appointed to the Council.

In the representations which we have received from various organisations and individuals, two relevant though not necessarily related arguments have been advanced for the introduction of bilingualism in these Councils, namely:

(a) that the general public should be able to follow meaningfully the proceedings of the open meetings;

(b) that non-English speaking but capable members of the community should be eligible for election or appointment.

Seen in the light of the desire to encourage the community to be more aware of the affairs of Hong Kong, we consider that interpretation facilities should be provided at the open meetings of these two Councils for the convenience of the general public and to enable them to listen to speeches and debates in these Councils. This recommendation is based on the principle that the whole community ought to have complete access to the proceedings of the Councils either by personal attendance or through radio and television and that the value of such an innovation should not be measured by the number of spectators in the public gallery at any particular time.

In considering this particular aspect, we have to examine whether Cantonese alone (as advocated by the vast majority of the representations received), Cantonese and Mandarin, or Mandarin alone should be adopted. In this connection, we note from the statistical figures in the Report of the Census, 1961, that Cantonese was the usual language of 79% of the Hong Kong population and it was understood by 95% of the population. We have no further information on these figures. Consequently, we have no doubt that Cantonese would at the present moment have more relevance and reality for the population as a whole and accordingly conclude that interpretation facilities for the open meetings of the Legislative Council and Urban Council should be confined to English and Cantonese only. This does not, however, rule out the possibility of introducing Mandarin in years to come and this should be kept under review.

As it is essential that the efficiency of the proceedings of the Councils should be maintained, we believe that simultaneous interpretation facilities should be introduced, as opposed to consecutive interpretation which is both tedious and time-consuming . . .

Our examination of bilingualism in these two Councils would not be complete without mentioning the proposition that bilingualism could make non-English speaking members of the public eligible to serve on them. A change in this direction would render it necessary not only to provide simultaneous interpretation facilities for all closed meetings of the Councils' Sub-Committees and Select Committees but also to prepare papers and to keep minutes, etc. in both languages efficiently and effectively. This, we feel, would impose for the time being too heavy a strain on local resources relating to interpreters and translators, particularly when there are other areas in which the wider use of Chinese in official business should be given priority.

c. The Population Transition

> But Hong Kong society was changing. One of the clearest indications of that was the decline in fertility in the 1970s. The traditional family put a premium on having many children, especially sons. Most Hong Kong families, packed into small shared flats and seeing upward mobility within reach (see DOCUMENT VII.e2 below) opted for few births. The Hong Kong population transition was a quiet movement. Social services provided reached their willing targets without much ado, as fertility dropped from 3.4 births per woman in 1971 to 2.00 in 1981.

DOCUMENT VII.c1: Fertility declines (source: Census and Statistics Department, Hong Kong, Demographic Trends in Hong Kong, 1971-82, *An Analysis Based on Vital Registration Statistics of Births, Marriages, and Deaths and on Census Results*, n.d., Hong Kong, p. 41)

The TFR*, defined as the sum of the age-specific fertility rates in a given year, represents the number of children that a woman would bear (ignoring mortality) if she

---

* Total fertility rate

Table 7.1
Total Fertility Rates and Net Reproduction Rates Per Woman, 1971-81

	1971	1972	1973	1974	1975	1976	1977	1978	1979	1980	1981
Total fertility rate	3.41	3.29	3.17	2.99	2.70	2.52	2.42	2.32	2.16	2.08	1.97
Net reproduction rate	1.63	1.55	1.50	1.42	1.26	1.18	1.14	1.09	1.01	0.98	0.93

were subject throughout her reproductive ages to the fertility rates prevailing in that year. This measure represents a hypothetical completed average family size if fertility were to remain constant at a given level. For a generation of women to replace itself each woman must produce on average one daughter who will survive to the end of childbearing age. This generally corresponds to an average completed family size of approximately 2.1 children in conditions of low mortality and allowing for such factors as the differential in the sex ratio at birth and infant and childhood mortality. As shown in the table the TFR fell from 3.4 in 1971 to just below 2.00 in 1981 — a level which would be insufficient for a generation to replace itself.

The NRR*, defined as the sum of the products of the age-specific fertility rates for female births and the female survival rates in a given year, represents the number of daughters who, according to the fertility rates prevailing in that year, would be born to a woman (allowing for mortality). If the NRR is one, women are exactly replacing themselves; if it is less than one, they are failing to do so. In 1981 women in Hong Kong were producing 7 per cent too few daughters to replace themselves.

d. New Hopes and Bold Beginning

In April 1966, even before the riots, the Hong Kong government had appointed a working party made up entirely of civil servants to consider the question of local administration.** The working party advised that changes should be implemented, but that they should consist primarily of introducing

---

* Net reproduction rate
** This the government probably did in response to initiative in the Urban Council to appoint its own ad hoc committee to advise on the future scope and functioning of the council. For details see *Government and Politics* pp. 129 to 136.

local councils of an advisory nature that were made up of both appointed and elected members. Minority opinions expressed in the report cast considerable doubt on the relevance of popular elections as a basis for representation. The riots that followed close upon the completion of the report quite changed the tone of the argument at high levels in government if not its content. Throughout the riots of 1967, many communal organizations had openly expressed their support for the Hong Kong government and their condemnation of violence and disruption. The Hong Kong government had possibly also come round to the view that the gap that had apparently been left unfilled by the ineffectiveness of traditional communal organizations had to be closed. The immediate answer was not an electoral reform, but the implementation of the City District Officers Scheme, and the extension from there, as Sir Murray Maclehose was appointed Governor in 1971, of making representation available to Hong Kong's 'grassroots' population. The reforms of the 1970s changed the tenor of communal representation in Hong Kong society. The Hong Kong government, having found traditional communal organizations wanting, dismantled its representational structure, revamped the Hong Kong community so that voluntary associations formed on a wider basis — the 'mutual aid committees' in resettlement estates were the pride of the Hong Kong government in this programme — might, in ways that seemed unclear to observers outside the Hong Kong government, to reflect the view of the Hong Kong population without the implementation of democracy.

DOCUMENT VII.d1: A programme for the 1970s (source: HE the Governor, in the Legislative Council, 18 October 1972, *Hong Hong Hansard, Reports of the Sittings of the Legislative Council of Hong Kong, Session 1973*)

Though it has been a busy year it has been a fascinating one. I have come back to a Hong Kong which is more developed and prosperous and of far greater stature than the one I knew 10 years ago. But also I find it more expectant of its Government.

In this first year I have been conscious of the need on the one hand to learn as much about everything as possible, and on the other to be selective on proposals for action. I have therefore concentrated on defining broad objectives in three fields where this seemed particularly necessary at this juncture — housing, education and social welfare.

...

I now turn to housing. There is no field in which Hong Kong's pressure of people has produced acuter problems or one in which the Government's response has been so vigorous or received such international acclaim. 1.6 million people have been housed at low rents in housing estates. Many of the later estates provide good examples of a solution to Hong Kong's particular problem of living at densities higher than anywhere else in the world. Most of the larger squatter colonies have disappeared. Much of the aging and dilapidated pre-war tenement property has been replaced in the process of private development. There has been some thinning out of over-crowding in old properties, and the rise in population in Kowloon and Hong Kong Island has been halted and slightly reversed.

But in spite of all this effort the problem remains. 300,000 people still live in squatter huts or temporary housing. Many units in resettlement estates are badly overcrowded, or have no separate wash places or lavatories. It is estimated that a further 310,000 people would need rehousing if all of those in shared private flats and tenements were to have a self-contained home, and few of these can afford the rents asked by private landlords. It is my conclusion that the inadequacy and scarcity of housing and all that this implies, and the harsh situations that result from it, is one of the major and most constant sources of friction and unhappiness between the Government and the population. It offends alike our humanity, our civic pride and our political good sense. Honourable Members might agree that in this city of rising standards and rising expectations it is not a situation we can accept indefinitely. Nevertheless it exists and will continue to exist unless we are prepared to take determined action over a considerable period.

The Housing Board and the Government departments concerned have therefore drawn up a plan. For planning purposes a target time is necessary, if only because any such plan must also provide for the annual natural growth of population. The target taken, which I repeat is as a basis for calculation, is 10 years and has as its objective to build on such a scale that, with the contribution of the private sector, there will be sufficient permanent self-contained accommodation in a reasonable environment for every inhabitant of Hong Kong. Such a target, if achieved, would lead to the virtual disappearance of squatter areas, eliminate overcrowding and sharing in both private and public housing, and in addition provide accommodation for those who have to be rehoused in consequence of development schemes and other situations where housing is offered to the homeless or unfortunate, and would also keep pace with the natural expansion of the population.

. . . .

For such a programme to succeed and to be acceptable to the potential inhabitants, three things seem to me essential.

First, good communications with the old urban areas. For Sha Tin this means a four-lane highway and tunnel and double tracking the railway to provide a ten-minute service. For Castle Peak it means a completely new motor road from Tsuen Wan.

Secondly, the housing in the new towns must be accompanied by a full ration of what is essential to modern life: medical, and secondary as well as primary educational facilities, parks and playgrounds, police stations, markets, fire and ambulance stations, community centres and much else.

Thirdly, there must be work, and so sites for private commercial and residential development. These towns in fact must be built as a whole. We have taken the first steps in this direction in the Lek Yuen estate at Sha Tin and in the third stage of the Lei Muk Shue estate at Kwai Chung.

Quite apart from the expansion of the main new towns in the New Territories, housing is also required for the rural areas and smaller New Territories townships, and also for boat squatter areas and for those who wish to live ashore. Plans are therefore in hand to provide a number of estates in these more remote areas. Although the number to be housed is only 30,000, it is a significant step that public housing is to be provided in places such as Tai O where nothing has ever been done in this respect before.

. . . .

I now turn to education. The objective of making free primary education available to all has been achieved. Your Government appreciates that what is now needed is to improve quality, and will exert itself in this respect.

But I think honourable Members will agree with the proposition that during the rest of the '70s the main thrust of our educational effort must be in secondary and technical education, not of course forgetting that increased secondary education carries with it the necessity for increasing correspondingly facilities in the tertiary field.

We are well on the way to achieving the present interim target of 3 years post-primary education for 50% of all children in the 12-14 year age group. Partial objectives, however necessary initially, make for distortion unless replaced by absolute objectives as soon as practicable. Our absolute objective of course is the provision of 3 years secondary education for all in the 12-14 year age group, and your Government proposes that we should address ourselves to this objective forthwith.

In recent months the Education Department and the Secretariat have worked hard on the practicalities and implications of such a change in objectives.

One must not under-rate the size of the operation involved, which requires the provision of 184,000 assisted places in forms 1-3 additional to those now available. About 20,000 of these extra places would be in pre-vocational schools. Some would be in government secondary technical schools, where numbers would be substantially increased.

A further recommendation is to double the percentage of places in secondary schools for the full 5-year courses leading to a Certificate of Education examination. This would require 55,000 places in forms 4 and 5 additional to those now available, and a substantial increase in the number of places in Government secondary technical schools is also planned.

In addition to these proposals for increased secondary education it is also hoped to provide 5 additional technical institutes by 1980 of which 2 should open in 1975.

To staff this expansion with teachers the output of the 3 existing colleges of education would be increased by 2,000 by 1976, and thereafter the construction of a fourth college or other means would be necessary.

As honourable Members will appreciate, an expansion of the extent proposed carries with it financial implications which the Government and they will wish to examine closely in due course. But it also implies the possibilities which are as exciting as they are far-reaching for our whole educational system. This hitherto has been based on the regrettable but inescapable assumption that there will be far fewer places available in secondary schools than students wishing to fill them. It has been this disproportion of places between primary and secondary schools that has lain at the root of the intensity of competition for the present Secondary Schools Entrance Examination with all that this implies for students, teachers and parents alike. It is arguable that it has also distorted both the curricula and teaching methods.

If therefore the proposals to increase the provision of secondary school places commend themselves to honourable Members, I think we should seize the opportunity to bring professional and public, as well as official, opinion to bear on the type of secondary education we should aim at in the new and less restricted circumstances, including the question of what examination system would be apropriate and what curricula. I suggest that the right time to do this is now at the start of the new programme.

I therefore propose to ask the Board of Education to advise me on these important issues as soon as possible and as a basis for its deliberations to submit to it the detailed plans which the Education Department has already drawn up. Amongst other things it would be valuable to have its advice on the speed at which it is practicable to plan to achieve this target. Connected with this is the extent to which they consider bisessionalism* appropriate as a permanent or interim measure. I might add that it is the view of the Government that an element of bisessionalism is essential if rapid progress is to be made.

Their view would also be valuable on the extent to which it is necessary to extend assisted places to all in the 12-14 year group. Clearly those must be assisted who could not otherwise afford to attend school, or the object of the reform would be frustrated; but what of those who could and would pay?

. . . .

I said earlier that an expansion of secondary education carried with it the necessity for an increase in the tertiary field. The demand for tertiary education in Hong Kong far outstrips existing facilities, and steps to increase these have been taken. This is both because a wider provision of tertiary education is good in itself, and because our society stands in urgent need of substantially increasing numbers of well qualified young people who can be trained for professional, technical, administrative and executive roles.

By 1974 the number of places in our two Universities will be some 6,000. This will mean that the Universities will have the capability of turning out about 1,600 graduates each year.

Plans are now in hand to raise the number of university places from 6,000 to 8,400 by 1978. The University and Polytechnic Grants Committee believes that an expansion of this order could be achieved without dilution of quality.

---

* The term 'bisessionalism' refers to the arrangement whereby students attend school in either the morning or the afternoon, so that school buildings may be used for two 'sessions' during the day.

This total is unlikely to be sufficient for our needs beyond the late seventies and in the eighties, and we are therefore already considering ways in which university education in Hong Kong can be further extended.

But the major expansion in tertiary education will be achieved by the new Hong Kong Polytechnic. It has had a slow start — perhaps inevitable in a wholly new venture — but under a dynamic Board I have every hope that it will achieve its target of 8,000 full-time and 20,000 part-time students by 1978. Together with the expansion of the universities this will mean that by 1978 tertiary education in Hong Kong will have been at least trebled.

. . . .

So to sum up, we envisage education facilities along the following lines: free primary education for all followed by secondary education for all to the age of 14; the latter to include an expanded pre-vocational or technical stream. At that point there will be on the one hand greatly expanded facilities for further secondary education leading to the Certificate of Education; on the other, young people will be able to choose between going into industry, or acquiring a qualification in a technical institute. Even if they go into industry, they will be able to benefit from the technical institutes through apprenticeship courses. In the post-secondary field we envisage a substantial expansion of tertiary education in the existing Universities and in the new Polytechnic. I might add that we hope that some young people who do not go through forms IV and V may nevertheless benefit from facilities for part-time instruction in the places of tertiary education.

. . . .

This brings me to social welfare. Inevitably I look back at the scene as it was 10 years ago when social welfare work was just emerging from the stage of an emergency operation to give assistance to the new influx of population in the 1950s.

I note that the economic and social progress achieved in the last 10 years has enabled a substantial advance to be made. For instance, a Government system of public assistance in cash has been introduced. In the community development field there is now a system of estate welfare buildings bringing together under one roof the welfare services for people living in resettlement estates. Family welfare services have been re-organized on a regional basis and their services integrated and made more comprehensive. Progress has been made in helping the disabled — some training centres have been opened, and a range of vocational and pre-vocational training facilities now exist. The probation and correctional services have been expanded and refined.

These are notable advances. While no one will claim that they measure up to the requirements of Hong Kong in either size or scope, they nevertheless do provide a sound base of carefully thought out and increasingly professional activity over a wide field. What I suggest is now required is firstly a comprehensive plan for orderly expansion, and secondly a corps of trained professionals to carry it out.

Let me take the second point first: the corps of professionals. I have found general agreement that the days are over when social welfare in Hong Kong was an emergency service where primary requirement was for enthusiasm, energy and devotion. These qualities are still called for and always will be, but now expertise and professionalism will be increasingly necessary.

Hong Kong has been well served by the social welfare departments of its two universities, but there is great need for training below the university level. The Government therefore proposes to establish an Institute for Social Work Training, providing two-year courses leading to a diploma or certificate. The institute will be open alike to those proposing to enter Government service or to work in the voluntary agencies . . .

So much for the people; now for the philosophy and the plan. In order to formulate these the Government set up new planning machinery, and in concert with representatives of the Hong Kong Council of Social Service and the voluntary social welfare agencies a white paper has been drafted. It is entitled: 'Social Welfare in Hong Kong: the way ahead', and will in its final form incorporate a complementary, detailed 5-year plan. I consider it a most valuable contribution. Its proposals represent a practical consensus of informed and experienced social welfare opinion on both the philosophy and the details of a carefully phased expansion programme.

The proposals envisage 4 main areas for development of which the first two are concerned with help in cash and the second two with help by service.

The first area covers assistance to those who through causes outside their control have not adequate means of support. This is the area in which the public assistance scheme already in existence is progressively proving its value. The second area is assistance in cash to what the paper describes as vulnerable. Groups which might be singled out as beneficiaries are the severely disabled and elderly infirm. But there are other groups, for instance the chronically sick or widowed mothers with young children, which might eventually be included in the scheme.

In respect of this area the paper makes the interesting proposal that financial support should be given to such groups regardless of their means — that is to say on proof of disability, just as people are eligible for public assistance on proof of poverty. It is maintained that in practice such a principle would not be abused and it would vastly simplify administrative procedures and costs. I am sure that honourable Members will wish to look closely at this aspect of the proposal, and I will be interested to hear their comments. While there is much to be said on either side, I hope that there will be general agreement firstly that extension of assistance to the disabled and infirm is a commendable objective to which we should now address ourselves; and secondly that the important thing is to get such a scheme going, and to learn from practical experience what administrative arrangements are ultimately most appropriate. The third area is provision of facilities for the disabled, so that there may be comprehensive services to meet their known needs in the field of training, employment and housing, particularly so as to help them to be independent and self-supporting members of the community. Here clearly employers will have a vital role to play. In this area the problem of providing for the elderly also bulks large. This is now being examined by a working party of members from the Government and the voluntary sector. The elderly should of course benefit both from public assistance and from the disability scheme I have already referred to. But the objective of the further services we have in mind would be to enable them to remain in the community as long as possible. The objective for the elderly might be described as care within the community. Finally the plan contains comprehensive proposals for extending the existing limited network of community and social centres operated by the Social Welfare Department to cover the whole of Hong Kong. Considerable expansion of social and recreational facilities, primarily through the voluntary agencies, is also envisaged.

. . . .

I would like at this point to say a word about social security. It is an emotive phrase, and means different things in different countries. But basically it should mean that provision by the state enables people to live secure in the knowledge that they and their children will be protected from the worst effects of adversity. In some countries it has been codified in a comprehensive unified system. Though this has not been done in Hong Kong we are nevertheless in a fair way to having such provision by the state. I have just referred to what is already being done and what it is proposed will be done in the field of what we call social welfare. But to this should be added our medical services, as no one need now pay more than a small fee for treatment either at a clinic or in hospital — and fees are remitted for the needy. Added also should be our educational system which provides free primary education, and in which nobody is deprived of secondary or tertiary education because of lack of means. Add also the provision of low rent Government housing on a scale unknown elsewhere in the world for those with low incomes. I find this a very extensive system of social security based on the principle of assistance for those in need. There is nothing else quite like it anywhere in the world. It is something characteristic of and unique to Hong Kong, something we may be proud of and something on which we may build with confidence as our resources allow.

I wish here to add another general point about the Government's attitude to payment for services provided by the tax payer such as housing, secondary and tertiary education, and so on. We are all agreed that these needs should be provided as cheaply as possible, as our means allow. But if, and I repeat if, we are ever faced with a choice between having the means to provide the infrastructure, that is to say the houses, the schools, the universities and the staff to work them on the one hand, and of providing them free or almost free on the other, I am sure that honourable Members, and indeed the people of Hong Kong, would agree that at this stage of our development, while we have a population that is predominantly young and active, the first call on Government should always be to provide the physical infrastructure leaving for later — and as our resources are available — the lowering of payments by those benefiting who are able to pay.

DOCUMENT VII.d2: Rebuilding grassroot society (source: HE the Governor, Address in the Legislative Council, 16 October 1974, *Hong Hong Hansard, Reports of the Sittings of the Legislative Council of Hong Kong, Session 1974*)

But I would like to speak about what the public — those at the receiving end of crime — have done. The creation of 1,500 mutual aid committees, with the accompanying superstructure of area committees, is not only a considerable administrative achievement, but indicates the great need that these organizations fill. There was indeed, a void: a void which was as dangerous for the Government as it was unwelcome to the ordinary citizen, who was left without means of influencing conditions outside his own front door. Some of these committees are more effective than others, but they have done much to discourage crime in their own areas. In many cases they have installed alarm systems, and engaged watchmen to patrol the premises, and they constitute a new deterrent to criminals that can be made increasingly effective and is very welcome to police and public alike.

I always leave meetings with mutual aid committees encouraged by the knowledge that in this field attitudes are changing fast. We have many good citizens willing to give a lead on how the people of a neighbourhood may help each other and help the community by making their own areas safer, cleaner and better to live in.

DOCUMENT VII.d3: The new Hong Kong Society (source: Mr Denis Bray, Secretary for Home Affairs, Address in the Legislative Council, 29 November 1973, *Hong Kong Hansard, Reports of the sittings of the Legislative Council of Hong Kong, Session 1973*)

Sir, in a review of any sort the dominant theme is change and in Hong Kong there is seldom a lack of change to contemplate. The physical environment changes with startling rapidity, and judging from the speeches earlier this afternoon this will continue, but my theme to-day is social change. Social change seems to be emerging as one of the most dramatic developments of the early seventies.

Our older society, prized loose from its stable clan structure, was made up of individuals more concerned with material well being than social awareness. Public services of a makeshift sort were accepted with gratitude for security was what they wanted. As the children of the post-war settlers have grown up we have been reminded that they expect more — that the makeshift services good enough for their parents are not good enough in the more prosperous society their parents have created. Services have been improved and long term plans drawn up.

But it has only recently become clear that the most important change in society is not its increasing wealth nor its increasing expectations of Government performance but its new sense of purpose.

The new society no longer expects everything to be done for it by a paternalistic Government. It is a society on the move, prepared to act on social issues with the same vigour that the old refugee society displayed in the pursuit of private prosperity.

How else can one explain the public response to the two campaigns of social awakening — Clean Hong Kong and Fight Violent Crime? Litter strewn streets are an obvious manifestation of social indifference. Before the 'Clean Hong Kong' campaign we were four million lap sap chungs*. The publicity and the strengthening of cleansing services were indispensible parts of the campaign but even the cleanest street can become litter strewn in a few hours. The effort required of each person was only a little restraint but it involved restraint by everybody, all the time. This was forthcoming.

Violent crime posed a completely different problem. We were not a society of four million criminals. Indeed only a very small fraction of the population has ever seen a violent crime being committed. Reporting crime, dialling 999, raising a hue and cry all required a more positive effort than refraining from throwing litter about. Nobody knew when they might be expected to make this effort.

I should like to be able to parade a table of reliable statistics about the state of crime illustrating the success of the campaign but I cannot. The trouble about crime statistics is that criminals do not send in accurate statistical returns. Over a short period when there is likely to be a steady proportion of unreported crime we can draw conclusions about trends from figures of reported crime. But if an extensive publicity campaign is mounted to encourage reports of crime, if four or more new reporting centres are set up, if reporting procedures are simplified, and if the public responds in this as it has shown itself willing to do in other social causes then the one thing we can be sure of is that the proportion of unreported crime will decline. There was even a drop in reported crime during the intensive part of the campaign when the police did everything they could to put men on the beat. But this drop has not been maintained partly, we suspect, because crimes are reported instead of being shrugged off. The statistics show, for instance a disproportionate increase in the number of small robberies reported — robberies which would not have been reported had the campaign not taken place. It is also happening that when criminals are caught and found to be responsible for a string of other crimes many of these other crimes were discovered only after the criminal had been caught. Caches of stolen goods used to be found which could not be returned because their theft had not been reported. There is less of this now.

When we get a longer series of monthly figures reflecting the new higher rate of crime reporting we shall be surer of our conclusions on the underlying figures of actual crime. In the meantime I believe we should be encouraged by greater public confidence. Last winter people were beginning to stay off the streets at night, to keep their children at home and walk in fear of attack. This is not the case to-day. Reports from City District Offices, opinion surveys, and police contacts all reflect a strengthening of public confidence in law and order. Just as the cleaner streets we can see for ourselves are a sign of the success of the 'Clean Hong Kong' campaign so a strengthening of confidence which we know of ourselves is the true measure of the success of the 'Fight Violent Crime' campaign.

---

* Literally, 'litter bugs', reference to people who litter.

Even so we still have far too many robberies and other violent crimes. The police must be given the men to deal with them. The immediate current object of the 'Fight Violent Crime' campaign is to recruit more men and women into the regular police. The first two weeks of the current recruitment campaign produced 1,649 young people who wished to join the Police. On past performance we would expect one out of seven applicants to measure up to police standards. Many more are needed and I am most grateful that honourable Members have expressed a desire to help find the people who can do this work which is of such vital importance to our community.

. . . .

I said that I believed a fundamental change was taking place in society — that the community was developing a new sense of purpose. If this is so what should our reaction be?

> Three main initiatives seem to be required:
> first we must let people know what we are thinking;
> second we must make it easier for people to formulate and present their views; and
> third we must make sure that these expressions of opinion are taken into account.

On the first point my honourable Friend, MR LOBO, asks that the green paper system be more widely used. Having come recently from the New Territories where all sorts of policy issues are freely discussed with rural leaders I do not find the proposal new or alarming. Green papers, reports of advisory bodies and findings of consultants are frequently published before decisions are taken. More informal methods of arising [*sic*] ideas and proposals could be developed (for instance a good many ideas have been aired this afternoon) and I should like to give further thought to this. There are obviously limits - my honourable Friend, the Financial Secretary would in all probability not really wish to air his budget proposals before presenting them to honourable Members in the Finance Bill. Nevertheless I would like to think that we can air more proposals involving a choice of courses open to us so that there is an opportunity to shape policy more closely to public aspirations.

On the second point we do start with a basic structure which enables people to formulate and present their views. At the centre we have a broad range of advisory bodies which are no doubt capable of further sophistication. I am however more concerned with the very much more widespread network of committees that has been reinforced during the 'Clean Hong Kong' and 'Fight Violent Crime' campaigns. My honourable Friend, Mr CHEONG-LEEN, proposed District Consultative Committees but these were first set up informally five years ago when the CDO scheme was introduced. As a part of the two campaigns these informal committees have been established as more formal City District Committees. In addition there are the Area Committees and the grass roots organizations of over 1,000 Mutual Aid Committees.

In the New Territories the Rural Committees and village organizations are quite new and were set up in support of these major campaigns. But I certainly hope they will provide the means whereby people can put forward their views of anything they like. I hope these institutions will develop further before we look for yet more new types of organization. In addition we do hope to improve our own opinion gathering methods. Proposals to strengthen the system are now being drawn up.

On the third point, the responsibility for taking public opinion into account rests on all officials and unofficials concerned with policy decisions. In addition a special responsibility rests on the holder of my post to ensure that public opinion is presented and considered at all levels.

DOCUMENT VII.d4: The ideology, goals and structure of the CDO scheme (source: Ambrose Yeo-chi King, 'Administrative Absorption of Politics in Hong Kong: Emphasis on the Grass Roots Level', in Ambrose Y.C. King and Rance P.L. Lee, eds. *Social Life and Development in Hong Kong*. Hong Kong: Chinese University Press, 1981, pp. 138-142)

The CDO [City District Office] scheme was launched with great fanfare and publicity in mid-1968, immediately after the climax of the 1967 riots. A government-sponsored intensive image-building campaign was successfully carried out to convince the public that the CDO Scheme is something which is genuinely of and for the people. The ideology of the CDO Scheme is a 'service ideology': service for the Government; service for the community; and service for the individuals. These are explicitly stated in the Directive to City District Officers.

The explicit goals of the CDO Scheme are many-sided. It is designed to be a political communication agent, a community organizer, a trouble-shooter for the people. To put it in more general terms, the CDO Scheme is aiming to counteract the tendency of the metropolitan Government toward centralization and departmentalization. The establishment of the CDO Scheme is to make one person or one office which the residents could recognize as 'the government' in their district.

The CDO scheme was approved by the Hong Kong Government in early 1968. It was decided that ten CDOs would be established in the whole metropolitan area. By the end of the same year five CDOs had been established: Eastern, Western, Wanchai, Mong Kok, and Yau Ma Tei. The other five, subsequently opened by the end of 1969, were Central, Kwun Tong, Sham Shui Po, Kowloon City, and Wong Tai Sin.

The CDO Scheme is under the general supervision of the Secretariat for Home Affairs. Directly under the Secretary for Home Affairs are two deputies. One is in charge of the traditional duties of the former Secretariat for Chinese Affairs - newspaper registration, trust fund, liquor licensing, tenancy matters, etc. The other is responsible for the CDO Scheme. Under him are two City District Commissioners, one responsible for the four CDOs on Hong Kong Island, and the other for the six CDOs in Kowloon.

The organizations of the ten CDOs are the same. The City District Officer is the head of the office. Under him are two sections: Internal and External, each headed by an Assistant City District Officer. The Internal Section deals mainly with administrative matters, and the External Section with field or 'liaison' duties. The number of other staff varies with individual offices. There are usually five to eight Liaison Officers assigned to each office. One is invariably assigned to the Public Enquiry Counter, and a greater part of the rest to the External Section. There are two to four Liaison Assistants in each office to assist the LOs [Liaison Officers].

The CDO at Work in Kwun Tong Community

How has the CDO Scheme actually performed at the district level? How has the idea of the CDO Scheme been transformed into action? We have selected Kwun Tong District for our study. Kwun Tong District, one of the ten City Districts of metropolitan Hong Kong, is one of the most rapidly developed urban communities in Hong Kong.

The CDO is not an ordinary functionally-specific administrative organization; rather, it is a multifunctional political structure. What are the functions of the CDO in the Kwun Tong District? According to our findings, during the three-month period of June to August 1971, the CDO's activities involve such things as commenting on the District's development planning; helping to clear out huts and hawkers; building a playground for children; helping in relief of typhoon victims; organizing festival celebration: administering the Fat Choy Special Aid Fund; handling 'individual and family cases'; answering public enquiries; and administering statutory declarations, etc. The CDO's activities are indeed highly functionally-diffuse. They involve just about everything occurring in any local community, ranging from political to very mundane affairs.

One of the CDO's major functions is to facilitate communication between the governors and the governed, including the input of intelligence about 'public opinion' to the decision-makers in the government. The CDO is required to produce a report entitled 'The Anatomy' of his District within six months of his appointment. In the 'Anatomy' thorough information about the peculiarities of the social and economic structure of the district as well as its personalities is expected to be included. The CDO is often asked by various departments to give comments on intended actions, such as the Development Town Plan of the Public Works Department, and other Government organizations ask it to gather information on social needs for decision-making. For example, the CDO has conducted a 'survey' on the needs of the ferry service on behalf of the UMELCO (Unofficial Members of the Executive and Legislative Councils). The methods used to gather intelligence, besides 'survey' conducting, are the District Monthly Meeting, the Study Group and 'Town Talk'.

The CDO holds regular Monthly Meetings which involve a fairly stable group of local leaders, leaders of Kaifong Associations, Multi-Storey Building Associations (MSB), District Associations, the business and industrial sector, etc.; the representatives of field agencies of Government departments are also present. The Monthly Meeting is the primary mechanism of the CDO for collecting the opinions of local leaders on any issue concerning the Government and the public. From the minutes of the meetings, we find that members present voice their opinions on the procedure of reporting crime to the police, on the improvement of recreational facilities in the district, etc. The CDO is designed to extend the Government's consultation circle at the centre to a much wider circle at the peripheral and district level.

The Study Group is rather ad hoc in nature. The people invited to discuss in the Study Group vary from one occasion to another, depending on the topics discussed. The discussants include industrialists, school principals, hawkers, shop owners, taxi-drivers, factory workers, students and others. Sometimes the subjects discussed might include not only matters of a specific nature but also matters of common concern such as traffic problems, corruption, petty crimes, smoke from restaurants, clearance of refuse, Chinese as an official language, etc.

The 'Town Talk' mechanism is not officially included in the CDO Scheme, but it is believed to be one of the most important channels for soliciting public opinion by the CDO. It is probably true that the Monthly Meeting or the Study Group are, in practice if not in theory, geared primarily to reach local leaders rather than the ordinary man. The Town Talk is in a sense more oriented toward the 'man in the street'. The CDO has no specific instructions on whom to consult. As one respondent reported, comments were noted down from casual conversation with whomsoever they happened to talk to, on official or private terms. It emphasizes not the quantitative but the qualitative aspect of the opinions expressed by the people. The key word is 'people'; several officers interviewed repeatedly and separately asserted that the present 'trend' was contacting the 'man-in-the-street'.

A second function of the CDO is to articulate the demands made known to them through the Monthly Meeting, the Study Group and Town Talk by people from different walks of life, as well as demands channelled through newspapers and outside 'requests'. Moreover, interests are articulated by the CDO's self-initiative, based upon its knowledge of the needs and attitudes of the residents of the community. The interests articulated by the CDO are both minor in nature and all-embracing. According to our findings in the period under analysis, the CDO made comments on multi-storey building car parks, cooked food stalls, hawker bazaars, a mini-bus station, a refuse collection centre, and a clinic with regard to the Kowloon Bay Development Plan. The CDO's interest articulation is limited in the sense that it has only a recommendation function.

With respect to the redressing of grievances, it has been expressly denied by the Chairman of the Urban Council that the CDOs are ombudsmen. The CDO is certainly not an ombudsman in the original Scandinavian sense which guarantees his independence as an instrumental officer of the legislature. The CDO is not independent. However, the public image of the CDO as an ombudsman is prevailing, and it is, furthermore, clearly stated in the Report of the CDO Scheme. The CDO's grievance redressing activities can be classified into two major types: redressing of grievances for groups and for individuals. The first type arises out of events affecting a large number of people, such as a clearance operation. This type of grievance redressing is relatively rare; in Kwun Tong District there were only two instances. One was the Shun Lee Chuen Clearance in which villagers whose huts were due to be demolished demanded compensation from the Government through the CDO; the other was the Typhoon

Rose case in which the victims of Sam Ka Chuen demanded a reassessment of the decisions of the Resettlement Department. By contrast, the individual cases in the same period were very large in number, totalling 256. Of these, family disputes accounted for 152, housing 37, and traffic accidents and compensation 24. In all cases it was the clients who took their complaints to the CDO for assistance.

The CDO referred the two group cases for consideration by the departments responsible but they were not favourably reviewed because the departments concerned thought their demands were not in compliance with government policies. In this respect, the CDO could do very little, but it did 'explain' the government policies to the two groups in a more personal way. As for the individual cases, 204 out of 256 cases received were recorded to have been settled. In handling individual cases, the CDO acted as a middleman between parties in deputes. When individual grievances arose from a Government decision, the CDO could not reverse the original decision, but it had the 'power' to bring the case to the responsible departments for a second look, although often all that the CDO could do was 'talk things over', and 'give advice'.

Another function of the CDO is a special set-up called the Public Enquiry Service Counter, usually manned by an Executive Officer, a clerk, and clerical assistants. The PES set-up is designed to familiarize people with the government bureaucracy. The Hong Kong metropolitan Government has become more and more technical, complicated, and fragmented; the ordinary people are often bewildered by the intricacy of governmental operation. There exists a kind of 'information gap' between the Government and the people. The PES is apparently a useful mechanism to bridge this 'information gap', and this is evinced in its enormous use by the people. The number of enquiries received per month by the CDO's PES counter increased from 991 in September 1970 to 5,472 in April 1971. The enquiries cover a wide range of information concerning personal documents, land and housing, employment, taxes, duties and fees, family welfare, education, traffic, medical, and other miscellaneous things.

Another important political function of the CDO may be called political socialization and recruitment. The CDO, in this regard, provides a framework for participation by 'responsible' local sectors. Most of the CDO's efforts are geared to structuring the channels of participation of two major categories of people - youth and 'local leaders'. Different institutional mechanisms have been created to co-opt and socialize them in CDO-sponsored community activities. The Monthly Meeting is the most formal forum. During the three months under study, other mechanisms and activities relating to socialization and recruitment were used. For example, with the help of the Lion's Club and the Army, student volunteers were mobilized to assist in constructing a playground and jetty at Kowloon Bay; they initiated and sponsored, with the support of local prominent people from Kaifongs, schools, and business firms, district-wide sports activities; they worked through voluntary associations in organizing and promoting recreational and festival activities. All these activities were apolitical in terms of their manifest functions; they were primarily recreational in nature. However, these activities were not sheer structuring of leisure time for the local leaders and the youth; they served to channel participation in a 'right' way, to develop community-oriented civic consciousness, to transform the young people into 'good citizens' and future community leaders, and to create a political culture which is supportive of the political structure of Hong Kong.

DOCUMENT VII.d5: Mutual Aid Committee offices (source: Janet Lee Scott, *Action and Meaning: Women, Participation in the Mutual Aid Committees, Kowloon*. Cornell, Ph.D. 1980, pp. 41-45)

The establishment of an office for the M.A.C. [Mutual Aid Committee] is a big event, for most members consider it important to have one. There are many reasons for this. First, the setting up of an office proclaims to all that an M.A.C. has been established for the building or the block and that the residents have worked hard and have cooperated to reach this goal. Also, the office indicates a strong and successful committee, one that is thriving and should be noticed by the M.A.C.s of other blocks or units. This can be seen more clearly where there are connected blocks sharing a common entrance on the ground level. If each block has an M.A.C. but only one has an office, the other committees will spare no effort trying to establish one, too.

Most of the M.A.C. offices that I visited were found in the public housing estates. Private housing M.A.C.s are less likely to have offices, a point to return to later. These offices are usually located on the ground floor, or occasionally, a vacant room on an upper floor will be turned over to the M.A.C. by the Housing Department. Committee members will not let the lack of a room stop them from having an office. If necessary, they will collect the materials and build one themselves in odd spaces: the air space in the center of the block, the area near or under the stairs, an unused storage room.

Once established, the room is nicely decorated. A partial description of one estate office will give some idea of typical arrangement:

> The room itself, in an upper floor, seemed newly opened. Tiled with new brown ceramic tile, it was encircled along the walls with wooden folding chairs with red padded seats. The walls themselves were hung with bright banners, formal paintings of Chinese horses, and a new blackboard. Two fans, one overhead and one floor fan attached to the wall, keep the room cool. Walls painted green. At one end, a folding table covered with coloured oilcloth, and behind it, a new cream-coloured metal desk with vases and pots of flowers. On the wall behind the desk, framed souvenirs and mementoes, a new wall clock. Near the window, a new television set sits on a stand also holding an array of drinking glasses, cups and thermos bottles.

The decoration of the office may be meager, the size may be small; no matter, the important thing is to have one. Still, not all of the estate-based M.A.C.s have them, but there are more there than in private buildings. A major reason for this is the lack of space. Private contractors rarely include extra rooms in their designs, so few buildings have spaces that could be rented or used. I once visited one office in a private building that had been converted from a storage room. Two ladies there showed how they had decorated the room with crepe paper, put up pictures, gathered tables and chairs, and had a telephone installed. They were quite pleased and proud of the result. Another committee, feeling the lack, took over part of the roof of their building to set up a recreation area. While not an office in the strictest sense, it was intended to be a gathering spot for committee members, and was furnished with items donated by members. This lack of space is keenly felt and mentioned, together with the problem of few social activities, as a major reason for residents not getting together more often, or even for not becoming acquainted.

When the time comes to open the office formally, a special celebration and ceremony may be held to mark the occasion. If possible, it is good to have an important figure officiate and give the main speech; the City District Officer of the Wong Tai Sin District, has performed this task for some of the M.A.C.s in the Tze Wan Shan Estate. Other dignitaries, officials, and officers of nearby M.A.C.s are also invited. In more than one office are framed photographs of its opening ceremony, attended by many public figures. One chairman showed me, with some pride, a clipping from an overseas Chinese newspaper describing the opening ceremony for her M.A.C office. She then insisted that my assistant and I add our signatures to the red commemorative banner that was to hang in the room.

The activities centreing around these offices are informal, yet recognized by the residents. The offices are especially busy in the estates and more so if they are located on the ground floor, where they are conveniently placed for the constant stream of passers-by. It is at the office that the patrol teams gather and the officers meet to plan activities. Depending on room size, the subcommittees may also use it for their meetings and the yearly elections are held there. It is a clearing area for announcements; notices from the District Office and other organizations are placed there for people to read. The office is staffed by at least one person, often an older gentleman, while one or more of the officers are usually present. These office helpers (it is unclear whether they are paid) answer the phone, take messages, give out information, and make themselves generally useful.

Telephone numbers and addresses of the residents are usually kept in the office, a practice which makes it easier to contact someone. A good percentage of the office traffic is accounted for by people coming in to use the telephone, or to leave messages or packages for someone in the building. Older residents of the building, mostly the old men, congregate around the office to watch television (which many committees buy for their offices) and relax*. There is always a group of them there, spending the day with their friends, chatting and nibbling. Younger residents, teenagers, are found less frequently, but they do come in just to see 'what is going on.' The M.A.C. uses the

---

* 'The section on old people congregating at the M.A.C. Office should really read, both old men and old women congregate there .... Great numbers of ah paus [old women] sit there all day gossiping and watching the residents go by.' — Author's communication to Ed.

office to store its equipment (patrol team helmets and sticks, party decorations, extra cups and materials) and display its memorabilia; banners, trophies, letters and photographs are all displayed with pride.

Given all this, it is not surprising that the committees will not only strive to obtain an office, but to keep one. At the time of this study, numerous committees in Wong Tai Sin and Tze Wan Shan Estates were angry over increased rents for these offices by the Housing Department. Some of these committees felt that the increase was too much and that they could not pay. Moreover, such a facility should not, they felt, be taxed at all as it was part of an officially established programme and backed by the District Office. With evident frustration some committee members told me that such a move would jeopardize the committee itself. At that point, possession of an office is more than a point of pride; it is part of the existence of the committee.

e. Hong Kong Workers

> Hong Kong's people did not seek change by putting pressure on the Hong Kong government. Hong Kong families looked inwards as they made their bid to improve themselves in the very competitive Hong Kong economy.[*] Hong Kong workers did not join trade unions, seldom went on strike, had few ideas about how their jobs might improve, but they seemed agreed in one aim, and that was that their children should move out of the poverty trap. They expected better education for their children to be an answer to upward mobility, and, if education for all their children together was beyond reach, then a family strategy should come into play so that the daughters might work to contribute to family income that would allow the sons to be educated. For many families, in the industrious Hong Kong of the 1970s, this strategy paid off, but it also implied that upward mobility tended to be associated with the natural family cycle and that, at least, among the poorer majority, it was the long-time resident, rather than the fresh immigrant, who would see its benefits.

DOCUMENT VII.e1: Employees' expectations for themselves and their children (source: H.A. Turner, *The Last Colony, But Whose? A Study in the Labour Movement, Labour Market and Labour Relations in Hong Kong.* Cambridge: Cambridge University Press, 1980, pp. 195-197)

The Hong Kong workers in the sample did not, in general, appear to have high aspirations for themselves, or resemble the aggressively ambitious petty-capitalists so

---

[*] S.K. Lau calls this 'utilitarianistic familism' in his *Society and Politics in Hong Kong*, Hong Kong: Chinese University Press, 1982.

frequently described by writers such as England and Rear[*]. When asked what kind of work they hoped to be doing in five years' time, the sample displayed a low level of personal aspirations. Over half of the sample (55%) wished to keep their present job, and of those that named another type of work (276 respondents), 83 chose some kind that would involve a sideways or downwards move. A further 39 respondents replied that they hoped to be out of the labour market by that time and 147 did not know what kind of work they would like to do. Only 123 respondents out of the total sample (13%) hoped to have improved themselves in five years' time by either securing a more prestigious job or by going into business on their own account.

The respondents' replies to a follow-up question specifically on whether they had considered starting a business within the next five years confirms the previous finding. Less than a third (31%) of the sample had seriously considered this, a surprisingly low figure considering the great number of small businesses in Hong Kong and their rapid turnover. Finally, the respondents' modest level of personal aspirations is further confirmed by their replies to the question on attendance at vocational classes (night school). The 21% of the sample attending such classes seemed to be definitely on the low side considering the age distribution of the sample, the pressing shortage of places in full-time post-secondary education institutions in Hong Kong and the preoccupation, so commonly found in developing societies, with formal educational qualifications.

There was little difference within the sample on the question of respondents' hopes for five years ahead, with the exception (to a limited extent) of government employees. Thus 24% of government employees aspired to jobs with higher prestige than their present job, compared to 9% of Cantonese firm employees, 9% of Shanghainese firm employees and 13% of UK firm employees. On the specific question of starting in business, there was a perceptible difference this time by skill level, with 37% of white-collar workers having considered this, compared to 18% of unskilled workers.

There was more variation within the sample in the case of further education. The proportions of white-collar workers (36%), government employees (34%) and employees of very large firms (32%) attending vocational classes of some kind were higher than the average (21%). Respondents in the 20-29 years group (32%) were also more likely to attend, together with, as might be expected, a larger proportion of the under-20 group (40%).

Despite their tendency to have limited aspirations for themselves, the workers in the sample had high aspirations for their children. When asked if they would like a son of theirs to do a job similar to their own when he grew up, the vast majority of the workers in the sample (89%) replied that they would not. When asked what job instead they would like a son of theirs to get, 80% of the white-collar workers with a definite

---

[*] J. England and J. Rear, *Chinese Labour Under British Rule: A Critical Study of Labour Relations and Law in Hong Kong*, Oxford: Oxford University Press, 1975.

preference opted for a technologist, professional or managerial type job and a further 6% for their son's running a business. Only 14% named a job that was at their own lower white-collar/technician level. The blue-collar workers were equally ambitious in relative terms. Thus, 56% of the blue-collar workers with a definite preference named either a technologist, professional or managerial type job, 30% named a lower white-collar/technician type job and a further 4% opted for having a business. Only 10% named a manual job.

The workers were prepared, moreover, to financially support a son through the educational process so that he could obtain the type of job either they hoped he would get, or the job the son himself preferred. Ninety-six percent of the sample would support a son for three years of secondary school and 94% for five years; 80% would support a son for a full-time three year university or polytechnic course. While equal proportions of all groups would financially support a son for three or five years of secondary school, there were some differences when it came to supporting a son for a university-style education. White-collar workers (96%) were more willing to do so than unskilled workers (72%) and respondents in the 20-29 years age group (93%) were considerably more willing to do so than those in the 50 years and over group (58%), thus showing that these workers were again more ambitious — this time on their son's behalf.

DOCUMENT VII.e2: Dutiful second daughter (source: Janet W. Salaff, *Working Daughters of Hong Kong: Filial Piety or Power in the Family?* New York: Columbia University, 1995, pp. 48–70; this book was first published by Cambridge University Press in 1981)

Mae Goh was 22 in 1973. Her solid build, her hair fixed in an outdated ear-length coif, tightly curled, her broad face with its calm, serious demeanour, and the plain, conservative gaberdine pants and knit skirts and tops she wore gave her the look of a hardworking, no-frills woman. This impression was appropriate, because Mae was a pivotal contributor to her family economy. Mae singlemindedly devoted herself to her family, and she derived her self-esteem from this care and attention.

The Goh household consisted of Father, Mother, and six siblings. Father was a low-paid clerk and First Brother was a delivery boy for a well-known retail comprador firm in Hong Kong. Mae and First Sister, Hua, were factory workers. The three youngest children, all sons, were students in 1973. The Goh family aspired to upgrade itself economically by drawing upon the wages of the three eldest children, and in so doing advance the education and hence the careers of the three youngest. Although ambitious for a working-class family, those plans were attainable as long as no unforeseen crisis occurred to weaken the family earning power. All family members had become keenly aware of the importance of coordinating their working efforts and pooling their individual earnings. Self-upgrading the household by multiple wage earning was the Goh family's strategy that had long guided Mae's behaviour.

Home

Mae was a Ch'iu-chaonese born in a village near the port city Swatow, northeast of Hong Kong in Kwangtung province. Father brought his mother and younger brother along with Hua and Mae with him to Hong Kong on a fishing boat in 1951. The Hong Kong government lacked the facilities to receive the incoming wave of refugees from the newly founded People's Republic, and families like the Gohs initially had to manage with rudimentary, makeshift accommodations. Upon their arrival, the Gohs purchased an overpriced, ramshackle squatter's hut from a petty entrepreneur who had nailed it together from old crates. The squatter huts were crammed together on a Kowloon mountainside which teemed with impoverished refugees. Within months their hut was badly burned by a fire that swept the squatter complex, and although the Goh family escaped unscathed, they had no other recourse but construction of a second shack similar to the one they had evacuated. Eventually the community was provided with a pump with running water, one communal outhouse for every 100 families, and cement walkways. Primary schools were built in the neighbourhood by missionary societies, but few other community services were available in the squatter area, which the government considered temporary.

In fact, the Gohs remained in this squatter area for nearly a decade, during which three sons were born, before the family was finally resettled in two rooms in Lok Fu resettlement estate, where the sixth, and last, child was born. Government-built resettlement estates were a relatively inexpensive form of housing for the Goh family, but their facilities were rudimentary. Their two 10' by 12' rooms, standard for the time, were allotted on the basis of 24 square feet per adult (6' by 4'), and they had a nine-member household. Children were allocated only one-half of the 'adult' space, so resettlement estate families had to curtail the physical movement and indoor play of their youngsters. Simple home industries like plastic flower assembling and piecework sewing were permitted in the rooms. Shops, schools, churches, a playground, and even factories were contained in the basements and on the rooftops of the Gohs' block of flats. This older estate in which Mae lived lacked indoor plumbing and water taps and private kitchens. The outdoor balcony was the sole walkway on each floor. Here the Goh family cooked, stored water, hung clothes, washed children, and socialized with the neighbours. There was a common stall-type toilet on every floor, laundering and bathing areas, as well as a common water spigot, where the family filled its water jars.

One of the Gohs' rooms was partitioned into three sleeping areas: the first for the two elder girls and Grandmother, the second for the three eldest brothers, and the third for the parents and youngest child. The other room served as their living room and contained a long side-board that held a matching tea service, a large Kewpie doll, and a telephone. A wall of the room was dominated by the 23-inch television set. A refrigerator was placed against the second wall, and the sewing machine took up yet another wall. The dining table, which filled the central floor space, doubled as the evening study area for the boys. Calendars advertising the fishing gear sold at Father's workplace adorned the walls.

By the 1970s, the Goh family could afford a more spacious flat and was put on a waiting list for a government-built low-cost housing unit. But Mae was relatively satisfied with her estate apartment, despite its obvious shortcomings, because of its proximity to her place of work. She explained, 'Living here is quite convenient. We have the market just downstairs, and transportation to work is easy. The only bad thing about this place is security. Just the other day a restaurant on the next block was robbed of sixteen hundred dollars, and not long before that a fellow was robbed in the staircase. Also, there are a lot of peeping toms here. The management installed doors on the toilet stalls only a few months ago. Before that, it was really horrible. There was no privacy at all. And they still haven't done anything about the bathing area yet. A friend of mine had to scream for help not long ago when she was bathing — someone was peeping at her. Now I have to go early to bathe, when there aren't too many people hanging around the bathing area. Also, it's very dangerous to walk around the estate very late, and so I usually try to get back before eleven. If I come home after that, then I ask Mother to be my guard.'

The Goh family tolerated these cramped, difficult accommodations because they were a decided improvement over the squatter shacks in which they had lived for many years. Also, this future-focused family concentrated its meager funds on the younger children's education and preferred not to squander its money on housing, which apart from short-term comfort promised few returns of the family investment. Nevertheless, the need for space and physical security were increasingly pervasive concerns, and by this time the Gohs could afford to search the private housing market for a modest alternative to the older resettlement estate apartment. While waiting for a government-financed low-cost housing apartment, the Gohs rented an inexpensive two-room flat in the Kowloon Walled City, a district not far from their estate home. Several of the Goh family members moved to the Walled City and others remained in the estate rooms, which began to seem comparatively spacious.

Parents

Mrs. Goh was a large-boned, rather stout woman, broad shouldered and easygoing. Her childhood was spent in a village near the city of Swatow, and like all of the mothers in my sample she matured during the economic depression and the turbulent years of China's war with Japan and the civil war. Mrs. Goh never attended school and at age 18 entered an arranged marriage with a neighbouring villager whose father was a trader in small wares. After two children were born, the Gohs emigrated by sea to Hong Kong. At first, Mrs. Goh's mother shared a squatter home with the family, but she and Mrs. Goh were continually at loggerheads, and the older woman finally moved to a one-half room resettlement estate apartment nearby.

Mrs. Goh was required to cook, sew clothes, shop daily for food bargains in the open-air marker, and take the youngest child to and from the nearby kindergarten, so she never had time to undertake employment outside the home. Her main diversions were chatting with her neighbours and watching television, and she gained pleasure from being with her family. Mrs. Goh never attended the cinema because she was not able to understand either the Mandarin dialect of contemporary Hong Kong films or the Chinese subtitles. At home, however, Mr. Goh cleared away the table and washed the supper dinner dishes so that Mother could view her favorite television soap opera after dinner.

Observing her children develop and doing her best for them was a source of fulfillment for this dedicated mother. Mrs. Goh made it clear to me that she was distressed by the large size of her family and revealed that she originally had wished to have fewer children. She had taken herbal contraceptive formulas in an effort to prevent her sixth birth. Later she blamed herself for the consequences: 'My youngest son has been in the hospital several times, and as you see he has no appetite. Mother-in-law says that the child is sickly because of the herbal medicines that I drank.' Mother's attempt at rudimentary birth control indicated that she never ceased attempting to control her life, although the action she took was not effective.

A slightly built man, Mr. Goh had a broad face, and Mae proudly pointed out their physical resemblances: 'Many times I've been walking down the street and people have stopped me to ask, 'Are you Goh's daughter?' We look so much alike!' Father clerked behind the counter in a small Ch'iu-chao trading firm that exported Chinese fishing nets to Ch'iu-chao traders in Thailand and Singapore. He dressed neatly in a white shirt and gray slacks, in contrast to the blue and black garb of the manual workers. Father's status on the job was low, and as jack-of-all-trades (or, as he put it, a 'many-kick-foot') he was required to toil long hours and sometimes all night as counterman, stockboy, and watchman.

This was Father's first steady work in Hong Kong, and he had remained at the same firm for over 20 years. The manager spoke the same Ch'iu-chao dialect, and Father felt loyal to the firm. When Father first obtained this position he earned only $40 a month[*], and after 20 years (with annual raises of $4), his income reached $120, a probable ceiling. Father's earning would soon be topped by the wages of his sons, who would, he fervently hoped, do much better than he in the world of work. By 'better' he meant higher wages and shorter hours in a steady white-collar position. A modest man, Father had never complained to his manager about his low pay. Hua and Mae both wished that Father could find a position with improved wages and hours, but they realized that it was impossible for a man his age to change his line of work. The girls loyally insisted that the firm did not pay Father his worth, and they endeavoured to make up for it by contributing their earnings to the family. Although Eldest Son had already taken a job as a delivery boy in a grocery store, paying somewhat less than Father's job but with shorter hours, hopes were pinned on Second Son, who would be promoted through technical college by dint of the family's efforts and who would vindicate Father's expectations.

---

[*] All dollar values in this entry have been converted by the author to the U.S. dollar at approximately HK$5 to US1.

Education

Such an expectation was realistic because neighbourhood schools were accessible to working-class children residing in the resettlement estate. The Gohs obtained small sums of money from missionary societies to pay the school fees and sent all six children to school. Each successive child attended a bit longer, paving the way psychologically and socially for the improved schooling of the next-younger sibling.

The primary school that the sisters and brothers attended enjoyed a modest reputation. It was a private missionary school, with a curriculum oriented toward the Secondary School Entrance Examination taken by all Hong Kong primary graduates. The pupils were taught in vernacular Cantonese, but Mandarin was the medium of written exercises, which the pupils rarely learned to proficiency. Mae's parents chose the school because of its proximity to home, low tuition fees, and the fair-minded reputation of its principal, a missionary who was outspokenly critical of the political and economic conditions that Hong Kong working-class people endured. 'It's a good school. It's close, too. The headmistress is a good person who's done a lot for people like us,' commented Mae.

Hua left school after primary 2 to work in a light bulb factory at 20c per day, but Mae completed primary 6 before going out to work. Mae proudly included her graduation from primary school among her major accomplishments. First Brother, the third child, obtained 3 years of secondary schooling, after which he held several jobs, including factory worker and delivery boy. The family pinned its economic hopes upon the fourth child, who was studying to enter a postsecondary technical institute, and the fifth, a form II pupil (the second year of secondary school). The sixth was still in primary school.

The two sisters deeply regretted their inadequate education, which they attempted to remedy by attending night school after work. At great physical cost and with few tangible results, Mae sat in a crowded classroom every night vainly attempting to absorb the rudiments of English grammar and a few facts of European history. She recalled 'Hua and I rushed right to school from work. We never had time to eat dinner. I used to buy a bread roll and eat it when the teacher turned his head to write on the blackboard. It was really tiring! But I enjoyed it because that's where I met my best friend I-ling, as well as A-li and some other friends. Although we have all dropped out of class by now, we still keep up our friendships.'

Mae then enrolled in part-time English lessons at the Caritas (Catholic) Youth Centre, where we first met in 1973, and various other classes as well — folk singing, European cooking, and social dancing. At the end of 1974 she re-enrolled in nightly classes, favoured by Mother as a means to improve her job opportunities. However, Mae candidly admitted that such an evening school, which provided no recognized certificate for its graduates, would not greatly elevate her job options, and she continued mainly to make more friends and for the contact with organized knowledge.

Mae and Hua ended their formal schooling for self-proclaimed 'economic reasons', but the reasons for which their parents sent them to work were based on conventional definitions of the elder daughters' obligations. The family's undoubted need for cash, coupled with norms limiting women's education and the ease of factory employment for young girls, made inevitable the sacrifice of their further education in favour of the family's economic needs. Nevertheless, the girls' education as far as primary level should be viewed as an assertion of a woman's right to learn. Hua and Mae themselves saw it that way. Secondary education was psychologically and sociologically remote for working-class girls of their age at the time. The sisters learned to read whereas their mother had not, and their formal education, however limited, distinctly increased their employment and social opportunities.

Because school provided extrafamilial experiences, it had a lasting value beyond the formal curriculum. Mae and Hua came into contact with other women their age, and their participation in the age-graded classes stimulated a consciousness of the common bond that unites youth. They also became aware of their ability to achieve on their own apart from their family, which paved the way for their assumption of continued responsibility for their own friendships, leisure-time activities, and jobs after leaving school.

Mae at work

In both large factories and small workshops, all of Mae's jobs consisted of repetitive operations: electronics assembling, seaming garments, and fusing the seams of plastic bags. Mae found small workshops preferable to larger factories because the personal proximity of the workshop owner meant he was aware of and could appreciate Mae's hard work on his behalf. Mae responded best to such personal calls upon her effort.

Mae invited me to visit one place of work, a small plastic bag factory in a narrow, two-floor tenement building within earshot of the busy Kai Tak Airport, with neither heating for the damp winter air nor air conditioning for the intense summer hear. The plastic bags were printed on the first floor, and Mae and three other women cut the bags to size and seamed three edges in the loft. They worked from a fifty-pound roll of plastic, unwinding it by hand, pulling one end under the arm of a machine that resembled an electric paper cutter; then the electrified arm dropped and seamed a bag. These actions took a few seconds but could not be mechanized because one machine could not handle the many sizes and shapes of bags, and as Mae further remarked, 'We girls are cheaper than machines.' Mae was paid on a piecework basis, $1 for 1,000 plastic bags, which represented 2 hours of seaming at a fast pace. She preferred piecework because of the flexible working hours and the lure of higher earnings than on a fixed wage. However, Mae earned at most $19-$20 for a 6-day week in 1973.

Before joining this workshop in 1973, Mae had tried her hand at several other jobs typically performed by women. In 1970 she left a relatively low-paying electronics factory for a slightly better wage in a plastic bag factory, where she learned the shortcuts from her sister Hua, who was already employed there. Mae quit that factory because a defective automatic machine she had been using to seam the bags emitted electric shocks and she burned her hand. The management refused to repair it, blaming Mae for handling the machine poorly. Mae commented, 'After I left, my replacement received such a serious shock that she was sent to the hospital, and only then did the management send someone to fix the machine.' Soon after that, Mae attended an evening class where she learned wig assembly. She paid $18 for the class, but shortly after she had acquired the skill, the artificial hair industry collapsed.

In 1973 alone, Mae worked in three separate establishments. Attracted by the promise of 2c more per 1,000 plastic bags (for 2 hours of work), Mae phoned in 'sick' to the shop I visited and tried out another workshop that offered higher pay. However, the manager of the new workshop broke his word and reduced the wage to the cheaper rate prevailing on the labour market. Conceding that they had lost the dispute with the management, almost all of the women who worked there left for other shops, and Mae joined them, returning to the first plastic bag plant. But she was soon laid off due to a shortage of plastic materials, which the manufacturers imported from Japan but whose local supply was temporarily being hoarded by larger factories. For several weeks Mae worked only a few hours a day in her workshop, supplementing that with work in a larger factory with an adequate supply of materials. A few months later, the small workshop suddenly closed its door when the owner absconded with the funds. Mae turned to another type of work altogether: seaming garments.

Mae did not undertake these job changes lightly, because they were costly in time and money lost. On her first day in the plastic bag workshop that I visited Mae earned only $1.60 because she had not yet learned how to use that particular seaming machine. On her second day there she earned $2.40. 'Still too low!' she complained - she was aiming for the $3.50-per-day wage that was her usual ceiling. Mae did not find the transportation to the new shop convenient either, and she walked a round trip of 70 minutes between home and work to save 8c bus fare each way.

Mae attributed her poor and irregular working conditions, the frequent layoffs, and lack of work security to the personalities of the employers operating in the competitive economic situation in Hong Kong. Her naivete of the local employment situation was grounded in a basic incomprehension of the international capitalist division of labour and Hong Kong's dependent role in this division of labour. Accordingly Mae stated the reason that the manager would not pay her the extra 2c per 1,000 bags was his 'stinginess,' whereas the next manager was 'all right.' Though he laid off the workers without pay or warning when he ran out of materials, this was 'not his fault,' but was due to the 'competition among workshops for plastics.' Mae was not critical of the government, and she rarely read newspapers. Regarding a then-current teachers' strike, Mae said vaguely, 'It's hard to know who is right, the government or the teachers.'

Mae was unaware of the location of the export markets for the products she manufactured. She showed me a large yellow plastic bag she had finished on which was written, 'Have a safe Hallowe'en, from your Esso dealer,' embossed with a picture of a witch riding a broomstick. She did not know what Hallowe'en was. I thought it ironic that Mae had lost one of her jobs in a dispute over 2c for 2 hours of work, and yet the bags she seamed had so little value that they were to be given away with the purchase of a tank of gas. Mae thought her firm also finished bags for Mexico, 'because the words look like Spanish.' (It seemed more likely to me that the bags bore the emblem of a chic boutique in New Haven or Chicago.)

Despite her shallow understanding of Hong Kong exporting practices, Mae manifested an undirected but vital response to her poor working conditions in the willingness to change jobs. Although her frequent job shifts were reflex responses to work problems, from which Mae fled instead of altering, she at least demonstrated an active rather than passive stance. Hua, in contrast, was considerably less resourceful and remained in one factory for over 10 years. 'I have considered changing jobs, ' Hua said, 'but I don't know any other trade. Also, I'm different from Mae, who changes jobs frequently. It's not worth it! You'll just have to change again later.'

Mae felt responsible for her family's economic station. Very close to her parents emotionally, Mae willingly subordinated her personal goals to their view of family needs. She saw very few contradictions between her personal work ambitions and the economic needs of the family. Mae had no personal work goals, but she would labour as hard on their behalf as she could. For that reason, it was not easy to discuss with Mae her 'future career ambitions,' a somewhat abstract concept that suggested a freedom of choice between work and marriage or between careers that she did not feel empowered to make. Whenever I raised this topic, Mae responded that she intended to do 'the usual thing' expected of young women - to work, see her brothers through school, then marry and continue until her own children arrived.

In this context, Mae's work goals were limited to the realistically attainable paycheck, friendly coworkers, and time for leisure. Elder sisters worked not only to improve their family's economic situation but also to attain a greater sense of independence and to spend small sums of money on themselves. They were relatively satisfied with their paychecks because they were an improvement over the recent past. Hua recalled that at age ten she earned only 20c daily in a light bulb factory, and even then the employer did not even pay all of her pitifully low wages. 'The management sometimes delayed paying me because I was under age and too afraid to complain, until Mother would go and raise hell.' Although consumer prices were considerably lower then (Hua paid only 10c for a meal and 2c for bus fare), the Goh family considered itself worse off in those days. On the contrary, Mae's 1973 daily wage of close to $3.50 was a decided improvement, even with the rise in prices. This decade-long gradual wage increase committed workers like these two women to tedious factory jobs because they helped alleviate family poverty and want.

The widening of the family's horizon's that followed its solution of the critical problems of shelter and hunger committed the offspring to work even longer for the common good. The stagnation of real wages from 1972 to 1974 further strengthened the girls' commitment to work, because they were still expected to elevate their family's living standards.

Improvement of the young women's work situations was discouraged by the family, the international division of labour (with Hong Kong workers performing labour-intensive, low-skilled manufacturing work), and the educational system. The Goh family encouraged daughters to study only when the training did not interfere with their current earning power. Although some of Mae's friends preferred jobs in which they learned new skills, few such jobs were available, and since most women were enjoined to remit their wages weekly, they invariably abandoned ideas of job training and upgrading in favor of higher-paying piecework machining. As a result, these two sisters and their friends were fixed in a work routine at an early age, and they could acquire other skills only at the fringe of their working routines, in evening school. Their brothers, however, who were expected to contribute significantly to their parents' support, even after marriage, were more likely to undertake low-paying apprenticeships for several years or to remain in school longer, to ensure themselves better prospects for the future. Although an employed married daughter still contributes small sums from her wage packet to her own parents, she is not obliged to do so. This gives rise to the relative lack of concern for the daughter's future career opportunities, a carry-over from the patriarchal traditions of Chinese culture, which severely restricted those young women's chances for remunerative work after marriage.

Mae disliked her work but had no future job plans. Mae believed that the only kind of job advancement for a woman was to study sewing and tailoring skills in evening class and then leave the factory to become a tailor. Her friend I-ling did just that, but Mae rejected that idea. 'What other kind of job could I have?' she asked rhetorically. 'I don't know how to do anything else, and I don't like to sew!' Mae held a conventional notion of women's proper sphere. Pointing to the man who ran the machine that painted the logo on the plastic bags, Mae said, 'Only men do that. Of course it's better paying than seaming work, but your hands get dirty when you handle that equipment.' After the small plastics workshop closed its doors, Mae turned to garment manufacturing despite her distaste for sewing.

The truncation of Mae's ambitions was consistent with the limited employment opportunities available in Hong Kong. For example, in the electronics industry, Mae's first job setting, the transnational corporations assign only a narrow spectrum of labour-intensive assembly jobs to their Hong Kong plants. But the reasons for the limited career mobility in factories and shops were little fathomed by Mae or Hua. The educational system encouraged neither an understanding of the international political economy in which Hong Kong was situated nor the necessary technical training for women in those highly skilled factory jobs that did exist. Nor did the factory ever train Mae for its supervisory or management posts, which were filled by male graduates of technical institutes, and these technical colleges would not accept students like Mae and her friends with only primary school education. Some of Mae's peers attended private evening school in English, hoping to improve their service girls' qualifications, but the classes were for the most part poorly taught.

However, a few factory women were selected as 'lead girls'. Two of Mae' friends, A-li and Kitty, advanced to such positions. At first both hesitated, doubting their ability to direct others, but ultimately A-li took the job. The second firmly rejected the position of section leader, stating, 'I was afraid that when I had 'm.c.' [menstrual cramps] I would not be able to work or give orders,' thereby revealing her agreement with the prevailing dictum that 'anatomy is destiny'. Thus, feelings of self-limitation and lack of social support, rooted in their subordinate position in the family, the workplace, and the educational system, undermined the determination of Mae and other women to compete for the few opportunities for advancement open to factory hands.

Neither Mae nor her elder sister Hua compared their jobs unfavourably with those of their brothers, since they felt that men and women 'naturally' held different types of jobs. Instead, they contrasted their work experiences with those of women of their social class in earlier generations. In so doing they realized that opportunities to work had broadened considerably compared to even the recent past. The speed of economic change was exemplified by the fact that Mae's mother had never worked outside the home whereas her daughters held semiskilled factory jobs. Hua had remained for years at an unsatisfying job in the plastic bag workshop, whereas Mae, 2 years her junior, more easily transferred from one factory to another. The generational comparison that Mae made was thus rooted in reality. The increased importance of single-sex peer groups further underlined the young woman's identification with other women like herself and suggested the inevitable contrast with women older and younger than herself.

Family relationships

Mae's paid labour input to the family economy was a continuation of her earlier unpaid work at home. It was assumed that the elder children in large families would take responsibility for everyday tasks, and Mae and Hua fulfilled this expectation. Many jobs fell to them before they were adolescents, because of their mother's busy involvement with toddlers and infants. Hua and Mae hauled water daily and cooked, cleaned house, and washed clothes.

After they joined the paid labour force, the two sisters continued to view their primary goal in working as the elevation of their family's living standard. Even though Mae's earnings varied with her frequent changes of employer and the length of her work week, she generally contributed close to three-quarters of her wages to her family. Mae and Hua accounted for over two-fifths of the family income in 1973, a relatively high proportion, because their father earned so little.

Hua and Mae clearly understood the centrality of their earnings, which helped the family purchase essentials: rent and food for the entire family, medical expenses, and education for the younger children. Rent for public housing was low, but utilities (including telephone) were expensive. Food comprised a substantial portion of their budget. Sociologists usually interpret a high proportion of family budget spent upon food as a trait of poverty, but there was little doubt that the Goh's meals improved in substance and appeal as their income enlarged. They could afford meat or fish daily, to eat out as a group in restaurants one or more Sundays a month, and occasionally to bring cooked food from stalls to eat at home.

Mae and Hua visited private physicians for minor ailments and they purchased Chinese herbal medicines when ill. The two sisters' income also enabled the Gohs to pay for Second Brother's education when he failed to qualify for a government scholarship. As the family income rose with several members working, more consumer goods were purchased. The television set, electric rice cooker, electric fan, small refrigerator, and sewing machine were all considered necessities in Hong Kong and could normally only be purchased by means of the children's additions to the family wage. Thus, according to Mae, her family came to enjoy a relatively comfortable existence only when there were more workers than dependents. 'Then,' Mae said with obvious satisfaction, 'our family was finally on its feet!'

For a family of daughters, this relatively comfortable life was necessarily of limited duration. Several years before Hua became engaged to Lan Bing in 1973, some of her income had been put aside for her dowry, and when Hua married at age 25, she could no longer contribute to the family budget. Mae's earnings became even more important than before.

Mother and Father took the daughters' income for granted, and the two sisters had little say about how their earnings were spent. Mae recommended that her younger brother attend her old primary school, and since her parents had little experience with educational institutions, they followed her advice. This did not signify their acceptance of a decision-making role for Mae. Nevertheless, Mae felt that her income contribution to the family did not go totally unrecognized, because she gained more freedom in her personal life. As long as she made the expected contribution to the family budget, Mae was freed for peer relationships of her own choosing, and thus she attained her goals in work: time to spend in activities with her friends. Mae legitimately withheld a part of her earnings for her own clothes and for outings with friends, such as Sunday tea and movies, which she could afford only when she was employed full-time.

Mae shared her mother's opinions about the importance of enlarging the family wage, and hence there were few conflicts over the money Mae spent on herself. She gave an example: 'I had to go to a wedding banquet and had to pay night school fees at the same time. So I talked it over with my mother. I said, 'To be a person, which, after all, reflects upon the family, I must give money at the banquet. Furthermore, my schooling might be beneficial to me in getting jobs in the future.' Mother agreed that both expenses were reasonable, and so we agreed that I would give less money to the family for several weeks.' Indeed, Mae could recall only one recent conflict with Mother over expenses. She wished to consult a Chinese herbal doctor about her cold, and her mother protested at the extra cost. But because Mae herself considered it a reasonable use of her earnings, she saw the herbalist anyway and paid for it herself.

Although Mae remitted most of her money to her family, she spent her leisure time as she wished. After she entered the labour force she performed little housework. Her mother did most of it, and even her younger brothers helped out. Mae was at liberty to spend her spare time visiting friends, attending courses, and going on outings. But Mother found it unthinkable that Mae might ever move away from home and rent a room by herself, if only because of the drop in family income this would entail. In agreement with her mother's viewpoint, Mae never seriously entertained such an option.

Although the sisters gained little authority in the family through their wage contribution, they gained considerable status as 'good daughters' from that contribution and increased their sphere of freedom. Mae valued that enlarged personal sphere highly, especially when she contrasted her position to that of women of earlier generations, who had lower status and considerably fewer personal options.

Peers

Young people form a substantial and visible part of Hong Kong life. Adolescents comprise a large sector of the population, and organizations like schools, factories, and clubs that draw members from teenagers and young adults thereby promote interaction among youths. Consequently, Hong Kong youths have many experiences in common and are aware of their status in society. After leaving primary school, where Mae and Hua first participated in meaningful activities with others their age, the sisters entered large factories with other girls also recruited from school. Ever since, the two sisters have worked side by side with other women of their age, and they freely turned to peers for assistance with job-related problems.

Friends helped the sisters locate work; Mae herself was an important link in the job information network. One evening during the wage dispute with the manager of the plastics workshop, I arrived at Mae's home to find her on the phone. A friend and former coworker had just phoned the name of a newly opened workshop that was hiring women to seam plastic bags. Next, several of her current coworkers telephoned to receive that information. This situation was not unique to Mae, and her friends also kept in touch with their former workmates at picnic reunions or on the phone to exchange job intelligence. The express purpose of such reunions was social but expanding channels of information was also important.

When I spent a day in Mae's workshop, the informal assistance she afforded her workmates was obvious. Mae twice stopped her plastic bag seaming to help two women next to her push and lift the 50-pound roll of plastic to their benches. The cooperation of two or three workers was not only necessary to perform mechanical tasks but it was also the means of learning the job, and in fact Hua had taught Mae to seam the bags. 'Otherwise I'd go too slowly while I was learning and wouldn't earn much,' Mae explained. She did not appear to begrudge the time such cooperation cost her, all the more striking given the rapid pace at which she resumed her piecework seaming, perhaps because she anticipated a future need for the assistance of workmates herself.

Work is just one identity-forming activity, and becoming an adult in Hong Kong involves learning many more social roles. Mae and her sister, having taken on heavy obligations at an early age, lacked an opportunity to enjoy an 'irresponsible adolescence' during which they could test out adult roles. This testing is especially important in a society like Hong Kong that is undergoing rapid social change, because youths cannot learn all their expected behaviour from adults. Friends teach each other about clothes, dating, Western films, picnics, and work opportunities. And youths look to the work setting for friends.

Mae's oldest friends were former workmates. Her photo album contained three major sets of picture, of which friends from work were an important part. One group of pictures showed three girls posing in different settings. The more recent of these were wedding photos. Mae explained that the three girls had been employed in the large plastic factory where Hua and Mae worked, and all five became fast friends. She asked me excitedly, 'Do you recognize me? This is my sister, and that is a friend who married two years ago. She has a baby now. That other woman married just last year. Now we hardly meet. Actually, our "group" has only three who are unmarried, and pretty soon my sister will marry, too. Then the only other maidens left will be me and the other girl in the picture.' Mae pointed to a young woman in the snapshot who she called Kitty. Mae and Kitty went out together to film shows and teahouses and visited me at my apartment for lunch. When the other women married, Mae rarely saw them, and she and Kitty became inseparable.

Mae relied upon formal recreational groups for new experiences. The youth activities sponsored by missionary and other welfare associations enabled young workers like Mae to make the transition to a youth-oriented culture with many links to the West. The missionary societies set out to provide 'something constructive' for young Hong Kong working people with spare time and money. Their Western-originated peer activities filled the cultural vacuum.

Mae joined those activities with enthusiasm and was a responsible leader of her peer group just as she was a leader at home or in the workshop. Whenever an outing was planned, invariably it was Mae who compiled the list of participants and collected money from them. She arranged for each person to make or purchase food for the parties of my English class. When I return to Hong Kong for brief visits, it is Mae who I phone in order to contact the other former language class members, their sisters, and friends.

The Hong Kong way of life is also influenced by the mass media. A decade ago the media barely reached the working girls, but their presence has since become pervasive. Like other Hong Kong youths, Mae saw films almost once a week, watched television several hours a day, and read fashion and movie magazines frequently. What is the message of the media for Mae and her friends? When flown across the ocean do products and behaviour that portray Western centrifugal society directly influence the centripetal Hong Kong way of life?

Studies of the media's impact upon North American viewers' behaviour find, first of all, that people are likely to be influenced personally by ads if the product or advertised behaviour counters no important social norm. A related consideration is that when persons who are important in the viewer's milieu (what sociologists call reference groups) use or advertise the product, the viewer will be more likely to adopt it. Advertisers, well aware of this phenomenon, deliberately associate consumer products in their commercials with images of powerful people and opinion leaders to suggest that viewers can become just as powerful if they simply buy the goods.

Accordingly, Mae and her family are likely eventually to adopt the consumer goods they view on television but are not likely to accept the human relationships portrayed in the media, because only the former accord with the fundamental norms of Hong Kong society. For most of the women in Mae's milieu, the purchase of goods is limited chiefly by the amount of money available. Thus the most visible impact of the media was in the areas of fashion and entertainment, to which there was little parental opposition. As long as they had some money, Mae and her friends purchased clothes or records that were advertised.

The marriage and family relationships viewed in films made and influenced by Hollywood contained elements of behaviour congruent with family norms, such as dating patterns, the wedding dress, and honeymoons. Hong Kong youths were encouraged by the media to date, and those who did not know the modern customs and codes of dating could learn from the movies or press. For several years one local magazine, *Lover* (Ai-lu), gained popularity by capitalizing on this phenomenon. Many of the articles and letters to the editor concerned the meaning and cultivation of 'love', and local starlets depicted the new marriage style in the magazine's pages. *Lover* thus profitably assumed the role of sounding board and contemporary authority on dating and boy-girl dilemmas faced by young working women.

The cinema presented various complex dating situations and solved them in Western fashion. The dilemmas presented in such films surrounding the institution of romantic love captivated Mae and her friends. The favorite films were *Love Story*, *The Graduate*, *The Young Ones* (a Taiwan film), and a Hong Kong film from the 1960s, *The Prince and the Maid*. The plots of these films featured a couple in love whose marriage was opposed by their parents. The films showed that love triumphed over parental objections based on status, but the successful romance ended in the death of the bride (except in *The Graduate*.) Mae and her friends identified emotionally with the celluloid couples' love affairs and thought it tragic when the brides died.

However, the impact of the cinema upon Mae's behaviour was limited by the fundamental differences between the styles of courtship and marriage portrayed on the screen and Hong Kong family norms. Hua was introduced by friends to a young man she liked well enough to marry, but their relationship was successfully opposed by her parents. In this situation Mae sided with the parents and not with 'romantic love'. Thus there was no opposition to these young women's adoption of clothes, grooming styles, and consumer goods that they saw on the screen. Such consumer goods countered few fundamental family norms. However, when it came to matrimony, the media-portrayed family dramas that advanced the children's right to act as independent individuals when choosing a mate fell on hostile ground.

The mass media are also especially effective when there are conflicting expectations among the groups that comprise the viewers' social environment. If people with contradictory social roles wish to reduce the discomfort or even pain caused by competing demands upon them, and if a product or behaviour is presented by the media as the means to resolve such role dilemmas, then such media can become very persuasive.

Superficial media portrayals of family life and Western marriage that omit much of the reality and portray only the gloss may possibly encourage young Hong Kong women in their conflicts with the older generation. Asked about the discrepancy that remains, however, between their vicarious enjoyment of love matches in Western films and their reluctance to counter their parents' opinions, A-li, a friend of Me, explained, 'Oh, we think that the Western way is really the best! We really want to learn how they do it, even if we ourselves can't always follow that way just yet.' The women adopt Western marriage values as portrayed by the media only if their families support them. Perhaps when the conflict of social opinion regarding their expected behaviour intensifies even further, Mae, A-li, and other friends will adopt the centrifugal marriage pattern of the media programs.

Dating and marriage

Mae did not have a boyfriend and rarely met eligible bachelors at work. This did not distress her, however. She once dated a man she met through friends in the factory. She recalled, 'The fellow did not phone me after that one time, so I guess he didn't want to keep up the relationship. Anyway, I'm too young to marry!'

When the time did come to marry Mae did not want Mother to arrange the match. Mae told of the way Mother interceded in Elder Sister's marriage plans: 'The person Hua is marrying is her second boyfriend. She met the first one on her own through a factory friend. Mother didn't like him and called him a 'teddy boy'.'

'Was he really a 'teddy boy' in your opinion?' I asked Mae.

'Well, he looked a bit like one, but the main problem was that he was not Ch'iu-chao. And so Mother arranged a marriage with Lam Bing, a Ch'iu-chao like us. Mother and Hua visited someone's home to meet Lam Bing. He answered a few questions, but both he and my sister were too shy to say much.'

Lam Bing turned out to be a low income earner. 'With the baby coming they have lots of money troubles. As for me, I prefer to accept complete responsibility for my choice, otherwise later I might blame mother!'

Mae intended to marry a person with whom she was 'compatible'. Having participated in peer activities for several years, she valued the kind of marriage in which her husband would hold similar ideas and would be as much a companion to her as her friends had been. Since Mae and her parents saw things in much the same way, however, she did not exclude the possibility that a man introduced to her would become compatible. Compatibility could develop given enough time.

Mae's accommodation to members of the older generation did not extend to living with them after marriage. Mae and Hua both recalled Mother's long dispute with Paternal Grandmother, which was only resolved when the old lady was provided with her own quarters. Mae explained it this way, 'Despite the fact that Mother is very easygoing in nature, Grandmother was too conservative. There was no real ill will between them, but they always argued over their different ideas.' That instance of generational conflict was impressed deeply upon the two sisters and they swore not to live with their own future mothers-in-law.

When Hua married in late 1973, she and Lam Bing first rented a small room near her mother-in-law's residence. Lam Bing stressed the limits of his obligation to his mother: 'We need not live together. So long as we give my mother the first choice of living near her, as opposed to living near my wife's mother, that's enough. Neither side wishes to do more than that. We don't really get along, and Mother herself wishes to preserve her independence.'

When the Lam's first child was born, Bing's face-saving attitude could no longer be maintained. A relative was sorely needed to care for their baby so that both parents could work. Mrs. Goh was willing to take over care of the child and so the couple moved into the Goh's Lok Fu resettlement estate apartment with Mother. At that point there were too many people in the Lok Fu flat, and Mae obligingly went to live with her aunt and uncle in their resettlement estate apartment. Finding that their small flat was still overcrowded, Mae's parents rented a two-room apartment in a nearby tenement in a district known as Kowloon Walled City, where rents were cheap.

Domestic arrangements for the Goh family

March, 1973
A. Mother, Father, and six children live in two rooms in Lok Fu resettlement estate, Kowloon. Hua, the eldest daughter (age 25), is engaged to Lam Bing.
B. Father's brother and his wife and children live in another resettlement estate. Their child occasionally comes to spend the night with the Goh family, and the Goh children often stay with them.

September, 1973
A. Mother, Father, and five children live in the same resettlement estate.
B. No change.
C. Hua has married, and she and Lam Bing rent a room in an apartment on Hong Kong Island. Hua is pregnant.
D. Lam Bing's mother lives near the Lams with her brother's family. Mother Lam eats with her brother's family and assists them with child care.

September, 1975
A. Residence unchanged, but now Hua's baby stays with Mother Goh. Mae has moved out.
B. Mae moves to the resettlement estate room of her aunt and uncle.
C. Hua and Lam Bing live during the week in their rented room. On weekends the couple returns to the Gohs' Kowloon resettlement estate rooms to be with their child.
D. No change.

September, 1976
A. The Goh family (Father, Mother, Mae, and four brothers) moves into a private two-room tenement flat in Kowloon Walled City. Mother continues to care for Hua's child.
B. Mae moves out of her uncle's place, back to her family.
C. Hua, Lam Bing, and paternal grandmother Goh live in the Lok Fu resettlement estate rooms vacated by the Goh family.
D. No change.

After Hua married and had a child, Mae's earnings were more important than ever, and Mother was apprehensive about her possible marriage. Mae had anticipated gaining such centrality in the family wage-earning unit, and so at the time of her sister's engagement she emphasized to me her plans to remain single until Second Brother completed his schooling and went to work: 'Mother said I can marry whomever I wish, but even after I find someone I must postpone the marriage for several years. With Elder Sister married, we can't afford to lose another income just now!'

Realizing that her marriage was an event that concerned the family as a whole, Mae did not worry about being without a boyfriend. At the age of 22, she was not yet considered an 'old maid.' Because her parents and peers understood that Mae was meeting family obligations, and because those obligations were equally incumbent upon Mae's friends, little pressure was exerted to find a spouse. Mae's relative unconcern over being single was also related to the eventual possibility of arranging a marriage should she approach age 30 with no prospect in sight. At our last meeting, however, she was not yet considering this eventuality. She gained status from meeting her family obligations and she enjoyed opportunities to interact with friends. Neither would be possible if she were to marry.

Summary

As second daughter in a family of six children who were growing up while the family was in straitened circumstances, Mae was trained to put her family's definition of its economic needs before her own desires. The theme of Mae's life was that she not only accommodated the needs of her family but realized her own desire to enjoy peer-group experiences. Both were possible through Mae's factory employment. Her duties to her family did not prevent Mae from enjoying peer activities, and her loyal fulfillment of her family's expectations gave her more independence to pursue friendships.

f. Transforming the Rural Family

As always in Hong Kong's history, for a substantial number of people, settling into urban life in Hong Kong implied a break with the rural past. In the 1970s, the trend of urbanization was rapidly reaching many New Territories villages. Some came under its impact earlier than others, some villages had to move to make way for urban development while others remained in situ, as it were, as three-storey houses built in the style of the 'Spanish villa' took over the village landscape, but none was spared from the booming city. One should not jump to the conclusion that urbanization necessarily resulted in the nuclear family. The villagers of Kwan Mun Hau, noting the changes to their lifestyle, clung on to the values of the joint family.

Kwan Mun Hau Village was originally located on the shore near what is now the town centre of Tsuen Wan. The population accepted compensation from the Hong Kong government and moved to the new Kwan Mun Hau Village on the hillside in 1965. The author of the following entry lived in the new village for eighteen months from November 1968.

DOCUMENT VII.f1: Some explanations of changes in household size, structure, and process (source: Elisabeth L. Johnson, *Households and Lineages in a Chinese Urban Village*, Ph.D. thesis, Cornell University, 1976, pp. 296-320)

Kwan Mun Hau households are now larger, on the average, than they were 30 years ago. The large joint household is almost a phenomenon of the past, however, with only one such household presently existing in the village, although a number of joint property-households exist. There are now more stem family households than there were a generation ago, and fewer nuclear family households. There has so far been little tendency to divide stem households into nuclear ones, but potentially joint households have, with one exception, divided. Households continue to be organized patrilineally for the most part, although there are a few exceptions.

The explanatory variables discussed below are those first set out in the Introduction to this thesis, which presents those hypotheses relating family change and economic development which have been proposed by other authors.

(1) Demographic changes. The larger size of contemporary Kwan Mun Hau households must be explained by the demographic changes resulting from the village's involvement in the urbanization and modernization process. Particularly important is the fact that Kwan Mun Hau has become part of the urban milieu without the migration of individuals or families from the village. There is now virtually no migration of individuals out of the village, one couple from household 6 and three brothers of ego in household 18 being the only exceptions. A few households from each of the lineages have moved elsewhere in Hong Kong, to China, or abroad. Both lineages also have households living in Hoi Pa Village, which was adjacent to old Kwan Mun Hau, but this is nearby, within the city. In contrast, it was a common pattern during and especially prior to the 1930s for individual men from village households to work either in the urban areas of Hong Kong or abroad. In most cases they still retained property and economic ties with their households, and those who worked in urban Hong Kong could return at intervals, but those who went abroad could return only rarely, if at all. The dangerous nature of the work they engaged in (mining, railroad building) must have meant that they often did not survive to return. Both short- and long-term migration must have resulted in decreased fertility because they meant the separation of married couples. With the early development of Tsuen Wan in the 1930s, such migration became unnecessary because local employment opportunities developed. The separation of married couples because of the demands of employment is now unknown. In contrast, the large number of single-person households among outsiders in Kwan Mun Hau suggests that migration has either disrupted marriages or prevented them from being made. Likewise, the relatively small size of outsider households and their simpler structure points to the disruptive effects of migration, for in many cases relatives were either left behind in China or scattered by separate migration and the

search of employment and housing in Hong Kong. The property base of such households would also have been lost through land reform and the nationalization of businesses in China.

There is little evidence for changes in marriage patterns in Kwan Mun Hau that would result in changes in household size, structure, or process. Marriage remains nearly universal and the average age at marriage appears not to have changed in the last 30 years, although women marrying during the 1920s and before were probably more likely to marry in their late teens, especially those who were married as small daughters-in-law*. The fact that the husband-wife bond is now more solidary because of the prevalence of introduced and self-arranged marriages among younger people, suggests that wives have more influence on the timing of household division, and that the nuclear family may tend to be more of a separate unit in relation to the rest of the household. Some property-households are unusually large at the present time because the men have made polygynous marriages, but such households are not always coresidential. Polygynous marriages have often served to increase the number of children born to a man and thus the size of the property-household. As they are apparently declining in popularity, this change should have a negative effect on household size in the future.

The most striking demographic change in Kwan Mun Hau during the past 30 years has been the decline in mortality, due primarily to the availability of modern preventive and curative medicine. Whereas before about 1945, approximately half the children born did not survive, the death of a child is now extremely rare. The decline in the occurrence of adult deaths also means a decline in early widowhood, which has a positive effect on fertility. The number of children born has probably increased slightly due to improved fecundity (related to diet and medical care) and the decrease in widowhood. This is difficult to discern, however, because of the fact that children born since the Occupation have virtually all survived, resulting in very large families for women who bore children between 1945 and 1965. The pattern has now been altered by the fact that modern means of birth control became readily available in about 1965. Before that time, one or two village women were sterilized and one used a diaphragm, but most used abortion or nothing. Since about 1965, contraception has become not only available, but also known and accepted, so that many (although not all) younger women are choosing to bear no more than about four children. This means that many households will not have the large numbers of children characteristic of those in which the children are presently reaching adulthood; but low mortality means that virtually all will be assured of having the number of children they wish. There is therefore less need to adopt children into the household than there was in the past, as the need to adopt would result only from sterility (or possibly from failure to bear sons) rather than from child mortality.

---

* A 'small daughter-in-law' was a young girl growing up in her husband-to-be's family, having been given away in marriage by her own parents at an early age.

Demographic changes have meant that the general pattern of household change has been:

(a) Before 1940, most large households were joint, formed by the postponement of division. There were many small households, nuclear in structure, consisting only of a couple (or widow) and a small number of children. Seven of eighteen households had more adults than children, when 'children' is defined as unmarried people less than 30 years of age.

(b) By about 1955-1960, there were many households which were large because large numbers of children had been born and were surviving, and the proportion of adults was relatively low.

(c) Many families are now limiting the number of children born, so that although there will be more children than in the pre-1940 families (only two households of nineteen have more adults than children) there will be fewer in the stage (b) families and the proportion of adults will gradually increase.

There is now emerging the potential for the formation of many joint households in the village, as most households have more than one male in the younger generation (see Table 7.2). Whether and in which households this occurs depends on a complex of other factors.

Table 7.2
Survival of More Than One Brother to Adulthood, by Household

Household	Age less than 30*	Age 30-50	Age 50+
1	yes	no	no
2	–	no	no
3	yes	yes	yes
4	–	yes	yes
5	yes	no	yes
6	yes	yes	no
7	no	yes	no
8	yes	–	yes
9	yes	no	no
10	yes	no	?
11	yes	no	no
12	no	no	yes
13	no	no	no
14	yes	–	yes
15	yes	yes	yes
16	yes	yes	–
17	yes	no	yes
18	no	yes	yes
19	–	yes	no

(2) Changes in Property and Economy. With the urban development of Tsuen Wan, the economy of Kwan Mun Hau has changed profoundly. Before about 1960, household subsistence derived at least in part from agriculture. Before 1945 rice and vegetables were grown and pigs raised; the surplus of these products, and pineapples and pine trees, provided a source of cash income. Later, rice ceased to be grown and households either switched to growing vegetables or abandoned agriculture altogether, except for the raising of pigs and chickens for subsistence and cash. The bulk of the agricultural work was done by women, who also earned cash income as labourers (ego in household 19, who also ran small businesses), employees in shops, government, or business; or worked as managers of small businesses, or large ones. By the 1930s, men no longer went abroad to work. Most households therefore drew part of their subsistence from their commonly-held agricultural property, but also depended on cash, earned by men and women in outside employment. This is probably typical of the Hakka in South China.

I do not know enough about Kwan Mun Hau agriculture to be sure what kind of household structure might be most functional in this situation. . . . It may be that agricultural activities were more easily carried out by a group of women than by a woman working alone. According to one woman (age 60, household 4):

> Although we were three daughters-in-law in my family, it was still not enough to do all the farm work. The older one did agricultural work, one looked after the cows, and I carried pig food.

She went on to say that the older women in the household did the housework. It would have been virtually impossible for a woman at that time to manage the agricultural work without a woman in the senior generation to look after the household and children. I heard of one case in which a woman had no mother-in-law and had to lock her small son in the house all day while she farmed. His deviant personality (he is the wife-beater described in Chapter 4*) may in part result from this treatment. Thus, from the women's point of view, the stem family household, at a minimum, was essential.

From the point of view of men, most were so dependent on cash income from outside employment that I see no functional advantage in joint household organization except in those cases in which family property and the earnings of members were sufficient to form and develop large family businesses. The only example of this in the sample and, to my knowledge, in the village is household 3 (and possibly household 14). To keep such businesses undivided has a clear functional advantage; but in terms of household structure, there is no reason why the joint owners should not divide to live, as they have in fact done.

Likewise, in the present Kwan Mun Hau economy, I see no apparent functional value to the joint household. Many households derive their principal support from

---

* Not included here – Ed.

rents, while in some of these and all others men work as employees, labourers, or managers of small or large businesses. The time-schedule demands of outside employment (jobs held mainly by poorer men and highly-motivated wealthy ones) may mean that men are not available in the household to handle crises or manage affairs, (one man, household 11, mentioned this as a problem) but as they work nearby this does not seem to be a problem seriously affecting family unity. Women are accustomed to taking charge. Some young and middle aged women now work in factories; others, and older women, stay at home to manage the household. The stem family household has functional value in this situation. Resident grandmothers can readily care for the children of working mothers.

It has been argued that during the urbanization process, as households become dependent on outside earnings rather than on the exploitation of their common property, conflicts may develop between brothers in a joint household because of their differential earning power and contribution to the household. Two informants mentioned this as a problem.

> In the past, we maintained joint households because we respected the senior members of the family who wanted everyone together, and the income of labourers was similar to that of others so there were no disputes over finances. Now incomes vary a lot, so those who earn more are not willing to benefit the others. So for selfish reasons brothers prefer to separate. So, now it means to earn a living separately but to keep the property intact. In the past, the father usually collected all the incomes and managed the finances.
> (man, age 56, household 8)
> In the past everyone did farm work. They did the same work for the same income. But now they do different work. The younger generation have better education so they have many different professions and different incomes which lead to different ideas within the same generation, so sons must live separately.
> (man, age 34, household 12)

I know of no households in which this is presently a problem, but there is only one joint household. It may have been the cause of disputes which led to divisions in other households. Kwan Mun Hau households have for years been dependent on cash earned elsewhere, but there probably was less possibility in the past for large differentials among brothers' earnings. From my observations, I would say that differential earning capacity at present results primarily from ability and/or personal choice, rather than a choice on the part of the family to educate one son better than another. Girls are often supported less than boys in their education, but as far as I could see boys are offered fairly equal opportunities, unless they are unable or choose not to study longer. The norm is strong for older siblings to contribute their earnings to the household and help support the education of younger siblings.

The nature of property owned by Kwan Mun Hau households has changed, with the development of Tsuen Wan, from agricultural land, house land, houses, and businesses to houses in the village, buildings in the city, urban building land, and businesses. Some families still have farm land, but it is generally unused or occupied by squatters and will yield no income until it is sold. When the village moved, agricultural and house land were exchanged for houses in the new village and, for those who had a surplus, for building land in the city. Almost half the village families did not have enough land to cover the full cost of their new houses, and had to take ten-year interest-free loans from the government. In some cases, the houses obtained may have been sufficient for their needs and the loans taken to meet the cost of additional houses, but in most such cases the families would not only have to pay off the loans but also would have no extra houses to rent out. Those who did not take loans are at an advantage, not only because they have had no loans to pay off but also because most have extra houses to rent out or land on which to build rent-producing buildings. This process must have increased economic differentiation in the village. Families with more than one son and only the house in which they live as property, having given up their agricultural land, will have nothing to divide among their sons but that house.

Thus, certain of the wealthiest households now have a large property base which produces income for members and can be divided among the family sons. The poorest families have only their own houses, but no income-producing property, and nothing to divide. I would expect the property to be a unifying force in wealthy households, although this would not prevent the brothers from dividing to live unless used by their father as a threat or inducement to stay together, his economic power reinforcing his authority. If a division of property were desired, urban land and buildings (but not businesses) could probably be more easily divided among brothers, with less loss of efficiency, than could agricultural land in the past.

(3) Housing Space. A variable directly related to property ownership is the availability of housing space. Shortage of housing space can either force or prevent the development of joint households. One informant (man, age 32, household 19) said the latter was a problem in the old village, while another cited the former problem:

> In the old village we wanted to divide to live but had no more space. We were not allowed to build more houses or add a floor as the government planned to move the village . . . We divided to live when the village moved. Many divided then because there is a lot of room here. For example, one brother can live upstairs and one downstairs. Brothers live close together. In the old village, all the family members crowded into one house.
> (man, age 56, household 8)

Now housing space is presently a problem for some families and potentially a problem for most. It is not possible either to add on to present houses (which are built according to a common plan) or to build new houses in the village, because the village owns only the land occupied by the houses and that immediately surrounding it, i.e., the terraces and sidewalks. Those poorer families who own only one floor or one house now generally have enough space to live, although some do not. Household 16 did not after the second brother married. Some are very crowded, with ten or twelve people living on one floor. If a household owns only one floor, it cannot be partitioned into more than three rooms, or four at the very most, and each nuclear family must have its own room, at a minimum, as well as allowing a common room for eating. As sons from the often numerous families in these households marry, they must either stay together under extremely crowded conditions, rent adjacent housing (if they are fortunate enough to find some available) and continue to eat together, or divide to live, with one or more nuclear families renting or buying housing either in the village or in the city. I saw one family face this crisis as the oldest son married. The family owns one floor and has three sons and two daughters. The mother looked desperately for nearby housing to rent and was finally able to rent a floor in a house two doors away, so the family was able to continue to eat together. The son moved into the family home with his wife and some of his siblings moved to the rented quarters.

Wealthier families (or at least those with more property, although their cash income might be low), may have enough space to form joint households, if the houses owned are adjacent. This would mean that they have to stop renting these houses to tenants, and thus lose a source of income. Household 6, which is not wealthy but has two houses, lives on three floors of two adjacent houses and thus has an adequate number of bedrooms as well as a large living room. If the houses owned are not adjacent, this may prevent the development of a joint household, although there is sufficient space for all brothers. The married sons of ego in household 3 live elsewhere in the village, although the children of one live with ego. His second house is not adjacent to the first. He said:

> In the past the Hung lived in joint households because the houses were large. My old house had ten rooms, with the three brothers together, but now the houses are small so we must separate. If so many people were together it would be like a chicken coop or a pigeon cage.
> (man, age 55, household 3)

The process of dividing to live is made relatively simple by the fact that each floor of the new houses was built with its own kitchen and bathroom. No new kitchen has to be built, as it would have been in traditional houses, although the family may decide to build a stove in the new kitchen. Thus ego in household 7 and his brother divided easily because each floor of their house was already a complete living unit.

In summary, restrictions on building new housing and shortages of housing space will make it imperative for most poorer families to divide to live as sons marry. All except perhaps one son will have to leave the parental home and possibly the village to find housing. Wealthy families may not be short of space, but the fact that the houses they own may not be adjacent may necessitate dividing to live. Because the houses readily divide into separate living units the process is facilitated.

(4) Legal changes and government intervention. Without government intervention, and the village leadership's response to the government offer to move

the village, Kwan Mun Hau would almost certainly be dispersed by now. Its location in a rapidly-growing city means that there have been restrictions on land use and on building since the development plan was first made, however. Inability to expand village housing may in the not too distant future result in the dispersal of many village families, as they find housing elsewhere in the city. The villagers are unable to use their increasing wealth to build new or bigger village houses to accommodate joint families, as did ego in household 3 while in the old village.

Informants mentioned that many families divided to live at the time of the move, although I knew of only one such case. A number of divisions of property-households took place at that time, however, at the urging of the District Office, in order to simplify the problems of compensation for house and agricultural land.

Some informants asserted that Hong Kong law is at variance with village customary law, which complicates property division. There is no way that people can avoid involvement of the government in property division, as all land transactions must be registered with the District Office. According to one man:

> If brothers get along well, they can negotiate a settlement themselves, asking for help from elders or the village head. Now even if it is settled that way they must go to the District Office to register it. But British law states that each brother should have an equal share, so this may lead to conflict between brothers, or between brothers and the law. Therefore there may be disputes either because the brothers are not friendly or because they want to follow law rather than custom. This can become very complicated, and can lead to a loss of friendship between brothers.
> (man, age 32, household 1)

If such problems are common, they may delay the division of property-households, but would not prevent brothers from dividing to live. Present Hong Kong law makes it possible to go against customary law in the inheritance or division of their property if they so wish. They are now able to write wills and designate heirs. Ego in household 3 has done so. I suspect this may be to limit or cut off the inheritance of one son, with whom he allegedly has had conflicts.

In one respect, the *absence* of government intervention may foster the development of more complex households. There is no government pension plan in Hong Kong, and social security provisions for those without support are minimal. There are few nurseries for the care of the children of working mothers, and the quality of care is not uniformly good. In this situation, the stem family provides valuable services for dependent family members.

> In foreign countries there are pensions for old people but in Hong Kong there are none, so usually children are responsible for their parents. Also, the concept of the family is more important for Chinese people.
> (man, age 41, household 9)

(5) Authority patterns. The maintenance of a joint household demands the presence of a strong authority figure in the senior generation who can command respect and obedience, according to several informants. Although older people are still respected, they no longer have the power within the household which they held a generation ago, and relationships are more egalitarian. One reason may be that the household property is less important as a source of support than it was, and in some cases is nonexistent, except for the house in which the family lives. It is more difficult for a household head to control income that is derived primarily from members' earnings, although unmarried members, at least, normally contribute their incomes to the household. Most younger men (except those who live primarily off the family property) have the potential ability to separate from the household because of their own earning power.

> In the past we respected our parents and had to live with them. If not, we would be gossiped about. People would say: 'He cares only for his wife and not for his parents.' Now as people find jobs outside they may live separately, but still must support their parents.
> (man, age 40, household 6)
>
> In the past the young people had to obey any decision of the old and could never reject it because the old people kept the money and the property. But now they have learned a lot and can earn a lot of money and prefer to do what they want, not what the old people like. We can't do anything about it. Times have changed. But I don't like the change.
> (man, age 67, household 15)

Not having seen the previous situation, I cannot make this comparison, but I saw no evidence of any rebelliousness among the younger men, not much desire to leave the parental household or the village. Nor was I aware of any flagrant violations of parental authority. Instead, parents seem to have voluntarily ceded some of their authority. Few would presume to attempt to arrange a son's marriage, for example. I asked the men in the interview sample whether they would choose their sons' occupations, and without exception they said that this choice should be made by the sons in accordance with their interests.

> I wouldn't force my son. We will see what his interests are. I will wait until he is in middle school to discuss it with him.
> (man, age 34, household 12)
>
> My sons should follow the occupations they like. They shouldn't go into my business if they don't want to.
> (man, age 55, household 3)

Thus, the present relationship of the old to the young is not heavily authoritarian. The old are treated with respect but, because of changing values and the loss of much of their former control over their sons' livelihood, they neither ask nor expect complete conformity to their wishes.

(6) Attitude change. One would expect that traditional values regarding the household might be undermined by the fact that villagers now receive modern education and associate with outsiders in school and at work, as well as in the village itself. They also receive heavy doses of Western values through the omnipresent television, although this is a very recent development.

There is considerable diversity of opinion as to the desirability of joint households, and as to personal preference for stem or joint households. I asked informants whether they would like to live with their sons after they marry. Of nine men (three in the interview sample are already living with sons), two would like to live with their married sons.

> It's best to separate people as far apart in age as my grandmother and myself. The old learned everything in the past; the young know new things. I don't want to live with old people but I would like to live with my sons after they marry. But it depends on them. Lots of disputes can arise from age differences. I prefer three generations together, not married brothers together.
> (man, age 34, household 11)

Six men would not like to live with their married sons.

> I prefer that my son separate after marriage because his way of thinking will be different. I like the idea of living separately but eating together. If the father doesn't have enough houses, they must be bought or rented. I prefer to eat together, because it then seems like a better family relationship.
> (man, age 34, household 12)

> We agricultural Chinese must give help to our parents and support them. The best way is to live separately, perhaps giving one or two children to the old people so it won't be so quiet. I prefer that my son live separately, although I have only one. He could perhaps return once a week to eat. The generations' ways of thinking are different. Disputes could easily arise between mother-in-law and daughter-in-law, especially when the men work outside the house.
> (man, age 45, household 7)

This latter informant said that he and his wife disagree on this issue, as his wife wants to live with their only son. Three men mentioned disputes between women as a possible source of conflict in a joint or stem household. One said that women now prefer to separate because they are better educated than in the past.

One informant can see good reasons both for remaining with his sons and for living separately from them.

> I never thought about whether my sons should live with me but my wife said

> it is better for them to move out and be independent and learn more from society. Furthermore, frictions might arise. . . I really would like a joint household. An old person likes help from his descendents. I don't know whether to consider my sons' future or myself.
> (man, age 54, household 14)

Several informants, both men and women, suggested that it would be beneficial to their sons to separate from the household, as they would then have to take more responsibility; or that the fact that they had separated would prove that they were capable of managing. Conversely I suspect that one reason why household 6 stays together is that two of its members seem incapable of earning a living on their own. The second son is unmarried and works irregularly at some marginal occupation, while the first has not worked for ten years, apparently because of his illness. Their mother complained bitterly about their incompetence. The family's only cash income, apart from rents, is that earned by the first son's wife and by the third son, although his remittances are intended only to support his wife and children.

Of twelve women informants (two not asked), five are already living with married sons. Of the remainder, four would like to live with their sons, although one of these is rather uncertain.

> My son could live with me or move out. It doesn't matter. When you take a daughter-in-law, you would like her to live with you, but now many Hakka people live separately. It depends whether they like old people or not. . . . I would like my sons to stay but I will have to see how they are. I don't know how they will be. If they are capable they can move away with their wives.
> (woman, age 32, household 11)

One said that this is the general Hakka custom. Two women said definitely that they would not like to live with their sons, one because she fears conflicts. The other said:

> I don't prefer to live with married sons. If they move away, it shows they are capable. I prefer that they separate. Married sons will have their own families. They should care for them more than their parents.
> (woman, age 44, household 16)

One woman (age 51, household 8) has no opinion, saying it is too far in the future to say.

When asked whether a joint household is good, four men said that it is not and five that it is.

> I don't like a joint household. It is held together by the old people and causes disputes between brothers and between their wives. You must have a large

> house, which is impossible now. Now we don't like it.
> (man, age 41, household 9)

> I prefer a joint household. The old people can help with the children and the young people can work. Old people prefer to stay with their sons and grandsons. But now the young people after marriage want to separate.
> (man, age 67, household 2)

One man was apparently referring to a joint property-household rather than a residential household.

> I like a joint household, in which the families live and eat separately but come together when they wish.
> (man, age 45, household 7)

Interestingly, two men who expressed a preference for the joint household said they preferred not to live with their married sons. They were evidently referring to a general value favouring the joint family, rather than their personal preference.

Of nine women asked this question, two do not favour the joint household.

> The joint household is not good, as lots of conflicts occur. It is very hard for the old people. Therefore if I had several sons I would separate them. Usually the sisters-in-law don't get along well. If there is work to be done, they wait for others to do it... If I had several sons I would live with whichever daughter-in-law was best. It is customary in the village that at property division the widow gets a share, so mine would go to whomever I live with. Without that, who would want to live with old people? (woman, aged 48, household 9)

Seven do favour the joint family household, although most qualified their answers by saying that it is good if it is harmonious or if there is a strong household head.

> A joint household is good. If the relationship between the men is good, that between the women will be. Then you will have people to talk with of the same experience and age. (woman, aged 62, household 1)

In summary, informants are divided in their expressed preferences. Opinions are far from unanimous that joint households are good, or that it is best to live with married sons. Many informants perceived a change to values favouring the stem or even nuclear family household; but most expressed the expectation or at least the hope that even if their sons live separately they would continue to give them financial support and help. This was sometimes expressed in strong normative terms, as an important Chinese value.

g. The New Poor

In 1980, unemployment stood at 3.8 percent of the work force in Hong Kong.* Wages were rising; who remained poor but the aged and the handicapped? The case was most strongly made by photographs reprinted in the Hong Kong newspapers of elderly men living in bed spaces fenced by metal wire. Social benefits being introduced by the Hong Kong government in the 1970s went some way to alleviate their distress, but money could not buy the isolation felt by the poor and elderly who had migrated from home into a competitive society.

DOCUMENT VII.g1: The living conditions of the poor and elderly (source: Dr Ho Kam-fai, Address in the Legislative Council, 23 October 1980, *Hong Kong Hansard, Reports of the sittings of the Legislative Council of Hong Kong, Session 1980/81*. Hong Kong: Government Printer)

A joint survey conducted by the Hong Kong Council of Social Service and the Social Welfare Department estimated that by 1979, 67,500 elderly people would be living in 'substandard and often inhuman living conditions' that is, 16,200 living in bed spaces, verandahs and staircase landings; 4,500 living in roof shacks, basements and attics; 9,500 living in other non-domestic housing; and 37,000 in temporary structures.

In 1978, a survey undertaken by a group of Chinese University students projected that about 10,000 people were living in boarding houses in various parts of Hong Kong and Kowloon, including Tsuen Wan. About 40% of the inhabitants were above 60 years of age. They lived on three-decker bunks, which were fenced in by chicken wire, and they were sensationally known as 'caged men'. The average boarding house measured 900 square feet, including kitchen and toilet, and was occupied by 63 inhabitants, thus the average living area per person was about 15 square feet. Living conditions were appalling: — over-crowded, unventilated, squalid and dark. Almost half of the elderly inhabitants suffered from varying degrees of physical and mental disorder. Roughly 80% of the elderly lodgers came to Hong Kong before 1960; a great majority of them did not have relatives here and lived on public assistance. To make matters worse, these lodgers were not protected by the Landlord and Tenant (Consolidation) Ordinance, because the boarding houses were registered for non-domestic use. The current boom in real estate might heighten their fears of being evicted, because the landlords may take procedure to repossess the properties for redevelopment.

---

* Lok-sang Ho, 'The Hong Kong economy: a 1985 review,' in Alex Y.H. Kwan, ed. *Hong Kong Society*, Hong Kong: Writers and Publishers' Cooperative, 1989, p. 51, citing Hong Kong government statistics.

h. As They Kept Coming

Gradually, but only gradually, Hong Kong had to put a limit on the number of immigrants from China who would be allowed to stay. Locking out prospective immigrants did not stem the flow, but it must have reduced its size. It must also have given a new meaning to being a Hong Kong resident, indicated by the possession of an identity card issued by the Hong Kong government that from 1974 all Hong Kong residents were required by law to carry. People continued to come, but some were now legal and others illegal. They could have made yet another new underclass.

DOCUMENT VII.g1: Locking out illegal immigrants (source: *South China Morning Post* 24 October 1980)

This appears to be the first time Hong Kong has resorted to a total lock-out of all illegal immigrants from China. Until the early 1950s people were free to come and go between China and the Colony.

This tradition of free movement dated back to the Treaty of Nanjing, which secured Hong Kong for Britain in 1842.

In 1953 the Hong Kong Government reluctantly began restricting the flow of people by making it necessary for people to possess valid exit documents from China before they could enter the Colony. On the other side of the border, the authorities also exercised exit controls. But many people entered Hong Kong by clandestine means. The population increased from 1.8 million in 1949 to 2.3 million in 1957.

By the late 1950s the Government described the numbers of illegal immigrants — mostly arriving by sea — as a 'serious' problem.

The problem turned into a nightmare in April 1962 when there was a sudden relaxation of controls on the China side of the border. Hundreds and then thousands of people swarmed across the border each day. It was a time of widespread famine in China following the disastrous agricultural policies of 'the great leap forward.' Hunger and the search for a better life propelled the would-be settlers across the border. The influx reached its peak on May 23, 1962, when 5,620 immigrants were arrested in the frontier area.

Hong Kong's hard-pressed security forces sent back to China as many illegal entrants as they could catch, after questioning them, giving them a meal and allowing them to rest. There was strong public sympathy for the hungry captives returned by truck and train to famine-stricken Guangdong province and New Territories villagers made several attempts to set them free. At the end of May, the Chinese authorities reimposed normal border controls as suddenly as they had relaxed them six weeks earlier. In that period 62,400 people had been repatriated but an estimated 60,000 had succeeded in sneaking illegally into Hong Kong...

For the next 13 years if illegal immigrants successfully got past guards on China's side of the border, they were allowed to stay in Hong Kong unless they were suspect politically. There was little or no attempt at repatriation. If people were caught entering illegally they were usually charged with an immigration offence, detained for a week or so and then set free.

By the late 1960s, however, the number of legal and illegal immigrants entering Hong Kong began to worry the Government once more. Among the new arrivals were former overseas Chinese who had rallied to an invitation in the 1950s to 'return to the motherland.' They were now disillusioned with life in China and wanted to get back to their old homes in Southeast Asia. China was allowing them to leave.

The numbers of legal arrivals soared from about 100 a day in the late 1960s to 500 and 600 a day in 1973-4. It was estimated, moreover, that for every person entering legally three or four were arriving illegally — giving a total of about 2,000 people a day.

The Government made representations to China. On December 1, 1974, Hong Kong reversed its 'open door' policy and began sending back illegal immigrants captured while trying to enter the Colony.

For illegals, the one major loophole was that if they managed to 'touch base' — to reach their families in Hong Kong — they were allowed to stay permanently. The loophole has meant, at a conservative estimate, that Hong Kong has at least 200,000 extra people today.

The Government's announcement yesterday amended the six-year-old repatriation policy to close the loophole. The tide of public sympathy so evident when hungry illegal immigrants were rounded up and repatriated in 1962, has apparently turned.

CHAPTER EIGHT

AFFLUENCE AND BEYOND

The 1980s and 1990s will be remembered as a time of anomaly. The decision reached by the governments of the United Kingdom and of the People's Republic of China in 1982 on the return of Hong Kong to China in 1997 altered the fundamentals of Hong Kong's existence. The economic restructuring of China with its impact on the expansion of trade and industry, especially in the Pearl River Delta, brought Hong Kong unprecedented prosperity. The impact was immediate. The Hong Kong government abandoned representation through appointment in favour of public elections. The number of Hong Kong people who sought to emigrate soared. But Hong Kong people became affluent, hopeful of long-term prospects in China but cautious of the immediate consequence that political change might bring to their livelihood and their children's career opportunities. Whatever optimism they held was temporarily repelled by the Tiananmen Incident in June 1989. Nevertheless, as the wheels of history turned on, they prepared for the future.

a. Out of Apathy

No observer had anticipated the events that took place at Tiananmen in Beijing and none the spontaneous reaction of Hong Kong people. Until then, no incident in Hong Kong's history had rallied 40,000 people onto the street, let alone half a million. Whatever the means by which the Hong Kong government might choose to reach the Hong Kong population, the support in the rallies demonstrated that psychologically, Hong Kong's politics was never far from China's politics. At heart, Hong Kong people were Chinese.

DOCUMENT VIII.a1: Unprecedented mass support (source: Emily Lau, 'Out of apathy', *Far Eastern Economics Review* 1 June, 1989, pp. 17-18)

The Chinese government's attempted crackdown on the student pro-democracy movement has spurred Hong Kong's mass political awakening. Almost 40,000 people braved the winds and rain of Typhoon Brenda on 20 May to rally . . .

The 20 May demonstration which provided the first glimpse of local people's strong reaction to events across the border, took place in a city almost immobilised by a typhoon. The demonstrators attended a rally and then marched to Peking's [Beijing's] quasi-diplomatic representative in Hong Kong, the Xinhua news-agency, to protest against the crackdown. The following day, a crowd estimated by police at over half-a-million flooded the streets and a rally was held in a local race course, which is opposite the Xinhua offices.

Initially, pro-Peking groups were reluctant to support the students, but as the situation in Peking and other parts of China deteriorated, leftist trade unions, teacher organizations, newspapers and even some staff at Xinhua, pledged their support for the students. Some local NPC [National People's Congress] delegates and members of the Chinese People's Political Consultative Conference, a political advisory group, urged Peking not to use force against the students and to lift the blackout on live televised news and on foreign correspondents conducting interviews on the streets of Peking . . .

One ironical impact of China's turmoil in Hong Kong, has been the apparent change of stance on the part of some conservative industrialists. Hong Kong businessmen such as tycoon and Basic Law Drafting Committee member Li Ka-shing, who had opposed the development of democracy locally, have voiced support for the students. Industrialist Stephen Cheong, a staunch opponent of direct elections, now called for speedier democratic changes. Businesswoman Veronica Wu of the New Hong Kong Alliance, a newly formed political party representing business people and professionals, said if political reforms were implemented in China, the pace of political developments in Hong Kong also could accelearte . . .

The huge demonstrations in Hong Kong also have shown up the inefficacy of the pro-democracy lobby, which has been trying in vain to galvanize the masses for the past few years. The most successful rally they organized managed to attract about 7,000 people, while the usual turnout had been about 500.

b. Rich and Poor

Affluent Hong Kong lived with the luxury that the 1980s could provide the 'yuppie' generation the world over. As affluence was transformed into job opportunities, the flow of immigrants from the neighbourhood continued; the neighbourhood was now no longer confined to south China, but in the 1980s it was to include noticeably the Philippines and Vietnam.

In the 1980s, many Filipinos were recruited to work as domestic maids in Hong Kong families. The Vietnamese came as refugees; they were confined to closed camps and most were re-patriated to Vietnam.

DOCUMENT VIII.b1: An affluent generation (source: Census and Statistics Department, Hong Kong, *Hong Kong 1986 By-Census, Summary Results*, Hong Kong: Census and Statistics Department, 1986, pp. 15-21)

Educational attainment of the population has improved markedly over the past 10 years. The improvement was particularly significant in the higher levels of education (matriculation and tertiary education).

Table 8.1
Educational and Economic Characteristics of the Hong Kong Population

Educational Attainment of Population

Educational Attainment	1976	1981	1986
No schooling/kindergarten	18.5 %	15.5 %	13.8 %
Primary	47.1	39.9	35.3
Secondary	29.2	36.3	39.5
Matriculation	2.0	3.7	5.4
Tertiary education			
Non-degree course	0.7	1.9	2.4
Degree course	2.5	2.7	3.6
Total	100.0	100.0	100.0

School Attendance of Population

Age Group	1976	1981	1986
3-5	60 %	83 %	92 %
6-11	98	98	99
12-16	79	84	93
17-18	44	45	56

Labour Force

	1976	1981	1986
Population aged 15 and above	3 077 700	3 749 100	4 149 100
Economically active population	1 922 500	2 503 800	2 753 800

(Table 8.1 cont)

(Table 8.1 cont)

Participation of Population in Labour Force

Year	Male	Female
1976	80.4 %	43.6 %
1981	82.5	49.5
1986	80.9	51.2

Median Age of Labour Force

Year	Male	Female	Overall
1976	35.5 years	28.1 years	33.1 years
1981	33.3	28.8	31.8
1986	34.3	30.3	32.9

Occupational Distribution of Working Population

Occupation	1976	1981	1986
Professional, administrative and managerial workers	7.5 %	8.5 %	11.7%
Clerical and related workers	9.6	12.0	14.5
Sales workers	11.4	10.3	11.7
Service workers	14.8	15.6	16.4
Production and related workers, transport equipment operators and labourers	52.2	50.7	43.4
Others	4.5	2.9	2.3
Total	100.0	100.0	100.0

Income from Main Employment

Monthly income from main employment	1976	1981	1986
Under HK$ 1,000	71.8 %	18.7 %	6.4 %
HK$1,000-1,999	21.0	49.6	21.8
HK$2,000-2,999	3.8	18.2	29.8
HK$3,000-3,999	1.6	6.6	18.4
HK$4,000-4,999	0.4	2.6	8.3
HK$5,000-5,999	0.5	1.3	4.6
HK$6,000-7,999	0.4	1.1	4.4
HK$8,000-9,999	0.2	0.5	2.1
HK$10,000 and over	0.3	1.4	4.2
Total	100.0	100.0	100.0

Median monthly earnings from main employment	1976	1981	1986
At current prices	HK$ 742	1,516	2,573
At 1976 prices	742	1,010	1,125

An increasing proportion of children aged 3-5 were attending kindergarten and nursery, 92 per cent in 1986 as compared with 60 per cent in 1976. The rate of school attendance for children aged 6-11 was close to 100 per cent. The attendance rate for the age group 12-16 and the age group 17-18 has risen from 79 per cent to 93 per cent and from 44 per cent to 56 per cent respectively, as a result of improvements in school attendance at the secondary level of education and matriculation. The smaller increase in the rate for these two age groups between 1976 and 1981 can be explained by the inflow of young immigrants, who had a lower tendency to attend school.

The population aged 15 and above in 1986 increased by 10.7 per cent over 1981 and the labour force increased by 10 per cent. As a result, the labour force participation rate decreased slightly from 66.8 per cent in 1981 to 66.4 per cent in 1986.

The labour force participation rate for males showed a slight increase over the years 1976-86, falling back from a peak in 1981. The high male participation rate in 1981 can largely be explained by the significant inflow of young male immigrants (there was a higher tendency among these immigrants to seek work). The labour force participation rate for females, on the other hand, increased steadily during the 10-year period. The increasing trend in the female rate was partly due to the inflow of young female immigrants (again who had a higher tendency to seek work) before the change of immigration policy and partly due to increasing female participation in the labour force.

With the inflow of immigrants largely subdued, the labour force grew older again in 1986 as a result of the aging of the population.

Over the past 10 years, there was a significant change in the occupational pattern of the working population. In 1976, over half of the working population were production workers; in 1986, the figure was 43.4 per cent. The proportion of those in professional, administrative and managerial occupations has risen from 7.5 per cent to 11.7 per cent. The proportions in clerical and service occupations have also increased appreciably.

Incomes from employment for workers increased substantially during the years 1976-86. In 1976, more than nine-tenths of workers earned less than $2,000 a month; in 1986, the figure was 28.2 per cent. The median monthly earnings, calculated at 1976 prices, increased from $742 in 1976 to $1,010 in 1981 and to $1,125 in 1986, indicating that real income from main employment grew at an average annual rate of 7.0 per cent between 1976 and 1981 and at a rate of 2.2 per cent between 1981 and 1986.

DOCUMENT VIII.b2: When even the posh can go lean (source: Michael Taylor, 'Gloom at the Top, Hong Kong's Poshest Shops Face Leaner Times', *Far Eastern Economic Review* 4 October, 1990 pp. 79-80)

Sales came early this year to some of Hong Kong's most glitzy upmarket shops, stayed longer, and ended only after dramatic discounts finally cleared the shelves of designer products. For shoppers, the bargains confirmed Hong Kong as a place to spend money fast. But for luxury goods retailers, the prolonged sales season revealed a market in crisis.

It is not easy to quantify the problem, but the anecdotal evidence is unmistakable: the sector is struggling to pay for soaring overheads out of stagnating turnover.

Gucci's general manager in Hong Kong, K. Yasui, says, 'Margins are under greater pressure than ever before. It's a survivor's game.' Upmarket department store Lane Crawford will be hard put to match its earnings forecast, warns president Frederick Doe, though business is 'not disastrous.' The general manager of a top European prestige goods retailer, accustomed to 30% growth a year, is happy just to be wringing marginal turnover growth out of the market. The managing director of a high-class retail chain with some 40 outlets in Hong Kong just says, 'It's really bad.'

The sales season demonstrated that. Normally, Hong Kong's summer sales last for a couple of weeks in July. This year, the first sales signs went up in June, and some have yet to come down. Lane Crawford's Doe speculates that an impromptu sales season may materialise in October, though not, he stresses, at Lane Crawford.

The immediate crisis is the result of long-term trends and short-term accidents, global influences and local pressures. 'When you have so many small factors, it starts to affect people's psychology,' says a director of one of Hong Kong's largest upmarket retail chains.

Monet Schemm, general manager of Louis Vuitton in Hong Kong, says, 'The slowdown started with the decline of the yen in early 1989, followed by Tiananmen Square, the decline of the stockmarket, another period of decline in the yen and, today, the Middle East crisis. Customers have obviously become more cautious.'

Rents in Hong Kong's prime shopping areas are the second or third most expensive in the world. Typically, rents will swallow 15-20% of a prestige shop's turnover, though they vary enormously in Central, the territory's main shopping and commercial area. Hong Kong Land's The Landmark complex commands the highest rent renewal rates, up to HK$300 (US$42.3) per sq.ft. a month; space across the road has recently been fetching just HK$120 per sq.ft.

One director at a major Landmark tenant says, 'You can't get rent reductions. But we have negotiated a reasonable increase — last year the landlord was talking about 100% increases.'

Lane Crawford's Doe says: 'In the past shopkeepers have paid whatever rents are being asked in order to get into prime locations. Some of the rents are simply unsupportable.'

Dickson Concepts has about 40 retail outlets in Hong Kong and has in the past paid top dollar for the locations it wants. Nevertheless, it treats each shop as a separate profit centre, closing those that lose money. This year it relocated two shops in Central to cheaper premises nearby.

It is not alone. Nicholas Brooke, partner of property consultants Levett & Bailey, says: 'We know of two retail chains at the top end which are looking at each and every outlet.'

For some retailers there is nowhere else to go. Yasui of Gucci, which is based in

The Landmark, says: 'We have to be in a prime location in Central.' Gucci's rents are estimated to be among the highest in the territory at HK$300-500 per sq. ft. a month.

But the basic problem is stagnating demand. For some luxury retailers, the story begins and ends with the relative weakness of Hong Kong's tourist industry. Tourists account for 70-80% of Gucci's business, which the company believes is typical at the top end of the market. Louis Vuitton does not disclose its tourism dependency, but rivals assume it is all but total. Tourists account for half of Dickson Concepts' Hong Kong retail business — two-thirds of it Japanese and another 15-20% Taiwanese.

Dickson Concepts' chairman Dickson Poon once remarked that the number he kept the closest eye on was the number of Japanese tourists.

The news from the Hong Kong Tourist Authority [Association] is not encouraging: though in the first half of the year, 3.5% more Japanese tourists arrived in Hong Kong (compared with the same period in 1989), at HK$4.9 billion, they spent 3.4% less. In the same period, the average Japanese tourist spent HK$7,706 during his stay, 6.7% less than last year. Spending per day fell 6.4% to HK$2,612. Worst of all, the average Japanese tourist cut his shopping budget by 8%.

The days of tour coaches disgorging hungry hordes of Japanese into the Louis Vuitton showroom may be numbered, for as far as luxury retailing is concerned, there is a clear long-term trend of Hong Kong losing its comparative advantage over Japan.

Hong Kong's luxury retail sector has long been a major beneficiary of Japan's byzantine distribution system, which has kept prices of luxury goods vastly higher in Tokyo than in Hong Kong. Dunhill conservatively claims price differentials amount to 'about 35%, as a rule of thumb.'

However, the Japanese distribution system is under attack, particularly in the context of US-Japanese trade negotiations, and Japanese retailers have come under pressure from the Ministry of Trade and Industry to bring their prices more into line with the rest of the world. At the same time, European luxury goods suppliers are keen to escalate Hong Kong prices to Tokyo levels, and pocket the difference.

For much of the year, Hong Kong's diminishing comparative advantage over Tokyo was exacerbated by a weakened yen. At the beginning of the year, the exchange rate was HK$1:¥18.47, but by April the Japanese currency had slumped to ¥20.45. Japanese tourists found their yen budget slashed by more than 10%.

In addition, Japan's April 1989 imposition of a 3% sales tax had the perverse effect of lowering the price of European luxury goods, as it was accompanied by the abolition or reduction of high import duties.

But if the first half of 1990 saw the comparative impoverishment of the Japanese tourist, it also saw the dramatic emergence of the free-spending Taiwanese shopper. Total Taiwanese spending in Hong Kong's shops shot up by 44.8% to HK$3.3 billion in that period, making the Taiwanese tourist the second-largest source of shopping income after the Japanese. Total spending per head rose 41% to HK$5,145, and spending per day rocketed 56.7% to HK$2,404.

From the luxury goods retailers' point of view, the Taiwanese is the ideal tourist: statistics reveal him skimping on his hotel bill to conserve his spending money.

The Taiwanese visitor spends a far greater proportion of his money shopping than any other tourist, 65.8% compared with the Japanese tourist's 58.1%, and a global average of 51.6%. The average Taiwanese tourist spent HK$3,385 in Hong Kong's shops in the first half of the year, 58% more than the corresponding period last year.

But hopes that the Taiwanese would sustain the market died with the collapse of regional stockmarkets in the wake of the Gulf crisis. The 'wealthy effect' took a swift toll. 'The August stockmarket crash has had an impact — from mid-August, there has been a dearth of Taiwanese customers,' one luxury goods retailer says. His lament is echoed by Yasui of Gucci: 'Those rich people have lost a lot of money.'

The upshot is that retailers have been thrown back on demand from the wealthier ranks of Hong Kong's 5.7 million population. In theory, local demand should be buoyant. Not only have wages rocketed, but negligible real interest rates offer little incentive to Hong Kong people to leave the money in the bank. Those companies which have not previously targeted the local market have been pleasantly surprised. Dunhill says it has doubled its sales to Hong Kong customers this year, while Louis Vuitton claims 'a healthy growth in sales to local clients.'

But other retailers, with a greater local market exposure, tell of local demand falling sharply after the collapse of stockmarkets. Joyce Boutiques, which generates about 65% of its turnover from the local market, in the prospectus for its forthcoming listing admits that 'sales for the month of August . . . were lower than for the corresponding month last year,' despite having increased its retail floorspace.

A director of a large Hong Kong high-end retail chain is blunter: 'When the stockmarket went down, it affected local customers' psychology: people are saying 'Emigrate first, and then spend like hell'.'

Coming on top of damaged consumer psychology has been a de-Centralisation of Hong Kong shopping. This year has been a bonanza for Swire Properties' Cityplaza — an increasingly up-market shopping mall based several miles from Central. The change in local shopping habits is precisely measurable, since Cityplaza rents are based on the level of turnover.

David Mahoney of Swire Properties says, 'We know exactly what the turnover of our clients is. Year on year, the improvement this year for Cityplaza as a whole is approximately 40%. Last year it was 28%.'

Hong Kong's resilience is regularly astonishing, so it is too early to tell whether the luxury goods sector will recover its profitability. But the crisis has prompted speculation that Hong Kong might be overshopped, as far as luxury goods outlets are concerned. 'There are too many shops for the market to support — a lot of firms do fairly well, and a lot go bankrupt,' Doe of Lane Crawford warns, though he is confident about his own company's expansion plans.

Asia is now said to be the largest market for luxury goods, and, outside Tokyo, Hong Kong is the major shop window. European suppliers' designs on the territory have been intensified, retailers say, by the problems afflicting major US retailers. An excess supply of European goods must affect the price of prestige.

Luxury retailers are fittingly snooty about the company they keep, and segment the market into divisions of prestige. 'We pretty much recognise each other,' says the general manager of one indisputably 'first division' supplier. 'When the third and fourth division firms start moving in, you know the place is getting badly overshopped.' On this analysis, Singapore is 'definitely overshopped' while Hong Kong is only 'probably overshopped.'

Nevertheless, not all is gloom. First, the market is buttressed by Hong Kong's luxury hotel infrastructure; hard-pressed hoteliers will continue to find ways to bring potential shoppers into the territory. And at the very top end of the market, life continues as normal. Rolls-Royce has sold all its 1990 Hong Kong allocation of 36 cars, and has secured another nine for the territory this year. Luxury retailers are not expected to be among the buyers.

DOCUMENT VIII.b3: At the bottom-end of the wage scale (source: Extracted from Working Party on New Arrivals, Community Development Division, Hong Kong Council of Social Service, and Social Sciences Department, Lingnan College, *Report on the Social and Economic Adaptation of the Chinese New Arrivals in Hong Kong*, 1985)

The respondents were relatively young with the median age of 29 and mean of 31. Specifically, 70.4% of the respondents ranged from 18-34 years of age.

Concerning their sex, 67.4% of the respondents were male and 32.6% of them were female.

54.1% of the respondents were married, 44.8% single, and 1.1% widowed or divorced.

Taking the distribution of sex of the respondents into account, it was found that there were more males in the single group (48.3%) and more females in the married group (59.5%).

The majority of the respondents, 65.3% have been residing in Hong Kong for 3-1/2 years to less than 6-1/2 years.

Most of the respondents came from rural areas in Mainland China (59.0%), 25.9% from towns, and 15.1% from cities.

68.6% of the respondents came from Guangdong Province of Mainland China, and 23.1% from Fukien [Fujian].

Among the respondents, 56.3% of them were legal immigrants from Mainland China and 43.7 were illegal.

Almost all (98.9%) of the illegal immigrants came from Guangdong Province of Mainland China.

When we take their sex into consideration, it is found that there were more male illegal immigrants and more female legal immigrants.

Findings also indicate that illegal immigrants were younger than the legal immigrants. The data shows that the proportion of illegal immigrants was higher in the age groups of 18-24 and 25-29.

A substantial proportion of the respondents (61.5%) resided in private housing, 14.1% in public housing, 12.6% in wood squatter, and the rest (11.9%) in quarters, stone squatters and others.

Among those living in private housing, 58.3% were renting a room, 17.7% renting a flat, 16.9% self-owned, and the rest 7.1% were either by instalment or renting a bed. Of these living in the public housing, the majority of them were living in temporary housing (49.1%) and public estate (46.4%).

Bearing in mind that the standard per capita floor space for public estates in Hong Kong is 50 sq.ft., a large proportion of the respondents (57.1%) lived below that standard.

Most of the Chinese new arrivals were factory workers (38.5%) engaged in textile, electronic and garment industries; then skilled workers (21.7%) e.g. carpenters, electricians and masons; catering workers (8.5%) e.g. waiters, cinema-guides; and construction workers (6.2%). Only a few (4.7%) of them were clerical, managerial, professional workers and salesmen.

The distribution of the current monthly salary of the respondents is shown in Table 8.2. It is found that 73.2% of the working respondents' monthly salary ranged from HK$1,500 to 3,499 with the mean of HK$2,522.70 and median HK$2,400.

Table 8.2
Distribution of Current Monthly Salary of the Respondents

Monthly salary	Number	%
Less than 500	2	0.3
500-999	11	1.6
1,000-1,499	61	8.8
1,500-1,999	129	18.5
2,000-2,499	163	23.4
2,500-2,999	104	14.9
3,000-3,499	114	16.4
3,500-3,999	50	7.2
4,000 or above	62	8.9
Total	692*	100.0

* 12 cases of 'no answer', 2 cases of 'don't know' and 129 cases of 'not applicable' are excluded.

Generally speaking, language is one of the areas which affects adaptation, for it influences communication between local residents and immigrants, opportunities for making friends, understanding the habits and customs of the new society and also some life opportunities such as job-hunting and prospect of job promotion.

The focus of the following discussion on language problem is mainly on Cantonese and English. It is because Cantonese is the major medium of communication and is more crucial to new arrivals' social life adaptation. On the other hand, English is more crucial to new arrivals' job-searching and promotion.

Although 68.7% of the respondents came from Guangdong Province, still 49.5% of them claimed that they did not know how to speak Cantonese, and 10% could only speak a little during their early arrival.

The effects of poor ability to speak Cantonese might lead to difficulties in making new friends. Those new arrivals who could not speak or could speak only a little Cantonese might have more difficulties in making new friends than those who could.

Non-Cantonese speaking respondents were more likely to make friends with Chinese immigrants than those Cantonese speaking respondents. On the contrary, those Cantonese speaking respondents were more likely to make friends with Hong Kong local residents.

Finally, when we asked those non-Cantonese speaking respondents how they learn Cantonese after arrival in Hong Kong, we found that very few of them (0.7%) learn Cantonese by attending language courses. Most of them learn by just talking with colleagues (37.2%), watching television (27.0%) and talking with friends (20.7%).

We asked the new arrivals if they were being discriminated against in the following aspects:

(1) job-hunting
(2) salary and fringe-benefits
(3) prospect of job promotion
(4) educational or professional qualification
(5) making friends with local residents

The first four aspects relate to job opportunities and the last one is concerned with social life.

The response of new arrivals revealed that most of them did not find themselves being discriminated against. Only some feel being discriminated against in the aspect of job hunting (38.0%) and recognition of professional qualification (27.3%).

DOCUMENT VIII.b4: Why were people poor in Hong Kong? (source: Nelson W.S. Chow, *Poverty in an Affluent Society, a Report of a Survey on Low Income Families in Hong Kong*, Hong Kong: Department of Social Work, Chinese University of Hong Kong, 1982, pp. 96-97)

We admitted that we had adopted a rather novel design to measure poverty. When we first began our research, we were not sure whether this approach would ever come up with useful information to help us establish a poverty line relevant to the situation in Hong Kong. We were indeed very much excited when our deprivation index indicated that a deprivation threshold did exist and a proportion of households could reasonably be considered to be living in poverty. If our findings were valid, the poverty line that existed in Hong Kong in mid-1981 was a monthly income (a monthly expenditure should be more accurate as the amount denoted what the household needed to spend) of $2,000 to $2,199 for a household and $400 to $499 for a single person. A household has an average size of four members. According to the preliminary results of the 1981 Census, 9.5 percent of the households received a monthly income of less than $1,000 while a further 19 percent received less than $2,000. Since no information had yet been released regarding the sizes of the households having less than $2,000 monthly incomes, we had no way of calculating the actual number of families or persons who were deprived in their living styles.

Why were people poor in Hong Kong?

There is certainly no single reason which causes poverty. At the time of our survey, unemployment was certainly not the major cause of poverty. Even among the five percent of households which reported having unemployed members, few of them had only one working person. Near-to-full employment situation in Hong Kong had undoubtedly helped many families to live above the poverty line. Nevertheless, the prevalence of more than one working member in the household indicated that the earnings of only one person was generally insufficient to support a family. In other words, considering the standard of living in Hong Kong, the personal wages were generally low so that many families could only lift themselves out of poverty by having more than one member working. (In our sample, the median monthly income was $2,609 while the median monthly earnings of employed person was $1,505.)

Thus those families having only one working member often found themselves in dire conditions and some even had to be partially dependent on public assistance. From the analysis of public assistance families in our sample, we also found that they usually had less working members and the percentage of unemployed persons was higher than that of other households. Our understanding was that these families often failed to benefit from the near-to-full employment situation in Hong Kong as they had only aged members or members who were almost unemployable.

To summarize, though unemployment was listed as the number one threat causing hardship, its impact had very much been atttenuated by the fact that most families usually had more than one working member. Those families which had no employed member, such as those consisting of only aged persons, were most vulnerable to poverty.

DOCUMENT VIII.b5: Immigrants for hire (source: Translated from Kenichi Ohashi, 'Feilubin guangchang : feiyong zai zhongqu de juhui' (Filipino Square': Meeting place of Filipino servants in Central District) in Lu Dalue and Daqiao Jianyi (Kenichi Ohashi) eds. *Chengshi jiechu — Xianggang jietou wenhua guancha* (Urban touch — observations of street culture in Hong Kong), Hong Kong: Shangwu 1989, pp. 173-197)

At the end of 1987, 39,100 Filipinos were resident in Hong Kong. This was the largest group among foreign residents in Hong Kong. Among these people, 34,422 were given permission to stay in Hong Kong as 'domestic servants.' Since 1974, when the Immigration Department formally accepted the application of overseas domestic servants to work in Hong Kong, and with political, social and economic changes in Hong Kong and the Philippines, the number of female Filipino servants employed in Hong Kong had annually increased. The increase had been particularly noticeable since 1980. Female Filipino servants became so common that it might be thought that 'all Filipinas were female servants.'

As the number of female Filipino servants increased, it became more and more obvious since the mid-1970s that Central District was becoming their 'meeting place.' The Filipinos in Hong Kong, unlike other immigrants, did not settle into their own residential district. Instead, they created an informal holiday meeting place. I think this development can be accounted for by their peculiar pattern of migration. Firstly, most of them are single women. Even among the small minority who are married, few have come to Hong Kong with their husbands. Secondly, they have moved to Hong Kong on what may be referred to as 'contractual migration,' for they return to the Philippines upon the completion of their contracts. Thirdly, most of them live in the households of their employers. Given these peculiarities in their migration, we can say, looking at their meeting place from their vantage point, that their holiday meeting in Central is particularly meaningful.

In October 1986, the behaviour of Filipino people in public places in Central on holidays attracted attention as a result of the 'Statue Square problem.' The problem arose because they littered the public places in Central, and as a result, it was suggested that they should be driven out of those places. The suggestion carried a somewhat racist overtone. With the view of doing something about this problem, religious organizations and Filipino government organizations reviewed the situation, and suggested that a centre be set up to substitute for their current 'meeting place.' However, so far, Central has remained their 'meeting place.' Nevertheless, since this problem has arisen, some buildings on the edge of Central have intensified their security arrangements, and installed 'No entry' signs or rope barriers at entrances, staircases and open-air places. These notices are written in English and Tagalog. Obviously, they are meant for the Filipinos meeting nearby.

In a survey on Filipina servants conducted by C. French, responses received show that aside from church, public places in Central were the places they went to most frequently when they had their days off.* This pattern is confirmed by case studies on how Filipina servants spend their days off. The patterns is: church in the morning and the public places in the afternoon. We may conclude from this that both the church and public places are extremely meaningful to them.

Although Filipina servants use the word 'square' to refer to their 'meeting place,' this does not mean that they only meet in Statue Square. From the writer's survey, among the places where their meetings are held, aside from Statue Square (where

---

* Carolyn French, *Filipina Domestic Workers in Hong Kong*, Ph.D. thesis, University of Surrey, 1986.

2,038 people met), are Chater Garden (where 1,149 met), the City Hall gardens (where 532 people met), and Blake Pier (where 410 people met). On the day the survey was conducted, 5,410 Filipino people met in the 'meeting places' in Central.

How do the Filipino people who meet at the 'meeting places' in Central understand and handle these 'places'? What meaning is given these places so that they may become their squares?

Carina has come to Hong Kong for six months. She works as a domestic servant for a Chinese family in Western District. She has a 'base' in an ice-cream shop at World Wide House on Peddar Street. Every Sunday, she spends her time from 10.00 in the morning to 6.00 in the evening around her 'base' in Central. Although she knows that Statue Square is a great meeting place for Filipino people, she says because rope barriers have been put up on the edges of the square, it is difficult for a new-comer like her to keep a place there. Moreover, the square is a complicated place. Every now and then the police come along to inspect identity cards. So, she does not go there very often. She chooses her 'base' where she can spend a day quietly by herself. Moreover, that place faces the sun; it is bright and sunny. There are shops in the International Arcade that deals in goods for Filipino people. She has her meals and does her shopping there. She spends her day off reading magazines, writing letters, and talking to her friends. Three weeks ago, she met her friend Maria. When she was here on her own, Maria came over and said, 'Are you a Filipino?' After that, they chatted. They talked about their families in the Philippines and their lives in Hong Kong. Because she is older than Maria, Maria asks her advice on a lot of things.

Josephine has come to Hong Kong for two years. She works as a domestic servant in a Chinese family in the New Territories. She tends to meet her friends on the eastern side of Statue Square, in front of the former Supreme Court. The Hong Kong and Shanghai Bank is a landmark for her, and for that reason, she knows about the bank. She has friends who stay in Chater Garden. She often goes up to World Wide House for her shopping. She comes to Central on the Star Ferry. When she goes to the World Wide House, she goes through Prince's Building as a short cut. Occasionally, she has a snack or her lunch in the fast-food restaurants in Prince's Building. As for the washroom, she uses the ones in Chater Garden or Beaconsfield House.

Josephine was born on Luzon Island. She speaks Ilokano but she knows some other Filipino dialects. It is said that the Filipina servants at Statue Square are divided into little groups according to their places of origin in the Philippines. From the dialects they speak, they know where one another comes from. The ones who were born in Luzon meet mostly in Statue Square and Chater Garden, concentrating to the north of Statue Square. Many of them were born in the middle region of Luzon. If one looks at it from the point of view of dialect distribution, the situation is this: the ones in Chater Garden speak Ilokano, the ones to the south of Statue Square speak Ilokano and Ifugao, and the ones to the north speak Pampanga [Bangjiagai] and Tagalog.

Margie has come to Hong Kong for eight months. She spends most of her Sundays in the church, and so she does not have a 'meeting place' in Central. However, because she passes through Central on her way to church, she makes use of the service of a 'money changer' in Statue Square. She does it there because its rates are good. Because she changes her money there quite often, she has come to know the women who run it very well. She says they are people who have married Pakistani people in Hong Kong and so are not working as domestic servants.

The 'meeting place' of Filipina domestic servants in Central is really a colourful place. They chat, eat and drink, party, write and read letters, and they even do business — their clients are other Filipino people in the Central District. They sell magazines, food, ornaments; they look for boy friends, and they conduct religious worship. On a few occasions, Statue Square was also where they held political demonstrations.

Moreover, the Central District is also the largest arena where Filipino people exchange information. The people who sell their services, entertainment and leisure magazines in 'moving newstands' contribute to this activity. Filipino people learn about their own country from these magazines, and this information becomes the most suitable topics of their casual conversation. Conversing, after all, is the most important activity for the exchange of information at the square. Besides, there is plenty of business for the 'photographers' that take pictures on the charge of two dollars. They have a picture taken there and send it home to their friends and relatives to show them how cheerful they look.

The square has become a part of Hong Kong that is close to the Philippines. The Filipino people enjoy their own culture there, and this aspect of Hong Kong life should be valued. They eat food they buy from the shops or that they have themselves brought, they sing Filipino songs to guitar accompaniment, their cassette recorders play Filipino music, from tapes that can be bought all over the place in the 'stalls' at the square. More important than any of this is that they can converse in their own language there, rather than in English or Cantonese.

DOCUMENT VII.b6: The VMs [Vietnamese Migrants] (Source: Andrew Li and David Todd, *Report of Justices of the Peace on the Inquiry into the Events Surrounding the Removal of Vietnamese Migrants from the Whitehead Detention Centre on 7 April 1994*, Hong Kong, 1994. pp. 12–17)

Whitehead is situated at Wu Kwai Sha Tsui, Shatin, New Territories. It has a scenic view of Tolo Harbour to its north and Ma On Shan to its south. The new residential developments at Ma On Shan characteristic of an affluent Hong Kong overlook the centre.

The centre was built as a 'closed camp' for VMs and is designated as a place of detention udner the Immigration Ordinance for them.

Whitehead consists of 10 sections and a school complex. Each section is surrounded by a 5.6 meter high mesh fence and a perimeter fence of equal height surrounds Section 1 to 8. A perimeter concrete road also surrounds Sections 1 to 8. Another road known as the Main Road (approximately 500 meters in length and 5.5 meters in width) bisects this area separating Sections 1 to 4 from Sections 5 to 8. The main CSD [Correctional Services Department] offices are on the south on a hill (or knoll) looking over Sections

1 to 8 on the north and Sections 9 and 10 on the south. In front of the offices, a road runs along the length of this hill, overlooking the sections below which house the centre's inmates.

The dormitories vary from one or two storeys in height in Sections 1 to 8 whilst single storey Romney huts are built in Sections 9 and 10. Each dormitory is partitioned into halves. Within each Section, there is office accommodation for the UNHCR (United Nations High Commission of Refugees) and NGOs (Non-government organizations).

Section 7 is situated in the middle of Whitehead, at the foot of the hill on which the centre's administration offices are located. From the road bisecting the centre, one enters through a Main Gate into an enclosed area which forms the common lodge for entry into Sections 7 and 8 ('the Main Gate Lodge'). From the Main Gate Lodge, there is an entrance gate to Section 7 and another entrance gate to Section 8.

From the Main Gate Lodge, there are also separate entrance gates to the Administrative Block (adjacent to Section 7) and the Clinic, Immigration Block and Kitchen (adjacent to Section 8). They serve both sections but are fenced off from them. Sections 7 and 8 are administered as one unit by Whitehead staff. Welfare services within the Sections 7 and 8 unit are provided by the UNHCR's Social Services Section, Hong Kong Christian Aid to Refugees, the Save the Children Fund, and International Social Services. There is also a fenced passage through the Main Gate Lodge which connects Sections 7 and 8. This provided free access during the daytime between the two sections, allowing the inmates to intercommunicate and circulate freely between both sections. But this passage has been sealed off since 27 March, 1984.

From the entrance gate into Section 7, one enters into an open courtyard. There is a row of lavatories on the right of the entrance gate. At the far end of the courtyard is a washing area for clothes. There are two rows of huts. One row consists of 7 huts. Of these, 1 hut houses a single-storey recreation hall and a food issue hall; 5 huts are single-storey dormitories and 1 two-storey hut accommodates NGOs. The parallel row consists of 6 huts with 5 single-storey ones for dormitories and 1 two-storey one for NGOs.

The dormitory huts are 33.5 meters long, 12.5 meters wide, and have pitched, 'A'-shaped roofs which are 4.3 meters high at the centre-ridge and 3.3 meters high at the eaves. Corrugated metal ceiling panels below the roof give a uniform ceiling height within the dormitory huts of 3.3 meters. Bunks inside the dormitories are 3-tiered, with the bed board of the top tier a little less than 1 meter from the ceiling panels. Each dormitory hut is partitioned at its mid-section, thus dividing each hut into two separate dormitories each having one entrance — i.e. at either end of the hut. The mid-section partition does not allow access between the two halves of the hut. There is a 2 meter wide lane between each row of huts, and a 1 meter wide gap overhead between the eaves of adjoining huts.

Each dormitory (i.e. half hut) has the capacity to accommodate 90 persons, in 30 triple bunks. In practice, 70 to 80 persons are accommodated in each dormitory.

The 10 sections at Whitehead comprise: (a) Sections 1 to 8, housing between them the main VM population; and (b) Sections 9 and 10 which house VMs who have opted for voluntary repatriation and are awaiting return to Vietnam.

As at 28 March 1994 the total VM population at Whitehead was 15,339 including 340 in Section A and 136 in Section B. The total population of Sections 1 to 8 was 14,863 of whom 4,754 (32%) were under the age of 14 years.

As far as Section 7 is concerned, it housed a total population of 1,526 (including 483 under 14 years old) comprising: (a) 750 males (including 242 under 14 years old); and (b) 776 females (including 241 under 14 years old). They are virtually all from the Northern part of Vietnam, mostly from Hai Phong.

c. The Local People Emigrate

> In the jittery years after the joint declaration by the British and the Chinese governments on the return of Hong Kong to China in 1997, many Hong Kong people emigrated. The opinion was expressed often that Hong Kong was being depleted of its skilled workers and professionals. But it was also noticed in the 1990s that many who had emigrated returned, and many more, who had obtained the right of abode abroad, remained in Hong Kong.

DOCUMENT VIII.c1: How many emigrate? (source: Legislative Council, 12 April, 1989, *Hong Hong Hansard, Reports of the Sittings of the Legislative Council of Hong Kong, Session 1988-89*)

Mrs. Chow asked: Will Government inform this Council of the basis of estimation for the number of 42,000 Hong Kong people emigrating in 1989 as stated in the Government's submission to the Foreign Affairs Committee on emigration; what is the breakdown of the figure by countries of destination and how the figures compare with those in the last three years?

Secretary for Administrative Services and Information: Sir, in estimating the extent of emigration, the Government relies on three main sources of information:

(a) applications for Certificates of No Criminal Conviction (CNCC) processed by the Royal Hong Kong Police Force, which are required by most destination countries;
(b) visas issued by the main destination countries, according to statistics provided by their Consulates or Commissions in Hong Kong; and
(c) statistics on the balance of movement of Hong Kong residents (other than those in and out of China) provided by the Immigration Department.

Based on these sources and allowing for the various time intervals in the emigration process, the breakdown by country of destination for the last three calendar years, and forecast for the current year, is as follows:

Year	Canada	USA	Australia	Others	Total
1986	5,615	7,742	4,441	1,191	18,989
1987	16,254	7,411	5,208	1,125	29,998
1988	24,588	11,777	7,846	1,606	45,817
1989	16,400	12,800	10,900	1,900	42,000

DOCUMENT VIII.c2: Uncertainty and its impact (H.A. Turner, Patricia Fosh, Ng Sek Hong, *Between Two Societies: Hong Kong Labour in Transition*, Hong Kong: Centre of Asian Studies, University of Hong Kong, 1991, pp. 103-106)

The immediate point of this discussion is that 1989 clearly plunged Hong Kong society — and the future of its economy — into a state of great uncertainty. Though here we confine ourselves to the labour market effects. Even before the June events and their aftermath,[*] evidence had accumulated that a very large proportion of Hong Kong's people would emigrate before 1997 (if only to acquire residential and working rights in other countries, from which they might perhaps return to await the outcome of Chinese sovereignty with a refuge established against disappointment). Territory surveys showed that some 30 percent of families had at least one member with overseas residential rights already, with the proportion among professional people rising to 40 percent. Even among the employees in our own first sample survey of 1985, when less than a third thought it yet time to consider the then recent Anglo-Chinese Agreement's possible personal effects seriously, about one-sixth expressed anxiety at the prospect and a similar percentage owned to specific plans to leave.

In 1988, however, 45,000 people actually emigrated, mostly from the professional and entrepreneurial classes, and this outflow accelerated sharply in '89. Surveys by professional associations of their members have shown majorities who now intend to join it, and at time of writing scarcities of such qualified workers as doctors and accountants have already become a matter of concern. In July '89 — before the UK government's decision to give British passports with residence rights to around 250,000 Hong Kong citizens — one of the present writers estimated that by 1997 well over a million would have established such rights in other countries (particularly in North America and Australasia), often with pleadable rights for relatives. Informed local agencies have estimated higher figures.

All this suggests that around a quarter of Hong Kong's population, including many of its more skilled employees, are at least affected by an active exploration of overseas prospects, if they are not already involved in plans for removal. And although the administration has increased Hong Kong's planned output from higher education, with

---

[*] See DOCUMENT VIII.a1.

other agencies making emergency arrangements to train their own local specialists, it is not clear how far such measures would stay the outward flow rather than adding to it: Hong Kong has already become a rewarding recruiting ground for other countries that wish to attract scarce skills — or capital. It is this process, incidentally, that makes it rather unprofitable for us to attempt to trace the recent course of employee differentials further than we have: clearly, the upper labour market now has a new element of fluidity; for some scarce cadres, apparently, firms have found it necessary to engage expatriate workers at higher pay to replace local specialists withdrawing.

The major points here, however, are twofold: one, that whatever the other economic effects of the approaching change of sovereignty, the supply situation of qualified, managerial and entrepreneurial skills is likely of itself to represent a growingly adverse factor as 1997 nears; and two, that the mass of lower-skilled manual workers and white collar employees, who lack both qualificatory and personal resources for international mobility, are most likely to suffer from any economic deterioration ensuing from loss of such proficiencies. Moreover, other factors may aggravate these employees' exposure. In late '89, the Deputy Director of the PRC State Council's Hong Kong and Macau Affairs Office expressed a common Chinese sentiment, describing Hong Kong as a 'land of treasure'. Many PRC commercial and economic agencies (not all of which, under recent devolutions, are under close Central Government control) may well find it attractive to establish delegations and enterprises there — and the present representation of PRC undertakings in Hong Kong does not seem to have been notable for generosity in its employment terms or in its interpretation of local labour regulations: much less, for any special regard of union opinion. Moreover, although the reported Draft Basic Law confirms Hong Kong's high ratification of ILO Conventions (high, that is compared only to the PRC), the possibility of future moves to update Hong Kong's standing in this respect seems unclarified. Perhaps most important, however, is the uncertainty surrounding future immigration from the PRC to Hong Kong.

In many developing countries, the great cities have been magnets to the rural poor of their hinterlands, with consequences in terms of urban unemployment, poverty, overcrowding and social problems which are only too well known. The international border between Colony and mainland, however, permitted immigration to the Territory to be controlled at figures which were — despite a persisting minor seepage of illegal entrants — broadly within the absorptive capacities of Hong Kong's housing and public service programmes, and particularly of its labour market. It is by no means clear that this inwards pressure will be so closely regulated under a common sovereignty; and the effects of large admissions of workers accustomed to much lower standards of living upon the condition of Hong Kong's present labour force are readily foreseeable.

Of course, many of these things may not happen — or may not happen on the potentially disturbing scale which in 1990 seems possible. And there could be offsetting factors: Deng Xiaoping once said that he could wish China had eight Hong Kongs, but it does not; and its current economy and directive philosophy provide no obvious basis for another seven's early creation. If the political considerations that dominated the PRC's relations with Hong Kong after June '89 subside: if the Anglo-Chinese compromise of early '90 on the development of Hong Kong's representative system, and the subsequently-adopted Basic Law for the Hong Kong SAR [Special Administrative Region], after all provide (despite the '85 Agreement's ambiguities) sufficient formal guarantee of a reasonable and stable autonomy for the Territory, and if the PRC's own treatment of the latter over the transitional decade or so indicates that Hong Kong's acquired traditions of personal and communicative freedom, honest and open administration, and commercial liberalism will in fact be preserved — Hong Kong will at least have considerable attractions for foreign enterprises as a base for market relations with China, and for new growth of entrepot trade. Given an acceptable stability, a return migration of the qualified and enterprising is possible; and given some return to economic reformism in mainland China, it is even possible that Hong Kong may resume its recently-disturbed role as, effectively, China's main source and practical school of economic modernisation.

However, these are all 'ifs' — and meanwhile the only certain probability appears to be a great deal of uncertainty: which will take some years to resolve, and will be accompanied by disturbances to Hong Kong life and employment of which the residual employee majority will be Hong Kong's continuing recipients. It is unfortunate, perhaps, that the major public controversy on Hong Kong's future since mid-'89 should have been (in effect) between, on one side, a China now weighing economic considerations as secondary to those of political control — and on the other side, recently-emerged groups of political liberals in Hong Kong itself who were first concerned to secure a maximum advance to elective internal government before sovereignty's transfer. How far the mass of Hong Kong workers have been touched by this controversy remains unclear; but their own interests in the transition have been submerged by the constitutional conflict (assertion in the drafting Committee, for instance, that the Basic Law need include no right of collective bargaining because the practice was not customary in Hong Kong appears to have passed unchallenged). Plainly, this mass interest remains without adequate spokesmen.

d. The Survival of Customs

> Traditions continued in Hong Kong. Collective values did not easily erode. It had been predicted that the nuclear family might take over; but social surveys discovered that many held onto traditional family values. The clienteles at temples in Hong Kong saw no decline, traditional religious rituals continued to be practised as they had always been.

DOCUMENT VIII.d1: Family values (source: Lee Ming-kwan, 'Family and social life', in Lau Siu-kai, Lee Ming-kwan, Wan Po-san and Wong Siu-lun eds. *Indicators of Social Development: Hong Kong 1988*, Hong Kong: Hong Kong Institute of Asia-Pacific Studies, The Chinese University of Hong Kong, 1991, pp. 43-44)

A widely held view regarding family change in Hong Kong is that values and norms associated with the traditional Chinese family have been replaced by those more indicative of the nuclear family. In the survey, we try to find out whether this is true. More specifically, the survey tries to establish the attitudes of Hong Kong people towards the following traditional norms and values:
a. Newly married couples should live with their parents;
b. Children should not leave their elderly parents unsupported;
c. Siblings should continue to give help to one another even after they have their own families;
d. Daughters are different from sons because sooner or later they will be married and leave home. Sons remain ones' sons;
e. Men go to work; the home is the rightful place for women.

It is commonly believed that traditional norms and ideals such as these have become eclipsed by an alternate set which favour neolocal residence for the newly married, reduced obligations to kin and relatives, equal rights for sons and daughters to descent and inheritance, and a more liberal attitude towards husband-wife sex role differentiation.

These beliefs are not entirely confirmed by the findings. As many as 62.1% of the respondents agreed that newly married couples should live away from their parents. There are, however, nearly a quarter (23.2%) of them who were not sure if this was always right, and one-seventh (14.7%) who disagree.

There is also split response to the statement: 'Children are not necessarily obliged to support their parents.' About half (54.2%) of the respondents disagree with the statement. There are, however, a quarter (26.3%) who agree and one-fifth (19.6%) who have the attitude that the norm is relative to situations.

The attitude towards fulfilling obligations to one's siblings is, on the other hand, unequivocal, as 93.1% of the respondents agree that married brothers and sisters should continue to give help to one another. Only 1.9% disagreed.

The majority (74.3%) of the respondents also disagree that sons and daughters should have different rights and statuses.

Lastly, on husband-wife sex-role differentiation, there is a split response. Two-fifths (40.8%) of the respondents support the more traditional thinking about the arrangement of sex roles, i.e. women attending to domestic matters and men to business matters. The rest either disagree (47.5%) or have second thoughts (11.8%) about this.

The picture emerging from these findings is that although the nuclear family is very much an ongoing reality, people have not entirely given up all traditional family norms and ideals. They expect siblings to perform obligations, but are less insistent about supporting their parents. Many believe that sons and daughters should not be treated differently, but would think twice when asked to depart from traditional sex-roles. Under the label 'nuclear family' there is therefore a complex mix of values and norms which do not entirely accord with one another. Thus possibilities of family conflict arise from value dissensus.

DOCUMENT VIII.d2: Cognitive play (source: Chien Chiao, 'Cognitive play: some minor rituals among Hong Kong Cantonese, (1)', *East Asian Civilizations*, No. 2, 1983, pp. 138-140)

In comparison with other Hong Kong Chinese rituals, *da xiaoren* [beating the small person] in relatively simple. Still, one has to bring food, various 'fu' [talisman] or 'credentials', paper cut figures including that of *xiaoren* [little person] as well as of *guiren* [noble person] and mock paper money and gold or silver bullion (thick squares of rough paper bent into bowl shape). When the ritual begins, two candles and three sticks of incense are lit, food is displayed, then the small person paper figure wrapped in the 'small person paper' is fiercely beaten with a shoe or pierced into pieces with a sword while a chant is being sung. Then paper 'credentials' are rolled and waved over the recipient's body before they are burnt together with mock paper money and other paper goods. Finally two small pieces of plano-convex shaped wood which are known as '*bei*' (*pui*) or 'cup' are thrown to the ground to find out whether the ritual is a successful one.

A person may hold this ritual himself, or for three or four Hong Kong dollars which is about sixty or eighty cents in the US currency, have a professional performer to perform for him. There are also individual variations in the performances. For one thing, the 'small person' paper wrapping can be either beaten with a shoe or pierced with a short sword. What is left after beating or piercing may be just left on the ground or burnt. In a still fancier way, they may be put on a small paper-folded boat and burnt together.

Cross-road is a favorite place to hold the ritual. It may also be held at a White Tiger altar. Images of the White Tiger are usually made of stone and found under altars to the major gods. Such altars only exist in small temples where the professionals who are usually men known as nan'm lao (nan-mo loa) or chanting fellow may perform the ritual at a small fee (about five to ten Hong Kong dollars). A special place for the ritual is the Lover's Stone Park in the mid-level area on Hong Kong Island. On the sixth, sixteenth and twenty-sixth days of each lunar month, many 'Beating the Small Person' rituals are held right below the Lover's Stone, a pointed stone formation which becomes a popular fetish.

e. How Satisfied Have Hong Kong People Been?

Were Hong Kong people happy through their increasing affluence? Hong Kong people had had their dreams and had had to face a reality. They had had hopes as well as apprehensions. The crux to the problem, as sociologist Thomas W.P. Wong argues in the passage below, lies in the patterns of class structure and social mobility in Hong Kong. It is interesting and fitting, as Hong Kong society reaches the 1990s, for the question of class to be raised. Hitherto, the fluid population had been characterized by the inflow and outflow of people. As the settled population and its offspring take over economic opportunities, it is fitting that internally generated social classes should come to dominate Hong Kong's social structure.

DOCUMENT VIII.e1: Discourses and dilemmas (source: Thomas W.P. Wong, 'Discourses and dilemmas, 25 years of subjective indicators studies', in Lau Siu-kai, Lee Ming-kwan, Wan Po-san and Wong Siu-lun, eds. *Indicators of Social Development, Hong Kong 1990*, Hong Kong: Hong Kong Institute of Asia-Pacific Studies, Chinese University of Hong Kong, 1992, pp. 239-268)

If there is an impending sense of crisis in recent commentaries on the future of Hong Kong, it could not have been more systematically formulated and pursued than in the works of I. Scott and S.L. Wong.* However, as we shall see, the two formulations differ in their tenor and their conclusion. In his attempt to uncover the origins and implications of the loss of autonomy, brought in train by the signing of the Joint Declaration, and then the promulgation of the Basic Law, Scott basically sees the current crisis as one of legitimacy. The legitimacy of the colonial government has been much eroded, and things have certainly not been helped by its general 'resort to subterfuge,' when it comes to matters like the speeding up of democratisation of the polity. In our view, such an argument, leaving aside the diatribes against the attempts from the colonial and the Chinese government to curb or frustrate constitutional reforms, and, thereby, causing frustration, very much hinges on the interpretation of the political wishes and sentiments of the populace. But obviously the matter does not stop here. For the keystone of Scott's case lies in the loss of the moral basis of the colonial authority. To us, such a basis can only be empirically understood, and that means a systematic and longitudinal picture of the socio-political ethos is imperative. Scott interpreted traditional apathy among the Hong Kong people as a sign of confidence or consent, while the current apathy is one of disillusionment. Has there been such a change? Is it the case that such disillusionment is particularly felt among the young and the educated, the middle class? Elsewhere, we have raised our objections to these commentaries (for ultimately, that is what they are) on the grounds that they

---

* I. Scott, *Political Change and the Crisis of Legitimacy in Hong Kong*, Hong Kong: Hong Kong University Press, 1989; 'Opening speech,' in J.C.Y. Lee, et.al., eds. *Politics and 1991 Elections in Hong Kong*, Hong Kong: Department of Public and Social Administration, City Polytechnic of Hong Kong, 1992; S.L.Wong, 'Prosperity and anxiety in Hong Kong reexamined,' in S.K. Lau, M.K. Lee, P.S.Wan and S.L. Wong, eds. *The Development of Social Indicators Research in Chinese Societies*, Hong Kong: Hong Kong Institute of Asia-Pacific Studies, 1992, pp. 217-238; *Emigration and stablity in Hong Kong*, Occasional Paper No. 7, Hong Kong: Social Science Research Centre and Department of Sociology, University of Hong Kong, 1992; S.L. Wong and S. Yue, 'Satisfaction in various life domains,' in S.K. Lau, et.al. eds., *Indicators of Social Development: Hong Kong 1988*, pp. 1-24.

are empirically unsubstantiated.* For our purpose here, the lacunae in Scott points to the need to explore various dimensions of the normative system that may underlie the fundamental political orientations, and that may help to explain the emergent, more context-bound, political wishes and sentiments of the Hong Kong people. We believe that a survey of the past subjective indicators findings on relevant themes may contribute to that purpose.

In comparison with Scott, S.L. Wong sees the current crisis in a very different light. Wong begins with the social issue of emigration. Contrary to the more conventional view, he does not join the chorus of the alarming call brought on by the emigration waves of recent years. Instead, he argues that the present pattern of emigration is in fact 'part and parcel of the stability and prosperity of Hong Kong'. On the one hand, the alleged negative effects of emigration, such as brain drain and the more intangible phenomenon of anomie and moral hazards, are, in his view, either unfounded or exaggerated. On the other hand, the emigration evinces a 'traditional' refugee mentality as well as an activation of social networks, albeit now on a global level, both of which have served to build up the successful Hong Kong experience, and which will do so in the future. We feel that Wong probably has a case in his evaluation of the negative effects of emigration. What we want to take him to task for concerns the concept of 'refugee mentality.' For it is obvious that here Wong is embarking on a discussion of the nature of the Hong Kong identity, its formation, and its relation to the Hong Kong experience and the Hong Kong way of life. Politically, the prevalence of refugee mentality means that there is some *a priori* acceptance, or better, tolerance, of the colonial authority; the older generation escaped from one political regime not to endorse and trust another (alien) one, but to make a living for themselves and their offspring. As Hong Kong develops, the new generation may develop a sense of Hong Kong identity, which, in Wong's judgement, identifies more with Hong Kong as a way of life than with Hong Kong as a place of residence. When this is coupled with a prevalent and long-existing sense of political powerlessness, and a belief in self-help and personal liberty, refugee mentality reduces the problem of legitimacy, *pace* Scott (and we agree), 'into an academic issue'. The mentality immunises the Hong Kong people from ideological exhortations and political passions.

Economically, the refugee mentality 'creates a spirit of enterprise and engenders economic dynamism.' In Wong's judgement, this is the positive, and more important, effect the mentality has on the stability and prosperity of the society. The essential precariousness of the refugee proves to be a driving force for greater diligence, better education, and worldly/cosmopolitan orientations. If Hong Kong is in crisis, emigration does not add to it; quite the reverse, the implication of Wong's argument is that it reveals an ethos and forces which undergird and strengthen the social order. Our

---

* T.W.P. Wong and T.T.Lui, *From One Brand of Politics to One Brand of Political Culture*, Occasional Paper No. 10, Hong Kong: Hong Kong Institute of Asia-Pacific Studies, 1992.

question is: can 'refugee mentality' capture all the nuances and dimensions, and, as it were, the life and times, of the Hong Kong identity? It is obvious that Wong has emphasised the economistic, and economically dynamic, side of such identity. What other strands and components would a fuller conception of this identity consist of? Again, we believe that a review of past subjective indicators studies will go some way to constructing that fuller conception.

...

In the following review,* we have distinguished themes for which the findings have revealed striking changes from the ones where there has been an equally impressive degree of continuity and persistence. We can see that, in respect to the areas of life satisfaction (or generally quality of life), perceptions of openness and opportunities in the society, and sense of improvement and confidence, there have been significant and positive changes.

It is quite evident that there has been an important change in the degree of subjective well-being. In Mitchell's study, the Hong Kong people were unhappy with their social status and life in general; 32 per cent of the respondents felt economically deprived, and 57 per cent worried many times or sometimes about money. Thirty per cent said nothing in life gives satisfaction. On all these counts, the Hong Kong Chinese in the 1960s represented the worst (pessimistic, precarious) case among the other ethnic groups and societies in the study. However, recent findings show a much greater degree of satisfaction. In SI [Social Indicators Study] 88, 75 per cent of the respondents were satisfied with family life, 59 per cent satisfied with their work.

While we have little doubt that the improvement in such subjective well-being arose from the successful development of the society, which we, in another context,

---

* The following surveys are cited in the tables to follow:
R.E. Mitchell 1967, The Urban Family Life Survey, urban Hong Kong, N=3,966, aged 18 and above (Mitchell 1967); J.S. Hoadley 1967, Survey of Chinese University students, N=254 (Hoadley 1967); D.C. Chaney and D. Podmore 1969, Young adults study with a sub-sample drawn from Hopkins's housing survey, urban Hong Kong, N=1,123, aged 15-29 (Chaney & Podmore 1969); A. King 1971, Life quality study, as part of S. Shively's Kwun Tong Industrial Community Research Programme, N=1,065, aged 18 and above (King 1971); S. Millar 1974, The Biosocial Study, urban Hong Kong, N= 3,983, aged between 20 and 59 (Millar 1974); S.K.Lau 1977, urban Hong Kong, sub-sample drawn from Millar's biosocial survey, N=550, aged between 20 and 59 (Lau 1977); S.K. Lau and H.C. Kuan 1985, Ethos of Hong Kong people study, Kwun Tong area, N=792, aged 18 and above (Lau 1985); S.K. Lau 1986, Pilot study of Social Indicators Project, Kwun Tong, N=539, aged 18 and above (Lau 1986); S.K. Lau et.al. 1988, the first Social Indicators Study, Hong Kong-wide survey, N=1,662, aged 18 and above (Soc. Indic. Stud. 1988); T.W.P. Wong and T.L. Lui 1989, A Benchmark Study of Social Mobility, Hong Kong-wide, N=1,000 (male household heads), aged 20 to 64 (Wong and Lui 1989); S.K. Lau et.al. 1990, the second Social Indicators study, Hong Kong-wide, N=1,957, aged 18 and above (Soc. Indic. Stud. 1990), S.K. Lau, *Society and Politics in Hong Kong*, Hong Kong: The Chinese University Press, 1982 (Lau 1982).

Table 8.3
Life Satisfaction (%)

	Mitchell 1967	Millar 1974	Lau 1986	Soc. Indic. Stud. 1988	Stud. 1990
Per cent dissatisfied with life	40	10	15		3
Per cent who worried most about money	27		18		
Per cent who worried most about work	20		31**		
Per cent unhappy with current social status	33∞			15	

** This category in fact includes 'job, education, and prospects.' It would be reasonable to expect a much lower percentage for work if there is disaggregation of the category.
∞ Mitchell's option is 'quite or very unhappy,' while the category in Soc. Indic. Stud. 1988 is 'dissatisfied/very dissatisfied.'

called the 'Hong Kong experience'*, a more specific indicator of the optimism and confidence is the perception of openness and opportunities as the Hong Kong people took advantage of the structural changes in the society. Again, we find quite remarkable changes.

Table 8.4
Openness and Opportunities in Society (%)

	Mitchell 1967	Chaney & Podmore 1969	Lau 1977	Lau 1982
Per cent who saw much chance of upward mobility	50**	63°		60¥
Per cent who opted to stay in Hong Kong despite opportunities elsewhere	23		53	

** Chances for a working class boy to become a medical doctor are good or excellent
° Agree that Hong Kong is a land of opportunity. Like Lau 1982, the response is from young people.
¥ Most of the respondents are under 35 years old.

---

* T.L. Lui and T.W.P. Wong, 'Class, inequality and moral order: a perspective on Hong Kong in transition,' (in Chinese), unpublished paper, 1992.

We think it is particularly noteworthy that there is an increasing identification with Hong Kong as a land of opportunity and for career development. More than half of the respondents in 1977, in contrast to 23 per cent in 1967, opted to stay in Hong Kong, despite opportunities elsewhere. Although we do not have more recent findings on this count, the returning of emigrants to Hong Kong in the past few years, other than reflecting personal strategies and conditions in the global economy, seems to give some credence to the existence of a normative belief of openness and opportunities. And when this belief is coupled with positive evaluations of mobility experience, the result is greater confidence and a degree of personal efficacy.

Table 8.5
Evaluation of Mobility Experience and Personal Efficacy (%)

	Mitchell 1967	Lau 1985	Lau 1986	Soc.Indic. Stud. 1988
Per cent who see themselves as having higher status than parents	31		37	44
Per cent who see themselves as having lower status than parents	36		11	12
Per cent who feel they cannot control their life	53	54*		

* This is in response to the question: 'Do you agree that in face of future uncertainties, we can only adjust as best as we can?' This figure represents the proportion who agreed or strongly agreed. On the surface, it seems there is a similar fatalistic strand in the response, as in Mitchell's finding. But one should note that 80 per cent of Lau's respondents also strongly disagree or disagree with the statement that 'whether one will be successful or not is determined by fate, it is useless to make the effort'.

On the whole, we could then say that to the extent that the earlier studies captured important facets and facts of the, as it were, formative years of the Hong Kong experience, the changes since then have been towards a more satisfied, optimistic and self-assured direction. The relatively high degree of structural and exchange mobility in the society, as uncovered in a recent study, no doubt constitutes the societal reasons — the success and the satisfaction — for such changes in the normative orientations and belief systems. But a more detailed examination of the past survey studies also discloses important areas where continuities and persistence exist making for less complacency and optimism. We specifically refer to the areas of personal pessimism in relation to career development or prospects, strain and frustration arising from a realistic or stoic appraisal of society, and the perception of the future and meaning of life and work.

We have pointed elsewhere to the discrepancy between the optimistic belief in social openness and the pessimistic appraisal of one's work situation and career prospects.[*] We can also find a similar pessimistic orientation in the 1960s.

Table 8.6
Pessimism in Relation to Work (%)

	Mitchell 1967	Lau 1986	Soc. Indic. 1988	Stud. 1990
Per cent who see the chance for career development as great	16		7	12
Per cent who are satisfied with work	25	25*		37

* When probed in details about specific aspects of work, Lau's respondents had much more satisfaction from say the work nature, but were much less so when it came to promotion prospects, welfare, etc.

The pessimistic assessment of chance for career development is also evident in other studies. A study of clerical workers showed that nearly 40 per cent of the respondents saw little or no promotion prospects in their job. And 76 per cent of the respondents in the Social Indicators Studies 1990 survey could see little or no chance of finding a better job than the one they were holding, a finding not significantly affected by background characteristics. As for the liking for job, Mitchell titled the relevant chapter 'No job in Work,' only one quarter of his respondents expressed that they liked their job very much. So it may be that the relatively low level of job satisfaction and the pessimism in career development are related, but what concerns us is the continuity of such evaluations. Apparently upward social mobility or improved 'quality of life' has not ameliorated or eliminated such anxieties and whatever precariousness that may be entailed by them. Could it be that there are other structural and normative strains underlying the formation of the Hong Kong identity or way of life?

In relation to the strain arising from perceptions of social divisions and political situation, again, we find a persistent trend. The sense of political powerlessness is clear and is the subject of much discussion. We, however, feel it necessary to relate such sense of powerlessness to the way the Hong Kong people perceive the society and the

---

[*] T.W.P. Wong, 'Inequality, stratification and mobility,' in S.K. Lau, et.al. eds. *Indicators of Social Development*, pp. 145-172, and 'Social indicators and the social mobility experience of Hong Kong,' (in Chinese) in S.K. Lau, et.al. eds., *Development of Social Indicators Research*, pp. 161-174.

Table 8.7
Strain Arising from Perceptions of Society (%)

	Mitchell	Chaney & Podmore	King	Lau	Wong & Lui
	1967	1969	1972	1977	1989
Per cent who felt could do nothing about unjust government or society			82	91	
Per cent who felt employees were being taken advantage of	25*	61°			31¥

* Mitchell's question was: 'Do you think that people having your qualifications and work experience should be paid more, or about the same, as you are receiving now?'
° Chaney and Podmore's question was: 'Do you think that working people are fairly and equally treated by their employers, or that employers sometimes take advantage of them?'
¥ The question in the social mobility survey was this: 'Do you agree to the view that if bosses are to make profits, they have to exploit workers?'
It is obvious that these three questions tap quite differently the respondents' sense of distributive justice. We provide these figures to serve as general indicative signposts.

polity; in other words to the meanings, definitions, images — and the struggles over them — embedded in social behaviour and normative orientations. The values and beliefs involved in issues like distributive justice or moral economy are as pertinent to our understanding of political apathy (à la Lau) or political awareness (à la Scott) as a single piece of information on political efficacy. Thus, on the one hand, we could gauge the nature and amount of strain and frustration from Hoadley's study in which he saw significance in the fact that half of the Chinese residents he interviewed in the turbulent year of 1967 expressed negative orientations towards the police, the government, etc.* Similarly, it is a noteworthy indicator of powerlessness or fatalism that 71 per cent of Mitchell's Form 5 students saw the Hong Kong government as understanding not very well/not at all the people's needs. But, on the other hand, we should also note the implications when 66 per cent of the young workers interviewed by Lau and Ho in 1978 wanted to see their fellow workers have colour television sets before they themselves did, rather than to see unknown people earning millions.* What kind of distributive standard and meaning is involved here? And why is it that there is this apparently deep-rooted and long-standing sense of inequality and injustice?

---

* J.S. Hoadley, 'Hong Kong is the lifeboat: notes on political culture and socialization,' *Journal of Oriental Studies* vol. 8, 1970, pp. 206-218.

Table 8.8
Strain Arising from Perceptions of Society (%)

	Mitchell 1967	Lau 1985	Lau 1986	Soc. Indic. Stud. 1990
Per cent who gave centrality to work	21*		19°	
Per cent who felt it was pointless to plan ahead		45¥		33#

* The 'centrality of work' in Mitchell's study is an index composed of scores given to three questions on work.
° Lau's question was whether one would give up one's present job if a fortune befell: the figure is the percentage of respondents who would stick with present job.
¥ This refers to the proportion of people who felt they did not have the capability to plan and prepare for the future.
#This refers to the proportion of people who felt it was pointless to plan ahead.

Our last area concerns the perceptions of the future and the meaning of work. The findings over the past two decades again reveal continuities rather than change.

The issue of meaning of work is different from the one of job satisfaction. Even if there is some indication that the latter is on the rise (see earlier table), the Hong Kong people seem to have kept an invidious view of work. We hypothesise that this is due to a basic pragmatic strand in the work ethos of the Hong Kong people, which, more often than not, is clouded by the debate on instrumentalism in the local literature. While, for instance, Turner et.al. (1980) highlighted the collectivistic and non-money-driven aspects in the Hong Kong workers' approach to work (also concerned with welfare, work relations, and help from workmates or supervisor in case of difficulties), in an attempt to criticise England and Rear (1975), both parties, in our view, read too much positive and substantive significance into the idea of instrumentalism (or specifically, money-mindedness). Chiang perhaps was closer to the mark when she remarked:**

> Instrumentalism could be rooted in the very nature of job degradation in factories so that money becomes the only desirable feature of work. Instrumentalism could also be an expression of the need of workers to help themselves and their families to survive in a highly competitive and rapidly changing society.

---

* S.K. Lau and K.F. Ho, *Social Accommodation of Politics: The Case of the Young Hong Kong Workers*, Occasional Paper No. 89, Hong Kong: Social Research Centre, 1980.
** C.S.N. Chiang, 'Women and work: case studies of two Hong Kong factories,' M.Phil. dissertation, University of Hong Kong, 1984, citation from p. 19.

Thus, not only is there a fluid meaning to instrumentalism (dependent on its 'embeddedness' in various domains of life or social references), instrumentalism in a specific, narrow context probably signifies more a resigned, somewhat fatalistic, attitude towards work. Mitchell's Hong Kong respondents may have, in comparison with other Chinese and ethnic societies, most likely chosen the money aspect of their work, yet a sizable number of them did not agree that in their work they were just 'putting in time.' In response to the debate on instrumentalism in the industrial relations studies, one could say that money and meaning are compatible, just as instrumentalism is compatible with collectivism. Much hinges on the different contextual concerns and the different levels of relevance and primacy the ascertained orientations and values are located.

Thus the meaning of work and its bearing on industrial and work attitudes remain to be explored. But to go back to our concerns, if we could agree that the relatively low level of centrality given to work is indicative of both a specific (and thus temporal) dislike of one's present job and a more diffused (and perhaps more deep-rooted), cynical or invidious reaction to work in general, then the findings seem to suggest continuity rather than positive changes.

There is no gainsaying that, in the above exercise, much is still found wanting. The incomparability (not to mention the problem of interpretability of the findings itself) of some of the questions in the surveys is troubling, to say the least. Yet, we remain confident enough to try out various ideas on the changes the Hong Kong society has undergone, as they are reflected at the plane of the normative and belief territory of the people. Such scouting of the terrain, as it were, seems to have produced the following paradoxes. On the one hand, there is a strong belief in the openness and opportunities in the society, and in individual effort. On the other hand, there is also a sense of low personal efficacy, of pessimism, especially in relation to one's work, career development and politics. Similarly, while there is an unmistakable increase in satisfaction derived from life in general, with less worries about money and employment, there is also a sense of precariousness, of strain and frustration, and of injustice and inequalities in the society. We tend to see such 'contradictions' as more apparent than real. A social history of the hopes and frustrations of the Hong Kong people remains to be written, yet we believe there are structural reasons for the paradoxes. As a first step, the social mobility study in 1989[*] demonstrated that while there was truth to the Hong Kong dream, viz. upward mobility made possible by occupational structural changes and the pay-offs to efforts, the reality was that there was also persistent and emergent inequalities in chances of mobility, with the class structure exhibiting important trends towards rigidity and closure. Once we take the coexistence of the dream and the reality seriously, the 'contradictions' are then intelligible. Indeed, we

---

[*] Possibly as reported in Thomas W.P. Wong and Tai-lok Lui, *Reinstating Class: a Structural and Developmental Study of Hong Kong Society*, Occasional Paper No. 10, Social Sciences Research Centre and Department of Sociology, University of Hong Kong, 1992.

see them as providing a useful vantage point to understand the nature and formation of the Hong Kong experience, and a pivotal area where order and unrest in the future could be examined.

We hope that it is now plain to the reader that if we are to have a dialogue with Scott and Wong, this is probably the way we would respond. There is little evidence for Scott's case. If anything, there is more support — sense of political powerlessness, long persistence of general political concern, etc. — for the *quid pro quo* mentality as being more truthful to the reality than the legitimacy argument. Through our review, we have better ideas about the various dimensions involved in the normative system that may underlie the fundamental political orientations. A further thematization of the findings in terms of 'distributive justice,' 'moral economy' and some such areas will reveal that there are sources for both pragmatic acceptance of life-fate and moral/political outrage. With regard to Wong, the import of our survey is that the Hong Kong identity cannot possibly be captured by the 'refugee mentality' concept alone. Both analytically and substantively, the contents break the seams of the concept, and demand to speak in multiple 'languages': pragmatism, fatalism, cynicism..., depending on the context, the domain of life, the degree of primacy of livelihood, the level of generality, and so on. Perhaps not until the full nature of this 'polyglot' creature is understood could one deliberate, proclaim or pontificate on the subjective territory of the Hong Kong people and its implications for unrest and crisis, for growth and survival, or the fissure and the tenacity of the society.

INDEX

accountants, 134, 283, 368
apprentice, 77, 78, 188, 189, 202, 263, 288, 305, 327

boat population, 31, 50-1, 271; see also Tanka
Bray, Denis 2, 311
Burial Fund, 78, 80

caged men, 348
charity, 21-2, 128, 140-5 passim, 209, 211, 212, 227, 234-7, 265; see also Tung-wah Hospital and Po Leung Kuk.
China Mail, 28, 54, 61, 90, 91, 95, 100-8 passim, 133
Chinese Chamber of Commerce, 122, 141, 145, 192, 211
Chinese Communist Party, 150, 160
Chinese custom, 8, 17, 33, 112, 149, 237-48, 370-2; see also *mui-tsai*
Chow Shou Son, 117, 118-9, 156, 157
Christian missions and Christianity, 20, 52, 86, 102, 103, 113, 114, 138, 199, 233, 248, 371
citizenship, 48
City District Office, 310, 311, 312, 313, 314

Clean Hong Kong Campaign, 3, 309, 310
cockloft, 10, 36, 40, 181, 183, 185
Confucian Society of Hong Kong, 122, 123
Contractors and sub-contractors, 74-83 passim, 120, 126, 188, 189, 194, 201-2, 205, 249, 266, 315
coolies, 10, 18, 26, 30, 42, 48, 114, 129, 152, 181, 183, 187, 189, 201, 261
corpses, 131, 181, 235
Cultural Revolution, 2, 9, 10, 291, 296

Deng Xiaoping, 9, 369
drains, 33, 37, 38, 40, 251

elderly, 141, 177, 306, 347, 348, 371
Elliot, Elsie 2, 286
employment of children, 196, 197, 198, 200, 202
Eurasian, 4, 49, 50
European Reservation, 46, 55; see also Peak

family life, 30, 175, 203-4, 254, 265-8, 319-35, 335-47
Fight Violent Crime Campaign, 3, 309, 310
Fung Ping-shan, 6, 117, 133-146

General Chamber of Commerce, 117, 119, 123, 127-133
grassroots, 2, 4, 301, 307
guerrillas, 209
guilds, 61, 73-7, 78-3, 84, 185, 186, 189, 190, 196

Hakka, 32, 196, 271, 339, 346
hawkers, 42, 184, 201, 202, 211, 235, 255, 261, 312, 313
Hennessy, Sir John Pope, 22, 23, 55
Ho Kai, Sir Kai 4, 6, 63-9 passim, 85-8, 90-104 passim, 120
Ho Tung, Sir Robert 95, 110-6, 117, 119-121, 226, 282
Hoklo, 32, 271
Hong Kong government, 1-13 passim, 85, 118, 133, 146, 150,
 educational policies, 51-2
 handling of strikes in 1920s, 149-50, 162-6, 169-74, 192-5
 housing policies, 204-7, 250-3, 255-6
 policies on illegal immigrants, 349-50, 365-7
 purchase of rice 1919, 151-6
 revenue 1897-1926, 159
 riots of 1960s, 286-93
 sale of women, 174-5
 social programme in 1970s, 301-11;
 use of Chinese, 296-9
 See also City District Office, Legislative Council, Mutual Aid Committee, Urban Council
Hong Kong identity, 374, 375, 378, 382
Hong Kong University, 55, 112, 123, 140, 142, 145, 188, 373
housing
 Chadwick report 1882, 33-46
 Ho Kai's defence of Chinese houses, 87
 cubicles, 183-190 passim
 overcrowding, 203-4

subsidized housing, 204-5, 250-3
tenement in Wanchai, 256-60
housing in 1970s, 301-3

immigrants, 16, 17, 58, 183-91, 249-50, 272, 348-50, 359-61, 362-5, 365-7
income, salary and wages, 28, 50, 74-6 passim, 88, 147, 156-8, 163-5, 174, 181, 183-90 passim, 276, 279-80, 287-8, 322, 325-6 passim, 354-5, 360, 361-2
Indian, 52, 53, 146-8, 155
internment camp, 209, 210, 228, 232

Jardine, Matheson & Co., 119, 124, 146

Kang Yu-wei, 92-108 passim
ketchup, 25
Kowloon Walled City, 255, 321, 334
Kuomintang (Guomindang), 9, 191, 194

Language, 112, 122, 133, 271, 323-4, 361, 365
 Chinese as official language, 296-9
 Chinese to study their own language, 54
 cost of bilingual education, 294-6
 demand for English education, 53;
 Japanese, 226
 keeping of accounts in English, 283
Lau Chu Pak, 4, 117, 119, 121, 122, 123, 282
Legislative Council, 61, 85, 90, 114, 120, 122, 125, 129, 249, 251-3, 297-9, 301-11, 348, 368
literacy, 272 ff.
importance of women to become literate, 138
Lo, Sir Man-kam, 4, 85, 249, 251

Macau, 135, 139, 173, 223, 233, 292, 369
Maclehose, Sir Murray 2, 301
Man Mo deity, 60, 61, 62

Marriage Ordinance, 242, 243, 247
mui-tsai, 8, 174-80, 202
Mutual Aid Committee, 301, 307, 310, 315

New Territories, 52, 57, 154, 209, 211, 242-3, 264, 273, 302-3, 310-1, 335-47, 364
newspapers, 115, 212, 225, 291 ff., 313, 325, see also *China Mail, South China Morning Post.*

opium, 18, 19, 24, 25, 88, 90, 123, 124, 130 ff., 136, 146-7 passim, 151, 159, 171, 183, 212

Peak, 6, 49, 55, 116, 190, 197, 302
pirates, 17, 18
plague, 108, 120
Po Leung Kuk, 8, 62-73, 81, 114, 120, 123, 139, 140, 209, 227
police, 19, 60, 150, 163, 181, 198, 214, 217, 286, 289, 290, 291, 302, 307, 309, 310, 313, 352, 364, 379
population
    1876-1881, 23
    City of Victoria 1881, 31
    1911, 48-9
    urban 1911, 51
    1914 and 1941, 149
    total civil population 1897-1926, 158
    1931, 202-3
    1957, 249
    1966, 268-74
    population transition 1971-81, 299-300
Portuguese, 19, 23, 49, 50, 52, 54, 100

riots, 285
    1919, 154
    1956, 9, 233
    1966, 285, 286
    1967, 286

Sanitary Board, 4, 85, 86, 88, 114, 120, 122, 196
Shanghai, 7, 20, 94, 95, 96, 100, 103, 104, 108, 110, 117, 119, 120, 123, 125, 126, 128, 131, 141, 143, 147, 150, 154, 155, 161, 162, 163, 166, 167, 169, 170, 174, 180, 188, 192, 195, 196, 211, 212, 215, 275, 279, 280, 364
Shek-lau deity, 58,
South China Morning Post, 85, 107, 108, 109, 110, 213, 350
strikes, 4, 9, 82-3, 149-50, 160-74, 182, 191-3, 195, 317, 325
Sun Yat-sen, 86-110 passim, 150

Tanka, 18
temple, 57, 58, 60, 61, 85, 148, 190
Tiananmen, 351, 356
Triad, 191, 192
Tse Tsan Tai (Xie Zantai), 88-110,
Tung-wah Hospital, 6, 27, 61, 62, 83, 84, 85, 113, 120, 123, 138, 139, 145, 154, 209
typhoon, 135, 154, 312, 352

Urban Council, 60, 196, 199, 297ff., 313

vaccination, 22, 27
veranda, 33, 38, 46, 213, 217, 220, 221, 222, 251, 257, 258, 265, 348

working hours, 76, 199-200, 202, 183-90, 324

Yeung Ku-wan (Yang Quyun), 86-104 passim
Yung Wing, (Weng Hong) 101-10 passim